LIVING AND WORKING

IN

BRITAIN

A SURVIVAL HANDBOOK

by

David Hampshire

SURVIVAL BOOKS • LONDON • ENGLAND

First published 1991
Second Edition 1996
Reprinted 1996, 1997

Survival Books Limited, Suite C, Third Floor
Standbrook House, 2-5 Old Bond Street
London W1X 3TB, United Kingdom
☎ (44) 171-493 4244, Fax (44) 171-491 0605
E-mail: info@survivalbooks.net
Internet: survivalbooks.net

British Library Cataloguing in Publication Data.
A CIP record for this book is available from the British Library.
ISBN 1 901130 50 9

Printed and bound in Great Britain by Page Bros. (Norwich) Ltd., Mile Cross Lane,
Norwich, Norfolk NR6 6SA, UK.

ACKNOWLEDGEMENTS

My sincere thanks to all those who contributed to the successful publication of this book, in particular the many people who took the time and trouble to read and comment on the numerous draft versions, including Karen (my researcher and proof-reader) and John Verheul, Janet Macdonald, Ken Maxwell-Jones, Linda Hull, Kitty Strawbridge, Peter Turner, Pat & Ron Scarborough, Verena Dangerfield, Pat and Mike Grey, Veronica Orchard, Julia Thorpe, Jane and Philip Read, and Linda and Michael Osborn. Also a special thank you to Jim Watson for the superb cover and cartoons.

What Readers and Reviewers Have Said About Survival Books

When you buy a model plane for your child, a video recorder, or some new computer gizmo, you get with it a leaflet or booklet pleading 'Read Me First', or bearing large friendly letters or bold type saying 'IMPORTANT - follow the instructions carefully'. This book should be similarly supplied to all those entering France with anything more durable than a 5-day return ticket. – It is worth reading even if you are just visiting briefly, or if you have lived here for years and feel totally knowledgeable and secure. But if you need to find out how France works then it is indispensable. Native French people probably have a less thorough understanding of how their country functions. – Where it is most essential, the book is most up to the minute.

Living France

We would like to congratulate you on this work: it is really super! We hand it out to our expatriates and they read it with great interest and pleasure.

ICI (Switzerland) AG

Rarely has a 'survival guide' contained such useful advice – This book dispels doubts for first-time travellers, yet is also useful for seasoned globetrotters – In a word, if you're planning to move to the USA or go there for a long-term stay, then buy this book both for general reading and as a ready-reference.

American Citizens Abroad

It's everything you always wanted to ask but didn't for fear of the contemptuous put down – The best English-language guide – Its pages are stuffed with practical information on everyday subjects and are designed to complement the traditional guidebook.

Swiss News

A complete revelation to me – I found it both enlightening and interesting, not to mention amusing.

Carole Clark

Let's say it at once. David Hampshire's *Living and Working in France* is the best handbook ever produced for visitors and foreign residents in this country; indeed, my discussion with locals showed that it has much to teach even those born and bred in *l'Hexagone*. – It is Hampshire's meticulous detail which lifts his work way beyond the range of other books with similar titles. Often you think of a supplementary question and search for the answer in vain. With Hampshire this is rarely the case. – He writes with great clarity (and gives French equivalents of all key terms), a touch of humor and a ready eye for the odd (and often illuminating) fact. – This book is absolutely indispensable.

The Riviera Reporter

The ultimate reference book – Every conceivable subject imaginable is exhaustively explained in simple terms – An excellent introduction to fully enjoy all that this fine country has to offer and save time and money in the process.

American Club of Zurich

What Readers and Reviewers Have Said About Survival Books

What a great work, wealth of useful information, well-balanced wording and accuracy in details. My compliments!

Thomas Müller

This handbook has all the practical information one needs to set up home in the UK – The sheer volume of information is almost daunting – Highly recommended for anyone moving to the UK.

American Citizens Abroad

A very good book which has answered so many questions and even some I hadn't thought of – I would certainly recommend it.

Brian Fairman

A mine of information – I might have avoided some embarrassments and frights if I had read it prior to my first Swiss encounters – Deserves an honoured place on any newcomer's bookshelf.

English Teachers Association, Switzerland

Covers just about all the things you want to know on the subject – In answer to the desert island question about *the one* how-to book on France, this book would be it – Almost 500 pages of solid accurate reading – This book is about enjoyment as much as survival.

The Recorder

It's so funny – I love it and definitely need a copy of my own – Thanks very much for having written such a humourous and helpful book.

Heidi Guiliani

A must for all foreigners coming to Switzerland.

Antoinette O'Donoghue

A comprehensive guide to all things French, written in a highly readable and amusing style, for anyone planning to live, work or retire in France.

The Times

A concise, thorough account of the DOs and DON'Ts for a foreigner in Switzerland – Crammed with useful information and lightened with humourous quips which make the facts more readable.

American Citizens Abroad

Covers every conceivable question that might be asked concerning everyday life – I know of no other book that could take the place of this one.

France in Print

Hats off to Living and Working in Switzerland!

Ronnie Almeida

IMPORTANT NOTE

Britain is a diverse country with many faces, a variety of ethnic groups, religions and customs, and continuously changing rules, regulations (particularly with respect to social security, the National Health Service, education and taxes), interest rates and prices. Note that a change of government in Britain can have far-reaching effects on many important aspects of life. **I cannot recommend too strongly that you check with an official and reliable source (not always the same) before making any major decisions, or taking an irreversible course of action. However, don't believe everything you're told or read (even, dare I say it, herein).** Useful addresses and references to other sources of information have been included in all chapters and in **Appendices A and B**, to help you obtain further information and verify details with official sources. Important points have been emphasised, **in bold print**, some of which it would be expensive, or even dangerous, to disregard. **Ignore them at your peril or cost.** Unless specifically stated, the reference to any company, organisation or product in this book doesn't constitute an endorsement or recommendation. Any reference to any place or person (living or dead) is purely coincidental. There's no such country as Britain.

CONTENTS

1. FINDING A JOB   19

QUALIFICATIONS	23
EMPLOYMENT SERVICE	24
JOBCENTRES	25
RECRUITMENT CONSULTANTS	25
CONTRACT JOBS	26
PART-TIME JOBS	27
TEMPORARY & CASUAL JOBS	27
HOLIDAY & SHORT–TERM JOBS	28
VOLUNTARY WORK	29
WORKING WOMEN	30
JOB HUNTING	31
SALARIES	33
SELF-EMPLOYMENT	34
TRAINEES & WORK EXPERIENCE	36
AU PAIRS	37
WORKING ILLEGALLY	38
LANGUAGE	39

2. WORKING CONDITIONS   41

TERMS OF EMPLOYMENT	42
CONTRACT OF EMPLOYMENT	46
EMPLOYMENT CONDITIONS	48

3. PERMITS & VISAS   63

ENTRY CLEARANCE	65
WORK PERMITS	69
SETTLEMENT	82
DEPORTATION	82

4. ARRIVAL   85

IMMIGRATION	86
ENTRY REFUSAL	87
PASSPORT STAMPS	88

CUSTOMS 89
POLICE REGISTRATION 92
COUNCIL TAX REGISTRATION 93
EMBASSY REGISTRATION 93
FINDING HELP 93
CHECKLISTS 94

5. ACCOMMODATION 97

RELOCATION CONSULTANTS 98
BUYING PROPERTY 100
RENTED ACCOMMODATION 101
UTILITIES 107
HEATING 116

6. POST OFFICE SERVICES 119

BUSINESS HOURS 121
LETTER POST 121
PARCEL POST 125
IMPORTANT DOCUMENTS & VALUABLES 127
MISCELLANEOUS SERVICES 129
MAIL COLLECTION 129
CHANGE OF ADDRESS 130
POSTAL ORDERS 130
NATIONAL SAVINGS ACCOUNTS 131

7. TELEPHONE 133

TELEPHONE COMPANIES 134
PHONE INSTALLATION & REGISTRATION 135
CHOOSING A PHONE 136
STANDARD TONES 137
USING THE TELEPHONE 138
BT NETWORK SERVICES 140
INFORMATION & ENTERTAINMENT NUMBERS 141
BT CALL RATES 142
BT TELEPHONE BILLS 143
INTERNATIONAL CALLS 144
PUBLIC TELEPHONES 146
MOBILE TELEPHONES & PAGERS 148

TELEGRAMS, TELEX & FAX 150
DIRECTORIES 151
THE INTERNET 153
MOVING HOUSE OR LEAVING BRITAIN 153
MALICIOUS CALLS 153
EMERGENCY NUMBERS 154
SERVICE NUMBERS 155

8. TELEVISION & RADIO 157

STANDARDS 159
TELEVISION STATIONS 160
TV LICENCE 163
SATELLITE TELEVISION 164
CABLE TELEVISION 166
VIDEOS 166
RADIO 167

9. EDUCATION 171

STATE OR PRIVATE SCHOOL? 173
STATE SCHOOLS 174
SPECIAL EDUCATION 186
PRIVATE SCHOOLS 187
HIGHER EDUCATION 192
FURTHER EDUCATION 197
LANGUAGE SCHOOLS 198

10. PUBLIC TRANSPORT 203

TRAINS 205
UNDERGROUND TRAINS 213
BUSES 215
FERRIES & LE SHUTTLE 219
TIMETABLES & MAPS 221
TAXIS 221
AIRLINE SERVICES 223

11. MOTORING 229

VEHICLE IMPORTATION 231
VEHICLE REGISTRATION 232
BUYING A CAR 234
TEST CERTIFICATE 239
SELLING A CAR 240
DRIVING LICENCE 241
CAR INSURANCE 243
ROAD TAX (VEHICLE EXCISE DUTY) 247
GENERAL ROAD RULES 248
BRITISH DRIVERS 253
BRITISH ROADS 255
TRAFFIC POLICE 256
MOTORCYCLES 256
ACCIDENTS 257
DRINKING & DRIVING 259
CAR THEFT 260
PETROL 262
SPEED LIMITS 263
GARAGES & SERVICING 265
ROAD MAPS 266
CAR HIRE 267
MOTORING ORGANISATIONS 269
PARKING 270

12. HEALTH 275

EMERGENCIES 278
NATIONAL HEALTH SERVICE (NHS) 279
PRIVATE HEALTH TREATMENT 281
DOCTORS 282
DRUGS & MEDICINES 285
HOSPITALS & CLINICS 287
CHILDBIRTH 289
DENTIST 290
OPTICIAN 292
COUNSELLING 293
DRUG & ALCOHOL ABUSE 294
SEXUALLY-TRANSMITTED DISEASES 295
BIRTHS & DEATHS 296

13. INSURANCE 299

INSURANCE COMPANIES 301
INSURANCE CONTRACTS 303
SOCIAL SECURITY 303
NATIONAL INSURANCE 306
PENSIONS 308
ACCIDENT INSURANCE 313
PERMANENT HEALTH INSURANCE 314
HEALTH INSURANCE 315
DENTAL INSURANCE 318
LONG-TERM CARE INSURANCE 318
BUILDINGS INSURANCE 319
HOME-CONTENTS INSURANCE 321
PERSONAL LIABILITY INSURANCE 323
HOLIDAY & TRAVEL INSURANCE 323
MOTOR BREAKDOWN INSURANCE. 325
CAR INSURANCE 325

14. FINANCE 327

BRITISH CURRENCY 329
FOREIGN CURRENCY 330
CREDIT RATING 331
BANKS 332
BUILDING SOCIETIES 333
SAVINGS ACCOUNTS 336
CASH & DEBIT CARDS 338
CHARGE & CREDIT CARDS 340
OVERDRAFTS 343
LOANS 343
MORTGAGES 345
COUNCIL TAX 350
VALUE ADDED TAX (VAT) 351
INCOME TAX 352
CAPITAL GAINS TAX 362
INHERITANCE TAX 363
WILLS 364
COST OF LIVING 366

15. LEISURE 369

TOURIST INFORMATION 371
HOTELS 372
BED & BREAKFAST 374
SELF-CATERING 375
YOUTH HOSTELS 376
CARAVANS & CAMPING 378
MUSEUMS & ART GALLERIES 378
GARDENS, STATELY HOMES, PARKS & ZOOS 379
CINEMAS 380
THEATRE, OPERA & BALLET 381
CONCERTS 383
SOCIAL CLUBS 385
DISCOTHEQUES & NIGHTCLUBS 385
GAMBLING 386
PUBS 388
RESTAURANTS & CAFÉS 390
LIBRARIES 393

16. SPORTS 395

SPORTS & LEISURE CENTRES 397
SOCCER 398
RUGBY 400
CRICKET 401
SNOOKER & BILLIARDS 402
MOTORSPORTS 402
SKIING 403
CYCLING 403
HIKING 405
MOUNTAINEERING, ROCK-CLIMBING & CAVING 406
RACQUET SPORTS 407
SWIMMING 409
WATERSPORTS 410
AERIAL SPORTS 411
FISHING 412
GOLF 413
GYMNASIUMS & HEALTH CLUBS 414
MISCELLANEOUS SPORTS 415

17. SHOPPING 419

COMPETITION 422
SHOPPING HOURS 423
SHOPPING CENTRES & MARKETS 423
FOOD & SUPERMARKETS 424
DEPARTMENT & CHAIN STORES 427
CLOTHES 428
NEWSPAPERS & BOOKS 429
FURNITURE 431
HOUSEHOLD APPLIANCES 432
SECONDHAND BARGAINS 432
HOME SHOPPING 433
SHOPPING ABROAD 435
DUTY-FREE ALLOWANCES 436
THE CONSUMERS' ASSOCIATION 437

18. ODDS & ENDS 439

BRITISH CITIZENSHIP 440
CLIMATE 441
CRIME 442
GEOGRAPHY 444
GOVERNMENT 444
LEGAL SYSTEM 448
MARRIAGE & DIVORCE 451
MILITARY SERVICE 452
THE MONARCHY 453
PETS 454
POLICE 457
POPULATION 458
RELIGION 459
SOCIAL CUSTOMS 460
TIME DIFFERENCE 461
TIPPING 462
TOILETS 463

19. THE BRITISH 465

20. MOVING HOUSE OR LEAVING BRITAIN 477

MOVING HOUSE   478
LEAVING BRITAIN   479

APPENDICES   483

APPENDIX A: USEFUL ADDRESSES   484
APPENDIX B: FURTHER READING   490
APPENDIX C: WEIGHTS & MEASURES   492
APPENDIX D: MAP OF BRITAIN   496
APPENDIX E: SERVICE DIRECTORY   498

INDEX   499

SUGGESTIONS   509

ORDER FORM   512

AUTHOR'S NOTES

- The term Britain, as used in this book, embraces Great Britain (the island comprising England, Wales and Scotland) and Northern Ireland. Its official name is the United Kingdom (UK) of Great Britain and Northern Ireland. Northern Ireland is the former province of Ulster which remained part of the UK when the Irish Free State was established in 1921. The British Isles is the geographical term for the group of islands which includes Great Britain, Ireland and many smaller islands surrounding Britain. When referring to the Irish Republic (Eire) I have used the name Ireland. Although Britain is officially referred to as the United Kingdom, I have generally kept to the shorter term Britain except when using official names or titles.

- I have attempted to be specific regarding information applying to Britain as a whole and things that apply to England, Wales, Scotland or Northern Ireland only. I apologise in advance to those whom I have offended by including them under the banner of Britain when I should have been more specific.

- Frequent references are made in this book to the European Union (EU), which comprises Austria, Belgium, Denmark, Finland, France, Germany, Greece, Ireland, Italy, Luxembourg, the Netherlands, Portugal, Spain, Sweden and the United Kingdom, and the European Economic Area (EEA), which includes the EU countries plus Iceland, Liechtenstein and Norway.

- All times are shown using the continental 24-hour clock, e.g. 10 a.m. is shown as 1000 and 10 p.m. is shown as 2200 (see also **Time Difference** on page 461).

- Unless otherwise stated, all prices quoted usually include VAT at 17.5 per cent. Prices should be taken as estimates only, although they were mostly correct at the time of publication.

- His/he/him also means her/she/her (please forgive me ladies). This is done to make life easier for both the reader and (in particular) the author, and *isn't* intended to be sexist.

- All spelling is (or should be) English and not American.

- Warnings and important points are shown in **bold** type.

- Lists of Useful Addresses and Further Reading are contained in **Appendices A** and **B** respectively.

- For those unfamiliar with the Imperial system of weights and measures, metric conversion tables are included in **Appendix C**.

- A map of Britain (showing the counties) is included in **Appendix D**.

- A **Service Directory** containing the names, addresses, telephone and fax numbers of companies and organisations doing business in Britain is contained in **Appendix E**.

INTRODUCTION

Whether you're already living or working in Britain or just thinking about it – this is **THE BOOK** for you. Forget about all those glossy guide books, excellent though they are for tourists, this amazing book was written especially with you in mind and is worth its weight in bangers (sausages). *Living and Working in Britain* is designed to meet the needs of anyone wishing to know the essentials of British life including immigrants, temporary workers, businessmen, students, retirees, long-stay tourists, holiday home owners and even extra terrestrials. However long your intended stay in Britain, you will find the information contained in this book invaluable.

General information isn't difficult to find in Britain and a multitude of books are published on every conceivable subject. However, reliable and up-to-date information specifically intended for foreigners *Living and Working in Britain*, isn't so easy to find, least of all in one volume. My aim in writing this book was to help fill this void and provide the comprehensive *practical* information necessary for a relatively trouble-free life. You may have visited Britain as a tourist, but living and working there's a different matter altogether. Adjusting to a different environment and culture and making a home in any foreign country can be a traumatic and stressful experience, and for most people, Britain is no exception.

You need to adapt to new customs and traditions, and discover the British way of doing things, for example finding a home, paying bills and obtaining insurance. For most foreigners in Britain, finding out how to overcome the everyday obstacles of life has previously been a case of pot luck. **But no more!** With a copy of *Living and Working in Britain* to hand you will have a wealth of information at your fingertips. Information derived from a variety of sources, both official and unofficial, not least the hard won personal experiences of the author, his family, friends, colleagues and acquaintances. *Living and Working in Britain* is a comprehensive handbook on a wide range of everyday subjects and represents the most up-to-date source of general information available to foreigners in Britain. It isn't, however, simply a monologue of dry facts and figures, but a practical and entertaining look at life in Britain.

Adapting to life in a new country is a continuous process and although this book will help reduce your beginner's phase and minimise the frustrations, it doesn't contain all the answers (most of us don't even know the right questions!). What it *will* do is help you make informed decisions and calculated judgments, instead of uneducated guesses and costly mistakes. **Most important of all it will help you save time, trouble and money, and repay your investment many times over.**

Although you may find some of the information a bit daunting, don't be discouraged. Most problems occur once only and fade into insignificance after a short time (as you face the next half a dozen!). The majority of foreigners in Britain would agree that, all things considered, they relish living there. A period spent in Britain is a wonderful way to enrich your life, broaden your horizons and hopefully please your bank manager. I trust this book will help you avoid the pitfalls of life in Britain and smooth your way to a happy and rewarding future in your new home.

Good luck!

David Hampshire
April 1999

1.

FINDING A JOB

Finding a job in Britain isn't always as difficult as the unemployment figures may suggest, particularly for qualified and experienced people seeking work in the major cities. In fact, many Europeans find that the opportunities in Britain far outweigh those in their home countries. However, if you don't automatically qualify to live or work in Britain, for example by birthright or as a national of a European Union (EU) or European Economic Area (EEA) country (see page 22), obtaining a permit is usually more difficult than finding a job.

Immigration: Britain is a small country with a relatively large population, high unemployment among the young and middle-aged, and an expensive social security (welfare) system, all of which make immigration something of a sensitive issue. Consequently the government has greatly reduced the number of non-EU foreigners allowed to settle in Britain over the last few decades. However, foreigners are to be found in Britain in large numbers in almost every walk of life. There are large ethnic groups from a number of commonwealth countries and a sizeable number of foreigners from most EU countries, North America and other countries, together totalling some 3.5 million. The total workforce in Britain is around 25 million people (including 6 million part-time workers), of whom 55 per cent are men.

Employment Prospects: You shouldn't plan on obtaining employment in Britain unless you have a firm job offer, special qualifications and/or experience for which there's a strong demand. If you want a good job, you must usually be well qualified and speak fluent English. If you plan to arrive in Britain without a job, you should have a detailed plan for finding employment on arrival and try to make some contacts before you arrive. It's difficult to find work in rural areas and it isn't easy in cities and large towns unless you have skills or experience that are in demand. Many people turn to self-employment or starting a business to make a living, although this path is strewn with pitfalls for the newcomer.

Before moving to Britain to work, you should dispassionately examine your motives and credentials. What kind of work can you realistically expect to do? What are your qualifications and experience? Are they recognised in Britain? How good is your English? Are there any jobs in your profession or trade in the area where you wish to live? Could you work as self-employed or start your own business? The answers to these and many other questions can be quite disheartening, but it's better to ask them *before* moving to Britain than afterwards.

Unemployment: While still unacceptably high, Britain's unemployment rate of around 6 per cent in early 1999 was lower than most other EU countries. However, some analysts claim the real 'unemployment' figure is much higher when the 'economically inactive' are included in the jobless numbers. Unemployment varies from region to region and is much higher than the national average in some regions, particularly in areas where the emphasis has been on traditional manufacturing, employing semi-skilled or unskilled workers. These regions include parts of northern England, Scotland, Wales, Northern Ireland and the inner cities, where there's a significant number of long-term, middle-aged unemployed.

During the last decade, employees have been hit by a combination of recession and 'restructuring', as many companies slashed their workforces in order to become 'lean and mean' and compete more effectively. An ominous sign in recent years has been the export of service jobs to third world countries by some companies, which, if it catches on, could lead to massive job losses. During the recession companies quickly realised that they could operate with smaller workforces and today Britain's largest employers are continually reducing their workforces. Manufacturing has been in turmoil in the last few years during which it has been hard hit by the high value of the pound, relatively high interest rates and a slump in Asia and other overseas markets. It also suffers from low investment, lack of skills, intense global competition and a lack of strategy for the future. An estimated 500,000 manufacturing jobs are set to be lost in the next few years (according to a forecast based on Treasury statistics) and even once bullet-proof industries are feeling the pinch and slashing their workforces.

Unemployment is no respecter of age or experience and managers in their 40s and 50s who are made redundant are finding it increasingly difficult to find jobs. Many secure professions such as banking, insurance and the civil service no longer offer 'jobs for life'. Nobody is immune from unemployment – accountants, bankers, computer experts, doctors – all have felt the chill wind of unemployment in recent years. For today's manager, job security comes from having saleable skills (constantly updated with further education and training) and a portable pension to go with them.

Age Discrimination: Many senior employees in their 40s and 50s who lose their jobs are lucky to find new employment. In today's job market, too old to work begins around 45 in some professions and the 'rubicon' employment age has fallen from 50 to something like 38. In today's competitive world you can even be too old for some jobs before you reach your 30s, particularly if you're a mature student (many companies have an age limit of around 25 for graduate trainees). There's also a bleak outlook for youth unemployment, with unemployment among 16 to 24-year-olds running at around 15 per cent. Young working-class males are in crisis when it comes to finding employment and there are four times more unemployed men between the age of 18 to 24 than women. Many youths have no job prospects whatsoever and an increasing number are turning to crime as a 'career'. Companies are swamped with an average of 100 applications for each place on their graduate schemes and many graduates are forced to take menial jobs. Around a quarter are still unemployed six months after graduation and many are forced to take jobs without pay to gain experience.

Changing Workforce: The jobs lost in the last decade were generally well-paid skilled and semi-skilled manufacturing jobs, which have largely been replaced by poor quality, low-paid jobs or part-time and temporary jobs with few or no benefits. Employment experts believe that the era of secure full-time employment with comprehensive employee benefits and lifetime guarantees has gone forever. This trend is supported by the increasing number of full-time jobs that have been replaced by part-time (mostly for women), freelance and contract labour at lower wages and with no benefits (some 500,000 managers and professionals work part-time or on contract). Only around a third of employees have the security of a full-time job (down from 55 per cent in 1975), while a further third survive in the twilight world of contracts and casual work.

Education & Training: The inability of British schools and training centres to provide the skilled workforce necessary for today's marketplace is an increasing concern among employers. Britain currently has one of the least educated and most poorly trained workforces in the western world. The lack of qualified and trained staff bodes ill for Britain's future in an increasingly high-tech world and in the face of fierce international competition. Many experts believe Britain's future, like that of most western countries, is as a high-skilled, high-productivity economy, leaving labour-intensive tasks to the fast-growing population of the developing world. Britain still produces far too much 'industrial cannon fodder' rather than the technicians and engineers necessary for the international trade war now being fought from computer terminals.

Working Hours: Although the British don't have a reputation for hard work abroad, many Britons are workaholics, particularly among the managerial and professional classes, and most Britons see themselves as hard-working. British employees work the longest average hours in the European Union and 12-hour days and work-filled evenings aren't uncommon. Redundancies and cost-cutting have increased the pressure on employees, particularly on white-collar workers, many of whom now do the work of two or more people. Stress due to overwork is an increasingly common complaint and accounts for the loss of around two million working days a year.

Commuting: Britain is a nation of commuters and it's nothing for people to commute 80 to 160km (50 or 100mi) or even further by car, train or bus to work and back each day, although this is becoming increasingly difficult on Britain's clogged roads and overcrowded railways. People living in rural areas travel an average 40 per cent further to work than city-dwellers. Commuting is, however, expected to reduce considerably by the new millennium, when there's expected to be a huge increase in the number of people tele-working (working from home via telephone, modem, fax and computer). Nowhere will this be more welcomed than in the City of London, with its chronic rush-hour problems and general poor quality of life. Some 25 per cent of full-time employees currently work from home at least some of the time and this is expected to rise to at least a third in the next few years.

Industrial Relations: There has been a huge reduction in strikes in the last decade, which are now rare, particularly in the private sector (what few strikes there are occur in the public service). Anti-union legislation brought in by the Conservative government in the '80s actually helped strengthen the trade union movement, which is now a model of democracy. Unions must ballot members before undertaking industrial action and have grown in popularity since they ditched their confrontational stance with employers. High unemployment has also been a boon to employers and has discouraged employees from striking.

Further Reading: There are numerous books written for those seeking a job in Britain including *Get That Job* (Bay Books), *Finding the Right Job* by Anne Segull and William Grierson (BBC), *The Job Search Manual* by Lina Aspey (Management Books 2000) and *How to Find the Perfect Job* by Tom Jackson (Piatkus). There are also numerous magazines and newspapers, many of which are dedicated to particular professions, industries or trades.

Britain and the European Union

Nationals of all European Economic Area (EEA) countries (Iceland, Liechtenstein and Norway plus the European Union members which comprise Austria, Belgium, Denmark, Finland, France, Germany, Greece, Ireland, Italy, Luxembourg, the Netherlands, Portugal, Spain, Sweden and the United Kingdom) have the right to enter, live and work in Britain or any other member state without a work permit, providing they have a valid passport or national identity card and comply with the member state's laws and regulations on employment.

EEA Nationals are entitled to the same treatment as British subjects in matters of pay, working conditions, access to housing, vocational training, social security and trade union rights, and immediate dependants are entitled to join them and enjoy the same rights. EU legislation is designed to make it easier for people to meet vocational training requirements in other member states. There are, however, still practical barriers to full freedom of movement and the right to work within the EU, for example some jobs in various member countries require job applicants to have specific skills or vocational qualifications, and qualifications obtained in some member states aren't recognised in others. Other more practical barriers include housing availability and cost, and the transfer of pension rights. There are also restrictions on employment in the civil service, when the right to work may be limited in individual cases on the grounds of public policy, security or public health.

In the last ten years there has been a huge gulf between the British government and many other EU states on a wide range of issues, as the British Conservative government went from lukewarm endorsement to open hostility to closer European monetary and political union. Britain has always been a somewhat reluctant member of the EU and originally pinned its future on the now defunct European Free Trade Association (EFTA), the Commonwealth and its 'special relationship' with the US – anything except Europe where logic has always dictated its future lay. Fears of loss of 'sovereignty' were voiced by members of the government and others and served to influence many Britons against the closer integration of Europe (except for the young, who are generally enthusiastic).

Britain chose to remain outside the Euro currency (€) group of 11 countries (Austria, Belgium, Finland, France, Germany, Ireland, Italy, Luxembourg, the Netherlands, Portugal and Spain) along with Denmark and Sweden (Greece didn't qualify) when the Euro was launched in January 1999. However, since the election of a more pro-European Labour government in 1997, Britain's relations with its EU partners has improved and it looks increasingly likely that it will join the Euro around 2002 after a referendum.

QUALIFICATIONS

The most important qualification for working in Britain is the ability to speak English fluently (see page 39). Once you have overcome this hurdle you should establish whether your trade or professional qualifications and experience are recognised in Britain. If you aren't experienced, British employers expect studies to be in a relevant discipline and to have included work experience. Professional or trade qualifications are required to work in many fields in Britain, although these aren't as stringent as in other EU countries.

Theoretically, any qualifications recognised by professional and trade bodies in one EU country should be recognised in Britain. However, recognition varies from country to country and in some cases foreign qualifications aren't recognised by British employers or professional and trade associations. All academic qualifications should also be recognised, although they may be given less prominence than equivalent British qualifications, depending on the country and the educational establishment. A ruling by the European Court declared that when examinations are of a similar standard with just certain areas of difference, then individuals should only be required to take exams in those particular subjects.

All EU member states issue occupation information sheets containing a common job description with a table of qualifications, which are published in the various languages of the member states. These cover a large number of trades and professions and are intended to help someone with the relevant qualifications look for a job in another EU country. In many jobs and trades, member states are already required to recognise qualifications and experience obtained elsewhere in the EU. To obtain a comparison of British qualifications and those recognised in other EU countries contact the Qualifications and ITOs Branch, Department of Education and Employment, Moorfoot, Sheffield S1 4PQ (☎ 0114-2753275).

EMPLOYMENT SERVICE

The Employment Service is an executive agency of the Department of Education and Employment and its job is to provide help for those who have been unemployed for over six months and other unemployed people who require help, such as the disabled or disadvantaged. It's also responsible for paying Jobseeker's ('unemployment') Benefit to the unemployed, through unemployment benefit offices. The Employment Service has two main methods of assisting the unemployed: by placing people directly in jobs and by offering guidance and counselling so that people can find the best way to return to employment, e.g. through education or training. The Employment Service operates Jobcentres (see below), where jobs and training courses are advertised, and provides a number of programmes and training initiatives to help the unemployed find jobs.

These include a Back to Work Bonus, Employment on Trial, Jobclubs, Jobfinder's Grant, Jobmatch and the New Deal scheme introduced in 1998. The New Deal programme provides advice, support, training and direct work experience for youths aged 18 to 24 and those aged 25 or over who have been claiming Jobseeker's Allowance for two years or more. It's open to all EU nationals and non-British applicants are estimated to comprise some 10 per cent of the total. Information can be obtained from Jobcentres (☎ 0645-606 2626, Internet: www.newdeal.gov.uk). The Employment Service publishes a wide range of publications that are available from Jobcentres.

European Employment Service: The Employment Service is also responsible for SEDOC in Britain, which is the European system of exchange of applications and vacancies for work overseas. Under SEDOC the employment services in each member state exchange information on job vacancies on a monthly basis. Members include most EU countries and Norway, although applicants from non-EU countries need a work permit to work in Britain and other EU countries (as do EU nationals to work in non-EU countries).

Details are available in all local Employment Service offices in each country, where advice on how to apply for jobs is available. All Employment Service offices have access to overseas vacancies held on the National Vacancy Computer System (NATVACS) and the Oracle Jobfinder service. Applicants are required to complete two ES13 application forms, either in response to advertised vacancies or to make a general application, which is valid for six months. Overseas applicants seeking a job in Britain can make a direct application to the Employment Service in Britain, through their local employment service or by applying directly to the Department of Education and Employment, The Overseas Placing Unit, 4th Floor, Skills House, 3/7 Holy Green, Sheffield S1 4AQ.

JOBCENTRES

Jobcentres (written as one word) are government offices where local companies advertise for employees and where the unemployed can obtain information about government employment and training schemes. The vast majority of jobs advertised in Jobcentres are manual or low paid and they don't usually include managerial or professional positions (or jobs for 16 to 18-year-olds which are advertised in careers' centres). Jobs are displayed on boards under headings such as building, clerical, domestic, drivers, engineering, factory, hairdressing, hotel and catering, industrial, motor trade, nursing, office, receptionists, temporary, shops and latest vacancies (where new vacancies are initially posted).

Jobcentres are generally self-service, although staff are on hand to provide advice and help when required. If you find a job which is of interest, write down the reference number and take it to one of the staff, who will tell you more about the job and arrange an interview if required. You can register with a Jobcentre by completing a card and providing details of the kind of job you're looking for. If the Jobcentre doesn't deal with your profession or industry, they should be able to tell you about other sources of information. When a job comes in that matches your requirements, you will be informed. However, don't rely on this method but check the boards regularly, as new jobs are displayed each morning and good jobs don't remain vacant for long. You can usually check on new vacancies by telephone. Many cities have their own employment centres or 'job shops', where jobs with the local city or borough council are advertised.

RECRUITMENT CONSULTANTS

Private recruitment consultants (or head-hunters) and employment agencies abound in all major cities and towns in Britain (in London they outnumber pubs), and are big business. Most large companies are happy to engage consultants to recruit staff, particularly executives (head-hunters account for around two-thirds of all top level executive appointments in Britain), managers, professional employees and temporary office staff (temps). Most agencies specialise in particular fields or positions, e.g. computer personnel, accounting, executives and managers, sales staff, secretarial and office staff, catering, engineering and technical, nursing, industrial recruitment and construction, while others deal with a range of industries and professions. Some agencies deal exclusively with temporary workers such as office staff, baby-sitting, home care, nannies and mothers' helps, housekeeping, cooks, gardeners, chauffeurs, hairdressing, security, cleaners, labourers and industrial workers. Nursing agencies are also fairly common (covering the whole range of nursing services including physiotherapy, occupational and speech therapy and dentistry), as are nanny and care agencies.

Agencies, which must be licensed by local councils, don't usually charge employees a fee, but receive a fee of from one to four months salary from employers, plus a flat fee in many cases. Some agencies act as employers, hiring workers and contracting them out to companies at a hourly rate. Employees are paid an hourly rate, which may include paid public and annual holidays after a qualifying period. Agencies must deduct PAYE income tax (see page 355) and National Insurance contributions (see page 306) if employees don't have their own limited company. Many agencies also employ freelance staff on a contract basis, e.g. accountants, computer personnel, nurses, technical authors, draughtspersons and engineers (see **Contract Jobs** below).

Employment agencies make a lot of money from finding people jobs, so providing you have something to offer, they'll be keen to help you (if you're a computer expert, you may get trampled in the rush to find you a job). If they cannot help you, they'll usually tell you immediately and won't waste your time. A list of agencies specialising in particular trades or professions is available from the Federation of Recruitment and Employment Services, 36-38 Mortimer Street, London W1N 7RB (☎ 0171-323 4300). To find your local agencies look in the Yellow Pages under 'Employment Agencies'. Many local newspapers have an 'Employment Agency Directory'. Jobs are also advertised on TV teletext and via the Internet.

CONTRACT JOBS

Contract or freelance jobs are available through many employment agencies in Britain that specialise in providing workers for companies for a limited period. Many contract positions are for specialists in a wide range of fields including accountancy, computing, engineering and electronics, although there's also a strong market in providing cleaning, catering, maintenance and manual workers. Rates vary considerably, e.g. from £5 an hour for clerks up to £50 an hour or more for an exceptional computer specialist. Contract work may entail sub-contracting through a contract company or working directly for a particular company.

Contractors may work at home or on a client's or contract company's premises. Sub-contractors in the building industry require a special permit in order to be classed as self-employed. The potential for home-based work in Britain is huge, particularly within the computer industry, which is keen to exploit the number of computer professionals (particularly women) wishing to work part-time from home. There are many newspapers and magazines for contractors such as *Freelance Informer* and *Computer Contractor* (jobs are also advertised on the Internet).

Many employment agencies in Britain specialise in supplying contract staff to major companies, many of whom contract out non-core support work from cleaning to computing, rather than hire full-time employees. Employees of most British consultant companies are permanent company employees, although they often work full-time for another company on a contract basis. Contract workers who wish to be self-employed must have a limited company (the most common choice for long-term contractors), otherwise PAYE tax (see page 355) and National Insurance contributions (see page 306) must be deducted from payments by their employer, e.g. an employment agency. When necessary, agents may provide computer training for qualified applicants.

Non-EU employees of foreign companies who are living and working in Britain temporarily require a work permit (if applicable), which must be obtained by their British employer (unless employment is for a brief period only). However, many British companies avoid the need for work permits (and save money) by contracting computer programming and other information technology jobs to overseas companies (e.g. in Eastern Europe and Asia) where labour is much cheaper.

PART-TIME JOBS

Part-time jobs are available in most industries and professions and are common in offices, pubs, shops, factories, cafes and restaurants. Many young foreigners combine part-time work and study, for example improving their English or studying for a trade or professional qualification. Most part-time workers are poorly paid and rates were previously often well below the minimum wage of £3.60 an hour (£3 for those under 22), which is the least you should now receive. Part-time employees, officially classified as those working less than 16 hours a week, also have little protection from exploitation by employers, although some employers give part-time employees the same rights as full-time employees. Some companies operate a job share scheme, where two or more people share the same job. Many jobs listed below under **Temporary & Casual Work** are also available on a permanent part-time basis. See also **Recruitment Consultants** on page 25.

TEMPORARY & CASUAL JOBS

Temporary and casual jobs differ from part-time jobs in that jobs are usually for a fixed period only, e.g. from a few hours to a few months, or work may be intermittent. People employed in temporary, seasonal and casual jobs comprise around 5 per cent of the workforce. Some 65 per cent of British companies use temporary staff at some time, mostly in the summer when permanent staff are on holiday, and usually in clerical positions. Employers usually require your national insurance number (see page 306) and sometimes a P45 tax form (see page 356). For information regarding your legal obligations, contact your local Inland Revenue or Department of Social Security (DSS) office. Many employers illegally pay temporary staff in cash without making any deductions for tax or national insurance (see **Working Illegally** on page 38).

Casual workers are often employed on a daily, first come, first served basis. The work often entails heavy labouring and is therefore intended mostly for men, although if you're a female weightlifter there's no bar against the fairer sex. Pay for casual work is usually low and is almost always paid cash in hand. Temporary and casual work includes the following:

- Office work, which is usually well paid if you're qualified and the easiest work to find due to the large number of secretarial and office staff agencies.

- Work in the building trade, which can be found through industrial employment agencies and by applying direct to builders and building sites.

- Jobs at exhibitions and shows, including setting up stands, catering (waitresses and bar staff) and loading and unloading jobs.

- Jobs in shops and stores over Christmas and during sales' periods.

- Christmas jobs for the post office.

- Gardening jobs, both in private gardens and in public parks for local councils. Jobs may be advertised in local newspapers, on bulletin boards and in magazines. Local landscape gardeners and garden centres are also often on the lookout for extra staff, particularly in spring and summer.

- Market research, which entails asking people personal questions, either in the street or house to house (ideal job for nosy parkers).

- Modelling at art colleges; both sexes are usually required and not *just* the body beautiful.

- Security work offering long hours for low pay.

- Nursing and auxiliary nursing staff in hospitals, clinics and nursing homes (who are usually employed through nursing agencies to replace permanent staff at short notice).

- Newspaper and magazine distribution.

- Courier work (own transport required, e.g. motorcycle, car or van).

- Labouring jobs in markets.

- Driving jobs, including coach and HGV (truck) drivers, and ferrying cars for manufacturers and car hire companies.

- Miscellaneous jobs as cleaners, baby-sitters and labourers, are available from a number of agencies specialising in temporary work, e.g. Industrial Overload and Manpower.

Temporary jobs are also advertised in Jobcentres (see page 25). See also **Recruitment Consultants** on page 25.

HOLIDAY & SHORT-TERM JOBS

Holiday and short-term jobs are provided by numerous organisations in Britain, ranging from a few weeks up to six months. Before coming (or arranging to come) to Britain for a working holiday or short term job, it's essential that you check that you're eligible and will be permitted to enter Britain under the existing immigration and employment regulations (see **Chapter 3**). You may be required to obtain a work permit and/or entry clearance (see page 65). You should check the documentation required with a British Diplomatic Post in your home country well in advance of your visit. If you plan to study full-time in Britain and to work during your holidays, you don't require a work permit, but must first obtain permission from the Department of Education and Employment through your local Jobcentre (see page 25). You must also provide satisfactory evidence from your college, polytechnic or university that the employment won't interfere with your studies.

The Central Bureau for Educational Visits & Exchanges (c/o British Council, 10 Spring Gardens, London SW1A 2BN, ☎ 0171-389 4383) is the national office responsible for providing information and advice on all forms of educational visits and exchanges. They publish a number of books including *Working Holidays*, an annual guide to job opportunities in over 100 countries, which is recommended reading for anyone seeking a holiday job in Britain. Students from North America can consult the Council of International Educational Exchange (CIEE), 205 East 42nd Street, New York, NY 10017 (who represent the Central Bureau in North America), regarding temporary jobs in Britain. The following organisations can also help you find holiday and short-term jobs in Britain:

Student Exchange Employment Programme (SEEP) is a reciprocal scheme allowing British students to work in the USA for four months during the summer and

American students to work in Britain for up to six months at any time of the year. In the USA contact CIEE (see address above). The programme is administered in Britain by the British Universities North America Club (BUNAC), 16 Bowling Green Lane, London EC1R 0QH (☎ 0171-251 3472), who organise jobs in both Canada and the USA.

Vacation Work (9 Park End Street, Oxford OX1 1HJ, ☎ 01865-241978) publish *Vacation Traineeships for Students*, an annual guide to short-term opportunities for students, sixth formers and school leavers interested in obtaining work experience or training during their vacation period. Another Vacation Work publication is the *Directory of Summer Jobs in Britain*, which lists job opportunities throughout Britain, including the salary, hours, conditions and the qualifications necessary.

Central Services Unit (Crawford House, Precinct Centre, Manchester M13 9EP) publish *Vac Work* containing details of vacation work and sandwich placements (the British eat a lot of sandwiches), training and other kinds of employment for undergraduates during their vacations. The main list is published in January and supplements are produced throughout the year.

Many other holiday jobs (as opposed to voluntary jobs) are available in a range of occupations including couriers and representatives (e.g. in holiday camps), domestic staff in hotels, farmhands, supervisors and sports instructors, teachers, youth leaders, secretaries, nurses and shop assistants. A wide range of contacts for these and other jobs are listed in *Working Holidays* mentioned above.

VOLUNTARY WORK

The minimum age limit for voluntary work in Britain is between 16 and 18 and most organisations require good or fluent English to be spoken. No special qualifications are usually required and the minimum length of service varies from around one month to one year (often there's no maximum length of service). Handicapped volunteers are also welcomed by many organisations. Voluntary work is unpaid, although meals and accommodation are usually provided and some also pay pocket money. This may be insufficient for your out-of-pocket living expenses (entertainment, drinks, etc.), so you should ensure that you bring enough money with you.

It's essential that before coming to Britain for any kind of voluntary work, you check whether you're eligible and whether you will be permitted to enter Britain under the immigration and employment regulations. You may be required to obtain a visa or other entry clearance (see **Chapter 3**), so check what documentation is required with a British Diplomatic Post in your home country well in advance of your planned visit. The usual visa regulations apply to voluntary workers and your passport must be valid for at least one year. For temporary employment in international workcamps, farm camps, other voluntary jobs and au pair positions (see page 37), a work permit isn't usually required, but a letter of invitation from the voluntary organisation or your employer must be produced. This letter doesn't provide entitlement to any other kind of paid work in Britain.

International workcamps provide the opportunity for people from Britain and many other countries to live and work together on a range of projects including building, conservation, gardening and community projects. Camps are usually run for periods of two to four weeks between April and October. Normally workers are required to work for six to seven hours a day, five or six days a week. The work is usually quite physically demanding and accommodation, which is shared with fellow slaves, is normally fairly basic. Most workcamps consist of 10 to 30 volunteers from several countries and English is generally the common language. Volunteers are usually required to pay a registration fee, pay for their own travel to and from the workcamp, and may also be expected to contribute towards the cost of their board and lodging. An application to join a workcamp should be made through the appropriate recruiting agency in your home country.

Information about volunteering can be obtained from the National Association of Volunteer Bureaux, New Oxford House, 16 Waterloo Street, Birmingham B2 5UG (☎ 0121-633 4555) and the National Centre for Volunteering, Regents Wharf, All Saints Street, London N1 8RL (☎ 0171-520 8900). There are a number of books for volunteers in Britain including *Working Holidays* and *Volunteer Work* published by the Central Bureau for Educational Visits & Exchanges (see address on page 28). The National Youth Agency (17-23 Albion Street, Leicester LE1 6GD, ☎ 0116-285 6789) publish *A Guide to Voluntary Work Opportunities*, *Sparetime Sharetime*, *Workcamps? Why Bother?* and the *Volunteer Express*. The *International Directory of Voluntary Work* (Vacation Work) is a guide to 400 agencies and sources of information on short to long-term voluntary work in Britain and worldwide.

WORKING WOMEN

Women make up around 45 per cent of the workforce in Britain, including 85 per cent (some 4.5m) of part-time employees. A woman doing the same or broadly similar work to a man in Britain and employed by the same employer, is legally entitled to the same salary and other terms of employment. As in most western countries, although there's no *official* discrimination, in practice this often isn't the case. On average women earn 20 per cent less than men, although the pay gap between the sexes is narrowing, particularly in senior positions. In recent years employers have been trying harder to retain their female staff and many are setting up crèches and even 'granny' crèches (for parents) to discourage employees from leaving.

Although women are breaking into the professions and the boardroom in ever-increasing numbers, they often find it difficult to reach the top, where the old-boy network thrives. The main discrimination among women executives and professionals isn't in salary or title, but in promotion opportunities, as many companies and organisations are loathe to elevate women to important positions (partly due to fears that they may leave and start a family). This invisible barrier is known as the 'glass ceiling'. Although 'the best man for the job is often a woman', this isn't always acknowledged by employers, many of whom still prefer the standard male candidate aged between 28 and 38.

Job Clubs (organised by Jobcentres) provide help for unemployed women to secure jobs and training opportunities, become self-employed or gain access to higher education. A leaflet entitled *Employment Training for Women* is published by the Employment Service and available from Jobcentres. Self-employment among women in Britain has increased steadily during the last decade (around 30 per cent of new companies are started by women), particularly among black and Asian women, despite the fact that banks and other financial institutions are reluctant to provide finance.

JOB HUNTING

When looking for a job in Britain, it's advisable not to put all your eggs in one basket as the more job applications you make, the better your chances of finding the right job. Contact as many prospective employers as possible, either by writing, telephoning or calling on them in person. Whatever job you're looking for, it's important to market yourself correctly and appropriately, which depends on the type of job you're after. For example, the recruitment of executives and senior managers is handled almost exclusively by consultants, who advertise in the British quality national press (and also abroad) and interview all applicants prior to presenting clients with a shortlist. At the other end of the scale, manual jobs requiring no previous experience may be advertised at Jobcentres, in local newspapers and in shop windows, and the first suitable able-bodied applicant may be offered the job on the spot.

When writing for a job, address your letter to the personnel director or manager and include your curriculum vitae (CV), and copies of all references and qualifications. Note, however, that writing for jobs from abroad is often a hit and miss business and it's probably the least successful method of securing employment. If you're applying from abroad, it's advisable to tell prospective employers when you're available for interview and to arrange as many interviews as you can fit into the time available. Your method of job hunting will depend on your particular circumstances, qualifications and experience and the sort of job you're looking for, and may include the following:

- Visiting a local Jobcentre in Britain (see page 25). This is mainly for non-professional skilled and unskilled jobs, particularly in industry, retailing and catering.

- Checking the TV teletext job service and the Internet and other bulletin boards. The Internet has hundreds of sites (such as taps.com and topjobs.net) for jobseekers including corporate websites, recruitment companies and newspaper job advertisements (you can use a search engine to find them). An estimated 1.5 million people use the Internet for recruitment purposes.

- Contacting private recruitment consultants and employment agencies (see page 25).

- Obtaining copies of British daily newspapers, most of which have 'positions vacant' sections on certain days. The quality daily and Sunday newspapers (see page 429) all contain 'vacancies' sections for executive and professional employees, and also have job advertisements dedicated to particular industries or professions, e.g. the computer industry, teaching and the media. Most local and national newspapers are available in the reading rooms of local libraries in Britain, so you don't need to buy them. Jobs are also advertised in industry and trade newspapers and magazines. British newspapers are also available abroad from international news agencies, trade and commercial centres, expatriate organisations and social clubs (although they don't always contain the 'appointments' or 'situations vacant' sections).

- Applying to international and national recruiting agencies acting for British companies. These companies chiefly recruit executives and key managerial and technical staff, and many have offices worldwide and throughout Britain.

- Applying to foreign multinational companies with offices or subsidiaries in Britain and making written applications directly to British companies. You can obtain a list of companies working in a particular field from trade directories, such as *Kelly's* and *Kompass*, copies of which are available at reference libraries in Britain (they may also be found at British Chambers of Commerce outside Britain). If you have a professional qualification that's recognised in Britain, you can write to a British professional organisation for information and advice (addresses are obtainable from British Chambers of Commerce or British Council offices abroad).

- Putting an advertisement in the 'Situations Wanted' section of a local newspaper in Britain or a newspaper in an area where you would like to work. If you're a member of a recognised profession or trade, you could place an advertisement in a newspaper or magazine dedicated to your profession or industry.

- Networking, basically getting together with like-minded people to discuss business, which is a popular way of making business and professional contacts in Britain. It can be particularly successful for executive, managers and professionals when job hunting.

- Asking relatives, friends or acquaintances working in Britain, if they know of an employer looking for someone with your experience and qualifications.

- Applying in person to British companies (see below).

If you're already in Britain, you can contact or join expatriate social clubs, churches, societies and professional organisations, particularly your country's chamber of commerce. Many good business contacts can be made among expatriate groups.

Personal Applications

Your best chance of obtaining some jobs in Britain is to apply in person, when success is often simply a matter of being in the right place at the right time. When looking for a job it isn't necessarily *what* you know, but *who* you know. Many companies don't advertise but rely on attracting workers by word of mouth and their own vacancy boards. Shops often put vacancy notices in their windows and newsagents may also display job advertisements from employers on a notice board, although these are generally for temporary or part-time help. It's advisable to leave your name and address with a prospective employer, and if possible a telephone number where you can be contacted, particularly if a job may become vacant at a moment's notice. Advertise the fact that you're looking for a job, not only with friends, relatives and acquaintances, but also with anyone you come into contact with who may be able to help. You can give lady luck a helping hand with your persistence and enterprise by:

- cold calling on prospective employers;
- checking wanted boards;
- looking in local newspapers;
- checking notice and bulletin boards in large companies, shopping centres, embassies, clubs, sports centres and newsagents;
- asking other foreign workers.

When leaving a job in Britain it's advisable to ask for a written reference (one isn't usually provided automatically), particularly if you intend to look for further work in Britain or you think your work experience will help you obtain work in another country.

SALARIES

It can be difficult to determine the salary you should command in Britain and getting the right salary for the job is something of a lottery. Salaries can also vary considerably for the same job in different parts of Britain. Those working in London and the south-east are the highest paid, mainly due to the higher cost of living, particularly accommodation (although the disparity between the north and south of England has narrowed in recent years). Usually salaries are negotiable and it's up to each individual to ensure that he receives the level of salary and benefits commensurate with his qualifications and experience (or as much as you can get!). Minimum salaries exist in some trades and professions, but generally it's every man for himself! Salaries in some companies, trades and professions (particularly public sector government employees), are decided by national pay agreements between unions and the government.

Your working hours (see page 49) in Britain may be different from those in other countries and will vary depending on your profession and where you work. Most executive, professionals and 'white-collar' workers (those that don't get their hands dirty), officially work between 35 and 38 hours a week, particularly in London and other major cities. Factory and other 'blue-collar' (manual) workers (those that find it *difficult* to keep their hands clean) usually work from 37.5 to 40 hours a week, while many work much longer hours when overtime is included (although there's now a maximum 48-hour week under EU regulations).

There's usually a huge disparity between the salaries of the lowest and highest paid employees in Britain, which is much wider than in most other European countries. At the bottom end of the scale, some 15 per cent of employees earned less than £3.50 an hour before the minimum wage of £3.60 an hour (£3 an hour for those aged below 22) was introduced on 1st April 1999 (many believe that it's still too low). At the other extreme, executive and managerial salaries have been increasing in leaps and bounds and are now similar or higher than in many other European countries. The average salary of the chief executives of Britain's 100 top companies is over £500,000 a year, plus performance-related bonuses, share options and perks such as chauffeured company cars (corporate 'fat-cat' abuse of salaries and perks is more prevalent in Britain than in any other industrialised country).

Salaries for some professionals' have also soared in recent years, e.g. top commercial lawyers can earn over £1 million a year! In contrast, middle managers in Britain are relatively poorly paid by international standards. In the last decade private sector salaries have increased at a much faster pace than those in the public sector, with which there's a burgeoning pay gap. This has made it increasingly difficult for local authorities to recruit and retain staff and there are thousands of nursing and teacher vacancies throughout the country.

For many employees, particularly company directors and senior managers, their 'salary' is much more than what they receive in their monthly pay packet. Many companies offer a number of benefits (known as perks) for executives (which often continue into retirement) and managers. These may include a free company car (possibly with a chauffeur); free health insurance and health screening; paid holidays; private school fees; cheap or free home loans; rent-free homes; free rail season tickets; free company restaurants; non-contributory company pensions; share options; interest-free loans; free tickets for sports events and shows; free subscriptions to clubs; and 'business' conferences in exotic places (see also **Managerial & Executive Positions** on page 46). The perks of board members in many companies make up almost 50 per cent of total remuneration (to keep it out of the hands of the taxman). In addition, executives often receive huge golden handshakes should they be sacked or resign, which can run into £millions.

SELF-EMPLOYMENT

Anyone who's a British citizen, an EU-national or a permanent resident (see page 64), can work as self-employed in Britain, which includes partnerships, co-operatives, franchise and commission-only jobs or a private business (for the regulations regarding non-EU nationals see **Chapter 3**). Unlike most other EU countries, there are few restrictions and little red tape for anyone wanting to start a business or work as self-employed in Britain. One of the government's main initiatives for reducing the number of unemployed has been to encourage people to start their own businesses.

The number of self-employed has risen dramatically in the last decade and is some 3.5 million (around 15 per cent of the workforce), the highest in the European Union. Much of the reduction in unemployment in recent years has been as a result of self-employment or jobs created by small companies. Redundancy (and the difficulty in finding full-time employment) is often the spur for over 45's to start their own business. Those aged 45 to 55 account for some 20 per cent of new business start-ups (although many are hollow 'consultancies', where professionals eke out a living on commission) and over 20 per cent of all men over 45 are now self-employed. **However, self-employment isn't a panacea for unemployment.** Over half of the self-employed work from home and a further third work in construction or retailing.

Research: For many people, starting a business is one of the quickest routes to bankruptcy known to mankind. In fact, many people who open businesses would be better off investing in lottery tickets – at least they would then have a chance of getting a return on their investment! **Most experts reckon that if you're going to work for yourself you must be prepared to fail.** The key to starting or buying a successful business is exhaustive research, research and yet more research (plus innovation, value for money and service). It's absolutely essential to check out the level of competition in a given area, as a saturation of trades and services is common in many areas.

Finance & Cash Flow: Most people are far too optimistic about the prospects of a new business and over-estimate income levels (it often takes years to make a profit). Be realistic or even pessimistic when estimating your income and overestimate the costs and underestimate the revenue (then reduce it by up to 50 per cent!). While hoping for the best, you should plan for the worst and have sufficient funds to last until you're established. New projects are rarely, if ever, completed within budget. Make sure you have sufficient working capital and that you can survive until a business takes off. British banks are extremely wary of lending to new businesses, especially businesses run by foreigners (would you trust a foreigner?). If you wish to borrow money to buy property or for a business venture in Britain, you should carefully consider where and in what currency to raise finance. Under-capitalisation is one of the main reasons for small business failures, which isn't helped by the routine late payment of bills.

Payment: Late payment of bills is the scourge of small businesses in Britain. The average small firm waits up to 80 days for an invoice to be paid (big companies get paid an average of 35 days earlier), one of the longest periods in the EU. Not surprisingly many small businesses are bankrupted by late payers. Under new legislation, small companies have the right to claim interest on the late payment of bills, although most companies dare not for fear of losing business.

Loans & Overdrafts: British banks are reluctant to lend to small businesses without security and were blamed by many businessmen for prolonging the recession and bankrupting sound businesses by calling in loans and withdrawing overdraft facilities at a moment's notice. British banks probably have the worst record of refusing loans to sound businesses in the western world. During the recession in the '90s, relations between small businesses and banks reached an all-time low and although they have since improved, they are still terrible.

Information & Professional Advice: A wealth of free advice and information for budding entrepreneurs is available from government agencies, local councils and the private sector. Many books are published on self-employment and starting your own business including *Starting Your Own Business* and *Which? Guide to Earning Money From Home*, both published by Which? Books. Libraries are an excellent source of information about starting a business. The Employment Service (see page 24) publishes a 'Jobhunt' booklet entitled *Be Your Own Boss* and a magazine entitled *Home Run* (☎ 0181-846 9244) is published for homeworkers.

A number of local authority agencies and government departments provide free professional advice and assistance on starting and running a business, including finance and borrowing; marketing and selling; setting up and naming a company; bookkeeping and tax; premises and employment; advertising and promotion; patents and copyright; equipment and computing. These include the government run Small Firms Service and Business Enterprise or Business Advice Centres, financed by county councils. To find your local business enterprise or advice office, consult your local phone book or Yellow Pages.

The Small Firms Service (or the Scottish or Welsh Development Agencies in Scotland and Wales) offer information, signposting (to put you in touch with the right people), confidential counselling and business development services. The last two services are provided in consultation with business counsellors. The Small Firms Service produces an information pack entitled *Working for Yourself*. If you wish to start a business in the London area, a comprehensive booklet about enterprise aid entitled *Getting Started*, is available from the London Enterprise Agency (LEntA), 4 Snow Hill, London EC1A 2BS (☎ 0171-236 3000).

Grants, Low-Interest Loans and Training: There are a number of schemes designed to assist people (particularly young people) in starting a business including Livewire, Enterprise Training, the Enterprise Allowance Scheme, the Prince's Youth Business Trust and the London Enterprise Agency. Local, county and borough councils offer a variety of low-interest loans and grants, e.g. London Linc (Local Investment Networking Company). The government also provides a number of financial incentives and training schemes for those who wish to go it alone. Many county youth and community services run self-employment projects for young people, e.g. those aged 16 to 25. Ask your local Careers Centre for information.

Buying A Business: Businesses and franchises are advertised for sale each week in *Daltons Weekly, Exchange & Mart* and weekly and Sunday newspapers (e.g. the *Sunday Times*). There are also franchise magazines such as *What Franchise*. However, you should be wary of franchises, which usually take many years to make a profit (often the only ones who get rich are the franchise companies).

Miscellaneous: If you're self-employed, you must pay your own income tax and National Insurance class 2 and class 4 contributions (see page 306). To work as a self-employed sub-contractor in the building trade, you must have a sub-contractor's tax certificate card, without which an employer must deduct 25 per cent for standard tax and National Insurance contributions (see page 306). The Inland Revenue publish many leaflets for the self-employed that come under the general title of *Tax and Your Business* including *Starting your own business* (CWL1). Note that anyone who's self-employed and whose taxable turnover exceeds £50,000 a year, must register for Value Added Tax (see page 351). Depending on the type of work you're engaged in, you may need to adhere to local regulations (e.g. noise, safety and hygiene) and you may need to take out insurance against accidents at work or against damage to a third party's property.

Postscript: Whatever people may tell you, starting your own business isn't easy (otherwise most of us would be doing it). It requires a lot of hard work (self-employed people work an average of ten hours more a week than employees), usually a sizeable amount of cash (many businesses fail because of lack of capital), good organisation (e.g. bookkeeping and planning) and a measure of luck – although generally the harder you work, the more 'luck' you will have!

TRAINEES & WORK EXPERIENCE

Nationals of most countries are permitted to work in Britain as trainees or to gain practical work experience under the Training and Work Experience Scheme (TWES). The scheme is intended to give greater flexibility to British companies 'to assist their international business and trading links whilst maintaining adequate safeguards for British and EU nationals'. It's also designed 'to assist the emerging democracies of Eastern and Central Europe by helping their citizens gain valuable training or work experience in the UK'.

Applications for training are considered even if the training is available in the applicant's home country. Training usually applies to professions or occupations in which the training leads to the acquisition of occupational skills or professional qualifications. Trainees must be aged between 18 and 54 and work experience applicants between 18 and 35 years (who must also be at the start of their careers). The training or work experience must be for a minimum of 30 hours a week and for a fixed length of time. Work experience is normally limited to a maximum of one year, although in exceptional circumstances it can be extended to two years. Trainees occupy full-time positions with a normal salary and conditions of employment for similar on-the-job training in the area.

Work experience differs from trainee positions in that it doesn't usually result in a formal qualification, the worker doesn't fill a full-time position, and wages are paid in the form of pocket money or a maintenance allowance and are much less than would be paid to an ordinary employee (unless a statutory minimum wage is applicable). Applications are considered even when applicants have no previous employment related to the intended work experience, providing they have relevant qualifications and the work experience is closely related to their future career.

Although the training and work experience scheme is intended to develop applicants' industrial and commercial experience, a secondary objective is to improve their knowledge of the English language (where applicable), although applicants must have an 'adequate knowledge' of English before they're accepted. Applicants may not transfer from training or work experience to full employment in Britain and aren't permitted to work under the main work permit scheme for at least two years after the completion of their training or work experience. Trainees must sign an undertaking to return to their home countries once they have completed their training or work experience.

For information about how employers can apply for permission to employ someone under the trainee and work experience scheme, see **Trainees & Work Experience** on page 76.

AU PAIRS

Single people aged between 17 and 27 are eligible for a job as an au pair in Britain. Those aged under 18 need their parents written approval. Note that male au pairs are also permitted under EU regulations and many families now prefer them (although the British government was slow to accept them). The au pair system provides you with an excellent opportunity to travel, improve your English, and generally broaden your education by living and working in Britain.

Au pairs are usually contracted to work for a minimum of six months and a maximum of two years. You may work as an au pair on a number of separate occasions, providing the total period doesn't exceed two years. It's also possible to work for two or three months in the summer. Au pairs in Britain must usually be nationals of a European country (see the list on page 79). Au pairs who are nationals of EU countries can enter Britain with the minimum of formalities. Non-EU nationals must have a letter from the au pair agency or family confirming their invitation to work in Britain as an au pair, plus a letter confirming that they've had a recent medical examination. Au pairs from non-EU countries and those staying for longer than six months, must register with the police within seven days (see page 92).

Au pairs you receive free meals and accommodation and have their own room. You're required to pay your own fare to and from Britain, although some families pay towards the fare home for au pairs staying six months or longer. You may also be entitled to a week's paid holiday for each six month's service. In some families, au pairs holiday with the family or are free to take Christmas or Easter holidays at home, but you should ask permission before making arrangements to return at these times. Most families prefer non-smokers (smokers aren't popular and aren't accepted by some families) and girls with a driving licence (so you can take little Cecil or Penelope to public school in the family Rolls-Royce!). Working hours are officially limited to five hours a day (morning or afternoon), six days a week (a total of 30 hours), plus a maximum of three evenings a week baby-sitting. You should have at least one full day and three evenings a week free of household responsibilities and should be free to attend religious services if you wish. Au pairs are paid the princely (princessly?) sum of around £40 pocket money a week (possibly more in London), which means you stand little chance of getting rich unless you marry a wealthy Briton.

Au pair positions must be arranged privately, either directly with a family or through a private agency (there's no official government agency). There are dozens of agencies in Britain specialising in finding people au pair positions (both in Britain and abroad), all of which are licensed and inspected by the Department of Education and Employment. Some agencies offer a two-week trial period, during which either the au pair or the family can terminate the arrangement without notice. Write to a number of agencies and compare the conditions and pocket money offered. Agencies must provide a letter of invitation clearly stating your duties, hours, free time and pocket money (which must be shown to the immigration officer on arrival in Britain). **Agencies aren't permitted to charge au pairs a fee, which is paid by the family.**

Unfortunately abuses of the au pair system are common and you may be expected to work long hours and spend many evenings baby-sitting, while the family are out enjoying themselves. If you have any questions or complaints about your duties, you should refer them to the agency through which you found your position (if applicable). You're usually required to give notice if you wish to go home before the end of your agreement, although this won't apply if the family has abused the arrangement.

A useful book for prospective au pairs planning to work in Britain or abroad is the *Au Pair and Nanny's Guide to Working Abroad* by Susan Griffith & Sharon Legg (Vacation Work). A leaflet RON 2(AP) entitled *Information about Au Pairs* is available from the Home Office, Immigration and Nationality Directorate (IND), Block C, Whitgift Centre, Croydon CR9 2AR (Internet: www.homeoffice.gov.uk/ind/hpg. htm).

Note that it's possible for responsible English-speaking young women (without experience or formal training) to obtain employment as a 'nanny'. Duties are basically the same as an au pair, except that a position as a nanny is a real job with a real salary!

WORKING ILLEGALLY

There are hundreds of thousands of people working illegally in Britain (including many children), although only a small percentage are foreigners. The vast majority of illegal workers are British or foreign nationals who have the right to work in Britain, but who fail to declare their income (or total income) to the Inland Revenue. The illegal labour market (usually called the black economy) thrives in Britain and is estimated to be worth up to £20 billion a year. It's also estimated that around 10 per cent of unemployment claims are fraudulent. Although some unscrupulous employers use illegal labour in order to pay low wages for long hours and poor working conditions, many employers prefer to use casual or temporary labour.

It's strictly illegal for non-EU nationals to work in Britain without a work permit or official permission. If you're tempted to work illegally, you should be aware of the consequences as the black economy is a risky business for both employer and employee. A foreigner found working illegally is usually fined and deported, and may be refused future entry into Britain. Non-payment of income tax or National Insurance are criminal offences in Britain and offenders are liable to large fines and imprisonment. **Employees without permits have no entitlement to government or company pensions, unemployment benefits, accident insurance at work and no legal job protection.**

LANGUAGE

English is the most important and most widely spoken language in the world and is spoken by some 1.5 billion people as their first or second language. It's the world's lingua franca and is the language of the United Nations antechamber, international peacekeeping, world banking and commerce, air traffic control, academic research, computers (particularly the Internet), space travel, scientific discovery, news gathering and world entertainment. It's also essential for anyone planning to spend some time in Britain. If you're planning to live or work in Britain you will need to speak, read and write English well enough to find your way around Britain, e.g. dealing with government officials, public transport and shops, and to understand and hold conversations with the people you meet. Your English proficiency is particularly important if you have a job requiring a lot of contact with others or which involves speaking on the telephone or dealing with other foreigners, who may speak their own 'dialect' of English.

It's particularly important for students to have a high standard of English, as they must be able to follow lectures and take part in discussions in the course of their studies. This may also require a much wider and more technical or specialised vocabulary. For this reason, most universities and colleges won't accept students who aren't fluent in English and many require a formal qualification, e.g. a pass at GCSE or the Cambridge proficiency examination. Prospective students can assess their English fluency by taking the English Language Testing Service (ELTS) test at British Council offices in over 80 countries.

Whether you speak British or American English (or some other form) is usually irrelevant, although some foreigners have a problem understanding the British (who often don't understand each other) and even Americans initially have some problems understanding the natives (many British still believe the best way to communicate with foreigners is to SHOUT). The main difference between standard British English and standard American English is in the spelling (English spelling is a minefield) and pronunciation, plus a 'few' colloquialisms thrown in to confuse the issue. There are many regional accents in Britain, which is the way people pronounce their words, but few dialects, where a unique vocabulary, grammar and idiom is employed. The English spoken by television and radio newsreaders is usually referred to as 'Standard English'.

Some English (or British) people believe they have an historical claim on the English language and don't like foreigners 'mucking about with it'. However, there are four times as many English speakers in the United States as in Britain and more people speak English as a second-language (e.g. in India and many African countries, where English is used to communicate across national language barriers) than the number in mother-tongue countries. If you wish to improve your English before starting work or a course of study in Britain, there are English-language schools throughout the country where you can enrol in a part-time or full-time course lasting from a few weeks to a year (see **Language Schools** on page 198).

In Wales, certain schools teach Welsh (the 'language of heaven') as a compulsory subject, which has caused some discord among non-Welsh parents who aren't always happy that their children must learn Welsh. Some 90,000 people, mainly in the north-western Highlands and islands of Scotland, speak Gaelic, which is still taught in schools in these areas. Irish is taught as an optional subject in Northern Ireland.

2.

WORKING CONDITIONS

Working conditions in Britain are largely dependent on an employee's individual contract of employment and an employer's general employment conditions. Some aspects of your working conditions described in this chapter are prescribed by law and although many employers' pay and conditions are more generous than the statutory minimum, a substantial number of employers still offer pay and conditions that are actually illegal. Britain originally opted out of the social chapter agreed between the European Union (EU) countries at Maastricht in 1991, but the Labour government which was elected in 1997 promptly signed up to it (so British workers now have the same rights as those in other EU countries). However, it's feared that the new laws (coupled with a government 'Fairness at Work' initiative) will create problems for small companies. In recent years an increasing number of employers have been taken to employment tribunals and this is expected to escalate.

There's often a huge disparity between the working conditions of hourly paid workers and salaried employees (i.e. monthly paid), even between those employed by the same company. As in most countries, managerial and executive staff generally enjoy a much higher level of benefits than lower paid employees. Employees hired to work in Britain by a foreign (non-British) company, may receive a higher salary (including fringe benefits and allowances) than those offered by British employers. Citizens of EU member states working in Britain have the same rights as British nationals, for example with regard to pay, working conditions, vocational training and trade union membership. The employment conditions of non-EU nationals are generally the same as British nationals, although their employment is usually subject to the granting of a work permit and its renewal.

Detailed individual rights of employees are contained in a series of booklets and leaflets published by the Department of Education and Employment, available from Jobcentres and unemployment offices.

TERMS OF EMPLOYMENT

Negotiating an appropriate salary is only one aspect of your remuneration, which for many employees consists of much more than what they receive in their pay packet. When negotiating the terms of employment for a job in Britain, the checklists on the following pages should prove useful. The points listed under **General Positions** below apply to most jobs, while those listed under **Managerial & Executive Positions** (on page 46) may apply to executive and top managerial appointments only.

General Positions

- Salary
  - is the total salary adequate, taking into account the cost of living in Britain (see page 366)? Is it index-linked?
  - does it include an allowance for working (and living) in an expensive area (e.g. London)?
  - how often is the salary reviewed?
  - does the salary include commission and bonuses (see page 49)?
  - does the employer offer profit-sharing, share options or share-save schemes?

- is overtime paid or time off given in lieu of extra hours worked?
- is the total salary (including expenses) paid in pounds sterling, or is it paid in another country (in a different currency) with expenses for living in Britain?
- Relocation expenses:
  - are relocation expenses or a relocation allowance paid?
  - do the relocation expenses include travelling expenses for all family members?
  - is there a maximum limit, and if so, is it adequate?
  - are you required to repay your relocation expenses (or a percentage) if you resign before a certain period has elapsed?
  - are you required to pay for your relocation expenses in advance (which may run into £thousands)?
  - if employment is for a fixed period, will your relocation expenses be paid when you leave Britain?
  - if you aren't shipping household goods and furniture to Britain, is there an allowance for buying furniture locally?
  - do relocation expenses include legal and estate agent's fees incurred when moving home?
  - does the employer use the services of a relocation consultant (see page 98)?
- Accommodation:
  - will the employer pay for a hotel (or pay a lodging allowance) until you find permanent accommodation?
  - is subsidised or free, temporary or permanent accommodation provided? If so, is it furnished or unfurnished?
  - must you pay for utilities such as electricity, gas and water?
  - if accommodation isn't provided by the employer, is assistance in finding suitable accommodation given? What does it consist of?
  - what will accommodation cost?
  - while living in temporary accommodation, will the employer pay your travelling expenses to your permanent home? How far is it from the place of employment?
  - are your expenses paid while looking for accommodation?
- Working Hours:
  - what are the weekly working hours?
  - does the employer operate a flexi-time system (see page 50)? If so, what are the fixed (core time) working hours? How early must you start? Can you carry forward extra hours worked and take time off at a later date (or carry forward a deficit and make it up later)?
  - are you required to clock in and out of work?
  - can you choose either to take time off in lieu of overtime worked or to be paid for it?

- Part-Time or Periodic Working:
  - is part-time or school term-time working permitted?
  - are working hours flexible or is part-time working from home permitted?
  - does the employer have a job-sharing scheme?
  - are extended career breaks permitted with no loss of seniority, grade or salary?
- Leave entitlement:
  - what is the annual leave entitlement? Does it increase with age or length of service?
  - what are the paid public holidays?
  - is free air travel to your home country or elsewhere provided for you and your family, and if so, how often? Are other holiday travel discounts provided?
  - how much paid maternity/paternity leave is provided?
- Insurance:
  - is health insurance or regular health screening provided for you *and* your family? What does it include (see page 315)?
  - is free life assurance provided?
  - is accident or any special insurance provided by your employer?
  - for how long is your salary paid if you're ill or have an accident (see page 313)?
- Company pension:
  - is there a company pension scheme and what (if anything) is your contribution (see page 308)?
  - are you required or permitted to pay a lump sum into the pension fund in order to receive a full or higher pension?
  - what are the rules regarding early retirement?
  - is the pension transferable (portable) and do you receive the company's contributions in addition to your own? If not, will the employer pay into a personal pension plan?
  - is the pension index-linked?
  - do the pension rules apply equally to full *and* part-time employees?
- Employer:
  - what is the employer's future prospects?
  - is his profitability and growth rate favourable?
  - does he have a good reputation as an employer?
  - does he have a high staff turnover?
- Women:
  - what is the employer's policy regarding equal opportunities for women?

- how many women hold positions in middle and senior management or at board level (if the percentage is low in relation to the number of women employees, perhaps you should be wary if you're a career woman)?
- does the employer have a policy of reinstatement after child birth?

● Training:

- what initial or career training does the employer provide?
- is training provided in-house or externally and will the employer pay for training or education abroad, if necessary?
- does the employer have an on-going training programme for employees in your profession (e.g. technical, management or language)? Is the employer's training recognised for its excellence (or otherwise)?
- will the employer pay for a part or the total cost of non-essential education, e.g. a computer or language course?
- will the employer allow paid day release for you to attend a degree course or other study?

● What are the promotion prospects?

● Does the employer provide a free nursery or subsidised crèche for children below school age or a day care centre for the elderly (granny crèche)?

● Are free or subsidised English language lessons provided for you and your spouse (if necessary)?

● Is a free or subsidised employee restaurant provided? If not, is a lunch allowance paid? Is any provision made for shift workers, i.e. breakfast or evening meals?

● Is a travel allowance paid from your British residence to your place of work?

● Is free or subsidised parking provided?

● Are free work clothes, overalls or a uniform provided? Does the employer pay for the cleaning of work clothes (both workshop and office)?

● Does the employer offer cheap home loans, interest-free loans or mortgage assistance? Note that a cheap home loan can be worth £thousands a year.

● Is a company car provided? What sort of car? Can it be used privately, and if so, does the employer pay for petrol?

● Does the employer provide any fringe benefits such as subsidised in-house banking services, car discount scheme, cheap petrol, travel discounts, product discounts, sports and social facilities, or subsidised tickets for social and sports events?

● Do you have a written list of your job responsibilities?

● Have your employment conditions been confirmed in writing?

● If a dispute arises over your salary or working conditions, under the law of which country will your contract be interpreted?

Managerial & Executive Positions

- Is a 'golden hello' paid, i.e. a payment for signing a contract?
- Is private schooling for your children in Britain paid for or subsidised? Will the employer pay for a boarding school in Britain or another country?
- Is the salary index-linked or protected against devaluation and cost of living increases? This is particularly important if you're paid in a foreign currency that fluctuates wildly or could be devalued. Are you paid an overseas allowance for working in Britain?
- Is there an executive (usually non-contributory) pension scheme? British executives lead the world on pensions, most of whom retire on about 90 per cent of their net pre-retirement earnings (in stark contrast to people on average pay, who receive among the worst pensions in Europe).
- Is a housing allowance paid or a rent-free house or company flat provided, e.g. when working late in town?
- Are paid holidays provided (perhaps in a company owned property) or 'business' conferences in exotic places?
- Are costs incurred by a move to Britain reimbursed? For example, the cost of selling your home, employing an agent to let it for you or for storing household effects.
- Will the employer pay for domestic help or towards the cost of a servant or cook?
- Is a car provided *with* a chauffeur?
- Are you entitled to any miscellaneous benefits such as club membership, free credit cards, or tickets for sports events and shows?
- Is there an entertainment allowance?
- Is extra compensation paid if you're made redundant or fired? Redundancy or severance payments (see page 60) are compulsory for all employees in Britain (subject to length of service), but executives often receive a *very* generous 'golden handshake' if they are made redundant, e.g. after a takeover.

CONTRACT OF EMPLOYMENT

Under British law a contract of employment exists as soon as an employee proves his acceptance of an employer's terms and conditions of employment, e.g. by starting work, after which both employer and employee are bound by the terms offered and agreed. The contract isn't always in writing, although under the Employment Protection (Consolidation) Act 1978 (as amended) an employer must usually provide employees (working 16 or more hours a week) normally employed in Britain with a written statement containing certain important terms of employment and additional notes, e.g. regarding discipline and grievance procedures. A written contract of employment usually contains all the terms and conditions agreed between the employer and employee.

You usually receive two copies of your contract of employment (which may be called a 'statement of terms and conditions' or an 'offer letter'), both of which you should sign and date. One copy must be returned to your employer or prospective employer, assuming you agree with the terms and want the job, and the other (usually the original) is for your personal records. There are usually no hidden surprises or traps for the unwary in a British contract of employment, although as with any contract, you should know exactly what it contains before signing it. If your knowledge of the English language is imperfect, you should ask someone to explain anything you don't understand in simple English (British companies rarely provide foreigners with contracts in a language other than English). Your contract of employment (or statement) must contain the following details:

- name of the employer and employee;
- the date employment begins and whether employment with a previous employer counts as part of the employee's continuous period of employment;
- job title;
- salary details, including overtime pay and piece-rates, commission, bonuses and agreed salary increases or review dates;
- when the salary is to be paid, e.g. weekly or monthly;
- hours of work;
- holiday and public holiday entitlements and pay;
- sickness and accident benefits;
- pension scheme details;
- probationary and notice periods (or the expiry date, if employment is for a fixed period);
- disciplinary and grievance procedures (which may be contained in a separate document).

If there are no agreed terms under one or more of the above headings, this must be stated in the contract. Any special arrangements or conditions you have agreed with an employer should also be contained in the contract. If all or any of the above particulars are contained in a collective agreement, an employer may refer employees to a copy of this, including other documents such as work rules or handbooks, wage regulation orders, sick pay and pension scheme conditions, and the rules relating to flexible working hours and company holidays. Before signing your contract of employment, you should obtain a copy of any general employment conditions (see below) or documents referred to in the contract and ensure that you understand them.

Employment is usually subject to satisfactory references being received from your previous employer(s) and/or character references. In the case of a school leaver or student, a reference may be required from the principal of your last school, college or university. For certain jobs, a pre-employment medical examination is required and periodical examinations may be a condition of employment, e.g. where good health is vital to the safe performance of your duties. If you require a work permit to work in Britain, your contract may contain a clause stating that 'the contract is subject to a work permit being granted by the authorities'. Employees must usually be notified in writing of any changes in their terms and conditions of employment, within one month of their introduction. Details of contracts of employment and conditions are contained in the Department of Education and Employment booklet *Written statement of main terms and conditions of employment* (PL700).

EMPLOYMENT CONDITIONS

The term employment conditions (as used here) refers to an employer's general employment terms and conditions (including benefits, rules and regulations) that apply to all employees, unless otherwise stated in individual contracts of employment. General employment conditions are usually referred to in employment contracts and employees usually receive a copy on starting employment (or in some cases beforehand). Employment conditions are explained in this chapter or a reference is made to the chapter where the subject is covered in more detail.

Validity & Applicability

Employment conditions usually contain a paragraph stating the date from which they take effect and to whom they apply.

Place of Work

Unless there's a clause in your contract stating otherwise, your employer cannot change your place of work without your agreement. Note that the place of work refers to a town or area of a large city, rather than a different office or a new building across the street. Some contracts state that you may occasionally be required to work at other company locations.

Salary & Benefits

Your salary is stated in your contract of employment and salary reviews, overtime rates, piece and bonus rates, planned increases and cost of living rises may also be included. Only general points such as the payment of your salary into a bank account and the date of salary payments are usually included in employment conditions. You should usually receive an itemised pay statement (or wage slip), either with your salary if it's paid weekly in cash, or separately when your salary is paid monthly into a bank account.

Salaries in Britain are generally reviewed once a year, although the salaries of professional employees and all employees in some businesses may be reviewed every six months. The salaries of new employees may also be reviewed after six months. Annual increases may be negotiated individually by individual employees, by an independent pay review board or by a union (or unions), when the majority of a company's employees are members (called collective bargaining). Generally you're better off if you can negotiate your own salary increases. A percentage of your annual salary increase is usually to compensate for a rise in the cost of living (*always* applicable in Britain), although some employees (particularly in the public sector) may receive pay rises below the annual rate of inflation.

Commission & Bonuses

Your salary may include commission or bonus payments, calculated on your individual performance (e.g. based on sales) or the company's performance as a whole, which may be paid regularly (e.g. monthly or annually) or irregularly. Some employers pay all employees an annual bonus (usually in December), although this isn't normal practice. When a bonus is paid it may be stated in your contract of employment, in which case it's obligatory. In your first and last years of employment, an annual bonus is usually paid pro rata if you don't work a full calendar year.

Some employers operate an annual voluntary bonus scheme, based on each employee's individual performance or the company's profits (a profit-sharing scheme), although this may apply only to senior management and professionals. If you're employed on a contract basis for a fixed period, you may also be paid an end-of-contract bonus. When discussing salary with a prospective employer, take into account the total salary package including commission, bonuses and benefits such as a company car or a low-interest home loan. In industry, particularly in small firms, production workers are often paid on bonus or 'piece-work' rates, based on their productivity.

Working Hours

Working hours in Britain vary depending on your employer, your position and the type of industry in which you're employed. For example, the official working week in most manufacturing industries is around 37.5 to 40 hours, while many office employees work 35 to 38 hours a week (a 35-hour week is usually referred to as 9 to 5 or 0900 to 1700). At the other end of the scale, some employees in hospitals, security, catering and hotels may work up to 100 hours a week, although the average in these fields is between 50 and 60. However, under the EU social chapter, to which Britain is now a signatory, the maximum working week is now 48 hours (averaged over 17 weeks). For reasons of safety, employees must have rest breaks during the day and a daily rest period of 11 consecutive hours and a weekly rest period of 24 hours. Night-shift working is limited to eight hours a night, averaged over 17 weeks.

In practice the British work the longest average hours in the EU. Only some 30 per cent of workers work less than 40 hours a week and one in three people work over 40 hours a week (although only one in ten is contracted to do so). Shop floor (blue-collar or manual) workers in many companies are required to clock in and out of work, while white-collar (e.g. office) workers may not be, even when working in the same building. Employees caught cheating the clock are liable to instant dismissal.

If a company closes between Christmas and New Year or on other unofficial holidays, you may be required to compensate for this by working extra hours each week. If applicable, this is stated in your employment conditions. Your working hours may not be increased above the hours stated in your employment conditions without compensation or overtime being paid. Similarly, if you have a guaranteed working week, your hours cannot be reduced (i.e. short-time working) without your agreement. Your hours also cannot be changed without your agreement unless there's a clause (sometimes referred to as a 'mobility clause') in your contract. In reality an employer is unlikely to change or reduce your hours without agreement, if he wants to retain your goodwill and services. If you refuse short-time working and are subsequently dismissed, you can usually regard yourself as being made redundant (see page 60), in which case you should receive compensation.

Overtime among blue-collar workers is considered a perk and not something to be avoided at all costs, as in some other countries. Often one of the first questions a worker asks about a job is, "how much overtime is available?" Overtime is a lucrative bonus in some jobs, while in others it's a matter of economic necessity, without which many workers would find it difficult to survive. In between these two extremes many salaried employees are required to work long hours for no extra pay, e.g. NHS junior hospital doctors and most managers and executives. Note that the hours of work of most goods or passenger vehicle drivers are strictly controlled by law. In general, working hours are a matter of agreement between employers and employees and their representatives (e.g. unions).

Employers cannot normally require people to work excessive hours or unsuitable shift patterns likely to lead to ill health or accidents caused by fatigue. Many employers are instituting more flexible working hours and often permit employees to take part in job-sharing (where two people share a job), an annual hours scheme (where employees work an agreed number of hours a year), voluntary reduced time and working part of the time at home.

Flexi-Time Rules

Many British companies operate flexi-time working hours, particularly in offices. A flexi-time system usually requires all employees to be present between certain hours, known as the core or block time. For example from 0900 to 1130 and from 1330 to 1600. Employees may make up their required working hours by starting earlier than the required core time, reducing their lunch break or by working later. Only one in 50 workers now has an hour's lunch break, which is fuelling absenteeism and increasing lost working days due to stress. Most business premises are open from around 0700 to 1800 and smaller companies may allow employees to work as late as they wish, providing they don't exceed the legal maximum permitted daily working hours.

Overtime & Compensation

Working hours for employees who work a flexi-time system (see above) are usually calculated on a monthly basis. Companies usually allow employees to carry forward extra hours worked and take time off at a later date, or carry forward a deficit and make it up later. Payment may be made for overtime, depending on company policy or your employment conditions. Most companies pay overtime for work that's urgent and officially approved, and many prefer salaried (i.e. monthly paid) employees to take time off in lieu of overtime worked or expect them to work unpaid overtime. Middle and senior management employees aren't usually paid for overtime. When paid, overtime rates are usually the normal rate plus 25 per cent on weekdays and Saturdays, and plus 50 per cent on Sundays. Employees who work on public holidays may be paid double time (100 per cent supplement). In some industries and jobs, overtime terms and rates are agreed with a trade union.

Travel & Relocation Expenses

Your travel and relocation expenses to Britain (or to a new job in another area of Britain) depend on your agreement with your employers and are usually detailed in your contract of employment or conditions. If you're hired from outside Britain, your air fare (or other travel costs) to Britain is usually booked and paid for by your employer or his agent. You can also claim any additional travel costs, for example the cost of transport to and from airports. If you travel by car to Britain, you can normally claim a mileage rate plus the cost of the ferry or the equivalent air fare cost.

Most British employers pay your relocation expenses to Britain up to a specified amount. This may be paid as a percentage of your salary, a block allowance or specific expenses such as removal, legal and estate agent's fees only. The allowance should be sufficient to move the contents of an average house (castles aren't usually catered for) and you must normally pay any excess costs yourself. A company may ask you to obtain two or three removal estimates when they are liable for the total cost of removal. If you don't want to bring your furniture to Britain or have only a few belongings to ship, it may be possible to use your allowance to purchase furniture locally. Check with your employer. Generally you're required to organise and pay for the removal yourself. Your employer usually reimburses the equivalent amount in pounds sterling *after* you have paid the bill, although it may be possible to get him to pay the bill directly or make an advance payment.

If you change jobs within Britain, your new employer may pay your relocation expenses when it's necessary for you to move house. Don't forget to ask, as they may not always offer to pay (it may depend on how keen they are to employ you). See also **Relocation Consultants** on page 98.

National Insurance

State social security consists of National Insurance (NI) contributions that entitle you to a pension, unemployment and other benefits. NI contributions are compulsory for most residents of Britain and are usually deducted at source from your gross salary by your employer. For details see page 306.

Medical Examination

Many British companies require all prospective employees to have a pre-employment medical examination performed by a doctor nominated by them. An offer of employment is usually subject to an applicant being given a clean bill of health. This may be required for employees over a certain age only (e.g. 40) or for employees in particular jobs, e.g. where good health is of paramount importance for reasons of safety. Thereafter a medical examination may be necessary periodically (e.g. every one or two years) or may be requested at any time by your employer. Medical examinations are usually required as a condition of membership of a company health, pension or life insurance scheme. Some companies also insist on employees having regular health screening, particularly senior managers and executives.

Cars & Driving Licence

Many British employers provide senior employees such as directors, senior managers and professionals with a company car, although few jobs paying below around £20,000 a year offer a company car as a benefit unless it's necessary to do your job. If you're provided with a company car, you will usually receive full details about its use and your obligations on starting employment. If you lose your licence (e.g. through drunken driving) and are unable to fulfil the requirements of your job, your employment will usually be terminated (i.e. you will be fired), and you may not be entitled to any compensation. If a company car is provided, check what sort of car it is, whether you will be permitted to use it privately, and if so, who will pay for the petrol for private mileage. Some companies require employees to make a contribution towards the cost of providing a non-essential company car.

Note that using a company car for private use affects your tax position. Many companies offer employees a car allowance rather than provide a company car, which saves employees having to pay onerous taxes for a company car. Company cars are replaced on average every three years or after 112,000km (70,000mi). Most companies allow employees to buy secondhand company cars at advantageous prices.

Company Pension Fund

Around 95 per cent of medium to large companies provide a company pension fund for employees. Membership isn't compulsory, although most company pension funds offer much better terms than you can obtain privately, for example from a private pension plan. The amount you pay varies from nothing (non-contributory), reserved for senior staff, to between 4 and 8 per cent of your gross monthly salary, depending on your age and your employer's pension fund. See page 309 for information.

Accident Insurance

All employers, including even the smallest trader, are required to have occupational accident insurance for employees working on their premises, whether in a factory, office, shop, warehouse or residential accommodation. The reporting of injuries, diseases and dangerous occurrences was reinforced under new regulations that came into force in 1986. An employer is required to notify the appropriate authority immediately in the case of a death or serious injury as the result of an accident, and when anybody is off work for more than three days.

Although the primary responsibility for safety rests with the employer, employees are required by law to ensure that they co-operate with their employers and that they don't endanger themselves or anyone else by their acts or omissions. There are usually specific regulations for activities involving high risks, e.g. when operating electrical equipment and certain classes of machinery and the use of chemicals. Around 400,000 people are injured at work each year in Britain, including 500 fatalities and 12,000 serious injuries. For more information contact the local Health & Safety Executive office. For information about accident insurance see page 313.

Income Protection

Income protection in the event of sickness or an accident varies depending on your employer, your personal contract of employment, your length of employment and whether you're paid weekly or monthly. Most salaried employees (i.e. monthly paid) automatically receive sick pay when sick for a limited period. Usually you must have been employed for a minimum period before you're entitled to sick pay, e.g. 13 weeks, which may coincide with your probationary period. Employees paid weekly on an hourly rate, may not be paid at all for any illness lasting less than four days, after which time they receive Statutory Sick Pay (SSP).

Your employer may have an occupational sick pay (OSP) scheme, under which you receive your full salary for a number of weeks in the event of sickness or after an accident. OSP is often provided by employers as part of a company pension scheme, although only around half of small companies with less than ten employees and less than 50 per cent of all private sector companies have an OSP scheme. For more information see **Permanent Health Insurance** on page 314.

Miscellaneous Insurance

Other insurance provided by your employer is usually detailed in your employment conditions. This may include free life and health insurance, which also covers travel abroad on company business. Free life insurance is typically four times annual salary for top managers and directors. Some companies provide free membership of a private health insurance scheme, such as BUPA or PPP, although this may apply only to executives, managers and certain key personnel. Check that health insurance includes your family. Companies may also operate a contributory group health insurance scheme, offering discounted subscriptions for individual private membership.

Notification of Sickness or Accident

You're usually required to notify your employer as soon as possible of sickness or an accident that prevents you from working, i.e. within a few hours of your normal starting time. Failure to do so may result in you not being paid for that day's absence. You're required to keep your boss or manager informed about your illness and when you expect to return to work. For periods of less than seven days, you're usually required to provide a self-certificate of why you were absent on your return to work, although some employers may require a doctor's certificate. If you're away from work for longer than seven days, you're required to obtain a doctor's certificate (note that NHS doctors don't provide free medical certificates for absence from work due to sickness for periods of less than seven days).

Annual Holidays

Your annual holiday entitlement usually depends on your profession, position and employer, and your individual contract of employment. Holiday pay and entitlements are decided by individual or collective bargaining (e.g. by unions). Under EU rules, employees are allowed three weeks paid holiday a year, which increases to four weeks from 23rd November 1999. Most British companies grant employees four weeks paid annual holiday and around 25 per cent grant five weeks or more (the average is 23 days a year). Some employers give employees over a certain age, e.g. 50, an extra week's holiday, and offer additional holidays for length of service and for senior positions (but no time to take them!).

A company's holiday year may not correspond to a calendar year, but may run from 1st April to 31st March to coincide (roughly) with the financial year in Britain. Holiday entitlement is calculated on a pro rata basis (per completed calendar month of service) if you don't work a full 'holiday' year. Part-time staff may be entitled to paid holidays on a proportional basis. Usually all holidays must be taken within the holiday year in which they are earned, although some companies allow employees to carry them over to the next year.

Before starting a new job, check that any planned holidays will be approved by your new employer. This is particularly important if they fall within your probationary period (usually the first three months), when holidays aren't usually permitted. Holidays may usually be taken only with the prior permission of your manager or boss, and in many companies must be booked up to one year in advance. Most companies allow unpaid leave in exceptional circumstances only, when all your holiday entitlement has been exhausted. If you fall ill while on holiday, your holiday entitlement may be credited to you, providing you obtain a doctor's certificate. If you resign your position or are given notice, most employers will pay you in lieu of any outstanding holidays, although this isn't an entitlement and you may be obliged to take the holiday at your employer's convenience.

Public Holidays

Compared with many other European countries, Britain has few public or national holidays, usually referred to as bank holidays, as they are days on which banks are officially closed. Schools, businesses and many shops are also closed on public holidays. The British celebrate no national, independence or revolution day(s), and the only national religious holidays are Christmas and Easter. The following days are public holidays throughout Britain, except where noted:

January 1st	New Year's Day*
January 2nd	New Year's Bank Holiday (Scotland only)
March 17th	St. Patrick's Day (N. Ireland only)
March/April	Good Friday (the date changes each year)*
"	Easter Monday (Monday after Good Friday#)*
May	May Bank Holiday (first Monday in May)*
May	Spring Bank Holiday (last Monday in May#)*
July 12th	Orangeman's Day (N. Ireland only)
August	Summer Bank Holiday (first Monday in August – Scotland only)*
August	Summer Bank Holiday (last Monday in August)*
December 25th	Christmas Day*
December 26th	Boxing Day*

* national holidays
\# except in Scotland

If a public holiday falls on a weekend, there's usually a substitute holiday on the following Monday. An increasing number of British companies close down during Christmas and New Year, e.g. from around midday or 1700 on 24th December to the 2nd January. To compensate for this shutdown and perhaps other extra holidays during the year, employees may be required to work extra hours throughout the year, or may be required to take part of their annual holiday entitlement. Part-time staff are usually paid for a public holiday only when it falls on a day when they would normally be working.

If you're taken ill immediately prior to or immediately after a public holiday, you may be required to produce a doctor's certificate in order to be paid for the holiday period. You aren't required to work on public holidays unless otherwise stated in your contract of employment. When it's necessary to work on public holidays, you should receive the same or a higher rate of pay than is paid for working on a Sunday (e.g. double the normal rate) and/or time off in lieu. When employment involves working at weekends and on public holidays (e.g. shift working), you're usually recompensed in your basic salary or paid a shift allowance.

Compassionate & Special Leave of Absence

Whether or not you're paid for time off work or time lost through unavoidable circumstances (e.g. public transport strikes or car breakdowns) depends on your employer, whether you're paid monthly or weekly (e.g. with an hourly rate of pay), and not least, whether you're required to punch a clock. The attitude in Britain to paid time off depends on your status and position. Executives and managers (who admittedly often work much longer hours than officially required) have much more leeway regarding time off than a factory worker. All employees are allowed by law to take time off work for the following reasons:

- An expectant mother is entitled to 'reasonable' paid time off work for ante-natal care.

- A trade union official is entitled to paid time off for trade union duties and training for such duties, and employees may also be paid to attend union meetings during working hours. Similarly, a safety representative is allowed paid time off in connection with his safety duties.

- Time off for public duties such as service as a Justice of the Peace, juror or court witness, councillor or school governor, or as a member of a statutory tribunal or authority, although your employer isn't required by law to pay you.

- If you're made redundant, you're entitled to 'reasonable' paid time off to look for a new job or to arrange training in connection with a new job.

Many British companies also provide paid compassionate or special leave on certain occasions, which may include your own or a family marriage, birth of a child, or the death of a family member or close relative. The grounds for compassionate leave may be listed in your employment conditions.

Paid Expenses

Expenses paid by your employer are usually listed in your employment conditions. These may include travel costs from your home to your place of work, which (if applicable) may consist of a second class rail season ticket or the equivalent in cash (paid monthly with your salary). Companies without a company restaurant or canteen may pay employees a lunch allowance or provide luncheon vouchers. Expenses paid for travel on company business or for training courses may be detailed in your employment conditions or listed in a separate document. Most companies pay a mileage allowance to staff who are authorised to use their private motor vehicles on company business (but check that business use is covered by your car insurance).

Probationary & Notice Periods

For most jobs there's a probationary period, which may be two weeks for hourly paid employees and three months for salaried (monthly paid) employees. Your notice period normally depends on your method of salary payment, your employer, your profession and your length of service, and is detailed in your contract of employment and employment conditions. Probationary and notice periods apply equally to employers and employees. Most monthly paid employees have a one month (or four-week) notice period which takes effect after any probationary period. This may remain the same for the first four years of service. From four to 12 years continuous service, there may be an extra week's notice for each whole year of service. After 12 years service, the notice period may be three months or 12 weeks (unless your individual contract specifies a longer period). The notice period may be longer for executive or key employees, e.g. three or six months, or may be extended after a number of years service, in which case it will be noted in your employment conditions.

Unless otherwise stated in your contract of employment, there's a legal minimum notice period for full-time employees, depending on your length of service. For the first four weeks of service, there's no statutory minimum and you aren't entitled to notice unless otherwise agreed. After four weeks service you're entitled to one week's notice. After two years continuous service it's increased to two weeks and is extended by another week for each subsequent year of continuous service, up to a maximum of 12 weeks notice after 12 years service.

If an employer doesn't give you the required notice in writing, he's liable to pay you in full for the period of official notice (see **Discipline & Dismissal** on page 59). If you resign your job, you must usually do so in writing. If you resign or are given notice, your company may not require you to work your notice period, particularly if you're joining a competitor or your boss feels that you may be a bad influence on your colleagues. However, if he doesn't want you to work your notice, he must pay you in full for the notice period, plus any outstanding overtime or holiday entitlement.

If an employer goes bankrupt and cannot pay you, you can terminate your employment without notice, but your employer cannot legally do this. Other valid reasons for an employee *not* to give notice are assault or abuse on him or a colleague by the employer and failure to pay or persistent delay in paying an employee's salary. As the law stands, you can usually leave a job without giving notice and the chances of your employer having any legal rights worth enforcing are negligible. However, you may lose any bonuses or other monies owed to you, plus any possibility of receiving a good reference.

Education & Training

Education and training provided by your employer may be stated in your employment conditions. This may include training abroad, providing that it's essential for your job (although you may need to convince your employer). It's in your own interest to investigate courses of study, seminars and lectures that you feel will be of direct benefit to you and your employer. Most employers give reasonable consideration to a request to attend a course during working time, providing you don't make it a full-time occupation. In addition to relevant education and training, employers must also provide the essential tools and equipment for a job (although this is open to interpretation). It's compulsory for companies to provide appropriate and adequate safety and health training for all employees (see **Accident Insurance** on page 313).

If you need to improve your English ability, language classes may be paid for by your employer. If it's necessary to learn a foreign language in order to perform your job, the cost of language study should be paid by your employer. An allowance may be paid for personal education or hobbies (flower arranging, kite flying or break-dancing) which aren't work related or of direct benefit to your employer (unless he's in the flower, kite or dance business).

Pregnancy & Confinement

Time off work for sickness in connection with a pregnancy is usually given without question, but it may not be paid unless authorised by a doctor. You're guaranteed the right to 'reasonable' time off work for antenatal care without loss of pay, irrespective of how long you've been employed (usually a clinic or hospital appointment card must be produced). A pregnant or nursing mother cannot be required to work overtime and a woman cannot be dismissed because she is pregnant or for any reason connected with her pregnancy. If she's dismissed she has an automatic claim for unfair dismissal, irrespective of her length of service. It's also illegal to refuse a woman a job because she is pregnant, providing this doesn't prevent her from doing the job.

A mother cannot (by law) return to work during the first eight weeks after giving birth. Pregnant mothers are entitled to both maternity leave and pay, depending on the length of their employment (pregnant fathers aren't entitled to anything, but may qualify for the Nobel prize for medicine). Part-time employees aren't entitled to maternity leave and pay. All women irrespective of their length of service or hours of work are entitled to 14 weeks unpaid maternity leave (which may soon be increased to 18 weeks) and employment-related benefits such as private medical insurance, use of a company car and pension contributions must continue during this period. Some employers provide enhanced benefits including the payment of full salary for some or all of the maternity-leave period. At the end of the 14-week period you have the right to return to the same job and if you have worked for the same employer for over two years, you're entitled to return to the same or similar employment up to 40 weeks after giving birth. Most companies count periods of absence for maternity leave as continuous employment for the purpose of calculating an employee's number of years service, but not when calculating annual holiday.

Part-Time Job Restrictions

Restrictions on part-time employment for an employer other than your regular employer, may be included in your employment conditions. Many British companies don't allow full-time employees to work part-time (i.e. moonlight) for another employer, particularly one in the same line of business. You may, however, be permitted to take a part-time teaching job or similar part-time employment (or you can write a book!).

Confidentiality & Changing Jobs

If you disclose any confidential company information, either in Britain or overseas (particularly to competitors), you may be liable to instant dismissal and may also have legal action taken against you. You may not steal any secrets or confidential information (e.g. customer mailing lists) from a previous employer, but you may use any skills, know-how, knowledge and contacts acquired during his employ. If you make any inventions while an employee, they remain your property unless you sell them or a licence to your employer, or the invention was made as part of your 'normal duties', or you were specifically employed to invent, e.g. in research and development.

You may not compete against a former employer if there's a valid, binding restraint clause in your contract of employment. Your contract may also contain a clause defining the sort of information that the employer considers to be confidential, such as customer and supplier relationships and details of business plans. If there's a confidentiality or restraint clause in your contract that's unfair, e.g. it inhibits you from changing jobs, it will probably be invalid in law and will be unenforceable. If in doubt consult a solicitor (who's an expert in company law) about your rights. If you're a key employee, you may have a legal binding contract preventing you from joining a competitor or starting a company in the same line of business as your employer, and in particular, enticing former colleagues to join your company. However, such a clause is usually valid for one year only.

Acceptance of Gifts

With the exception of those employed in the public sector, employees are normally permitted to accept gifts of a limited value from customers or suppliers, e.g. bottles of wine or spirits or other small gifts at Christmas. Generally any gifts given and received openly and above board aren't considered a bribe or unlawful (although if you give your business to someone else in the following year, don't expect a 'bribe' next Christmas). You should declare any gifts received to your immediate superior, who decides what should be done with them. Most bosses pool all gifts and divide them among all employees. (If you accept a real bribe, make sure it's a big one and that you have a secret bank account.)

Long Service Awards

Most large companies present their employees with long service awards after a number of years, e.g. 15, 20 or 25 years. These are usually in the form of a gift such as a watch or clock (so you can count the hours to your retirement), presented to individuals by senior management. Periods of absence on maternity leave usually count as continuous employment when calculating your length of service.

Retirement

Your employment conditions may be valid only until the official British retirement age, currently 60 for women and 65 for men. If you wish to continue working after you have reached retirement age, you may need to negotiate a new contract of employment (you should also seek psychiatric help). If your employer has a compulsory retirement age, he isn't required to give you notice. However, it's illegal to have a lower *compulsory* retirement age for women than men or vice versa. Many companies present employees with a gift on reaching retirement age (e.g. the key to your ball and chain), the value of which usually depends on your number of years service.

Discipline & Dismissal

Most large and medium size companies have comprehensive grievance and disciplinary procedures, which must usually be followed before an employee can be suspended or dismissed. Some employers have disciplinary procedures whereby employees can be suspended with or without pay, e.g. for breaches of contract. Employees can also be suspended (usually with pay) pending investigation into an alleged offence or impropriety. Disciplinary procedures usually include both verbal and official written warnings. These procedures are both to protect employees from unfair dismissal and to ensure that dismissed employees cannot (successfully) sue their employer. If you have a grievance or complaint against a colleague or your boss, there may be an official procedure to be followed to obtain redress. If an official grievance procedure exists, it's usually detailed in your employment conditions.

Under normal circumstances, you cannot be fired in the first four weeks of an illness, in the eight weeks before you're due to give birth, or the eight weeks after giving birth. Instant or summary dismissal without any right to notice or salary in lieu of notice, is permissible only in exceptional circumstances for acts of gross misconduct. These may include refusing to work (without a good reason); cheating or stealing from your employer; competing with your employer; insulting your employer or colleagues; assault on your employer or a colleague; or drunkenness during working hours on your employer's premises (office parties excepted). You're entitled to written reasons for your dismissal and should ask for them if they aren't supplied voluntarily. They should in any case be supplied within two weeks of the request. If you're 'forced' to resign your position, in law you're deemed to have been dismissed 'constructively' and can claim unfair dismissal (this may also apply if your duties and responsibilities are drastically downgraded and you're asked to do more menial tasks, which may be designed to force you to resign).

If you believe you've been unfairly dismissed, you can take your case to the Advisory, Conciliation and Arbitration Service (ACAS) or the Equal Opportunities Commission. Protection against unfair dismissal includes a compensatory award, a basic award for lost redundancy up to a maximum amount, and a compensatory award, which is the amount the tribunal considers appropriate for the loss suffered by the employee as a result of the dismissal. Unfair dismissal awards are limited to a maximum sum (currently £15,000 but is to be increased to £50,000) depending on an employee's age and length of service, but sex discrimination awards are unlimited. A special award may also be made where unfair dismissal was due to an employee's membership or non-membership of a union, or when the tribunal made an order of re-engagement which was ignored.

Redundancy

The Redundancy Payments Scheme covers nearly all workers who are employed under a contract of employment, providing employees have at least two years continuous service and meet the conditions outlined below. The main exceptions are part-time employees who usually work less than eight hours a week and those who have reached retirement age and continue to work. You qualify for redundancy pay if you're dismissed wholly or mainly due to your job being phased out or when your employer wishes to reduce his workforce.

If you're made redundant, you're entitled to your normal notice period or pay in lieu of notice and are also entitled to redundancy pay. You're also usually entitled to reasonable time off work with pay to look for another job or arrange training. The amount of redundancy pay you receive depends on whether your employer pays the minimum required by law or more, either voluntarily or, for example, under pressure from trade unions. It may also be possible to take voluntary redundancy or early retirement and receive an early pension, e.g. in the case of ill health.

The Employment Protection (Consolidation) Act 1978 (as amended) states that an employee aged 18 to 65 (60 for women) who has worked 16 hours a week or more continuously for two years or eight or more hours a week continuously for five years, is entitled to a statutory redundancy lump sum payment. The amount payable is based on a sliding scale depending on your age, length of service and salary. The older you are, the more redundancy pay you will receive (pro rata). The basic payment is half a week's pay for each complete year of service after the age of 18 until age 22, one week for each year after the age of 22 until age 41, and one and a half weeks pay for each year after the age of 41 up to the age of 64.

There's a limit on the amount of a week's pay that may be taken into account, which is currently £220. The maximum amount payable is £6,600 (30 weeks at £220 per week) after 20 years service, which is the maximum period of employment taken into account. You normally receive your statutory redundancy payment at about the time you leave your job and it's usually tax-free (up to £30,000), although you should confirm this with a tax office.

Many companies engage an 'outplacement' consultant to assist employees who are made redundant. This includes advice and counselling on future job prospects, job hunting, state benefits, retirement, retraining, setting up in business and financial advice for employees who receive large redundancy payments. Executives, managers and key personnel may have a clause in their contract whereby they receive a generous 'golden handshake' if they are made redundant, e.g. after a takeover. The receipt of a redundancy payment, irrespective of the amount, doesn't affect your eligibility to claim Jobseeker's Allowance.

Disputes about redundancy payments can be decided by an industrial tribunal. For further information about redundancy payments contact your local Redundancy Payment Office (☎ freefone 0800-848489).

References

In Britain, an employer isn't legally obliged to provide an employee with a written reference. If you leave an employer on good terms, he'll usually provide a written reference on request. If your employer refuses to give you a written reference or gives you a 'bad' reference, it's advisable to ask your immediate boss or a colleague for a personal reference (failing that, write your own). In Britain, prospective employers usually contact your previous employer (or employers) directly for a reference, either orally or written. This can be bad news for employees as they have no idea what has been said about them and whether it was true or false. An employer is under no obligation (except perhaps morally) to provide a reference, but if he does, he cannot (legally) maliciously defame you, although should he do so, it's almost impossible to obtain legal address.

Trade Union Membership

British trade unions went through a bad time in the '80s under the Conservative government and have largely been legislated into toothless tigers. Many companies are now non-union and trade union membership fell by 30 per cent in the last decade to around seven million (and is still falling). The majority of union members are now professionals, managers and service providers rather than manual workers. In the '60s and '70s, the unions were their own worst enemies and they succeeded in losing many jobs as a result of their restrictive practices, belligerence and bloody-mindedness, by driving companies out of business (to say nothing of helping to drive the Labour Party into the political wilderness). Anti-union legislation has actually helped strengthen the trade union movement, which is now a model of democracy (unions must ballot members before undertaking any industrial action).

Whether you're better off as a member of a trade union depends on the industry in which you're employed. In most industries which recognise trade unions, members pay and conditions are decided by a process of collective bargaining between employers and trade unions. Employers aren't allowed to discriminate against an employee in selection, promotion, transfer, training or dismissal because he belongs or wishes to belong to a trade union. Certain employees of some companies may be required to join a union as a condition of employment when the employer operates a 'closed shop', which is a union membership agreement between the employer and one or more trade unions. On the other hand, many companies are non-union and don't officially recognise any trade unions, although individual employees may be union members. However, under new legislation employees have the right to union recognition if over half the workforce votes for it (a ballot is triggered when 10 per cent of the workforce call for it). A proposal under the government's 'Fairness at Work' legislation holds the prospect of companies with as few as 20 employees having to recognise and negotiate with trade unions (which could result in many small companies stopping employing full-time staff at 19).

Information about trade unions can be obtained from the Trade Unions Congress (TUC), Congress House, 22-28 Great Russell Street, London WC1B 3LS (☎ 0171-636 4030).

3.

PERMITS & VISAS

Before making any plans to live or work in Britain, you *must* ensure that you have the appropriate entry clearance (e.g. a visa) and permission, as without the correct documentation you will be refused permission to enter the country. If you're a national of a non-EEA country (see page 22) you may need to obtain *entry clearance*, e.g. persons intending to stay permanently, coming to work or who are visa nationals (see page 67). **If you're in any doubt as to whether you require clearance to enter Britain, enquire at a British Embassy, High Commission or other British Diplomatic Mission (collectively known as British Diplomatic Posts) overseas before making plans to travel to Britain.** Note that in some countries, entry clearance can take some time to be granted due to the high number of applications to be processed.

Britain's immigration laws are among the most draconian in the western world and there are strict regulations regarding the entry of foreigners seeking political asylum or those who intend to look for work illegally. With the exception of those who aren't subject to immigration controls (e.g. EEA citizens and Commonwealth citizens with a parent born in Britain), the onus is on anyone coming to Britain to *prove* that he won't break the immigration laws. You must 'satisfy the immigration officer' that you qualify under the immigration rules, which may depend on your nationality and the economic situation in your home country. Immigration officials aren't required to prove that you may break the immigration laws and can refuse you entry on the grounds of suspicion only. If you're refused entry, you will be 'removed' and sent back to your home country at your own expense (this isn't the same as deportation and doesn't automatically prevent you returning at a later date). You will be given the reason in writing and may appeal, but only *after* your departure if you don't have prior entry clearance (see page 65).

Nationals of some non-Commonwealth and non-EEA countries who have been given permission to remain in Britain for more than six months or who have been allowed to work for more than three months are required to register with the police (see page 92). When applicable, this condition is stamped in your passport, either on entry or by the Immigration and Nationality Directorate (IND) of the Home Office when granting an extension of stay. The Home Office (called the Interior Ministry in many countries) has the final decision on all matters relating to immigration.

Immigration is a complex subject and the information in this chapter is intended only as a general guide. You shouldn't base any decisions or actions on the information contained herein without confirming it with an official and reliable source, such as a British embassy. Permit infringements are taken seriously by the authorities and there are penalties for breaches of regulations, including fines and even deportation for flagrant abuses. The police and immigration authorities have the right to arrest anyone 'reasonably suspected' of being an illegal alien and can obtain search warrants to enter homes or places of employment. The penalties for harbouring illegal aliens are severe and prison sentences of up to seven years and heavy fines can be imposed on offenders. Carriers (i.e. airlines and shipping lines) are fined £2,000 plus costs for each passenger they land who doesn't have valid documentation (especially visas). The government also plans to introduce tough penalties for coach and lorry drivers who unwittingly bring illegal immigrants into the country.

The latest information about immigration, permits and visas can be obtained from the Immigration and Nationality Department (which publishes leaflets and booklets regarding all immigration categories), local law centres, Citizens Advice Bureaux and community relations councils. At the time of writing, the immigration service had introduced a new Integrated Casework Directorate and a restricted service was also being operated by the Public Enquiry Office in London. All applications for permits or visas should be sent to the Immigration and Nationality Directorate (IND), Block C, Whitgift Centre, Croydon CR9 2AR (Internet: www.homeoffice.gov.uk/ind/hpg.htm). The appropriate telephone number depends on the type of enquiry: general enquiries about immigration rules and procedures (☎ 0870-606 7766); requests for immigration application forms (☎ 0870-241 0645); and enquires about individual cases already under consideration (0870-608 1592).

ENTRY CLEARANCE

With the exception of EEA nationals, other foreigners entering Britain may need entry clearance from the Home Office or a British Diplomatic Post in their country of residence, *before arrival in Britain*. Entry clearance in the form of a visa or entry certificate also applies to visitors from certain countries and to returning residents who have been abroad for over two years. Entry clearance is issued for a single entry or may allow multiple entries for a number of years, e.g. one to five (a fee is payable depending on the type of entry clearance issued).

Unless there are special reasons or circumstances, you should always apply for entry clearance before arrival in Britain, consisting of one or more of the following:

- **visa** (for visa nationals);
- **entry certificate** (for a non-visa Commonwealth citizens, also known as semi-visa nationals);
- **letter of consent** (for a non-visa, non-Commonwealth citizen);
- **work permit** (which may count as entry clearance for non-visa nationals).

Entry clearance is necessary to enter Britain for the following reasons:

- settlement as the dependant of a person living there ('settlement' is the term used for permanently resident foreigners living lawfully in Britain with no time limit on their stay);
- as a person of independent means;
- to undertake employment;
- as a spouse seeking to join his or her partner;
- as a fiancé(e) wishing to enter for marriage and settlement;
- for business purposes;
- any family member coming with or to join a person in any of the above categories.

In addition to the above list, nationals of a visa country (see page 67) need a visa to enter Britain for any purpose. Persons entering Britain for employment must usually have a work permit (see page 69) issued by the Department of Education and Employment. Non-visa nationals with a work permit may require no other entry clearance. When applying for entry clearance, you must produce documentary evidence that you meet the requirements of the immigration rules for whatever category you're applying. Evidence may include any of the following, as applicable:

- A work permit sent to you by your prospective employer.

- A letter from a bona fide university, polytechnic, college or school, stating that you have been accepted on a full-time course of study and that you have paid your fees in full (or have been awarded a grant or scholarship).

- Evidence that your qualifications for a job or a course of study are genuine and satisfactory, e.g. certificates, diplomas and references.

- Evidence that you will be able to support yourself and any dependants during your stay in Britain without recourse to public funds, e.g. a bank statement, letter from a bank or other evidence of financial support, or in the case of a student, a letter from a sponsor or scholarship agency. The term 'public funds' refers to the following state social security benefits (see page 303): Income Support; Jobseeker's Allowance; Family Credit; Child Benefit; Housing and Council Tax Benefit; Housing and Homelessness Assistance; and any Disability Allowance.

- If your stay is for a limited period only, you may be required to give an assurance that you will leave Britain at the end of that period.

Entry clearance is also required for any dependants you're bringing with you or who will join you in Britain. You must prove that you're married and that you can support your dependants as well as yourself. Failure of your dependants to obtain entry clearance may mean that they will be refused entry into Britain. When applying for entry clearance, you must complete forms requiring your first names (Christian or forenames), family name (surname) and your date of birth. If these terms are unusual in your country, establish how you would like your name and date of birth to be written in English, and **always complete all forms in the same way.** This is particularly important for those whose written language isn't in Roman script (e.g. Arabic, Chinese or Russian).

If you're refused entry clearance, you will be given the reason in writing with instructions on how to appeal against the decision, which must be made within three months. **If you're refused entry clearance, don't travel to Britain as you will be refused entry.** Note that entry clearance *doesn't* guarantee you entry into Britain. Reasons for refusing entry to someone *with* entry clearance include deceiving the authorities to obtain entry clearance (e.g. an undisclosed criminal record); a change of circumstances since the entry clearance was granted; a decision by the authorities that your presence in Britain isn't conducive to the public good (someone likely to ferment trouble); or when it's believed you will become a charge on public funds. **Note, however, that anyone who arrives in Britain with entry clearance and is refused entry has the right of appeal (see page 65), and cannot be sent back until the appeal has been heard.**

Those intending to remain in Britain for longer than six months are normally referred to a medical inspector for an examination at their port of entry. Those who give medical or health treatment as the purpose of their visit or who appear to be in bad health, may also be medically examined. In certain circumstances, admission can be refused on medical grounds. Applicants for settlement as dependants from Commonwealth countries are required to have a medical examination before entry clearance is issued. However, the spouse and dependent children under 18 of a resident cannot be refused entry, but can be required to undergo medical treatment in Britain. Au pairs are also required to obtain a medical certificate before arriving in Britain (including a chest x-ray), stating that they are in good health and free from contagious diseases. **In all correspondence or contact with British consular officials or the Home Office, ensure that you fully understand everything and seek help if you aren't absolutely certain.**

Visas

Nationals of certain countries, officially called 'visa nationals', require a visa (an official stamp in their passport) to enter Britain, irrespective of the purpose of their visit, e.g. holiday, residence or employment. **If you need a visa and arrive without one, you will be sent back to your home country at your own expense.** Visitors' visas are issued for a maximum stay of six months and are never extended beyond this period. If you want to stay longer you must leave and apply for a new visa. Visa nationals aren't permitted to change their status.

In 1999, nationals of the following countries *required* a visa to enter Britain: Afghanistan, Albania, Algeria, Angola, Armenia, Azerbaijan, Bangladesh, Belarus, Benin, Bhutan, Bosnia-Herzegovina, Bulgaria, Burkina, Burma (Myanmar), Burundi, Cambodia, Cameroon, Cape Verde, Central African Republic, Chad, China, Comoros, Congo, Cuba, Djibouti, Egypt, Equatorial Guinea, Ethiopia, Gabon, Georgia, Ghana, Guinea, Guinea-Bissau, Haiti, India, Indonesia, Iran, Iraq, Jordan, Kazakhstan, Kirgizstan, Korea (North), Laos, Lebanon, Liberia, Libya, Madagascar, Mali, Mauritania, Moldova, Mongolia, Morocco, Mozambique, Nepal, Nigeria, Oman, Pakistan, Philippines, Romania, Russia, Rwanda, Sao Tome e Principe, Saudi Arabia, Senegal, Somalia, Sri Lanka, Sudan, Syria, Taiwan, Tajikistan, Thailand, Togo, Tunisia, Turkey, Turkmenistan, Uganda, Ukraine, Uzbekistan, Vietnam, Yemen and Zaire. With the exception of Croatia and Slovenia, nationals of the territories of the former Yugoslavia also require a visa.

If your leave to remain expires while you're in Britain and you haven't applied for an extension, you're committing a criminal offence and could be fined up to £2,000, sent to prison, and/or recommended for deportation (see page 82). If you're deported, it will be extremely difficult, if not impossible, for you to return to Britain. If you're a visa national and are planning a trip abroad, you will require a new visa from a British Diplomatic Post unless you're visa exempt or hold a multiple-entry visa.

From 16th May 1991 anyone granted leave to remain in Britain for longer than six months benefits from an extended visa exemption scheme. Under this scheme you don't require a visa if you depart from Britain and return within the period of your original leave to remain. You are, however, liable to examination at the port of entry to confirm that you qualify for re-admission. Before leaving Britain, ensure that your passport doesn't need renewing and that your leave to remain won't expire within the next few months. If your leave to remain is due to expire within around two months of your planned return, you should renew it before leaving Britain. You should make your application in person, as a postal application usually takes some time to be processed.

Applications for a visa to re-enter Britain must be made in person to the Immigration and Nationality Directorate, Public Caller Unit, Block C, Whitgift Centre, Croydon CR9 2AR (or another passport office) or in writing to the Correspondence Unit at the above address. Check the business hours before calling.

If you don't have time to obtain a visa before leaving Britain or your multiple-entry visa expires while you're abroad, you must apply for a new visa from a British Diplomatic Post before returning to Britain. For this you will require the same documentation that was necessary to obtain your original entry clearance. On your return to Britain, you may be required to show evidence of your reason for coming to Britain and that you have sufficient funds to support yourself and any dependants (this also applies to non-visa nationals with limited leave to remain in Britain).

If you're a visa national living in Britain, you may also need a visa to visit other countries. The *Guide to International Travel* (ABC Travel Guides) contains up-to-date information on visa and other travel requirements for all countries. Information about visa requirements is available from the Correspondence Unit, Immigration and Nationality Directorate (IND), Block C, Whitgift Centre, Croydon CR9 2AR. You can also check with any travel agency or your country's embassy or consulate in Britain. Applications must be made in advance, visas are valid for one to three months only, and they are often expensive. It can take weeks or even months to obtain a visa for some countries, particularly some African and Middle Eastern countries, during which time the embassy may retain your passport. Note that there are companies in major cities that obtain visas for a fee.

Entry Certificate

An entry certificate is required by non-visa national, Commonwealth citizens coming to work or settle in Britain. If you're a national of one of the countries listed below and are coming to Britain to work or settle, you **must** obtain special entry clearance in the form of an 'Entry Certificate', which like a visa consists of an official stamp in your passport. If you're refused entry to Britain for any reason, an entry certificate entitles you to an immediate right of appeal in the same way as a visa.

An Entry Certificate is issued by a British Diplomatic Post and is required by nationals of the following countries: Anguilla, Antigua, Ascension, Australia, Bahamas, Barbados, Belize, Bermuda, Botswana, Brunei, Canada, Cayman Islands, Cyprus, Dominica, Falklands, Gambia, Gilbert & Ellice Islands, Grenada, Grenadines, Guyana, Indonesia, Jamaica, Kenya, Kiribati, Leeward Islands, Lesotho, Malawi, Malaysia, Malta, Mauritius, Montserrat, Namibia, Nauru, New Hebrides, New Zealand, Papua New Guinea, St. Helena, St. Lucia, St. Vincent, St. Kitts & Nevis, Samoa, Seychelles, Sierra Leone, Sikkim, Singapore, Solomon Islands, Swaziland, Tanzania, Tongo, Trinidad & Tobago, Tristan da Cunha, Tuvalu, Uganda, Vanuatu, Virgin Islands, Western Samoa, Zambia and Zimbabwe.

Letter of Consent

A letter of consent is required by non-visa, non-Commonwealth citizens (of all countries that aren't listed above under visas or entry certificate) wishing to enter Britain for the reasons stated below. A letter of consent is issued by a British Diplomatic Post abroad and is required by the following persons:

● the spouse, children or other dependants of a person settled in Britain;

● the spouse or children under 18 years of age of a person admitted to Britain for employment or for self-employment;

- a fiancé(e) seeking to enter for marriage to a person settled in Britain (and planning to settle in Britain);
- persons entitled to permit-free employment;
- doctors and dentists coming to take up research or postgraduate training positions in hospitals;
- persons coming to establish themselves in business or self-employment, whether in a new or an existing enterprise;
- persons of independent means;
- writers and artists.

If a person who requires a Letter of Consent arrives without one, he may be refused permission to enter Britain. Any non-visa national, both Commonwealth and non-Commonwealth, may apply for entry clearance when it isn't compulsory under the immigration laws, e.g. when coming to Britain to visit or study. Note that the refusal of optional entry clearance, doesn't mean that you will be refused entry to Britain, but you will probably have difficulty entering Britain if you arrive without it. The refusal rate for optional entry clearance abroad is much higher than refusals at British ports or airports.

An application for a Letter of Consent should be made well in advance of your proposed date of travel and should be accompanied by the relevant documentary evidence. Where admission is sought as a dependant, evidence in the form of a birth and/or marriage certificate should be produced. If false representations are made or material facts concealed in order to obtain a Letter of Consent, or your circumstances have changed since it was issued so as to negate your claim to admission, you may be refused entry.

WORK PERMITS

It's difficult to obtain entry clearance to work in Britain if you don't qualify under a permit-free category (see below), particularly if your prospective employer is located in an area of high unemployment. A work permit must be obtained by an employer for a named worker and is always issued for a specific job for a specified period. Permits are issued providing no other person who's already allowed to live and work in Britain can be found to do the job, which must be proven by providing copies of advertisements and explaining why any applicants (who don't require a work permit) weren't suitable.

Vacancies must be advertised in the local, national and European press, as well as in any appropriate trade and professional journals. The salary and conditions of employment offered must be equal to those prevailing for similar jobs; the qualifications and experience must be exactly what's required; and they must usually have been acquired outside Britain. Employees should usually be aged between 23 and 54 (inclusive) for most occupations and applicants are normally expected to have an adequate knowledge of the English language. The lower age limit doesn't apply to sportsmen and sportswomen, and neither limit applies to artists and entertainers.

An employer must apply for a work permit at least eight weeks before he expects the prospective employee to start work in Britain by completing form OW1, available with explanatory leaflet OW5 from Jobcentres. After completion the form must be sent with documentary evidence of the applicant's qualifications and experience (including original references), the job description and evidence of advertising (plus full details of any replies received), to the Department of Education and Employment, Overseas Labour Section (W5), Moorfoot, Sheffield S1 4PQ (☎ 0114-840224 for an application form), **for overseas workers living abroad.**

If the overseas worker is already living in Britain, the application must be made to the Home Office, who will decide whether to refer it to the Department of Education and Employment. When an application has been approved for a Commonwealth citizen living in a Commonwealth country, the permit is sent to the prospective employee via the British government's representative there. For other countries, the permit is sent to the employer to forward to the prospective employee abroad. Work permits are issued to persons in the following categories:

- those holding recognised professional qualifications;
- administrative and executive staff;
- highly qualified technicians with specialised experience;
- other key workers with a high or scarce qualification in an industry or occupation requiring expert knowledge or skills;
- highly skilled and experienced workers for senior posts in hotel and catering work. They should have successfully completed full-time training courses of at least two years at an approved educational establishment abroad (or, exceptionally, have other relevant specialised or uncommon skills and experience);
- established entertainers, including self-employed entertainers coming to fulfil engagements (age limits don't apply);
- sportsmen and sportswomen who meet the appropriate skills criteria; professional sportsmen and sportswomen taking part in competitions of international standing don't normally require permits. The lower age limit of 23 doesn't apply.
- those coming for a limited period of training or work experience (see page 76);
- others if, in the opinion of the Secretary of State for Education and Employment, their employment is in the national interest.

Spouses and children under 18 wishing to accompany or join a work permit holder in Britain must obtain entry clearance from the nearest British Diplomatic Post to where they live, before travelling to Britain. **Failure to do so may mean they are refused entry.** A work permit holder must be able to provide accommodation and support his dependants in Britain without the use of public funds and must state this in writing. Permit holders aren't permanently restricted to the particular job for which their permit was issued, but are expected to remain in the same occupation. The consent of the Department of Education and Employment (the Department of Economic Development in Northern Ireland) is required to change jobs.

A work permit is valid for entry into Britain within six months of its date of issue and is usually issued for a period of one year unless limited to a shorter period. Permits valid for one year can usually be extended on application to the Home Office. It's difficult to obtain permission to employ someone who's already in Britain and who came here for a reason other than employment, e.g. as a visitor or a student. First the Home Office must decide whether his conditions of stay allow him to take employment, or if not, whether the conditions can be changed. Shortly before completing four years employment in Britain, work permit holders may apply to the

Home Office for the removal of the time limit on their stay, called 'settlement'. When the time limit is removed, you may take any employment without referral to the Department of Employment or the Department of Economic Development (Northern Ireland).

It's strictly forbidden for any non-EEA national to work in Britain without permission. If you're discovered working without a permit or permission, you're liable to deportation or prosecution, which could lead to a heavy fine or even imprisonment. If you have permission to remain in Britain (e.g. to study) this will probably be terminated. Certain categories of people can work full or part-time without a work permit, e.g. the wife of a work permit holder or a student (see page 77), although permission is necessary in some cases. A number of leaflets concerning work permits are published by the Department of Education and Employment and are available from Jobcentres or the Department of Education and Employment in Britain, including *A Guide for Workers from Abroad - Employment in the United Kingdom* (OW17).

Permit-Free Categories

The following people *don't* require a work permit to work in Britain:

- British nationals with the right of abode in Britain.

- Nationals of European Union (EU) and European Economic Area (EEA) countries.

- Commonwealth citizens with a parent born in Britain. A 'certificate of entitlement to right of abode' (or patriality certificate) is required from a British Diplomatic Post before arrival in Britain. Commonwealth citizens with a grandparent born in Britain don't have the right of abode there, but may obtain entry clearance to come to Britain, in which case they'll be admitted for a four-year period, after which they can apply for settlement (see page 82).

- Commonwealth citizens aged 17 to 27 seeking a holiday job and not intending to use public funds. Two years is the maximum period permitted as a working holidaymaker (see page 73).

- Religious ministers, missionaries and members of religious orders. Members of religious orders teaching in an institution of their own order don't require a permit, but if they are otherwise engaged in teaching, a permit is required.

- Doctors and dentists coming to take up research or post-graduate training positions in hospitals. If they're coming to take up 'ordinary' posts, they require a work permit.

- Sole representatives of foreign companies in Britain.

- Representatives of overseas newspapers, news agencies and broadcasting organisations, on long-term assignment to Britain.

- Private servants (aged 16 or over) of members of diplomatic missions.

- Employees of a foreign government or an international organisation of which Britain is a member.

- Teachers and language assistants under a scheme approved by the Department of Education and Employment.

- Persons permitted to set up in business as self-employed (see page 34).

- Certain categories of seamen under contract to join a ship in British waters or the operational staff of foreign-owned airlines.

- Seasonal workers at agricultural camps under approved schemes, voluntary workers and au pairs. A seasonal or voluntary worker must have been given entry clearance specifically for that purpose, otherwise an 'employment prohibited' stamp (see page 88) also includes seasonal or voluntary work.

Note that although people who qualify under the above categories don't require a work permit, they may still require entry clearance (unless they are EEA nationals).

EEA Nationals

If you're an EEA national, you can enter Britain in order to take up or seek employment, set up in business or become self-employed, without a work permit. You can remain in the UK for as long as you wish without obtaining a residence permit or registering with the police, but must be able to support yourself and your family without assistance from public funds. You *may* apply to the IND for a residence permit (issued free of charge) that confirms that you have the right of residence in the UK under European law. You must, however, provide evidence that you can support yourself and any dependants in Britain and if you have made any claims on public funds during your stay your application may be refused.

Leave to enter for any purpose is initially given for a period of six months, but anytime during the six months after employment or study has commenced an application can be made for a residence permit. A residence permit is limited to the duration of the employment or study if less than one year, otherwise it's usually valid for five years. The spouse, children under 21, other dependent children, and dependent parents, grandparents and great-grandparents of an EEA national, are all granted permission to enter Britain for the same period. EEA Nationals who are issued with a residence permit for five years can apply for the time limit to be removed after four years in continuous employment, self-employment or business in Britain.

Applications for residence permits for EEA nationals should be made to the EC Group, European Directorate, Immigration and Nationality Directorate, Room 1204, Apollo House, 36 Wellesley Road, Croydon CR9 3RR (☎ 0181-686 0688).

Other British Nationals

In addition to British citizens with the right of abode in Britain, there are a number of British 'nationals' who don't have this right, termed 'other British nationals'. These persons are citizens of British colonies or former colonies, who were granted British citizenship in the days when it was the ambition of the British Empire to paint the whole world (atlas) pink, and bestow upon everyone the 'honour' of British citizenship (see also page 440). There are a number of categories:

British Dependent Territories Citizen (BDTC): Citizens of British colonies (e.g. Gibraltar) who have the right to citizenship of that country only, and who have been subject to British immigration law since 1962.

British National (Overseas): This is a special category created so that Hong Kong residents, who aren't regarded as Chinese citizens under Chinese nationality law, wouldn't be formally stateless when their BDTC status (see above) ended on 1st July 1997. It doesn't affect their lack of immigration rights.

British Overseas Citizens: People in former British colonies who were unable to gain citizenship of that country when independence was gained. These are mainly people of Indian and Chinese descent from East African countries, Malaysia and Singapore.

British Subjects: Mainly people born in a princely state in India, who weren't in India at the time of the passage of Indian independence and citizenship laws, and therefore didn't gain Indian citizenship.

British Protected Persons: People from former colonies or territories previously under the protection of Britain, who were unable to gain new citizenship on independence.

Any British national (except a BDTC) who enters Britain legally but for a temporary period, e.g. as a visitor, cannot in practice be deported, as he's effectively stateless and no other country would be under any obligation to receive him. A scheme called the 'special quota voucher' scheme allows 'other British nationals' to live in Britain, but only at a slow trickle rate. A British national (as defined above) who's granted permission to settle in Britain, must obtain entry clearance issued by a British Diplomatic Post before travelling to Britain. If he has dependants in Britain, he must show that he's able to support them without recourse to public funds.

Working Holidaymakers

The working holidaymaker scheme is an arrangement whereby (primarily) single persons aged from 17 to 27 can come to Britain on an extended holiday for a maximum period of two years. To qualify you must be a Commonwealth citizen, British Dependent Territories citizen or a British Overseas citizen. Married persons also qualify if a couple both qualify for entry as working holidaymakers and they intend to holiday together. Couples mustn't have dependent children who are five years of age or over or who will reach five years of age before they complete their holiday. You must have the means to pay for your return fare home and be able to support yourself without recourse to public funds.

During the two-year period you may take employment which is incidental to your holiday, i.e. part-time or casual employment. You may not engage in business, provide services as a professional sports person or entertainer, or pursue a career. You cannot take full-time work (classified as over 25 hours a week) even on a casual basis for more than half your stay, i.e. one year. Any time spent outside Britain during the two-year period counts towards the maximum two years allowed (from the date you were first given permission to enter Britain).

Entry clearance must be obtained from a British Diplomatic Post before travelling to Britain, as it isn't possible to arrive as a visitor and change your status to that of a working holidaymaker. However, a person who's in Britain for a temporary purpose, e.g. as a student, may be granted an extension of stay as a working holidaymaker.

Self-Employed Persons

If you wish to enter Britain to set up in business or self-employment and aren't an EEA national, you must obtain entry clearance (see page 65) in the form of a Letter of Consent (see page 68) specifically for that purpose, before arrival. To set up in business, you must show that you will be investing a minimum of £200,000 of your own money and that your business will create new, paid, full-time employment for at least two people already resident in Britain. You must also show that there's a genuine need for your services and investment; that you will be occupied full-time in the running of the business; and that you will be able to support yourself and your dependants from the profits of the business without recourse to public funds.

Incentives to set up in business are available to people from overseas on the same basis as they are to British nationals, including grants, training assistance and government factories for rent or lease. Financial assistance is available for manufacturing investment that's judged to be particularly beneficial to the British economy. Both British government and EEA financial incentives may be available for businesses established in areas where there's high unemployment or other economic problems (designated 'assisted areas'). A business person with the appropriate entry clearance may be accompanied by his or her spouse and any children under 18, who will initially be admitted for one year providing they also have entry clearance. Annual extensions are granted, so long as the immigration rules continue to be met and settlement is normally granted after four years residence (see page 82). If you don't qualify as a businessman or as a self-employed person with special talents or skills, e.g. an entertainer, artist, sportsman or sportswoman, it's difficult to obtain permission to enter Britain and work as a self-employed person. See also **Self-Employment** on page 34.

Investors

A non-EEA national who has the sum of £1 million under his control and disposal, and who intends to live in Britain permanently, can obtain permanent leave to remain. Entry clearance is required (see page 65). An investor must plan to invest at least £750,000 in British government bonds or in the share or loan capital of British companies.

Spouses

The spouse of a non-EEA national with permission to live or work in Britain is granted entry clearance, providing the marriage is genuine, both partners intend to remain married and have actually met (the marriage cannot be arranged blind, as many are in Asian countries), they have somewhere to live and can support themselves without recourse to public funds. The spouse mustn't be under the age of 16. An application for entry clearance must be made to a British Diplomatic Post before travelling to Britain. The spouse of a non-EEA national entitled to work in Britain, is also eligible to work there, although if he enters alone, his passport may be stamped to prohibit him from working. This can usually be changed on application to the Home Office. On arrival in Britain, the spouse is given permission to stay and work for 12 months. Towards the end of the 12-month period, providing the couple are still married and intend to live together, the spouse may apply to remain in Britain permanently. A parent of a child resident in Britain with access rights granted by a British court can enter Britain providing he has entry clearance for this purpose.

Fiancé(e)s

The fiancé(e) of a non-EEA national settled in Britain, who wishes to enter for marriage and settlement, must obtain entry clearance in the form of a Letter of Consent (see page 68) from a British Diplomatic Post before travelling to Britain. Applicants must satisfy officials that a marriage will take place within a 'reasonably short time of their arrival in Britain' (usually six months) and that the **'primary purpose of marriage isn't to obtain entry or remain in Britain'**. Both marriage partners must also intend to live together permanently and must have actually met. 'Marriages of convenience' to foreigners aren't illegal unless performed for money, and in any case, don't give foreigners the right to enter or remain in Britain. You must also show that you won't use public funds and that you have access to funds and accommodation in Britain. Regulations are strictly enforced for men coming from the Indian subcontinent and for women from countries such as the Philippines and Thailand (where agencies operate a lucrative business providing wives for western men). People from other countries generally have fewer problems.

If you're permitted entry to Britain as a fiancé(e), you will initially be granted entry for six months in order to get married, during which time you're forbidden to work. If you enter Britain for a purpose other than marriage, e.g. as a tourist or student, and subsequently get married to someone who has permanent resident status in Britain, you may eventually also be granted resident status. However, you should ensure that your leave to remain in Britain hasn't expired before you get married, as if it expires within a few days or weeks of your marriage the authorities may think that you got married solely to remain in Britain (they're a suspicious lot), and can refuse you permission to remain. After marriage you must write to the IND who require:

- your passport;
- your spouse's passport or birth certificate;
- your marriage certificate;
- evidence that you can support your spouse and provide accommodation;
- a letter requesting leave to remain in Britain as the spouse of a British citizen or of someone with permanent residence.

After marriage you're initially permitted to stay for 12 months with no restrictions on working and after 12 months you're eligible to apply for settlement (see page 82). Note that foreigners with limited leave to remain in Britain who get married to a British or EEA national or a British resident, thus acquiring the right to remain in Britain, often find themselves subject to intense scrutiny by the immigration authorities. This is because an estimated 10,000 foreigners enter into marriages of convenience each year in order to remain in Britain ('professional' brides charge around £2,000 a time).

Children

Children under 18 (including natural children, step-children and adopted children) are granted permission to remain in Britain when both their parents are temporarily resident in Britain or have been granted permission to settle. An application for entry clearance for children must be made to a British Diplomatic Post before travelling to

Britain. If one parent only is resident in Britain, he (or she) must show that he has sole responsibility for a child's upbringing or that serious or compelling family or other circumstances render their exclusion undesirable. In practice it's usual for a child under 12 to be allowed to join a lone parent, particularly the mother, in Britain. Children over 18 must usually qualify for entry clearance in their own right, although special consideration is given to unmarried daughters under 21 with no close relatives in their own country.

Relatives

Only non-EEA nationals who are settled in Britain (permanent residents) may bring in relatives other than a spouse or children under 18. However, the widowed mother or father of a British resident may be granted entry clearance, providing he or she is over 65, or both parents, if one is over 65. In certain circumstances, relatives over the age of 18 (sons, daughters, sisters, brothers, uncles, aunts, and parents and grandparents under 65) may be permitted entry if they are largely dependent upon a British resident and meet the requirements. A resident must be able to support and provide accommodation for his dependants (without recourse to public funds), who must have been financially dependent on their relatives in Britain for some time before coming to Britain, and must usually have no close relatives in their own country.

It's possible to enter Britain as a visitor and change to dependant status, although a dependant who wishes to come to Britain to join parents or other relatives should seek the appropriate entry clearance before arrival, rather than pose as a visitor and seek to change status afterwards. If the immigration department suspects that your motive in coming to Britain was as a dependant and not as a bona fide visitor, your application may be refused.

Part-Time Employment

Generally no distinction is made between full and part-time employment by the immigration authorities, and whether you can work at all in Britain generally depends on what has been stamped in your passport. Spouses are usually given initial permission to remain for one year, with no restrictions on employment and no requirement to obtain a work permit. Students must obtain permission to work part-time from their college or educational institution (see **Students** on page 77) and their local Jobcentre. Voluntary workers (see page 29) don't require a work permit, but unless a person is given entry clearance specifically for voluntary work, an 'employment prohibited' stamp (see page 88) will apply.

Trainees & Work Experience

Under the training and work experience scheme, foreign nationals can work in Britain as trainees or gain practical work experience in a subject they have been studying, either in Britain or abroad. An employer must obtain a trainee or work experience permit and show how the training or work experience he offers will be useful. Trainee positions are for a predetermined length of time and although permits are usually initially issued for one year, they may be extended for a maximum period of up to three years. The maximum period for work experience is normally one year, which in exceptional circumstances can be extended by a further year. Applications should be made at least eight weeks in advance of the anticipated start date. For more information about eligibility see **Trainees & Work Experience** on page 36.

Although training and work experience are different categories, the application procedure is the same. The prospective employer must obtain form WP2 and guidance leaflet WP2 (notes) from the Department of Education and Employment, Overseas Labour Section, C Block, Porterbrook House, Moorfoot, Sheffield S1 4PQ, which contains sections to be completed by both the employer and the prospective trainee.

The employer must confirm (if applicable) that the applicant intends to leave Britain after his training period, as anyone issued with a permit as a trainee or for work experience must leave the country at the end of their training or work experience period. An overseas trainee or work experience applicant can bring his spouse and dependent children aged under 18 to Britain. After returning abroad, a trainee is expected to put to use the skills learned in Britain for at least two years, before an application under the main work permit scheme will be considered. Visitors are no longer permitted to switch to the training and work experience scheme after arrival (although students may be allowed to do so).

Students

Overseas students who are non-EEA nationals are permitted to enter Britain for the duration of a course, providing they have been accepted at a bona fide educational establishment and intend to leave Britain at the end of their course of study. Your course must be full or mostly full-time and must occupy a minimum of 15 hours a week during the daytime (0900 to 1700). You cannot combine a variety of part-time courses in order to make up the required 15 hours study per week and evening courses don't qualify as full-time study. Your fees must have been paid in full and you must show that you can financially support yourself and, in the case of married students, your spouse and children under 18 years of age (if accompanied by them), without recourse to public funds. You must prove that you're married by producing a marriage certificate. If your country of residence has strict foreign exchange controls, it's important to make arrangements for banking facilities in Britain or for money to be sent to you.

The spouse of a student and children under 18 years of age aren't permitted to work unless they have been given leave to enter or remain in Britain for 12 months or more. If you haven't decided what or where you wish to study, it's possible to obtain special entry clearance to enter Britain as a prospective student for up to six months in order to find a college and enrol there. When you have arranged everything, you can then apply for an extension of your permit.

On arrival in Britain you must have a letter from the college or school where you have been accepted as a student, stating your study hours, the length of your course and that you have paid (or can pay) your fees. If the immigration officer suspects that the course is merely a subterfuge to enable you to enter and remain in Britain, he can refuse you entry. The authorities may also check that you're attending classes. If you're permitted to enter Britain to study, you will usually be granted permission to remain for the period of your course or at least one year, unless you're enrolled in a short course.

If you wish to extend your permission to remain, you must apply to the Home Office and provide the same documentary evidence that was necessary for your initial application. You must show that you're progressing naturally from one course to another and not spending an exceptional length of time on one course. If you're a visa national and wish to leave Britain (e.g. for a holiday) during your study period, you must apply for a re-entry visa before leaving. You will need a letter from your college or school stating that you will be continuing with your studies on your return.

Students may usually apply to their local Employment Service Office (Jobcentre) to obtain permission to take part-time (evenings and weekends up to a maximum of 20 hours a week) or full-time holiday employment. You shouldn't rely on finding part-time work in order to help pay for your course or living expenses, as it may be impossible. If you find a part-time job, no suitable British resident must be available to do it, it mustn't interfere with your studies and you must receive the normal rate of pay. When you have found a job, you must obtain form OW1 (and explanatory leaflet OW5) from a Jobcentre. Your prospective employer must complete form OW1, which you then take to your local Jobcentre with your passport, police registration certificate (if applicable), and a letter from your school or college stating that the job won't interfere with your studies. You must apply for a permit for each separate job. A Jobcentre can give permission for the employment providing there's no suitable local resident available to fill the vacancy, and the wages and conditions of employment offered are equal to those prevailing for similar work in the area. Note that a student who works illegally in Britain risks prosecution or deportation.

If you need to do practical work experience during a sandwich course (which consists of full-time study with periods of full-time training and experience in industry and commerce) an application must be made to the Department of Education and Employment, Overseas Labour Section, Moorfoot, Sheffield S1 4PQ (☎ 0114-259 4074). The application must be made by your college on your behalf. Once you have been given permission to work as part of your course, you can change work experience jobs as often as necessary without re-applying for permission, providing you remain enrolled on the course. You must still, however, apply for permission to do part-time work unconnected with your course (see above). If you're prohibited from working in Britain, you must first apply to the Home Office to have the prohibition lifted before your college can apply for permission for practical work experience. However, this doesn't apply if you have a restriction on taking employment. Postgraduate students who aren't prohibited from working, can undertake teaching and demonstration work, providing it doesn't exceed six hours a week.

Overseas students aren't permitted to work in Britain after completing their studies unless there are exceptional circumstances, e.g. a student is highly qualified in a field of work where there's an acute shortage of skills. Students who have studied in Britain may be permitted to gain a further qualification as a trainee or to gain work experience (see page 36). Note, however, that student nurses are no longer permitted to switch to work permit employment after qualification. Doctors and dentists who have studied in Britain may be granted an extension for postgraduate training, providing they have limited or full registration with the General Medical Council or General Dental Council. Extensions are granted for one year at a time up to a maximum of four years. Graduates may be eligible for a position as a postgraduate research assistant at the end of their course (e.g. to study for a PhD), although this is granted in exceptional circumstances only.

If you enter Britain as a visitor and aren't a visa national (see page 67), it may be possible to obtain permission to extend your stay in Britain in order to study, although the authorities may be suspicious that your real purpose in coming to Britain was to study (and not as a genuine visitor). A visa national who enters Britain as a visitor, cannot obtain permission to study in Britain and must leave Britain and apply for a student visa in his home country. If you're unsure about anything regarding your status as a student in Britain, ask your student union or college principal, or contact the United Kingdom Council for Overseas Student Affairs (UKCOSA). UKCOSA (see address on page 88) is a registered charity established in 1968 to promote the interests and meet the needs of overseas students in Britain and those working with them as teachers, advisors and in other capacities.

Prospective students and those planning to study for less than six months (and their dependants) have no right of appeal against refusal of entry clearance and refusal of leave to enter, although they receive a detailed explanation of why their application was refused and can make a second application.

Au Pairs

Unmarried girls (or women) aged from 17 to 27 are admitted as au pairs for a period (or aggregate period) of up to two years. They must have no dependants in Britain and must be nationals of a European Economic Area (EEA) country or Andorra, Bosnia-Herzegovina, Croatia, Cyprus, the Czech Republic, the Faroe Islands, Greenland, Hungary, Macedonia, Malta, Monaco, San Marino, the Slovak Republic, Slovenia, Switzerland or Turkey. Nationals of Bosnia-Herzegovina, Macedonia and Turkey must obtain a visa from a British Diplomatic Post before travelling to Britain.

Non-EEA nationals must produce a letter from a host family confirming their invitation to work in Britain as an au pair. Immigration require a medical certificate (including a chest x-ray) confirming that you're in good health and free from contagious diseases. EEA nationals staying for longer than six months *may* apply for a residence permit from the Home Office on form EEC1. Non-EEA nationals must register with the police (see page 92) within seven days if they have been instructed to do so by the entry stamp in their passport. Au pairs from non-EEA countries aren't permitted to take any other kind of work during their stay in Britain. For further information see page 37.

Persons of Independent Means

Non-EEA nationals who wish to live but not work in Britain require entry clearance in the form of a Letter of Consent (see page 68) before arrival in Britain. To qualify you must be aged at least 60 and have under your control and disposal in the UK an income of not less than £25,000 a year. You must also be able to show that you're able to support and accommodate yourself and your dependants indefinitely without working and without recourse to public funds. Your presence must be in the best interests of Britain (whatever that means) or you must have close ties with Britain, e.g. close relatives, children attending school or periods of previous residence in Britain. If you're prohibited from working in Britain this also applies to members of your family and any dependants. Persons of independent means are usually admitted for an initial period of one year and qualify for settlement (see page 82) after four years continuous residence. Pensioners and students who are EEA nationals have the right of residence in any EEA country, providing they can prove they have sufficient income not to become a burden on the host country and have private health insurance.

Medical Treatment

A foreign national who wishes to enter Britain for medical treatment must satisfy the immigration officer that he has been accepted for consultation or treatment as a private patient, and must produce documentary evidence that he can pay for the treatment and support himself while undergoing it. A letter stating the medical treatment required must be endorsed by a registered medical practitioner holding an NHS consultant position. Persons who give medical or health treatment as the purpose of their visit, may be medically examined on arrival in Britain before being permitted entry. Anyone suffering from a communicable (contagious) disease may be refused entry, which is a throwback to the days when fears regarding TB were common. Visitors aren't permitted to enter or remain in Britain to receive treatment on the National Health Service.

Visitors

Non-EEA nationals can visit Britain for a period of up to six months, although there's nothing to stop anyone leaving Britain for a few days after remaining for six months, and then returning for another six months (providing you're able to satisfy the immigration officer that you're a bona fide visitor). However, if immigration officers think that you're spending more time in Britain than in your country of origin (or residence) or are really living in Britain, entry will be refused. If applicable, you still need entry clearance (see page 65) to enter Britain. The passports of visitors who aren't entitled to work in Britain are stamped with 'employment prohibited', which is strictly enforced (see page 88).

Visitors may be required to convince immigration officers that they will stay for a limited period only and won't attempt to find work in Britain. You may be asked to show proof that you can support yourself financially during your stay or that you have relatives or friends who can support you, and to show a return ticket or the money to buy one. Immigration officers sometimes employ double standards and immigration advice agencies report that many black and Asian visitors are refused admission, without proper account being taken of compassionate reasons why they should be permitted to remain in Britain. British residents can provide a letter of sponsorship for a visitor explaining their relationship to the applicant, the purpose of the visit and where the visitor will be staying. This is primarily intended for those who plan to provide support and accommodation for a visitor, who wouldn't otherwise be able to support himself in Britain.

Visitors are usually given permission to stay for six months, even when planning a short visit only. If you're given permission to stay for less than six months on entry, you can apply to extend your stay up to a maximum of six months in total. If you want to establish temporary residence for longer than six months *and* believe you're eligible under the immigration rules, you should apply at a British Diplomatic Post *before* coming to Britain.

Frequent visitors (e.g. business people) can apply for a multiple-entry visitor's visa valid for two years. A non-EEA national may transact business during a visit, but may not take paid or unpaid employment or self-employment, or engage in business or any professional activity. Business visitors may attend trade fairs, conferences, short classroom training courses and meetings, providing such activities are essential for fact-finding purposes as recipients of services or briefings by British businesses.

Visitors have no right of appeal against refusal of entry clearance and refusal of leave to enter, although they can make a second application after receiving an explanation why their application was refused.

Refugees

The only people who don't need to apply for refugee status on arrival in Britain are those whose status has already been decided abroad under the terms of the United Nations convention. Otherwise you will be granted refugee status in Britain only if you can prove that you have 'a well-founded fear of persecution in your own country for reasons of race, religion, nationality, membership of a particular social group or political opinion'. If you arrive in Britain seeking asylum, you should apply for it immediately on arrival. Anyone granted political asylum is automatically given refugee status. If you're already in Britain and political events in your home country make it impossible or dangerous for you to return there, you can apply for asylum in Britain. Asylum seekers may be fingerprinted and in certain circumstances may be detained while their application is being decided.

If you don't receive a decision to your application within six months (there's usually a huge backlog of cases), you can apply for permission to work in Britain. While an application for asylum is pending, you're unable to travel abroad, although if you're granted asylum you can apply for a United Nations Travel Document. After being granted asylum, you're given leave to remain in Britain for four years with no restrictions on employment and are entitled to the same social security benefits as British nationals. Your wife and children under 18 may join you in Britain and after four years you can apply for indefinite leave to remain (ILR) or settlement (normally a formality). The Home Office won't stamp your passport, but will send you a letter explaining your rights as a refugee. If you were required to register with the police (see page 92) before being granted refugee status, this will remain unchanged.

If you're refused asylum, you may be granted 'exceptional leave to remain' (ELR) for one year, after which it will be extended for a further three years until you're eventually granted settlement, usually after seven years. There are no restrictions on employment and after four years you may be allowed to bring your family to Britain, providing financial support and accommodation is available. ELR is often granted when the Home Office believes there's no threat of persecution, but finds humanitarian grounds to allow a person to remain, often because of war or civil unrest in their country of origin. Those granted ELR aren't entitled to a mandatory monetary award, but can claim Income Support (see page 305) if they aren't working or studying.

The number of foreigners seeking asylum in Britain has risen dramatically in the past decade and there were some 60,000 applications for asylum in 1998 alone (only Germany has received more applications in the last decade). Bogus 'economic refugees' (particularly eastern Europeans) have been arriving in their thousands in recent years, drawn by the relatively high social security benefits in Britain. (Tens of thousands of illegal immigrants are also 'on the run' in Britain after evading the authorities.) Since the Asylum and Immigration (Appeals) Act became law in July 1993, refusals have risen to over 75 per cent of all decisions, although applicants who are refused asylum have the right of appeal. For information about the rights of refugees in Britain contact the Refugee Council, 3 Bondway, London SW8 1SJ (☎ 0171-582 6922).

SETTLEMENT

Settlement is the name given to the status of permanent residence in Britain, which means you can stay in Britain indefinitely, without any restrictions on working or the need for a work permit. A foreigner married to a British citizen is granted settlement status after one year. Foreign nationals who have held a residence permit for four years and who have been in continuous employment, self-employment or business in Britain, can apply for settlement. If you've stayed in Britain legally for ten years and don't qualify under the normal rules, you can apply for settlement on the grounds of the length of your stay. In this case the granting of settlement status will depend on a number of factors including whether you have established a way of life in Britain and have strong ties with the country; have been in trouble with the law or have a criminal record; have spent long periods abroad; and have strong family ties in Britain.

If you're a student, you should wait until the end of your studies before applying for settlement status. If you make an application for settlement as a student and are refused, you will be unlikely to be permitted to extend your leave to remain as a student. This is because the Home Office will take an application for settlement as a sign that you don't intend to leave Britain when you've completed your studies. Settlement is also granted to the spouse of anyone who qualifies for settlement, providing both partners have been resident in Britain on the same temporary status for the same period.

A permanent resident can leave and enter Britain freely, so long as he doesn't remain out of Britain for more than two years at a time. Permanent residents who remain abroad for longer than two years may still qualify to return to Britain as residents, for example if they have strong family ties there or have lived there most of their lives. In this case an application for entry clearance must be made at a British Diplomatic Post. However, returning residents must make it clear that they are returning for the purpose of settlement. If they say that they are leaving again soon, they may be admitted as visitors only and will have great difficulty in regaining settlement status (so make it clear that you're returning home to stay). A settled foreign national can eventually apply for British citizenship (see page 440).

DEPORTATION

Any infringements concerning work permits, entry clearance, overstaying leave to remain and police registration, are taken seriously by the authorities. If you break the immigration laws, the Home Secretary can issue a deportation order sending you back to your own country (at your own expense). The grounds for deportation include:

● illegal entry into Britain;

- failure to comply with your conditions of entry (e.g. working without a permit or official permission);
- overstaying your leave to remain without obtaining an extension;
- conviction of a criminal offence for a person over 17 (when deportation is recommended by the court);
- your presence isn't considered to be in the public's interest;
- being the dependant of a deportee.

Anyone breaking the immigration law also faces a fine of up to £2,000 and up to six months imprisonment. If, in the opinion of the immigration authorities, someone entered Britain illegally or by deception, then he can be ejected from the country under a process called **removal**, without a court or appeal process. Police and immigration officers have the right to apprehend (without a warrant) anyone whom they 'reasonably suspect' to be in breach of the immigration law.

4.

ARRIVAL

On arrival in Britain to take up employment or residence, your first task will be to battle your way through immigration and customs, which fortunately for most people present no problems. Non-EEA nationals must complete a **landing card** on arrival in Britain, which are distributed on all international flights to Britain and are available from the information or purser's office on ships and ferries. For information regarding permits and visas see **Chapter 3**. British customs and immigration officials are usually polite and efficient, although they may occasionally be a 'trifle overzealous' in their attempts to deter smugglers and illegal immigrants (so it pays to be *very* nice to them). You may find it more convenient to arrive in Britain on a weekday rather than during the weekend, when offices and banks are closed.

Britain isn't a signatory to the Schengen agreement (named after a Luxembourg village on the Moselle River where the agreement was signed) which came into effect on 1st January 1995 and introduced an open-border policy between certain member countries. These now comprise Austria, Belgium, France, Germany, Greece, Iceland, Italy, Luxembourg, the Netherlands, Portugal, Spain and Sweden. Britain isn't a member and has no plans to join, ostensibly because of fears of increased illegal immigration and cross-border crime such as drug smuggling. Therefore anyone arriving in Britain from a 'Schengen' country must go through the normal passport and immigration controls, both on arrival in the UK and when entering a Schengen country from the UK.

In addition to information about immigration and customs, this chapter contains checklists of tasks to be completed before or soon after arrival in Britain and when moving house, plus suggestions for finding local help and information.

IMMIGRATION

When you arrive in Britain, the first thing you must do is go through **Passport Control**, which is usually divided into two areas: 'EU/EEA Nationals' and 'All Other Passports'. Make sure you join the right queue or you may waste a lot of time. Passport control is staffed by immigration officers, who have the task of deciding whether you're subject to immigration control, and if so, whether or not you're entitled to enter Britain. You must satisfy the immigration officer that you're entitled to enter Britain under whatever category of the rules you're applying to enter. Present your passport to the immigration officer with the following, as applicable:

- entry clearance (visa, entry certificate or letter of consent);

- a work permit (which may count as entry clearance for non-visa nationals);

- a completed 'landing card' (all non-EEA nationals);

- a letter from a bona-fide educational establishment stating that you have been accepted on a full-time course of study;

- a letter stating you have been offered a position as an au pair, trainee or voluntary worker;

- evidence that your qualifications for a job or a course of study are adequate, e.g. certificates or diplomas;

- evidence that you will be able to support yourself and any dependants during your stay in Britain without recourse to public funds (see page 66), e.g. a bank statement or letter from a bank, or evidence of financial support such as cash, travellers cheques and credit cards;

● if your stay in Britain is for a limited period only, you may need to give an assurance that you will leave at the end of that period.

Note that if you leave Britain for any reason after your initial entry, e.g. for a holiday, you will be required to produce the same documents for re-admission. EU nationals are given a form IS120 by the immigration officer on arrival, which must be produced if you remain in Britain longer than six months. If you're entering Britain from a country other than an EEA member state, you may be required to have immunisation certificates. Check the requirements in advance at a British Diplomatic Post abroad before arriving in Britain.

The immigration officer may also decide to send you for a routine (and random) health check, before allowing you to enter Britain. After the health check you must return to immigration to have your passport stamped. Britain has strict regulations regarding the entry of foreigners whose reason for seeking entry may be other than those stated. Generally the onus is on anyone visiting Britain to *prove* that he's a genuine visitor and won't infringe the immigration laws. The immigration authorities aren't required to establish that you will violate the immigration laws and can refuse your entry on the grounds of suspicion only.

The treatment of foreigners by immigration officers varies, but some people complain of harassment and have trouble convincing officials that they are genuine visitors (or whatever), e.g. blacks and Asians, particularly those from the Indian sub-continent (immigration officers are trained to assume that everyone who isn't an EEA national is trying to enter Britain illegally). Young people may also be liable to interrogation, particularly those travelling lightly and 'scruffily' dressed. It's advisable to carry international credit and charge cards, traveller's cheques, return or onward travel tickets, student identity cards, or a letter from your employer or college stating that you're on holiday. Visitors arriving from 'exotic' regions (e.g. Africa, South America, the Caribbean, the Middle and Far East) may find themselves under close scrutiny from customs officials looking for drugs.

Be extremely careful how you answer seemingly innocent questions (immigration officials *never* ask innocent questions) from the immigration authorities at your port of entry, as you could find yourself being refused entry if you give incriminating answers. Whatever the question, never imply that you may remain in Britain longer than the period permitted or for a purpose other than that for which you have been granted permission. For example, if you aren't permitted to work in Britain, you could be asked: "Would you like to work in Britain?" If you reply "Yes", even if you have no intention of doing so, you could be refused entry.

ENTRY REFUSAL

If you're refused entry into Britain, your legal position will depend on whether or not you obtained entry clearance (see page 65) before arrival, as described below:

With Entry Clearance

If you're refused entry and have entry clearance (i.e. a visa, entry certificate, letter of consent or work permit), you cannot immediately be sent back to your home country, but will be permitted to make an appeal (in the first instance to an independent adjudicator) and allowed to remain in Britain until it has been heard. You will be given the reasons for the refusal in writing and will be told how to make an appeal against the decision. You should contact the Immigration Advisory Service (IAS), 2nd Floor, County House, 190 Great Dover Street, London SE1 4YB (☎ 0171-357 7511) immediately, who will help you make your appeal. If you're a student, you can also contact the United Kingdom Council for Overseas Student Affairs (UKCOSA), 9-17 St. Albans Place, Islington, London N1 0NX (☎ 0171-354 5210, 1-4pm, Mondays to Fridays).

The appeal process can take up to several months before a decision is made. If you entered Britain to work or study, you should continue with your plans, but it wouldn't be wise to make any long-term commitments (like paying for a long course of study or signing a long lease on a property), in case you lose your appeal and must leave Britain. Your action pending an appeal may depend on the advice you receive from the IAS (or other agencies), regarding the strength of your case and the likely outcome of your appeal.

Without Entry Clearance

If you have no entry clearance, you will either be asked to return to your home country immediately or will be given a short period of temporary admission (from 24 hours to a week or more) until a final decision is made. If you aren't granted temporary admission, you may be held in a detention centre, e.g. at Heathrow airport, or you may be permitted to stay in private accommodation. If this happens to you, contact the Immigration Advisory Service (IAS) immediately, by telephoning the local representative (the IAS has representatives at all major international airports). Don't do anything until you have been advised by the IAS, who may be able to make a representation on your behalf to prevent you being deported. If you're granted temporary admission, you will be given a date and time when you must report back to immigration (if you aren't held in an immigration detention centre). You must surrender your passport to the immigration officer and provide him with an address where you will be staying, where you must remain.

The period of temporary admission is to allow you time to provide the necessary evidence to support your case for entry into Britain. If at the end of the period of temporary admission, you're unable (with the help of IAS or another agency) to provide the evidence required or you cannot convince immigration to allow you to stay, you should leave Britain voluntarily. If you refuse to leave voluntarily (or if you go into hiding), you will be detained and forcibly removed, which will probably make it impossible for you to enter Britain in future. If you leave voluntarily, there's no bar on re-entry, providing of course you can satisfy the immigration officials on your return. Contact anyone necessary before leaving. You can appeal against the refusal within 28 days, but only after you have returned to your home country.

PASSPORT STAMPS

If you're granted entry to Britain (officially called **leave to remain**), the immigration officer will put a stamp in your passport, which determines how long you may remain in Britain, if you can work, and whether you're required to register with the police (see page 92). **Your passport stamp is important and may be one of the following:**

Stamp	Restrictions
Leave to enter the United Kingdom, on condition that the holder does not enter or change employment paid or unpaid without the consent of the Secretary of State for Employment, and does not engage in any business or profession without the consent of the Secretary of State for the Home Department, is hereby given for/until *date*. The holder is also required to register at once with the police.	Limited leave to enter with a restriction on taking employment and the requirement to register with the police.
Leave to enter the United Kingdom, on condition that the holder does not enter or change employment paid or unpaid and does not engage in any business or profession, is hereby given for/until *date*.	Limited leave to enter with a prohibition on taking employment and no requirement to register with the police.
Leave to enter the United Kingdom is hereby given for/until *date*.	Limited leave to enter with no restrictions on taking employment and no requirement to register with the police.
LEAVE TO ENTER FOR SIX MONTHS EMPLOYMENT PROHIBITED.	Limited leave to enter on a visit with a prohibition on taking employment.

If you enter Britain to work, live or study, you will usually be given **leave to remain** for one year. Don't be concerned if you plan to stay longer, as you will be able to extend this later, providing your circumstances remain the same. If you're unsure about the meaning of the stamp in your passport, contact the IAS (see address on page 88) for information and advice.

CUSTOMS

When you enter Britain to take up temporary or permanent residence, you can usually import your personal belongings duty and tax free. Any duty or tax due depends on where you came from, where you purchased the goods, how long you have owned them, and whether duty and tax has already been paid in another country. Note that there are no restrictions on the importation of goods purchased tax and duty paid in another European Union country, although there are limits for certain goods, e.g. beer and wine (see page 435).

All ports and airports in Britain use a system of red and green 'channels'. Red means you have something to declare and green means that you have nothing to declare (i.e. no more than the customs allowances, no goods to sell and no prohibited or restricted goods). **If you're <u>certain</u> that you have nothing to declare, go through the 'green channel', otherwise go through the red channel.** Customs officers make random checks on people going through the green channel and there are stiff penalties for smuggling. If you're arriving by ferry with a motor vehicle, you can affix a green or red windscreen sticker to your windscreen, which helps customs officers direct you through customs.

A list of all items you're bringing in is useful, although the customs officer may still want to examine your belongings. If you need to pay duty or tax, it must be paid at the time the goods are brought into the country. Customs accept cash (sterling only); sterling travellers' cheques; personal cheques and eurocheques supported by a cheque guarantee card; Mastercard and Visa; and some ports and airports also accept debit cards. If you're unable to pay on the spot, customs will keep your belongings until you pay the sum due, which must be paid within the period noted on the back of your receipt. Postage or freight charges must be paid if you want the goods sent onto you.

Your belongings may be imported up to six months prior to your arrival in Britain, but no more than one year after your arrival, after transferring your residence. They mustn't be sold, lent, hired out or otherwise disposed of in Britain within one year of their importation or of your arrival (whichever is later), without first obtaining customs authorisation.

If you're shipping your personal belongings (which includes anything for your family's personal use such as clothing, cameras, television and stereo, furniture and other household goods) unaccompanied to Britain, you *must* complete (and sign) customs form C3, obtainable from your shipping agent or HM Customs and Excise (see address below), and attach a detailed packing list. If you employ an international removal company, they will handle the customs clearance and associated paperwork for you. Any items obtained in Britain or within the EU can be brought into Britain free of customs and excise duty or VAT, provided:

- any customs duty, excise duty or VAT was paid and not refunded when they were exported from Britain (or the EU in the case of customs duty);
- they were in your private possession and use in Britain before they were exported;
- they haven't been altered abroad, other than necessary repairs.

The personal belongings you're allowed to bring into Britain duty and tax free depend on your status, as shown below.

Visitors or Students Resident Abroad

If you're a **visitor**, you can bring your belongings to Britain free of duty and tax without declaring them to customs providing:

- all belongings are brought in with you and are for your use alone;
- they are kept in Britain for no longer than six months in a 12-month period;
- you don't sell, lend, hire out or otherwise dispose of them in Britain;
- they're exported either when you leave Britain or before they have been in Britain for more than six months, whichever occurs first.

If you're unable to export your belongings when you leave Britain you must apply to the nearest Customs and Excise Advice Centre for an extension.

In addition to the above, students attending a full-time course of study in Britain can permanently import their clothing and household linen, study articles and household effects for furnishing their accommodation.

People Moving or Returning to Britain

If you're moving or returning to Britain (including British subjects) from outside the EU, you can import your belongings free of duty and tax providing you have lived at least 12 months outside the EU. Your possessions must have been used for at least six months outside the EU before being imported. Tax and duty must have been paid on all items being imported (this isn't applicable to diplomats, members of officially recognised international organisations, members of NATO or British forces, and any civilian staff accompanying them). Articles must be for your personal use, must be declared to customs, and you mustn't sell, lend, hire out or otherwise dispose of them in Britain within 12 months, without customs authorisation.

People with Secondary Homes in Britain

If you're setting up a secondary home in Britain, you can bring normal household furnishings and equipment with you free of duty and tax if you usually live in another EU country. If you give up a secondary home outside the EU, there's no special relief from tax and duty for importing belongings from that home. If you have lived outside the EU for at least 12 months you can import household furnishings and equipment for setting up a secondary home free of duty, **but not free of value added tax (VAT), which is levied at 17.5 per cent.**

To qualify, you must either own or be renting a home in Britain for a minimum of two years, and your household furnishings and equipment must have been owned and used for at least six months. Articles must be for your personal use, must be declared to customs, and you mustn't sell, lend, hire out or otherwise dispose of them in Britain within 24 months without customs authorisation. If goods are imported separately a customs form C33 must be completed.

Further Information

Information regarding duty-free allowances (e.g. alcohol and tobacco) can be found on page 436; goods obtained tax-paid in the EU (page 435); the importation of vehicles (page 231); and the importation of pets and animals (page 454). Information concerning customs regulations is contained in a number of booklets, called *Notices*, for personal belongings and household effects (Notice 3); private motor vehicle (Notice 3A); pleasure craft or boats (Notice 8 or 8A); people moving to Britain after marriage (Notice 4); inherited goods and vehicles (Notice 368); antiques (Notice 362); vehicles for business use (Notice 115); and motor vehicles, boats or aircraft from elsewhere in the EU (Notice 728).

Copies of the notices listed above can be obtained from customs offices or from HM Customs and Excise, Excise and Inland Customs Advice Centre, Southbank, Dorset House, Stamford Street, London SE1 9PY (☎ 0171-928 3344). Customs and excise can also provide detailed information regarding the importation of special items.

Prohibited & Restricted Items

The following items are prohibited or restricted, although some may be imported with a special licence:

- Controlled drugs (e.g. opium, heroin, morphine, cocaine, cannabis, amphetamines, barbiturates and LSD), explosives (including fireworks and toy caps), firearms (including gas pistols, electric shock batons and similar weapons), explosives and flick knives. The holder of a British firearm or shotgun certificate may import a weapon into England, Wales or Scotland, in his accompanied or unaccompanied baggage. If no certificate is held, the weapon will be retained by customs until a certificate or temporary permit is produced. Note that it's now illegal to own a handgun in Britain and the ownership of other guns has also been curtailed.

- Most animals and all birds, whether alive or dead (e.g. stuffed) and certain articles derived from protected species including ivory, reptile leather, fur skins and goods made from them. **It's a criminal offence to attempt to smuggle an animal into Britain and it's almost always discovered.** Illegally imported animals are either exported immediately or destroyed and the owners are *always* prosecuted. They face (and invariably receive) a heavy fine (e.g. £500) and/or up to a year's imprisonment (see also **Pets** on page 454).

- Some horror comics and pornographic (obscene) books, magazines, tapes, videos and films.

- Meat, poultry and most of their products (whether cooked or not), including ham, bacon, sausage, paté, eggs and milk. Certain fish or fish eggs are prohibited.

- The importation of certain plants is prohibited, although it's a complicated matter. The latest regulations can be obtained from the Ministry of Agriculture, Fisheries and Food, Plant Health Administrative Unit, Foss House, 1-2 Peasholme Green, Kings Pool, York YO1 2PX (☎ 01904-455191/2).

- Non-approved radio transmitters and cordless telephones.

If you're caught trying to smuggle any goods that aren't duty and tax free, customs may confiscate the goods, and if you hide them in your car, they can confiscate that also! If you attempt to import prohibited items you may be liable to criminal charges or deportation.

POLICE REGISTRATION

Foreigners over 16 may be required to register at their local police station within seven days of arrival if they:

- are non-EEA and non-Commonwealth nationals;
- have limited permission to enter Britain;
- have been granted an extension of stay by the Home Office;
- have been allowed to work in Britain for more than three months;
- have been given leave to remain in Britain for longer than six months.

Registration also applies to the dependants over 16 of anyone required to register, including those who turn 16 while living in Britain. **When required, registration is indicated by the immigration stamp in your passport** (see page 88). You must report to the police station nearest to where you're staying within seven days, even when you're staying in temporary accommodation. You will require your passport, two passport-size photographs (black and white or colour) and the fee. In the greater London area, all residents must register at the Aliens' Registration Office (Metropolitan Police), 10 Lambs Conduit Street, London WC1N 3NX (☎ 0171-230 1208). Business hours are 0900 to 1630 Mondays to Fridays and you should expect to wait a long time (unless you're first in the queue).

Details such as your name, address, occupation, nationality, marital status and the date your permission expires, are entered in a green booklet called a 'police registration certificate'. It's advisable to take a copy of your marriage and birth certificates with you. If the police registration certificate isn't given to you on the spot, you may need to surrender your passport, which will be returned to you later with your certificate. Make a photocopy or a note of the certificate's number, date, and place of issue, in case you lose it (in which case the fee must be paid again). You should inform the authorities of any change in your situation within seven days, e.g. if you change your address or extend your leave to remain in Britain.

You're required to carry your police registration certificate with you at all times, but not your passport. It's advisable to take your police registration certificate with you when travelling abroad, as this will make re-entry into Britain easier. It should be surrendered to the Immigration Officer if you're travelling abroad for longer than two months. Note that unlike many other Europeans, Britons aren't legally required to prove their identity on demand by a policeman or other official. There are proposals to introduce a compulsory national identity (ID) card, although this has met with stiff opposition from civil liberty groups.

COUNCIL TAX REGISTRATION

All residents or temporary residents of Britain are required to register with their local authority or council for council tax purposes soon after arrival in Britain or after moving to a new home, either in the same council area or a new area. For information see page 350.

EMBASSY REGISTRATION

Nationals of some countries are required to register with their local embassy or consulate as soon as possible after arrival in Britain. Registration isn't usually mandatory, although most embassies like to keep a record of their nationals resident in Britain (if only to help justify their existence) and it may help to expedite passport renewal or replacement.

FINDING HELP

One of the biggest difficulties facing new arrivals in Britain is how and where to obtain help with day-to-day problems. For example, finding a home, schools, insurance requirements and so on. This book was written in response to this need. However, in addition to the comprehensive information provided herein, you will also require detailed local information. How successful you are at finding help will depend on your employer, the town or area where you live (e.g. those who live and work in the London area are much better served than those living in a rural village), your nationality and your English proficiency. Obtaining information isn't a problem, as there's a wealth of data available in Britain on every conceivable subject. The problem is sorting the truth from the half-truths, comparing the options available and making the right decisions. Much information naturally isn't intended for foreigners and their particular needs. You may find that your friends, colleagues and acquaintances can help, as they are often able to proffer advice based on their own experiences and mistakes. **But beware!** Although they mean well, you're likely to receive as much false and conflicting information as you are accurate (not always wrong, but possibly invalid for your particular area or situation).

Your local council offices, library, tourist information centre and Citizens Advice Bureau are excellent sources of reliable information on almost any subject (see page 450). Some large employers may have a department or staff whose job is to help new arrivals or they may contract this job out to a relocation consultant (see page 98). There are expatriate clubs and organisations for nationals of many countries in most areas, many of which provide detailed local information regarding all aspects of living in Britain, including housing costs, schools, names of doctors and dentists, shopping and much more. Clubs produce data sheets, booklets and newsletters, and organise a variety of social events which may include day and evening classes ranging from local cooking to English-language classes. One of the best ways to get to know local people is to join a social club, of which there are hundreds in all areas of Britain (look under 'Clubs and Associations' in your local Yellow Pages).

Embassies and consulates usually provide information bulletin boards (jobs, accommodation, travel) and keep lists of social clubs for their nationals, and many businesses (e.g. banks and building societies) produce books and leaflets containing valuable information for newcomers. Local libraries and bookshops usually have books about the local area (see also **Appendix B**).

CHECKLISTS

Before Arrival

The following checklist contains a summary of the tasks that should (if possible) be completed before your arrival in Britain:

- Obtain a visa, if necessary, for all your family members (see **Chapter 3**). Obviously this *must* be done before arrival in Britain.

- If possible, visit Britain prior to your move to compare communities and schools and arrange schooling for your children (see **Chapter 9**).

- Find temporary or permanent accommodation and buy a car. If you purchase a car in Britain, register it and arrange insurance (see pages 232 and 243).

- Arrange for shipment of your personal effects to Britain.

- Arrange health insurance for your family (see page 315). This is essential if you won't be covered by the National Health Service on your arrival in Britain (see page 279).

- Open a bank account in Britain and transfer funds (you can open an account with many British banks overseas). It's best to obtain some British currency before your arrival in Britain as this will save you having to change money on arrival.

- Collect and update your personal records including those relating to your family's medical, dental, educational (schools), insurance (e.g. car insurance), professional and employment (including job references) history.

- Obtain an international driver's licence, if necessary.

- Obtain an international credit or charge card, which will be invaluable during your first few months in Britain.

Don't forget to bring all your family's official documents including birth certificates, driver's licenses, marriage certificate, divorce papers, death certificate (if a widow or widower), educational diplomas and professional certificates, employment references, student ID cards, medical and dental records, bank account and credit card details, insurance policies and receipts for any valuables you're bringing with you. You also need the documents necessary to obtain a residence or work permit (see **Chapter 3**), plus certified copies, official translations and numerous passport-size photographs.

After Arrival

The following checklist contains a summary of tasks to be completed after arrival in Britain (if not done before arrival):

- On arrival at a British airport or port, have your visa cancelled and passport stamped, as applicable.

- If you don't own a car, you may wish to rent one for a week or two until you buy one locally (see page 234). Note that it's difficult to get around in rural areas without a car.

- Register for the council tax at your local town hall (see page 350).

- Register with your local consulate (see page 93).

- Do the following within a few weeks of your arrival:

  - register with your local social security office (see page 303);
  - open an account at a local bank and give the details to your employer (see page 334);
  - arrange schooling for your children (see **Chapter 9**);
  - find a local doctor and dentist (see **Chapter 12**);
  - arrange whatever insurance is necessary (see **Chapter 13**) including:
    * health insurance (see page 315);
    * car insurance (see page 243);
    * home-contents insurance (see page 321);
    * personal liability insurance (see page 323)

DUN
SEARCHING

5.

ACCOMMODATION

In most regions of Britain accommodation (both to rent and buy) isn't difficult to find, depending of course on what you're looking for. There are, however, a few exceptions, e.g. London, where property at an affordable price is in high demand and short supply, and where rents (in relation to average salaries) can be astronomical. Particularly hard hit are those on low incomes, pensioners, the unemployed, single parents, students and the young. Accommodation usually accounts for around a third of the average British family's budget, but can easily rise to 40 or 50 per cent in high cost areas and when interest rates are high.

Home ownership has increased considerably in the last decade due to easier access to home loans and government encouragement to council house (housing owned by local authorities) tenants to purchase their homes. Home ownership is, however, unevenly spread throughout Britain and is only some 50 per cent in Scotland compared with 70 per cent in Wales and around 75 per cent in England. The average age of first-time buyers in Britain is around 26, one of the lowest in the world (compared, for example, with around 37 in Germany). Britons also have the highest level of ownership of second homes in Europe. There are around 2.5 people per household in Britain and 25 per cent of households consist of one person only, a figure that's expected to rise considerably in the next ten years (most new homes are built for single occupation). Four out of five people in Britain live in houses rather than apartments (flats).

Britain had a booming house market in the '80s, which culminated in average prices rising by 30 per cent annually in 1988/89, when the most desirable properties rose by 50 to 100 per cent in a single year! However, during the recession in the late '80s and early '90s Britain experienced an unprecedented collapse in property values, resulting in almost two million households with negative equity (where the amount owed on the mortgage exceeds the value of a property). Negative equity was widespread in the south-east (where over 25 per cent of owners were affected in some areas), although there was virtually no negative equity in Scotland and Northern Ireland. The shock of falling home values hit the British particularly hard, as they traditionally see buying a house as an investment rather than a home for life (as is common in most of the rest of Europe).

In recent years there has been a strong recovery in property values in most regions. In 1998 prices were rising by up to 30 per cent a year in some parts of London, although the average rise was between 5 and 10 per cent, and prices actually fell or remained flat is some areas. Despite the problems in recent years, property remains an excellent long-term investment. The huge demand for new homes has led to an increasing amount of land being swallowed up by buildings (the worst affected area is southern England) and it's estimated that one-fifth of England will be built on by the year 2050.

RELOCATION CONSULTANTS

If you're fortunate enough to have your move to (or within) Britain paid for by your employer, it's likely he will arrange for a relocation consultant to handle the details. There are generally three types of relocation consultants in Britain: corporate relocation agents (whose clients are usually large companies), commercial property agents and home-search agents, who act for individuals. The larger relocation consultants may provide all three levels of service, while smaller companies may have just a few staff and offer a home-search service only. Companies that are members of the Confederation of British Industry (CBI) can use the CBI's relocation services.

Relocation consultants usually charge a registration (or administration) fee of £200 to £300, payable in advance. The fees charged by consultants vary widely and may range from £250 to £500 a day for accompanied viewing of properties and other amenities. If finding a house is part of the service, a fee of 1 or 2 per cent of the purchase price is normal, with a minimum charge of around £750. To arrange the sale of an employee's house, provide a bridging loan, advise on mortgages, schools and insurance, and help a spouse find a job, a relocation consultant may charge a company from £1,000 to £2,000. Home-search companies are becoming increasingly common and will undertake to find the home of your dreams. This can save buyers considerable time, trouble and money, particularly if you have special or unusual requirements. Some specialise in finding exceptional residences costing upward of £250,000 and can save buyers money by negotiating the price on their behalf.

Finding accommodation for single people or couples without children can usually be accomplished in a week or two, depending on the area, while families usually take a bit longer. You should usually allow at least two months between your initial visit and moving into a purchased property. Rental properties (see page 101) can usually be found in two to four weeks, depending on the location and your requirements. There are relocation consultants in all parts of the country, most of which provide the following services:

House Hunting: This is usually the main service provided by relocation consultants and includes both rented and purchased properties. Services usually include locating a number of properties matching your requirements and specifications, and arranging a visit (or visits) to Britain to view them.

Negotiations: Consultants will usually help and advise with all aspects of house rental or purchase and may conduct negotiations on your behalf, organise finance (including bridging loans), arrange surveys and insurance, organise your removal to Britain and even arrange quarantine for your pets (see page 454).

Schools: Consultants can usually provide a special report on local schools (both state and private) for families with children. If required, the report can also include private boarding schools in Britain.

Local Information: Most consultants will provide a comprehensive information package for a chosen area including information about employment prospects, state and private health services, local schools (state and private), estate agents, shopping facilities, public transport, amenities and services, sports and social facilities, and communications.

Miscellaneous Services: Most consultants provide advice and support (particularly for non-working spouses) both before and after a move, orientation visits for spouses, counselling for domestic and personal problems, help in finding jobs for spouses and even marriage counselling (moving to another country puts a lot of strain on relationships).

Although you may consider a relocation consultant's services expensive, particularly if you're footing the bill yourself, most companies and individuals consider it money well spent. You can find a relocation consultant through the Association of Relocation Agents, PO Box 189, Diss IP22 1PE (☎ 08700-737475, e-mail: info@relocationagents.com) or look in the Yellow Pages under 'Relocation Agents'.

If you just wish to look at properties for rent or sale in a particular area, you can make appointments to view properties through real estate agents in the area where you plan to live and arrange your own trip to Britain. However, you must make *absolutely certain* that agents know exactly what you're looking for and obtain property lists in advance.

BUYING PROPERTY

Buying a house or apartment in Britain has traditionally been an excellent investment, although this was severely tested in the '90s during much of which a property investment was anything but as safe as houses! However, most people still find buying preferable to renting, depending of course on how long you're planning to stay in Britain and where you're planning to live. If you're staying for a short term only, say less than two years, then you may be better off renting. For those staying longer than two years, buying should be the better option, particularly as buying a house or apartment is generally no more expensive than renting and you could make a nice profit.

Prices: Apart from the obvious things such as size, quality and land area, the most important factor influencing the price of a house is its location. A three-bedroom, semi-detached house costing £50,000 in the north of England or Scotland, will usually cost at least 50 per cent more in the south-east. In early 1999, the average price of a house in Britain was around £70,000, which was the same as ten years previously at the height of the property boom (it fell to around £60,000 in 1995). As with most things, higher-priced houses, e.g. over £250,000 (which outside London are usually termed executive or prestige homes by estate agents), generally provide much better value for money than cheaper houses, with a proportionately larger built area and plot of land, better build quality, and superior fixtures and fittings. Most semi-detached and detached houses have single or double garages included in the price.

There are few bargains when it comes to buying properties and although you may be able to negotiate a reduction of 5 per cent or possibly 10 per cent (particularly if someone is looking for a quick sale in a buyer's market), there's usually a good reason if a property is substantially cheaper than other similar properties. Although it isn't always advisable to look a gift horse in the mouth, you should generally be suspicious of a bargain. On the other hand, most sellers and estate agents price properties higher than the market price or the price they expect to receive, knowing that prospective buyers will try to drive the price down, so always haggle over the price (even if you think it's a bargain). This is, in fact, one of the few occasions in Britain when you're expected to bargain over the price, although you should try to avoid insulting the owner by offering a derisory amount. Note that most house sales are part of a chain of sellers and buyers (around seven or eight isn't uncommon) and only one link needs to fail to jeopardise a whole series of sales. If you're a foreigner and a first-time buyer (at least in Britain), you will be delivered from the dreaded chain and may also be eligible for special terms offered by many lenders to first-time buyers (see page 345).

Contracts: When buying property in England, Wales or Northern Ireland, prospective buyers make an offer subject to survey and contract. Either side can amend or withdraw from a sale at any time before the exchange of contracts (when a sale is legally binding). In a seller's market, gazumping (where a seller agrees to an offer from one prospective buyer and then sells to another for a higher amount) is rampant and *isn't illegal*. There are proposals to speed up the home buying process (from a few months to a few weeks), which would reduce the risk of gazumping, although many people believe that following the example of Scotland (see below) and many other countries is the only way to stamp it out altogether. On the other hand, in a buyer's market a buyer may threaten to pull out at the last minute unless the seller reduces the price (called 'gazundering').

There's no gazumping in Scotland as neither side can pull out once an offer has been made and accepted. In Scotland, when you wish to purchase a property your solicitor will contact the seller's solicitor and note your interest. Once the seller's solicitor has had sufficient interest, he'll usually fix a closing date, by which time all offers must be submitted in writing. Once your offer in writing is accepted, it's legally binding and you cannot pull out. Therefore it's vital that you have a survey done (and have the necessary finance) before making an offer in Scotland. The problem with this system is that each prospective buyer must have his own survey done, which has prompted a proposed change in the law where the seller is responsible for having a survey done prior to selling a property (an excellent idea).

Information: There are numerous other books on the subject of buying a home including *Buying a Home in Britain* by your author David Hampshire (published by Survival Books in summer 1999) and *Which? Way to Buy, Sell and Move House* by Alison & Richard Barr (Which? Books). There are also many magazines published in Britain for homebuyers including *What Mortgage, Mortgage Magazine, What House* and *House Buyer*, which contain the latest information about mortgages and house prices throughout Britain. Homebuyer Events Ltd., Mantle House, Broomhill Road, London SW18 4JQ (☎ 0181-877 3636) organise regular property shows in Britain (which include overseas homes). All building societies and banks publish free booklets for homebuyers, most of which contain excellent (usually unbiased) advice.

RENTED ACCOMMODATION

Rented accommodation is the answer for people who don't want the trouble, expense and restrictions involved in buying a house, or who are staying in Britain for one or two years only (when buying isn't usually practical). Unlike most European countries, there isn't a strong rental market in Britain (less than 10 per cent of private properties are rented in Britain, compared with around 20 per cent on the continent), where families have traditionally preferred to buy rather than rent. However, there are still some two million people living in private rented accommodation in Britain. There's a chronic shortage of rental properties in many areas, particularly in London and other major cities, and rental properties with three or more bedrooms located in good areas are in short supply everywhere. Furthermore, rental accommodation can be prohibitively expensive and the quality of properties often leaves a lot to be desired, particularly at the lower end of the market. **You should be aware that renting accommodation is a jungle in Britain, which has one of the most unregulated letting markets in Western Europe (with little or no consumer protection against unscrupulous agents and landlords).**

One of the reasons for the unpopularity of renting in Britain is that it has traditionally been relatively easy to obtain a 95 or even 100 per cent mortgage with repayments over 25 or 30 years. This means that it's usually cheaper or no more expensive to buy a home in Britain than it is to rent. According to research done by

Abbey National Bank, renting is around 35 per cent more expensive than buying a home over the long term and people who rent a house 'waste' an average of some £85,000 over 25 years! Owners can also make a tax-free profit (or a tax-free loss!) in a relatively short period as no capital gains tax (see page 362) is paid on the profits from the sale of your principal home. Many people who cannot afford to pay a high mortgage often let a room (or rooms) to reduce the cost.

The Housing Act 1988 deregulated new lettings in the private sector. From January 1989 new lettings have generally been of two kinds: an **assured tenancy** with a long-term security of tenure or an **assured shorthold tenancy** for a fixed period of at least six months (see **Rental Contract** on page 106). These changes were intended to encourage greater choice and competition in the rental market. Unlike many other countries, 95 per cent of rental properties in Britain are let furnished. The reason is historical, as until January 1989 landlords had much greater protection under the law if properties were let furnished, although this is no longer the case. The furniture and furnishings in many rental properties varies from fair to terrible, except for the rare luxury property (with an astronomical rent) that's let for a fixed term by owners who are spending a period abroad.

Rental property can usually be found in two to four weeks in most areas, with the possible exception of large houses (four or more bedrooms), which are rare and *very* expensive. Family accommodation in particular is in short supply in London, with the possible exception of luxury homes with astronomical rents. Most people settle for something in the suburbs or country and commute to work. Note, however, that if you need to travel into a city centre (particularly London) each day, you should be prepared to spend at least an hour or more travelling each way. Unfurnished houses and apartments are difficult to find anywhere and were normally rented on payment of a large fee (which could be £thousands), which was nominally for 'fixtures and fittings', but was in fact just a way of selling the tenancy (known as 'key money'). This is still practised but is rarer nowadays.

Most rented property is let through letting agencies or estate agents, who charge between £25 and £150 for 'administration', taking up references, drawing up tenancy agreements and carrying out an inventory. You must usually pay one month's rent in advance, depending on the type of property and the rental agreement, plus a deposit against damages equal to one to two months rent. When you agree to rent a property you're usually asked for a holding deposit of between £50 and £200 before an agreement is signed (this should go towards your rent but is often simply an additional fee). Some letting agents (e.g. in London) charge an up-front fee of around £100 to house hunters with the promise of finding them accommodation, in return for which they simply supply a list of 'vacant' properties often just taken from newspapers. Many agents employ a wealth of scams and rip off both the tenant and the landlord at every opportunity.

Agents usually have a number of properties available for immediate occupancy and lists are normally updated weekly. You should have no problem finding something suitable in most areas if you start looking at least four weeks prior to the date when you wish to take occupancy. Most letting agents require a reference from your employer (or previous employer if you have been less than one year with your current employer), and bank and credit references, or in the case of a company let, copies of audited accounts and status. Agents may ask to see a foreign resident's police registration certificate (see page 92).

Your deposit should be put into a savings account in the names of the renter and the agent or landlord, although this is rare (if it isn't and the letting agent goes bankrupt, you will lose your deposit). If possible, you should deal only with a member of the Association of Residential Letting Agents (ARLA) or the National Association of Estate Agents (NAEA), both of which insist that members have a bonding scheme or professional indemnity cover to safeguard rental income and deposits. However, agents are totally unregulated in Britain and you often have no option but to deal with 'cowboys'.

Local Housing Aid or Advice Centres offer advice concerning finding somewhere to live and usually handle both private and council house problems. Contact your local council for information. A Citizens Advice Bureau can also offer advice regarding the legal aspects of letting and a tenant's rights. In some towns and cities there are council-run housing aid centres, where you can obtain free advice on housing problems. There are also a number of useful books published detailing the legal rights and duties of both landlords and tenants including the *Which? Guide to Renting and Letting* (Which? Books).

Single Accommodation

Finding accommodation that doesn't break the bank is a huge problem for young single people and students (and anyone not earning a fortune). For many the solution is a bedsit, flatlet, lodgings or sharing accommodation with others, officially termed 'houses in multiple occupation' (HMOs). Single accommodation also includes hostels (including student and youth hostels), guesthouses, lodgings, bed & breakfast and cheap hotels, although these usually provide relatively expensive temporary accommodation only. Don't expect any 'luxuries' in inexpensive accommodation as the standard is generally poor, particularly in areas with high demand.

The standard of rental accommodation is at its worst in HMOs such as bedsits, studios, shared houses and properties with shared facilities. In an English House Conditions Survey in 1996 it was estimated that around 20 per cent (much higher in London and other major cities) of all privately rented homes were unfit for human habitation. In fact at the bottom end of the market Britain has among the worst rental accommodation in Western Europe which may include faulty plumbing, poor sanitation, decrepit furniture, insect and rodent infestations, dangerous wiring and unsafe gas appliances. There's little or no control over landlords who get away with 'murder', although legislation has been proposed which will lay down minimum standards and include a registration scheme.

You must be over 18 to hold a tenancy agreement and young people usually find it harder to find a rental property than more mature people, due to the usual arguments that the young are unreliable, noisy, poor, itinerant and untidy (etc.). If you're seeking cheap accommodation, you may find it more difficult in September when the new term starts and students are looking for accommodation (if you're a student see also page 196). Before taking on long-term accommodation, you may wish to check the council tax rate in the area (see page 350).

Bedsits: If you prefer to live on your own but don't want to pay a lot of rent (who does?), the solution may be a bedsit (also called a studio). A bedsit usually consists of a furnished room in an old house, where you live, eat, sleep and sometimes cook. If separate cooking facilities are provided, you must usually share them with someone else (or a number of people). You must also usually share a bathroom and toilet, provide your own linen (sheets, blankets and towels), and do your own laundry and cleaning. Bedsits offer plenty of privacy but can be lonely and depressing. A single bedsit costs from around £40 in the provinces and from £60 a week in London. Double bedsits are also available costing from around £60 in the provinces and from £75 a week in London. Slightly up market from a bedsit is a flatlet or studio flat, which may have its own bath or shower and toilet, and sometimes a separate kitchen or kitchenette (a tiny kitchen). The rent for a studio apartment is around 50 per cent higher than for a bedsit.

Lodgings: Another possibility is to find lodgings (also called digs) in a private home, which is becoming increasingly common as many people are forced to take in lodgers to pay their mortgages. This is similar to bed and breakfast accommodation (see page 374), except that you're usually treated as a member of the family and your rent usually includes half-board (breakfast and an evening meal). In lodgings you have less freedom than a bedsit and are required to eat at fixed times, but will at least have some company. Lodgings are often arranged by English-language schools for foreign students. A boarding house is similar to lodgings where the owner takes in a number of lodgers and may provide half-board or cooking facilities. Lodgings or a room in a boarding house cost from around £45 in the provinces to £60 a week in London, for a room with breakfast. With breakfast and an evening meal, the cost ranges from around £60 in the provinces to £75 a week in London.

Shared Accommodation: This is another answer to high rents, particularly in major towns and cities, and is popular among students and the young. Sharing usually involves sharing the kitchen, bathroom, living room and dining room, and may also include sharing a bedroom. Sharing also usually means sharing all bills (in addition to the rent) including electricity, gas and telephone, and may also include sharing food bills and cooking. Some landlords include electricity and gas in the rent. The cleaning and the general upkeep of the house or apartment is also usually shared. As always when living with others, there are advantages and disadvantages of shared accommodation, and its success depends on the participants' ability to live and work together.

If you rent a property with the intention of sharing, make sure that it's permitted in your contract. The cost of sharing a furnished apartment varies considerably depending on the size, location and amenities. A rough guide is from around £40 (single) to £60 (double) in the provinces and from £60 a week in London with your own bedroom. Note that shared accommodation in many areas is in old, run-down houses, where even the living and dining rooms have been converted into bedrooms. Many people advertise for flatmates in local daily and evening newspapers. Often you will be sharing with the owner, which can be a bit inhibiting. Flat-sharing is particularly common in London, where many newspapers and magazines contain advertisements for flat-sharers, e.g. the *Evening Standard*.

For information about college accommodation see page 196 and for information about temporary accommodation including hotels, bed and breakfast, self-catering and youth hostels, see **Chapter 15**.

Rental Costs & Standards

Rental costs vary considerably depending on the size (number of bedrooms) and quality of a property, its age and the facilities provided. Not least, rents depend on the neighbourhood and the region of Britain, and are generally lowest in Scotland,

Northern Ireland, Wales and the North of England, and highest in London and the south-east. Rents are also lower in rural than urban areas. As a general rule, the further a property is from a large city or town, public transport or other facilities, the cheaper it will be (obvious really, isn't it?). Rents are high, particularly when you consider that renting can cost more than buying a home in many areas. Average rental costs for furnished apartments and houses in the south-east (outside London and the M25 motorway) are shown in the table below:

No. of Bedrooms	Monthly Rent (£)
bedsit/studio	200 to 450
1	350 to 600
2	400 to 800
3	500 to 1,200
4	600 to 2,000 +++

The rents shown above are for good quality modern or renovated properties and don't include properties located in the central area of large towns, in major cities or in exclusive residential areas, for which the sky's the limit. In London, rents are at least 50 per cent higher than the minimum shown above, while in some remote country areas they may be lower. Rents for desirable houses with four or more bedrooms are £3,000 or £4,000 per month in many areas. It may be possible to find cheaper, older apartments and houses for rent, but they are rare, generally small and don't usually contain the conveniences that are standard in a modern home, e.g. no central heating or double glazing (heating in old houses can be highly eccentric). If you like a property but think the rent is too high, try to negotiate a reduction or ask an agent to put your offer to the owner.

Kitchens normally contain an oven with a grill, refrigerator (small), fitted kitchen units, and occasionally a dishwasher and a separate freezer. Many houses don't have basements or utility rooms, so washing machines (usually provided) and dryers are located in the kitchen. Many houses have lofts and garages that are often used for storage. Most have baths (but not enough hot water to fill them) and may have a separate shower or an *en suite* shower or bathroom. Often shower attachments are run off a bath and don't have a separate pump (which means that the water trickles out). Bathrooms occasionally contain a bidet. In general, British plumbing is better than that found in many countries (although Americans won't be impressed). All modern houses have central heating (see page 116), although it's rare at the bottom end of the market. An airing cupboard (linen closet) is common and usually contains the hot water boiler. Unfurnished apartments and houses usually have light fittings in all rooms, although there may be no bulbs or lampshades. Fitted wardrobes in bedrooms are rare and curtain rails aren't provided unless they are built-in. Most houses, whether furnished or unfurnished, are fully or partly carpeted.

Many rental properties are old houses, particularly in London and other large cities, that have been modernised and divided into apartments. At the bottom end of the market, many properties have dreadful furnishings, e.g. flowery wallpaper which may 'match' the equally awful three-piece suite, with sickly green carpets and brown bathroom suites (or vice versa). Up market (i.e. expensive) property may, however, be furnished to a high standard. In furnished accommodation you usually need to provide your own bedding and linen, although crockery, kitchen utensils and most household appliances are usually provided. It may be possible to 'throw out' the owner's or landlord's tatty furniture and replace it with your own (but you may have to pay to move and store it).

Rental Contracts

When you find a suitable house or apartment to rent, you should insist on a written contract with the owner or agent, which is called a tenancy or rental agreement. Make sure that you obtain a rent book, which is used to record all payments you make. If you don't have a rent book, always pay by cheque and insist on a receipt. Your contract may include details of when your rent will be reviewed or increased, if applicable. When you wish to leave rented accommodation you must give at least one month's notice in writing, unless it's within the first six months of an assured shorthold tenancy (see below), in which case you must pay the rent to the end of the period. If your landlord wants you to leave, the notice he must give you depends on your agreement with him and whether your tenancy is covered by the law. It's a criminal offence for your landlord to harass you in any way in an attempt to drive you out. Under the Housing Act (1988) the following kinds of rental agreements and tenancies were created, most of which provide tenants with fewer rights than previously and make evictions easier for landlords:

Assured tenancy: An assured tenancy is a tenancy for an indefinite period and doesn't need to be in writing. The landlord cannot live on the premises and providing you pay the rent and take care of the property, you cannot be asked to leave. Your landlord must apply to a county court and must have a good reason to evict you, e.g. unpaid rent, damage to the property or its contents, or you must have otherwise broken your contract with him. However, if he offers you similar accommodation, needs the property for himself, or a mortgage lender needs vacant possession in order to sell it, a court may serve you with written notice to leave. The rent cannot be increased until one year after you first agreed the rent and if you don't agree with the increase you can ask the council's Rent Assessment Committee to set a fair rent.

Assured shorthold tenancy: An assured shorthold tenancy is a tenancy with a fixed time limit of not less than six months, for which a written rental agreement is necessary stating clearly that it's an assured shorthold tenancy. You cannot terminate your agreement (or be evicted) during the first six months and thereafter you or your landlord must give two months notice in writing to terminate the agreement. Under an assured shorthold tenancy you have the right in certain cases to ask the Rent Assessment Committee to set a fair rent.

No agreement: If you haven't an agreement with your landlord, you're protected in law and have the same rights as an assured tenancy (see above) if your landlord doesn't live on the premises. Always try to obtain a tenancy agreement and retain evidence of all payments to your landlord. If after taking up residence you're offered a holiday let, licence agreement or tenancy with board and service, you should refuse and contact a Citizens Advice Bureau for advice. These agreements provide you with no security and few legal rights as a tenant.

Flat-sharers: The law regarding flat-sharing is more complicated and it's simpler when one person is the tenant and sub-lets to the others, which must be permitted by the tenant's agreement. It's possible for all sharers to be joint tenants with one tenancy agreement or individual tenants with individual tenancy agreements. Whatever the agreement, you should have only one rent book and pay the rent in a lump sum. It's usually the occupants' responsibility to replace flatmates who leave during the tenancy.

Fair Rents: A tenant in an assured shorthold tenancy can ask the local Rent Assessment Committee for help in ensuring that his rent isn't too high, although this may not apply to someone with a written assured tenancy. Your complaint will be investigated and your rent could be lowered or raised (if it's decided the rent is too low). If you have been overcharged, the landlord can be ordered to repay the excess as far back as two years. Information concerning rent allowances, rent rebates, fair rents and housing benefits is contained in a series of free housing booklets published by the Department of the Environment and available from rent (registration) offices, local authorities, Citizens Advice Bureaux and housing advice centres.

Deposits: Usually a deposit equal to one or two months (the maximum permitted by law) rent must be paid for an assured shorthold tenancy. This should be repaid when you leave, providing there are no outstanding claims for rent, unpaid bills, damages or cleaning. Always check the contract to find out who holds the deposit and under what circumstances it will be returned, and obtain a receipt. Note than many agents and landlords will go to almost any lengths to avoid repaying a deposit and tenants in Britain lose £millions to landlords and letting agents who refuse to repay deposits when a lease has expired. Often the landlord will make a claim for 'professional' cleaning running into hundreds of pounds, even when you leave a place spotless. If the landlord fails to return your deposit you should threaten legal action and if this has no affect you should take him to the small claims court (see page 448).

Don't sign a contract unless you're sure you fully understand all the small print. Ask one of your British colleagues or friends for help, or obtain legal advice. British law (actually English or Scottish law) usually prevents you from signing away all your rights; nevertheless, it pays to be careful. If you have any questions regarding your rental agreement or problems with your landlord, you can contact your local Citizens Advice Bureau for advice (see page 450). They will check your rental agreement and will advise you of your rights under the law.

UTILITIES

Utilities is the collective name given to electricity, gas and water companies (and usually also includes telephone companies). All Britain's utility companies have been privatised in the last decade or so, which was quickly followed by increased prices and worse service. However, in the last few years most people have been able to choose their electricity and gas supplier and the increased competition has led to lower prices, with many companies promising savings of around 10 per cent to switch companies. Many companies now provide both electricity and gas and offer contracts for the supply of both fuels, often called 'dual fuel', which may result in a discount (although you may be better off buying from separate companies). You can find the cheapest supplier of electricity and gas on the Internet (www.buy.co.uk), although you should carefully compare rates, standing charge and services before changing your supplier.

Electricity

The electricity supply in Britain is 240 volts AC, with a frequency of 50 hertz (cycles). This is suitable for all electrical equipment with a rated power consumption of up to 3,000 watts. For equipment with a higher power consumption, a single 240V or 3-phase, 380 volts AC, 20 amp supply must be used (in Britain, this is installed only in large houses with six to eight bedrooms or industrial premises). Power cuts are rare in most parts of Britain, although some areas experience many a year. Electricity companies pay compensation for a power cut lasting longer than 24 hours, but nothing for cuts of less than 24 hours (which includes 99.9 per cent of cuts).

If you move into an old home in Britain, the electricity supply may have been disconnected by the previous electricity company and in a brand new home you will also need to get the electricity connected. In the last few years householders have been able to choose their electricity company from among British Gas, Eastern Energy, Eastern Electricity, East Midlands Electricity, Independent Energy, London Electricity, Manweb, MEB, Northern Electric & Gas, Norweb, Scottish Hydro-Electric, Scottish Power, SEEBOARD, Southern Electric, SWALEC, South Western Electricity and Yorkshire Electricity. Most companies cover the whole country, while a few cover certain regions only. To have the electricity reconnected and the meter read, for which you should allow at least two days, you must choose an electricity company and complete a form. There's usually a charge for connection. If you're in Britain for a short stay only, you may be asked for a security deposit or to obtain a guarantor (e.g. your employer). You must contact your electricity company to get a final reading when you vacate your home.

Power Rating: Electrical equipment rated at 110 volts AC (for example from the USA) requires a converter or a step-down transformer to convert it to 240 volts AC, although some electrical appliances (e.g. electric razors and hair dryers) are fitted with a 110/240 volt switch. Check for the switch, which may be located inside the casing, and make sure it's switched to 240 volts *before* connecting it to the power supply. Converters can be used for heating appliances but transformers, which are available from most electrical retailers, are required for motorised appliances (they can also be purchased secondhand). Total the wattage of the devices you intend to connect to a transformer and make sure its power rating *exceeds* this sum.

Generally all small, high-wattage, electrical appliances, such as kettles, toasters, heaters and irons, need large transformers. Motors in large appliances such as cookers, refrigerators, washing machines, dryers and dishwashers, will need replacing or fitting with a large transformer. In most cases it's simpler to buy new appliances in Britain, which are of good quality and reasonably priced, and sell them when you leave if you cannot take them with you. Note also that the dimensions of British cookers, microwave ovens, refrigerators, washing machines, dryers and dishwashers may differ from those in most other countries. All electrical goods purchased in Britain must conform to British safety standards. If you wish to buy electrical appliances, such as a cooker or refrigerator, you should shop around as prices vary considerably (see **Household Appliances** on page 432). The British Electrotechnical Approvals Board (BEAB) label indicates that an electrical appliance has been tested for compliance with the appropriate safety standards by an independent approval organisation.

Frequency Rating: A problem with some electrical equipment is the frequency rating, which in some countries, e.g. the USA, is designed to run at 60 Hertz and not

Britain's 50 Hertz. Electrical equipment *without* a motor is generally unaffected by the drop in frequency to 50 Hz (except television sets, see page 159). Equipment with a motor may run okay with a 20 per cent drop in speed, however, automatic washing machines, cookers, electric clocks, record players and tape recorders are unusable in Britain, if they aren't designed for 50 cycle operation. To find out, look at the label on the back of the equipment. If it says 50/60 Hertz, it should be okay. If it says 60 Hz, you may try it anyway, **but first ensure that the voltage is correct as outlined above.** If the equipment runs too slowly, seek advice from the manufacturer or the retailer. For example, you may be able to obtain a special pulley for a tape deck or turntable to compensate for the drop in speed. Bear in mind that the transformers and motors of electrical devices designed to run at 60 Hz will run hotter at 50 Hz, so make sure that equipment has sufficient space around it for cooling.

Fuses: Most apartments and all houses have their own fuse boxes. Fuses may be of three types: wire, cartridge fuses or circuit breakers. Older houses may have rewireable fuses, although these are rare nowadays. Cartridge fuses are found in few houses these days and are colour coded to signify their rating. Circuit breakers are usually fitted to modern houses (and houses that have been modernised) and consist of circuit breakers, which, when a circuit is overloaded trip to the 'off' position. When replacing or repairing fuses of any kind, if the same fuse continues to blow, contact an electrician – **never attempt to use fuse wire or fit a fuse of a higher rating than specified, even as a temporary measure.** When replacing fuses, don't rely on the blown fuse wire or fuse as a guide, as it may have been wrong. If you use an electric lawn-mower or power tools outside your home or in your garage, you should have a Residual Current Device (RCD) installed. This can detect current changes of as little as a thousandth of an amp and in the event of a fault (or the cable being cut), will disconnect the power in around 0.04 seconds.

Plugs: Regardless of the country you have come from, all your plugs will require changing, or a lot of expensive adapters will be required. Modern British plugs have three rectangular pins (which are of course unique to Britain) and are fitted with fuses as follows:

Fuse Rating (amps)	Colour	Watts
1 (or 2)	green	shaver adapters (2-pin) only
2	white	standard lamp
3	red	maximum 750
5	grey	750 to 1,250
13	brown	1,250 to 3,000

All plugs in Britain are 'approved', e.g. shown by an ASTA or BSI symbol on them, which means they have passed an independent test before being offered for sale. Moulded plugs must be fitted to electrical appliances sold in Britain. Items such as audio and hi-fi equipment, electric blankets, radios, table lamps, soldering irons, televisions (some manufacturers recommend a 5-amp fuse) and slow cookers up to 720 watts, should be fitted with a three-amp fuse (red). Most other heavier domestic items (e.g. iron, kettle, toaster, vacuum cleaner, washing machine, electric fire, refrigerator, freezer, tumble or spin drier, dishwasher, lawn mower) between 1,250 and 3,000 watts need a 13-amp fuse (brown). If you aren't sure what sort of fuse to use, consult the instructions provided with the apparatus. The fuse rating (amps) is calculated by dividing the wattage by the voltage (240). Note that for maximum safety, electrical appliances should be turned off at the main wall point when not in use (in Britain the DOWN position is ON and the UP position is OFF).

Wiring: Some electrical appliances are earthed and have a three-core wire. Britain conforms to the standard European colour coding for wiring. The blue lead is neutral and connects to the left pin of the plug marked 'N'; the brown (or red) lead is the live lead and connects to the right (fused side) pin of the plug marked 'L'; if present, the green and yellow lead is the earth and connects to the centre (top) pin of the plug marked 'E'. **Always make sure that a plug is correctly and securely wired, as bad wiring can prove fatal.** Never use a two-pin plug with a three-core flex. If you have old wiring or sockets which accept round pin plugs, ask an electrician about the correct plugs and wiring to use. Leaflets about safety, plugs, fuses, and wiring are available from electricity companies.

Bulbs: Electric light bulbs were traditionally of the Edison type with a bayonet fitting, which is unique to Britain (the British pride themselves on being different). To insert a bulb you push it in and turn it clockwise around 5mm. However, nowadays bulbs (and lamps) with a screw fitting are also widely available. **Note that bulbs manufactured for use in the USA must never be used in Britain, as they will explode.** Low-energy light bulbs are also available and are more expensive than ordinary bulbs, although they save money by their longer life and reduced energy consumption. Bulbs for non-standard electrical appliances (i.e. appliances not made for the British market) such as refrigerators, freezers and sewing machines, may not be available in Britain (so bring extras with you). Plug adapters for imported lamps and other electrical items may be difficult to find in Britain, so it's advisable to bring a number of adapters and extension cords with you, which can be fitted with British plugs.

Safety: Only a qualified electrician should install electrical wiring and fittings, particularly in connection with fuse boxes. You should use an electrical contractor who's approved by the National Inspection Council for Electrical Installation Contracting, Vintage House, 36-37 Albert Embankment, London SE1 7UJ (☎ 0171-564 2323), a list of which is obtainable from your local electricity company's showroom. Always ask for a quotation for any work in advance and check the identity of anyone claiming to be an electricity employee (or any kind of 'serviceman') by asking to see an identity card and checking with his office. Most electricity companies carry out free visual checks of domestic installations. Special controls can be fitted to many appliances to make their use easier for the disabled and the blind or partially sighted (e.g. studded or Braille controls).

Electricity is the most expensive method of central heating and is up to 50 per cent dearer than other forms of central heating and hot water systems, particularly gas. To reduce bills and obtain the maximum benefit from your heating system, your home should be well insulated (see **Heating** on page 116). Cooking with electricity costs the average family up to three times as much as with gas. For further information and a wide range of electricity brochures, contact your local electricity company's showroom.

Complaints: If you have any complaints about your electricity bill or service, contact your local electricity company. If you don't receive satisfaction contact the Office of Electricity Regulation (Offer), Hagley House, Hagley Road, Edgbaston, Birmingham B16 8QG (☎ freefone 0800-451451 or 0121-456 2100) or the Electricity Consumer Council, 5th Floor, 11 Belgrave Road, London SW1V 1RB (☎

0171-233 6366). There are also regional offices. For information about bills, see **Electricity & Gas Bills** on page 112.

Gas

Mains gas is available in all but the remotest areas of Britain. However, you may find that some modern houses aren't connected to the mains gas supply. If you're looking for a rental property and want to cook by gas, make sure it already has a gas supply (some houses have an unused gas service pipe). If you move into a brand new home you must have a meter installed in order to be connected to mains gas (there may be a charge for this depending on the gas company). In some remote areas without piped gas, homes may have a 'bottled gas' (e.g. Calor Gas) cooker. If you buy a house without a gas supply, you can usually arrange to have a gas pipeline installed from a nearby gas main. You're usually connected free if your home is within 25 metres of a gas main, otherwise a quotation is provided for the cost of the work involved. A higher standing charge is made for properties in remote areas.

Gas was previously supplied by British Gas throughout Britain and was the monopoly supplier to some 19 million homes. However, since May 1998 everyone in England, Scotland and Wales has been able to choose from up to 26 gas supply companies. Depending on where you live, up to 17 companies may compete for your business including Amerada, Beacon Gas, British Fuels, British Gas, Calortex, Eastern Natural Gas, Energi from Norweb, London Electricity, Midlands Gas, North Wales Gas, Northern Electric & Gas, ScottishPower, Southern Electric Gas, SWALEC Gas, York Gas and Yorkshire Electricity. In 1998 almost all the new companies were cheaper than British Gas and some three million households had left British Gas for one of its competitors. If your new home already has a gas supply, simply contact the company of your choice to have the gas supply reconnected or transferred to your name (there's a connection fee) and the meter read. You must contact your gas company to get a final meter reading when you vacate a property.

Gas is the cheapest method of central heating and is estimated to be up to 50 per cent cheaper than other forms of central heating and hot water systems, particularly if you have a high efficiency condensing boiler. Gas companies may install gas central heating and delay payments for a period, e.g. six months. Note, however, that to reduce bills and obtain the maximum benefit from your heating system, your home must be well insulated (see **Heating** on page 116). Cooking with gas costs the average family around two-thirds less than with electricity. There are also a range of other gas appliances, including gas tumble dryers, which are cheaper to run than electric dryers. If you wish to purchase gas appliances, such as a gas cooker or a gas fire, you should shop around as prices vary considerably (see **Household Appliances** on page 432).

Gas appliances, wherever purchased, can be fitted by independent gas fitters (who offer the fastest service) or your gas company. If you use an independent gas fitter, choose one who's registered with the Council for Registered Gas Installers (CORGI), 1 Elmwood, Chineham Business Park, Crockford Lane, Basingstoke, Hants. RG24 8WG (☎ 01256-372300). Contact CORGI for the names of members in your area or ask your regional Gas Consumers Council office. Special controls can be fitted to many appliances to make them easier to use by the disabled and the blind or partially sighted (studded or Braille controls).

Gas central heating boilers, water heaters and fires should be checked annually, particularly open-flued water heaters, which are illegal in bathrooms (faulty gas appliances kill around 30 people a year and are fairly common in cheap rented accommodation). Free gas safety checks are carried out for those over 60, the disabled and those living alone who receive a state disability benefit. You can take out a service contract with your gas company, which includes an annual check of your gas central heating system, boiler and appliances. Without a service contract a repair or routine service could take anything from a few days to a few weeks. Private companies and engineers also maintain gas appliances and may be cheaper than gas companies. Always ask for a quotation for any work in advance and check the identity of anyone claiming to be a gas company employee (or any kind of 'serviceman') by asking to see an identity card and checking with his office.

Note that gas installations and appliances can leak and cause explosions or kill you while you sleep. If you suspect a gas leak, first check to see if a gas tap has been left on or a pilot light has gone out. If not, then there's probably a leak, either in your home or in a nearby gas pipeline. Ring your local gas service centre (listed under 'Gas' in the phone book) immediately and vacate the house as quickly as possible. Gas leaks are extremely rare and explosions caused by leaks even rarer (although often spectacular and therefore widely reported). Nevertheless, it pays to be careful. British natural gas has no natural smell (which is added as a safety precaution) and is non-poisonous. You can buy an electric-powered gas detector which activates an alarm when a gas leak is detected.

For further information and a wide range of gas brochures, contact your local gas company. If you have a complaints about your gas bill or service and you don't receive satisfaction from your gas company, you can contact the Office of Gas Supply (Ofgas), Stockley House, 130 Wilton Road, London SW1V 1LQ (☎ 0171-828 0898) or the Gas Consumers Council, Abford House, 15 Wilton Road, London SW1V 1LT (☎ 0171-931 0977). See also **Heating** on page 116.

Electricity & Gas Bills

Electricity and gas companies usually levy a standing quarterly charge for supplying the service, reading meters and billing, which is added to your actual or estimated consumption and billed as described below. Some companies guarantee prices for a number of years when you buy gas and electricity from them. Value added tax at 5 per cent is applicable to domestic electricity and gas bills.

Electricity: Electricity consumption is charged in units (when bills are paid by direct debit), one unit being equal to one kilowatt (1,000 watts) of electricity. Electricity companies offer a range of tariffs, some of which apply only to homes with night storage heaters and overnight immersion water heaters, when electricity is charged at a lower night tariff (for which a special meter may need to be installed). In addition to night storage and hot water heaters, economy periods can also be used to run washing machines, tumble dryers and dishwashers, e.g. with a timer.

Gas: Most electricity and gas consumers use a credit meter, where you're billed quarterly in arrears for the gas used and pay by direct debit. British Gas levies a standing charge of 7p per day for customers on the standard credit tariff and 1.295p per kWh. Rates are around 15 per cent higher if you pay by cash or a cheque more than ten days after the bill date (rather than by direct debit). Gas bills have fallen by around 20 per cent since competition was introduced in 1996 and in 1998 the average household could save up to £60 a year by switching from British Gas to another supplier. The Gas Bills Hotline (☎ 0845-600 4050) of *Which?* magazine provides an analysis of your gas costs from new companies for £6.95.

Meter Reading: At least every second electricity or gas bill is an estimate (shown by an 'E' or 'A' by the 'Present' meter reading), as meters are read every six months only. If nobody is at home when the meter-reader calls, you can give the electricity or gas company the meter reading on the card provided or on the back of your bill, otherwise you will receive an estimated bill until the next time the meter is read. Some houses have an outside meter box which can be read at any time by the meter reader. Electricity and gas companies are supposed to demand a meter reading if the meter hasn't been read for one year.

You should insist on actual rather than estimated meter readings in order to avoid overpaying or receiving unexpected 'catching-up' bills. In some cases you may receive an actual bill after an estimated bill has been sent out. Always check bills, e.g. by checking against your meter reading, and question bills that are too high. If a bill is in dispute, pay the part that isn't in dispute, i.e. what you normally pay, and question the rest. If you receive an unusually large bill or aren't happy with the size of your bills (who is?), you can ask the electricity or gas board to check your meter. When moving house, you should give notice in writing to have a final meter reading or to empty a coin box.

Payment: Bills can be paid in a variety of ways, including post (e.g. by cheque); in cash or cheque at electricity shops and offices; via a bank or building society credit transfer or by direct debit mandate; or at a post office. Customers who pay by direct debit receive a discount of up to 15 per cent. Note that if you're a new customer without a previous payment record, you may be required to pay a deposit (e.g. £100) if you don't pay your bill by direct debit. If you pay your electricity or gas bill via a budget payment scheme, payments are estimated on your previous year's consumption. At the end of the year, what you have paid is compared to your actual consumption and you receive either a rebate or a bill for the difference. Keep a record of all bills paid for future reference.

Pre-Payment Meter: If you don't have a credit meter, you will have a pre-payment meter, where electricity and gas is paid for in advance, usually by inserting £1 coins in a meter (meters may also be key or token operated). Electricity Key Budget Meters are operated by an electronic key, with which you can purchase 'electricity' for £1 to £50 (in £1 units) from vending machines in (or outside) electricity company shops. There's an emergency credit facility which allows you to use up to £5 of electricity when there's no credit on your key. There's an additional quarterly charge for customers with a pre-payment meter. If you move into a house with a pre-payment meter, you can have it changed to a credit meter free of charge. Those who have difficulty paying fuel bills are often offered pre-payment meters, although a monthly payment plan is a better choice, providing of course you can meet the payments.

If you live in rented accommodation such as a bedsit, your landlord will probably resell electricity to you via a pre-payment meter, the maximum price of which is set by the electricity company. Make sure you aren't overcharged (a booklet is provided by gas and electricity companies). For more information obtain a copy of a leaflet entitled *Landlords, Tenants & Electricity Charges* (published by Offer) from the address above or your local electricity company.

Disconnection: If you don't pay your bill a warrant may be obtained from a judge or magistrate to cut off your supply. The electricity and gas industries publish a leaflet entitled *Paying Electricity and Gas bills*, which tells you how to obtain help if you cannot pay a bill. All electricity and gas companies publish a *Code of Practice* on the payment of bills by domestic customers. Most pensioners are protected from disconnection during the winter months. Anyone who's in financial difficulty should contact their local electricity or gas company as soon as possible, who will try to come to an arrangement over any outstanding bills and may recommend a direct payment or pre-payment scheme.

If you're threatened with disconnection and cannot pay your bill, you should obtain immediate advice, e.g. from a Citizens Advice Bureau. If you're disconnected, you must wait two to three days to be reconnected after paying your bill, pay a reconnection charge and may be asked to pay a security deposit. Note that an electricity or gas company cannot disconnect you for non-payment of a bill that isn't for the supply of electricity or gas, e.g. a bill for a repair or other work.

Water

The water industry in England and Wales was privatised in 1989, when ten regional water companies were created to provide water and sewerage services (there are also a further 18 local water-only companies). You're unable to choose your water company (as you are your electricity and gas companies), which have a monopoly in their area. Less than 10 per cent of households in England and Wales have water meters, where you're billed for the actual water used (plus a standing charge). For all other households, water and sewerage rates are based on the rateable value of a property (although rates were abolished in April 1990 and have been replaced by the council tax). In Scotland, fresh water is charged as an addition to the council tax (which includes sewerage) and in Northern Ireland, water and sewerage are paid as part of the domestic rates (there's no council tax).

Supply: Britain's climate has fluctuated from one extreme to another in recent years with floods in winter and droughts in summer. Due to a shortage of reservoirs, many areas of Britain (particularly the south-east) experience an acute water shortage during prolonged periods without rain (e.g. around a week), resulting in water having to be rationed and the use of hose-pipes and sprinklers and car washing banned. (It seems inconceivable there can be a water shortage in a country where it never seems to stops raining!) The ever-spiralling demand for water (which is expected to rise by 20 per cent by the year 2020) has also had an alarming affect on Britain's waterways and wildlife in the last decade.

Wastage & Conservation: The British are notoriously wasteful of water and there's very little conservation and few homes have water meters. The average garden sprinkler uses 200 gallons of water an hour, which is enough to last a family of four for two days. Many people believe that the quickest way to reduce water shortages is to encourage people to conserve water and reduce wastage, e.g. by making water meters compulsory in all homes and charging consumers for the actual water used (although the bulk of the charges for water are for maintaining the infrastructure and have nothing to do with the cost of the actual water). Water companies could also reduce wastage through leaks, estimated to amount to some 25 per cent of the total supply, and build more dams and reservoirs. In recent years profits have been diverted into salary increases for water bosses and shareholders' pockets, rather than invested in infrastructure improvements (water companies have also invested billion of pounds in unrelated businesses).

Water Meters: Water companies in England and Wales will in future be able to decide whether they charge a flat (licence fee) rate for all customers, or charge for the actual amount of water used, calculated by a water meter. Presently you can have a water meter fitted voluntarily in England and Wales, although this isn't possible in Scotland and Northern Ireland. Most industrial customers have water meters. The cost of having a water meter installed varies considerably, depending on your water company (the industry watchdog, Ofwat, gives a benchmark figure of £150). If you have a property with a high rateable value and low water consumption, you would probably benefit from having a meter installed (some people recoup the cost of the meter in a single year). However, for most customers there's no incentive to install a meter as it would result in higher bills. Most new houses are fitted with water meters.

Bills: Water companies include an annual standing charge of from £25 to £40 (for both water and sewerage), which is the same for all properties, plus a variable charge based on the rateable value of your property if you don't have a water meter. If you have a water meter installed, water is charged by the cubic metre. Bills, which usually include sewerage (except in Scotland), are sent out annually and can usually be paid in full, in two six-monthly payments or in ten instalments. In some areas water and sewage are handled by separate companies and homeowners receive bills from each company. Since water privatisation in 1989, water bills have increased by some 40 per cent in real terms. The cost of water varies depending on the local water authority, with the most expensive water companies charging almost double the cheapest. The average unmetered annual water and sewerage bill in 1998-99 was around £250.

Payment: Water bills can be paid by direct debit from a bank account (for which there's usually a rebate), which means that you aren't required to remember when they are due. If you don't pay your water bill, you will receive a reminder ('Final Notice') and if this isn't paid immediately, the full annual amount usually becomes due. If you persistently failed to pay your bill, water companies could previously apply to a county court for permission to disconnect your supply, which happened to tens of thousands of households each year. However, it's now illegal to cut off the water supply to a home.

Quality: The quality of tap water in Britain varies depending on the region. Although drinking water is among the cleanest and safest in the world, it doesn't measure up to EU standards in all areas. Water bills are expected to rise even further to fund improvements in drinking water quality. In recent years there have been a number of scares about the poor quality of drinking water in some areas, some of which were a result of accidental contamination of the water supply. There are also concerns about the number and level of chemicals contained in water, particularly aluminium, lead (usually from old lead water pipes) and nitrates, although some (like chlorine) are added as part of the water treatment process.

In some areas, homeowners have reported tap water infestations, such as freshwater shrimps or water fleas (the water companies don't charge extra for the 'on tap' food supply). Water companies are loath to admit liability for illness caused by the water supply, as the cost of compensation and clean-up can run into £millions. If you have a tap connected to a garden hose, a washing machine or a dishwasher, or a shower with a flexible pipe over the bath, you must fit a non-return valve that stops pollution from dirty water siphoning back into the mains supply. A non-return valve can be plumbed in or you can buy one which screws directly onto a tap. If you're concerned about the quality of your tap water, contact your local water company or the Drinking Water Inspectorate, Floor 2/a2 Ashdown House, 123 Victoria Street, London SW1E 6OE (☎ 0171-890 5956).

Water in Britain is usually hard, particularly in the south-east, due to a natural excess of magnesium and calcium compounds. Although hard water is generally good to drink, you need a copious supply of decalcification liquid to keep your kettle, iron and other apparatus and utensils clean. Note that water from some taps may be unsafe to drink as it comes from storage tanks. Stainless steel pots and pans will stain quickly when used to boil water, unless they are cleaned soon after use. Distilled water or water melted from ice from your refrigerator or freezer, should be used in some electric steam irons. Tap and shower filters must be decalcified regularly.

Before moving into a new home you should enquire where the main stop-valve or stopcock is, so that you can turn off the water supply in an emergency. If the water stops running for any reason, you should turn off the supply to prevent flooding from an open tap when the supply starts again. Contact your local water company if you have a problem reconnecting your water supply, as it could have been turned off by them.

If you need a plumber, e.g. as a result of a burst pipe, you may be able to get a recommendation or a list of names from your local water company, which may help prevent you being ripped off. When employing a plumber always ask what the minimum call out charge is (it's usually around £1 million plus £500,000 an hour for labour). Britain is famous for the eccentricity of its plumbing, although many burst pipes could be avoided by lagging. If you have a complaint which you cannot resolve with your water company, you should contact you local Customer Service Committee or the Office of Water Services (OFWAT), Centre City Tower, 7 Hill Street, Birmingham B5 4UA (☎ 0121-625 1300).

HEATING

Around 80 per cent of British homes have central heating (including all new homes) or storage heater systems, many of which also provide hot water. Central heating systems may be powered by oil, gas (the most common), electricity or solid fuel (e.g. coal or wood). Whatever form of heating you use, you should ensure that you have good insulation including double glazing, cavity-wall insulation, external-wall insulation, floor insulation, draught-proofing, pipe lagging, and loft and hot water tank insulation, without which up to 60 per cent of heat goes straight through the walls and roof. Many companies advise and carry out home insulation, including gas and electricity companies, who produce a range of leaflets designed to help you reduce your heating and other energy bills.

The cost of heating your home varies depending on a number of factors, not least the fuel used, the size of your home and the length of time your heating is switched on. Most people in Britain switch their heating on for limited periods only (using timer controls), e.g. for a few hours in the morning before the occupants go to work or school, and from around 1600 or 1700 when children or parents come home until the family goes to bed. During the day and at night, many people turn the heating off, which is why many British houses are so cold during the daytime in winter. In order to reduce heating bills, many people selectively heat certain rooms only or parts of a house.

The cheapest method of central heating is gas, which is estimated to be up to 50 per cent cheaper than other forms of central heating and hot water systems, particularly if you have a high-efficiency condensing boiler. Many homes have storage heaters that store heat from electricity supplied at the cheaper off-peak rate overnight and release it to heat your home during the day. In an apartment block is heated from a central system, radiators are usually individually metered, so you pay only for the heating used. If you wish to install heating in your home, you should use a company that's a member of the Heating and Ventilating Contractor's Association, 34 Palace Court, London W2 4JG (☎ 0345-581158 or 0171-229 2488), who operate a guarantee scheme for domestic heating.

You can reduce your heating and other energy bills by saving energy. For information contact your gas or electricity company, local Energy Advice Centre (☎ freefone 0800-512012). Wasting Energy Costs the Earth (PO Box 200, Stratford-upon-Avon CV37 9ZZ. National Energy Services, ☎ 01908-672787) will provide details of energy surveyors in your area who will perform an energy survey for £50 to £100 depending on the size of your property.

Note that central heating dries the air and may cause your family to develop coughs. Those who find the dry air unpleasant can purchase a humidifier to add moisture to the air. Humidifiers that don't generate steam should be disinfected occasionally (to prevent nasty diseases) with a special liquid available from chemists.

6.

POST OFFICE SERVICES

There's a post office in almost every town and village in Britain, offering a wide range of services, most of which are described in this chapter. The post office provides over 100 different services, which, in addition to the usual post office services provided in most countries, include a number of unique services. The term 'post office' is used in Britain as a general term for three separate businesses: the Royal Mail, Post Office Counters Limited and Parcelforce (formerly Royal Mail Parcels). Girobank plc, the former post office banking division, still operates from post offices, but is now owned by Alliance & Leicester Giro. For the sake of simplicity and to avoid confusion, the term 'post office' has been used throughout this chapter to refer to all these services.

Inland mail refers to all mail to addresses in Great Britain, Northern Ireland, the Channel Islands and the Isle of Man. Of some 19,000 post offices in Britain, only around 600 are operated directly by the post office. The remainder are franchise offices or sub post offices run on an agency basis by sub-postmasters (which don't offer all the services provided by a main post office). Plans to privatise the post office have been abandoned, although it has been accused of back-door privatisation with the transfer of many post offices (even in quite large towns) from the high street to supermarkets, stationery stores, newsagents and other shops.

In addition to postal services, the post office also acts as an agent for a number of government departments and local authorities (councils), for example, the sale of television licences (exclusive to post offices), national insurance stamps and road tax. You can also pay many bills at a post office including electricity, gas, water, telephone, cable, store cards, mail-order bills, council tax, rent payments and housing association rents. The post office is also the largest chain of outlets for national lottery tickets and a distribution centre for social security leaflets. The post office provides bureaux de change facilities in most branches (although you may need to order foreign currency) and an expensive international money transfer service in conjunction with Western Union International. It charges 1 per cent commission on the purchases of travellers' cheques and foreign currency with a minimum fee of £2.50, which is lower than most banks (see **Foreign Currency** on page 330). The post office will also buy back foreign currency free of commission.

The post office (founded in 1635) is the last bastion of the old state sector and like all nationalised companies it's over-staffed and inefficient in some areas. Despite this, it provides one of best postal services in the world, delivering some 75 million letters and packets a day to around 26 million addresses. Services have improved considerably in recent years and it's now one of the world's most modern and automated post offices offering a vast range of services compared with most foreign post offices. The Royal Mail even has an office in New York (offering a cheaper and faster international service than the US postal service) from where it ships mail in bulk to London and sends it onto other international destinations. However, overseas rivals are also muscling in on Royal Mail services and a number of overseas groups handle mail in Britain.

Private sector couriers are able to handle only time-sensitive and valuable mail, subject to a minimum fee of £1. The courier industry, particularly in London and other major cities, is growing by some 20 per cent a year and Britain is a major centre for international air courier traffic. Major companies include Federal Express, DHL, UPS and TNT, plus the post office Parcelforce service. The post office produces a wealth of free brochures about postal rates and special services, most of which are available from any post office. It also has a helpline (☎ 0345-223344) and an Internet site (www.royalmail.co.uk).

A *Mini Mailguide* is available from post offices containing information about all Royal Mail products and services. A more comprehensive **Mailguide** for business users is available for £25 and can be obtained on free trial for 14 days. Ask at any post office. The Post Office publishes a *Customer Charter* outlining the standards it aims to meet. If you have any complaints regarding any post office service, you should complain in writing to your local Post Office Advisory Committee listed in the phone book, or you can contact the Post Office Users' National Council, 6 Hercules Road, London SE1 7DN (☎ 0171-928 9458). Complaints about lost or damaged mail must be made on form P58 *Enquiry about a missing or damaged letter or parcel*, available from any post office.

BUSINESS HOURS

Post office business hours in Britain are usually from 0900 to 1730, Mondays to Fridays, and from 0900 to 1230 on Saturdays. In small towns and villages there are sub post offices (usually part of a general store) which provide most of the services offered by a main post office. Sub post offices usually close for an hour at lunchtime, e.g. 1300 to 1400, Mondays to Fridays, and usually also close on one afternoon a week, usually Wednesday. Main post offices in major towns don't close at lunchtime. There are post offices at major international airports, some of which are open on Sundays and public holidays. In major cities, some post offices have extended opening hours, e.g. the Trafalgar Square branch in London, open from 0900 to 2000 Mondays to Saturdays.

LETTER POST

The post office provides a choice of first and second class domestic mail delivery (further evidence of the British preoccupation with class). The target for the delivery of first class mail is the next working day after collection and the third working day after collection for second class. Some 95 per cent of first class mail is delivered the next day, although some letters fail to arrive until weeks after posting (probably those that are delivered by rail). It's unnecessary to mark mail as first or second class, as any item which is posted with less than first class postage is automatically sent second class.

International letters, small packets and printed papers (both airmail and surface) are limited to a maximum of 2kg (1kg for Cambodia) and up to 5kg for books and pamphlets. Second class mail mustn't exceed 750g (£1.45), although there's no limit for first class mail. This means that parcels weighing between 750g and 1kg must be sent by first class mail. Parcel mail standard service costs £2.70 for up 1kg, which is more expensive than first class mail (£2.50 for 1kg). Inland postage rates have been frozen for three years and the cost of sending a 2nd class letter was actually reduced from 20p to 19p in April 1999. To ensure delivery the next day, first class mail should be posted by 1700 for the local area (e.g. a letter posted in the south-east of England to any address in the same region) or by 1300 for other parts of Britain excluding Northern Scotland. The cost of posting a letter or postcard in Britain is shown below:

		Countries		
Item	UK*	EU	Other Europe	Rest of the World
Surface letter up to 20g		26p	30p	30p
Surface letter up to 60g	26p/19p	56p	56p	50p
Airmail letter up to 10g	-	-	-	43p#
Airmail letter up to 20g	-	-	30p	63p#
Postcards	26p/19p	26p	30p	37p

* The two rates are for first (26p) and second (19p) class mail. Postcards are charged at the same rate as letters within Britain.

\# Airmail rates for letters to destinations outside Europe (rest of the world) are divided into two airmail zones, depending on the distance. For letters above 20g, rates vary.

Note that letters to Europe (Western and Eastern Europe, including Cyprus, Turkey and the USSR) are prepaid at surface rate, but are sent by airmail when this will result in earlier delivery. Domestic and international postal charges are listed in leaflets available from any post office. Further information can be obtained by writing to Postage Rate Leaflets, Freepost, Newcastle-upon-Tyne, NE85 2BR.

General Information

Note the following when posting letters in Britain:

- All airmail letters (including letters for European destinations) should have a blue airmail label affixed to the top left hand corner available from post offices, or 'PAR AVION - BY AIR MAIL' should be written or stamped on items. Most international mail to addresses outside Europe can be sent either by surface mail (or an economy rate), airmail or by express 'Swiftair' mail.

- Airmail letters to Europe take an average of from 2.5 days to Denmark, Norway and Switzerland and up to seven days to Italy and some other countries (which gives an excellent indication of the relative efficiency of European postal services). Airmail to other destinations usually takes four to seven days. Surface mail takes up to two weeks to Europe and up to 12 weeks outside Europe. Underpaid airmail items may be sent by surface mail or will incur a surcharge. Leaflets are published in September listing the latest mail posting dates for Christmas for international mail (forces, surface and airmail).

- It's possible to send international mail weighing up to 2kg by 'Swiftair' express mail to over 140 countries worldwide. A surcharge of £2.70 is made in addition to the normal airmail postage. Pre-paid envelopes (Swiftpacks) valid for anywhere in the world are available in three sizes, standard DL (10cm x 21.5cm/maximum weight 50g), CF (16.5cm x 23cm/100g) and C4 (23cm x 33cm/150g) costing £3, £3.25 and £4 respectively. Average delivery times to selected worldwide destinations are shown in a leaflet available at post offices. Note that you cannot rely on the Swiftair average delivery times to some countries (there are no guarantees).

- There's at least one mail delivery a day from Mondays to Saturdays in all areas of Britain and in many areas there are two deliveries a day (morning and early afternoon) from Mondays to Fridays. Mail can also be collected from post offices. If you want a first class letter to reach its destination on the next working day, you must ensure you catch the latest recommended posting time.

- Inland mail, including parcels and registered packets, can be sent **Cash on Delivery (COD)**, where the addressee pays a specified amount to the postman on delivery. The fee in addition to postage is £1.25 (95p for contract customers). The COD service covers items valued up to £350, although sums over £50 are collected on post office premises only (the postman doesn't want to get mugged). Cheques are accepted only with a cheque guarantee card.

- You can receive mail free of charge via the main post office of any town in Britain through the international **Poste Restante** service (where mail is addressed to any main post office) for a maximum of three months. Mail sent to a Poste Restante address is returned to the sender if it's unclaimed after 14 days (or one month if sent from abroad). Identification is necessary for collection, e.g. a passport.

- If you send a letter with insufficient postage it will usually be delivered, although all unpaid and underpaid letters are treated as second class mail. Where an item is unpaid or underpaid at the applicable second class postage rate, the addressee is charged the amount of the under postage plus a fee of 15p (which also applies to parcels). There's a surcharge of 25p on all unpaid or underpaid mail from abroad, in addition to the amount of the underpayment. If the post office is unable to deliver a letter it's returned to the sender with a sticker stating the reason why.

- Post boxes are red and are usually free-standing, but may be set into (or attached to) a wall. Main and sub post offices have post boxes outside and main post offices also usually have them inside. Collection times are shown on all post boxes. Mail is usually collected several times a day from Mondays to Saturdays and once on Sunday from main post offices, indicated by a yellow strip on the collection plate (or the location of the nearest Sunday collection box is shown). At main post offices there may be separate post boxes for local mail (towns are usually listed on the box), 2nd class mail, 1st class mail and abroad, meter or pre-franked mail and a special box for first day covers.

- Aerogrammes (pre-printed airmail letters) are available from post offices and stationery stores, and usually include postage, which is the same to all countries. They aren't necessary for European destinations as all mail is sent by air. Aerogrammes cost 36p each or £1.99 for a pack of six. Pictorial aerogrammes are also available at £2.99 for a pack of six. Pre-paid envelopes are available in various sizes for inland mail costing 30p (DL size) for first class letters and 24p for second class letters weighing up to 60g.

- If you want to increase your chances of receiving a reply or simply wish to save a correspondent money, you can send an **international reply coupon** (60p each). These are exchangeable at post offices abroad for postage stamps equivalent to the basic surface letter rate to Britain.

- In Britain most mail is sorted by machine, which is facilitated by the use of full and correct postal addresses (omitting all punctuation). All letters should have the postcode (zip code) after the city or county, which allows addresses to be identified down to part of a street or in some cases to an individual address, for example:

  Reginald Percy Wilberforce-Smith
  99A High Street
  Wombledon
  Surrey WO1 9XY
  United Kingdom

- If you don't know your postcode or want to find someone else's code, you can consult Postcode Directories at main post offices or telephone 0345-111222 or check post office's Internet website (www.royalmail.co.uk). Postcodes can be used as an identity mark for your property. Note that United Kingdom (UK) is preferred by the post office to Britain or Great Britain (or England, Scotland, Wales or Northern Ireland). A list of the correct local postal addresses is given in section one of all phone books. Thompson Local Directories (see page 151) include a list of post codes for all addresses in major cities and towns. A Royal Mail approved *Postcode Atlas of Great Britain and Northern Ireland* (Bartholomew) is available from bookshops. You should write your address on the back of mail so that it can be returned to you if it's undelivered.

- Stamps can be purchased from vending machines located outside most post offices, in stores and shops, and at major tourist attractions. Books of four or ten first or second class stamps are also sold at post offices and by over 40,000 shops (e.g. stationers, newsagents and general stores) throughout Britain. International stamp books with airmail stickers are also available from post offices and other outlets. Non-value indicator stamps marked with 1st or 2nd are valid indefinitely (even when prices change) for inland mail up to 60g in weight (or in part payment for heavier items). They can also be used as full or part payment for items to EU countries, but not to other international destinations. A new stamp for Europe with just an 'E' and the Queen's head on it was introduced in 1999.

- Like many countries, Britain provides special services for philatelists through special post office philatelic shops. Many main post offices also have post shops for philatelists and special 'First Day Cover' post boxes. Brochures describing special stamps and first day covers produced for philatelists are available from main post offices. For more information contact the British Philatelic Bureau, Freepost, 20 Brandon Street, Edinburgh EH3 0HN (☎ 0131-550 8989). The Royal Mail also operates the Royal Mail Young Collectors Club (Freepost. Northampton NN3 1BR) for young stamp collectors, and an international pen pal club (anything to sell stamps) for children aged 9 to 16. For information write to Hola!, Dept. 1, Freepost AT398, Camberley, Surrey GU17 7BR.

- There are concessionary postage rates for mail to and from members of HM Forces. Rates are listed in a *HM Forces Letter Rates* leaflet available from post offices.

- Literature for the blind up to 1kg in weight can be sent free by airmail to Europe. For mail weighing from 1kg to 7kg there's no charge for the first kg, but each 50g (or part thereof) above 1kg costs 1p. Airmail for the blind outside Europe costs 10p up to 500g, 20p over 500g and up to 1kg, and 20p for each kg over 1kg and up to 7kg. All international surface mail for the blind is free up to 7kg. Special 'Literature for the Blind' labels (P4558) are available from the Royal National Institute for the Blind, 224 Great Portland Street, London W1N 6AA (☎ 0171-388 1266).

• If you're going to be away from your home for up to two months, you can have your mail held by the post office and delivered on the day of your choice. The 'Keepsafe' scheme costs £5 for up to two weeks, £8 for three weeks, £10 for four weeks and £15 for up to two months. A form is available from your local post office and a week's notice is required.

PARCEL POST

The standard inland parcel service is operated by Parcelforce and handles around 1 million parcels and packages every day, 95 per cent of which are delivered within three working days to any address within Britain. There are four different services depending on how fast you want a parcel delivered: delivery AM (morning), by close of business, scheduled and economy. Note that there are restrictions on the size of parcels, depending on the service. Parcel post includes the following services:

Small Packets: An airmail small packet service is available to all countries with a limit of 2kg (except for Cuba, Myanmar and Papua New Guinea, where the limit is 500g). You must write 'SMALL PACKET' in the top left-hand corner on the front of the packet. An 'Airpack' service is provided for sending small packages (such as videos, books, photos, cassettes and clothes) weighing up to 500g. A padded envelope with a self-adhesive strip (including a customs form) is provided for a fee of £2.49 to Europe and £4.99 to the rest of the world. You may include a letter only if it relates to the contents of the packet.

Printed Papers: Unsealed commercial items (e.g. advertising material), non-personalised direct mail, calendars and literary items (e.g. books, newspapers and periodicals) up to 5kg in weight can be sent at a reduced 'Printed Paper' surface mail rate. Items should be marked 'Printed Papers', mustn't contain personal letters and taped messages, and must be packed so they can be easily opened for examination, e.g. with string or plastic tags (or have a transparent window through which the contents can be scrutinised). There's also a special airmail printed paper rate, although some items (e.g. newspapers and periodicals) must be registered with the post office. See the leaflet entitled, *The easy way to mail abroad*. When sending a small packet or printed papers, 'Small Packet' or 'Printed Papers' (as applicable) should be written above and to the left of the address, and the sender's name and address should also be written on the back of the parcel.

Standard parcel delivery usually takes three days to any address in Britain, including Saturday deliveries. The standard service for inland parcels costs £2.70 up to 1kg, £3.65 for 2kg, £5.65 for 4kg, £6.15 for 6kg, £7.05 for 8kg, £7.55 for 10kg and £8.85 for 15kg to 30kg (the maximum permitted weight). Note that some post offices don't accept parcels weighing over 10kg. Compensation for loss or damage is limited to £20 per parcel, providing you complete a **Certificate of Despatch** when you send your parcel. Higher compensation is possible by paying a **Compensation Fee** of 75p (£150 compensation) or £1.30 (£500 compensation) and completing a **Compensation**

Fee Certificate of Despatch. Domestic parcels can measure up to 1.5m in length and a total of 3m when length and girth are combined.

Parcelforce Worldwide is a guaranteed delivery service that's available from all main post offices for urgent parcels and from any post office for economy parcels. There are a number of UK next day services including **Parcelforce by 9am, Parcelforce by 10am** and **Parcelforce by Noon,** all of which guarantee delivery by the time specified to all major UK business centres and to most of the rest of Britain and outlying areas soon after. Insurance against loss, damage and consequential loss is provided up to £500. Parcels must be signed for on arrival. The minimum fee for **Parcelforce by 9am** is £27.30 (up to 10kg plus £1.05 per extra kg) and for **Parcelforce by Noon** it's £16.70 (up to 10kg plus 85p per extra kg). **Parcelforce 24 and Parcelforce 48** provide a guaranteed next-day (£13.15 up to 10kg) or two-day delivery (£10.50 up to 10kg) to 95 per cent of all British business addresses.

Parcelforce Standard, International Standard and International Economy Services provide a parcel service to some 240 countries and territories worldwide. The **Standard** service (from £12.85 for parcels weighing up to 500g to selected EU countries) takes from three working days to Europe and from five working days to the rest of the world. The **Economy** service (from £10.80 for parcels weighing up to 500g to Canada and the USA) takes from ten working days to Europe and from 20 working days to the rest of the world. There's no economy service to mainland western European countries and some other countries. Compensation is provided up to £5,000 per consignment for International Datapost and Parcelforce 24, and £250 for International Standard. There's no automatic compensation for the International Economy service. The international maximum parcel weight and size varies from country to country up to a maximum of 30kg, although the majority of countries set a limit of 20kg. Parcels over 10kg and up to 25kg are accepted only at main post offices. Parcelforce International publish a leaflet giving the *Recommended Last Posting Dates for Christmas*. For further information regarding Parcelforce International, ☎ freefone 0800-224466.

Datapost International provides a guaranteed 'timetabled' express international delivery service to over 200 countries worldwide, usually up to a maximum weight of 20kg (some up to 30kg). Parcels sent via Datapost take 24 hours within Europe and from one to four days to other regions, depending on the destination. Mail can be handed in at post offices or collected from the sender's address. The cost is from £25.85 for parcels weighing up to 500g to EU countries. Compensation is provided up to £5,000 per parcel. All services with a guaranteed delivery time offer a money-back guarantee in the event of late delivery.

Customs Declaration: Parcels and small packets sent to international addresses outside the European Union (except Andorra, Canary Islands, Gibraltar and the Vatican City) must be accompanied by a customs declaration label (CN22 for values up to £270 and CN23 for goods valued above this amount). If an item being sent is of 'no commercial value' (NCV), you should write this on the customs form under 'value'. Forms are available from post offices. Parcels can also be sent by **Franc de Droits (FDD),** which enables the sender to prepay customs and other charges that otherwise must be paid by the addressee. This also expedites customs clearance abroad. A yellow FDD label must be affixed to the left of the address.

Wrapping Parcels: A booklet entitled *Wrapping up Well* is available from post offices, describing how to pack goods for sending through the mail. When sending drawings, large photographs, paintings, or anything which will be damaged if bent,

sandwich them between stiff cardboard. Apparently in the 'good ol' days' when mail went by coach, you could send a box of eggs through the mail without them being scrambled. Nowadays stickers such as BREAKABLE, THIS WAY UP, FRAGILE and HANDLE WITH CARE are a dead give away and an open invitation for a game of 'drop the parcel'. Cardboard boxes called Postpaks, padded ('jiffy') bags and a range of 'pack & wrap' wrappings are available from post offices and most department and stationery stores. A booklet entitled *Prohibited & Restricted Goods* lists what *cannot* be sent through the mail. You can send quite large objects by parcel post, but it's advisable to enquire before packaging your mother-in-law for shipment to Outer Mongolia (just to make sure she arrives safely and *isn't* returned).

Leaflets are published in September listing the latest mail posting dates for Christmas for international 'economy' parcels, which are roughly between 1st October (e.g. Australia) and 20th November, depending on the country (USA around 23rd October). Parcelforce publish a booklet, *The Complete Guide to Parcel Deliveries*, available from post offices. For further information about Parcelforce services ☎ freefone 0800-224466 or write to Parcelforce, PO Box 30, Stratford-upon-Avon, Warwicks CV37 9BR.

IMPORTANT DOCUMENTS & VALUABLES

The post office provides a number of services for the delivery of important documents and valuables:

- A **certificate of posting** is available free on request at any post office counter. A number of items can be listed on one leaflet. A maximum of £26 (100 times the cost of first class postage) is payable in compensation for the loss or damage of ordinary letters or parcels, for which a **certificate of posting** has been obtained. Without this certificate the post office isn't liable to pay compensation, unless you have insured an item or taken out consequential loss compensation (see below). There's no compensation for money or jewellery sent by ordinary post.

- If you're sending money, jewellery, valuable documents or anything needing a guaranteed next day delivery, you should use **registered mail**. There are two classes of registered mail, ordinary registered for items valued up to £500 and 'registered plus' for items valued up to a maximum of £2,200. The fee for ordinary registered mail is £2.70 for mail weighing up to 2kg plus 30p compensation premium per item and first class postage. For items weighing over 2kg and up to 10kg the fee is £3.80 inclusive of postage. The fee for registered plus mail is £3.30 for items valued up to £1,500 and £3.60 for items valued up to £2,200 (weighing up to 2kg), plus first class postage. You receive a receipt for registered mail, which must be signed for on delivery (although the signatory doesn't need to be the addressee).

  Special registered envelopes are available in three sizes for sending valuables through the post: small (156mm x 95mm/£3.30), medium (203mm x 120mm/£3.80) and large (292mm x 152mm/£4.20). The fee includes compensation up to £500 and first class postage for up to 60g. If you're sending a registered or registered plus item within Britain that's worth more than its face or material value, you can pay for **consequential loss compensation**. This provides cover where the late delivery or loss or damage of an item would involve you in additional expense in excess of the cost of replacement. You can insure an item from £1,000 (fee £1.20) up to a maximum of £10,000 (fee £3). Fees are in addition to the registered mail fee.

- **Advice of delivery** is available for a fee of 31p when sending inland registered, recorded or insured items. Proof of delivery must be requested at the time of posting. Signed evidence of delivery is returned to the sender, but not from a named individual.

- **International registered** mail provides compensation of up to £500 or £2,200, plus airmail postage. The service is available to a limited number of countries only, some of which have different compensation levels (listed in a leaflet entitled *International Priority Services*). Proof of posting is provided and a signature is obtained on delivery. Optional advice of delivery is available for a fee of 40p payable at the time of posting.

- If you wish to have a record of delivery of a letter, you can send it by **recorded delivery** to inland addresses for a surcharge of 60p (plus first or second class postage). Enter the addressee's name and address on the 'Recorded' slip, the bottom part of which will be date stamped and returned to you as a receipt. The post office must obtain a signature for mail sent by recorded delivery, although the signatory doesn't need to be the addressee. **Don't send valuables or money by recorded delivery.** If a recorded or special delivery item (see below) is lost or damaged, you may receive compensation equal to 100 times the cost of first class postage.

  An **international recorded** service is available for £2.50 per item plus airmail postage (some countries also accept recorded mail sent by surface mail). Proof of posting is provided and a signature is obtained on delivery. Optional advice of delivery is available for a fee of 40p at the time of posting. International recorded delivery entitles you to compensation of up to £25 for loss or damage.

- A **Special Delivery** service is provided for £3.20 for items weighing up to 100g, which guarantees delivery by noon the next day (Mondays to Fridays) to most UK destinations. Other rates are £3.50 (up to 500g), £4.60 (1kg), £5.85 (2kg) and £13.50 (10kg). Pre-paid C5 and C4 envelopes are available up to 500g. A form must be completed and a receipt is provided. A signature is collected on delivery (you can also check the delivery by calling 0345-001200 after 1pm on the day of delivery). The standard compensation is £250, which can be increased to £1,000 for an additional 30p or to £2,500 for an additional £1.35.

- Parcels can be insured with the **compensation fee** facility for values above £22. The compensation fee is applicable only to inland parcels and costs 45p for compensation up to £75, 55p up to £140, 75p up to £250 and 95p up to £400. You must complete a green 'compensation fee' form. Money, which includes coins, banknotes, stamps, postal orders and gift vouchers, shouldn't be sent by this service (see 'registered envelopes' above).

- **International insurance** is provided for the insurance of valuable items from £150 to £1,500, in steps of £150. It costs from £1.75 (for compensation up to £150) up to £3.85 (for compensation up to the maximum limit of £1,500). Check in advance whether this service is available to the addressee's country.

Confirmation of Delivery: To confirm delivery of registered, registered plus, special delivery and recorded items you can telephone 0645-272100 between 0800 and 1800 Mondays to Fridays and 0800 to 1400 on Saturdays, and quote your receipt number. For a small charge you can also request a copy of the delivery signature.

Claims: Should you need to make a claim, it should be made within 12 months of posting. For lost or damaged mail, you must complete a form (P58) available from any post office. A return address must be written on the back of all mail sent by registered, special delivery or recorded mail.

MISCELLANEOUS SERVICES

- The post office provides a range of savings stamps (mostly used by pensioners, who buy stamps when drawing their pensions), designed to help people budget for their regular 'bills' including TV licence, road tax, telephone, council tax, water, electricity and gas. Stamps usually cost £1 each and are affixed to special cards. These stamps aren't recommended for most people, as no interest is paid or free bonus stamps provided (which means you provide the post office with a free loan) and if you lose your stamps, you've lost your money.

- Main post offices sell sterling travellers cheques in denominations of £20, £50 and £100 and provide *bureaux de change* facilities.

- Royal Mail International services mustn't be used for the transmission of dangerous substances. Most of these are fairly obvious and include such things as explosives, gases, flammable liquids and solids, oxidising substances, poisonous (toxic) and infectious substances, radioactive materials, corrosive dyes and other miscellaneous dangerous goods. A full list is provided in the *Royal Mail International* booklet.

- A Freepost address or business reply service (pre-paid) is available for a licence fee of £27.50 per year. An international business reply service is also available from main post offices.

MAIL COLLECTION

If the postman calls with mail requiring a signature or payment when you aren't at home, he'll leave a collection form. These include recorded delivery, registered letters, surcharged items, special delivery/express, cash on delivery, insured items, perishable goods or a parcel which is too bulky to be left. If you receive mail from abroad on which customs duty or VAT is payable, this is collected by the post office (sums over £50 are collected only at post offices). You can choose to collect an item which couldn't be delivered or you can complete the bottom part of the collection form and instruct the post office to:

A. Allow someone else to collect it on your behalf (identity must be shown).

B. Have it redelivered on a date of your choosing.

C. Have it delivered to another address, e.g. a business or a neighbour.

Present the collection form at your local 'Letter Delivery Office', the address of which is printed on the form. Check the opening hours in advance as some are open for collections only in the mornings, e.g. 0800 to 1200, Mondays to Fridays and 0800 to 1100 on Saturdays. Identification may be required to collect mail, e.g. a driving licence or passport, preferably with your address on it (which should be the same as that on the item to be collected). Mail is retained for three weeks, with the exception of recorded delivery mail, which is retained for one week only.

You can have your mail stored in a private box at most post offices for £52 a year (£42 for six months). Collection must usually be made during normal opening hours, although boxes at main post offices can be accessed 24 hours a day. You can also hire a private box for parcels at a Parcelforce delivery depot.

A private courier company *must* obtain a signature for all deliveries and if you aren't at home, they will leave a form asking you to contact them about re-delivery.

CHANGE OF ADDRESS

Your mail can be redirected to a new or temporary address in Britain for a charge of £6 for one month, £13 for three months, or £30 for a year or double these charges to an address abroad. All letters are redirected to inland addresses by first class mail (whether or not they were originally sent by first class mail). A 'home mover pack' is provided as part of the redirection service consisting of address and response books, ten change of address cards, ten pre-printed new address labels, and personalised stationary with envelopes. Information about mail redirection is available by calling 0345-777888. Parcelforce (see page 125) also operate a redirection service for parcels (☎ freefone 0800-224466).

A *Royal Mail Redirection Service* form (P944), available from post offices, must be completed at least five working days before you wish redirection to begin (it can be completed up to three weeks in advance). The redirection can also be arranged by post or phone and the fee paid by cash, cheque or giro transfer. If you require an extension, a further form P944 must be completed. Mail can also be redirected from a Post Restante address, but usually for one month only.

If you receive mail for the previous occupants of your home, or any mail which comes through your letter box that isn't addressed to you, you have two choices what to do with it (the third is to throw it away, which is illegal!). You can send it onto the addressee by crossing out the address, writing the new or correct address and dropping it in a post box, without a stamp. If you don't know the addressee's new address you can cross out the address and write 'Address Unknown' and drop it in a post box.

POSTAL ORDERS

Postal orders are a convenient and safe way of sending small amounts of money by mail to people who don't have cheque accounts (bank, building society or Girobank). **You should never send cash through the post, either within Britain or internationally, except by registered mail** (see page 127). Postal orders can be purchased for any amount from 50p to £20, although there's no limit to the cash value you can buy. A fee is payable depending on the value: 25p for values from 50p to £1, 44p from £2 to £4, 58p from £5 to £7, 66p from £8 to £10, 80p for £15 and 85p for £20. Stamps can be affixed up to 49p to make up exact amounts. Postal orders are valid for six months from the last day of their month of issue.

Enter the name of the payee on both the postal order and the counterfoil. You may also enter the name of the post office where the postal order is to be cashed if the payee doesn't have a bank account. If the payee has a bank account, an additional safeguard is to cross the postal order by drawing two parallel lines vertically across it. This means that it can no longer be cashed at a post office and must be paid into a bank account (uncrossed postal orders can also be paid into a bank account). If you make a mistake, don't try to rub it out or alter it as this will result in payment being refused. Return the postal order and counterfoil to your post office and ask for a replacement postal order to be issued (a further fee is payable).

Postal orders can be cashed in around 50 (mostly Commonwealth) countries and dependencies worldwide, and are usually cheaper than sending an international cheque. For inland use, postal orders are an expensive way of paying your bills, particularly when a cheque drawn on most current accounts incurs no bank charges (providing you stay in credit). They should be used only when you or the recipient doesn't have a bank, building society or Girobank account. See the post office leaflet entitled *The handy way to send cash today*.

NATIONAL SAVINGS ACCOUNTS

In addition to Girobank, the post office also operates the National Savings Bank, which manages a total of around 20 million accounts. The national savings bank operates savings accounts only and doesn't provide lending facilities. Customers are issued with a bank book in which all deposits and withdrawals are entered. There are two main types of account, an ordinary account and an investment account.

The **ordinary account** allows you to save in amounts of £10 or more and to withdraw up to £100 a day on demand. If you have used an ordinary account for at least six months at a particular post office, you can apply for a regular customer account and have your daily withdrawal limit (at a named post office) increased to £250. A regular customer account also entitles you to withdraw up to £100 in cash at any other post office if you hand in your bank book or £50 if you wish to retain your book. Interest rates vary depending on the balance maintained. A higher rate is paid to those who maintain a balance of at least £500, providing the account is open for a whole calendar year. Interest is paid annually at the end of the year and the first £70 of annual interest is tax-free (£140 for a joint account). Children aged over seven can open their own accounts.

The **investment account** is intended mainly for non-taxpayers, as it provides tax-free interest. Interest is paid annually at the end of the year and a month's notice must be given before making a withdrawal. The minimum deposit is £20 and the maximum £100,000. Other national savings investments include tax-free savings certificates (paying either a fixed rate of interest or a lower fixed rate of interest combined with index-linking); taxable income, first option and pensioners bonds; and government stock (gilts). National savings premium bonds are a popular form of saving where 'interest' is paid in the form of cash prizes of up to £1 million chosen by lottery (see page 387). For general information call National Savings (☎ freefone 0800-868700).

7.

TELEPHONE

Around 90 per cent of homes in Britain have a fixed-line telephone and the country is also a world leader in the use of mobile phones. All telephones have Subscriber Trunk Dialling (STD) and all private telephones are on International Direct Dialling (IDD), which means that you can make calls to most countries directly without going via the operator. Most telephone exchanges have been converted to digital operation in the last decade which allows customers with tone phones to access a wide range of 'network' services such as call diversion and call waiting.

The cost of making telephone calls in Britain has reduced considerably in the last few years, in particular the cost of long-distance and international calls (even ET could afford to phone home these days). International calls are made even cheaper by many indirect access providers who buy time from British Telecom (BT) and other companies and re-sell it to their customers (see page 145). The average telephone bill has halved for many users in the last decade.

New Codes: Homes across Britain are to have their telephone numbers changed from 1st June 1999 (just four years after the last shake-up). Area codes that will change include London (see below), Belfast (new code 028+90 before existing six-digit numbers), Cardiff (029+20), Coventry (024+76), Portsmouth (023+92) and Southampton (023+80). The 0171 code (inner London) will change to 020+7 and the 0181 code (outer London) to 020+8. Other codes in Northern Ireland besides Belfast will also be affected. The old codes will continue in use until 22nd April 2000. You can check number changes on the Internet (www.numberchange.org) or by calling 0808-224 2000.

Note that the general emergency telephone number throughout Britain is 999 (see also page 154)

TELEPHONE COMPANIES

The telephone system in Britain is dominated by British Telecom (BT), created with a 25-year licence (to print money) in 1984 when the state-owned telephone system was privatised. In 1991, the government ended the duopoly of BT and Mercury, and opened up the telecommunications market to national and international competition. Britain is at the forefront of telecommunications technology and other European countries lag behind when it comes to telecoms liberalisation (although most countries have now privatised their former public monopolies). Over 100 companies are licensed to operate telecoms services in Britain and the market is very competitive, therefore it's important to shop around and compare rates in order to save money.

Users can choose between BT, cable companies, radio-based networks and a large number of indirect operators. In recent years cable (TV and phone) companies have proliferated and now cover some 11 million homes. To find out which cable phone company operates in your area ☎ 0990-111777. Radio-based companies include Ionica, Atlantic Telecom and Scottish Telecom, all of which operate in restricted areas but are planning to increase their coverage. With indirect companies you need to dial a code before each number you call or call a free number to obtain a dialling code.

The major companies include ACC Telecom*, AT&T*, Atlantic Telecom, BT*, Cable & Wireless*, The Cable Corporation, CableTel, ComTel, Eurobell, First Telecom*, Ionica, Kingston, Scottish Telecom, Telewest and Yorkshire Cable (* =

national operators). In 1998, Ionica, Eurobell and Kingston offered the largest savings for most users, but are available in certain parts of the country only. ACC Telecom is among the cheapest national indirect companies and Scottish Telecom offers the cheapest direct service. The savings depend on how large your monthly bill is, when you make most calls and what sort of calls you make (e.g. local, national or international). Connection costs range from free up to around £30. Also shop around the Internet, e.g. www.toll.co.uk, which provides tariff calculators for both terrestrial and mobile phone services.

Most households still use BT for their phone services, although considerable savings can be made by switching to another company. Note, however, that whether a particular company or scheme is cheaper depends on how much you use the phone, and when and where you call most frequently. One reason many people stick to BT is because it isn't yet possible to have a 'portable' number in Britain, i.e. a number that can be transferred from BT to a cable company or vice versa, although this is planned. This is a serious drawback for business users, many of whom retain their BT lines for incoming calls and use cable or other carriers to make outgoing calls. **Anybody who makes a lot of international calls should investigate the companies mentioned on page 145.**

Contact your local telecoms advisory service or the Cable Communications Association for details of local telephone service providers. For information about cable service providers in Britain, contact the Telecommunications Users' Association, Woodgate Studios, 2-8 Games Row, Barnet, Herts. EN4 9HN (☎ 0181-449 8844).

PHONE INSTALLATION & REGISTRATION

Before moving into a new home, check whether there's a telephone line and that the number of lines or telephone points is adequate (most new homes already have phone lines and points in a number of rooms). If a property has a cable system or other phone network (see above), you could decide not to have a BT phone line installed. If you move into an old house or apartment (where you aren't the first resident) a telephone line will probably already be installed, although there won't be a phone. If you're moving into a house or apartment without a phone line, e.g. a new house, you may need to apply to BT for a line to be installed.

BT's target for residential line installation is four working days, depending on the area and the particular exchange. The installation of a new line (to an address where there wasn't previous a service) is £99 and to take over an existing line costs £9.99 or is free of charge if you move house and take over a working phone line on the *same day* as the existing customer moves out. If a property has an old-style phone point (which cannot be unplugged), it should be replaced with a new-style linebox or master socket. This can be done by BT only and it's illegal to do it yourself or get anyone other than a BT engineer to do it. Once you have a BT linebox or master socket, you can install as many additional sockets as you like, but you shouldn't connect more than four telephones to one telephone line. You can install additional sockets yourself by buying DIY kits from BT or a DIY shop, or BT can install them for you (although their labour charges are astronomical). BT sell a wide range of extension kits, sockets and cords.

New residential subscribers, particularly tenants in rented property, may need to pay a deposit. BT uses a vetting system to determine whether or not new customers should pay a deposit by contacting a credit reference agency. If you're a new arrival in Britain or have been abroad for some years, BT may charge you a deposit, which they will retain for a maximum of a year (providing you pay your bills on time). Interest is paid on deposits. You can appeal against the demand for a deposit to your local district general manager. Alternatively new customers may be asked to agree a maximum bill limit with BT, which eliminates the requirement to pay a deposit. If this level is exceeded before the end of the quarter, BT will contact you to agree a course of action.

The procedure for having a telephone connected or installed is as follows:

1. Ring BT's customer service (ServiceCare) on 150, who will send you a form to complete.

2. Complete and send the form to your local district office (listed on the form).

3. If there's a deposit to pay, BT will inform you and it must be paid before a line is installed or connected.

4. When BT has received your application (and deposit, if applicable) they will schedule a date for the installation of your phone line and notify you by post (you will receive a 'job number'). If it's simply a matter of having an existing line reconnected, BT should be able to do this on or before the date requested. If you're moving to a new address within the same area code, it's usually possible to retain your existing number.

CHOOSING A PHONE

You aren't required to rent a phone from BT and can purchase a phone from a wide range (many in a variety of colours) offered by BT and other retailers. The quarterly rental for a BT phone is a minimum of £4.99, which means in one year you will have paid for the price of a basic telephone (the cheapest BT phone costs £19.99). The advantage of renting a BT phone is that they will fix it free of charge if it's faulty and you can change phones as often as you wish. With a cheap purchased phone, it's cheaper to throw it away and buy a new one than have it repaired. **Before buying a phone it's wise to compare prices and features, which vary considerably.** All telephones used in Britain must be approved, indicated by a label with a green circle. Non-approved equipment (which may be indicated by a red triangle) is also sold in Britain, but it's a criminal offence to use it as it could damage the phone system.

The price of a phone usually depends on its quality, country of origin and not least its features. All modern phones offer tone dialling, which permits faster dialling (the number is dialled immediately you enter the last digit) and also supports the BT network services listed on page 140. These phones have asterisk (*) and hash (#) buttons and play musical notes when you dial. Some phones can be switched between tone dialling and the old analogue system.

A non-BT, standard, one-piece phone (with the keys on the handset) costs from £10 to £15, while an all-singing, all-dancing model costs between £30 and £40. Typical features include a built-in loudspeaker (so you can talk and listen without using the handset); on-hook dialling; number memory facility; last number re-dial; mute or 'secrecy' button; LCD display (so you can check the digits entered); hands-free operation; timer or call cost counter; lock; and an intercom system. You can even buy a videophone, which allows two callers to see each other on a small screen. However, picture quality is poor and a conversation is often plagued by voice delays.

Cordless phones are popular and standard models can be operated up to 100 or 200 metres from their base unit. If you're thinking of buying a cordless phone, note that they rely on mains power and therefore are useless if there's a power failure. There's also a new European standard for cordless phones, called Digital Enhanced Cordless Telecommunications (DECT), which have a 300 metre range and a base unit that can drive up to six phones. You may also consider a telephone with a built-in answering machine (see also **Call Minder** on page 140). Answering machines (like all electronic equipment) are becoming increasingly sophisticated and the latest machines offer a variety of features including fast erase, monitoring/screening, two-way conversation recording, cue and review, answer only, paging, logging of time and date, digital talking diary, call screening, music, memo facility, and remote message retrieval (which allows you to listen to your messages from almost anywhere in the world, simply by ringing your home phone number). Machines with two tapes are best (one for announcements and one for messages).

You can try the latest BT phones at BT shops (see your local phone book) and business communications centre, where advice and demonstrations are available. BT publish a wide range of booklets and leaflets including *In Touch*, a catalogue of BT products and services. For information about products and services you can also ☎ freefone 0800-800150. However, compare phones and equipment available from high street shops before buying, and if possible, test them before buying. Some retailers provide an unconditional money-back guarantee for a limited period.

For those with special needs, a variety of special phones and attachments are available. If you live or work in a noisy environment, a headset can be purchased allowing hands-free operation. Special handsets are available for the blind (with a nodule on the figure 5) and extra large key pads for the partially blind. Phones fitted with a flashing light, loud ring, a built-in amplifier or an inductive coupler (for those with behind-the-ear hearing aids) are available for the hard of hearing (highly recommended for politicians). BT publish a *Guide for people who are disabled or elderly*, which can be obtained by calling 150 or your local BT sales office.

Finally, for those who dread receiving phone bills, BT offer a range of payphones and cardphones, although they are *very* expensive. You can also arrange to have a phone barred from making outgoing calls. See also **Mobile Telephones & Pagers** on page 148.

STANDARD TONES

Standard telephone tones (the strange noises phones make when they aren't connected to a subscriber) are provided to indicate the progress of calls. Note that tones in Britain may be completely different from those used in other countries. There's sometimes a pause before you hear a tone, so hold on for a few seconds before replacing the receiver to allow the equipment time to connect your call. The following standard tones are used in Britain:

Ringing Tone: Previously the ringing tone of a phone was fixed (although tones vary from phone to phone). However, you can now have personalised numbers on the same phone, with each user having his or her own personalised distinctive ring (so you know instantly whether a call is for you). There's a quarterly fee for this service.

Dial tone: A continuous high pitched hum which is heard when you lift the receiver. This indicates that the phone is connected to the network and you can start dialling.

Ringing tone: A repeated burr indicates that the dialled number is ringing.

Engaged tone: A single tone repeated at short intervals means that the dialled number is busy (engaged). Try again after a few minutes. An engaged tone sometimes means that the lines of the exchange you're dialling are engaged and not the number you're calling. Try again after a short interval. Sometimes you will hear a recorded message telling you that "All lines are busy, please try later."

Unobtainable: A continuous steady tone means that you have dialled a number which isn't in use or is temporarily out of service or out of order. Check the code and number and dial again. If unsuccessful, check the number with directory enquiries or that it's in service by calling the operator.

In some cases you will hear a recorded announcement, for example when an area code or number has been changed. To listen to typical examples of tones ☎ freefone 0800-789456.

USING THE TELEPHONE

Using the telephone in Britain is much the same as in any other country, with a few British eccentricities thrown in for good measure. When dialling a number within your own exchange area, dial the number only, e.g. if you live in Toy Town and wish to dial another subscriber in Toy Town. When dialling anywhere else the area code must be dialled before the subscriber's number. When telephone numbers are printed, they may be shown as any of the following: Toy Town 1234, 01567-1234 or Toy Town (01567) 1234, the recommended method. One problem when the area name isn't shown is that you may not know whether a number is in the local area or at the other end of Britain (although you can always ask the operator). When dialling a number in Britain from overseas, you dial the international access code of the country from which you're calling (e.g. 00), followed by Britain's international code (44), the area code *without* the first 0 (e.g. 1567 for Toy Town) and the subscriber's number. For Toy Town 1234, you would dial 00-44-1567-1234.

When answering the telephone, you should give the area code and number (01567-1234) followed by your name or a company name. Many people, however, just pick up the phone and say "hello" or some such greeting ("yeah?"). Telephone numbers are usually dictated one digit at a time on the phone, except for repeated numbers, e.g. 11 or 222, which are given as double one or treble two. Zero is usually read as the letter 'O' (oh). If you get a bad line, e.g. you're unable to hear the caller or the caller is unable to hear you, or a crossed line where you can hear voices in the background, the connection may improve if you dial the number again.

Free Numbers: Free numbers, called freefone by BT, have a prefix of 0800 (BT), 0500 (Mercury) or 0321 (Vodaphone). They are usually provided by businesses who are trying to sell you something or having sold you something, provide a free telephone support service. Some companies have a freefone name rather than a number, in which case you can phone the operator (100) and ask for the freefone name.

Local & National Call Numbers: Numbers with the prefix 0345 (BT), 0645 (Mercury) and 0845 (various operators) are charged at the local rate, irrespective of where you're calling from. Numbers with the prefix 0990 (BT), 05415 (Mercury) and

0870 (various operators) are charged at the national rate even when you're calling locally.

New Telephone Codes: At the moment it's difficult to know what kind of phone (or even a pager) you're calling and what it's costing. In future a number's prefix will tell you what type of number it is; for example 00 (international dialling), 01/02 (national area codes), 03 to 06 (these are reserved for future use), 07 (mobiles, pagers and personal numbers), 08 (freefone & special rate services) and 09 (premium rate services).

The following (expensive) operator services are also available:

ADC (Advice of Duration & Charge) Call: A call can be timed and the charge given by the operator by asking for an ADC call. Although it's useful when you aren't using your own phone and must pay for the call, it's expensive. ADC calls cost £1.80 plus the cost of the operator connected call, which is much (much) higher than the cost of a direct-dialled call. **If you're calling from a tone phone you should use Charge Advice** (see page 139).

Alarm Call: An alarm call costs £2.70 (it's cheaper to buy an alarm clock).

Personal Call: You can make an international personal call or person to person call, where you start paying for the call only when the person required comes on the line. This service costs £5 plus the cost of the operator connected call. It's much cheaper to make a brief call to find out whether the person you wish to speak to is available.

Reverse Charge Call: A reverse charge, transferred or collect call, is where the person being called agrees to pay for the call. Useful when you've no change, the payphone won't accept your coins or when you're calling your mother-in-law. The charge for international calls is made whether you're making or receiving a reverse charge call. Note that making reverse charge call from abroad to Britain is *very, very* expensive, as it's charged at the operator connected call rate. This service costs £1.80 plus call charges.

Line Faults: If you have a BT line, faults must be reported to BT on 151 for domestic users and 154 for business users. When you report your phone out of order, ask for a reference number so that you can verify the number of days it's out of service, as you may be able to claim compensation. Faults should be repaired within two working days under the BT 'Customer Service Guarantee' and if this isn't achieved BT will pay a daily compensation rate up to a maximum of £1,000 per line for residential customers (providing you can prove that you have lost money as a result of the fault). Most faults are fixed within one working day. To claim compensation, call 150 or write to the Claims Manager of the office which sends your telephone bill. BT operates a free priority fault repair scheme for those who are disabled or chronically sick.

BT Chargecard: Direct-dialled calls and calls via an international operator can be made with a free BT Chargecard to over 200 countries and to Britain *from* over 100 countries using the BT Direct service. Direct-dialled BT Chargecard calls are 5 per cent cheaper than BT payphone rates, although if you call via the operator there's an additional service charge of £1.50 for UK calls (even local calls) and 50p for international calls. Calls from payphones are charged at BT public payphone rates (see page 146). BT Chargecards can be used to dial direct from any tone phone, which includes all BT payphones and most private phones, although they cannot be used from mobile phones.

When using a BT Chargecard from abroad you may be charged an astronomical sum, e.g. over five times the cost of using a local pay phone! If Chargecard calls need to be made via the operator, they are always dearer than making a direct-dialled call. Chargecards are also prone to security risks, both in Britain and when used abroad. Although they offer convenience, it comes at a high price, which is fine **providing someone else is picking up the tab**. For information about the BT Chargecard ☎ freefone 0800-345144.

BT NETWORK SERVICES

The following BT network or select services are available to subscribers with a tone phone connected to a digital exchange, which includes most BT customers. If you subscribe to Mercury or Energis you can still use most network services and most cable companies offer similar services.

Call Barring allows you to bar or block outgoing or international calls, or specific numbers such as access to premium rate services (see **Information & Entertainment Numbers** below). It costs £7 a quarter.

Caller Display allows you to see the number of callers and decide whether you want to speak to them. In order to use Caller Display you need to buy or rent a CLI adapter costing £49.99 with an LCD display that shows and stores the numbers of callers and keeps a record of up to 50 incoming numbers. Alternatively you can buy a special BT Relate 1000 Caller Display phone (£89.99) incorporating a display screen. This allows you to create a personal 20-number directory that will display any names (e.g. Mum, Uncle Tom, Fred, Mary) you choose to be associated with numbers. Caller display costs £4 a quarter.

If you don't want your number to be displayed you can dial 141 in front of any number you dial. Customers can also block their number from ever being displayed (or given out) by ☎ freefone 0800-801471 or 150 and making a request. When 141 is used or a customer has blocked their number permanently, the message 'number withheld' is displayed on the caller display. Note that people may refuse to answer calls when 'number withheld' is displayed (and if everybody withheld their number before dialling the system would cease to function). Caller Display doesn't work with Mercury, cable company lines or mobile phone calls.

Call Diversion allows you to automatically divert calls from your own phone to another phone (in Britain or abroad) where you can be reached, e.g. from home to office or to a mobile phone. To divert calls you dial *21*, the number to where you want calls to be diverted (code and subscriber's number), followed by #. To reset call diversion dial #21#. Call Diversion costs £7 a quarter and there's a three-month free trial.

Call Minder is an answerphone service (at the local telephone exchange) which will even take messages while you're using the phone and answer two calls at once. It can record a total of 15 minutes or 30 messages. You dial 1571 to retrieve messages, when (if you have any new messages) you receive a recorded message telling you this when you pick up your phone, e.g. 'This is BT Call Minder . . . You have two messages. Please call to collect them.' Message retrieval is free and messages can be retrieved from any tone phone in Britain or abroad. Call Minder costs £6 per quarter and there's a three-month free trial.

Call Return allows you to find out the number of the last person to call you, whether you answered the phone or not. You dial 1471 and a recorded announcement will give you the number. If you don't want your number passed on in this way, you can dial 141 before any number you ring. To return the call of the last person to call you, dial 1474 and the number is dialled automatically. Call Return is a free service.

Call Waiting tells you (via a beep on the line) if another call is trying to get through to you when you're already on the phone and allows you to swap between the calls. There's an introductory offer of £3 a quarter for the first year, after which it costs £4 a quarter.

Reminder Call allows you to make alarm calls. To use it you dial *55*, followed by the time required using the 24-hour clock, e.g. 0730, followed by #. For example to be called at 0700 dial *55*0700#. It costs 20p per use or £6 per quarter.

Ring Back tells you the cost of calls. To use it you dial *40*, the number you're calling, followed by #. When you hang up the exchange phones back and tells you how much the call cost. It costs 10p per use or £6 per quarter.

Ring Me Free allows someone to call you free of charge and bill the cost to your phone bill (so don't give the number to telephone salespersons). It costs 10p per use.

Three-Way Calling allows you to hold a three-way conversation (one party can be abroad). It costs 50p per use or £4 a quarter.

For more information or to order network services ☎ freefone 0800-334422.

INFORMATION & ENTERTAINMENT NUMBERS

The use of premium rate information and entertainment numbers has increased considerably in recent years and include numbers with the prefixes 03311, 03313, 03314, 0336, 0338, 0880, 08364, 0839, 0881, 0891, 08941, 08942, 08943, 08944, 0895, 0897, 08975, 0898, 09301, 09305, 09309 and 0991. The rate for premium rate numbers, which must be shown when they are listed or quoted, is a minimum of 39p at cheap rate and 49p at all other times, e.g. 0839 numbers. Calls to 0897 numbers cost £1.49 per minute at all times. Call rates for numbers with the above prefixes are listed in a BT leaflet *UK call prices*. They are huge money-spinners for the companies and are beloved by TV and radio competitions, which although the prizes may look attractive, are nothing compared to the revenue generated by the phone lines. **If you use these numbers frequently you can go bankrupt!**

Information numbers (e.g. those beginning with 0891) offer a wide range of recorded information on practically any subject. For example you can play games, listen to your horoscope or a story, obtain motoring or weather information, or improve your sexual performance. Most 'bulletins' last around three minutes, making the cost of a standard rate call £1.47. The majority of information service companies provide a free service directory. Numbers beginning with 0898 or 0338 offer services with an adult theme (such as sex chat lines) and can include live conversation. A personal identification number (PIN), available free from BT, is required for customers wishing to use adult services.

Some people have received huge telephone bills, which include calls to national and international sex-lines that they haven't made. It's extremely difficult to prove that you (or a family member) didn't make these calls, even if you can show that you were out of the country at the time! Although BT deny it, it's possible for someone to gain access to your line and to make calls at your expense. To prevent this happening you can use Call Barring (see page 140) to bar access to premium rate numbers or block international dialling from a private phone.

If you have a complaint about information and entertainment numbers, you can contact the Independent Committee for the Supervision of Standards of Telephone Information Services (ICSTIS), Alton House, 177 High Holborn. London WC1V 7AA (☎ freefone 0800-500212).

BT CALL RATES

BT remains by far the largest telephone company in Britain and therefore its call rates are listed here for comparison purposes. They are NOT meant as an endorsement of BT, which charges some of the highest rates in Britain. BT charges for all calls, including local calls, for which there's no standard flat-rate charge or a number of free calls. BT levy a quarterly line rental fee of £26.77 for a residential line (there's a £1 reduction when your is bill paid by direct debit) or £12.72 for those who come under the Light User Scheme. VAT (at 17.5 per cent) is applicable to line rental and all calls, and is included in all rates shown unless otherwise noted. For a large percentage of BT's customers, the line rental fee accounts for over half their bill.

BT have three charge rates for self-dialled, domestic calls from ordinary lines (not payphones or mobile phones), depending on the time and day. **Daytime Rate** is in operation from 0800 to 1800, Mondays to Fridays; **Evening and Nightime Rate** is from 1800 to 0800, Mondays to Fridays; and **Weekend Rate** from midnight Friday until midnight Sunday. Note, however that BT charges a minimum of 5p for all calls, therefore your cheap weekend local call will need to be five minutes in length to take advantage of the 1p a minute rate. Some companies (e.g. One.Tel) offer national calls for 4p a minute at all times and are therefore cheaper during the day.

Tariff/Cost Per Minute (1998)

* Type of Call	Daytime	Evening/Night	Weekend
Local	4p	1.5p	1p
Regional	8p	4p	3p
National	8p	4.2p	3p

* Local calls are calls within your local call area, regional calls are up to 56km (35mi), and national calls over 56km.

Special Rates: BT and other telephone companies offer a range of tariffs and discount schemes, although it's difficult to compare their value for money and most offer relatively small savings. BT's special tariffs include:

Automatic Discounts: BT provides an automatic discount of 5 per cent for direct-dialled calls costing between £58.75 and £293.75 and an 8 per cent discount for calls costing over £293.75.

Light User Scheme: If you make few calls and just want a phone so people can call you, this is for you. Your bill for calls must be under £10.81 a quarter (including VAT) and you receive a rebate on your line rental of 12.89p (excluding VAT) for every 10p your call bill is below £10.81. The maximum rebate is £13.94 (excl. VAT). BT makes no concessions to pensioners as for example in Belgium, France, Germany and Ireland.

Friends & Family: BT customers can save 10 per cent on direct-dialled calls to ten nominated numbers (including one international and one mobile number) plus an extra 10 per cent to a 'best friend's' number. Friends and family can be combined with PremierLine or Option 15 (see below). Mercury operate a similar service under their SmartCall scheme.

Option 15: If your quarterly bill for direct-dialled calls is over £31 (including VAT) you will save 11 per cent on all direct-dialled calls plus 5 per cent off calls made to mobile phones and premium rate numbers (e.g. information and entertainment services). The fee for Option 15 is £3.39 a quarter. Note that you may be better off with Premier Line (see below).

Premier Line: Provides 15 per cent savings on all direct-dialled calls plus 5 per cent off calls made to mobile phones and premium rate numbers (e.g. information and entertainment services). There's an annual fee of £24 (£6 a quarter). To make it worthwhile you need to spend over £45 (including VAT) on direct-dialled calls a quarter.

Operator-Connected Calls: One of the most expensive people you can phone in the whole world is your local telephone operator (it's cheaper to visit someone personally by taxi than make a call via the operator). **The minimum period charged for an operator connected call is three minutes, so even the cheapest three minute local call via the operator costs a fortune.** However, if a call has to be made via the operator because a dialled call has failed, the cost is roughly the same as a dialled call (although the minimum charge period is still three minutes).

BT publish a leaflet entitled *UK call prices*, listing all their domestic call rates.

BT TELEPHONE BILLS

You're billed every quarter (three months) by BT for your line rental, phone rental (if applicable) and calls, when you're sent a blue *Telephone Account* plus a 'Statement'. If applicable, the telephone connection fee is included in your first bill. BT provides free itemised bills to all customers on demand that include the number called, the date and time, the duration and the call cost. Customers can choose to have all calls itemised or some only.

BT Phone bills can be paid by budget account (to spread bills evenly over 12 months); quarterly direct debit; by post using the envelope provided; at your bank (complete the form provided) or a post office; and at a BT phone shop. The best way for most people to pay their phone bill is monthly via a budget account or quarterly from an interest-bearing bank or building society account. With quarterly direct debit, your account is debited 14 days after you receive the bill. BT sells £1 telephone stamps (available from BT shops and post offices) to help spendthrifts save for their phone bills. Note, however, that these pay no interest and if you lose them, you've lost your money.

If you don't pay your phone bill within around 14 days of receipt, you will receive a red *Reminder of Payment*, after which you will have another 14 days in which to pay it. If you don't pay your bill within this period, your phone will be disconnected, usually without any further notification. You may, however, receive a further 'Important Notice' reminder, which may give you a further few days to pay your bill, **but don't count on it.** If you're cut off, you may have to wait up to a week to have your phone reconnected after paying your bill. You must also pay a reconnection fee (in your next bill) and may be required to pay a deposit against future bills. Elderly and handicapped persons can apply to be listed under a 'Protected Service Scheme', whereby they name someone who will be told if a bill remains unpaid after a reminder. BT will delay cutting off the service so that the named person can deal with it, which prevents, for example, someone returning from hospital to find that their phone has been disconnected.

If you have a query about your account, phone account enquiries on 150. If you feel that your bill is incorrect (e.g. too high) you shouldn't pay it, but should ask to have it checked by your local telephone manager. Unfortunately (despite thousands of cases that prove otherwise) BT believe that their billing system is infallible and it's almost impossible to prove that you didn't run up the bill or to get BT to admit that there's a fault in their system. BT doesn't, however, discriminate against the private phone user and a large number of companies also complain that their bills are wrong due to mistakes. One investigation found that many companies were overcharged for calls and rental, as well as for equipment and engineering. We aren't talking about peanuts here, as many companies have been overcharged by tens of thousands of pounds (no wonder BT makes such large profits!). If you don't have a fully itemised bill, it's almost impossible to prove that you didn't make calls charged to you.

If you're in dispute with BT over your phone bill (as many people seem to be at some time or other) you shouldn't be disconnected, although if only part of your bill is in dispute, **you should pay the part that isn't in dispute to avoid being cut off.** BT will disconnect a private customer who refuses to pay his bill indefinitely (companies with large bills usually receive better treatment). If you cannot obtain satisfaction from your local BT area manager (the phone number is on your bill) or district general manager, you should contact the secretary of your national Advisory Committee (the address is listed in your phone book under 'Code of Practice for Consumers'). Two independent organisations also deal with complaints about the telephone service: The Telephone Users Association, Woodgate Studios, 2-8 Games Road, Barnet, London EN4 9HN (☎ 0181-449 8844) and the Office of Telecommunications (Oftel), 50 Ludgate Hill, London EC4M 7JJ (☎ 0345-145000). As a last resort you can go to legally binding arbitration if your dispute is for less than £5,000.

Mercury: Mercury customers receive two bills. One from BT for line rental and local calls, and an itemised bill from Mercury for long-distance and international calls. Mercury will provide separate codes when two or more people are using the same phone, so that you can see how much each person has spent (or you can use different codes to separate private and business calls). Mercury also allows customers to choose between monthly and quarterly bills. It has a 24-hour, 365 days-a-year customer assistance number (freefone 0500-500194) dealing with bill enquiries, complaints, faults and other matters concerning service.

INTERNATIONAL CALLS

All private telephones in Britain are on International Direct Dialling (IDD), allowing calls to be dialled direct to over 190 countries and reverse charge calls (collect) to be made to some 140 countries. To make an International call, dial 00, the country code, the area code **without** the first zero (with a few exceptions such as Italy) and the subscriber's number. Dial 155 for the international operator to make non-IDD calls, credit card calls, person-to-person and reverse charge calls (which aren't accepted by all countries). Dial 153 for international directory enquiries. The codes for the major cities of many countries are listed in phone books in section three 'International

Information', including the time difference (one sure way to upset most people is to wake them at 0300 hours).

BT charges for dialled international calls from ordinary lines are based on charge bands (1 to 16), which are shown in phone books with international dialling information. In 1999, sample weekend rates (with Friends & Family – BT's lowest) were 24p per minute to Australia, 18p to France and Germany, 14p to Ireland, 42p to Japan, 52p to South Africa and 16p to the USA. International charges are listed in a BT leaflet entitled *International call prices*. **Note that rates are much higher during the daytime from Mondays to Fridays. Using an alternative company to BT, e.g. an indirect access company (below), can result in huge savings.**

Indirect Access Companies: The cheapest companies for international calls are usually indirect access companies (previously termed 'callback' companies as you needed to ring a number and receive a call back to obtain a line). Nowadays you simply dial a freefone number to connect to the company's own lines or dial a code before dialling a number. They may offer low rates for all calls or just national and international calls. Some charge a subscription fee. Calls are charged at a flat rate 24 hours a day, seven days a week. Some companies allow you to make calls from any tone phone (even abroad), while others restrict you to a single (e.g. home or office) number. Calls may be paid for with a credit (charge or debit) card, either in advance when you must buy a number of units, or by direct debit each month. Alternatively you may be billed monthly in arrears.

Low cost companies have devastated BT's share of the international market in recent years, particularly transatlantic calls, which isn't surprising when you consider the savings that can be made. For examples One.Tel (☎ 0845-308 1878) charges a flat rate of 6p per minute to the USA, 9p to Australia, Canada, France, Germany and Ireland, 10p to New Zealand, 15p to Japan and 30p to South Africa (these rates aren't applicable to mobile phones or payphones). Compare these rates with BT's above. Isn't competition wonderful? Most other indirect access companies such as Alpha Telecom (☎ freefone 0800-279 0000), AXS Telecom (☎ freefone 0800-358 2223), Callmate (☎ freefone 0800-376 3000), First telecom (☎ freefone 0800-458 5858), Primus (☎ freefone 0800-036 0003) and Swiftcall (☎ freefone 0800-769 0200) have similar rates to One.Tel. It's possible to buy a box that you connect between your phone and wall socket that automatically routes long-distance and international calls via the cheapest carrier. Telecom Plus' Service Plus service costs £23.50 to join plus £1.76 per month, in addition to call costs and the cost of the switching box.

Home Country Direct: Many European countries subscribe to a Home Country Direct service that allows you to call a special number giving you direct and free access to an operator in the country you're calling. The operator will connect you to the number required and will also accept credit card or reverse charge calls. The number to dial is shown in phone books in the International code section. You should be extremely wary of making international reverse charge calls to Britain using BT's UK Direct scheme, as you will pay at least double the cost of using a local payphone. For information about countries served by the Home Country Direct service call international directory enquiries on 153.

International Calling Cards: You can obtain an international telephone calling card from telephone companies in many countries that allow you to make calls from abroad and charge them to your telephone bill in your home country. American long distance telephone companies (e.g. AT&T, MCI and Sprint) compete vigorously for overseas customers and all offer calling cards allowing foreign customers to bill international calls to a credit card. AT&T's Worldplus Service allows you to make calls from almost any phone in over 45 countries (☎ freefone 0800-220679 for information).

The benefits of international calling cards are that they are fee-free; calls can be made to/from most countries; calls can usually be made from any telephone, including hotel telephones; and calls are made via an English-speaking operator in America (foreign-language operators are also available). Most important of all, call charges are often based on the 'callback' system and are charged at American rates (based on the cost between the USA and the country you're calling from and to), which is usually much cheaper than calls made via local telephone companies. Some companies offer conference calling facilities that allow you to talk to a number of people in different countries at the same time. Other features may include a 'world office' facility that allows you to retrieve voice and fax messages at any time, from anywhere in the world. Note that if you do a lot of international travelling, it's advisable to have a number of phone cards, as the cheapest card often depends on the countries you're calling from and to.

For information about IDD, codes and general information about direct dialling overseas (including a free copy of *The everyday guide to phoning abroad*) ☎ freefone 0800-800856. For information about BT international products and services ☎ freefone 0800-272172, and for information about Mercury international services ☎ freefone 0500-500194 (24 hours). BT provide a translation service for a wide range of languages (call 0171-492 7222 for information and bookings). See also **The Internet** on page 153.

PUBLIC TELEPHONES

Most public telephones (officially called 'payphones') permit International Direct Dialling (IDD) and international calls can also be made via the operator. Payphones in Britain were traditionally located in the famous red telephone boxes, which have been replaced in the last decade by sterile 'vandal-proof' steel and glass booths containing push-button payphones. Many payphones aren't enclosed and some offer little protection from the elements and surrounding noise (although if they remain in working order, most people will be happy). New payphones are easier to use than the old ones, for example handsets are set at a lower, more convenient height for those in wheelchairs and they're fitted with an 'inductive coupler' for wearers of post-aural hearing aids. They also have a wider entrance to provide access for the disabled and wheelchair users. There are also private 'call shops' in major cities where you can buy a pre-paid calling card and make calls in comfort.

Payphones in Britain are operated by British Telecom and IPM, and accept coins (BT only), Phonecards (BT and IPM) and credit cards (BT and IPM). Cards are replacing cash in payphones and various new payment cards have been introduced in recent years. Since installing new payphones in the last decade, BT claims that over 95 per cent (almost 100,000) are in working order at any one time. Public payphones are widely available in all cities and towns in Britain, in public streets; inside and outside post offices and railway stations; and in hotels, pubs, restaurants, shops and other private and public buildings. If you're driving, finding a payphone is usually easy, but finding somewhere to park is a different matter altogether.

To make non-IDD calls, chargecard calls, person-to-person and reverse charge (collect) calls, dial 100 for inland calls or 155 for international calls. Not all payphones accept incoming calls, so check for a sign before asking someone to call you back. Some payphones may display the words '999 calls only' (emergency calls), which means you will be unable to make an ordinary call, but may be able to dial the operator (100) and make reverse charge and BT chargecard calls. Emergency 999 calls are free from any payphone. Some public payphones at airports, ports, main railway stations and some main post offices are reserved for international calls, shown by a sign. Directory enquiry calls (see page 152) are free from a payphone (so make all your enquiry calls from them).

Charges for dialled inland calls from payphones are calculated in units of 10p which is the minimum charge. This means the cost of a call from a payphone is double the minimum cost (5p) from a private phone. Operator connected calls from payphones are roughly double the cost of dialled calls and should be avoided if at all possible. Most payphones are push-button operated and accept all coins except for 1p and 5p (i.e. 10p to £2). You'll need at least £1 to make an international call or a Phonecard with at least ten units left on it (see below). Note, however, that payphones should be avoided at all costs when making international calls, as the rates are prohibitively high.

When using a payphone, partly used coins are lost, but wholly unused coins are returned when you hang up the receiver. Payphones also have a 'follow on call' button which is visible when you pick up the receiver. If you still have unused coins in credit, you can press this button and make another call using the remaining credit. If the display flashes, insert more coins until the flashing stops. It's advisable to insert relatively small coins unless you're calling long distance. Instructions for using payphones are as follows:

1. Lift the handset and wait for the dialling tone (a high pitched hum). If you don't hear a dialling tone, the telephone is out of order.

2. Insert the minimum call charge of 10p (or more for long distance calls), a Phonecard or a credit card. When you have inserted at least 10p the credit display will show how much you have in credit and stop flashing. If you're using a Phonecard or credit card, you will be instructed when to dial.

3. Dial the number required.

4. When your credit is exhausted, the credit display will start flashing again and a warning tone will be given on the line. You have ten seconds in which to insert more coins (or a new Phonecard) before the call is disconnected.

5. Replace the handset and any completely unused coins will be returned. If you still have credit for partly used coins, you can press the 'follow on call' button and make another call using the remaining credit. Otherwise any credit will be lost, so it pays not to insert too many 50p or £1 coins. If you're using a Phonecard or a credit card, don't forget to take it with you.

If you have difficulties phone the operator on 100. British Telecom produce a multi-language leaflet for visitors from overseas in English, French, German, Italian, Japanese and Spanish entitled *How to call home from the UK*, and individual leaflets for certain countries.

Private Payphones: Be wary of using private payphones, e.g. those located in pubs, restaurants, hotels, shopping centres and petrol stations. The charge rate for these phones is set by the owners, many of whom charge extortionate rates. The call charge should be displayed on all private payphones, although most don't (would you advertise to your customers that you're ripping them off?). You should also avoid using hotel-room phones, when fees can be astronomical. Some hotels even charge a fee to connect guests to freefone numbers used to make chargecard calls.

Phonecards: To make life easier for those without pockets full of coins, who have trouble handling coins or who don't carry cash (dirty, vulgar stuff), BT provide payphone Phonecards which can be purchased from BT shops, post offices, newsagents and kiosks, off licences, garages and railway station booking offices, or anywhere the green and white Phonecard sign is displayed. Phonecards are available in £2, £5, £10 and £20 denominations (indicated in units of 20, 40, 100 and 200). With a Phonecard you can make calls from some 35,000 BT Phonecard payphones (indicated by a Phonecard sign), some of which also accept coins.

The Phonecard is inserted in a special slot and the cost of calls and the remaining value (number of 10p units) on the card is indicated on a digital display. It's advisable to carry a Phonecard because when you need to use a coin-operated payphone there's usually a queue (the British love queuing), but Phonecard phones are often unoccupied. Reverse charge (collect) and credit card calls can also be made from Phonecard payphones. BT Phonecards are produced in a number of designs and topical themes to encourage collectors (some BT Phonecards fetch high prices among collectors).

Credit Card Payphones: Credit or chargecard payphones, which usually accept Access, American Express, Diners Club, Mastercard and Visa cards, are provided at airports and main railway stations, but tend to be even more expensive than coin-operated or Phonecard payphones (and therefore should only be used in an emergency). There's a minimum charge of 50p when using a credit card payphone (BT and IPM). A large number of London's licensed taxis, called taxifone cabs, are fitted with metered passenger payphones accepting all leading credit cards (taxifone cabs can be booked in advance). A BT chargecard can be used to make calls from payphones, but there's a high charge.

MOBILE TELEPHONES & PAGERS

Britain has among the highest number of mobile phone users in Europe (over 10 million in 1998), which is expected to double by 2006. In addition to being a necessity for travelling business people, a car telephone is a vital status symbol for yuppies and the young. Some car manufacturers fit phones in their cars as standard equipment, particularly to attract women drivers (a mobile phone is useful when you break down or have an accident). On the negative side, mobile phones are now so widespread that many businesses (e.g. restaurants, cinemas, theatres, concert halls, etc.) ban them and some even use mobile phone jammers that can detect and jam every handset within 100m. **In recent years there has been widespread publicity regarding a possible health risk to users from the microwave radiation emitted by mobile phones.**

There are four digital mobile phone companies in Britain: Cellnet, Vodafone, One-2-One and Orange, all of which cover most of Britain (maps showing the areas covered are available). There's little discernible difference between the two major companies, Cellnet and Vodafone, although you should check out the reception in your local area, particularly if you live or work in a remote rural area. Some companies (particularly Vodafone) have been criticised for their poor reception in many areas of the country (and even worse customer service). Subscribers can buy a

GSM phone, which can be used in many countries worldwide including much of western Europe, Australia, Hong Kong, South Africa and parts of the Middle East. You must have a contract with a 'roaming' agreement if you wish to use your mobile phone abroad and should check the countries your service provider has contracts with.

Buying a mobile phone is an absolute minefield as, not only are there four networks to choose from, but dozens of tariffs covering connection fees, monthly subscriptions, insurance and call charges. Before buying a mobile phone, shop around and compare phone prices and features; installation and connection charges; rental charges; and most importantly, charge rates. One way to do this is via buy.co.uk (www.buy.co.uk) on the Internet, who provide a mobile phone calculator. The cheapest phones usually carry hefty running costs and tie the customer to long contracts with heavy penalties for breaking a deal. An alternative to taking out a contract is to buy a 'pre-pay phone', where you buy the phone for around £70 (usually includes 'free' call vouchers) and buy vouchers for line rental and call time. There's no contract, no monthly charges and no bills. Vouchers have a serial number that you enter into your phone to top up its credit. Note that although they are extremely popular, pre-pay phones aren't cheap and high charges outweigh any advantages (although they are good for those who make few calls but want to be able to receive calls).

Phones are sold by retail outlets such as BT shops, specialist dealers (e.g. Carphone Warehouse, The Link, People's Phone and Phones Direct) and department and chain stores (e.g. Dixons and Tandy) and supermarkets (some banks even offer free phones to induce students to open accounts), all of whom have arrangements with service providers or networks to sell airtime contracts along with phones. Don't rely on getting good or impartial advice from retail staff, some of whom know little or nothing about phones and networks (one old joke is that the difference between Clint Eastwood and a mobile phone seller is that Clint isn't a real cowboy). Always deal with an independent company that sells a wide range of phones and can connect you to any network.

Retailers advertise almost daily in magazines and newspapers, where a wide range of special offers are promoted. There are many different phones available and prices vary considerably, although you should expect to pay around £50 for a 'standard' phone. The cost is usually subsidised and retailers and network providers recoup the cost through line rentals and call charges. Before buying a phone, compare battery life, memory number capacity, weight, size and features which may include alphanumeric store, automatic call back, unanswered call store, mail box, call timer, minute minder, lock facility and call barring.

Note, however, that the network you connect to is far more important than the type of phone you buy. The most important point is where you're going to use it, followed by when, how often and whether you will make mostly local or long-distance and international calls. Don't be influenced by a cheap phone when the real costs lie in high call and line rental charges. Generally the higher the connection and line rental charges, the lower the cost of calls. If you make a lot of calls select a tariff with low call charges. Conversely, if you make few calls or need a phone mostly for incoming calls, choose a tariff with low monthly costs. Bear in mind that the web of tariffs are primarily designed to confuse customers! Note that many users regret buying a mobile phone or at least the one that they bought or the network they signed up with. Once you sign a contract you're usually stuck with the same phone for at least 12 months. Since 1st January 1999 it has been possible to transfer your mobile phone number between operators and you can also have a personal fax number and direct faxes to any fax machine.

Costs: It's impossible to quote rates here as there are too many options and they change too frequently (a price war erupted in 1998 as companies sought to increase or maintain their share of the market). **Mobile phones aren't a cheap option!** National peak call rates are typically four times BT rates (8p per minute) and eight times those charged by direct dial companies such as One.Tel (4p per minute). BT charges for calls to mobiles from fixed-line phones are 32p per minute (daytime rate), 22p per minute (evening/night-time) and 10.5p (weekend). The difference is even more dramatic when you compare the cost of international calls. Mobile phone companies were accused of overcharging customers by an estimated 20 per cent in 1998 (particularly calls from fixed-line phones to mobiles, which comprise around 50 per cent of calls involving mobile phones) and were ordered to reduce their charges by Oftel (the industry watchdog). British users are charged up to twice as much as those in some other European countries and line rental alone can cost as much as £30 a month before you make a single call.

Car Phones: When buying a mobile phone for car use you should choose one which provides hands-free use and on-hook dialling, i.e. where you don't need to hold the handset to use it. You can also get a phone with voice-activated dialling, where key words such as 'office' or 'home' will dial the appropriate number for you. Note that you can be prosecuted for using a hand-held phone while driving (classed as 'inconsiderate driving'), which has resulted in a number of fatal accidents.

Security: Theft of mobile phones is a huge problem and stolen mobile phones are usually reprogrammed (cloned) to make free calls abroad (although new phones are supposedly clone-proof). Mobile phones should never be left in cars. It's advisable to insure a phone for its real value, as if it's stolen you will be billed for its replacement cost, not what you paid for it. All phones are provided with a unique serial number which allows their use to be blocked if they're stolen and phones can be programmed to stop users making certain calls, e.g. international calls.

Pagers: There are three main pager networks in Britain: BT, PageOne and Vodazip (covering different parts of the country), plus all four mobile phone companies. Pagers can be used as a 'cheap' alternative (a one-time, up-front fee of under £90) to mobile phones and can be used to receive messages rather than just an alarm that instructs you to call a pre-designated number. However, you must return a call by phone. There are basically three types of pagers: alpha numeric messages, numeric messages and tone-only (which works like an answer machine where you dial a number to obtain a message).

Before buying a mobile phone (or pager), check the reviews and comparison tests in surveys conducted by *Which*? magazine (see page 437), and *What Cellphone* and *What Mobile* magazines

TELEGRAMS, TELEX & FAX

There's no longer an inland telegram service in Britain, where you could send a message from a post office or a telephone line and have it delivered by hand (by a motorcycle telegram boy) the same day. This has been replaced by a **Telemessage** service which is available both in Britain and the USA (where it's delivered as a mailgram the following working day). A Telemessage can be dictated over the phone by dialling 190 or can be sent by telex. Providing it's sent before 2200 (1900 on Sundays and public holidays) the message is delivered by post the following day (except on Sundays). The cost within Britain is £8.99 for the first 50 words and £4.99 for each additional 50 words or part thereof (the name and address is free!). International Telemessages cost £5.49 plus 65p or 75p per word, depending on the destination, e.g. 65p to the USA. A special greetings card can be used for special occasions. International telegrams can be sent by telephone or telex to most countries and are delivered the same or the next day. They are charged on a per word basis, depending on the country of destination.

Telex is the largest dedicated text message network in the world, with over 100,000 subscribers in Britain and over two million worldwide in over 200 countries. BT publish *The Telex Book* containing a complete list of all British subscribers, available in paperback, hardback or on microfiche. Fax (or facsimile) is available to virtually all IDD destinations and is the fastest growing area of international traffic, with the number of machines doubling each year. Fax costs are billed in the same way as telephone calls and an A4 page is transmitted in around 60 seconds to almost anywhere in the world. British Telecom publish an annual official *UK Facsimile Directory* and provide international directories for over 50 countries. An order form for telex and fax directories is provided at the back of phone books.

Mobile phone and portable computer users can use a portable fax, which allows fax transmissions to be made from virtually anywhere in Britain. ISDN (integrated services digital network) lines allow you to send data, such as information held on computers, on a phone line at high speed and virtually error free, e.g. an A4 page takes around four seconds to send. BT business communication centres provide 'faxbureau' facilities, as does the Royal Mail via fax centres. The Royal Mail also provides a fax/courier service called 'Faxmail', where messages are delivered the same day to most British addresses and to many destinations worldwide. Shop around when buying a fax machine as prices vary considerably. **Beware of bogus bills from publishers of international telex and fax directories, who send companies invoices for £hundreds for unsolicited entries in trade and business directories.**

DIRECTORIES

British telephone subscribers, both business and private, are listed in directories, called 'phone books', which are divided into local areas (BT introduced smaller directories in 1995 covering more local areas). If you don't have the latest local phone book when you move into a new home, you can get one free from your local BT phone shop. Phone books for adjacent areas may also be provided free (for information ☎ freefone 0800-800150). Since 1995, when smaller directories were issued, business and private subscribers have been listed separately. Private subscribers are usually listed under the name given when applying for a telephone, followed by their initials. If you want more than one entry in your local phone book, e.g. when a husband and a wife both retain their family names or when two or more people share a telephone, there's a quarterly charge for each extra entry and a charge each time a new phone book is published (approximately every 18 months). New phone books are delivered to subscriber's homes. Each phone book is divided into the following sections:

Section 1: Useful Information. Includes a map of the area and a list of towns covered by the phone book, BT service numbers, BT service information, dialling tones, local postal addresses, free calls to BT service and customer offices, useful local numbers (e.g. hospitals), number changes and charge information.

Section 2: Local & National Codes. Contains instructions and codes for local and national calls, and charging information.

Section 3: International Codes. Includes instructions, codes and other information regarding international calls. International time differences are shown in relation to Greenwich Mean Time (GMT), which is British time from October to March. From March to October British Summer Time (BST) is in use, which is GMT plus one hour (see also page 461).

Section 4: Business & Residential Numbers. Contains the names, addresses and telephone numbers (with codes) of all subscribers within the area covered by the phone book. Business and residential numbers are listed separately in alphabetical order. The introduction explains how entries are formulated.

Section 5: Consumer Advice. Includes a code of practice for consumers, information about selling by telephone, a list of BT publications and an order form.

Yellow Pages: In addition to subscriber phone books, business directories called *Yellow Pages* are published covering all regions of Britain. Yellow Pages in Britain are widely used and are indispensable to most subscribers. They contain a local route planner and town maps, telephone information and national helplines. Subscribers are listed under a business or service heading (in alphabetical order) for the area covered. If you don't have the latest local Yellow Pages when you move into a new home, you can obtain a free copy from your local BT phone shop. Yellow Pages for areas other than your local area cost £5 each (paperback only) and can be ordered using the order form in any copy of Yellow Pages (or ☎ freefone 0800-671444). New Yellow Pages are delivered to subscriber's homes. All phone books and Yellow Pages are available in public reference libraries and via the Internet (e.g. www.yell.co.uk).

Thomson Local Directories are available for most of southern and central England and the most populous areas of northern England, Scotland and Wales (covering over 80 per cent of British households). They contain local community information (e.g. helplines, government departments, leisure, premiums lines, with maps and post office postcodes), a main directory of businesses and suppliers, and an alphabetical index of all local businesses included in the directory. For a free copy contact Thomson Directories, Thomson House, 296 Farnborough Road, Farnborough, Hants. GU14 7NU (☎ 01252-555555). Directories are available for other areas (other than where you have a phone) for £5.50 per copy.

Other Directories: Useful local telephone numbers are also listed in local monthly guides published by councils and chambers of commerce. BT publish **Business Pages** for a number of regions (including London), which are phone books for business people (☎ freefone 0800-671444). For those who can never find anything in the phone book or Yellow Pages, there are **Talking Pages** (☎ freefone 0800-600900), the classified telephone directory from Yellow Pages for businesses, shops and services throughout Britain. Telephone numbers can also be obtained over the Internet (e.g. www.freepages.co.uk).

Directory Enquiries: Calls to BT directory enquiries (192) cost 35p for up to two numbers. Mercury charge 21p per call plus 48p per minute at weekends and 36p a minute at all other times. Other companies will be able to offer director enquiry services in future, which should reduce the cost. Enquiry calls for the blind, disabled and from payphones are free. BT provides a free directory enquiries helpline (☎ freefone 0800-700200). If you want directory enquiries to find a number for you, you must usually know the town or city of the person or business whose number you require. International numbers for most major cities in the world can be obtained from directories in central reference libraries in major towns and cities.

THE INTERNET

The success of the Internet is built on the ability to view and collect information from computers around the world by connecting to a nearby service for the cost of a local phone call. If you have correspondents or friends who are connected to the Internet, you can make long-distance and international 'calls' for the price of a local phone call. Internet users can buy software or use Internet services such as IDT Net2Phone (www.net2phone.com) and Creative WebPhone (www.netspeak.com) that effectively turns your personal computer into a voice-based telephone. All you need is a sound card, a microphone, a modem, and access to an Internet provider (there are dozens of providers in the UK, some of which provide free Internet access).

Most systems work more like a sophisticated two-way radio than a telephone and aren't as efficient as using a phone. However, all you pay is the cost of a local call to your Internet provider and even this call is free in some areas where local cable phone companies provide free local off-peak calls. Once on the Internet there are no other charges, no matter how much distance is covered or time is spent online. However, because internationals call costs have fallen dramatically in recent years the savings are no longer significant.

There are many magazines for Internet users in Britain including *Internet*, *Net*, *Internet Today* and *Net User*.

MOVING HOUSE OR LEAVING BRITAIN

When moving house or leaving Britain you must notify your telephone company, preferably at least 14 days in advance (for BT dial 150). When moving house and remaining within the same code area, you may be able to retain your existing number. Don't forget to have the telephone line disconnected when moving house, otherwise the new owners or tenants will be able to make calls at your expense. **It's particularly important to notify a company well in advance if you're leaving Britain and want to get a deposit repaid.**

MALICIOUS CALLS

If you receive malicious or obscene phone calls, BT gives the following advice:

1. Remain calm. Try not to encourage the caller with an emotional response; remember it's your telephone and you're in control.

2. Do not enter into any conversation. Simply place the handset down beside the telephone and ignore it for a few minutes before replacing it gently.

3. If the caller phones repeatedly, don't say anything when you pick up the handset; a genuine caller will speak first.

4. If the calls are silent, don't attempt to coax the caller into speaking; just replace the handset gently if no-one speaks.

5. Don't ever give out any details about yourself or your family unless you're absolutely sure that you know and trust the caller.

Tell your children not to give any information to strangers and that if anyone asks for their parents when they aren't at home, they should say that 'you're unable to come to the telephone at the moment' (e.g. in the bath/shower), and *not* to tell callers that you aren't at home. If you need assistance in dealing with malicious calls or if you're receiving persistent malicious calls call BT (☎ freefone 0800-666700). BT can arrange for the operator to intercept all your calls. Another possibility is to subscribe to BT's Caller Display service (see page 140) which allows you to identify callers before answering the phone. As a final resort you can obtain a new unlisted number. BT publish a leaflet entitled *Malicious calls*. One rather drastic way to deter malicious callers is to blow a loud, piercing whistle down the phone!

Note that it's an offence to make malicious or nuisance calls in Britain (telephone salespersons please note). If you want to reduce the number of unsolicited sales calls you receive (who doesn't), you can register with Telephone Preference Service (TPS) by completing a form provided by BT. After you register with the TPS none of the Direct Marketing Association's 500 members should contact you.

EMERGENCY NUMBERS

There's only one national emergency number in Britain, the 999 service, which is for police, fire and ambulance emergencies, plus coastguard, cave and mountain rescue services. Emergency 999 calls are free from all telephones, including payphones. When you dial 999 the operator will ask you which emergency service you require ("Emergency, which service please?") and you will immediately be switched through to that service. You must state clearly your name, location and give a brief description of the emergency. Some payphones are reserved for emergency 999 calls only, shown by a flashing '999 calls only' message.

In addition to providing an emergency transport service for those in urgent need of medical attention, the ambulance service also deals with the victims of accidents such as drowning, asphyxiation (lack of oxygen), choking, electrocution, serious burns and hanging. They are your best bet when faced with a life or death situation. In addition to attending fires, the fire service attends traffic accidents, natural and man-made disasters, and extricates people who are trapped (e.g. in a building). Note that the fire brigade may charge for special services, such as supporting a house that's in danger of collapse as a result of subsidence (or rescuing a cat from a tree!). A new emergency code, 112, was introduced throughout the EU in 1992 to help foreign visitors and is used in addition to the existing 999 number.

The **Samaritans** provide a confidential and anonymous counselling service in times of personal crisis. Local numbers are available in section one (Useful Information) of your phone book, along with numbers for other organisations offering free help and advice such as Alcoholics Anonymous. Local hospitals are also listed here. See also **Emergencies** on page 278 and **Counselling** on page 293.

SERVICE NUMBERS

The following BT service numbers are listed in section one of phone books, where other local useful numbers are also listed, and can be called from anywhere in Britain (except where noted).

Number	Service
100 (1)	Operator Services
150	Residential Customer Service (including sales and accounting enquiries and general complaints)
151	Residential Fault Reporting
152	Business Customer Service (see 'Residential Customer Service' above)
153	International Directory Enquiries
154	Business Fault Reporting
155	International Operator (non IDD, person-to-person, reverse charge and credit card calls)
190	Telemessages and International Telegrams
191	Any Other Enquiries (not listed here)
192	Inland Directory Enquiries
193	Mercury fault reporting
194	Mercury sales enquiries
195	Mercury billing enquiries

NOTE

1. The operator makes calls which cannot be made by STD or IDD, takes inland and international telemessages and telegrams (see page 134), makes calls or sends messages to someone on board a ship via BT's maritime services, and assists you if you're having difficulty making a call. The operator also provides the operator services listed on page 139.

8.

TELEVISION & RADIO

Watching television (TV), referred to colloquially as the 'box' or 'telly', is Britain's most popular pastime (or a national epidemic, depending on how you view TV). This unsocial disease has all but replaced all those boring things like talking, listening to music, exercise, visiting people (particularly people without TVs), or generally doing anything which might exercise the brain or the body (perish the thought!). Most British homes have at least one TV and over 60 per cent have more than one (25 per cent have three or more), and 80 per cent have a video recorder.

Many families have a TV in every room except the toilet, particularly in children's rooms where TVs (and computers) serve as tranquillisers for overactive kids, i.e. anytime when they're awake. In households where TV reigns supreme, the box is far more influential with children than parents. Although the TV may well have killed off conversation, in deprived households with only one TV it does wonders for arguments (about which programme to watch). The average Briton is glued to the box for over 15 hours a week or 33 (24-hour) days a year (surprisingly, homes with cable and satellite TV watch little more than those receiving terrestrial TV only). Interactive TV services are the latest offering for couch potatoes and include home shopping and banking, educational programmes, computer games, and videos on demand.

While still producing a surfeit of nonsense (e.g. inane quiz shows and soaps, otherwise known as 'tabloid' TV) to cater for the TV junkies, British TV (and British produced TV programmes) is generally recognised as the best, or least worst, in the world. British TV companies produce many excellent programmes including documentaries; wildlife and nature programmes; serialised adaptations of novels; TV films; situation comedy; and variety shows, which are sold throughout the world. Other excellent programmes include current affairs, serious music, chat shows and sports coverage. Some three-quarters of Britons get their main information about the world from TV News, although the presentation is becoming more showbiz (newscasters are stars in their own right). Some critics complain that there's too little live TV, where comedians fluff their lines, jugglers drop their balls and dancers fall about (although there are plenty lots of live chat shows). Explicit sex is becoming commonplace and has led to the Broadcasting Standards Council trying to ban gratuitous sex scenes.

Most families in Britain own a video recorder, not simply to watch video films, but also to tape their favourite TV soaps such as Coronation Street, Eastenders, Neighbours, The Bill, Home and Away and Brookside, which are easily the most popular programmes in Britain (now joined by the National Lottery draw). Despite the generally high quality of TV programmes, Britain still has an active 'Campaign for Quality Television' to keep TV companies on their toes. Competition between the British Broadcasting Corporation (BBC), Independent Television (ITV) and satellite TV companies is keen (particularly regarding sports coverage), although Britain experiences nothing like America's ratings' 'wars'.

BBC television has been broadcasting regularly since 1936 and introduced a second station (BBC2) in 1964. The first regular commercial programmes began in London in 1955, followed by two more national commercial TV stations (Channel 4 in 1982 and Channel 5 in 1997). In addition to the five national TV channels, there are also many cable and satellite stations, both of which have taken off in a big way in the last few years. Satellite TV is the only choice for those who wish to watch foreign language TV.

TV Guides: TV programmes (terrestrial, satellite and cable) are listed in daily newspapers (Saturday newspapers also include Sunday programmes) and weekly guides such as *The Radio Times* (published by the BBC), *The TV Times, What's On TV* and *TV Plus*. Free TV guides are also provided with most daily and weekly newspapers. Regional ITV programme variations are shown in national newspapers, although not all newspapers list all satellite and cable programmes. Satellite TV (see page 164) programme listings are published in yet more guides including *Satellite Times* and *Satellite TV*. Programmes can also be displayed via teletext TV information systems, Ceefax on BB1 and BBC2 and Oracle on ITV channels. BBC radio programmes can also be displayed via BBC teletext.

STANDARDS

The standards for TV reception in Britain aren't the same as in many other countries. TVs and video recorders manufactured for use in the USA (NTSC Standard) and continental Europe, won't function in Britain due to different transmission standards. Most European countries use the PAL B/G standard, except for, you guessed it, France, which has its own standard called SECAM. All British channels broadcast on 625 lines ultra-high frequency (UHF) and about 99 per cent of the population live within the transmission range. The British standard is a modified PAL-I system, where the audio signal is shifted to avoid the buzz plaguing the conventional PAL system when, for example, transmitting subtitles or other white areas.

If you bring a TV to Britain from the USA or the continent, you will get either a picture or sound, **but not both.** A TV can be converted to work in Britain, but it's usually not worth the trouble and expense. If you want a TV and video recorder (VCR) that will work in Britain and other European countries (including France) and/or the USA, you must buy a multi-standard model. Some multi-standard TVs also handle the North American NTSC standard and have an NTSC-in jack plug connection allowing you to playback American videos.

Digital TV: All major terrestrial stations are now available in both digital and analogue and from November 1998 around 60 per cent of viewers have been able to receive digital TV through an aerial (this is expected to increase to 90 per cent by the end of 1999). However, in order to receive digital TV you need a separate decoder or an integrated TV (with a built-in decoder). In addition to providing a superior picture, better (CD) quality sound and widescreen cinema format (with a digital TV), digital TV also allows for interactive services, digital text and interactive TV.

Video: VCRs manufactured for non-British markets are unusable in Britain and recordings made for the North American market are unplayable in Britain (although NTSC standard video machines and TVs are useful for playing NTSC standard videos and video games in Britain). Video recordings made on a PAL VCR can usually be played back on any other PAL VCR with both sound and vision. Most modern VCRs have a feature called 'Videoplus +' which allows you to record programmes simply by entering a 'Video Pluscode' (shown in most programme listings).

Teletext: When buying a TV in Britain, you will find it advantageous to buy one with teletext (or 'fastext' an improved version), which apart from allowing you to display forthcoming programme listings, also provides a wealth of useful and interesting information including news, weather, sport, travel, financial, consumer and entertainment. Two teletext information services are available on British TV:

Ceefax (BBC) and **Oracle** (ITV). Both systems also provide subtitles for selected programmes for people with hearing problems, which are indicated in programme listings (usually by a star). Satellite stations also provide teletext services.

TV Models: The price of a TV varies considerably depending on its make, screen size, features and, not least, the retailer (shop around). A 20in (51cm) colour TV with an FST (flatter squarer tube) screen, stereo sound (useful for stereo broadcasts, including satellite TV), remote control, Fastext and a SCART socket (a standard plug for making connections between televisions, videos and satellite receivers), costs between £350 and £450. A basic portable colour TV can be purchased from around £100, while a state-of-the-art 23in (59cm) colour TV with Fastext and Nicam digital stereo sound, costs from around £500. Nicam is a new high quality, digital stereo sound system, developed by the BBC, ITV and the TV/video manufacturers and provides a dramatic improvement in TV sound comparable to compact disc. Note that not everyone can receive Nicam sound, so check the availability in your area before buying a Nicam TV.

Widescreen digital TVs (with a built-in digital decoder) vary considerably in quality and cost from around £700, but will inevitably become cheaper as more models become available and the demand increases. TV addicts can add dolby surround sound (with a Dolby pro logic amp with a built-in decoder and separate speakers) and create cinema sound effects. If money is no object you can buy a TV with a flat or plasma screen costing up to £15,000! Other recent innovations include LaserDisc and Video CD systems, although these are expensive when compared with VHS video and a waste of money for most people. If you have a TV, VCR and a satellite receiver, you can buy a special remote control for around £50 that will operate all three.

Second-hand TVs: There's an active market in secondhand TVs and videos (and most other things) in Britain, so should you wish to sell your old telly to buy one with all the latest bells and whistles (or because you're leaving Britain), you will have no problem. Second-hand colour TVs can be bought from retailers, rental companies and through advertisements in local newspapers from as little as £50. **Note that dealers are best avoided as their prices are usually ridiculous.** Be wary of retailers who offer a derisory £50 for your old TV in part exchange for a new one. Not only is your old colour TV likely to be worth more than £50, the price of a new TV may also be uncompetitive.

Rental TV: TV rental is fairly common in Britain and is mostly offered by specialist national rental companies (e.g. Granada and Radio Rentals), although some local TV and radio shops also rent TVs. It's always cheaper to buy than rent a TV or video over a long period. Some people are tempted to rent by the ever-changing technology, although you should bear in mind that rental TVs are rarely the latest models and the minimum rental period is usually 12 or 18 months. Renting a TV in Britain is a habit carried over from the '50s and '60s when few people could afford to buy a TV outright. **Today renting hardly ever makes economic sense.**

TELEVISION STATIONS

In most city and rural areas, five TV stations can be received: BBC1, BBC2, ITV3 (independent television), Channel 4 and Channel 5. In areas where two ITV3 stations overlap, viewers can usually receive both stations. Under the Broadcasting Act 1990, the ITV channel was officially renamed Channel 3 (shown as ITV3 in this book), thus allowing all channels to be referred to by a number. The BBC channels carry no advertising and are publicly funded through an annual TV licence (see page 163), the sale of the *Radio Times*, and the trading activities of BBC Enterprises. With the exception of Wales, where many Welsh-language programmes are broadcast, and regional news broadcasts, BBC programmes are the same throughout Britain. All terrestrial TV stations now broadcast for 24 hours a day, as do many satellite and cable stations. Programmes on BBC begin at odd times (e.g. 6.20, 8.05), depending on the length of programmes, as they aren't subject to commercial breaks. ITV programmes usually start on the hour or half hour. The terrestrial TV audience in Britain is fairly evenly divided between BBC and ITV.

BBC1 shows mainly general interest programmes including light entertainment, a breakfast news and chat show, children's programmes, national and local news with weather reports, films (without commercial breaks, therefore ideal for video copies), popular series (including American and Australian soaps and other imported programmes), chat shows, current affairs, documentaries, comedy, plays, and live and recorded sport. The BBC1 has lost ground to ITV3 in recent years, particularly in news coverage, although its current affairs programmes, such as *Panorama*, are still among the best.

BBC2 caters more for minority interests and the intellectual or discriminating viewer, although it also shows general interest programmes. These include the open university and schools programmes in the early mornings, documentaries, international films, travel and wildlife programmes, serious drama, foreign films with subtitles, art and history, rock and classical music (e.g. the BBC Proms concerts), live sports and hobby-oriented programmes (e.g. cookery and gardening). In *Newsnight*, BBC2 has the best daily in-depth current affairs and news programme. The launch of digital TV in 1998 heralded the introduction of three new digital BBC channels: BBC News 24, BBC Choice (the first new general channel from the BBC for 35 years) and BBC Learning. Information about BBC TV is available on the Internet (www.bbc.co.uk).

ITV3 or Channel 3 companies (which vary from region to region) are financed by the proceeds from advertising and are usually referred to collectively as 'commercial television' (plus Channel 4 and Channel 5). From 1st January 1993 the licence holders for each ITV3 region have been decided by a controversial sealed-bid system, with the spoils going to the highest bidder. Licences run for ten years. There are 14 regional ITV3 companies covering the whole of Britain:

Name	Area
Anglia	East of England
Border	Northern England/Southern Scotland and Isle of Man
Carlton	London Weekdays
Central	East, West and South Midlands
Channel (CTV)	Channel Islands
Grampian	North of Scotland
Granada	Northwest England
HTV West	Wales and West of England
LWT	London Weekend
Meridian	South and Southeast England
Scottish	Central Scotland
Ulster	Northern Ireland
Westcountry	Southwest England

Yorkshire-Tyne Tees   Yorkshire and Northeast England

In addition to the above stations, there's also GMTV, which is broadcast nationally on all ITV3 stations from 0600 to 0925 and includes news, information, current affairs and light entertainment. London has two ITV3 stations, Carlton, which broadcasts from Mondays to Fridays, and London Weekend Television (LWT), which covers the weekend. All programmes are in English with the exception of the occasional foreign film with subtitles, some Welsh language programmes on HTV, and a few Gaelic broadcasts in Scotland. The ITV3 companies mostly produce their own programmes, but also buy them from abroad, particularly the ubiquitous American cops and robbers series and soaps.

ITV3 programmes are generally similar to those shown on BBC1 and consist mainly of general interest and sports programmes, but with more soaps and game shows. Given a choice, most people prefer to watch programmes without commercial breaks. However, although they can be obtrusive, most commercials are shown between programmes and breaks aren't anything like as frequent as in the USA. Watching a film can be a trial, but breaks are useful for toilet breaks and making a cup of tea. ITV3 produces some excellent news and current affairs programmes, including *World in Action* and many superb documentaries and drama series. News at 10, which was previously screened at 2200 on all ITV 3 channels, has now moved to 2300 and been shortened to 20 minutes (from 30 minutes). The early news slot has also moved from 1740 to 1830 and been increased from 20 to 30 minutes.

Channel 4 started broadcasting in 1982 as an alternative commercial channel, catering primarily to minority interests and showing educational programmes. According to the terms of its charter, Channel 4 programmes must be complementary to those on ITV3. It has a statutory duty to provide information, education and entertainment, and should cater for tastes and interests not normally provided on ITV3. Programmes are similar to BBC2 (although not as highbrow) and include many excellent documentaries; travel programmes; art and music; foreign films and series with subtitles; current affairs; in-depth evening news (1900); general interest series (often repeats of older series); and minority sports, some of which (such as American football) have established a large cult following. It has courted controversy in recent years by showing soft porn. In Wales, Channel 4 is the Welsh language channel, Wales S4C (Sianel 4 Cymru), which shows a majority of Welsh language programmes during peak viewing hours (1830 to 2200).

Channel 5: A new terrestrial general entertainment channel, Channel 5, went on air on 1st January 1997. It was initially available to around 75 per cent of homes, one in four of which required an extra aerial. Areas that don't receive channel 5 include most of the south-east and south-west, parts of East Anglia and much of Northern Ireland, Scotland and Wales, because nearby existing TV transmitters would interfere with channel 5's signals (although Channel 5 is offered on cable).

General Quality: The quality of programmes on British TV varies from terrible to excellent. The competition to buy foreign (e.g. American and Australian) programmes and exclusive rights to sporting events is fierce, particularly with the increased competition from satellite TV. Hopefully this will result in TV companies producing more of their own programmes, which, apart from being superior to much of the imported trivia, are also a lucrative export earner. The TV companies produce around 75 per cent of all programmes, a quarter of which are made by independent producers.

Complaints: If you wish to berate or praise the TV companies, they all welcome feedback from their viewers (particularly compliments). Letters to BBC television should be addressed to Viewer and Listener Correspondence, BBC Television Centre, Wood Lane, London W12 7RJ (☎ 0171-580 4468). You'll find the address of your local ITV3 company in your phone book. If you have a complaint, you could also try the Independent Television Commission (ITC), 33 Foley Street, London W1P 7LB (☎ 0171-255 3000), which is responsible for licensing and regulating all commercial (non-BBC) TV services in Britain including Channel 3 (ITV3), Channel 4, Channel 5, teletext, cable and satellite. The address of Channel 4 is 60 Charlotte Street, London W1P 2AX (☎ 0171-396 4444). If you wish to complain about a programme or an advertisement, you can also contact the Broadcasting Standards Commision, 7 The Sanctuary, London SW1P 3JS (☎ 0171-233 0544).

TV LICENCE

An annual TV licence (£97.50 for colour, £32.50 for black and white) is required by all TV owners in Britain. Registered blind people are generously offered a reduction of £1.25 on production of the local authority's certificate for the blind. The fee is linked to the cost of living and is subject to a three-year agreement under the BBC's charter. The licence fee, which is a compulsory tax to watch TV, is set to continue until at least the year 2001, although it may eventually be abandoned.

TV licences must be renewed annually and can be purchased from post offices or from TV Licensing, Freepost (BS6689), Bristol BS98 1TL (☎ 0990-226666). A 'Television Licence Application' form must be completed. The licence fee can also be paid by direct debit from a bank or building society account in one payment or in quarterly or monthly payments (which include a small premium). The post office operates a TV licence saving scheme for philatelists, through the purchase of £1 TV licence stamps. If you're leaving Britain, you can obtain a refund on any unexpired three-month period of a TV licence by applying in writing to Customer Services, TV Licensing, Freepost (BS6689), Bristol BS98 1TL.

A licence is required by anyone who has a TV or video (or has one installed) that can receive or record BBC, ITV, Channel 4, Channel 5, S4C, satellite or cable TV programmes. If a TV is used for video playback, as a computer monitor or to receive satellite TV only, the licence fee isn't payable. However, your TV must be incapable of receiving BBC and ITV channels, which can be done only by permanently disconnecting your TV aerial and tuner circuitry.

The licence fee covers any number of TVs (black & white or colour depending on the fee paid) owned by the licence holder, members of his family and domestic staff, at his main home. **The licence fee also covers a TV at a second home in Britain, providing that both TVs aren't used simultaneously.** If you have inadvertently paid for a licence for a TV in a second home, you're entitled to a full refund.

Non-Payment: Registration must be made within 14 days of installing a TV. The BBC use detector vans to check which homes have TVs and whether they have paid their licence fee (of course most people wouldn't dream of not paying). The BBC also runs 'ads' to shame/frighten people into buying a licence. You can be heavily fined (up to £1,000) for not having a TV licence and if you don't pay the fine you can be jailed. Hundreds are people are fined or jailed each year for licence-fee default (it's no wonder Britain jails more of its people than any country in Western Europe). An estimated 10 per cent of people in mainland Britain don't buy a licence. Note that shops selling or renting TVs must forward customers' names and addresses to the authorities.

SATELLITE TELEVISION

Although many people complain endlessly about the poor quality of TV in their home countries, many find they cannot live without it when abroad. Fortunately the advent of satellite TV in the last decade means that most people can enjoy TV programmes in English and a variety of other languages almost anywhere in the world. Britain is well served by satellite TV, where a number of satellites are positioned carrying over 200 stations broadcasting in a variety of languages.

Astra: Although it wasn't the first in Europe (which was Eutelsat), the European satellite revolution really took off with the launch of the Astra 1A satellite in 1988 (operated by the Luxembourg-based *Société Européenne des Satellites* or SES), positioned 36,000km (22,300mi) above the earth. TV addicts (easily recognised by their antennae and square eyes) are offered a huge choice of English and foreign-language stations which can be received throughout most of Britain with a 60cm (or smaller) dish and receiver. Since 1988 a number of additional Astra satellites have been launched, increasing the number of available channels to 64 (or over 200 with digital TV). An added bonus is the availability of radio stations via satellite, including all the national BBC stations (see **Satellite Radio** on page 168).

Among the many English-language stations available on Astra are Sky One, Movimax, Sky Premier, Sky Cinema, Film Four, Sky News, Sky Sports (three channels), UK Gold, Channel 5, Granada Plus, TNT, Eurosport, CNN, CNBC Europe, UK Style, UK Horizons, The Disney Channel and the Discovery Channel. Other stations broadcast in Dutch, German, Japanese, Swedish and various Indian languages. The signal from many stations is scrambled (the decoder is usually built into the receiver) and viewers must pay a monthly subscription fee to receive programmes. You can buy pirate decoders for some channels. The best served by clear (unscrambled) stations are German-speakers (most German stations on Astra are clear).

BSkyB Television: You must buy a Videocrypt decoder, an integral part of the receiver in the latest models, and pay a monthly subscription to receive all BSkyB or Sky stations except Sky News (which isn't scrambled). Various packages are available costing from around £12 to £30 a month for the premium package offering all movie channels plus Sky Sports. Subscribers are sent a coded 'smart' card (similar to a credit card), which must be inserted in the decoder to switch it on (cards are frequently changed to thwart counterfeiters). Sky subscribers receive a free copy of *SkyTVguide* monthly.

Digital Television: Digital TV was launched on 1st October 1998 by Sky Television (☎ 0870-424242) in the UK. To watch digital TV you require a Digibox and a (digital) Minidish, costing £200 including installation (the actual cost of the set top box is around £400 without the hefty subsidy paid by BSkyB). Customers must sign up for a 12-month subscription and agree to have the connection via a phone line (to allow for future interactive services). In addition to the usual analogue channels (see above), Sky digital TV offers BBC1 & 2 and Channels 4 and 5 (but not ITV3), plus many new digital channels (a total of 200 with up to 500 possible later). ONdigital (☎ 0808-100 0101) launched a rival digital service on 15th November 1998, which although it's cheaper than Sky digital, provides a total of 30 channels only (15 free and 15 subscription) including BBC1 & 2, ITV3, Channel 4 and Channel 5. Cable & Wireless also plan to launch a digital service in 1999. Digital TV will also be available via cable and terrestrial aerials in the near future. Contact your local TV store for further information and installation.

Eutelsat: Eutelsat (owned by a consortium of national telephone operators) was the first company to introduce satellite TV to Europe (in 1983) and now runs a fleet of communications satellites carrying TV stations to over 50 million homes. Until 1995 they had broadcast primarily advertising-based, clear-access cable channels. Following the launch in March 1995 of their Hot Bird satellite, Eutelsat hoped to become a major competitor to Astra, although its channels are mostly non-English. The English-language stations on Eutelsat include Eurosport, Euronews, BBC World and CNBC Europe. Other channels broadcast in Arabic, French, German, Hungarian, Italian, Polish, Portuguese, Spanish and Turkish.

BBC Worldwide Television: Although intended for an international audience, it's possible to receive the BBC Worldwide TV stations, BBC Prime (general entertainment) and BBC World (24-hour news and information) in Britain via the Intelsat VI and Eutelsat II F1 satellites respectively. BBC Prime is encrypted and requires a D2 Mac decoder and a smartcard (£75 plus VAT per year). BBC World is clear (unencrypted) and is financed by advertising revenue. For more information and a programming guide contact BBC Worldwide Television, Woodlands, 80 Wood Lane, London W12 0TT, UK (☎ UK 0181-576 2555). The BBC publishes a monthly magazine, *BBC On Air*, giving comprehensive information about BBC Worldwide Television programmes. A programme guide is also listed on the Internet (www.bbc.co.uk/schedules) and both BBC World and BBC Prime have their own websites (www.bbcworld.com and www.bbcprime.com). When accessing them, you need to enter the name of the country so that the schedules appear in local time.

Equipment: A satellite receiver should have a built-in Videocrypt decoder (and others such as Eurocrypt, Syster or SECAM if required) and be capable of receiving satellite stereo radio. A 60cm dish (to receive Astra stations) costs from around £150 plus the cost of installation (which may be included in the price). Larger (from 90cm) motorised dishes cost from £600 to over £1,000. Shop around as prices vary enormously. Systems can also be rented, although renting isn't good value for money. You can even get a 1.2 or 1.5 metre dish and receive hundreds of stations in a multitude of languages from around the world. If you wish to receive satellite TV on two or more TVs, you can buy a system with two or more receptors. To receive stations from two or more satellites simultaneously, you need a motorised dish or a dish with a double feed (dual LNBs) antenna. **When buying a system, ensure that it can receive programmes from all existing and planned satellites.**

Location: To receive programmes from any satellite, there must be no obstacles between the satellite and your dish, i.e. no trees, buildings or mountains (or anything else) must obstruct the signal, so check before renting or buying a home. Under current planning regulations most householders are permitted to erect one satellite dish aerial without planning permission, providing it's no bigger than 90cm. Dishes can be mounted in a variety of unobtrusive positions. You may need planning permission to install a satellite dish or antenna on a house depending on its size, height, position, the location of the property, and whether or not a dish is already installed. If in doubt contact your local council's planning department. Note that those living in conservation areas and in listed buildings are banned from erecting aerials on buildings (or may be required to mount them so they cannot be seen from public roads). In strong signal areas it's possible to mount a dish indoors, providing there's a direct line to the satellite through a window or skylight.

Programme Guides: Many satellite stations provide teletext information, which include programme schedules. Satellite programmes are also listed in most national daily newspapers, general TV magazines and satellite TV magazines such as *What Satellite, Satellite Times* and *Satellite TV* (the best), available from newsagents or on subscription. The annual *World Radio and TV Handbook* (Billboard) contains over 600 pages of information and the frequencies of all radio and TV stations worldwide.

CABLE TELEVISION

Cable television in Britain was originally confined to areas of poor reception (e.g. due to natural geographical features or high-rise buildings) or where external aerials weren't permitted. However, there has been an explosion in cable TV in the last decade and it's the fastest growing sector of the TV industry. Over ten million homes can now receive cable TV and there are around three million subscribers (although Britain still has a long way to go to match European countries such as Belgium the Netherlands and Switzerland, where 90 per cent of the populations has access to cable TV).

The new broadband cable systems can carry up to 30 channels including terrestrial broadcasts, satellite TV, channels delivered by videotape and local services. Most cable TV companies provide all the stations offered by satellite TV plus a few others, a total of up to 40 (possibly including local cable TV companies such as Channel One in London). There's an initial connection fee of around £25 for cable TV, and a subscription of around £15 a month for the basic package, up to £35 a month for a package including all the premium channels. One of the main advantages is that most cable companies offer inexpensive telephone services, possibly including free local off-peak calls, which can save you enough on your phone bill to pay for your cable TV. Digital TV services are to be introduced in spring 1999 and are expected to be cheaper than satellite digital TV as no extra equipment is necessary. Companies will also offer pay-per-view broadcasts, movies on demand, home shopping and access to the Internet.

Cable TV is controlled by the Independent Television Commission (see page 163). For information about cable TV contact the Cable Communications Association, 5ᵗʰ Floor, Artillery House, Artillery Row, London SW1P 1RT (☎ freefone 0800-300750).

VIDEOS

There are numerous video hire shops in Britain, which reached (or exceeded) saturation point in the early '90s. The British video market is the second largest in the world after the USA and Britain has the highest ownership of VCRs in Europe (around three-quarters of households). Many video shops are open until 2000 or even 2200, seven days a week. To hire a video you must usually be a member, for which shops require proof of your address and verification of your signature. If you're under 18, a parent is required to stand as a guarantor. Some video shops have a children's membership scheme with special deals for kids and cheap rental rates for children's films (although most kids are more interested in video nasties). Daily hire charges range from around £2 to £3, depending on the film rating (new top ten films are the most expensive) and the shop. There's usually no extra charge for weekend hire (e.g. Saturday to Monday) when a shop doesn't open on a Sunday.

Members are issued with a membership card which must be shown when hiring videos. Usually you can take out up to three or four films at any time, which must usually be returned by 1900 the following day. If you're late returning a film, you're charged an extra day's rental for each day overdue. If you lose or damage a film, you will be expected to pay for a replacement at retail price. Insurance against loss or damage is sometimes available for a one time payment, e.g. £5. Videos can also be hired from public libraries, where the cost is usually 50p or £1 a night for films or fiction and £1 a week for non-fiction. Most video shops also sell secondhand video films at reduced prices and newly released videos usually cost £9.99 (or £4.99 for older less popular films). Woolworths (the chain store) have a good selection of the latest videos for sale.

RADIO

Radio reception in Britain is excellent in most parts of the country, including stereo reception, which is clear in all but the most 'mountainous' areas (although FM reception isn't always good in cars). The radio audience in Britain is almost equally split between the British Broadcasting Corporation (BBC) and commercial radio stations (although the BBC has been losing listeners to commercial stations at an alarming rate in recent years). Community and ethnic radio is also popular in many areas and a number of universities and colleges operate their own radio stations. In addition to the FM or VHF stereo wave band, medium wave (MW or AM) and long wave (LW) bands are in wide use throughout Britain. Shortwave (SW) band is useful for receiving foreign radio stations. As in other countries, British radio stations scour the country (world?) to find brainless, incoherent, banal dimwits whom they can instantly turn into wallies of the radio waves, known as disc jockeys (some of whom achieve greater fame as even bigger prats on TV).

BBC Radio: BBC operates five network radio stations with easy to remember (if unimaginative) names: BBC Radio 1 (contemporary music, FM 97.6-99.8), BBC Radio 2, dubbed 'the opium of the people', (entertainment, culture and music, FM 88-90.2), BBC Radio 3 (classical music, jazz, drama, discussions, documentaries and poetry, FM 90.2-92.4), BBC Radio 4 (conversation, comedy, drama, documentaries, magazine programmes, news, FM 92.4-94.6, LW 198), BBC Radio 5 Live (news, current affairs and sports, MW 693, 909) and around 40 English BBC local radio stations with some 10 million listeners. There's no advertising on BBC radio stations, although it's the main source of income for commercial radio stations (the other is selling T-shirts). BBC radio is financed by the government and the revenue from TV licence fees, as no radio licence is necessary in Britain.

BBC radio programmes are published in national newspapers and Radios 1, 3 and 4 are broadcast both in stereo on FM and in mono on AM. BBC radio programmes are also listed on the BBC TV teletext information service. If you have any difficulty locating the BBC's stations, send an SAE to the BBC, Listener Correspondence, Broadcasting House, Portland Place, London W1A 1AA (☎ 0171-580 4468).

BBC World Service: The BBC World Service (the insomniac's station) broadcasts worldwide, in English and around 37 other languages, for over 770 hours a week (a *very* long week). Although mainly intended for listeners outside Britain, the BBC World Service can be received loud and clear in most parts of England. The

BBC World Service is the most famous and highly respected international radio service in the world, with regular listeners estimated at 120 million (give or take a few). The main aims are to provide unbiased news, project British opinion, and reflect British life, culture and developments in science and industry.

News bulletins, current affairs, political commentaries and topical magazine programmes form the bulk of its output, supported by a comprehensive sports service, music, drama and general entertainment. Broadcasts in English (24 hours a day) are supplemented by programmes of special interest to Africa, Southern Asia and the Falklands Islands at peak listening times. For programme and frequency information write to BBC World Service Publicity, PO Box 76, Bush House, Strand, London WC2B 4PH. General enquiries concerning BBC radio should be addressed to BBC Radio, Broadcasting House, Portland Place, London W1A 1AA (☎ 0171-580 4468). A BBC monthly magazine, *London Calling*, is available on subscription.

Commercial Radio: Commercial radio is hugely popular in Britain and is Britain's fastest growing entertainment medium. Most cities can now receive at least five commercial stations (over ten in London). However, there are still only some 200 commercial radio stations in the whole of Britain, compared with around 1,000 in France and Italy, and over 9,000 in the USA. The British are avid radio listeners and over 90 per cent of the population listens to the radio for 20 hours or more each week. Commercial radio is reported to have some 36 million listeners or almost 80 per cent of all adults.

Stations vary from large national stations with vast budgets and millions of listeners to tiny local stations run by volunteers with just a few thousand listeners. Stations provide a comprehensive service of local news and information, music and other entertainment, education, consumer advice, traffic information and local events, and provide listeners with the chance to air their views, often through phone-in programmes (talkzak). Advertising on commercial radio is limited to nine minutes an hour, but is usually less (although it sometimes appears to be endless, particularly on Capital FM). Britain has three national commercial radio stations: Classic FM (FM 100-101.9) Virgin Radio (popular music, FM 105.8, MW 1197, 1215) and Talk Radio UK (MW 1053, 1089), Britain's first 24-hour, national, speech-only commercial station. Britain's most popular commercial radio stations is Capital Radio (Capital FM and Capital Gold plus stations in Birmingham, Kent, Hampshire and Sussex), the world's largest metropolitan radio station with over 3 million listeners,

Digital Radio: Digital radio offers better sound quality, less interference and no frequency changing. It's available in around 60 per cent of Britain, which is expected to rise to 90 per cent by the end of 1999, although you need a special digital radio to receive it (it can also be received on a PC with a special digital card). All national BBC radio stations are broadcast digitally and new BBC digital radio programmes include BBC Radio 5 Live Sports Plus, BBC Parliament and BBC Xtra. Commercial radio has also gone digital with seven new national stations available only on digital. Digital One was awarded the franchise to launch a range of commercial radio channels and Classic FM, Virgin Radio and Talk Radio all broadcast digitally.

Satellite Radio: If you have satellite TV you can also receive radio stations via your satellite link. For example, BBC Radio 1, 2, 3, 4 and 5, BBC World Service, Sky Radio (a popular music station *without DJs*), Virgin 1215 and many foreign (i.e. non-English) stations are broadcast via the Astra satellites. Satellite radio stations are listed in British satellite TV magazines such as *Satellite Times*. If you're interested in receiving radio stations from further afield you should obtain a copy of the *World Radio TV Handbook* (Billboard).

9.

EDUCATION

B ritish schools have a mixed reputation; while the quality of state education varies widely, universities and other higher education institutions have an excellent international reputation and educate tens of thousands of foreign students a year from all corners of the globe. Full-time education is compulsory in Britain for all children between the ages of 5 (4 in Northern Ireland) and 16, including the children of foreign nationals permanently or temporarily resident in Britain for one year or longer. No fees are payable in state schools (schools maintained by local authorities), which are attended by over 90 per cent of pupils in Britain. The remainder attend one of the 2,500 private fee-paying schools in Britain that include American, international and foreign schools. Some 80 per cent of pupils stay on at school after the age of 16 or go onto higher education.

Most state schools (primary and secondary) are co-educational (mixed) day schools, with the exception of a few secondary schools that accept boarders. Private schools include both day and boarding schools and are mostly single-sex, although an increasing number of junior and some senior schools are co-educational. Admission to a state school for foreign children is dependent on the type and duration of the residence permit (see **Chapter 3**) granted to their parents. Your choice of state and private schools will vary considerably depending on where you live.

One of the most important decisions facing newcomers to Britain is whether to send their children to a state or private school. In some areas state schools equal the best private schools, while in others (particularly in neglected inner city areas) they lack resources and may achieve poor results. In general, girls achieve much better results than boys and immigrant children (e.g. from Asia) often do particularly well. Britain's education system has had a bad press in recent years and according to many surveys is falling behind the leading countries, particularly in mathematics and science. There's a dearth of vocational education and training in Britain, and general educational standards are inferior to those in many advanced industrial nations (e.g. Germany and Japan). In 1997 Britain ranked just 32nd out of 53 countries for the quality of its primary and secondary education (according to the World Economic Forum).

Many parents prefer to send their children to a private school, often making financial sacrifices to educate their children privately. Not so many years ago, private education was the preserve of the children of the nobility and the rich, although today around half of the parents of private school pupils were themselves educated at state schools. There has been a sharp increase in the number of children attending private schools in recent years due to the increasing affluence of the middle classes.

There's no legal obligation for parents in Britain to educate their children at school and they may educate them themselves or employ private tutors. Parents educating their children at home don't require a teaching qualification, although they must satisfy the local education authority that a child is receiving full-time education appropriate for his or her age, abilities and aptitudes (they will check and may test your child).

Further Information: The weekly *Times Educational Supplement* and *Scottish Education Supplement* (available from newsagents) contain up-to-the-minute news and opinion about education and schools in Britain, including management, governors, research and teaching posts. There are numerous books for parents faced with choosing a suitable state or private school including the Daily Telegraph *Schools Guide* and the *Good Schools Guide*. You can also consult an independent adviser such as Gabbitas Educational Consultants Ltd. (126-130 Regent Street,

London W1R 6EE, ☎ 0171-734 0161, Internet: www.gabbitas.co.uk), who can provide advice and information on any aspect of education in Britain. There are many education-related Internet sites including the national grid for learning (Internet: www.ngfl.gov.uk) BBC education (Internet: www.bbc.co.uk/education) and Eduweb (Internet: www.eduweb.co.uk). The Department for Education and Employment (DfEE) has a 'learning direct' telephone helpline for learning and career queries (☎ freefone 0800-100900).

An invaluable organisation for overseas students is the UK Council for Overseas Student Affairs (UKCOSA, 9-17 St. Alban's Place, London N1 0NX, ☎ 0171-354 5210) which is a registered charity established in 1968 to promote the interests and meet the needs of overseas students in Britain and those working with them as teachers, advisors or in other capacities. The British Council (which has offices in around 80 countries) provides foreign students with information concerning all aspects of education in Britain.

In addition to a detailed look at state and private education, this chapter also contains information about higher and further education and language schools.

STATE OR PRIVATE SCHOOL?

If you're able to choose between state and private education, the following checklist will help you decide:

- How long are you planning to stay in Britain? If you're uncertain then it's probably better to assume a long stay. Due to language and other integration problems, enrolling a child in a British school with a British syllabus (state or private) is advisable only for a minimum of one year, particularly for teenage children.

- Bear in mind that the area in which you choose to live may affect your choice of local school(s). Although it's unnecessary to send your children to the state school nearest your home, you may have difficulty obtaining admission to a state school if you don't live within its catchment area.

- Do you know where you're going after Britain? This may be an important consideration with regard to your children's schooling. How old are your children and what age will they be when you plan to leave Britain? What future plans do you have for their education and in which country?

- What age are your children and how will they fit into a private school or the British state school system? The younger they are, the easier it will be to place them in a suitable school.

- If your children aren't English-speaking, how do they view the thought of studying in English? Is teaching available in Britain in their mother tongue?

- Will your children require your help with their studies? Will you be able to help them, particularly with the English language (if it isn't their mother tongue)?

- What are the school hours? What are the school holiday periods? How will the school hours and holidays influence your (and your spouse's) work and leisure activities?

- Is religion an important consideration in your choice of school? In British state schools, religion is usually taught as a compulsory subject. Parents may, however, request permission for their children not to attend. Some voluntary-aided schools are maintained by religious organisations and they may make stipulations as to religious observance. Religion is an issue in every area of life in Northern Ireland, where even primary education is divided along religious lines. Religion is also a contentious issue among certain ethnic groups, such as Muslims, who believe that education should be single-sex (particularly for girls).

● Do you want your children to attend a co-educational (mixed) school? State schools are usually co-educational.

● Should you send your children to a boarding school? If so, should it be in Britain or in another country?

● What are the secondary and further education prospects for your children in Britain or another country? Are British educational; qualifications recognised in your home country or the country where you plan to live after leaving Britain?

● Does the school have a good academic record? All schools must provide exam pass rate statistics (e.g. GCSE and GCE A-levels) and a prospectus, which they may mail to you.

● What are the facilities for art and science subjects, for example arts and crafts, music, computer studies (how many computers?), science, hobbies, drama, cookery and photography? Does the school have an extensive library of up-to-date books (a good library is usually an excellent sign)? These should be listed in a school's prospectus.

● How large are the classes? What is the teacher pupil ratio?

Obtain the opinions and advice of others who have been faced with the same decisions and problems as you, and collect as much information from as many different sources as possible before making a decision. Speak to teachers and the parents of children attending schools on your shortlist. If possible, interview the head teacher before making a decision. Most parents find it's desirable to discuss the alternatives with their children before making a decision. (If it isn't already too late, you could always decide against children and save yourself a lot of trouble!)

All Local Education Authorities (LEAs) provide schools for children with special educational needs, including those with emotional and behavioural difficulties, moderate and severe learning difficulties, communication problems, hearing or sight impairment, or physical handicaps. There are, however, few special teaching facilities in Britain for gifted children (see **Special Education** on page 186). See also **Choosing a State School** on page 177 and **Choosing a Private School** on page 190.

STATE SCHOOLS

The term 'state' is used here in preference to 'public' and refers to non fee-paying schools controlled by Local Education Authorities (LEAs) and funded from state taxes and local council tax revenue (officially called maintained schools). This is to prevent confusion with the term 'public school', used in the USA (and Scotland) to refer to a state school, but which in England and Wales usually means a private fee-paying school. Private schools are officially referred to as independent schools in England and Wales.

If you live in a rural area, your LEA will be one of the 39 English or eight Welsh county councils. In large cities your LEA is the local borough council. All state schools have a governing body usually made up of a number of parent representatives and governors (appointed by the LEA), the head teacher and other serving teachers. In Scotland, education authorities must establish school boards (consisting of elected parents and staff members) to participate in the management and administration of schools. Most state schools have a Parents and Teachers Association (PTA).

Education Reforms: The state education system in England and Wales has been changing at a frenetic pace in the last few decades, which has led to a generation of curriculum chaos. Changes include the virtual abolition of the 11-plus examination (which was previously used to decide admission to higher secondary schools and which still exists in a few areas) and the introduction of non-selective comprehensive schools, where admission is irrespective of ability or aptitude. It's generally recognised that the introduction of comprehensive schools has raised the standard for the worst schools, while lowering the standards of some schools. Most state education is coeducational. In 1989 a new 'national curriculum' was introduced, which itself was revised in 1993.

The state school system in England and Wales has been going through a crisis for many years due to a lack of funding, crumbling infrastructure (the school repair bill runs into many £billions), and shortages of books (around a quarter of secondary schools are short of textbooks) and other equipment. Teacher morale is low due to low salaries (that have failed to keep pace with inflation); poor working conditions; a lack of professional recognition; stress; government interference and lack of consultation; cuts in education funding; and classroom disruption. Not surprisingly this has led to a shortage of teachers (the state school system has some 10,000 teaching vacancies), particularly in maths and science, and the situation is deteriorating. There are also around 35,000 vacancies a day due to sickness, training or maternity leave, that are temporarily filled by private supply teachers at an estimated cost of £300 million a year.

In recent years many schools have been forced to cut their teaching budgets, at a time when they should have been increasing them. Some schools have insufficient funds to buy books for the revised national curriculum and other essentials (Britain spends less on school books per pupil than most other EU countries). Some state schools, particularly primaries, rely on parents' and charity fund raising to provide essential equipment (e.g. computers), books and stationery, carry out building repairs and in some cases even pay teachers' salaries. Parents may be asked to make donations (some schools ask parents for monthly 'fees') of £100 a year or more per child and business sponsorship also raises £millions a year. Most schools have a 'school fund' to purchase equipment that schools cannot afford to buy out of their budgets. However, parents cannot be forced to pay for anything and all contributions are voluntary (many are for activities that take place wholly or mainly within school hours, e.g. school trips). Note that it isn't always the best-funded schools or those with the best facilities that achieve the best exam results.

One of the most heated debates in the last few years has been over large class sizes, although this problem is being addressed by the government and class sizes are falling (and classes tend to become smaller as pupils get older). Britain's state schools have nearly twice as many pupils per teacher as many other European countries. Private schools are quick to point out that their small classes lead to more individual instruction and better results, which is supported by studies in other countries. There's often a huge variation between education achievement in the same class and Britain doesn't have a system of holding back slow learners (e.g. for a year), as is widely employed in other European countries. However, many schools have re-introduced streaming, where pupils are taught in groups according to their ability. There's no stigma attached to streaming, which simply recognises that children learn at different rates and some are brighter than others.

Standards: Illiteracy is a problem in Britain (where some two million people have no ability to read and write functionally) and the decline in reading, writing and arithmetic among children is causing increasing concern. The standard of reading and writing is often weak at primary level, especially in deprived urban areas where social problems are rife. In recent years the gulf between the good and bad schools has widened (in both state and private schools). In the worst schools pupils have low expectations, no ambitions and aren't pushed to do their best. There can be a huge difference in examination results between schools, even those in the same area and good schools are said to be getting better, while bad schools are getting worse (in recent years failing schools have been threatened with take-over 'hit' squads).

There are three kinds of state school in Britain: Grant-maintained (GM) schools, county schools, and voluntary-aided and voluntary controlled schools.

Grant Maintained (GM) Schools: The 1988 Education Reform Act allowed primary and secondary state schools to opt out of LEA control and adopt Grant Maintained status, providing a majority of their governors and parents voted in favour. Grant maintained schools are self-governing and receive their finance directly from central government based on the number of pupils. Schools must manage their own budget and employ their own support staff, including caterers and cleaners. The previous government heavily promoted GM schools and offered inducements such as increased funding to persuade schools to opt-out.

Other Schools: Voluntary-aided and voluntary controlled schools provide both primary and secondary education, and are financially maintained by LEAs. The difference is that voluntary-aided school buildings are in many cases the responsibility of voluntary bodies (e.g. a church or a foundation) plus 15 per cent of the capital costs, e.g. for new building projects. Schools with C of E (Church of England) or Catholic in their name may be aided schools. County Schools are owned by LEAs and wholly funded by them. They are non-denominational (not church aided or supported) and provide both primary and secondary education. LEAs also provide schools for children with special educational needs (see **Special Education** on page 186). State schools in England and Wales are usually classified as follows:

Type of School	Age Group
Nursery	up to 5
Infant or 1st School	5 to 7 or 5 to 8
Junior or Middle	7 to 11 or 8 to 14
Primary	5 to 11
Secondary or	11 to 18 or 12/13 to 18
Secondary +	11 to 16
6th Form College	16 to 19

In some parts of England and Wales, the transfer age from 1st to Middle school and from Middle to Secondary school is one year later than shown above (i.e. 8 and 12 respectively instead of 7 and 11). This is under review by some LEAs (although controversial) in order to come into line with the Key Stages of the National Curriculum (see page 182) and make it easier for children to move to a school in another region (where applicable, information is published by county councils). In Scotland the transfer to secondary schools is made at age 12.

More information: The Advisory Centre for Education (ACE) Ltd., 1B Aberdeen Studios, 22 Highbury Grove, London N5 2DQ (☎ 0171-354 8318), provides information on all matters related to state education and operates a telephone advice line from 1400 to 1700 Mondays to Fridays (☎ 0171-354 8321). All county councils publish information and booklets for parents, as do most state schools.

Having made the decision to send your child to a state school, most experts advise that you stick to it for at least a year to give it a fair trial. It may take your child this long to fully adapt to the change of environment and the different curriculum, particularly if English isn't his mother tongue.

Choosing a State School

The quality of state schools, their teaching staff and the education they provide, varies considerably from region to region, LEA to LEA, and from school to school. If you want your children to have a good education, it's absolutely essential to get them into a good secondary school, even if it means moving house and changing your job. You have the right to express a preference for a particular state school and don't have to choose a school within your local LEA. However, priority is usually given to children with a family member already at a school, children with special family or medical circumstances, and to children living in a school's catchment area.

It's vital to research the best schools in a given area and to ensure that your child will be accepted at your chosen school, **before buying or renting a home**. Admission to most state schools is decided largely on the local catchment area and if you live outside a school's area your child may not be admitted. Note that homes near the best state schools are at a premium and prices in some areas have risen due to the high demand. In addition, some schools have been forced to reduce their catchment areas, thus excluding many children whose parents may have moved home specifically so their offspring could attend a particular school. Children can be denied the right to attend a school simply because they live on the wrong side of a street.

Parental choice was a cornerstone of educational reforms in the '80s, although many believe it's a charade as the money isn't available to fill the increased demand from parents for places at the best state schools. There are over one million surplus places in schools costing £millions a year to maintain, while children are falling over each other in the best schools (and parents are fighting to get their children accepted). You can appeal against a refusal, as thousands of parents do each year, although most are unsuccessful. Many parents are dissatisfied with their child's school place.

Note that an LEA is obliged to provide transport or pay travelling expenses only when the nearest state school is over 3km (2mi) for under-8s or over 5km (3mi) for over-11s. You can apply to change schools if you or your child wishes, but due to the possible disruption of your child's education this shouldn't be undertaken lightly.

There has never been so much information available about schools as there is today. To help you choose an appropriate school, all primary and secondary schools are required to publish a prospectus giving details of educational, religious and social attitudes. A list of schools in a given area can be obtained from county or borough education offices in England and Wales (listed in phone books). Secondary schools are also required to publish full details of their GCSE and GCE A-level results (see page 184). The government also publishes school performance tables. There are many books written to help you compare different schools including *Choosing a State School* by Caroline Cox (Hutchinson) and The Sunday Times *State Schools Book* (Bloomsbury), which details 500 of the best state schools throughout the country. *The Sunday Times* (and other newspapers) also publish education supplements to help parents choose a state (or private) school.

Admissions

You should address enquiries about admissions (enrolment) to state schools to the Chief Education Officer of the LEA or alternatively contact school secretaries or head teachers directly. If possible, enquiries should be made well in advance of taking up residence in a new area. All schools prefer children to start at the beginning of a term (see below). The school year in England and Wales normally begins in September and runs until July of the following year. In Scotland it generally runs from mid-August to the end of June and in Northern Ireland from September to June. Most local councils publish information regarding school admissions and information is also available from the local Education Department.

Terms & School Hours

The school year is usually divided into three terms (autumn, spring and summer, a throwback to when children helped with the harvest), which are separated by 14 weeks holiday. The mid-term (or half-term) is usually marked by a one-week break. The typical term dates are as shown below, although the dates and the length of holidays vary depending on the school and the area:

Term	Dates (1999/2000)
Autumn 1999	1st September to 17th December
(half-term	25th to 29th October)
Christmas break	18th December to 4th January
Spring 2000	5th January to 13th April
(half-term	21st to 25th February)
Easter break	14th April to 2nd May
Summer 2000	3rd May to 21st July
(half-term	29th May to 2nd June)
Summer break	22nd July to September

Terms are a flexible length to accommodate the main public holidays, e.g. Easter is always out of term time. Most schools also close for staff training on certain days, which are listed in the school schedule. School holiday dates are published by schools well in advance, thus allowing you plenty of time to schedule family holidays during official school holidays. Holidays shouldn't be taken during term time, although many parents ignore this and it isn't illegal. By law, parents are permitted to withdraw their children from school for up to two weeks a year without official permission.

However, it's unwise to take a child out of school, particularly when he should be taking examinations or during important course work assignments. The GCSE exams (see page 184) are scheduled for late May and June, and if your child misses an exam you may have to pay the fee *and* will have to pay again for him or her to take it later. The school day in state schools is usually from 0900 to 1200 and 1300 to 1530 or 1600, Mondays to Fridays. Some (usually secondary) schools keep what are termed 'continental hours', starting at 0830 and finishing at 1430 (with a short lunch break). There are no state school lessons on Saturdays in Britain.

Provisions & Uniforms

Most primary and secondary schools provide lunches (cafeteria self-service or buffet-style) for around £1 per day and parents are permitted to join their child for lunch in some schools. It may be necessary for pupils to order meals in advance and to book meals for a whole week, i.e. no meals on odd days. A child whose mother doesn't go out to work and who lives within walking or cycling distance of school, may go home for lunch. In Northern Ireland a midday meal is provided for all primary school children who wish to have one. Most schools allow children to take a snack for morning break, e.g. biscuit, apple or crisps (chips), and milk is on sale in some schools. Free milk and lunches are provided for pupils whose parents receive Income Support (see page 303), who may also be exempt from paying for travel and school outings. Note that all secondary schools provide covered cycle racks for pupils who cycle to school. Primary school children usually need the following items:

- school bag or satchel, or a small bag or box for a packed lunch;
- a pencil case with pencils, etc. (not obligatory);
- gym shoes (plimsolls), shorts, T-shirt and a towel for games and exercise periods;
- sports bag for above (if satchel is too small).

Although most state schools have a school uniform, the rules about wearing them may vary. In some schools it's obligatory, while in others they don't oblige pupils to wear them (rules may be more relaxed in infant and junior schools). Less well off parents, e.g. those claiming Income Support, can claim a uniform grant and some secondary schools may also help with the cost of uniforms. State schools went through a period in the sixties when school uniforms were unfashionable and were considered by educationalists to inhibit personality, in addition to being a burden on less well-off families (which is still the case).

In recent years many state schools, particularly comprehensive schools, have reintroduced school uniforms in an attempt to instil in students a sense of identity, discipline and pride in their school. Those in favour of uniforms also argue that they enhance a school's reputation and contrary to earlier belief, the children whose parents cannot afford good clothes don't stand out as everyone wears the same clothes.

Nursery & Pre-School

Attendance at a nursery school or kindergarten for children under five years of age isn't compulsory. All children must start compulsory schooling in the term following their fifth birthday. Around 50 per cent of all children aged three to five attend voluntary nursery school in Britain (although many more attend some sort of pre-school), which is one of the lowest provisions of nursery education in Europe (in Belgium and France it's 95 per cent). A new government scheme plans to provide part-time, 'early years' education for four-year-olds from the term following their fourth birthday (but it may involve payment of a fee).

Children from three to five years-old may be catered for in local state nursery schools or in nursery schools attached to primary schools; however, the provision of state nursery schools by LEAs isn't mandatory. Admission to nursery education is usually based on need and then on a first-come, first-served basis. Local authorities provide 500,000 places for four-year-olds in England and Wales. Nursery schools have no catchment area and you can apply to any number of schools, although you need to put your child down for entry as soon as possible.

The cost of private nursery school varies and is usually from £50 a week or £400 a term, although it can cost up to £5,000 a year. Some schools allow you to choose a number of morning or afternoon sessions, e.g. from £150 a term for two sessions a week, rising to around £400 a term for five full days a week. School hours vary but may be from 0900 to 1200 (morning session) and 1215 to 1515 (afternoon session). Children who attend nursery school all day usually require a packed lunch (a mid-morning snack and drink may be provided by the school). There are over 800 nursery schools in Britain using the world-famous Montessori method of teaching.

If you're unable to get your child accepted by a state-aided nursery school, you must pay for him to attend a private pre-school playgroup. These usually cost around £2 to £2.50 a session. Many playgroups accept children from age two, but stipulate that they must be toilet trained. These consist of informal and play facilities provided by private nursery schools and playgroups, organised by parents and voluntary bodies such as the Pre-School Playgroups Association, 69 Kings Cross Road, London WC1X 9LL. The Pre-School Learning Alliance (☎ 0171-833 0991) provides places for some 800,000 under five-year-olds. Children attend for between two and five weekly sessions of two and a half hours a day on average. Parents pay a fee each term and are encouraged to help in the running of the group. A playgroup doesn't generally provide education (just educational games) for under five-year-olds, although research has shown that children who attend nursery school are generally brighter and usually progress at a much faster rate than those who don't.

Nursery school is highly recommended, particularly if a child or its parents aren't of English mother-tongue. After one or two years in nursery school, a child is integrated into the local community and is well prepared for primary school (particularly if English isn't spoken at home). A number of books are available for parents who wish to help their young children learn at home, which most educationalists agree gives children a flying start at school.

Primary School

Primary education in Britain begins at five years and in state schools is almost always co-educational (mixed boys and girls). Primary school consists mainly of first or infants' schools for children aged five to seven (or eight), middle or junior schools for those aged seven to eleven (or eight to twelve) and combined first and middle schools for both age groups. In addition, first schools in some parts of England cater for children aged from five to eight, nine or ten, and are the first stage of a three-tier school system: first, middle and secondary. Some primary schools also provide nursery classes for children aged under five.

Primary education almost always takes place in a local school, although in some areas primary schools don't have a catchment area. Infant (or first) school pupils are usually given formal homework and parents are encouraged to help children with their reading, writing and maths. The average size of primary school classes is around 26, although over a million primary school children (around a third of the total) are taught in classes of over 30 pupils (this is supposed to end by September 2001). Middle schools, mostly in England, are also classified as primary schools and cover varying age groups from age 8 or 9 to 12 or 14, and usually lead to senior comprehensive (secondary) schools. Teaching time in primary schools is from 20 to 25 hours a week.

LEAs must provide a primary school place at the start of the term following a child's fifth birthday, although some admit children earlier. If a child attends a nursery class at a primary school, he will usually move up to the infants class at the same school, although it isn't compulsory. Entry to a primary school isn't automatic and parents must apply to the head for a place. In England and Wales, the transfer to secondary schools is generally made at 11 years, while in Northern Ireland it can be 11 or 12. In Scotland, primary school lasts for seven years and pupils transfer to secondary school at the age of 12. In a few areas children may take the 11-plus examination at age 11, which determines whether they go onto a grammar or high school, or to a secondary modern school (see **Examinations** on page 184).

Secondary School

Secondary schools are for children aged from 11 or 12 to 16 and for those who choose to stay on at school until age 18 (called 'sixth formers'). Most state secondary schools are co-educational, although there are many single-sex schools in Northern Ireland. Students are streamed in some secondary schools for academic subjects. The main types of secondary schools are:

Middle Schools: Although regarded as secondary schools, middle schools take children aged 8 or 9 who move onto senior comprehensive schools at 12 or 14.

Comprehensive Schools: Where admission is made without reference to ability or aptitude. Comprehensive schools provide a full range of courses for all levels of ability, from first to sixth year (from ages 11 to 18, although some cater for 11 to 16-year-olds only) and usually take students from the local catchment area. In some counties all secondary schools are comprehensive.

Secondary Modern Schools: Provide a general education with a practical bias for 11 to 16-year-olds who fail to gain acceptance at a grammar or high school. Like comprehensive schools, secondary modern schools cater for students from the local area.

Secondary Intermediate: Northern Ireland only. Equivalent to a comprehensive school.

Secondary Grammar Schools: Have a selective intake and provide an academic course for pupils aged from 11 to 16 or 18 years. In areas where the 11-plus examination is retained (see page 184), entry to grammar school is for the 25 per cent or so who pass.

High Schools: Are provided in some areas for those who pass their 11-plus exam, but aren't accepted at a grammar school.

6th Form College: A school where 16-year-olds (e.g. from secondary modern schools) study for two years for GCE A-levels. It also takes students from comprehensive schools catering for 11 to 16-year-olds.

Technical Schools: Provide an integrated vocational education (academic and technical) for students aged from 14 to 18. Schools take part in the Technical and Vocational Education Institute (TVEI) scheme, funded by the Manpower Services Commission (MSC).

City Technology Colleges: Specialise in technological and scientific courses for children aged 11 to 18 (see below). These are usually located in deprived parts of Britain.

Comprehensive schools are usually divided into five or seven-year groups, with the first year having the youngest children, e.g. 11-year-olds. At the age of 16 students can take GCSE examinations (see **Examinations** on page 184) or leave school without taking any exams. Children may leave school on the Friday before the last Monday in May of the school year if their 16th birthday falls between 1st September and 31st August of the academic year.

After taking their GCSEs, students can usually stay on at school for the sixth year (or transfer to a 6th form college) and spend a further two or three years studying for their A-level examinations, usually in order to qualify for a place at a university. They can also retake or take extra GCSEs or study for the B. Tech or GNVQ exams at a 6th form college. Around 40 per cent of all students stay on at secondary school to take A-levels. The average pupil/teacher ratio in most state secondary schools is around 21, although class sizes are over 30 in some schools. Teaching time is from 22 to 26 hours in secondary schools, but may be increased to boost exam results.

City technology colleges are state-aided and independent of LEAs and are a recent innovation in state education for 11 to 18-year-olds. Their aim is to widen the choice of secondary education in disadvantaged urban areas and to teach a broad curriculum with an emphasis on science, technology, business understanding and arts' technologies. Although initially received with hostility and scepticism by the educational establishment, technology colleges have proved a huge success.

Curriculum

The Education Reform Act of 1988 established the progressive introduction of a national curriculum in primary and secondary schools, for the years of compulsory schooling from 5 to 16. This means that children in all parts of Britain now receive the same basic education, which makes comparisons between how children are performing at different schools easier and facilitates transfers between schools. Prior to the national curriculum, head teachers (also called headmasters or headmistresses) in England and Wales were responsible for determining the curriculum in their schools in conjunction with LEAs and school governors.

The national curriculum (which has spawned a new language: curriculingo) was introduced over six years from autumn 1989 to summer 1995, ostensibly to bring Britain into line with Europe. It consists of nine subjects which all children must study at school: English, mathematics, science, history, geography, technology, music, art, physical education (PE) and a modern foreign language (in secondary schools from 11 years). English, mathematics and science are termed 'core' subjects, because they help children to study other subjects, and are compulsory up to GCSE level. Other subjects are termed 'foundation' subjects. The core subjects plus technology and a modern language are often referred to as the 'extended core'. In Wales, Welsh-speaking schools teach Welsh as a core subject and other schools in Wales teach Welsh as a foundation subject (although this has caused some dissension among English-speaking parents, when pupils are forced to learn Welsh against their parent's wishes). Religious education must be part of the curriculum and is decided locally. Parents can, however, decide whether their child takes part.

For each subject there are goals setting out what children should know and be able to do at each stage of their schooling. These goals are called attainment targets. There's also a description of what children should be taught to help them achieve attainment targets, called programmes of study. At the ages of 7, 11, 14 and 16, there's an assessment of how children are doing, compared with the attainment targets. Assessment is intended to show where children need extra help and where they are doing well, and to help them progress at an appropriate rate. Parents are regularly sent information about how their child has performed in tests and other assessments.

Schooling is divided into four **key stages** for different age groups, which help parents know what their children are learning at various ages. Parents receive a report containing the results of Standard Assessment Tests (SATs) at the end of each key stage (at ages 7, 11, 14 and 16), based on national attainment targets. The key stages are:

Key Stage	Age	Year Groups
1	5-7	1-2
2	7-11	3-6
3	13-14	7-9
4	14-16	10-11

In key stages 1 and 2, English, maths, science, technology, history, geography, art, music and PE are taught. In key stage 3 a modern foreign language is added. In key stage 4 compulsory subjects are English, maths, science, technology, PE and a modern foreign language (from September 1996). In stage 3 children aged 11 to 14 should have 20 per cent of their timetable free for subjects other than the statutory requirements, which increases to 40 per cent in stage 4. Other subjects may be taught in addition to the national curriculum and religious education, which are decided by individual schools. All schools are required to publish information in their prospectus and the governing body's annual report, about what's taught at the school. Children with special education needs also follow the national curriculum where possible.

In Scotland there's effectively a national curriculum for 14 to 16-year-olds only, who must study English, mathematics and a science subject, plus five other subjects. These form the core area and are supplemented by other activities which make up the elective area. Provision is made for teaching Gaelic in Gaelic-speaking areas. Standard tests are being introduced in English and mathematics for 9 and 12-year-olds. In Northern Ireland a curriculum common to all schools is being introduced with six broad areas of study, within which certain subjects will be compulsory, including religious education. All secondary school pupils will need to study a European language and the Irish language will be available as an additional modern language within the six areas of study. The assessment of pupils will generally be in line with those in England and Wales at the ages of 8, 11, 14 and 16.

The national curriculum has already been revised and is expected to be modified over the coming years to counter problem areas and to take into account the changing face of education and training in Britain. For further information contact the Qualification and Curriculum Authority, 29 Bolton Street, London W1Y 7PD (☎ 0171-509 5555). The government publish a number of books including *Education Reforms in Schools, Key Stages 1 and 2 of the National Curriculum* and *The National Curriculum*, all published by The Statenery Office.

Examinations

Prior to the introduction of comprehensive schools, the 11-plus examination was sat by all pupils in England and Wales at the age of 11, and was the major turning point in a child's schooling. The major objection to the 11-plus was that it decided a child's future education at too young an age and left little room for late developers (very few children who failed the 11-plus made it into higher education). However, the 11-plus hasn't quite passed into history and it's still taken by primary school pupils in a few areas, where those who pass go onto a grammar or high school. Those that fail attend a secondary modern school. Places at advanced secondary schools are limited, so in addition to achieving the required 11-plus pass mark, pupils also require a recommendation from their head teacher. It's possible to transfer from a high school to a grammar school, but it's rare.

In England, Wales and Northern Ireland, the main examination usually taken at age 16 after five years of secondary education is the General Certificate of Secondary Education (GCSE), introduced in 1984. The General Certificate of Education Advanced (A) level may be taken after a further two years of study. In Scotland the main examination is the Scottish Certificate of Education (SCE). SCE standard (ordinary) grade is taken after four years secondary education and the SCE Higher grade (highers) after a further two years. Passes in the GCE A-level and SCE Higher grade exams are the basis for entry to further education, and are recognised by all British and European universities and most American colleges. In recent years there has been a controversial debate over whether GCSE and A-level standards are falling, although GCSE and A-level results remain the best guide to a school's teaching standards. The following examinations are held in England, Wales and Northern Ireland:

General Certificate of Secondary Education (GCSE). In 1988 the GCSE examination replaced the General Certificate of Education (GCE) Ordinary-level and the Certificate of Secondary Education (CSE) examinations. The GCSE differs from its predecessors in that the syllabi are based on national criteria covering course objectives; content and assessment methods; differentiated assessment (i.e. different papers or questions for different ranges of ability) and grade-related criteria (i.e. grades awarded on absolute rather than relative performance). Coursework forms part of the assessment of GCSE results depending on the subject and the examination board, and can vary from 30 per cent to as much as 70 per cent. When children reach the end of the third year of secondary education they choose GCSE subjects with the help of teachers and parents (there's no restriction on entry to any examination).

GCSEs are sat at 16 or earlier but can be sat at any age by gifted children. Certificates are awarded on a seven-point scale, graded A to G (below which results are classified as 'U' or ungraded). Grades A to C are the equivalent of the old GCE O-level grades A to C, or CSE grade 1. Grades D to G are at least as high as that represented by CSE grades two to five. From June 1991, students who obtained GCSE D or E grades but wanted to stay on at school have been able to take the **Certificate of Further Studies (CFS)**, instead of retaking the GCSE. The CFS is a more practical examination for less academic students and is available in eight subjects. Generally five or six GCSE passes (grade A to C) are required by children who intend to take A-levels and go onto higher education.

Certificate of Extended Examination (CEE). The CEE comprises a number of single-subject examinations set and awarded by GCSE examining boards and taken a year after GCSE. Apart from English and mathematics, subjects are non-traditional and include social, environmental, technological, business and health studies.

Advanced levels (A-levels) and Advanced Supplementary levels. General Certificate of Education (GCE) Advanced level (A-level) examinations are usually taken two years after GCSE (at age 17 or 18) by those who wish to go onto higher education. A-levels are much the same as before the introduction of the GCSE examination, although the grading system has been changed. They are marked on a seven grade scale from A to E, N (narrow failure) and U (unclassified), for which a certificate isn't given. A-levels are usually taken in three subjects, although this may be increased to five. In recent years there has been a sharp rise in the number of A-level passes, particularly in top grades A and B, which has led to a call for tighter A-level standards. Many educationalists believe that exams and marking are deliberately being watered down in order to increase pass rates.

In 1987 **Advanced Supplementary level (AS-level)** examinations were introduced, which are open to full-time A-level students and others. An AS-level syllabus covers not less than half of the corresponding A-level syllabus (with not less than half the teaching time) and where possible is related to it. An AS-level is graded as half an A-level and therefore two AS-level passes are usually accepted as the equivalent of one A-level pass. AS-level courses are intended to supplement and broaden A-level studies and examinations are graded A to E (as for A-level grades). AS-level examinations have proved unpopular with schools and there's a high failure rate. Around five times as many students take A-levels as AS-levels and few students take both.

Scholarship levels (S-levels). Most examining boards allow the option of an additional paper of greater difficulty to be taken by A-level candidates, to obtain what is known as a Scholarship-level qualification. S-level papers are available in most traditional academic subjects and are marked on a three-point scale; grade A or 1 (distinction), grade B or 2 (merit) and unclassified.

Scotland has its own examination system, the **Scottish Certificate of Education (SCE)** standard (ordinary) and higher grade examinations. The standard grade (roughly equivalent to the GCSE) is taken at age 15 and the higher grade is usually taken at the age of 17 or 18. The Scottish Certificate of Sixth Year Studies (SCSYS) is a further qualification for pupils who stay on at school after passing the SCE higher grade. Some Scottish private schools set GCE A-levels as well as SCE higher grade.

The **Certificate of Pre-Vocational Education (CPVE)** is a nationally recognised award for 17-year-olds doing an extra year at school or college.

To gain acceptance to a university in Britain, a student usually requires at least two A-level passes (grades A to E). This is the minimum and to study some courses more passes and high grades are necessary, e.g. to study law and medicine you usually require three A grade passes, while the requirement for some other courses may be two B grade passes and one C. If you receive an unexpectedly low grade in an exam, you can appeal to your school. There's a fee for most appeals; however, if you're successful the fee is returned. If you're going to appeal, do so as soon as possible, as an A-level course, a college or university place, or a job may rest on the outcome.

Special concessions are made for dyslexic children taking GCSE and A-level exams, which allow them to use an amanuensis or word processor to write answers and to have exam questions read out to them or recorded on tape.

SPECIAL EDUCATION

Special education is provided for children with moderate or severe learning difficulties (e.g. a hearing, speech, or sight impediment, a physical handicap or autism) or a behavioural problem, which either prevents or hinders them from attending a mainstream school for their age group. However, whenever possible, children with special education needs (SEN) are educated in mainstream schools, in order to give them the same education as other children. There are around 2,000 SEN schools in Britain (both day and boarding schools), most of which are state schools operated and financed by LEAs.

There are, however, too few special schools and it's estimated that around a third of pupils with special education needs are educated in mainstream schools (although there are often educational and social reasons for this). Some special schools are run privately by voluntary bodies, which may receive a grant from central government for capital expenditure and equipment. Day-to-day running costs are met by the LEAs for pupils placed in voluntary schools. Some private schools provide education wholly or mainly for children with special education needs. Most LEAs provide an educational psychological service for children with behavioural problems.

Some LEAs provide special teaching and facilities for gifted children (those with very high IQs), although there's little provision for young geniuses. In the past, the only avenue open to most parents was to pay for private tuition or apply for a private school scholarship. Mensa, the society for the super-intelligent, has established the Mensa Foundation for Gifted Children, which helps to develop the potential of gifted children through special schools and individual counselling. For information write to Mensa, Freepost, Wolverhampton WV2 1BR. It's important to choose the best possible school for a talented or gifted child.

The Advisory Centre for Education (ACE) Ltd., 1B Aberdeen Studios, 22 Highbury Grove, London N5 2DQ (☎ 0171-354 8318), can answer questions and give advice on special education. Contact your local LEA for information about special schools in your area or write to the Department of Education and Employment (who publish a *Special Educational Needs* booklet) for a list of special schools throughout Britain. There are a number of books available for parents of children with special needs including *The Gabbitas Guide to Schools for Special Needs* (Kogan Page) and *Schools Catering for Dyslexia* (ISIS).

PRIVATE SCHOOLS

Private fee-paying schools in Britain are officially termed independent schools (although historically referred to as public schools) because they are independent of local or central government control. Britain is renowned for the quality and variety of its private schools which include such world-famous schools as Charterhouse, Eton, Harrow, Roedean, Rugby, Westminster and Winchester. Many private schools, including many of the most famous names, are run as charitable foundations. Schools may be owned by an individual, an institution or a company, and although traditionally the preserve of the wealthy, they attract an increasing number of pupils from less privileged backgrounds.

Around 50 per cent of parents who choose a private education for their children, were themselves educated in the state sector. There are some 2,500 private day and boarding schools in England and Wales, 150 in Scotland and around 15 in Northern Ireland, educating a total of some 550,000 children. Schools take pupils from the ages of 2 to 19 and include boarding and day schools (some are both), single-sex and co-educational schools. Some schools cater for special education needs (see page 186) and there are also private schools for gifted children in art, music, theatre or dance.

Among the private schools in Britain are many which follow special or unorthodox methods of teaching, for example Montessori nursery schools and Rudolf Steiner schools. All private schools in Britain must meet certain minimum criteria and be registered with the Department of Education and Science. Although fee-paying, most private schools aren't run for private profit and all surplus income is reinvested in the running of schools. Private schools receive no grants from public funds and are owned and managed by special trusts. Most schools have a board of governors who look after the school and its finances. The head is responsible to the governors, but usually has a free hand to choose staff and make day-to-day decisions.

Fees vary considerably depending on a variety of factors including the age of pupils, the reputation and quality of the school, and its location (schools in the north of England are generally cheaper than those in the south). Day school fees vary from around £500 to £2,000 a term (three a year) for pre-preparatory schools to £3,000 to £4,000 a term for senior boarding pupils. Fees aren't all-inclusive and additional obligatory charges are made, in addition to optional extra services. There are also commercial tutorial colleges or 'crammers', providing a one-term or one-year resit course for students who have failed one or more GCE A-levels. Fees are high and start at around £1,000 for a one-term, one A-level course, rising to as much as £8,000 for a one-year, three A-level course.

Private school fees tend to increase an average of 5 to 10 per cent annually (unless you're rich or someone else is paying, start saving *before* you have any children). Many companies and banks specialise in insurance and investment policies for parents planning to send their children to private school. Many senior and some junior schools provide scholarships for bright or talented pupils, which vary in value from full fees to a small proportion. Scholarships are awarded as a result of competitive examination.

Private schools range from nursery (kindergarten) to large day and boarding schools, and from experimental schools to traditional institutions. A number of independent schools are also available for religious and ethnic minorities, for example schools for Muslims, where there's a strict code regarding the segregation of boys and girls. Most private schools are single-sex, almost equally split between boys' and girls' schools, but there are a number of mixed schools (co-educational) and a number of boys' schools admit girls to their 6th forms (by which time sex education is part of the curriculum). The different types of private schools are shown in the table below:

Type of School	Age	Notes
All-Through	2-5 to 16-18	Cater for all ages from nursery to senior or sixth form
Pre-Preparatory	2 to 7	Equivalent to LEA nursery and infant schools. Usually attached to junior schools.
Junior/Preparatory	7 to 11+ or 13+	Lead to admission to senior schools at 11+ or 13+ when the CEE (see below) is taken
Senior	11-18 or 13-18	Sometimes have a lower school for pupils aged 11 to 13
Sixth Form	16+	Many senior schools admit students at 16+ usually to study for GCE A-levels.

Most private junior schools (also called preparatory schools) cater for boys from the age of 7 to 13 years, but some are for girls only and an increasing number are co-educational. Junior schools usually prepare pupils for the Common Entrance Examination (CEE) to senior private schools, which is a qualifying exam to test whether prospective pupils will be able to cope with the standard of academic work required. The CEE is set by the CEE board and is marked by the school which the pupil plans to attend. It's sat at 13 by boys and 11 to 13 by girls. Entrance to many schools is either by an exam (e.g. the CEE), a report or assessment, or an interview. Some senior schools don't require pupils to take the CEE or any other exam, but admit pupils after an interview.

Most private schools provide a similar curriculum to state schools (see page 182) and set the English GCSE (see page 184) and GCE A-level examinations. Some Scottish schools set the Scottish Certificate of Education (SCE) at standard (ordinary) and higher grades. Private school pupils can also take the International Baccalaureate (IB) examination, an internationally recognised university entrance qualification.

The advantages of private schools are manyfold, not least their excellent academic record. According to one survey, pupils at private preparatory schools are nine times more likely to achieve 100 per cent passes in the national tests (see page 184) than those at state junior schools. Three out of four children gain five or more GCSE ordinary level passes, more than half gain two or more GCE A-levels and more than two-thirds gain one or more. Although private school pupils make up less than 10 per cent of the total in Britain, they take 35 per cent of the top GCE A-levels and provide over 25 per cent of university students, i.e. a student from a private school is almost four times as likely to go onto university as a student from a state school. Some private secondary schools have a near 100 per cent university acceptance rate and half of all 'Oxbridge' (Oxford and Cambridge universities) entrants are educated at private schools.

Don't assume, however, that all private schools are excellent or that they all offer a better education than state schools. In the last ten years there has been a rapid expansion in private education, which some analysts believe has led to a reduction in standards in some schools. Some have expanded too fast and increased their class sizes considerably, particularly in areas of high demand, such as London and the southeast, and a number have been criticised by government ministers for their poor standards in recent years.

School uniforms are generally considered to be a mark of identity, pride and discipline in private schools (some 'public' schools such as Eton have a particularly eccentric mode of dress). Private schools provide a broad-based education (aimed at developing a pupil's character) and offer a varied approach to sport, music, drama, art and a wide choice of academic subjects. Their aim is usually the development of the child as an individual and the encouragement of his unique talents, which is made possible by small classes (an average of around 15 in senior schools and even less in many junior schools) that allow teachers to provide pupils with individually tailored lessons and tuition. Some private schools cater for special needs including gifted children and slow learners or those who suffer from dyslexia, although the latter are usually better provided for in state schools. Private schools also cater for parents requiring a single-sex school (girls often progress faster without the distraction of the opposite sex), boarding facilities and those who wish their children to be educated in the customs of a particular religious belief.

Make applications to private schools as far in advance as possible (before conception for the best schools). Obviously if you're coming from abroad, you won't usually be able to apply one or two years in advance, which is usually considered to be the best time to book a place. Note that it isn't usually simply a matter of selecting a school and telling the head when you will be bringing little Cecil or Gertrude along. Although many nursery and junior schools accept pupils on a first-come, first-served basis, the best and most excive schools have waiting lists or a demanding selection procedure. Most popular schools, particularly day schools in the greater London area and other cities, have long waiting lists. Don't rely on enrolling your child in a particular school and neglect other alternatives, particularly if the chosen school has a rigorous entrance examination. When applying you're usually requested to send previous school reports, exam results and records. Before enrolling your child in a private school, ensure that you understand the withdrawal conditions in the school contract.

Further Information: There are a number of guides to private schools in Britain including the *The Gabbitas Guide to Independent Schools* (Kogan Page), *The Equitable Schools Book* (Bloomsbury), published in association with *The Sunday Times* newspaper (contains independent reports on over 500 private schools), and *Choosing Your Independent School* published by the Independent Schools Information Service (ISIS), 56 Buckingham Gate, London SW1E 6AG (☎ 0171-630 8793), a guide to over 1,400 boarding and day schools in Britain and Ireland for boys and girls aged 2 to 19. ISIS also organise an annual national exhibition of independent schools. Another excellent guide is the *Independent Schools Yearbook: Boys' Schools, Co-educational Schools and Preparatory Schools* published by A & C Black, 35 Bedford Row, London WC1R 1JH (☎ 0171-242 0946). It contains details of governing bodies, staff, admission, entrance examinations, scholarships, and fees for major private secondary schools for boys and some preparatory schools.

In addition to private schools that follow a largely British curriculum, there are also American, international and foreign-language private schools in Britain. See also **Nursery & Pre-School** on page 180.

Choosing a Private School

The following checklist is designed to help you choose an appropriate and reputable private school in Britain:

- Does the school have a good reputation? Does it belong to any recognised body for private schools such as the Incorporated Association of Preparatory Schools? How long has it been established? Is it financially stable?

- Does the school have a good academic record? For example what percentage of pupils obtain good examination passes or go onto good universities? What subjects do pupils do best in? All schools provide exam pass rate statistics. On the other hand, if your child isn't exceptionally bright, you may prefer to send him to a school with less academic pressure (many students find the demands very stressful in some schools).

- What does the curriculum include (a broad and well-balanced curriculum is best)? Ask to see a typical pupil timetable to check the ratio of academic to non-academic subjects. Check the number of free study periods and whether they are supervised.

- Do you wish to send your children to a single-sex or a co-educational school. Many children, particularly girls, make better progress without the distractions of the opposite sex (although their sex education may be neglected).

- Day or boarding school? If you're considering a day school, what are the school hours? Does the school provide transport for pupils to and from home? Many schools offer weekly boarding that allows pupils to return home at weekends.

- Do you intend to send your children to a junior or senior private school only or both?

- How many children attend the school and what is the average class size? What is the ratio of teachers to pupils? Are pupil numbers increasing or decreasing? Check that class sizes are in fact what it says they are in the prospectus. Has the number of pupils increased dramatically in the last few years (which could be a good *or* a bad sign)?

- What are the qualification requirements for teachers? What nationality are the majority of teachers? What is the teacher turnover? A high teacher turnover is a bad sign and usually suggests under-paid teachers and poor working conditions.

- What extras will you be required to pay? For example optional lessons (e.g. music, dancing and sports), lunches, art supplies, sports equipment, school trips, phone calls, clothing (most schools have obligatory uniforms, which can be *very* expensive), insurance, textbooks and stationery. Most schools charge parents for every little thing.

- Which countries do most students come from?

- Is religion an important consideration in your choice of school? What is the religious bias of the school, if any?

- Are special English classes provided for children whose English doesn't meet the required standard? Usually if a child is under nine years of age it doesn't matter if his English is weak. However, children over this age aren't usually accepted unless they can read English fluently (as printed in text books for their age). Some schools provide intensive English tuition for foreign students.

- If you have decided on a boarding school, what standard and type of accommodation is provided? What is the quality and variety of food provided? What is the dining room like? Does the school have a dietician?

- What languages does the school teach as obligatory or optional subjects? Does the school have a language laboratory?

- What is the student turnover?

- What are the school terms and holiday periods? Private school holidays are usually much longer than state schools, e.g. four weeks at Easter and Christmas and ten weeks in the summer, and they often don't coincide with state school holiday periods.

- If you're considering a day school, what are the school hours?

- What are the withdrawal conditions, should you need or wish to remove your child? A term's notice is usual.

- What examinations are set? In which subjects? How do they fit in with future education plans?

- What sports instruction and facilities are provided?

- What are the facilities for art and science subjects, for example arts and crafts, music, computer studies (how many computers?), science, hobbies, drama, cookery and photography?

- What sort of outings and holidays does the school organise?

- What medical facilities does the school provide, e.g. infirmary, resident doctor or nurse? Is health and accident insurance included in the fees?

- What sort of discipline and punishments are imposed and are restrictions relaxed as children get older?

- What reports are provided for parents and how often? How much contact does the school have with parents?

- **Last, but not least, unless someone else is paying, what are the fees?**

Draw up a shortlist of possible schools and obtain a prospectus (some schools provide a video prospectus). If possible, obtain a copy of the school magazine. Before making a final choice, it's important to visit the schools on your shortlist during term time and talk to teachers and students. **Where possible, check the answers to the above questions in person and don't rely on a school's prospectus to provide the information.** If you're unhappy with the answers, look elsewhere. Having made your choice, keep a check on your child's progress, listen to his complaints and compare notes with other parents. If something doesn't seem right, try to establish whether the complaint is founded or not, and if it is, take action to have the problem resolved. Don't forget that you're paying a lot of money for your child's education and you should expect value for money. See also **State or Private School?** on page 173.

HIGHER EDUCATION

Post-school education in Britain is generally divided into higher and further education. Higher education is usually defined as advanced courses of a standard higher than A-levels (see page 184) or equivalent and usually refers only to first degree courses. Courses may be full-time, part-time or sandwich courses (nothing to do with food, but courses which combine periods of full-time study with full-time training and paid work in industry and commerce). Degree level courses are offered by 89 universities (48 old universities and 41 new universities which were formerly polytechnics), plus 15 Scottish central institutions and hundreds of Colleges of Higher Education (CHE), many of which provide teacher-training courses. Britain is internationally renowned for the excellence of its universities and other higher education establishments, which include the world-famous Oxford (12th century) and Cambridge (13th century) universities (collectively referred to as Oxbridge).

The age of admission to university is usually 18 (although they admit exceptional students at a younger age) and courses usually last for three years, although some last for four years. This is seen as a big advantage for foreign students from countries where courses often last much longer and results in British universities attracting almost 100,000 overseas students. There are also many American colleges in Britain, mainly in the London area. For information contact the Educational Advisory Service, The Fulbright Commission, Fulbright House, 62 Doughty Street, London WC1N 2LS, UK (☎ 0171-404 6994).

In the last decade there has been a boom in higher education in Britain and around 40 per cent of all school leavers now attend university. Since the early '80s the number of undergraduates has almost doubled to 1.5 million and today's 18-year-olds have a 60 per cent chance of going to university at some time in their lives. Many universities have lowered their entrance qualifications to attract more students and also because of falling standards among Britain's school leavers. In recent years there has been a debate about the 'dumbing down' of higher education, as some universities accept students who failed their A-levels to fill empty places (universities face financial penalties if they don't enrol sufficient students). Some universities also 'mark up' students who fail their exams and many people believe that the standards of today's degrees have been watered down and are far lower than they were 20 or 30 years ago. Some analysts even believe that Britain's hallowed Oxford and Cambridge universities are falling below the standards set by some other countries, particularly the USA.

Fees: From the 1998/99 academic year, British and EU students have had to pay up to £1,000 a year towards their tuition costs. Students whose parents earn less than £23,000 a year are exempt and there are also other special exemptions. LEA grants are to be replaced by student loans (see below) in the 1999/2000 academic year, which have been increased to help students meet these extra costs.

LEA Grants: Students receive a means-tested maximum grant (1998/99) of £2,225 in London and £1,810 elsewhere (£1,480 if living with parents) to help pay for living expenses. When the student's parents assessable annual income is below £15,000 the grant is paid in full. When parents' incomes are above £15,000 a year a reduced grant is paid and over £35,000 students don't receive a grant.

Student Loans: In an attempt to reduce grants (or at least limit increases) the government introduced a student loan scheme, whereby students can take out interest-free loans to supplement their grants. For the 1998/99 academic year, loans are available to British students as follows:

Rates*	Loan Limit	
	Years 1+2	Final Year
London	£3,145	£2,565
Provincial	£2,735	£2,265
Home-based	£2,325	£1,970

* There are three rates: students based in London, students based outside London (provincial) and students living at home (home-based).

Loans are repayable after the April following graduation, once your income is above the income threshold (which will be £10,000 a year in the year 2000). You pay 9 per cent of your income above the threshold, e.g. if your income is £18,000 a year, you would repay £60 a month (9 per cent of £8,000). Therefore the amount you repay each month is directly related to the level of your income. A free booklet entitled *Financial Support in Higher Education* is published by the Department for Education and Employment.

Other Grants: In addition to loans, students can apply for financial help from 'access funds' which colleges can distribute at their discretion to their most needy students. When you arrive at university, you will be informed about student loans and the access fund by your college administration department or the student union. Banks also offer students interest-free overdrafts, although these should be treated with caution. An increasing number of companies and professional organisations (plus the military) sponsor higher education, in return for a number of years service. Many students find it increasingly difficult to survive on their grants and some are forced to choose their university not on course preference, but on where they can more easily survive on their meagre resources.

EU Students: Grants covering fees and living expenses are also given to European Union (EU) nationals and their children working in Britain, and to officially recognised refugees and their children. EU nationals who are normally resident within the union area are eligible for grants (covering university fees only) on the same basis as British residents, but must pay their own living expenses. With the exception of these grants, authorities can only give grants covering fees and living expenses to students who have been resident in Britain (or the Channel Islands or Isle of Man) for the three years immediately prior to the first year of their course. The factors determining the size of a grant are complex (as is anything devised by civil servants), but it depends largely on a student's financial resources and those of his parents.

Non-EU Students: Overseas students from outside the EU must pay the full cost of their courses and living expenses. This includes non-EU, EEA nationals unless they have been migrant workers in the UK or are the child or spouse of an EEA migrant worker. There are, however, public and private scholarships and award schemes available to overseas students, particularly at postgraduate level. These are provided by the British government, the British Council, universities and individual colleges, and by a number of private trusts and professional bodies. Details of grants are available from around 80 British Council offices worldwide. Note, however, that even with a grant you must be able to support yourself during your studies.

Young people aged 16 to 18 who have been admitted into Britain with their families or otherwise, may be permitted to continue their education at school or at a post-school establishment provided by LEAs. Fees may be payable and students must have an adequate knowledge of English and show evidence of suitable entry qualifications. A foreign national over 18 years of age who wishes to study full-time in Britain on a course lasting longer than six months (and which will lead to a professional or educational qualification) must provide evidence of his educational qualifications and his financial means. Evidence must be given to both the educational establishment and to the immigration authorities (see page 77).

Cost of Living: The estimated annual living costs for students (excluding course fees) are around £6,000 a year in London and £4,000 in the provinces. Financial hardship has caused a big increase in student drop-outs in recent years, with one in eight students abandoning study for a job. Many universities have job clubs to help students supplement their income and around a third of students work their way through university. Overseas students studying in Britain for longer than six months are entitled to free health care from the National Health Service (see page 279). Students on shorter courses also benefit if their home country has a reciprocal health agreement with Britain, otherwise you should take out private health insurance.

Course Fees: Although course fees are set by individual institutions, they may take into consideration government-recommended fee levels. For home students and students from EU countries annual fees are set at three levels. EU students can obtain a booklet, *Investing in the Future: Help with tuition fees for European Union (EU) Students* (☎ 01325-391199 or freefone 0800-731 9133).

Entrance Qualifications: The usual minimum qualification for entrance to a university is a mixture of GCE A-levels and AS-levels (see page 184) or SCE highers (set in Scotland). Generally the better the university (or the better the reputation) and the more popular the course, the higher the entrance qualifications. Applicants usually need a minimum of two or three A-level passes and three GCSE passes (minimum grade C), including a foreign language and English and mathematics. The minimum entrance requirements are set by individual universities and colleges and vary considerably. The basic A-level entry requirement for most diploma courses is an A-level E grade and many colleges of higher education and universities accept students with a couple of A-level D grades. Universities and other institutions are usually flexible in their entrance requirements, particularly with regard to 'mature' students (anyone 21 or over) and those with qualifications other than A-levels. Some 20 per cent of university students are aged over 35.

Generally overseas students' qualifications which would admit them to a university in their own country are taken into consideration. However, passes in particular GCSE or A-level subjects (or equivalent) may still be required. Whatever your qualifications, all applications are considered on their merits. Some universities have been forced to lower entrance requirements, particularly for science and engineering courses, due to a drop in GCE A-level standards (some have also extended engineering courses from three to four years). All foreign students require a thorough knowledge of English, which will usually be examined unless a certificate is provided. British universities accept the international baccalaureate (IB) certificate as an entrance qualification, but an American high school diploma isn't usually accepted. Contact individual universities for detailed information.

Courses: The university academic year runs from September or October to June or July and is divided into three terms of 8 to 10 weeks. Students study a main subject plus one or two subsidiary subjects and specialise in their main subject for the first one or two years. The main subject is often subdivided into parts, each taught by a different professor or lecturer, e.g. mathematics may be subdivided into pure, applied, geometry and algebra. In some universities it's possible for students to design their own degree courses. Many students choose a sandwich course, which includes a year spent working in industry or commerce.

Degrees: The most common degrees awarded in Britain are a Bachelor of Arts (BA) and a Bachelor of Science (BSc). Bachelor's degrees are given a classification, the highest of which is an 'honours' degree, which is awarded when the course included extra detail in the main subject. The highest pass is a first-class degree, which is quite rare. Second-class degrees classified as 2.1 (very good) and 2.2 (average) are usual, while a third-class degree is poor. The lowest classification is a 'pass'. Second degrees are usually a Master of Arts (MA) or a Master of Science (MSc), which are awarded to Bachelor's for a one-year course in a subject other than their undergraduate subjects. Students who do post-graduate work in the same subject(s) as their undergraduate work, usually do a two-year Master of Philosophy (M-Phil) or a three-year Doctor of Philosophy (PhD) research programme. In some Scottish universities, a Masters degree is awarded as the first degree in arts subjects. Graduates who wish to qualify as teachers must do a four-year Bachelor of Education (BEd) degree course or a one-year post-graduate training course at a university or teacher's training college (known as a Postgraduate Certificate of Education/PGCE).

Applications: To apply for a place at university you should begin by writing to the Admissions Officer of selected universities, giving your personal details and asking for information. If you're encouraged by the reply, you must then apply formally. All applicants for entry to full-time, first degree (undergraduate) courses at British universities must be made to the Universities and Colleges Admissions Services (UCAS), PO Box 67, Cheltenham, Glos. GL50 3SF (☎ 01242-227788), who publish a handbook listing all universities, colleges and courses (over 100,000!). A useful book is the *UCAS University and College Entrance Official Guide*.

Applicants can apply for a maximum of six courses (which may be at six different universities), for which there's a fee of around £15. Note that the number of applicants per university place varies considerably from university to university. You would be wise not to make all your applications at universities where competition for places is at its fiercest (unless you're a genius). Most universities have between 10 and 15 applications per place available, with the most popular courses including medicine, law, and arts courses such as English. The university year usually begins in October, so you should make your application in autumn of the year before you plan to start your course (i.e. apply in the autumn of 1996 for entry in October 1997). UCAS accepts applications from 1st September of the previous year and the closing date is 15th December (15th October for Oxford or Cambridge universities, where applicants apply direct to colleges and may need to take an entrance exam). Those with a number of offers need to choose two by 15th May, otherwise they will be deemed to have rejected all offers of a place.

Late Applications: Late applications are considered until June of the entrance year and a 'clearing' scheme operates up to September for late applications. When A-level results are announced in August each year, the quality newspapers (broadsheets) publish details of degree and Higher National Degree (HND) vacancies at university colleges for those who haven't yet attained a place. This is also intended to assist those who may have done better or worse than expected in their A-levels, and may wish to seek a place at a 'better' university or who no longer qualify for their original choice. Many colleges also advertise their courses in national newspapers, particularly in educational supplements. The electronic education network **Campus 2000** operates until September 21st each year and is the primary source of up-to-date vacancy details.

College Accommodation: The cost of accommodation is a major factor for many students when deciding which university to attend and an increasing number of students stay at home and study locally because of the rising costs. Following acceptance by a college or university, students are advised to apply for a place in a hall of residence ('in hall') or other college accommodation, such as self-catering houses and apartments. Such accommodation is limited to around one-third of all students, although most universities accommodate all first year students. Students should write as soon as possible after acceptance to accommodation or welfare officers, whose job is to help students find suitable accommodation (both college and private). Some colleges guarantee accommodation to overseas students for the duration of their course. The cost of accommodation in halls of residence varies considerably and averages around £50 a week.

Private Accommodation: A large number of students rent privately owned apartments or houses, that are shared with other students, although in many areas this kind of accommodation is difficult to find and expensive (from around £35 a week in the provinces up to £80 a week in London). Another alternative is to find lodgings (or digs) where you rent a room in a private house with meals included (see also **Single Accommodation** on page 103). The British Council may be able to help you find accommodation in Britain (the address of your local office can be obtained from British Diplomatic Posts abroad). If you're studying in London contact the British Council, Accommodation Unit (☎ 0171-389 3003). The British Council information centre (10 Spring Gardens, London SW1A 2BN, ☎ 0171-389 4383) provides information and advice on studying in Britain for overseas students.

Open University: In addition to the traditional universities (where students attend all lectures at the university), Britain also has an Open University (OU). It has no central campus and most study work is done at home. The OU is one of the biggest success stories of British education and since its establishment in 1969 it has enrolled well over a million people. The Open University is, as the name suggests, open to all, irrespective of age, occupation, background or previous qualifications. There are no entry qualifications, no admission interview and no barriers of any kind, and courses are filled on a first-come, first-served principle. You simply need to be 18 or over, resident in Britain and be willing to do a lot of hard work!

Open university students study at home in their spare time (some lectures are broadcast on BBC radio and TV, often starting as early as 0600); however, you aren't left to struggle along on your own. The OU has a network of 13 regional centres and over 250 study centres throughout Britain, that are the bases for some 5,000 tutors and councillors whose job is to guide you through your studies. You also have the opportunity to meet fellow students at tutorials and residential summer schools. In addition to traditional degree courses, the OU offers short courses, self-contained study packs and post-graduate degrees. For further information contact the Central Enquiry Service, Open University, PO Box 600, Milton Keynes MK7 6YZ (☎ 01908-653231).

Student Bodies: All universities have a huge variety of societies and clubs, many of which are organised by the students union or council, which is the centre of social activities. Most college student unions or councils in England and Wales are affiliated to the National Union of Students. There are also students union bodies in Scotland and Northern Ireland. Most universities have excellent sports facilities that may also be open to the public. Wherever you're studying, take at least six passport-size photographs for student identity cards, hall and travel cards.

Further Reading: The Consumer Association (see page 437) publish a number of books for those planning to enter higher education including *Making the Most of Higher Education*, *Which Subject?* and *Which Career?* Other useful books include *The Student Book* by Klaus Boehm and Jenny Lees-Spalding (MacMillan), which contains everything you need to know about how to get into and survive university, and *The Times Good University Guide*. The *School Leaver & Which Course* magazine is available at Careers Centres. UKCOSA (see page 88) provide a wealth of information for prospective foreign university students in Britain.

FURTHER EDUCATION

Further education generally embraces everything except first degree courses taken at universities and colleges of higher education, although the distinction between further and higher education (see pages 197 and 192) is often blurred. Further education courses may be full or part-time and are provided at universities (e.g. part-time courses), colleges of technology, technical colleges (often referred to as 'tecs'), Colleges of Further Education (CFE), Adult and Community Colleges, and by numerous 'open learning' institutions. Each year half a million students attend further education courses at universities alone, which are often of short duration and job-related, although courses may be full or part-time and may include summer semesters.

Qualifications that can be earned through further education include GCSE, GCE A-level, the international baccalaureate, BTEC (e.g. higher national certificate and diploma), SCOTVEC, City and Guilds, bachelors and masters degrees, MBA degrees, and a range of other nationally and internationally recognised certificates and diplomas. New qualifications for school-leavers include National Vocational Qualifications (NVQs) and General National Vocational Qualifications (GNVQs).

The Business and Technical Education Council (BTEC) organises over 250 courses, designed with the co-operation of major companies in various fields, available in colleges, training centres and companies. BTEC (SCOTVEC in Scotland) courses are a combination of academic and practical, and cover everything from computer studies to engineering, caring to travel and tourism. BTEC trains over 200,000 new students each year and offers three course levels leading to the BTEC first, BTEC national, and BTEC higher national certificates and diplomas.

Many further education courses are of the open learning variety (as provided by the Open University, see page 196) where students study mostly at home. Institutions include some 50 correspondence colleges which offer literally hundreds of academic, professional and vocational courses, and enrol many thousands of students each year. Most correspondence colleges are private commercial operations, although there are a few exceptions, including the National Extension College (NEC), which has no entry qualifications. NEC courses are generally acknowledged to be among the best in open learning and include GCSE, A-levels, general education, business and skills, and personal development courses. For information contact the NEC, 18 Brooklands Avenue, Cambridge CB2 2HN (☎ 01223-316644).

Open learning courses in accounting, management, marketing, supervisory skills, small businesses, health and care, retailing, information technology, and engineering are run by the Open College (OC), which has regional offices in London, Manchester, Glasgow, Belfast and 80 local centres. The Open College of the Arts is an educational trust that caters for those wishing to develop their artistic abilities, but who wish or need to work from home. Courses include art and design, creative writing, drawing, painting, textiles, sculpture, garden design, photography, singing, the history of art, music and camcorders. For information write to the Open College of the Arts, Houndhill, Worsborough, Barnsley, South Yorkshire S70 6TU (☎ 01226-730495).

Some institutions such as the Open University (see page 196) and Warwick University Business School offer distance learning Master of Business Administration (MBA) courses for those who cannot or don't wish to study on a full or part-time, locally taught basis. There are around 70 institutions in Britain offering MBA courses, which together accept some 15,000 students (many from overseas). The Open University alone enrols some 10,000 managers each year, making it the largest business education institute in Britain. Many other business schools offer MBA courses covering subjects such as banking, business administration, communications, economics, European languages, information systems, management, marketing, public relations, and social and political studies. Fees for a full-time MBA at the London Business School are over £10,000 a year for two years (plus a further £10,000 a year in living costs).

The Adult Literacy & Basic Skills Unit (ALBSU), Commonwealth House, 1-19 New Oxford Street, London WC1A 1NU (☎ 0171-405 4017) was established in 1980 and is the national unit in England and Wales for literacy, numeracy and related communication skills. ALBSU also has a limited but important role in the development of English for Speakers of Other Languages (ESOL). ALBSU publish a wide range of information leaflets and booklets including a comprehensive *Publications* catalogue. General information about adult education and training is available free in many towns and cities from educational guidance units (usually part of the public library service) and adult guidance agencies.

In London, many further education courses are listed in *Full-Time Floodlight* and *Summertime Floodlight* (both published by Floodlight Publishing), London's guide to summer (April to August) courses.

LANGUAGE SCHOOLS

If you don't speak English fluently (or you wish to learn another language) you can enrol in a language course at one of over 5,000 language schools in Britain. Obtaining a working knowledge or becoming fluent in English while living in Britain is relatively easy, as you will be constantly immersed in the English language and will have the maximum opportunity to practice (the British aren't renowned for their proficiency in foreign languages). However, if you wish to speak or write English fluently, you will probably need to attend a language school or find a private tutor. Over 500,000 students come to Britain each year to learn English, 75 per cent from Western Europe, thus ensuring that EFL schools (over 1,000) are big business.

It's usually necessary to have a recognised qualification in English to be accepted at a college of higher or further education in Britain. In many areas there's an ethnic minority language service providing information and counselling in a variety of languages. These organise a wide range of English classes including home tuition, open learning and small classes, at beginner and intermediate levels.

There are English-language schools in all cities and large towns in Britain; however, the majority of schools, particularly those offering intensive courses, are to be found in the south. The largest concentration of schools is in London and the world-famous university towns of Oxford and Cambridge. There are also a large number of schools along the south coast of England, particularly in Brighton and Bournemouth. Edinburgh is the most popular location in Scotland. The British Tourist Authority (BTA) publish an annual directory, *Learning English*, of English-language schools, including state sector courses, and recognised and non-recognised schools (see below). The introduction is written in Arabic, Dutch, English, French, German, Italian and Spanish. A copy can be obtained free from BTA offices abroad or direct from the British Tourist Authority (see page 371).

You may find it advantageous to choose a school that's a member of Arels-Felco Ltd., the association of recognised English language teaching establishments in Britain. Arels-Felco incorporates ARELS (Association of Recognised English Language Schools) and FELCO (Federation of English Language Course Organisations), and is a non-profit association whose members are recognised as efficient in the teaching of English as a foreign language by the British Council. Members must follow the association's regulations and code of conduct, which include high academic standards and rules governing the welfare of students. Some members of Arels-Felco are registered as non-profit educational trusts (which means VAT isn't payable on fees) and many members cater for the handicapped, including blind, deaf and physically handicapped students. Arels-Felco publish an annual directory of members containing details of all courses, obtainable from Arels-Felco Ltd., 2 Pontypool Place, Valentine Place, London SE1 8QF (☎ 0171-242-3136).

Courses offered by schools that are members of Arels-Felco mainly fall into four categories: general English courses available all year round; courses for executives; junior (9+) holiday courses; and adult (16+) courses. Courses vary in length from one week to six months and cater for all ages from five (in special schools) through to senior citizens. The average class size is around 10 to 12, with 15 usually being the maximum. Most schools are equipped with computers, language laboratories, video studios, libraries and bookshops, and some even have their own restaurants and bars (to help loosen the tongue).

Most language schools offer a variety of classes depending on your current language ability, how many hours you wish to study a week, how much money you want to spend and how quickly you wish to learn. Full-time, part-time and evening courses are offered by many schools, and many also offer residential courses or selected accommodation with local families (highly recommended to accelerate learning). Courses that include accommodation (often half board, consisting of breakfast and an evening meal) usually offer excellent value for money. Bear in mind that if you need to find your own accommodation, particularly in London, it can be difficult and expensive. Language classes generally fall into the following categories:

Category	No. hours a week
compact	10 to 20
intensive	20 to 30
total immersion	30 to 40+

Most schools offer compact or intensive courses and also provide special English courses for businessmen, lawyers, journalists and doctors (among others), and a wide variety of examinations, all of which are recognised internationally. Course fees vary considerably and are usually calculated on a weekly basis. Fees depend on the number of hours tuition per week, the type of course, and the location and reputation of the school. Expect to pay £150 to £250 a week for an intensive course providing 20 to 30 hours of language study per week. A compact course usually costs around £80 to £100 per week and half board accommodation around £80 to £90 a week extra (more in London). It's possible to enrol at a good school for an all-inclusive (tuition plus half-board accommodation) intensive course for as little as £200 per week. In London and other large cities, students in private accommodation may need to spend more time travelling to classes each day.

Total immersion or executive courses are provided by many schools and usually consist of private lessons for a minimum of 30 to 40 hours a week. Fees can run to £1,000 a week or more and not everyone is suited to learning at such a fast rate (or has the financial resources). Whatever language you're learning, don't expect to become fluent in a short period unless you have a particular flair for languages or already have a good command of a language. Unless you desperately need to learn a language quickly, it's better to space your lessons over a long period. Don't commit yourself to a long course of study (particularly an expensive one) before ensuring that it's the correct one. Most schools offer a free introductory lesson and free tests to help you find your appropriate level. Many language schools offer private and small group lessons. **It's important to choose the right course, particularly if you're studying English in order to continue with full-time education in Britain and need to reach a minimum standard or gain a particular qualification.**

Many language schools offer special English classes for au pair girls costing from around £40 to over £150 a term, depending on the number of hours tuition per week. Most courses for au pairs include around four hours study a week. The school year begins in the middle of September and ends in June, and some schools accept au pairs only in the September and January terms (au pairs arriving after Easter may find it difficult to obtain classes). There are usually no classes for au pairs over the summer holiday period (June to mid-September). Among the best value-for-money English courses are those run by state colleges under the control of Local Educational Authorities (LEAs), the Department for Education and Employment, or the Scottish Education Department.

Most colleges offer full-time, part-time and vacation English courses for overseas students throughout the year, with fees ranging from around £20 to £80 a week. Many courses are cheaper for EU nationals and may even be free during the daytime for those aged under 18. Colleges usually arrange accommodation for students. A booklet containing a list of colleges and their courses (including courses for English language teachers) is available from the British Association of State English Language Teaching (BASELT), Secretariat, Cheltenham & Gloucester College of Higher Education, Francis Close Hall, Swindon Road, Cheltenham, Glos. GL50 4AZ (☎ 01242-227099).

You may prefer to have private lessons, which are a quicker but generally more expensive way of learning a language. The main advantage of private lessons is that you learn at your own speed and aren't held back by slow learners or dragged along by the class genius. You can advertise for a teacher in local newspapers, on shopping centre or supermarket bulletin boards, university or school notice boards and through your or your spouse's employer. Your friends or colleagues may also be able to help you find a suitable private teacher. If you're living in Britain and speak reasonable English but need conversational practice, you might consider enrolling in a part-time course at an adult education institute.

Many British universities hold summer and other holiday English language courses for foreigners, e.g. Birmingham, London and Oxford. For a programme contact the Secretary, British Universities Summer Schools, University of Oxford, Department for Continuing Education, 1 Wellington Square, Oxford OX1 2JA (☎ 01865-270378). The British Chamber of Commerce provides an English tuition advisory service in many countries and works closely with English schools, universities and institutions in Britain, covering all aspects of English language teaching. For information contact your local British embassy, consulate or high commission abroad. For an introduction to languages in Britain see **Language** on page 39.

10.

PUBLIC TRANSPORT

Public transport services in Britain vary from region to region and town to town. In some areas services are excellent and good value for money, while in others they are infrequent, slow and expensive. Britain has no unified general transport policy, particularly a long-term strategy that balances the needs of the public transport user against those of the motorist. Consequently, Britain has one of the most congested and ill-planned transport systems in Europe (exacerbated by the disastrous rail privatisation, which has driven even more people onto the roads). However, it isn't *always* essential to own a car in Britain, particularly if you live in a large town or a city with adequate public transport (and where parking is impossible in any case). On the other hand, if you live in a remote village or a town away from the main train and bus routes, it's usually essential to have your own transport. Public transport is cheaper if you're able to take advantage of the wide range of discount, combination (e.g. rail, bus, underground and ferry), season and off-peak tickets available.

Britain's transport 'system' is heavily weighted in favour of road transport and the level of public transport subsidies in Britain is among the lowest in Europe, e.g. in the European Union only Greece and Ireland invest less per head of population on their railways. Despite more people using public transport in London than in any other European city (London has the world's largest rail and tube network), it has the most expensive public transport of any capital city in Europe, with fares around four times those of Rome and some 15 (fifteen) times more expensive than Budapest. The percentage of travellers in Britain using public transport is, not surprisingly, very low, with some 90 per cent of all journeys made by car.

The poor services and high cost of public transport has made a huge contribution to the heavy road congestion, with traffic levels in the south-east and other heavily populated areas approaching saturation point. Apart from the environmental damage caused by the ever increasing number of cars on British roads, road congestion costs British business, billions a year, which, when added to the cost of road accidents, suggests a huge commercial benefit would be reaped from improved public transport. Many cities and counties promote the use of public transport instead of private cars, although trying to encourage people to travel by public transport has met with little success. One of the biggest problems facing Britain is that it's much cheaper to run a car than it is to use the railways. Most analysts believe the reverse must be true if Britain isn't to suffer almost permanent gridlock in its major cities in the next ten years.

Rising levels of traffic pollution are choking Britain's cities, where asthma and other bronchial complaints (which are aggravated by exhaust pollution) have increased hugely in recent years. Many experts believe the only answer is to pedestrianise town centres and severely limit traffic in town and cities (which is done in many European countries), while at the same time investing heavily in public transport systems. Although Britain killed off its trams (which in mainland Europe still perform an excellent role midway between a bus and a train) many years ago, a number of cities are building new metro, light rail transit and supertram systems, and banning cars from city centres.

A wealth of information is published by national and local public transport companies, local and county councils, and regional transport authorities, most of which provide a wide range of passes and fares for travellers. Many regions offer combined bus, train, underground (metro) and ferry passes, and offer special rates for children, students, young people, pensioners, families, the unemployed and those receiving social security benefits, in addition to off-peak travel reductions. Students can obtain an International Student Identity Card (ISIC), offering travel discounts in Britain and worldwide.

A guide to public transport (land, sea and air) for disabled people entitled *Door to Door* is available free from The Department of Transport, Building No. 3, Door to Door Guide, Freepost, Victoria Road, South Ruislip, Middx. HA4 0NZ. Other useful books include, *Out and About*, a travel and transport guide for the elderly published by Age Concern, and the *Guide for the Disabled Traveller* (Automobile Association). If you find it difficult to use public transport, either because of frailty or a disability, you should enquire whether your local council operates a 'dial-a-ride' or 'book-a-ride' service for residents. Free or reduced travel passes are available in most areas for senior citizens, the blind and the disabled, and many transport authorities publish information leaflets for disabled travellers (see also the **Disabled Persons Railcard** on page 212).

Although primarily intended for tourists, *Getting About Britain*, is a useful guide to public transport services and fares for the independent traveller. It's published three times a year and is available free from British Tourist Authority (BTA) offices abroad or on subscription from Getting About Britain, 21 Church Walk, Thames Ditton, Surrey KT7 0NP (☎ 0181-398 8332). Public transport information is also available via the television teletext information service, via the Internet (e.g. www.bargainholidays.co.uk) and from TravelCall (☎ 09001-910910, Internet: www.travelcall.co.uk) who claim to provide travellers with the cheapest, most direct and quickest routes for UK journeys.

TRAINS

The railway network in Britain is one of the most extensive in Europe with over 17,500km (11,000mi) of lines, some 2,500 passenger stations and around 15,000 trains a day. Britain pioneered railways and the Stockton and Darlington Railway (1825) was the first public passenger steam-powered railway in the world. In 1938 Britain set a world steam record of 126.5mph (203kph), although it now lags far behind its international competitors (incredibly trains on many routes were actually faster 100 years ago!). It has been estimated that France (TGV), Germany (ICE), Italy (Pendolino) and Japan (Bullet Train) are up to 20 years ahead of Britain in high-speed train technology, with trains routinely running at speeds of up to 200mph (321kph) or faster.

British Railways was nationalised in 1947 and has been in almost continual decline ever since due to serious financial neglect by a succession of governments. Over the years cuts in funding have led to a reduction in the size of the rail network (which is expected to be reduced even further in future as unprofitable lines are closed); a deterioration in the quality and frequency of services; massive increases in fares; and a lack of investment in the infrastructure and rolling stock.

Privatisation: In an effort to reduce government subsidies and as part of its privatisation doctrine, one of the Conservative government's last acts in office was to privatise British Rail. The privatisation of British Rail was completed in 1997 and passenger services are now operated by some 25 separate private companies. Other privatised companies include Railtrack, which is responsible for the tracks and infrastructure; rolling stock companies that lease locomotives and passenger carriages; freight service providers; infrastructure maintenance companies; and track renewal companies. The railway companies receive government subsidies to the tune of £1.6 billion a year, although this will drop to £926 million in the years 2003-4.

Since privatisation railway services in Britain have gone from bad to worse and resulted in higher fares, fewer services, poor connections, increased train cancellations, late trains (punctuality if one of the biggest problems), too few seats (overcrowding is widespread), narrower seats, closed ticket offices, unhelpful staff or a lack of staff, poor or no catering on trains, and a paucity of accurate information. Not surprisingly there's widespread public dissatisfaction, which resulted in almost one million complaints in 1998! In fact most observers believe that privatised rail services are even worse than official figures reveal and that Britain now has the worst (and most expensive) railways in Western Europe. **Note that in the last few years Britain's railways have been changing at an incredible pace and some of the information contained in this chapter may already be out of date by the time you read it.**

Trains in Britain are expensive and even if you're able to take advantage of special tickets, excursion fares, family reductions and holiday package deals, they are still usually dearer than buses (or private cars) over long distances. The harsh reality (accepted by every other western European country) is that it's impossible to run a comprehensive, quality rail service at a price people are willing to pay (or can afford) without huge public subsidies. Although services are expected to improve in the long term thanks to new investment programmes, most analysts believe that without increased state subsidies (or re-nationalisation) the only certain thing about Britain's rail service is that fares will continue to increase and services will be cut.

Types of Trains: Most trains consist of first (shown by a '1' on windows) and standard class carriages. Services categorised as suburban or local are trains that stop at most stations along their route, many provided by modern Sprinter and Super Sprinter class trains, with push-button operated or automatic doors. Long distance trains are termed express and InterCity, and stop at major towns only. Express services are provided by new 158 (158kph/98mph) class trains in some areas. InterCity 125 trains, so named after their maximum speed of 125mph (201kph), are the world's fastest diesel trains and operate on most InterCity services. New InterCity 225 (225kph/140mph) trains have been introduced on major routes.

All InterCity 125 and 225 trains are air-conditioned, have a buffet car in standard class and a restaurant car in first class, although the food has been criticised for its poor quality and high cost. During rush hours (before 0930 and from 1600 to 1900) trains are frequent on most routes, although it's best to avoid travelling during rush hours, when trains are packed. Although travelling by train may not always compare favourably on paper with air travel, it's often quicker when you add the time required to get to and from town centres and airports. Many towns and cities are served by half-hour or hourly services.

First Class: InterCity Pullman is the name given to the fastest first class and executive class services between London and major business centres in England and Wales. Executive tickets include a first class ticket, seat reservations, 24-hour parking, vouchers for a meal or refreshments on the train, and central zone tube tickets for London arrivals. Executive passengers can purchase vouchers for breakfast, lunch and dinner, which are served at your seat. Pullman lounges are available for all full fare first class or executive passengers at London's Euston and King's Cross stations, plus Edinburgh, Glasgow Central, Leeds and Newcastle stations, where phones, photocopiers, televisions and meeting rooms are provided.

Steam & Holiday Trains: Although the major operators no longer operate steam trains, Britain is still a Mecca for steam fans and private railway steam trains provide scheduled services in many parts of the country. Steam fans should obtain a copy of the yearbook of the Association of Railway Preservation Societies, *Railways Restored* by Ian Allan, which is a guide to over 100 steam lines, museums and static railway exhibits throughout Britain (many are operated by volunteers and provide limited scheduled services for tourists and railway enthusiasts). Many railway magazines (e.g. *Steam Railways*) are published in Britain and leaflets about steam trains and services are available from tourist information centres.

Trains can be hired for the day in most parts of Britain and some companies operate special day and longer trips for train enthusiasts in Pullman-style, first class, saloon coaches, many including travel on narrow-gauge railways. The ultimate (and the world's most expensive) nostalgic rail journey in Britain is on the *Royal Scotsman*. You can also book a trip on the famous Orient Express from London to Venice, which is one of the world's most popular train trips. If you're planning a holiday in Britain travelling by train, it will pay you to visit a travel agent, who will provide you with comprehensive rail information and a detailed itinerary at no extra cost.

General Information

- Many main railway stations offer a choice of restaurants and snack bars, although the standard of food often leaves much to be desired.

- Food and drink machines are provided at many stations.

- Some old trains have doors with no handle on the inside. To open the door from the inside you must open the window and turn the handle on the outside.

- It's prohibited to put your feet on seats or open the windows of air-conditioned carriages.

- Many large railway stations provide wash, shower and brush-up facilities, including hair dryers. Some also provide nappy (diaper) changing rooms. Most main line stations charge 10p to use a toilet.

- Most main stations have instant passport-size photograph machines.

- Public payphones (which accept Phonecards) are available on InterCity and express train services.

- There are car parks at most railway stations, where fees usually range from between £1 and £3 a day (some stations also have free car parks, while others are free at weekends). Season tickets are also available. Note that there's a high incidence of car theft (and the theft of articles from cars) at station car parks, so don't leave anything in your car and take precautions against theft (see page 260).

- Wheelchairs for disabled passengers are provided at major railway stations. Most trains have special facilities for the storage of wheelchairs, including all InterCity services.

- Some London railway stations, e.g. Victoria, have banks with extended opening hours.

- Special carriages are provided for non-smokers. The penalty for smoking in a non-smoking carriage (shown by a sign on the windows) is a maximum fine of £50.

- Railway companies often carry out engineering work affecting services, particularly at weekends. You're advised to check with local information offices before travelling. Planned engineering work may be detailed in timetables and train delays are also listed on television teletext services.

- Toilets are provided on trains on all but the shortest distance services (but shouldn't be used when a train is in a station).

- Travel insurance for rail passengers is available from main line stations.

- Luggage can be sent unaccompanied and can be insured. Many stations and airports have luggage lockers (£1.50 to £4 for up to 24-hours), left luggage offices (£2.50 to £3 for up to 24 hours) and luggage trolleys (although they're usually difficult to find). When using a luggage locker insert the correct money to release the key. Note the number of the locker (on the key) in case you lose the key. Railway porters are available at large stations.

- Bicycles can be sent between any two stations using local services, i.e. excluding express and InterCity services.

- It's possible to hire a car from all major stations (e.g. Hertz executive connections or rail-drive services) and if you book 24-hours in advance a car can be arranged to meet you at around 100 major stations at any time of the day or night. Cars can also be hired on the spot from some stations and left at other mainline stations. To make a Hertz InterCity reservation, contact your local travel agent or InterCity Business Travel Service.

Tickets

Railway operators offer a bewildering range of tickets depending on a variety of considerations, such as the day and time of day you're travelling, when you will be returning and how often you travel. The private railway companies operate diverse services ranging from local rural lines to major cross-country routes, many offering few standard services and tickets. Therefore with the exception of national InterCity services, some of the rail passes and tickets described in this chapter may be available only in certain regions, although most provide similar services. Ticket staff are supposed to provide you with the cheapest ticket available for your journey, although overcharging is commonplace (but less widespread than previously). Always double or treble check ticket prices before buying a ticket for a long-distance journey involving a number of railway companies.

There are two classes of travel on most routes, first and standard (or second) class. First class fares are around 50 per cent more expensive than standard class, which is used by the vast majority of travellers in Britain. Only single, day return and season tickets are issued for first class travel. One day Travelcard and AwayBreak tickets are issued for standard class travel only, but the holders of Network cards (see page 211) may purchase first class supplement tickets which are valid for the day on which the ticket is dated. At weekends and on public holidays you can upgrade a standard ticket to first class on all InterCity trains on payment of a supplement.

Children aged from 5 to 15 pay half the adult fare (except for apex, superapex and shuttle advance Intercity tickets, where no child fare is available) and children under five travel free (subject to a maximum of two children per fare-paying adult). Half fare up to a maximum of £4 single or £8 return is payable for a dog (except guide dogs for the blind, which travel free). All tickets and passes are described in leaflets available from any station.

A ticket must usually be purchased from a ticket office or machine before boarding a train. If a station is unstaffed, a ticket may be obtained from the conductor on the train (if there is one) or you must pay at your destination. In many areas, local public transport tickets can also be purchased at post offices, ticket agencies, travel agents and corner shops. At many stations there are ticket machines, although these sell tickets to a limited number of local destinations only. There are various types of machines, but you usually select your destination from those listed, select the ticket type required and then insert the amount displayed. Machines usually accept all coins from 5p to £1, plus £5, £10 and £20 notes. There are also machines selling 'permit to travel' tickets (for a nominal fee) indicating the boarding station and the time. You give the permit to the ticket inspector on the train or the ticket collector at your destination, and must pay the difference between the permit's cost and the fare.

Fare Evasion: Fare evasion is rife in Britain and costs around £50 million annually, particularly at undermanned stations. Note that ticket inspectors check tickets on many trains and staff carry out undercover operations to detect persistent fare evaders, who face heavy fines and possibly a prison sentence. In 1990 on-the-spot fines of £10 were introduced in some areas, although if you're discovered travelling without a valid ticket, you're normally required to pay only the full or correct fare for your journey. Fare-dodgers who don't pay their fines may be blacklisted and reported to credit agencies. If you're discovered travelling in first class with a standard ticket, you must pay the full first class fare, not just the fare difference. You must usually show your ticket (or surrender an expired ticket) to a ticket collector at your destination station.

Reservations: Seats can be reserved on all InterCity trains for £1 standard class and £2 first class, per single journey (although apex tickets include free reservations). If you're travelling in a group, you can make up to four reservations together for the same fee. InterCity reservations are free on some services or included in the fare. Seats can be reserved from two months in advance and up to two hours before a train departs (or from 1600 the previous day for early morning trains). InterCity seats can be booked from over 300 stations nation-wide or from a rail appointed travel agent. When booking, you should indicate any preferences such as smoking or non-smoking, window or aisle seat, or facing or back to the direction of travel.

It's advisable to reserve seats in advance on long journeys, particularly when travelling during holiday periods or at weekends. Don't sit in a seat with a reserved sign on it (unless it's yours). Note that a ticket doesn't guarantee you a seat (or even that a train will arrive). Special seats are reserved for the handicapped on most trains. Tickets can be ordered by phone and paid for with an Access, American Express, Switch or Visa card.

Season & Special Tickets

Many season and special discount tickets are available in Britain. These include family tickets, discounts for the young (16 to 25) and senior citizens, reduced price tickets for commuters and groups of ten or more, and special holiday and excursion tickets. Information is available from the information or ticket office at any railway station. If you're a regular train commuter, you can buy a weekly, monthly or annual point-to-point season ticket. A photograph is usually required for season tickets.

If you're planning to move to the country and commute to London or another city, check journey times and season ticket costs (which have been increasing hugely in recent years). Many commuters have moved back into town after successive fare increases and longer than expected travelling times (which were to have been reduced by electrification and the introduction of new trains). If you must commute long-distance by train, your best bet is to buy an annual season ticket or a ticket for as long a period as you can afford, preferably with an interest-free loan (which is also usually tax-free) from your employer. Apart from being cheaper, an annual season ticket protects you (for a short time) from incessant fare increases which invariably hit long-distance commuters hardest, and not least, from queuing to buy tickets. If you don't work a conventional nine to five working day, it's worth inquiring about off-peak tickets. **When buying annual, monthly or weekly tickets, take into account holidays and any other time spent away from your usual place of work, when calculating the savings compared with daily tickets.**

Refunds on annual season tickets aren't equivalent to the unused portion of the ticket. If you lose a season ticket it will be replaced free of charge, but don't lose it again, as it's replaced once only. Having lost your season ticket once, it would be an excellent idea to take out insurance against loss or theft. Note that magnets (such as those fitted to some handbags) can destroy the magnetic information strip on tickets, causing them to be rejected by automatic ticket machines. The following season and special tickets are available in most regions:

• A **Travelcard Season Ticket** can be purchased for periods of seven days, one month or a year, by commuters who work in the London area. A Travelcard ticket combines travel on trains, buses, the London underground (tube) and the Dockland Light Railway. Travelcards operate on a zone system and can be purchased for one zone or a number of adjoining zones (London and the surrounding area is divided into six zones), for which they provide unlimited travel during the specified period. A leaflet is available with details of zones and fares. You can also buy a season ticket for a station car park.

  A **Photocard** is required when you use a Travelcard season ticket, which can be obtained free from any railway station or underground ticket office on production of a passport-size photograph. Children under 16 require proof of age (no annual ticket is available). The savings on a monthly all-zone Travelcard compared to a weekly ticket are marginal (a few pounds) and an annual ticket costs the same as 40 weekly tickets. When you take into account annual holidays (e.g. five weeks) plus any other time spent away from your normal place of work (e.g. training and seminars), the annual ticket doesn't look much of a bargain (unless your employer pays for it). Annual season tickets offer convenience rather than large savings and you may be better off investing your money and buying weekly or monthly tickets. See also **Underground Trains** on page 213.

• A **group travel discount** of 25 per cent is available for groups of ten or more passengers of any age. Anyone under 18 is charged the half price child fare, which also qualifies for the 25 per cent reduction. Free group seat reservations are available. For journeys that go through London, underground travel between mainline stations is included in the fare. For destinations in central London, underground travel can be included in the cost for an extra charge.

- **Apex** (advance purchase excursion) return tickets are available for selected journeys. Bookings must be made at least seven days in advance and free seat reservations (obligatory) are provided. The return journey must be made within one month of outward travel and no break of journey or change of train is permitted. There are no reductions for Railcard holders or children. A cancellation fee of £5 is made for cancellations made seven or more days before the date of outward travel, or half the fare if less than seven days.

- **Motorail** services (where you and your car are transported by train) are provided on long-distance routes from Bristol to Edinburgh and London (Euston) to Aberdeen, Carlisle, Edinburgh, Fort William, Glasgow and Inverness. Only a day service is operated on the London-Carlisle route, a day and night service on the London-Glasgow route and night services only on all other routes. Fares are high. You may be better off driving and enjoying a few leisurely stops on the way, or taking a shuttle flight and hiring a car at your destination. Book as early as possible, especially during peak periods, which include all public holiday periods and most Fridays and Saturdays from May to October. Motor vehicle in transit insurance is available through Motorail reservation offices. Bookings can be made via Motorail (☎ 0990-502309).

- **Executive** and **Silver Standard** tickets are available for business travellers on certain routes, offering free car parking, meal and refreshment vouchers, free seat and/or sleeper reservations, free sleeper berths on some routes and free London central zone underground tickets. Executive tickets are first class only and a supplement of £5 is payable.

- Air-conditioned **Sleepers** are available on most InterCity overnight services between Scotland and London, the West Midlands, south-west England and the south Coast. Reservations should be made.

In addition to the above tickets, special fares are provided to exhibitions (e.g. the National Exhibition Centre in Birmingham), London day breaks on Saturdays and Sundays, and special InterCity day out, day return fares and rail tour excursions. In summer, InterCity holidaymaker trains link Scotland, the north and Midlands with resorts in Cornwall, Devon, Dorset and Hampshire. Leaflets are available from stations describing the various season and special tickets available.

Railcards & Network Cards

The cards described below aren't tickets, but annual passes that allow holders to purchase reduced fare tickets on InterCity and local trains. Note that rail and network cards cannot be used on all trains and services.

A **Young Persons (YP) Railcard** is available for those aged between 16 and 25 (full-time students aged 26 and over attending a British educational establishment for over 15 hours a week, 20 weeks a year, also qualify). The YP railcard costs £18 and is valid for one year from the date of purchase. It provides a one-third reduction on most fares and discounts on a Network Card and some ferry services. For travel before 1000 on weekdays there's a minimum fare. There's no minimum fare in July and August, on public holidays, at weekends and after 1000 on weekdays. To apply you require two passport photographs and must provide proof of age (birth certificate, passport, identity card, driving licence or student card with photo). In addition to your YP railcard, you will receive a photocard which you must sign. Both cards must be carried when travelling and the YP railcard isn't transferable.

A **Family Railcard** is available for £20 and is valid throughout Britain for one year from the date of purchase. It provides a 20 to 33 per cent reduction for most fares. Two adults can be named on the card and either can use it independently. A Family Railcard is valid for up to four adults (who all qualify for the discounts) and up to four children (aged under 16 at the time of purchase of the family railcard), who each travel for a £2 flat fare, irrespective of the distance. **Note that a 'family' group must consist of at least one child and one adult named on the railcard.** Adults and children needn't be related. A family or group day ticket for groups of one or two adults travelling with between one and four children (under 16) is also available.

A **Senior Railcard** is available to those over 60 for £18 a year (from date of purchase), offering a one-third reduction on most fares. Discounts are also available on some ferry services. Proof of age is required (passport, NHS medical card, birth certificate) when buying a Senior Railcard, which must be signed.

A **Disabled Persons Railcard** is available to those who are severely disabled. The card costs £14, is valid for one year from the date of purchase, and allows the holder and a travelling companion to travel at reduced fares (usually a one-third reduction). InterCity and express trains and modern local and suburban trains (e.g. Sprinter and Super Sprinter) have provision for most wheelchair-bound passengers to travel within the passenger cars. New trains are designed with handicapped travellers in mind, including spaces for wheelchairs and a washroom that accommodates wheelchairs. Guide dogs accompanying blind people travel free of charge. A leaflet entitled *Rail Travel for Disabled Passengers* explains the facilities provided and contains a railcard application form. Wheelchairs, disabled persons' toilets and reserved car parking spaces for disabled drivers are available at most mainline stations.

The **Network Railcard** provides a one-third reduction off most standard fares for the holder and up to three other adults who travel with him, anywhere within the London and SouthEast region. You can also take up to four children (under 16) at a flat rate fare of £1 each. The Network Card costs £20 and is valid for one year from the date of purchase. With a Network Card, you cannot travel before 1000 Mondays to Fridays, but can travel at anytime on weekends and public holidays.

An annual season ticket, including an annual London Travelcard (see page 210) purchased at a South West Trains station, is issued as a **Gold Card**. This provides the same conditions for leisure travel as the Network Card. A **Gold Card Partners Card** is available for £1 for a family member or friend. Subject to certain restrictions, Network and Gold Card holders can travel first class for £3 (child £1.50) for any distance on a single or return journey on the same day. Network cards and Partners Cards don't require a photograph but must be signed by the holder(s). All Network Cards can be used when buying other discounted tickets to obtain additional reductions.

If you find the wide range and variety of tickets and passes bewildering, it's hardly surprising. With such an abundance of season and special tickets, the only thing you can really be sure of is that unless you're travelling free, you may be paying too much for your ticket. You can no longer rely on railway staff to provide you with the latest information, as since the rail system was privatised different fares are often quoted for the same journey (particularly those involving a number of different rail companies). You may even be sold a ticket for a service that has been suspended or doesn't operate on the day you plan to travel!

Eurostar Passenger Services

The opening of the Channel tunnel in 1994 gave Britain a direct rail connection with the continental rail system, with the introduction of the Eurostar train service to Brussels and Paris. This threatens to drag Britain's railways screaming and kicking into the 21st century, although passengers will have to wait for high-speed trains on British soil. Since the start of Eurostar services an estimated 25 per cent of business travellers have switched from air to rail for journeys between London and Brussels and Paris. Airlines have tried to play down the affect that Eurostar has had on their business, although for many travellers Eurostar is cheaper overall when you take into account the cost of getting to and from airports. However, many analysts believe that Eurostar must undercut airlines and ferries significantly if it's to increase its share of travellers.

Eurostar trains run from London Waterloo International to Paris and Brussels at speeds of up to 185mph (on the continent!), taking around three hours to Paris. Meals in first class are complementary (i.e. you have already paid for them in the price of your ticket), although reports indicate that the food leaves much to be desired. There are a range of special fares (including discovery special, weekend return, apex weekend, pass holder (for holders of international rail passes), senior return, youths (under 26) and groups. For reservations ☎ 0345-303030. See also **Le Shuttle** on page 220.

UNDERGROUND TRAINS

The London underground railway system (or 'tube' as it's known locally) celebrated its centenary in 1990 and is internationally famous, ranking alongside the Paris metro and the New York subway. London's tube network covers the largest area of any underground rail system, with 391km (242mi) of track, of which around 171km (106mi) is underground, and 267 stations. It provides the quickest way to get around London. The tube operates from 0500 or 0530 until around 0030 (a notice of first and last trains is displayed at each station). If possible you should try to avoid travelling during the rush hours, e.g. around 0800 to 1000 and 1630 to 1830, when passengers are packed in like sardines (when travelling with children or friends hang onto them, as it's easy to become separated in the crush).

The tube runs to all areas of central and greater London and inter-connects with all London mainline stations. Platforms are reached from street level by lifts, stairs, or in central London, by escalators. When travelling on an escalator you should stand on the right (or alternatively, on the same side as everyone else). After a fatal fire at King's Cross underground station, **no smoking is permitted <u>anywhere</u> within the tube system.** To plan your journey, check the maps showing the zones and stations displayed at all stations, or obtain a free *Tube Map* from any underground or London railway station.

The tube has 12 lines (excluding the Docklands Light Railway), each with a different name and colour (e.g. the Central line is red, the Circle line is yellow). New lines have been built in recent years (e.g. the East London line) and existing lines (e.g. the Jubilee line) are being extended. Where lines cross *and* where there's an interchange station it's shown on maps by a circle. Check the line(s) you need to reach your destination and where you need to change before starting a journey. Once on board a train you can follow your progress on the map displayed in each carriage above the seats or at the ends of carriages (make sure you're travelling in the right direction!). Underground trains stop at all stations (apart from a few that operate during rush hours only) and the doors open and shut automatically.

The London underground system is divided into areas, called zones, central London being designated zone one. A standard ticket price is charged for travel within a zone, but as you cross into a second or third zone the price increases. For example, travel within one zone costs £1.40 (child under 16, 60p), rising to £3.40 (child £1.40) for a six-zone journey. You can also buy a book (carnet) of ten single tickets for zone one for £10. Tickets can usually be purchased at all underground stations and you should always buy a ticket before you start your journey, and keep it for inspection and collection at your destination. Children under five years of age travel free and those aged 5 to 15 travel at reduced rates, which are often less than half (around 40 per cent) of the adult fare. Children need a Child Rate photocard (available from station ticket offices, London Travel Information Centres and selected newsagents on production of a passport size photograph and proof of age) for travelcards valid seven days or longer, and 14 and 15-year-olds need a child rate photocard to purchase any child rate ticket. Photocards are issued free of charge.

Tickets are available from ticket machines, which accept all coins from 5p to £1 and £5 notes, and from ticket offices. There are a number of types of machines: in large machines you first select the ticket type and then select the station or zone(s) required (blue buttons), while smaller machines show only the ticket prices, so you must know the fare for your journey (shown on an alphabetical list). Machines are easy to use (if in doubt watch or ask someone). All machines give change, although if a machine is short of change the message 'EXACT MONEY ONLY' will be displayed. Often there are long queues at ticket offices, so *always* keep some change handy for machines or buy a season ticket. If you need to pay an excess fare, a special window is provided at some central London stations, otherwise you must pay the ticket inspector. New machines have been installed in over 2,000 newsagents throughout London to dispense Travelcards, bus passes and London Transport cards.

To gain access to platforms at most central London stations, a ticket must be inserted in an automatic gate. Don't forget to retrieve your ticket from the gate. If the gate 'eats' your ticket or doesn't open, a 'seek assistance' message will be displayed (ask a ticket inspector for help). Note that magnets, such as those fitted to some handbags, can destroy the magnetic information stripe on tickets, causing them to be rejected by automatic ticket gates. Take care, particularly if you have a season ticket. Rail tickets that include tube travel can also be used in these gates. You're subject to an on-the-spot fine of £10 for travelling without a valid ticket.

A **London Travelcard** is available which includes tube travel, most London buses (including some Green Line buses but excludes Airbuses and Night Buses), most National Railway services and the Docklands Light Railway (which is actually part of the tube system). Travelcards are based on a six-zone system. They can be bought from tube station ticket offices (one-day cards are available from some machines) and from rail stations within the tube network. A limited range of cards can also be purchased from some bus garages, selected newsagents and travel agents.

Travelcards are valid for one day, a weekend, a week, a month or any period up to one year. A photocard is required (see above) for seven day, one month and annual travelcards.

A one day travelcard costs from £3.80 for zones one and two and £4.50 for all six zones (£1.90 for a child, irrespective of the number of zones). Note that a one day travelcard can be used only after 0930 from Mondays to Fridays (but at any time on other days). If you wish to travel before this time you will need an LT card which is more expensive. A monthly travelcard for zone one costs £55 (child £21.20) and £134.10 (child £51.90) for all six zones. Payment for tickets can be made with personal cheques (with a guarantee card) and with Access, Visa or Mastercard for monthly and annual season tickets. There's no charge for dogs on the tube. Ticket prices are listed in a *Tickets* booklet available from ticket offices. Tube tickets can be purchased by disabled travellers at reduced rates after 0930 Mondays to Fridays and all day at weekends and on public holidays. A family or group day ticket for groups of one or two adults travelling with between one and four children is available for £3.60 for each adult and 60p for each child (valid for all zones).

A 24-hour travel information service for the tube and London buses is provided by calling 0171-222 1234 (24-hours). London Transport underground information is also provided on the television teletext service and the Internet (www. londontransport.co.uk). The London Transport Unit for the Disabled, 55 Broadway, London SW1H 0BD (☎ 0171-222 5600) publishes *Access to the Underground* for elderly and disabled passengers.

There are other underground urban railway networks in Glasgow, Liverpool, Manchester and Tyne and Wear (Newcastle). The latter is a modern light rapid transit (LRT) system 56km (35mi) in length with over 40 stations. Many other cities have plans for LRT or supertram systems.

BUSES

In Britain there are two main types of bus service: town and city services and long-distance, often referred to as coaches. Each region of Britain has its own local bus companies providing local town and country services. In large towns and cities, most bus services start and terminate at a central bus station and it can be confusing trying to find the right connection. If you need assistance ask at the bus station information office. Most bus companies provide free timetables and route maps, and many local district and county councils publish a comprehensive booklet of timetables and maps (possibly for a small fee) for all bus services operating within their boundaries. In many cities a night bus service is in operation. Timetables are also posted at major bus stops.

National long-distance bus services are listed in *Getting About Britain* distributed by the BTA (see page 371). Local bus companies organise special day trips and outings throughout Britain, plus European tours. Check that a holiday bus company is a member of the bonded Bus and Coach Council, which pays compensation should a member be unable to meet its commitments. London Transport bus information is listed on the television teletext service. See also **Timetables & Maps** on page 221.

The deregulation of bus services in 1986 allowed any bus company to operate on any route, and led to cut-throat competition and many companies going out of business. In the last few years the large operators have swallowed up many of their competitors (amid numerous claims of dirty tricks) and on many routes have established a monopoly or near monopoly. Stagecoach are the biggest bus company with around 25 per cent of the market, followed by FirstBus (Badgerline and GRT) and British Bus. The largest seven bus companies own some three-quarters of the industry.

Long-Distance Buses

A number of companies provide long-distance bus services in Britain. The major operator is National Express (NE) which provides a nation-wide service in England, Wales and Scotland (where service are operated in conjunction with its sister company Caledonian Express Stagecoach). Some local bus companies operate express bus services (which make a limited number of stops) within their area, e.g. London Transport's Green Line Coach service. Bus companies also operate sightseeing trips throughout Britain.

National Express serves over 1,400 major towns and cities nation-wide (daily with the exception of Christmas Day) and carries over 11 million passengers more than a billion miles a year. It operates a fast and reasonably priced hourly service to the most popular destinations which is much cheaper than train travel (what isn't?). Express buses are the cheapest form of long-distance travel within Britain and although journeys take up to twice as long as trains, fares are often 50 per cent lower. National Express coaches arrive and depart from Victoria coach station (☎ 0171-730 3499 for information) in London, which is a 10-minute walk from Victoria railway station.

National Express provides a wide range of tickets including standard single tickets, day return, economy return, discount economy return, economy advance purchase return, standard return, discount standard return, standard advance purchase return and standby fares. Ask the ticket office or travel agent what's the cheapest ticket for your journey. There's a discount of up to 30 per cent on most services for children (aged 5 to 15), senior citizens (over 60), young persons (16 to 25), full-time students (any age) and trainees. A senior coachcard and a young person or mature, full-time, student discount coachcard, costs around £10 a year. A passport size photograph and proof of age or student status is required. National Express offer a family discount card for around £15 a year, where adults pay the full fare and one child per adult card holder travels free, with a maximum of two adults and two children per journey (additional children pay full child fare). Children under the age of five who aren't occupying a seat travel free when accompanied by an adult fare-paying passenger. Groups of ten or more people travelling together qualify for discounts on most fares and season tickets are available for regular travellers.

A luxury Rapide service is provided from London to over 250 towns and cities, with reclining seats, toilet/washroom and a hostess light refreshments service. National Express buses serve London (Heathrow, Gatwick, Luton and Stanstead), Manchester and Birmingham airports, and a Rapide airlink service provides inter-airport links. Dogs aren't carried on Rapide services or any service where refreshments are provided. On other services there's a small charge for a single fare for a dog. National Express operate a Caledonian Express Stagecoach service from London to most major cities in Scotland.

International bus services are also available and include Eurolines, Supabus, Hoverspeed and Transline services, with regular buses to around 200 destinations in Europe and Ireland. Most international services operate from London Victoria Coach

Station, with domestic nation-wide connections, although some operate directly from the provinces.

Tickets can be purchased in advance at around 2,000 National Express agents (most travel agents) throughout Britain or from departure points. Assured reservations can be made for a small fee at least one day in advance and are recommended at busy times, on overnight services, when boarding at a suburban point, or when it's important that you travel at a particular time. Access or Visa card bookings are accepted and must be made at least five days in advance if the tickets are to be posted to you. Journeys may be broken, but tickets must be officially endorsed at the start of each journey. For information and tickets telephone 0990-010104 or 0990-808080 for credit/debit card bookings (credit card bookings can also be made via the Internet: www.nationalexpress.co.uk). You're requested to limit yourself to one suitcase on National Express buses (plus hand baggage), although this isn't obligatory. Smoking is permitted on single-decker buses at the rear of the bus and on double-deckers at the rear of the upper deck only.

Airbus, Airlink and Flightline bus services are provided at all international airports, including inter-airport bus services. Airbus services operate from London Euston and Victoria stations to Heathrow airport. All international and regional airports have bus services to local cities and towns. Some local bus companies provide saver cards for the young, e.g. those under 24, offering discounts of around 50 per cent for travel after 0900. Many other reduced fare tickets are available, including cheap day returns, season tickets, rover tickets and family tickets.

Rural and City Buses

Most counties and regions in Britain are served by one or more local bus companies (e.g. London and its suburbs are served by London Transport), which often operate both single and double-decker buses (including London's world-famous red buses). In many towns and cities, bus companies also use mini-buses. Services usually operate from around 0600 to 2400 and in major cities there's a also a night bus service, e.g. London has an excellent night bus service (with slightly higher fares than day buses) operating from 2300 to 0600. Like national bus companies, local bus companies organise local, national and international day trips and tours with pick-up points in local towns and villages. Buses are often slow during the day due to traffic congestion, particularly in major towns and cities, and it's often quicker to take a train, or in London (and a few other cities), the tube (see page 213). In rural areas, buses run infrequently, rarely to where you want to go and they usually follow a circuitous route that takes in the surrounding villages and towns. A direct journey taking say 15 minutes by car can easily take an hour or two by bus!

Buses throughout Britain are usually denoted by a route number, which is shown at bus stops and on buses. The destination of a bus is also shown on the front and sometimes also on the side or back (so you can see which bus you've just missed). Always check the route number and direction of a bus before boarding. If in doubt ask someone. There are both compulsory stops (called 'fare' stops) and request stops, where you must hail a bus by raising your hand if you want it to stop. When you want to get off a bus at a request stop, you must signal the driver by pressing a button or pulling a cord inside the bus, which activates a buzzer or bell in the driver's cab. Make sure you give the driver adequate time to stop and don't ring the bell just as you're approaching your stop. You usually get off a bus via the middle or back doors.

Most buses in Britain are one-person operated, where you either show your ticket or pay the driver when you get on. On some double-decker buses tickets are purchased from a conductor on the bus. Keep your ticket, as it may be inspected at any time during your journey. Fares in London and some other cities are based on a zone system, as for London tube trains (see page 213). In London, in addition to standard double-decker buses, Red Arrow single-decker buses operate frequent services between major railway stations in central London. On Red Arrow buses a flat rate fare is charged for both adults and children, which is inserted in a machine (no ticket is issued). Have the 210exact fare ready when boarding or buy a Travelcard (see page 210) or bus pass valid for the central fare zone. A Travelcard includes travel on most London buses, the London tube, south-east railways and the Docklands Light Railway. London Transport publish extensive bus guides (including maps) for all areas and operate a 24 hour information service (☎ 0171-222 1234).

A postbus passenger service combining delivery and collection of mail with stops on route to pick up passengers is provided in remote areas of England, Wales and Scotland by the Royal Mail. Services run two or three times a day from Mondays to Fridays and once on Saturdays. Services in England and Wales are listed in the *Postbus Guide* available free from libraries and tourist information offices or direct from Post Office Public Affairs, 30 St. James's Square, London SW1Y 4PX. For a timetable of postbus routes in Scotland write to the Public Relations Unit, West Port House, 102 West Port, Edinburgh EH3 9HS.

Most bus companies charge reduced rates (usually half fare or less) for children aged 5 to 15 and those under five travel free if they aren't occupying a seat (although some bus companies may limit the number of free children per adult). There's usually no charge for dogs, which are carried at the discretion of the driver or conductor (if the bus is already carrying a dog, they may refuse, although guide dogs are usually accepted). You're usually charged an additional full fare for non-collapsible baby carriages and prams. Senior citizens (over 60) and blind and disabled persons may be entitled to free or half fare travel in certain areas, but usually require a permit from the local district or borough council. Most bus companies provide bus pass or season tickets on most routes (weekly, monthly, annual), both point-to-point and unrestricted, for which a photocard is usually required. In some areas a 'Sunday Rider' or 'rambler' ticket provides unlimited Sunday travel on most local bus services (Sunday timetables are provided). Bus services on unprofitable routes are often subsidised by local councils and run as a public service, e.g. early morning commuter and hospital services.

From Mondays to Saturdays, services usually run at the same times each day. On Sundays and public holidays a restricted service is usually in operation, with the exception of Christmas and Boxing Days, when no services are normally provided. All buses have an official seating capacity and allow a certain number of passengers to stand when all seats are occupied, shown on a notice displayed in vehicles. Anything left on a bus can be reclaimed from the offices of the bus company, the largest of which have their own lost property offices. There may be a small charge for the return of property, depending on its value. If you find an article of lost property on a bus, you're required by law to hand it to the driver or conductor.

In central London, a special service for handicapped passengers uses small buses equipped with wheelchair lifts to connect Paddington, Euston, King's Cross, and Waterloo stations and the Heathrow/Victoria bus link. Free or subsidised door-to-door bus services are provided for the blind and handicapped in most areas.

Bus timetables (free or for a nominal fee) are provided by all bus companies and are available from transport companies and public libraries. See also **Timetables & Maps** on page 221.

FERRIES & LE SHUTTLE

Regular car and passenger ferry services operate all year round, both within the Britain Isles and to continental ports in Belgium, France, Germany, Holland, Iceland, Spain and various Scandinavian countries. The proportion of passengers travelling to and from Britain by sea has reduced considerably since the early '60s due to the reduced cost of air travel and competition from Eurotunnel (see page 220). The major ferry companies operating international services are P&O (which also operates as P&O Stena Line on some routes) and Brittany ferries, which dominates the routes in the western Channel (Caen, Cherbourg, Roscoff and St. Malo) with around 40 per cent of the market. Hoverspeed operates a hovercraft service from Dover to Calais and catamaran (Seacat) services on the same route plus Folkestone to Boulogne and Dover to Ostend. A larger Hoverspeed superseacat service operates from Newhaven to Dieppe.

Some ferry services operate during the summer months only, e.g. May to September, and the frequency of services varies from dozens a day on the busiest Dover-Calais route during the summer peak period, to one a week on longer routes. Services are less frequent during the winter months, when bad weather can also cause cancellations. Most Channel ferry services employ large super ferries with a capacity of up to 1,800 to 2,000 passengers and 700 cars. Ferries carry all vehicles, while hovercraft take all vehicles except HGVs, large trucks and buses. All operators except Hoverspeed offer night services, which may be cheaper. Berths, single cabins and pullman seats are usually available, and most ships have a restaurant, self-service cafeteria, a children's play area and duty-free shopping. Generally the longer the route, the better and wider the range of facilities provided, which often makes it worthwhile considering alternative routes to the Dover-Calais crossing. Although Dover-Calais is the shortest route and offers the most crossings, longer passages are generally less crowded and more relaxing, and fares are often lower.

On longer routes, most ships provide hairdressing, fast-photo developing, pools, saunas, live entertainment, cinemas and discos. Most ferries have a range of shops, including duty-free shops, which are huge money-spinners and the reason ferry companies offer such low winter fares (ferry companies make up to 50 per cent of their profits from on-board sales). However, duty-free (see page 436) is set to end in mid-1999 (although a reprieve is being considered by the EU), after which fares are expected to increase to compensate for the lost revenue. Most ferries offer day cabins with en suite facilities, which provide somewhere to leave luggage, shower and change, or just have a nap. When travelling on a cross-Channel ferry with your car, remember to take any items required during the crossing with you, as you aren't allowed access to the car decks during journeys. Many ships cater for children and mothers, and have play areas, baby-feeding and changing rooms. All major ferry operators offer a business class (e.g. P&O's club class) typically costing an extra £7 to £10 per person, per trip. It includes a quieter lounge; free tea, coffee and newspapers; and fax, photocopier and other facilities. Ferry companies also provide ship-to-shore telephone, telex, fax (shore only), and photocopiers on both ships and at ports.

It isn't always necessary to make a booking, although it's advisable when travelling during the summer peak period, particularly on a Friday or Saturday (and when you require a berth on an overnight service). Like air travel, ferry services are sometimes subject to delays due to strikes, out of service ferries, or simply the large number of passengers. If possible, it's best to avoid travelling during peak times. Check-in times depend on the particular crossing and are from 20 to 60 minutes for motorists and from 20 to 45 minutes for foot passengers. Comprehensive free timetables and guides are published by shipping companies and are available from travel agents (although it *much* quicker to book direct).

Fares: Peak fares are high, e.g. a standard Dover-Calais return with P&O for a vehicle up to 5m in length costs around £300 (£150 single) including the driver and one passenger. This drops to around £90 for a five-day return during the cheapest period. If you want a single ticket only, it may be cheaper to take advantage of a special offer and throw away the return ticket. Ferry companies offer a range of fares including standard single and return fares, apex fares, and 5 and 10-day returns. Children under four years old travel free and those aged from 4 to 14 travel for half fare. Students may be entitled to a small discount during off-peak periods. Bicycles are transported free on most services.

Whenever you travel always check for special offers. Last minute tickets can be purchased at up to 50 per cent discount from 'bucket' shops. P&O shareholders who own at least £600 worth of P&O concessionary stock receive a 50 per cent discount on Dover-Calais and Felixstowe-Zeebrugge crossings, and 40 per cent off Portsmouth-Cherbourg, Portsmouth-Le Havre and Portsmouth-Bilbao crossings. Some ferry lines have clubs for frequent travellers, e.g. the Brittany Ferries French and Spanish Property Owners Clubs, offering savings of up to 30 per cent on single and standard return fares. The Eurodrive Travel Club (☎ 0181-324 4000) claims to be able to obtain the cheapest rate for any ferry company.

Day Trips: A huge boost to ferry companies in the low winter season in recent years has been the explosion of low-cost shopping trips to Calais and Boulogne. However, this is having a detrimental affect on summer crossings, as many people baulk at paying up to £300 for a summer crossing when a winter trip costs as little as £10 return for a car and £1 for foot passengers! Most special offers are usually by coupon only, which are available in most daily newspapers during the winter (off-peak) season. Half of those who make return crossings from Dover to Calais are simply making day trips or one-night stays.

British Isles: Within Britain there are regular ferry services to the Isle of Wight, i.e. Portsmouth to Fishbourne and Ryde, Southsea to Ryde and from Lymington to Yarmouth. Car ferry services operate from England to Douglas (Isle of Man) from Heysham, Fleetwood and Liverpool. From Douglas there are regular services to Belfast and Dublin. Regular services operate from the west of Scotland to the Western Isles and to the Orkney and Shetland islands from the north and east of Scotland. Regular ferry services to the Channel Islands are operated from Poole, Torquay and Weymouth throughout the year. Services to Ireland operate between Stranraer-Larne, Fishguard-Rosslare, Holyhead-Dun Loghaire (for Dublin) and Swansea-Cork.

Le Shuttle: Eurotunnel started operating their shuttle car train service from Folkestone (access to the Eurotunnel terminal is via the M20 motorway, junction 11a) to Coquelles, near Calais, in 1995. The shuttle provides a 15-minute service during peak periods, taking just 35 minutes. One of the advantages (in addition to the short travel time) of Le Shuttle is that you can remain in your car isolated from drunken soccer fans and screaming kids. Fares are similar to ferries, e.g. a peak (summer) club class return costs around £340 and an off-peak (January to March) return £170, for a vehicle and all passengers. It's advisable to book in advance (☎ 0990-353535), although you should note that reservations are for a particular day, not a particular train or time. Don't expect to get a place in summer on the 'turn up and go' service, particularly on Fridays, Saturdays and Sundays. Demand is lighter on services from France to Britain, when bookings may be unnecessary. Trains carry all 'vehicles' including cycles, motorcycles, cars, trucks, buses, caravans and motorhomes. Vehicles carrying gas are banned.

One of the first things you should do after boarding a ship is to study the safety procedures (announcements are also made). Although travelling by ship within Europe is one of the safest means of transport, there have been a number of major ferry disasters on roll-on, roll over (ro-ro) ferries in recent years.

TIMETABLES & MAPS

All British public transport companies produce comprehensive national and local timetables, route maps and guides, although with Britain's often chaotic road traffic conditions and the railways' innumerable delays and cancellations, you would be wise to confirm times before travelling. A national timetable is published, although InterCity and local timetables stand a better chance of being accurate, as they're published more frequently. Most public transport services run frequently, particularly during rush hours. At major airports and railway stations, arrivals and departures are shown on electronic boards and VDUs. Bus timetables may be for individual routes, all routes operated by a particular company, or all routes serving a city, town or region. Bus timetables, which include all local bus company services, are often published by local or county councils and are available free (or for a nominal price) from bus companies, libraries and tourist information centres. Many county councils publish excellent public transport guides and maps (available from libraries, tourist centres, newsagents and council offices), which include all bus, rail and ferry transport services operating within the county.

National Rail publish the *Complete Great Britain Passenger Railway Timetable*, although it's largely a work of fiction (and in 1999 was printed with 35 days in March and 34 in April – not a good sign!). In some areas, combined timetables and guides are published including all local bus, rail, metro (underground) and ferry services. In Wales, timetables and guides are published in both English and Welsh. In London the number for general rail enquiries is 0990-848848 and for London Transport it's 0171-222 1234. London has 11 mainline rail stations serving different parts of Britain and no trains travel across London, so if your rail journey takes you via London you must change to your onward station (via tube, bus or taxi). For National Rail enquiries telephone 0345-484950.

TAXIS

Taxis are usually plentiful in Britain except when it's raining, you have lots of luggage or you're late for an appointment. There are two kinds of taxis in Britain, licensed taxis or cabs (abbr. of cabriolet) and private hire cars or minicabs. All taxis must be licensed by the local municipal or borough council and have a registered license number. Minicabs don't always need to be licensed, although most are. The main difference from the passenger's point of view, is that taxis can be hailed in the street and minicabs can only be booked by phone. In addition to taxi services, many taxi and minicab companies operate private hire (e.g. weddings, sightseeing), chauffeur and courier services, and provide contract and account services, e.g. to take children to and from school. Many taxi and minicab companies provide a 24-hour service with radio controlled cars.

Taxis aren't particularly expensive in Britain and are cheaper than in many other European countries. London taxis (officially called Hackney Carriages) cover an area of around 1,580km² (610mi²) and each cab has a license number plate and the driver (cabby) wears a badge bearing his driver number. There's a minimum charge of around £1.40 for roughly the first 500m or two minutes and around 30p for each additional 250m or minute (a lot of time is spent stuck in traffic). There are extra charges for additional passengers, baggage, and surcharges for evenings between 2000 and midnight, nights, weekends and public holidays. The fare from London-Heathrow airport (served by London cabs) to central London is around £30. There are also business class cabs in London with more luxurious seats, soundproofing and a telephone (and higher rates than standard cabs). In rural areas taxis charge around £2.50 a mile (1.6km). Taxi drivers expect a tip of around 10 per cent of the fare, although it isn't obligatory.

A licensed taxi is only legally required to take you to a destination within the district or borough in which it's licensed, e.g. in the London Metropolitan area a driver can refuse to take you further than 10km (6mi), while from London-Heathrow airport the radius is 32km (20mi). If the destination is outside the taxi's district, the driver can refuse the hire, but if he accepts he must either charge the fare shown on the meter or whatever fare has been agreed. There's a notice in most licensed taxis giving details of areas and the supplementary charges which may be levied at the time of the journey.

If fares have recently been increased and the meter hasn't been adjusted to the new rates, an 'additional fares' list is displayed inside the cab. Recommended fares for a number of destinations may be published in information booklets, e.g. the *Guide to Heathrow Airport* published by the British Airports Authority (BAA). Licensed taxis can ply for hire anywhere within their fare area and can be hailed on the streets, hired from taxi ranks (special waiting places for taxis), railway stations, airports and hotels, or can be ordered by telephone.

Minicabs: Minicabs usually have no meters, although if they do have a meter and are licensed by the local council, it must be set to the rates fixed by the local council. If a minicab has no meter, **you must agree the fare in advance when booking and confirm it before starting your journey.** Minicabs cannot be hailed in the street and it's illegal for them to tout for business (although they do, particularly late at night). Licensed taxis and minicabs must be insured for 'hire and reward', which means the driver is insured to carry fare-paying passengers. If a minicab is unlicensed it's unlikely to be insured for hire and reward. Note that there are no licensing requirements for minicabs in London, which means that minicabs may not be insured to carry fare-paying passengers. Local minicab companies can be found in the Yellow Pages. The London underground operates a 'Home-Link', 24-hour minicab service from tube stations to your home for a flat fare of £2.50 (within designated areas) for up to four passengers.

Don't use the services of private car drivers (always without meters) who may approach you at airport terminals or railway stations, as they are 'pirate' taxis and aren't licensed to ply for hire and aren't insured to carry paying passengers.

When travelling with large objects, mention it in advance when booking by telephone. New 'London-style' black cabs are designed to take wheelchairs and are common in London and other major cities (when booking by phone specifically ask for a wheelchair taxi, if required). In some areas there are low-fare schemes for the elderly and handicapped, using tokens or vouchers issued by local councils. In most London boroughs a Taxicard scheme is provided for disabled residents who cannot use buses and trains. Information about low-fare or Taxicard schemes can be obtained from local councils. Note that in some areas women are advised not to travel by minicab alone at night (ask the local police for advice).

Complaints: Complaints about service or hire charges can be made to the local taxi or minicab licensing office (if licensed). Complaints about London cabs can be made to the Public Carriage Office, 15 Penton Street, London N1 9PU (☎ 0171-230 1631/1632). Make a note of the taxi's license number, the driver's badge number, and the date and time of the incident. If you think you have been overcharged, obtain a receipt.

AIRLINE SERVICES

The airline business is extremely competitive in Britain, although it isn't cheap by North American standards, and British travellers enjoy the cheapest airline travel of any European country (the UK is the main crossroad for the world's long-haul airlines). In addition to the lowest scheduled fares, charter flights are available to most European destinations throughout the year for a fraction of scheduled airline fares. British Airways (BA) is Britain's national airline and is the western world's largest airline with flights to over 150 international destinations. BA claims to be the world's favourite airline and although some competitors may dispute this, they are certainly popular and have an excellent safety record (on the down side they have a poor punctuality record). BA is part of the Oneworld alliance that includes American Airlines, Canadian Airlines, Cathay Pacific, Finnair, Iberia and Qantas. A closer alliance (akin to a merger) with American Airlines was postponed due to demands by the European Union that it gave up a large number of its slots at Gatwick and Heathrow. Although it's one of the world's most profitable airlines, BA made a loss in 1999 due to increased competition from no-frills airlines and a downturn in business class passengers.

BA, along with Air France, operate Concorde supersonic aircraft, which jealous competitors once dubbed the fastest white elephant in the world. The main British intercontinental opposition to BA comes from Virgin Atlantic, which is consistently rated as one of the best airlines in the world, e.g. by readers of *Business Traveller* magazine. Virgin has pioneered new customer values and its upper class service includes a complementary chauffeur driven car to escort you to and from the airport (regardless of whether you live at Lands End or John O'Groats or anywhere in between), a free economy standby ticket (for your butler or maid), on-board bar and lounge, a choice of three meals, and a personal video walkman complete with a choice of 100 films. British Midland, Britain's second largest airline, has an excellent reputation for its standards of service and low fares, on both domestic and international routes, and is regularly voted Britain's top domestic carrier. Domestic air services are provided between British international and provincial airports by a number of airlines, including Air UK, British Airways, British Midland, Brymon Airways, Capital Airlines, Dan-Air Services, GB Airways (a BA franchise partner) and Jersey European Airways, most of which offer reduced off-peak and standby fares.

Like hotels, most airlines deliberately over book as an insurance against passengers who don't turn up or who cancel at the last minute. The EU has agreed a compensation scheme under which airlines are required to pay passengers denied boarding due to over-booking ('bumped' passengers), although compensation levels are strictly limited. BA, which claims 99 per cent of its flights are trouble-free, bumps around 10,000 passengers a year, although it at least pays some compensation (which is more than most airlines). **You should check-in at least two hours before an international flight, as if you arrive late you may get bumped.** Allow time for traffic delays, accidents and security checks, and check with airlines for up-to-date flight information. Catching a plane in Britain (apart from a domestic shuttle flight) *isn't* the same as catching a bus. If you're flying to the continent during a public holiday period or at any time during the summer (particularly on a charter flight), you should be prepared for a delay. However, flights times are also getting slower due to congestion, with flying times in 1998 slower than they were some 25 years earlier.

Useful publications for frequent air travellers include the Official Airline Guides (OAG) Worldwide *Pocket Flight Guide*, *The Complete Sky Traveller* by David Beaty (Methuen), *The Round the World Air Guide* by Katie Wood and George McDonald (Fontana) and the *The Airline Passengers Guerilla Handbook* by George Albert Brown (Blakes), which is nothing to do with hijacking, but a guide to how to fight your way through the airline jungle. Frequent fliers may wish to obtain a copy of the *Official Frequent Flyer Guidebook* (Airpress, Colorado Springs).

Air Miles is an enterprising scheme introduced in 1988 by British Airways, and supported by over 10,000 retail outlets, products and services across Britain, including petrol stations, car hire, hotels, department stores, banking services (e.g. savings accounts) and credit cards (NatWest). An American (Eli Broad) paid for a painting with an American Express card in 1994 and netted himself 2.4 million free air miles! Air Miles vouchers or stamps are provided with purchases, which can be exchanged for scheduled air tickets on any British Airways flight. Air Miles can also be used for package holidays (including hotel and car hire), travel within Britain with National Express, ferries and cruises, car hire, holiday discounts, hotels and days out in Britain. For full details contact Air Miles Travel Promotions Ltd., Airlink House, Hazelwick Avenue, Three Bridges, Crawley, West Sussex RH10 1NP (☎ 01293-513633).

Airports

There's a total of over 140 licensed civil airports in Britain, including many international airports, the most important of which are London-Heathrow, London-Gatwick, Manchester, Glasgow, Birmingham, Luton, Edinburgh, Belfast, Aberdeen, Newcastle, East Midlands and London-Stanstead (all handling over one million passengers a year). Many regional airports also operate a limited number of international flights (excluding flights to Ireland, which are widespread) including Bristol, Cardiff, Humberside, Leeds-Bradford, London-City, Lydd, Norwich, Southend and Teeside. Regional airports often have bargain fares to popular

European destinations. A number of smaller airports operate scheduled domestic flights to both regional and international airports.

National Express (see page 216) provide scheduled bus services to Heathrow, Gatwick, Manchester and Birmingham international airports from major cities. They also provide airport-to-airport services between these airports and Luton for passengers with inter-connecting flights. Air taxis, both helicopters and fixed-wing aircraft, are available from all major airports and many smaller provincial airports. All international airports have executive passenger lounges and publish free passenger information booklets. Major airports have direct rail or bus connections to local rail stations. British airports don't have comprehensive shopping centres open to non-travellers, as are common on the continent. Both short and long-term parking is available at most airports, although it's usually very expensive.

London's Heathrow airport is the world's busiest international airport, handling over 50 million passengers a year (terminal one alone handles 20 million passengers a year), which is expected to increase to over 80 million by 2016. Heathrow has four terminals (and is planning a fifth) and handles mostly scheduled flights. London's Gatwick airport is the world's second busiest international airport after Heathrow, handling over 25 million passengers a year. Gatwick has one runway only (although an additional runway is under consideration) and just two terminals, and is used extensively by charter airlines. Both Heathrow and Gatwick have excellent bus and rail connections to central London, the provinces and other British airports. Heathrow can also be reached by tube and via the high-speed, Heathrow Express direct rail connection from Paddington station taking just 15 minutes. Many of Britain's regional airlines are denied landing rights at Heathrow and Gatwick, and passengers are often forced to fly via the continent to pick up an international flight or must get to these airports by rail or road.

Flight information is available direct from airports and via the television teletext service. Thomas Cook publish a comprehensive *Airports Guide – Europe* containing detailed information about 75 major airports in Europe, including public transport serving airports.

Fares

Air fares to and from Britain are the most competitive in Europe and among the most competitive in the world. Competition between BA and Virgin (and American carriers) on Atlantic routes helps stimulate competition. BA and Virgin routinely match each others prices and usually knock a further £1 off (so they can claim that they're cheaper). BA triggered a price war in summer 1998 when it put two million cut-price tickets on the market (fares to 80 Worldwide destinations were slashed by up to £500) and Ryanair (an Irish airline based in Dublin but operating widely in Britain) gave away 500,000 tickets in a 'buy one get one free' promotion on certain routes. Stiff competition from US airlines has also shaken up the transatlantic fare structure. The low 'shoulder' period from Christmas to Easter is best for Transatlantic bargains (prices rise sharply again in the spring), when fares are cut by up to 50 per cent.

Deregulation in 1997 led to a spate of new low-cost airlines such as Debonair, Easyjet, Go (owned by BA) and Virgin Express, which have hit the profits of the major airlines and cemented Britain's position as Europe's low-cost, air travel hub. These airlines offer a no-frills service (some even operate without tickets) and undercut other airlines by charging for seats only. Meals and entertainment must be paid for separately. The biggest problem facing airlines trying to gain access to a new route is the allocation of takeoff and landing slots during peak times, which are jealously guarded by all national airlines (which is why new airlines must operate from less popular airports).

Most airlines provide a vast range of tickets depending on when you want to fly, how many nights you want to stay, how much notice you give, and whether you fly on a fixed (pre-booked) flight or an open ticket. Business tickets may range from standard, business return, day return, Eurobudget and Eurobudget return. If you've ever wondered why airlines spend so much time and money wooing business travellers, it's because a business class seat produces up to *seven* times the profit generated by an economy class seat. BA sets high business class fares on some routes, particularly on routes where there's little competition. The difference in price between economy and business fares are much greater in Britain than in most other European countries. BA is planning to introduce the world's first all business (Club) class planes on selected European and transatlantic routes in an effort to put higher-paying passengers on wider seats. In contrast, in recent years many companies have cut the cost of their travel budgets by ordering executives to travel economy and use low-cost airlines.

Leisure tickets may include apex and superapex, pex and superpex, excursion and super excursion, key and superkey, late saver and standby. Apex (advance purchase excursion) is the most common fare and must be purchased 7-30 days (depending on the route) in advance. Many airlines also offer discounts for youths, students and senior citizens. **If you're planning a trip abroad during school holidays book well in advance, especially if you're going to a popular destination, e.g. Paris or New York.**

Whatever your destination, it pays to shop around for the best deal (one of the best is a round-the-world ticket from about £800). The day of the week and the departure times of flights vary considerably between airlines and you can often save money by taking an off-peak or night flight (although night flights are best avoided). All airlines publish six-monthly or annual timetables. It's advisable to contact a travel agent who can provide you with comprehensive travel information, a detailed itinerary and all tickets at no extra cost. Also compare fares from a number of travel agents. However, you should be aware that some of the low cost flights and holidays advertised by travel agents are limited offers, restricted to certain dates and often include hidden extras. If you're a non-smoker and cannot stand to be anywhere near smokers, make sure you don't get the row next to them when booking your seat. Many airlines now ban smoking on short-haul flights and some have banned smoking on all flights.

Children under 12 years of age usually travel at 33 to 50 per cent of the adult fare (although there are no discounts on some routes) and have the same baggage allowance as adults. BA provides special stewardess services to look after children travelling alone, described in a *Young Flyer Service* brochure. BA also has a 'Flightrider Club' for children (who BA hopes will grow up into frequent business travellers). Most airlines don't charge for babies or infants who don't occupy seats, e.g. aged up to two or three years old, or charge a nominal fare only. BA charge 10 per cent of the adult fare if babies don't occupy a seat and they travel free on domestic flights. Free carrycots are provided and collapsible pushchairs or strollers can usually be stowed in the passenger cabin. Emergency supplies of baby food and nappies (diapers) are available on intercontinental flights.

Always make sure you fully understand any ticket restrictions. It pays to be wary of tickets offered by bucket shops (outlets which sell cheap airline tickets) and anyone who's not an IATA travel agent, as there's a lucrative trade in forged tickets. To find a cheap flight, check the classified advertisements in daily and Sunday newspapers (e.g. the *Sunday Times* and *Observer*) and entertainment magazines such as London's *Time Out*. The best deals for students are usually offered by STA Travel and Campus Travel. It's best to book holiday flights with a company with an Air Travel Organisers' Licence (ATOL) issued by the Civil Aviation Authority, as ATOL pays compensation should a member be unable to meet its commitments (☎ 0171-832 5620 for information). Holidays booked through a member of the Association of British Travel Agents (ABTA) are also covered by a bond system (☎ 0171-637 2444).

Britain introduced an airport departure tax on 1st November 1994, which is included in ticket prices. Passengers aged over two years on domestic flights and flights to EU countries (plus Iceland, Norway and Basle and Geneva in Switzerland) pay £5, and travellers to North America and all other destinations pay £10.

Baggage

The size, weight and number of items of hand baggage varies depending on the airline and the class of your ticket (most airlines allow first and business class passengers extra hand baggage). The baggage allowance on flights from Britain is usually 15kg for charter flights, 20kg for tourist class, and 30kg for business and first class passengers. Passengers are officially limited to one piece of hand baggage per person (excluding personal handbags and cameras), although this isn't usually enforced. The dimensions of hand baggage (length, breadth and height) when added together shouldn't total more than 115cm (45in). If an item is larger than 650mm (25in) wide and 500mm (19in) high, it will be searched by hand as it won't go through the X-ray machine. All additional bags should be checked in at the airline check-in desk for carriage in the aircraft hold. Always get a check-in stub for your baggage, as without it you cannot claim for compensation if it's lost or stolen. If passengers flying with BA in the UK have their baggage damaged in transit it will be replaced on the spot. **Always keep any valuables in your hand baggage and make sure your baggage is fully insured.**

Prohibited items and substances are listed in airport and airline information leaflets and guides including *Can I Take It?*, *Dangerous Articles in Baggage* and *Cabin Baggage* available from BA offices and appointed travel agents. If in doubt ask the airline with which you're travelling. Never pack electronic equipment such as personal computers and transistorised music systems in your hold baggage, but keep them in your hand baggage. If you have a portable computer, it's wise to have it checked by hand, as data could be erased or corrupted by powerful X-ray machines. Passengers are requested not to leave their baggage unattended at any time at British airports, as it may be stolen or taken away by security staff.

11.

MOTORING

British roads are among the most crowded in Europe (the south-east of England is the most congested region in Europe) and in Western Europe only Italy has more vehicles per mile than Britain. The most significant increase in the last two decades has been in the number of women drivers, which doubled between 1975 and 1993. However, Britain has a comparatively lower level of car ownership (around 400 per 1,000 people) compared with some other European countries. Traffic density in the major cities and towns is particularly high and results in frequent traffic jams.

During rush hours, from around 0730 to 0930 and 1630 to 1830 Mondays to Fridays, the traffic flow is painfully slow in many areas, particularly on busy motorways, e.g. anywhere on the M25 London orbital motorway, on the M1, M3 and M4 motorways into and out of London, and in and around most major cities. Most town centres are chaotic during rush hours, particularly central London, where the average traffic speed is around 10mph (it takes as long to cross most city centres in a car as it did 200 years ago in a horse and cart!). Journey times have doubled in the last ten years and Britain's motorists spend an average of around five days a year in jams, which are estimated to cost British industry £billion annually.

Traffic jams are also created throughout Britain by the pervasive roadworks, particularly in towns and on motorways (the most common sight on Britain's motorways are plastic traffic cones, the production of which is a huge industry). Traffic jams have spawned a number of navigation 'gadgets' to warn drivers of hold-ups in order that they may avoid them. However, although they warn of major jams, it's often impossible to divert to another route in time to avoid jams (in any case they are also jammed). Outside rush hours and towns, car travel is often trouble-free and you may even come across a motorist with a smile (rather than a scowl) on his face, although you may need to travel as far as North Wales or Scotland to see him.

Britain's road network suffers from the lack of investment in the railways, which has resulted in millions of tonnes of freight thundering through towns and villages, destroying roads and buildings, and polluting the environment. A greater investment in off-road public transport would also cut the number of private vehicles on roads, particularly in cities. Successive British governments have responded piecemeal to Britain's transport problems and have failed to strike a balance between investment in roads and public transport. Most motorists would like to see more investment in public transport to ease road congestion (and get all the **OTHER** motorists off the roads!).

Planners are finding it impossible to build enough roads to cater for the expected rise in traffic (the number of cars on Britain's streets is set to double in the next 25 years) and no sooner are new roads built than they immediately fill up and become overcrowded. The newest motorways (such as the M25 orbital motorway around London) are already hopelessly overcrowded because road planners badly underestimated the density of traffic and built too few lanes. The M25 (opened in 1986) was designed to handle 80,000 vehicles per day and already it averages around double this, rising to over 200,000 on some sections. Road-widening schemes are underway on many of Britain's main roads, which simply add to the traffic problems (at least in the short term).

One of the biggest problems created by road traffic is pollution (including noise pollution) which is strangling London and many other British cities, where levels of pollution are already well above international health limits on hot days. An intense public debate is under way in Britain about the best way to take Britain's transport system into the 21st century. Many experts believe that drastic measures are needed to curb car use by banning most traffic from city centres, while at the same time providing inexpensive, frequent and fast public transport between and within cities. There are already plans to ban cars from busy towns on days of heavy pollution, when asthmatics, bronchitis sufferers and the elderly are particularly at risk. There are also proposals to keep traffic out of villages and away from beauty spots in an attempt to stop traffic pollution destroying them.

There are around 3,500 deaths a year on British roads and over 300,000 injuries, which, although unacceptably high, are among the lowest casualties of any developed country (it's difficult to have an accident when you're stuck in a traffic jam). A quarter of deaths in road accidents involve drivers under the age of 25 (who hold 10 per cent of licences) and thousands of others are maimed for life. Britain has no speed restrictions for young and inexperienced drivers (as in many other European countries), who can also drive high-performance cars immediately after passing their driving tests. Women drivers have half as many accidents as men, but usually cover fewer miles.

Traffic information is available from British motoring organisations (see page 269) and via the television teletext service. The Automobile Association's 'Roadwatch' telephone information service provides the latest information on the state of the motorways (☎ 0336-401110) and main trunk roads throughout Britain. The AA also provides a wealth of other telephone information, including 'Weatherwatch'; roadworks; motoring law; hints and advice; new and used car information; and touring information (to receive a directory phone 01256-493747).

VEHICLE IMPORTATION

If you plan to import a motor vehicle or motorcycle into Britain, either temporarily or permanently, first make sure that you're aware of the latest regulations. Obtain a copy of Notice 3 (*Bringing your Belongings and Private Motor Vehicle to the United Kingdom From Outside the European Union*) or PI1 (*Permanent Import of Motor Vehicles into Great Britain*) from Her Majesty's Customs and Excise, CDE5 Southbank, Dorset House, Stamford Street, London SE1 9PY, United Kingdom (☎ 0171-620 1313). You must complete customs form C104F if you're importing your private vehicle for no more than six months in a 12-month period. If you're setting up home in Britain then you must complete form C104A. Forms are available from shipping agents or from the above address. Information is also available from motoring organisations (see page 269). The regulations also apply to the importation of boats and aircraft.

You should check whether you will be able to register and licence a particular vehicle in Britain and whether it can, if necessary, be modified to comply with British standards of construction, i.e. receive National Type Approval. Check with the manufacturer's export department, the British importers or the vehicle licensing authority in Britain that the vehicle you're planning to import meets the latest regulations. For further information obtain a copy of leaflet P11 from HM Customs and Excise at the above address. If you wish to import a car (except as a visitor), inform the customs staff on arrival in Britain. Whether you're required to pay import duty and car tax depends on how long you have owned the car and how long you have lived abroad. Duty is 10 per cent on cars, 8.6 per cent on motorcycles below 250cc and 7.8 per cent on motorcycles above 250cc, plus VAT at 17.5 per cent. There's a reduced rate of duty for vehicles imported from some countries.

A vehicle purchased abroad duty and tax-free may be imported and used in Britain only by a diplomat; a member of an officially recognised international organisation; or a member of NATO or British forces or the civilian staff accompanying them. Note that importing some 'exotic' foreign cars (most American cars) into Britain isn't advisable as you may have problems with servicing and spares, and if it's a monster, manoeuvring and parking on Britain's narrow roads can be difficult or impossible. Note that all cars registered in Britain over three years old must undergo an annual serviceability test (see **Test Certificate** on page 239). See also **Buying a Car Abroad** on page 236.

VEHICLE REGISTRATION

A vehicle registration document (V5) shows the registered keeper (the person who keeps the vehicle on public roads and not necessarily the legal owner) of a vehicle. It gives the keeper's name and address, the registration mark (number) and other details about the vehicle. A new registration document must be issued each time there's a change in the details printed on it, e.g. a change in the address of the keeper.

When you import a vehicle into Britain (either free of tax and duty or when duty and tax have been paid on importation) you will be given a Customs and Excise clearance form C&E 386. You'll also receive a Department of Transport notice PI1 *Permanent Import of Motor Vehicles into Great Britain* and leaflet V277, explaining the legal requirements you must satisfy in order to register a vehicle in Britain. Leaflet V100 contains notes about registering and licensing a motor vehicle and leaflet V355 tells you what you need to know about registering and licensing motor vehicles that haven't previously been registered in Britain. Both are available from post offices. If you wish to import a vehicle permanently after bringing it into Britain temporarily (e.g. as a visitor), you must contact your nearest customs and excise office. If you import a car on arrival in Britain or at a later date, you will require the following documents:

- the invoice, receipt, or bill of sale or transfer for the vehicle, made out in your name;

- the foreign registration document (either full or temporary) for the vehicle made out in your name;

- a green card or international insurance certificate made out in your name;

- if you have owned the vehicle longer than six months and wish to import it free of duty and tax, you will require proof of how long you have owned it.

When you have received customs clearance, you will be given form C&E 386, which you must take to the nearest Vehicle Registration Office (VRO) to get your vehicle registered and licensed. You will also need the following documents:

- A British insurance certificate or cover note (see page 243). A foreign insurance certificate, with or without a green card, isn't valid for a car registered in Britain which is kept by someone who's resident in Britain. You can drive on foreign registration plates with valid foreign insurance until such time as you have applied for British registration. If your foreign insurance isn't valid in Britain, you must obtain temporary insurance through an office of the AA or RAC motoring organisations (see page 269) at your port of arrival in Britain or, if this isn't possible, you must visit a local insurance office before driving in Britain.

● A current British test certificate (see page 239) if your vehicle is over three years old or a declaration of exemption. If your vehicle isn't old enough to require testing or is exempt, you will need an exemption certificate.

● The road tax fee (see page 247) for six or 12 months. The VRO will provide you with the tax disc on payment of the fee (cheques are accepted).

● If the vehicle was previously registered in Germany, the VRO will want to see evidence that the German number plates have been invalidated. Ask at a VRO for information.

● A completed form V55/5 (*Application for a First Licence for a Motor Vehicle and Declaration for Registration*), available from a post office or VRO.

The VRO will allocate you a registration number (corresponding to the year of manufacture of your vehicle), which you take to a garage to have British registration plates made and fitted to your vehicle. When the plates have been fitted, you must display your road tax disc inside your car windscreen (see page 247). Your vehicle registration document (V5) will be sent to you directly by the DVLC (Swansea) a few weeks later. If your vehicle has been admitted without duty and tax being paid, the vehicle registration document will be endorsed with the words 'Customs Restricted Until (*date*)'. This can be exchanged for a standard registration document when you have paid the duty or tax or after the one-year restriction period has expired.

If you're buying a new car from a garage in Britain, they will apply for a registration number on your behalf and fit registration plates. When you buy a used vehicle in Britain you should always be given the registration document. Note, however, that the document doesn't prove legal ownership and you should satisfy yourself that the seller either owns the vehicle or is entitled to offer it for sale. You should ask to see a bill of sale in the seller's name or other evidence, such as a hire purchase discharge document. **If you have any doubts about the ownership of a vehicle, you shouldn't buy it. For example if you're buying privately and the address on the registration document doesn't tally with the seller's address.**

When you buy a used vehicle, you must complete the back of the registration document ('Notification of Changes') and send it to the DVLC, Swansea SA99 1AR. If you buy a used vehicle without a vehicle registration document or you lose your document, you can apply for a new one using form V62 (available from post offices and VROs). If you change your address, you must complete the back of the registration document and send it to the DVLC at the above address. If you sell a vehicle registered in your name, you must complete the lower part of the registration document headed 'Notification of Sale or Transfer', detach it and send it to the DVLC. Keep a separate note of the buyer's name and address and give him the top part of the registration form. If your vehicle is stolen you must report it to the police, who'll notify the DVLC.

New British registration numbers are released twice a year by the Department of Transport, when a new prefix letter is issued. Thus you can (usually) tell the age of a car from it's registration number, which normally remains with it throughout its life. From 1999, there have been two number plate prefix changes a year on 1st March and 1st September (which was introduced to eliminate the mad August rush when prefix changes were made once a year). It's absolutely vital for some people to be seen driving a car with the latest registration, which leads to a mad scramble for new cars in March and September each year (although this isn't simply snob appeal, as the registration letter of a secondhand car affects its resale price).

If you want to give someone who has everything a present, you could consider buying him a personalised registration number. The ultimate 'one-upmanship' in Britain is to have your initials or name on your car number plate. Most of the best numbers (A1, RU12, FU2) have been snapped up years ago and are virtually priceless, but there are still hundreds for sale each week in publications such as *The Sunday Times*, *Exchange & Mart* and car magazines. A number of companies enjoy a lucrative business selling registration numbers, which can cost £thousands even for the most obscure numbers (the prices are ludicrous to the uninitiated). Numbers are also sold by auction. When you change cars (or buy a new number), you can have the registration number transferred to your new car by completing form V317 (available from a VRO) and paying an assignment fee.

The DVLA (who issue licence numbers) also cash in on this profitable business and allow motorists to create their own number when registering a new vehicle for a hefty fee. Call the DVLA enquiry line (☎ 01792-772151) for information. In future plates will incorporate the European Union (EU) blue star symbol (as in many other EU countries) and there are also plans to introduce EU number plates.

BUYING A CAR

After years of decline, the British car industry is now relatively profitable, although most major manufacturers are foreign-owned (American, French, German or Japanese). Most British cars exist in niche markets such as Aston Martin, Rolls-Royce, Morgan and TVR. Cars are dearer in Britain than in many other European countries, although you can obtain a discount off the list (book) price of most new cars. Whether you're buying a new or secondhand car, it's worthwhile considering a diesel-engined vehicle. Although diesel fuel is around the same price as unleaded petrol in Britain, diesels are cheaper to run (e.g. 35 to 40 per cent better fuel consumption) and have a much longer engine life.

Car sales are covered by the Misrepresentation of Goods Act 1967, which means that a seller cannot lawfully make false claims. If you buy from a dealer, you're additionally covered by the Sale of Goods Act 1979, which says a car must be of merchantable quality and good for the purpose intended. *Which?* magazine (see page 437) publish an annual *Which? Car* edition containing independent information on best buys, performance, comfort, convenience, reliability, trouble spots, running costs, safety, recalls, and new and secondhand prices. New and used car reports are available via the AA's telephone and fax information service (to order a free directory ☎ 01256-493747).

New Cars

Making comparisons between new car prices in different countries is often difficult due to fluctuating exchange rates and the different levels of standard equipment. Standard equipment may include electric windows and mirrors, central locking, electric sun roof, alloy wheels, stereo radio/cassette/CD, power steering, ABS, air bags, automatic transmission, leather or power seats, cruise control and air conditioning. Some manufacturers include many of these items as standard equipment, while others charge dearly for them as 'optional extras'. A catalytic converter is fitted as standard equipment to all petrol-engined cars sold in Britain. Paying for expensive optional extras on many cars is unlikely to increase the car's value when you sell it, although many cars are easier to sell with options such as power steering, central locking and electric windows. Note that capital depreciation is a greater threat than rust to a new car owner, as a car's value can drop by as much as 60 per cent within three to four years.

The manufacturer's list price includes the wholesale price, the dealer's profit, car tax and 17.5 per cent VAT on all these items. In addition you must usually pay for delivery (average £450), number plates (e.g. £25), a tank of petrol, floor mats, mud flaps and road tax (see page 247). Delivery charges have increased considerably in recent years and are a rip-off used to hike car prices (and are exclusive to motor vehicles). They can vary considerably for the same car depending on the supplier. When comparing prices, ask dealers for the on-the-road price, including delivery and the other charges listed above.

Another important aspect of buying a new car is the warranty period, during which major parts are insured against replacement. Many manufacturers now provide extended warranties of up to four years with unlimited mileage and most others offer an extended warranty for an annual fee (usually with a mileage limit). Some manufacturers offer three years (or longer) unlimited mileage or a limit of 96,000km (60,000mi). If you do a high annual mileage and change your car every two or three years, you would be well advised to buy a car with an extended warranty or pay for extra cover. Note, however, that warranties usually contain a range of get-out clauses for manufacturers.

Shop around and compare prices, discounts and incentives from a number of dealers. There has been a slump in sales to private buyers (rather than fleet sales) in recent years, which means that buyers can usually get a good deal. Free insurance, servicing and petrol are just some of the added incentives to buy offered in recent years. You can often get a good bargain by buying an old model that has been, or is due to be, replaced by a new model. When new registration numbers are issued (see page 232) is a good time to buy a new car with the previous year's registration number, which may be sold for £thousands below list price. One way to get a good price without haggling is to contact a company such as Woolwich Motorbase (☎ 0870-607 2727), which buys in bulk and deals directly with manufacturers.

Finance Deals: Dealers offer a range of finance deals that may be a better option than paying cash, particularly if you're offered a one or two-year, no-interest deal. Note, however, that most require deposits of up to 50 per cent. A plethora of deals are on offer and seven out of ten cars are bought on a leasing or hire purchase scheme. One such deal is called the 50-50 scheme, where you pay 50 per cent and drive for two years, after which you either pay the balance or hand the car back to the dealer and walk away. The most popular deals are personal contract plans (a combination of hire purchase and rental) which are offered by car manufacturers and some banks, and account for one in five of all car sales. Some manufacturers (e.g. Mitsubishi) were even offering a 'buy-one-get-one-free' deal in 1999, whereby they replaced your new car with another one after six months (but only once!).

Although not as cheap as no-interest finance packages, personal contract deposits are lower at 20 to 30 per cent. After deducting the deposit the manufacturer deducts the Minimum Guaranteed Future Value (MGFV) that he expects the car to be worth in two or three years time when the contract expires. The balance is divided into 24 or 36 equal monthly repayments and interest is charged on the MGFV and the amount outstanding. At the end of the two or three year period the customer can pay the MGFV or simply return the car to the dealer.

You can reject a new car if it's faulty, but you have only a few days or weeks in which to do so. If you buy a real 'lemon' you can have it inspected by a motoring organisation (see page 269) or a member of the Institute of Automotive Engineers (☎ 01543-251346), which usually provides irrefutable independent evidence in the event of a legal battle with the manufacturer.

Buying A New Car Abroad

New car prices in Britain are, according to most consumer organisations and the British government, a rip-off. British drivers pay up to 60 per cent more than their European counterparts for *exactly* the same cars, with most costing 30 to 40 per cent more in Britain than on the continent (you can make even larger savings on servicing!). A report by the government found that 60 out of 74 best-selling cars were more expensive in Britain than Europe (cars are even cheaper in the USA) and has initiated an investigation into car prices by the Office of Fair Trading. One survey sited examples such as the Ford Mondeo, which was found to be 58.5 per cent more expensive in Britain than Spain and a Nissan model selling for £9,000 in the Netherlands cost £15,000 around the corner from the British factory where it's made! Spurious arguments concerning equipment, exchange rates, higher taxes, etc., account for only a fraction of the difference is UK and continental prices.

Huge savings can be made by buying on the continent, although manufacturers try to prevent British buyers from doing so by refusing to provide dealers with right-hand-drive models (although this is illegal). British car dealers and manufacturers deliberately provide misleading and false information to discourage buyers from buying abroad, although the procedure is straightforward and simple, and any drawbacks are more than offset by the vast savings. The biggest savings can usually be made in Belgium and the Netherlands, although it depends on the make and model of car that you're buying.

One of the easiest ways to buy a car abroad is in conjunction with Broadspeed (☎ 0171-413 9940/9950) and the Stena Line (☎ 01233-646881 for reservations) travelling on the Harwich–Hook of Holland route. Broadspeed provide a complete buying package with buyers negotiating directly with Dutch dealers. Dutch prices include over 50 per cent tax, which makes the Netherlands one of the cheapest countries in Europe in which to purchase a car for export. All British buyers need to pay is UK VAT at 17.5 per cent. In early 1999, samples prices included a BMW 328i costing £28,145 in Britain (£22,610 in Holland including all taxes) and a Peugeot 306 costing £11,795 in the UK (£7,840 in Holland). The more expensive the car the bigger the saving, although the saving as a percentage of the total price is higher on cheaper models. You can also buy an import through many UK agents without leaving the UK, although it's cheaper to personally import a vehicle. A car can now be bought in the USA through an agent (previously the buyer had to personally import it) such as American Car Imports (☎ 0181-889 7500). The best buys are in the 4-wheel drive, sports and APV sections of the market. Note, however, that most US imports are available in left-hand-drive only.

You can obtain an estimate of the VAT you will need to pay by contacting HM Customs and Excise, Central Processing Unit, Postal Depot, Charlton Green, Dover CT16 1EH (☎ 01304-224379). You must notify customs within seven days of its arrival in the UK. Customs require the original purchase invoice, the foreign registration document and documents showing how and when you brought the vehicle to the UK, e.g. your ferry ticket. You will receive a bill for VAT, which must be paid within 30 days (you must keep your purchase invoice and VAT receipt for six years).

Used Cars

Used cars can be excellent value for money, particularly low mileage cars less than one year old, where the savings on the new price can be as high as 25 per cent. The minute a new car leaves the showroom it's usually worth 10 per cent less than the purchase price. Some models depreciate much more than others and often represent excellent secondhand bargains. If you intend to buy a used car in Britain, whether privately or from a garage, check that:

● it has a test certificate, if applicable (see page 239) and that its condition matches its declared age.

● it hasn't been involved in a major accident and suffered structural damage. If in any doubt, obtain a declaration that it's accident free, which should be obtained in writing.

● it's in good mechanical condition and check the bodywork in daylight, preferably with an expert (if you aren't one yourself).

● it hasn't been stolen or is subject to a leasing or hire purchase contract, in which case the original owner or lender can legally demand it back. Thousands of cars are sold each year before they are paid for. If in doubt, check with the Hire Purchase Information (HPI) register through a Citizens Advice Bureau.

● the official service coupons have been completed and stamped, and that routine servicing have been carried out regularly by an authorised dealer (mandatory for a manufacturer's warranty to be valid). It's best to buy a car with a full service history (fsh), that should also verify the mileage (see 'clocking' below).

● the price roughly corresponds to that shown in guides to used car prices (see below).

● the import tax and duty have been paid if it's an imported model (the registration document of a vehicle imported without tax and duty being paid, will be annotated with 'customs restricted until *date*').

● a written guarantee or warranty is provided (see below). The manufacturer's warranty is usually transferable to subsequent owners.

If you're buying a car from a dealer who's a member of the Society of Motor Manufacturers and Traders (SMMT), the Motor Agents Association (MAA), the Vehicle Builders and Repairers Association (VBRA) or the Scottish Motor Trade Association (SMTA), extra protection *may* be afforded (but don't count on it). Most garages provide a warranty on used cars, e.g. three to 12 months (unless it's covered by a manufacturer's warranty), although you should check what it includes and more importantly, what's *excluded*. You may be able to purchase an additional one to three years warranty, depending on the age and make of the car. The best warranties are supported by the manufacturer.

Most experts recommend that you don't buy a used car that you couldn't afford to run from new, although you could forego fully comprehensive insurance on an inexpensive vehicle. The higher the new price of a car, generally the more it will cost to repair and service. Many cars have *very* expensive parts that may need replacing including catalyst-equipped exhausts, ABS systems, engine control units, automatic gearboxes, electronically-controlled heaters, nose and tail cones, power-steering racks, dashboard electronics and power accessories. The more electronic gadgets a car has, the more there is to go wrong (the cost and fitting of replacement parts would deter many people from buying certain cars).

You can get a guide to the value of most secondhand cars from motoring magazines such as *What Car?*, *Motorists Guide*, *Parker's Car Price Guide* and *Used Car Prices & Information*, all of which are published monthly. Always do your own research in your area by comparing prices at dealers, in local papers (and free car magazines) and in the national press, e.g. *Exchange & Mart* and the *Thames Valley Trader*. Many private sellers are willing to take a considerable drop and dealers will also usually haggle over the price. The average annual mileage for a car in Britain is around 12,000 (19,311km) a year and cars with high mileage (e.g. 20,000mi/32,186km a year) can usually be bought for substantially less than the average price. A new innovation in recent years has been car 'supermarkets' (e.g. CarLand, ☎ freefone 0800-783 3366, Internet: www.carland.com) selling nearly-new or used models, mainly ex-fleet or ex-lease.

You must be extremely careful when buying a used car in Britain, whether from a garage or privately. Sellers use many ploys such as 'clocking' (winding back the odometer); false test certificates (most likely on older cars); and any number of ruses to hide major faults such as accident damage, rust or imminent engine failure. It's advisable to check a car's history before buying it to ensure that it hasn't been written off (e.g. a 'cut and shut', where two 'good' halves are cut and welded together making a death trap), stolen, disguised or the number plates changed. This costs around £25 and can be done by companies such as HPI Autodata (☎ 01722-422422) who maintain a register. Cars written-off in road accidents are also substituted by stolen cars, so it's advisable to check that the vehicle identification number matches the registration number. The mileage can usually be verified by buying a car with a full service history (fsh). **Complaints about secondhand car purchases regularly outnumber all other consumer complaints!**

You have a certain amount of protection in law, whether buying from a dealer or privately, although legally you're better off buying from a dealer. The Automobile Association (see page 269) publish a booklet entitled *The law about buying and selling a car*. For people who know little about cars, the Office of Fair Trading publish a booklet entitled *Used Cars*, which includes tips about buying, service and repair. If you buy a 'lemon' (a dud) you should take legal advice to find out whether you have a valid complaint.

Always check a car carefully (particularly the tyres which may be illegal) and take it for a test drive. It's advisable to obtain an independent inspector's report from a motoring organisation (see page 269) before buying, although this may not be possible with a private sale when a decision must often be made on the spot. Keep a copy of any advertisements which include a description and note any claims made by the seller. **Beware of dealers claiming to be private sellers (which is illegal). If the seller's name and address isn't the same as that in the vehicle registration document, you should be suspicious (it could also be stolen).**

In addition to buying a car from a dealer or privately, you can also buy a car from car auctions throughout Britain. These are, however, generally for the experienced buyer and the trade, who buy around 90 per cent of all cars sold at auction. ADT Auctions, one of the largest in Britain, produce a booklet for would-be buyers and sellers, available from any of their auction centres (see the Yellow Pages).

TEST CERTIFICATE

All vehicles (cars, motorcycles, motor caravans, light goods and dual purpose) that are over three years old must have an annual Department of Transport (DTp) test. This was previously called the Ministry of Transport (MOT) test or 'MOT test' and the name has stuck. Passenger-carrying vehicles with more than eight seats and taxis (excluding private hire cars) must be tested after they are one year old and there are also separate rules for goods vehicles over 1,525kg (30cwt), about which information can be obtained from a VRO.

Tests are performed by officially approved test centres, including local authorities and most large garages, many of which will test your car while you wait (although you may need to make a booking). Some garages do tests seven days a week and even provide a free collection and delivery service. The test usually takes 20 to 30 minutes, depending on the condition and cleanliness of your car, and includes all lights, steering and suspension, brakes (including the handbrake), tyres and wheels, seat belts and general items such as windscreen washers and wipers, horn, exhaust system and silencer, exhaust emission and vehicle structure (e.g. soundness of the bodywork). Tyres require 1.6mm of tread over 75 per cent of their width. The test has been made more stringent over the years and it's now difficult to get an old car to pass.

The official (maximum) cost of the test is around £30, although some garages charge less. When your car passes the test you will be given a 'Test Certificate' (VT20). If it fails, you receive an inspection report (VT30) listing the defects which must be corrected. If the tester completes the 'Warning' (section D) part of the test report, you're allowed only to drive it home, to a garage for repairs or to another testing station after repair. You can appeal against a test failure by completing form VT17 (available from any testing station) and sending it to the local Department of Transport office with the appeal fee within 14 days of failure. If a vehicle fails on minor points which can fixed within one day, no re-test is required. Otherwise a vehicle will need a full re-test. Usually if a failed vehicle is repaired by the garage which did the test, no further fee is payable.

You can have your car tested anytime, for example if you want to sell it. However, if it fails the test, even when it isn't due, you're unable to drive it until it has passed. It's an offence to use a vehicle on public roads without a valid test certificate. You're permitted only to drive it to a testing station where you have pre-booked a test in advance. Note that without a test certificate you cannot renew your road tax (see page 247). If you lose your test certificate, you can get a duplicate from the testing station which carried out the test, providing you have the serial number or the approximate date of issue.

It's unwise to buy a vehicle without a recent test certificate, even at a bargain price (which should make you even more suspicious), as many old cars fail their test. The standard of testing is variable, due mainly to a wide variation in the interpretation of test standards and it's unlikely that two testing stations will find the same faults on an 'old' car, e.g. one over five years old. Even buying a car with a new test certificate doesn't guarantee that it's in good condition (it has been estimated that some 50,000 test certificates are altered or completed fraudulently each year). It's easy for someone to obtain a false test certificate and many testers lose their licences each year due to issuing 'false' certificates. **A valid test certificate should never be taken as a guarantee of a car's roadworthiness, particularly as many aspects of a car's operation aren't tested, e.g. engine and gearbox.** Many garages fail cars for no apparent reason (other than to generate work for themselves!) and pass others that should have been failed and over half of all vehicles are tested incorrectly.

If you're buying a car privately without a guarantee, you would be advised to have an independent inspection carried out by a motoring organisation (see page 216). If you ask a garage (or anyone) to do a pre-test check on your car, don't ask them to repair it to test standard to get it through the test, as this could result in unnecessary expense. Ask them to take it for the test to find out what (if anything) needs fixing. Essential repairs recommended by a garage may not be the same as those officially required after a test. An MOT handbook on mechanical safety for cars and light vans entitled *How Safe Is Your Car* is issued by the Vehicle Inspectorate. Note that the police carry out roadworthiness spot checks on vehicles. **If your vehicle is found to be unroadworthy, the fact that you have a valid test certificate is irrelevant.**

SELLING A CAR

The main points to note when selling a car are:

● A potential buyer cannot test drive your car unless he's covered by your or his own insurance. You're responsible if someone drives your car with your permission without valid insurance.

● It's illegal to sell a car in an unroadworthy condition, unless you're selling it as a non-runner without a test certificate (see above). Never describe a car as being in a better condition that it is, e.g. excellent condition. If it's subsequently found to have any faults, you could be liable to reimburse the buyer or pay for repairs.

● Inform your insurance company. Either cancel your insurance or transfer it to a new car. Note that if you cancel your insurance, even for a short period, this may affect your no-claims discount when you take out insurance on a new car. When you sell a car, you're required to notify the motor vehicle registration office by completing the appropriate part of the vehicle registration papers (see page 232). The new owner of the car must also register his ownership with them (this is intended as a cross check of ownership).

● If you're selling your car privately you should insist on cash. It's usually a formality for the buyer to accompany you to your bank and make a cash transfer on the spot. There are confidence tricksters (crooks) who will, given half a chance, will happily give you a dud cheque and drive off with your car. Be wary of banker's drafts and building society cheques, which although as good as cash, may be counterfeit or stolen (some crooks try to pass them over a public holiday period when the banks are closed). If someone insists on paying by cheque, you should never allow them to take your car until the cheque has cleared. Don't allow a dealer or car auctioneer to take your car until a cheque has cleared, as cheques sometimes bounce after companies have ceased trading.

- Include in the receipt that you're selling the car in its present condition (as seen) without a guarantee, the price paid and the car's odometer (mileage) reading. The new owner may ask for a declaration in writing that the car is accident free, which applies to major accidents that have caused structural damage and not slight knocks.

- You can advertise a car for sale in local newspapers, on free local notice boards, in the Saturday or Sunday editions of national newspapers, and in many motoring newspapers and magazines. Among the best market places are the *Exchange & Mart* and the *Thames Valley Trader*. The best place to advertise a car depends on the make and value of the car. Cheap cars are probably best sold in local newspapers, while expensive and collectors cars are often advertised in the motoring press and in the broadsheet Sunday newspapers, such as the *Sunday Times*. Buyers will usually travel a long way to view a car that appears good value for money (if nobody phones, you will know why).

DRIVING LICENCE

The minimum age for driving in Britain is 17 for a motor car (up to 3.5 tonnes laden) or motorcycle over 50cc and 16 for a motorcycle (moped) up to 50cc, an invalid carriage and certain other vehicles. For commercial vehicles up to 7.5 tonnes laden, the minimum age is 18 and for heavy goods vehicles (HGV) it's 21. Driving licences are issued for certain categories of vehicles, e.g. category A is for a motorcycle, B is for a car, C is for a truck and D is for a bus. Holders of a full foreign driving licence or an international driving permit may drive in Britain for one year.

If you hold a licence from an EEA member state or a licence issued in Australia, Barbados, British Virgin Islands, Cyprus, Gibraltar, Hong Kong, Japan, Kenya, Malta, New Zealand, Singapore, Switzerland or Zimbabwe, you can obtain a British driving licence in your first year in Britain without taking a driving test. **If you don't apply during your first year, you aren't permitted to drive after this period until you have passed a driving test.** If you hold a licence issued by a country that isn't listed above, you must take a driving test during your first year in Britain. If you don't pass the driving test during your first year in Britain, you must apply for a provisional licence and drive under restricted conditions (e.g. with a qualified driver) until you have passed your test.

Some foreign licences (for example licences printed in Arabic or Japanese) must be translated into English or an international driving permit must be obtained before arrival. To apply for a British driving licence, you must obtain an application form (D1) and form D100 (which explains what you need to know about driver licensing) from any post office. An eye test certificate isn't required, although you must be able to read a number plate at 67 feet (20.5m) in daylight, with glasses or contact lenses, if necessary (you *will* be tested). Unlike most foreign driving licences, a British licence doesn't contain a photograph. Complete form D1 and send it to the DVLC, Swansea with the appropriate postcode (shown on the form) and the following:

- your foreign driving licence and, if applicable, an international driving permit (which are returned to you);
- a permanent address in Britain;
- a cheque or postal order for the fee (not cash or banknotes).

Your British driving licence will be sent to you around one week later and is valid until age 70. Don't forget to sign it. After the age of 70 it must be renewed every three years, providing you remain fit to drive. However, you must declare any health problems which might make you unfit to drive at any time and not just when applying for a licence. An international driving permit is required if you intend to drive in some countries. This may vary depending on which driving licence(s) you hold. Check with a British motoring organisation (see page 269).

An international driving licence, valid for one year only, is obtainable from British motoring organisations for £3, either in person or by mail. You must provide a passport-size photograph and the fee and complete a form giving details of your British, Northern Ireland or British Forces Germany (BFG) driving licence. Holders of a British or foreign car driving licence can ride a motorcycle of up to 125cc in Britain, without obtaining a special licence. For motorcycles over 125cc you must have a motorcycle licence (see page 256). Foreign licences issued by EU member states and certain other countries can be exchanged for a British licence within five years of becoming resident in Britain. Send your foreign licence to the Foreign Licence Section, DVLC, Swansea SA99 1AE, with a completed form D1TEST, the fee and your foreign licence.

If you change your permanent address in Britain, you must notify the DVLC as soon as possible by completing the section on the back of your British licence and returning it to the address shown. A new licence will be issued free of charge. You can be fined a maximum of £50 if you fail to notify the DVLC of a change of address. A new licence is issued for the sum of £11 for the following reasons:

- your licence has been lost, stolen, destroyed or defaced;
- to receive a clean licence after the expiry of endorsements (see below);
- to add or remove provisional motorcycle group D or add new groups to a full licence;
- to obtain a new licence after a period of disqualification;
- to exchange a Northern Ireland licence for a first GB licence.

A provisional licence is exchanged free for a full licence after passing a driving test. A policeman can ask to see your driving licence at any time and you must either produce it immediately or take it personally to a police station (named by you) within seven days. Driving without a licence or while disqualified attracts a heavy penalty. Court convictions for many motoring offences result in an 'endorsement' of your licence, which means you're given a number of penalty points. Most offences 'earn' a fixed number of penalty points (e.g. speeding usually merits three penalty points), but some are at a court's discretion. If you want to request a court hearing for a fixed penalty offence, you must usually do so within 28 days. If you don't pay a fine within the set period it may be increased dramatically. Some offences cannot be dealt with under the fixed penalty system and you must appear in court.

If you total 12 or more penalty points within three years, you're automatically disqualified (banned) from driving for a minimum of six months. If you already have points on your licence and points for a new offence would bring the total to 12 or more, you must go to court (as only a court can disqualify you from driving). If you have been disqualified in the past three years, you usually lose your licence for a minimum of one year (two previous disqualifications normally results in a two-year ban). You can be disqualified for a single offence such as drunken or reckless driving, which can also result in a prison sentence where injury or death resulted. Note that if you drive while disqualified, you can receive a prison sentence and have your car confiscated.

The length of time endorsements remain on a driving licence depend on the offence, e.g. it's 11 years from the date of conviction for offences involving drunken driving and four years for all other offences from the date of the offence or the date of the conviction. You can apply for the removal of a penalty point endorsement after three years from the date of the offence. You can also apply for a disqualification of four years or longer to be lifted after a minimum period of two years. You must apply for a new licence (using form D1) after a period of disqualification. Further information about driving licences can be obtained from the Customer Enquiries Unit, DVLC, Swansea SA6 7JL (☎ 01792-772151).

CAR INSURANCE

The following categories of car insurance are available in Britain:

Third party: The minimum cover which includes all public and private roads. In addition to the legal minimum, it includes cover for injury to other people caused by your passengers. Third party insurance provides the minimum legal cover in all EU countries plus the Czech Republic, Hungary, Norway, the Slovak Republic and Switzerland without a green card. Not all insurance companies offer third party car insurance.

Third-party, fire and theft (TPF&F): Known in some countries as part comprehensive, TPF&F includes (in addition to third party cover) loss or damage caused to your car and anything fitted to it by fire, lightening, explosion, theft or attempted theft. It usually includes broken glass.

Comprehensive: Covers all the risks listed under the two categories above plus damage to your own car, theft of contents (usually limited to £100 or £150), broken glass (e.g. windscreen replacement), personal accident benefits and medical expenses (e.g. £100 or £200). It also usually includes damage due to natural hazards, e.g. storm damage. Extra cover may be included free or for an additional fee and may include the cost of hiring a car if yours is involved in an accident or stolen, legal assistance, no-claims discount protection, and extra cover for a car stereo or phone.

Windscreen damage results in around 1.5 million claims a year, mostly due to stones thrown up by other vehicles on resurfaced roads. Comprehensive insurance may also cover you against loss when your car is in a garage for service or repair. Check a policy for any restrictions, for example you may not be covered against theft if your car isn't garaged and locked overnight. Most lenders usually insist on comprehensive insurance for leasing, contract hire, hire purchase and loan agreements.

Comprehensive insurance can be extended to include other vehicles not belonging to or hired to the policyholder, and any insurance policy can include other people to drive your car (either individually named or any driver). Note that comprehensive insurance generally covers you for only third party when you're driving a car that doesn't belong to you. Separate passenger insurance is usually unnecessary as passengers are automatically covered by all British motor insurance policies (people are injured in around 40 per cent of all accidents, yet two out of three don't bother to make a claim). Personal accident, medical expenses, clothing and personal effects cover, are usually included in comprehensive policies. Around two-thirds of British motorists have full comprehensive insurance.

Green Card: British motor insurance doesn't include a free green card (which extends cover to the countries listed above under **Third party**), which is usually available for a maximum period (e.g. three months a year) and is expensive. Note, however, that it isn't necessary to have a green card when driving in Western Europe, but without one you're covered only for the legal minimum third party insurance required by law.

Premiums

There's a competitive motor insurance market in Britain, which has been heightened in recent years by the proliferation of direct marketing and direct response insurance companies (e.g. Direct Line, Churchill Insurance, Eagle Star Direct and The Insurance Service), who are often able to offer cheaper insurance by cutting out the commission paid to traditional insurance brokers. However, there's no longer much of difference between premiums offered by direct-selling companies and traditional brokers. Car insurance is also offered by banks, motoring organisations, manufacturers (expensive) and a range of other companies.

The cost of motor insurance in Britain is quite high, although it's lower than in many continental European countries. The average premium has risen by around 25 per cent since 1994 (in some cases by as much as 50 per cent) and it's important to shop around for the best deal as quotes can vary by up to 50 per cent. *Everyone* **can save money by shopping around for their car insurance!** Some companies offer low premiums for certain categories of drivers, e.g. those age over 45 or 50 (with good driving records and family cars), low mileage drivers and women. Many insurers offer discounts of up to 15 per cent for those who pass an 'advanced' or 'defensive' driving test such as the Pass Plus training scheme (☎ 0115-901 2633).

If you have a collector's car, joining a specialist motoring group or club may entitle you to cheaper insurance, especially when the club is large, such as the MG Owners Club with 50,000 members. Some employers, trade associations or professional bodies provide cheaper insurance for employees and members, through agreements with insurance companies. Some manufacturers also organise special rates through a particular insurance company, but it isn't always a good deal. **Always obtain a quotation in writing before paying the premium or an instalment.** Bear in mind that the cheapest policy won't usually offer the best deal, particularly regarding the prompt settlement of claims (many insurance companies take a long time to settle claims).

It's often worthwhile using a broker who will shop around for the best deal, although some refuse to quote for young or high-risk drivers. Some brokers specialise in finding drivers with a bad claims record or driving convictions the cheapest cover, such as Motor Advice (☎ 0897-664422) or Insurance Selection (☎ 0171-639 9734). You can compare rates over the Internet, as most insurers have a website and there are also brokers (e.g. www.screentrade.co.uk) who will find a number of quotes. Many companies offer extra discounts when policies are purchased and paid for with a credit/debit card over the Internet. You should also check the regular surveys carried out by *Which?* magazine (see page 437) and financial magazines.

The cheapest insurance companies are often able to offer lower premiums because they simply cherry-pick the motorists least likely to make a claim. Usually they won't insure inexperienced motorists in powerful cars (which usually includes all 'sports' cars), anyone under 21 or over 74, and insist on a minimum number of years no-claims bonus (see below) and a clean licence (possibly with the exception of one speeding or parking offence). These companies may also not recognise a no-claims discount earned overseas with a foreign insurance company. Many insurers also have rigid restrictions regarding occupation (actors, musicians, sportsmen and journalists/writers and others are blacklisted by some insurers). An estimated one million motorists break the law and drive without insurance, as they are unable to obtain it or the cost is prohibitive.

The most important factor influencing premiums is a car's insurance group (although not all insurers place cars in the same group), which is calculated according to the new cost; the cost of spare parts, bodyshell and labour; repair times; and its performance. In addition to the car's insurance group (rated one to 20), other factors affecting the cost include:

● the type of insurance cover required;

● the make and type of car (and how expensive it is to repair);

● the age and value of the car;

● your driving experience and driving record (endorsements and disqualifications);

● your age, sex (some companies offer a discount to women) and occupation;

● what you use your car for, e.g. business or pleasure;

● your accident record and no-claims discount;

● who will drive the car besides the owner;

● your health (you may be required to pay an excess if you suffer from epilepsy or diabetes);

● where you live and whether your car is garaged overnight (Britain is split into regions for the purpose of assessing risks, with rural areas the cheapest and cities the most expensive);

● the number of miles you do a year (some policies offer reduced rates for those who do low mileage, e.g. less than 7,500mi/12,000km a year);

● any extras you require, such as a protected no-claims discount.

Premiums are usually higher for those who live in inner cities, where driving conditions are more hazardous (due to the sheer volume of traffic) and where there's a high risk of theft. Some insurers insist that a car (particularly a high-risk car) has an engine immobiliser, although if you have a tracking devices (see page 260) you may receive a discount of up to 20 per cent.

With comprehensive insurance, you can choose to pay a voluntary (sometimes compulsory) excess, for example the first £50, £100 or £200 of a claim, which will reduce your premium. You must make sure you state any previous accidents or driving offences when applying for car insurance, otherwise your insurer can refuse to pay out in the event of a claim. Drivers under 21 or 25, inexperienced drivers (holders of a licence for less than one or two years) and drivers with a bad accident record, must usually pay a compulsory excess. You're usually also required to pay an excess, e.g. £25, if you make a claim on your windscreen cover (which normally covers all glass), but this doesn't affect your no-claims discount. Drivers who have been banned for drunken or dangerous driving must usually pay at least double the standard premium for a number of years.

For a small extra premium, most insurance companies will cover you for the legal costs arising from road accidents (also available separately from British motoring organisations, but is more expensive). If you cannot live without a car, make sure that your policy will pay for car hire in the event of an accident or your car being stolen (or that you have separate 'uninsured loss' insurance to cover this). Special 'mobility' insurance is available to pay for the cost of alternative transport after a disqualification, medical revocation of your licence, or your inability to drive due to certain injuries.

Motor insurance policies are valid for one year from the date you're first insured. You must usually pay in advance, although some companies allow you to pay in instalments either monthly, quarterly or half-yearly by direct debit from a bank account, sometimes without incurring an additional charge (if there's an extra charge, check the APR, see page 343). You're given a 'cover note' to prove that you're insured until your insurance certificate is issued. Check that the details on the cover note are correct, particularly the type of cover required and the date and time it commences. Towards the end of your insurance period you will receive a renewal notice from your insurance company.

You aren't required to renew your car insurance with the same company, but may shop around for a better deal. **Note, however, that if you don't renew your motor insurance by the date due, your cover will cease automatically.** You can change your insurance company and policy whenever you like in Britain, for example by giving seven days notice and returning the certificate, whereupon you will receive a portion of your premium back, providing that you have made no-claims. If you're staying in Britain for a short period, check whether you can take out a fixed period policy, e.g. for three or six months.

No-Claims Discount

A foreign no-claims discount (or bonus) is valid in Britain, although many British insurance companies won't accept a no-claims discount earned overseas with a foreign insurance company. You must provide written evidence from your present or previous insurance company, not simply an insurance renewal notice. The maximum no-claims discount in Britain is usually 65 to 70 per cent, which is more generous than in many other countries. Some insurance companies offer an introductory discount. The no-claims discount offered by insurance companies is typically as shown below:

No. Year's No-Claim	Discount (Bonus)
1	30 per cent
2	40 per cent
3	50 per cent
4	60 per cent
5	65 to 70 per cent

Normally when you make a claim you lose two years no-claims discount (also applies to a claim for fire or theft), so it's sometimes cheaper to pay for minor damage yourself. Damage to glass doesn't affect your no-claims discount, but you're usually required to pay the first £25 of a claim. Most insurance policies offer a protected no-claims discount policy or allow you to insure your no-claims discount. This means that you can usually make one 'at-fault' claim within a certain period (e.g. three years) or two 'at-fault' claims (e.g. within five years), without losing any of your no-claims discount.

Some companies provide an extra no-claims discount or lower premiums for experienced motorists with a clean licence and an accident-free driving record. If you insure two or more vehicles, you can only claim a no-claims discount on one vehicle, although you may be given a discount on the premiums of other vehicles. Note that if you're uninsured for longer than two years, you will usually lose your entire no-claims bonus.

ROAD TAX (VEHICLE EXCISE DUTY)

Road tax (officially called 'vehicle excise duty' or 'vehicle license' – politicians love to invent alternative names for taxes, although they fool nobody), is required for all cars and costs the same irrespective of the type of vehicle, its engine size or power (a mini costs the same as a Rolls-Royce). This is currently £155 a year for a private car. However, a variable rate of road tax will be introduced from autumn 2000 based on the number of grams of carbon dioxide a vehicle emits per kilometre driven. Emissions are directly related to the size of a car's engine, so those driving cars with smaller engines will pay less and those with bigger engines more (cars will be divided into five bands). At the time of writing it wasn't known what the tax would be for each band. If you think tax on cars is high, spare a thought for the poor truck owner who pays £5,750 a year (compared with from around £300 to £2,000 on the continent) and Britain also has the most expensive diesel fuel in Europe!

Road tax is usually paid at a post office, where forms and information leaflets are available (spendthrifts can purchase special £5 road tax stamps to help save for their road tax). If you're registering a vehicle for the first time, it's possible to licence it for part of a month plus six or 12 months. To obtain your road tax disc, you must complete a *Vehicle licence application form* (V10). Notes about registering and licensing a vehicle are contained in leaflet V100 (a separate licence and form is required for a heavy goods vehicle). Take your completed form V10 to any post office with your vehicle registration document or a completed form V62 (see page 232); a valid insurance certificate or cover note (see page 243); a valid test certificate, if applicable (see page 239); a disabled exemption certificate, if applicable; and the payment (e.g. cash or cheque).

Some applications must be made at a Vehicle Registration Office (VRO), which are listed in leaflet V100. After paying your road tax, you receive a tax disc showing the registration number and the date to which duty has been paid. This must be displayed on the inside of the windscreen of your car on the left-hand side (top or bottom). It's usually inserted in a plastic holder available from garages and motor accessory shops.

Road tax cannot be transferred from one vehicle to another, although you can obtain a refund for each whole month it still has to run, e.g. when you sell a car or take it off the road. To do this you must remove the tax disc and take it with a completed form V14 (available from post offices) to any VRO or send it to Refund Section, DVLC, Swansea SA99 1AL. You should apply for an exchange tax disc if the taxation class of your vehicle changes, e.g. if you convert a car into a truck or motor caravan, or if you buy a vehicle with a licence which doesn't cover your use of the vehicle. If your tax disc has been lost, stolen, destroyed or spoilt in any way (e.g. the figures cannot be read), you can obtain a duplicate licence for a small fee. Complete form V20 and send it to a VRO.

In recent years there has been a clampdown on tax evaders. If a vehicle has been taxed since 1st January 1998 it must have a current tax disc or you *must* file a Statutory Off Road Notification (SORN) with the DVLC. If you use or keep a vehicle on a public road that isn't taxed, your subject to a fine of £1,000 or five times the unpaid tax, whichever is greater. If you fail to file a SORN the fine is also £1,000 and if you make a SORN declaration when a car is being used or kept on a road it could cost you £5,000 or two years in jail.

Many experts believe it would be far better to adopt the system used in a number of European countries, where registration plates are personal (transferred from car to car) and supplied by the authorities, **and you can obtain them only by paying road tax.** An even better and fairer scheme would be to abolish road tax altogether and include it in the cost of petrol. This would add only a fraction of a penny to the price of a litre and would ensure that those owning gas-guzzlers and who use the roads most would pay more. This is, however, unlikely as it would deprive the government of a tax opportunity and throw millions of civil servants (whose primary occupation is devising new taxes) out of work.

GENERAL ROAD RULES

The following general road rules and tips may help you adjust to driving in Britain and avoid an accident:

- Among the many strange habits of the British is that of driving on the left-hand side of the road (if everyone else drove on the left, the British would drive on the right!). You may find this a bit strange if you come from a country which drives on the right, however, it saves a lot of confusion if you do likewise. It's helpful to have a reminder (e.g. 'think left!') on your car's dashboard. Take extra care when pulling out of junctions, one-way streets and at roundabouts. Remember to look first to the *right* when crossing the road and drivers of left-hand cars should note that headlights should be dipped to the left when driving at night.

    If you're unused to driving on the left, you should be prepared for some disorientation or even terror, although most people have few problems adjusting to it. For many foreigners, the strangest custom is driving on the left-hand side of the road and some drivers have a real fear of driving on the 'wrong' side of the road. If this applies to you, the International Drivers Service (☎ 0181-570 9190) specialises in teaching foreigners how to survive on British roads. The traffic system, density and speed of traffic is also completely alien to many foreigners, particularly Americans.

- All motorists are advised to carry a warning triangle, although it isn't mandatory. If you have an accident or a breakdown (see page 257), you should signal this by switching on your hazard warning lights. If you have a warning triangle it must be placed at the edge of the road, at least 50 metres behind the car on secondary roads and at least 150 metres on motorways.

- In Britain there's no priority to the right (or left) on any roads, as there is in many European countries. At all crossroads and junctions in Britain, there's either an octagonal stop sign (solid white line on road) or a triangular give way sign (dotted white line on road), where a secondary road meets a major road. Stop or give way may also be painted on the road surface. You must stop completely at a stop sign (all four wheels must come to rest) before pulling out onto a major road, even if you can see that no traffic is approaching. At a give way sign, you aren't required to stop, but must give priority to traffic already on the major road.

- The different types of traffic signs in Britain can usually be distinguished by their shape and colour as follows:

  - warning signs are mostly triangular with **red** borders;
  - signs within circles with a **red** border are mostly prohibitive;
  - signs within **blue** circles but no red border give positive instructions;
  - direction signs are mostly rectangular and are distinguished by their background colour; **blue** for motorway signs, **green** for primary routes and **white** for secondary routes. Local direction signs often have blue borders with a white background. Signs with brown backgrounds are used to direct motorists to tourist attractions. All signs are shown in a booklet entitled *Know Your Traffic Signs* (see page 253).

- On roundabouts (traffic circles), vehicles on the roundabout (coming from your right) have priority and not those entering it. There are many roundabouts in Britain, which although they are a bit of a free-for-all, speed up traffic considerably and are usually preferable to traffic lights, particularly outside rush hours (although some busy roundabouts also have traffic lights). Some roundabouts have a filter lane which is reserved for traffic turning left. Traffic flows clockwise round roundabouts and not anti-clockwise as in countries where traffic drives on the right. You should signal as you approach the exit you wish to take. In addition to large roundabouts, there are also mini-roundabouts, indicated by a round blue sign. The British think roundabouts are marvellous (we spend most of our time going round in circles), although they aren't so popular in countries where traffic drives on the right. Roundabouts are particularly useful for making a U-turn when you discover that you're travelling in the wrong direction. The biggest roundabout in the world is the M25 motorway, affectionately known as the magic roundabout.

- On country roads, sharp bends are shown by signs and the severity (tightness) of a bend is indicated by white arrows on a black background (or vice versa); the more arrows the tighter the bend (so SLOW down).

- The wearing of seat belts is **compulsory** for all front and rear seat passengers (over one year of age) and children under 14 in rear seats must use seat belts or child restraints when fitted (although it makes sense to wear rear seat belts at all times irrespective of age). Seat belts or restraints must be appropriate for the age and weight of a child, as follows:

  - **under 1 year old (weighing less than 10kg):** a front or rear-facing baby seat with a built-in three-point harness in either the front (but not when the front seat is fitted with an airbag) or rear of a car;

  - **1 to 4 years old (under 18kg):** a rear-facing Renault Argonaute-style seat or a front-facing restraint with a built-in (e.g. five point) harness;

  - **3½ to 7 years old (15 to 25kg):** lap table (for use when only a lap belt is available);

  - **3 to 12 years old (15 to 36kg):** a three-point adult belt with a booster seat with head restraint.

  Special harnesses and belts are also available for the handicapped. Note that all belts, seats, harnesses and restraints **must be correctly fitted and adjusted, without which they may be useless.** Some child car seats have fatal flaws and many cars have seat belt straps that are too short for rear-facing baby seats. It's estimated that some two-thirds of child seats are wrongly fitted. The RAC (☎ freefone 0800-550055) produce a safety video entitled *There's No Excuse!*. If all available restraints in a car are in use, children may travel unrestrained (although this is extremely unwise).

- It's estimated that seat belts would prevent 75 per cent of the deaths and 90 per cent of the injuries to those involved in accidents who weren't wearing belts. Note, however, that lap belts fitted in the centre rear seat of many cars are dangerous and should be replaced. In addition to the risk of death or injury, you can be fined £50 for ignoring the seat belt laws. The vast majority of British people wear seat belts, due in no small part to a shocking (but effective) advertising campaign in the '80s called 'Clunk Click, Every Trip'. Note that it's the driver's responsibility to ensure that passengers are properly fastened. If you're exempt from wearing a seat belt for medical reasons, a safety belt exemption certificate is required from your doctor. The ultimate protection is supposed to be afforded by airbags, although a number of deaths have been blamed on them in recent years.

- Don't drive in lanes reserved for buses and taxis, unless necessary to avoid a stationary vehicle or obstruction, and give priority to authorised users. Bus lanes are indicated by road markings and signs indicate the period of operation, which is usually during rush hours only (although some lanes are in use 24 hours a day), and which vehicles are permitted to use them. Bus drivers get irate if you illegally drive in their lane and you can be fined for doing so.

- Headlights must be used at night on all roads where there's no street lighting, where street lamps are over 185 metres (200 yards) apart and on roads where street lamps aren't lit. You must use your headlamps or front fog lamps at any time when visibility is generally reduced to less than 100 metres. In Britain it's legal to drive on parking (side) lights on roads with street lighting (although they do little to help you see or be seen). Note that headlight flashing has a different meaning in different countries. In some countries it means "after you", while in others it means "get out of my way". It can even mean "I'm driving a new car and haven't yet worked out what all the switches are for". In Britain headlamp flashing has no legal status apart from warning another driver of your presence, although it's usually used to give priority to another vehicle, e.g. when a car is waiting to exit from a junction. Hazard warning lights (all indicators operating simultaneously) are used to warn other drivers of an obstruction, e.g. an accident or a traffic jam on a motorway (using them when parking illegally has no legal significance unless you have broken down).

- Front fog or spot lights must be fitted in pairs at a regulation height. Rear fog lamps should be used only when visibility is seriously reduced, i.e. to less than 100 metres, and shouldn't be used when it's just dark or raining. Unfortunately many British drivers don't know what fog lamps are for and use them when visibility is good, but don't use them (or any lights) in fog.

- The sequence of British traffic lights is red, red + amber (yellow), green, amber and back to red. Red + amber is a warning to get ready to go but you mustn't start moving until the light changes to green. Amber means stop at the stop line and you may proceed only if the amber light appears after you have crossed the stop line or when stopping might cause an accident. A green filter light may be shown in addition to the full lamp signals, which means you may drive in the direction shown by the arrow, irrespective of other lights showing.

  You may notice that many traffic lights have an uncanny habit of changing to green when you approach them, particularly during off-peak hours. This isn't magic or due to your magnetic personality. Around half of Britain's traffic signals are vehicle-actuated, where sensors between 40 and 150 metres from the lights (depending on the speed limit) are set into the road and change the light to green unless other traffic already has priority. Signals stay at green for a minimum of seven seconds, although it can be as long as one minute.

- At many traffic lights, cameras are installed to detect motorists driving through red lights (you receive notification around one month later and must *prove* that you weren't driving to avoid prosecution). In Britain, traffic lights are placed on the left side of the road at junctions and may also be duplicated opposite. You won't have to play hunt the traffic lights as on the continent of Europe, where lights are placed on the left, right or up in the air, and may present a multitude of confusing signals.

- Always approach pedestrian crossings with caution and don't park or overtake another vehicle on the approach to a crossing marked by a double line of studs or zig-zag lines. At pelican (pedestrian) crossings, a flashing amber light follows the red light, to warn you to give way to pedestrians before proceeding. **Note that pedestrians have the legal right of way once they have stepped onto a crossing without traffic lights and you must STOP. Motorists who don't stop are liable to heavy penalties.** Where a road crosses a public footpath, e.g. when entering or emerging from property or a car park bordering a road, you *must* give way to pedestrians.

- Britain lacks a rule of the road which compels slow moving vehicles (such as tractors or cars towing caravans) to pull over to allow other traffic to overtake. The AA states that a driver towing a caravan who sees more than six vehicles following him, should pull over and let them pass, but it isn't compulsory. Worse still, timid drivers who never overtake anything unless it's stationary, bunch up behind slow moving vehicles, thus ensuring that nobody can overtake without having to pass a whole stream of traffic (or forcing a gap).

- Fines can be exacted for a wide range of motoring offences, although on-the-spot fines *aren't* imposed in Britain. Convictions for most motoring offences means an 'endorsement' of your licence, which results in penalty points being imposed (see page 241). Serious offences such as dangerous or drunken driving involving injury or death to others can result in a prison sentence.

- Many motorists seem to have an aversion to driving in the left-hand lane on a three-lane motorway, which in effect reduces the motorway to two lanes. It's illegal to overtake on an inside lane unless traffic is being channelled in a different direction. Motorists must indicate before overtaking *and* when moving back into an inside lane after overtaking, e.g. on a dual carriageway or motorway. Learner drivers, pedestrians, cyclists and mopeds aren't permitted on motorways.

- White lines mark the separation of traffic lanes. A solid single line or two solid lines means no overtaking in either direction. A solid line to the left of the centre line, i.e. on your side of the road, means that overtaking is prohibited in your direction. You may overtake only when there's a single broken line in the middle of the road or double lines with a broken line on your side of the road. If you drive a left-hand drive car, take extra care when overtaking (the most dangerous manoeuvre in motoring) and when turning right. It's wise to have a special 'overtaking mirror' fitted to your car.

- The edges of motorways and A-roads are often marked with a white line with a ribbed surface, which warns you through tyre sound and vibration when you drive too close to the edge of the road.

- In Britain there are three main kinds of automatic railway level crossings: automatic half-barrier level crossings, automatic open crossings and open level crossings without gates or barriers. Always approach a railway level crossing slowly and **STOP**:

  - as soon as the amber light is on and the audible alarm sounds followed by flashing red warning lights (half-barrier level crossings and automatic open crossings)

  - as soon as the barrier or half-barrier starts to fall (if applicable) or the gates start to close

  - in any case when a train approaches.

  Many automatic and manual crossings have a telephone which can be used to contact the signalman in an emergency or to ask for advice or information. In remote areas, open level crossings have no gates, barriers, attendant or traffic lights. Some level crossings have gates, but no attendant or red lights. If there's a telephone, contact the signalman to check that it's okay to cross, otherwise providing a train isn't coming, open the gates wide and cross as quickly as possible. Close the gates after crossing. **Crossings without gates must be**

approached with extreme caution (including pedestrian railway crossings). Even a car that's built like a tank won't look so smart after a scrap with a 70-tonne locomotive.

- Be particularly wary of cyclists, moped riders and motorcyclists. It isn't always easy to see them, particularly when they are hidden by the blind spots of a car or when cyclists are riding at night without lights. **When overtaking, ALWAYS give them a wide . . . WIDE berth.** If you knock them off their bikes, you may have a difficult time convincing the police that it wasn't your fault; far better to avoid them (and the police). Drive slowly near schools and be wary of children getting on or off buses.

- A 'GB' nationality plate (sticker) must be affixed to the rear of a British registered car when motoring abroad. Drivers of foreign registered cars in Britain must have the appropriate nationality plate affixed to the rear of their car (not an assortment). Note that yellow headlights, which are fitted to all vehicles in France, are illegal in Britain (except for visitors) and should be converted.

- If you need spectacles or contact lenses to read a number plate 79.4mm high at a distance of 20.5m (67ft) in good daylight, then you must always wear them when motoring. It's advisable to carry a spare pair of glasses or contact lenses in your car.

- The police routinely prosecute motorists for using a mobile phone while driving (classed as 'inconsiderate driving'), although in itself it isn't illegal. It's one of the most common and hazardous driving habits in Britain and has resulted in numerous accidents, many fatal, and has been calculated to increase the risk of an accident by some 400 per cent (even hands-free phones are little safer as they all distract the driver's attention).

- A booklet published by the Department of Transport entitled *The Highway Code* (The Stationery office) contains advice for all road users, including motorists, motorcyclists and pedestrians. It's available for 99p from bookshops and British motoring organisations and is essential reading. Although *The Highway Code* shows many road signs commonly used in Britain, a comprehensive explanation is given in a booklet entitled *Know Your Traffic Signs*, available at most bookshops for £1.20. A free booklet entitled *On the Road in Great Britain* (in English, French, German, Italian and Spanish) is published by the Department of Transport and is available from British motoring organisations, travel agents and government offices.

BRITISH DRIVERS

Like motorists in all countries, the British have their own idiosyncrasies and customs. In general, Britons have a reputation for being good and considerate drivers, and most take their driving seriously. Most drivers are courteous and, unlike many other Europeans, are usually happy to give way to a driver waiting to enter the flow of traffic or change lanes. However, tempers are rising on Britain's overcrowded streets and road rage ('invented' in California), where drivers blow their tops and attack or drive into other motorists, is becoming more common. It's often provoked by tailgating, headlight flashing, obscene gestures, obstruction and verbal abuse, so be careful how you behave when driving in Britain. Although British drivers are generally law abiding (except with regard to speed limits), a recent survey found that millions would drive on the wrong side of the law if they thought they could get away with it.

A phenomenon known as 'motorway madness', where motorway driving turns normal people into lunatics, is widespread in Britain, where many drivers are afraid of motorways and have little idea how to drive on them. Common faults include poor lane discipline, undertakers (motorists who overtake on the inside), driving too fast in poor conditions (e.g. fog and heavy rain), and driving much to close to the vehicle in front. Many motorists in Britain (and most other countries) drive too close to the vehicle in front and have no idea of safe stopping distances. *The Highway Code* (see page 253) states that the safe stopping distance (including thinking distance, the time it takes for drivers to react) is 23m (75ft) at 30mph (50kph), 53m (175ft) at 50mph (80kph) and 96m (315ft) at 70mph (113kph).

These stopping distances are on dry roads, for cars with good brakes and tyres, in good visibility with an *alert driver* (if you're half asleep and driving an old banger on a wet or icy road, you had better not exceed 10mph, otherwise you will never stop in an emergency). Although these distances may appear generous, many other countries recommend longer stopping distances. If further proof is needed of how dangerous and widespread tailgating is, simply witness the statistics on the number of 'concertina' (multiple car) accidents in Britain, particularly on motorways in bad weather conditions. As a safety precaution, try to leave a large gap between you and the vehicle in front. This isn't just to allow you more time to stop, should the vehicles in front decide to get together, but also to give a 'tailgater' more time to stop. **The closer the car behind you, the further you should be from the vehicle in front.** Motorway police criticise motorists for driving too close, too fast and for not looking far enough ahead.

One thing most foreigners immediately notice when driving in Britain is the speed at which most people drive, which is often 50 per cent above the prevailing speed limit (unless you're on the M25, in which case you will be stationary). The exception to this rule is the ubiquitous 'Sunday driver', so-called because he rarely drives on any other day of the week and is never actually going anywhere but just enjoying the scenery (hence his maximum 20mph speed). You'll also notice that many motorists are reluctant to use their lights in poor visibility or until it's completely dark at night, and even then may use parking lights only in areas with street lighting. Sometimes it's just as well that people fail to use their headlights as many are badly adjusted and dazzle oncoming drivers (it's hard to believe they are ever checked during the annual serviceability test).

One of the biggest problems when motoring in towns and most residential areas in Britain, is the vast number of cars parked (legally or illegally) on roads. You'll often find that you must stop because your side of the road is completely blocked or because oncoming traffic isn't keeping over to its side of the road to allow you sufficient room to pass. Parked cars are also particularly hazardous when pulling out of busy junctions (many more of which should have roundabouts).

Take it easy when driving in winter. Although heavy snow is rare, particularly in the south, Britain has a lot of fog and ice, which make driving extremely hazardous (it also gets dark at around 1600 or even earlier in the north). Black ice is also common and is the most dangerous sort because it cannot be seen. When road conditions are bad, allow two to three times longer than usual to reach your destination (or better still take a train, if any are still running after privatisation!).

Despite their idiosyncrasies, British drivers are above average (average is bad) and more polite than most other drivers in Europe. Don't be discouraged by the tailgaters and road hogs as driving in Britain is less stressful than in many countries (apart from the jams). Most people who come from countries where traffic drives on the right quickly become used to driving on the 'wrong' side of the road. Just take it easy at first and bear in mind that there may be other motorists around just as confused as you are.

BRITISH ROADS

There are some 362,000km (225,000mi) of roads in Britain, including around 3,100km (1,950mi) of motorways. In general, the quality of British roads are excellent, although some main roads and motorways are in a poor condition due to being constantly chewed up by juggernauts and the heavy volume of traffic. Poor road design and shoddy workmanship has added to road problems and costs the British taxpayer £millions each year. Many suburban roads are full of potholes, particularly in London where some councils cannot afford to repair them. Roads in all areas are often badly repaired after being continually dug up by utility companies (telephone, electricity, gas, water, cable TV) and local councils, none of whom have spirit-levels. It's estimated that some 600,000 holes are dug each year in London's roads alone, which is around double the national average. Speed humps, known as 'sleeping policemen', are becoming a common sight on Britain's roads, particularly in residential areas, near schools, on private roads, in university grounds and in car parks. They are designed to slow traffic (or wreck your suspension) and are sometimes indicated by warning signs, as if you fail to slow down it's possible to turn your car over.

Britain has a smaller motorway network than many other western European countries and has no toll motorways, although trials are underway and tolls are expected to be introduced within the next few years. It's impossible to introduce toll booths as used on the continent and vehicles would be fitted with a 'transponder' which communicates with toll-charging gantries installed on motorways. Motorists will receive a monthly bill. Tolls are expected to create havoc on other roads as motorists desert motorways for A and B roads.

The Severn Bridge was privatised in 1991 and there are now two separate bridges. There's a toll charge of £4.80 for cars when crossing from east to west (Wales to England), which has prompted many people to leave the M4 at Swindon and drive through Gloucester into Wales (called 'rural rat-running', it includes many truck drivers who often ignore bridge weight restrictions).

Motorway travel in Britain is generally fast, although it's often slowed to a crawl by road works and the ubiquitous contra-flow, where two-way traffic occupies a single carriage. Motorways are generally accident free, except in fog and poor visibility, when multiple-vehicle accidents are frequent due to motorists driving too fast and too close (the police believe the general standard of motorway driving in Britain is abysmal). However, despite their high traffic density, motorways are Britain's safest roads, accounting for just 3 per cent of all casualties or 11 injuries per 100 million km, compared with over 100 injuries per 100 million miles in towns and around 35 in rural areas. By the year 2020 traffic on motorways is set to rise by between 50 and 100 per cent.

Emergency SOS telephones are located on motorways, where arrows on markerposts at the roadside indicate the direction of the nearest telephone. The hard shoulder on motorways is for emergencies only and you mustn't stop there simply to have a rest (for which you can be fined). Note also that the hard shoulder is a dangerous place to stop and many fatal accidents on motorways involve vehicles stopped there.

TRAFFIC POLICE

Police must have a reason to stop motorists in Britain, e.g. erratic driving or a defective bulb, although they can usually stop you on any pretext. Police cars sometimes display messages to motorists behind them via a panel inside their rear windscreen, e.g. 'Seatbelt', 'Reduce Your Speed', 'Do Not Pass', 'Accident Ahead' or 'Follow Me'. Police sometimes wear plain clothes and drive unidentified cars. If someone in plain clothes stops you, wait for identification to be shown before unlocking your car door or winding down your window. Never antagonise a police officer or make any smart cracks, as this is the fast lane to prosecution. If you remain courteous and obsequious you may be let off with a caution. If you think you haven't committed an offence and wish to contest it in a court of law, don't accept a fixed penalty notice, but ask for a full charge to be brought against you.

You aren't required by law to carry your car or motorcycle papers when motoring in Britain. However, if you're stopped by the police (for any reason) while driving, they may ask to see the following:

- driving licence (British if held);
- vehicle registration document (log book);
- test certificate (see page 239);
- insurance certificate (or an international motor insurance certificate, if you drive a foreign registered car).

If you don't have your papers with you when stopped by the police in Britain, you must take them personally to a police station (named by you), usually within seven days. They mustn't be sent by post.

MOTORCYCLES

Motorcycling is popular in Britain, both as a means of transport and as popular pastime (scooters and motorcycles have become fashionable again in recent years), with over one million motorcyclists. In recent years motorcycle accidents have been greatly reduced due to the compulsory wearing of helmets, better bikes and protective riding gear, better training, and defensive riding by bikers. In general, laws that apply to cars also apply to motorcycles. However, there are a few special points that apply to motorcyclists in particular:

- A moped with an engine capacity up to 50cc can be ridden at the age of 16 with a provisional licence (see page 241). A moped is defined as a 'motorised cycle' which has an engine of not more than 50cc. Anything larger is classified as a motorcycle. Note that the maximum legal speed a moped can be ridden is 30mph (50kph).

- A full motorcycle licence can be obtained at the age of 17 after passing a test.

- British standard (or equivalent) approved crash helmets are compulsory for both riders and passengers.

- It's illegal for a motorcycle rider with a provisional licence to tow a trailer or carry a pillion passenger (unless the pillion passenger holds a full motorcycle licence). To carry a pillion passenger, a motorcycle must be fitted with a dual seat and footrests.

- You must use dipped headlights, day or night.

- You must have valid third party insurance.

- You cannot ride a motorcycle over 250cc until you have held a full motorcycle licence for two years.

- Motorists with a full motor car licence (British or foreign) may ride a motorcycle (up to 125cc) without passing a test or obtaining a special licence. Unlike a motorcyclist with only a provisional licence, it isn't compulsory for a qualified motorist to take a riding test for a moped. An 'L' (learner) plate must, however, be displayed.

Insurance for motorcycles is high and similar to that for cars (see page 243). The cost of insurance depends on your age (riders under 25 pay *much* more), type and cubic capacity of your motorcycle, and the length of time you have held a licence. No-claims discounts are lower than for cars (the maximum is 20 or 25 per cent only) and policies usually carry an excess.

From July 1996 all learner riders throughout the EU have had to follow a course of training designed to take them safely through stages to a full licence. After an initial compulsory basic course, riders receive a provisional licence that allows them to ride bikes up to 12bhp for two years. After taking a test they will be limited to machines up to 33bhp for a further two years. 'Mature' riders aged 21 or over can qualify to ride larger bikes after accelerated training.

An MOT handbook on motorcycle safety entitled *How Safe Is Your Motorcycle* is produced by the Vehicle Inspectorate and the Home Office publish a leaflet *Put the Brakes on Bike Theft* (available from police stations and libraries). Essential reading for all bikers is *Sorry Mate, I Didn't See You* by Tim Monaghan (BBC). The AA operate a motorcyclist breakdown service (Rider Club) for motorcyclists (☎ freefone 0800-919595).

ACCIDENTS

Britain has a lower accident toll than most other European countries, although the death toll is still unacceptably high. It's generally recognised by the police and other experts that the majority of accidents could be avoided by improving driving standards (including less speed and less alcohol consumption by motorists), and the eradication of accident black spots through the redesign of roads and junctions. One of the most common causes of accidents, particularly on motorways, is drivers falling asleep. If you feel tired you should stop and rest immediately, as it's almost impossible to drive through it (this is such a serious problem that in future cars may be fitted with 'driver fatigue' warning lights). However, motorways are Britain's safest roads and 75 per cent of all road deaths happen on urban roads, which carry only 40 per cent of all traffic. Motorways carry 15 per cent and account for 6 per cent of road deaths.

If you're involved in (or cause) a car accident that results in injury to a person or a large animal (dog, horse, cattle, ass, mule, sheep, pig or goat) that isn't in your vehicle, or cause damage to any vehicle or property (apart from your own), the procedure is as follows:

1. Stop immediately. If possible move your car off the road and keep your passengers and yourself off the road. If you have an accident (or a breakdown) on a motorway, don't stay in your vehicle whatever the weather (even if parked on the hard shoulder) as there's a danger that another vehicle will run into you (a surprising one in eight of all motorway deaths occur on the hard shoulder). Wait on the embankment or nearby land (this also applies to stopping on other fast roads). Note that failing to stop after an accident or failure to give particulars or report to the police is a serious offence, for which there's a maximum fine of £2,000, a licence endorsement and eight to ten penalty points.

2. Warn other drivers of any obstruction by switching on your hazard warning lights (particularly on motorways) or by placing a warning triangle at the edge of the road at least 50 metres behind your car on secondary roads and 150 metres on a motorway. If necessary, for example when the road is partly or totally blocked, turn on your car's dipped headlights and direct traffic around the hazard. In bad visibility, at night, or in a blind spot, try to warn oncoming traffic of the danger, e.g. with a torch, or by waving a warning triangle up and down.

3. If anyone is injured, immediately phone 999 for an ambulance, the fire brigade (if someone is trapped or oil or chemicals are spilled) or the police. If an ambulance is called the police will come automatically. Emergency telephones are provided on motorways. Give first-aid only if you're qualified to do so. Don't move an injured person unless absolutely necessary to save him from further injury and don't leave him alone except to phone for an ambulance. Cover him with a blanket or coat to keep him warm.

4. You must call the police if there are any injuries, damage to a third party's property you cannot contact, or the road is blocked. If you think someone else involved in an accident is drunk or has otherwise broken the law (e.g. their vehicle is unroadworthy), you should call the police. The police normally breathalyse everyone involved in an accident as a matter of routine. Note that the police may refuse to attend an accident scene if nobody has been injured. Calling the police to the scene of an accident may result in someone being fined for a driving offence. In all cases you mustn't say anything which could be interpreted as an admission of guilt, even if you're as guilty as hell. Admitting responsibility for an accident, either verbally or in writing can release your insurance company from responsibility under your policy. In other words you must say nothing (not even 'sorry') or only that your insurance company will deal with any claims. Let the police and insurance companies decide who was at fault.

5. If either you or any other driver(s) involved decide to call the police, don't move your vehicle or allow other vehicles to be moved. If it's necessary to move vehicles to unblock the road, mark the positions of their wheels with chalk and measure the distance between vehicles. Take photographs of the accident scene if a camera is available (you can keep a throw-away camera in your car) or make a drawing showing the positions of all vehicles involved before moving them.

6. Check immediately whether there are any witnesses to the accident and take their names and addresses, particularly noting those who support *your* version of what happened. Write down the registration numbers of all vehicles involved (or possible witnesses) and their drivers' and owners' names, addresses and insurance details. Note also the identification numbers of any police present. You must (by law) give anyone with reasonable grounds for requiring them (e.g. the owner of damaged property) your name and insurance details, and the vehicle owner's name and address (if different).

7. If you're unable to give your insurance details to anyone with reasonable grounds for requiring them, you must report the accident in person to a police station within 24 hours. If you have caused material damage, you must inform the owner of the damaged property as soon as possible. If you cannot reach him, report the accident to a police station within 24 hours (this also applies to damage caused to other vehicles when parking). It's often advisable to report any accident involving another vehicle within 24 hours to avoid any repercussions later. If you have an accident involving a domestic animal (except a cat) and are unable to find the owner, it must also be reported to the police. This also applies to certain wild animals, e.g. deer. Make sure your visit is officially recorded by the police officer on duty and that you receive signed verification of your report.

8. If you're detained by the police, you aren't required to make a statement, even if they ask for one. If you do make a statement, don't sign it unless you're certain that you understand and agree with every word.

9. Lastly, you should report all accidents to your insurance company in writing as soon as possible, even if you don't plan to make a claim (but reserve your right to make a claim later). Your insurance company will ask you to complete an accident report form, which you should return as soon as possible (don't forget to sign it).

Many insurers will handle a claim for you, otherwise you will need to write to the other driver's insurance company yourself, giving details of your claim (but inform your insurance company). If your car is involved in an accident and the other driver isn't insured or cannot be traced, you may be able to claim from a compensation fund operated by the Motor Insurers' Bureau (MIB) and financed by insurance companies (☎ 01908-240000). The fund doesn't cover hit-and-run accidents where the driver cannot be traced. If successful you must pay the first £175 and each claim is limited to a maximum of £250,000 (for supercar owners). The Royal Society for the Prevention of Accidents (RoSPA), Cannon House, The Priory Queensway, Birmingham B4 6BS (☎ 0121-248 2000) and the Department of Transport publish various leaflets concerning car and motorcycle safety.

DRINKING & DRIVING

As you're no doubt well aware, drinking and driving make a dangerous cocktail. Around a tenth of all injury accidents (and over 500 deaths a year) result from driving with excess alcohol in the blood, and around 20 per cent of drivers and motorcyclists killed in accidents have alcohol levels above the legal limit. On Friday and Saturday nights between 2200 and 0400, around two-thirds of drivers and riders killed are over the legal alcohol limit. In Britain you're no longer considered fit to drive when your breath contains 35 micrograms of alcohol per 100ml or your blood contains 80mg of alcohol per 100ml (or 107mg per 100ml of urine).

For someone of average body weight, the recognised maximum they can drink and still remain under the limit is two pints of average strength beer or its equivalent. Anything more than two small beers or even a glass of wine may be too much for someone of slim build or someone unused to alcohol. Random breath tests aren't permitted in Britain. However, the police can stop any car at random under any pretext (e.g. to check that it isn't stolen) and ask the driver to take a breath test (particularly around Christmas and the New Year, when there's a crack-down on drunken driving). This involves simply blowing into a device which turns red if you fail the test. It's an offence to refuse to take a breath test, for which the penalty is the same as failing the test.

If you fail the breathalyser test, you're taken to a police station and be given a further test on a special analyser after around 20 minutes. If you're still over the limit, you have the right to request a blood or urine test, which may also be requested by the police. The police and most people choose blood tests. If a test wasn't requested by the police, you must pay a fee if you're found to be over the limit. Samples of blood or urine are put into separate containers, one of which is sealed and given to you for private analysis (should you so wish). Note that you can still be over the legal limit the morning after a heavy night's drinking and you can also be disqualified for driving while under the influence of drugs (cannabis smoked days before a test can show up in specimens and can result in a disqualification for driving while under the influence of drugs). You can also be convicted of being drunk in charge of a vehicle without actually driving it, which carries the same penalties as drunken driving.

If you're convicted of drunken driving you will lose your licence for a period (usually a minimum of six months), receive a heavy fine (maximum £5,000) and you can even be imprisoned for up to ten years if you cause an injury or death. Second offenders within a period of ten years are disqualified for three years. Drunken drivers must pay much higher insurance premiums after disqualification. Convicted drivers can take a hard-hitting course to get their licence back sooner (an idea borrowed from America). Courses last for 20 to 30 hours spread over five or six sessions and cost between £50 and £200. This results in reductions of up to 25 per cent in the period of disqualification and a discount of up to 40 per cent on the heavy insurance bills faced after a ban.

If you have an accident while under the influence of alcohol it could be expensive. Your car, accident and health insurance could all be nullified. This means you must pay your own (and any third party's) car repairs, medical expenses and other damages.

CAR THEFT

Over 500,000 cars are stolen each year in Britain (one every minute), which has the highest (per capita) number of stolen cars in Europe. Car crime is a huge and profitable business in Britain, costing £billions a year and representing around a third of all reported crime. It's estimated that some 70 per cent of stolen cars are broken up and sold for spares, while the rest are given a false identity and sold (many are exported to the Middle and Far East). One car in ten becomes a victim of 'autocrime' in England and Wales, and if you regularly park your car in a city street, you have a one in four chance of having it or its contents stolen. Having your car stolen means more than just taking a taxi home. It may mean weeks of delay sorting out insurance, extra time and expense travelling to work, possible loss of personal (maybe irreplaceable) possessions and loss of your insurance no-claims discount. It may also involve hiring a solicitor or going to court to re-claim your car after it has been sold by the thief (if a car is stolen and sold, it can be a nightmare getting it back).

If you drive a new or valuable car it's wise to have it fitted with an alarm, an engine immobiliser (preferably of the rolling code variety with a transponder arming key) or other anti-theft device, and to also use a visible deterrent such as a steering or gear change lock. This is particularly important if you own a car that's desirable to car thieves, which includes most new sports and executive cars, that are often stolen by professional crooks to order (although the most vulnerable cars are GTI hatchbacks which are often stolen and wrecked by joyriders – a British phenomenon). A reflection of the high rate of stolen cars in Britain is that it's standard practice for many new cars to be fitted with dead locks and sophisticated alarm systems (some cars such as the Jaguar XJ are, according to experts, virtually theft-proof). Professional thieves now steal cars by towing them or removing them on trailers rather than crack security devices. Needless to say, if you're driving anything other than a worthless wreck, you should have theft insurance (which includes your stereo and belongings).

Don't take unnecessary risks and always lock your car, engage your steering lock and completely close all windows (but don't leave pets in an unventilated car). Never leave you keys in the ignition, not even when filling up at a petrol station or in your driveway. Put any valuables (including clothes) in the boot or out of sight and don't leave your vehicle documents in the car or any form of identification. If possible avoid parking in commuter and long-term car parks (e.g. at airports and railway stations), which are favourite hunting grounds for car thieves. When parking overnight or when it's dark, park in a well-lit area, which helps deter car thieves.

Car theft has spawned a huge car security business in the (losing) battle to prevent or deter car thieves. These include a multitude of car alarms, engine immobilisers, steering and gear stick locks, personal wheel clamps, window etching with the car registration number, locking wheel nuts and petrol caps, and removable/coded stereo systems (a favourite target of thieves). A good security system won't prevent someone breaking into your car (which usually takes a professional a matter of seconds) or prevent it being stolen. What it will do is make it more difficult and may prompt a thief to look for an easier target. If you plan to buy an expensive stereo system, buy one with a removable unit or control panel/fascia (which you can pop in a pocket), but never forget to remove it, even when stopping for a few minutes (although thieves sometimes steal the back box, leaving you with a useless facia). Finally insure your car stereo for its full replacement value. One of the best deterrents may be to keep a pet cobra, tiger or fierce dog in your car. If all else fails, buy a Reliant three-wheeler, as no self-respecting crook would touch it! For complete peace of mind, particularly in London, you're better off using public transport.

The best security for a valuable car is a tracking device that's triggered by concealed motion detectors. The vehicle's movements are tracked by radio or satellite and the police are automatically notified and recover over 90 per cent of vehicles. Some systems can immobilise a vehicle while it's on the move (which might not be such a good idea!). Tracking systems include Securicor Trakbak (around £600 plus £150 installation and £120 annual membership) and Tracker

Network (note that some systems are more accurate than others). Many insurance companies offer a discount on comprehensive insurance (e.g. 20 per cent) when you have a tracking system fitted.

A lot of information is available on car security including *How to Buy a Car and Keep it* and *Keep Your Car Secure* published by Home Office Crime Prevention, Room 151, Queen Anne's Gate, London SW1H 9AT (☎ 0181-569 7000). If your car is stolen, report it to the police and your insurance company as soon as possible. Don't, however, expect the police to find it or even take any interest in your loss. Further information about car crime prevention can be obtained from your local police station or from the Home Office, PO Box 7000, Cirencester GL7 1RY (or ☎ 0171-273 4000).

PETROL

Two grades of petrol (or gas) are available in Britain: four star (97 or 98 octane and equivalent to continental super) and premium unleaded (95 octane). Super unleaded (98 octane) is also available at some petrol stations for high performance cars, although it's being phased out and may even be banned because of its higher benzene content. From 1st January 2000, 4-star leaded petrol will no longer be sold throughout the European Union. Some cars may need modification to run on unleaded fuel, which usually involves a simple adjustment to the ignition timing (although some may need hardened valve seats and the fuel pump and fuel-line seals changed).

Petrol is usually priced both in litres and gallons (despite decimalisation). The price varies considerably depending on local competition, the state of the world oil market (and whether war has broken out in the Middle East). In early 1999 the price was around 70p a litre for premium unleaded and 75p for super unleaded and 4-star leaded. After sharp tax increases in recent years, Britain now has among the most expensive petrol in Europe. Diesel fuel is available from around one-third of garages and costs around the same price as premium unleaded (and is around double the price on the continent).

The price of petrol varies little between the major oil companies, although small savings can be made by buying from supermarkets, which have around 20 per cent of the market. Shop around for the best buy as prices can vary. It's cheaper in England than other parts of Britain, although some towns with a lot of passing trade (e.g. Dover) are expensive. Prices must be displayed. As one observer commented, a sign of the increasing crime rate in Britain is that every time you stop for petrol you get mugged by a ruthless gang of criminals (the oil companies *and* the government). Many oil companies provide stamps or coupons which can be exchanged for gifts, although most motorists would prefer cheaper petrol. Over half of all motorists use unleaded petrol, although most cars could do so. Since October 1990, all new cars registered in Britain have been capable of running on unleaded fuel (in addition to leaded fuel, if applicable) and all new cars sold in Britain from 1993 have been fitted with catalytic converters. Most cars that aren't fitted with catalytic converters can run quite safely on unleaded petrol without any engine adjustments, and with the exception of high performance cars, it's unlikely to affect their performance.

If your car can run on unleaded fuel, it may be indicated by a label inside your petrol filler flap or be stated in your car's handbook. If in doubt ask a dealer, the British importer or your car's manufacturer (but get confirmation). **A car fitted with a catalytic converter must never be filled with leaded petrol.** To do so will damage the catalytic converter which is expensive to replace. To prevent errors, unleaded petrol pump pipes are coloured green and the nozzles of leaded petrol pumps in Britain are larger than those of unleaded pumps, and won't usually fit the petrol filler hole of a car fitted with a catalytic converter. Nevertheless, pay attention, particularly when a garage attendant is filling your car. Some unleaded pump nozzles are too large and won't fit the filler holes of cars fitted with catalytic converters, in which case you must use a funnel (or go to another garage). **Note that filling some cars, particularly high-performance cars, with unleaded petrol can damage the engine.**

The cleanest fuels of all are compressed natural gas (CNG) and liquefied petroleum gas (LPG). Most petrol engines can be converted to use both petrol and CNG/LPG (and can be switched between them). However, its availability is limited. For a list of outlets contact the LP Gas Association, Pavillion 16, Headlands Business Park, Salisbury Road, Ringwood, Hants. BH24 3PB (☎ 01425-461612).

Most petrol stations are open from 0800 to 2200 hours and on motorways they're usually open 24 hours. It's no problem finding a petrol station, as all towns usually have at least one. Signs on motorways indicate the distance to the next petrol station. When paying in self-service petrol stations, you simply tell the cashier your pump number (most pumps don't issue receipts). Outside normal business hours, some petrol stations have automatic pumps accepting £5 or £10 notes.

Note that most garages provide air (there may be a nominal charge of 10p or you may be given a token if you buy petrol), use of a car vacuum cleaner (fee around 10p) and a car wash (£2 to £6, depending on the type of wash chosen). Beware of car washes with wheels, which can be trapped under body parts and wreck them (e.g. spoilers). Most petrol stations also have a car wash and a shop selling a wide range of motoring accessories and other goods. In fact, the main business of many petrol stations isn't selling petrol, on which profit margins are minimal (except for the government!). Today's petrol stations are more like convenience stores and sell a wide range of confection, snacks, drinks (even beer, wine and spirits), pizzas, newspapers and magazines, and take in dry-cleaning (some even have cafés or their own bakery).

SPEED LIMITS

The following speed limits are in force for cars and motorcycles throughout Britain, unless traffic signs show otherwise:

Type of Road	Speed Limit
motorways and dual carriageways	70mph (113kph)
unrestricted single carriageway roads	60mph (97kph)
built-up areas (towns)	30mph (48kph)*
residential Roads	20mph (32kph) if signposted

* applies to all traffic on all roads with street lighting unless otherwise indicated by a sign.

Note that speed limits on British roads are marked in miles per hour not kilometres. When towing a caravan or trailer, speed limits on all roads (except those in built-up and residential areas) are reduced by 10mph (16kph). Cars towing caravans aren't permitted to use the outside (overtaking) lane of a three-lane motorway at any time. Speed limits for buses, coaches and goods vehicles not exceeding 7.5 tonnes are the same as when towing, except that the permitted speed limit on motorways is 70mph. Heavy goods vehicles (exceeding 7.5 tonnes) are permitted to travel at 40mph on single carriageways, 50mph on dual carriageways and 60mph on motorways.

You're forbidden to drive in the fast lane on motorways unless you're overtaking and you can be fined for doing so. Special speed limits on motorways are shown by illuminated signs and flashing lights, but aren't usually compulsory. You can be prosecuted for driving too slowly on a motorway. Mobile radar traps are regularly set-up around the country. If you're stopped by a following police vehicle, he must have followed you for at least three-tenths of a mile or be using a mobile radar device (e.g. a radar gun, which are in common use). The fitting and use of radar warning devices is illegal in Britain, although this doesn't prevent them being sold and widely used.

Roadside cameras are installed in many towns and residential areas, which may be indicated by a sign depicting a camera. They are also installed at traffic lights to detect motorists driving through red lights. However, only some 15 per cent of cameras are in operation at any time (due to the high cost of film) and many motorists take a chance on getting caught. New laser-guided, portable video cameras are being introduced capable of trapping three cars a second and working day and night (and they cannot be detected by radar warning devices). Over 250,000 motorists were prosecuted on the evidence of speed cameras in 1996.

There's a maximum fine of £400 for speeding, although the usual fine in a magistrates' court is around £50. Speeding fines usually depend on an offender's previous convictions and the speed above the limit. There's no consistency in the punishment meted out to speeding drivers and the size of the fine and the length of a ban often depends on your legal representation, your position and standing in the community, and the leniency or otherwise of the magistrate. Average fines vary from as low as £30 to over £150 in different parts of Britain. Fines for speeding vary from a fixed penalty of £40 for marginal speeding (e.g. up to 15mph above the limit), to £hundreds for speeding of 30mph or more above the limit, when you will almost certainly be prosecuted in court and may be disqualified from driving for a period.

If you're stopped for marginal speeding, you have the choice of paying a fixed penalty or going to court. If you go to court and lose, your fine is likely to be higher and you will also have to pay costs (so make sure you have a good case). Usually you're permitted to drive 10 per cent over the limit to allow for a speedometer error. So if you're clocked at 33mph in a 30mph zone, or 66mph in a 60mph zone, you won't usually be prosecuted for speeding. In addition to fines, driving licences are 'endorsed' for most motoring offences, using a points system. A fixed penalty for speeding carries three penalty points (see page 241).

Despite prosecutions and fines, speeding is common in Britain and many motorists have a complete disregard for speed limits, particularly on motorways, where speed limits are rarely enforced and a large number of people consistently drive over 100mph. It's estimated that two-thirds of drivers exceed urban speed limits and over 50 per cent of cars on motorways exceed 70mph. Needless to say, excessive speed is the major cause of accidents in Britain and is estimated to cause

1,000 deaths and over 75,000 injuries a year. A pedestrian is almost ten times more likely to die as a result of an impact from a car driven at 40mph than one driven at 20mph. However, many accidents are also caused by stationary and slow cars.

Note that in some areas (e.g. residential estates, private roads, school and university grounds, and car parks) there are speed humps, known as 'sleeping policemen', designed to slow traffic. They are sometimes indicated by warning signs and if you fail to slow down it's possible to damage your suspension or even turn your car over.

GARAGES & SERVICING

Garages in Britain are generally open from 0700 to 1830 and usually close for lunch between 1200 and 1300. Servicing and repairs at main dealers are expensive (particularly in major towns) and the cost of labour is usually around £30 to £40 an hour. Smaller garages are usually cheaper, although the quality of work is variable and it's best to choose one that has been personally recommended. Ask your friends and colleagues if they can recommend a garage close to your home or work place. However, if anything goes wrong (and it often does), you will have a better chance of redress with a main dealer or a garage that's a member of a trade association (such as the Retail Motor Industry Federation or the Scottish Motor Trade Association) or approved by a motoring organisation (see page 269).

Note that when a car is under warranty, it must usually be serviced by an approved dealer in order not to invalidate the warranty. The date or mileage at which services are due may be calculated from the previous service, and not according to the standard periods and mileage indicated in the service record. Check in advance. Most main dealers have 'set price' published fees for regular services and certain repairs. Many garages, including most main dealers, will provide a free replacement car while yours is being serviced, although you must book it in advance and arrange for comprehensive insurance. Some garages will collect your car from your home or office and deliver it after the service, or alternatively will drop you off at a station or local town and pick you up to collect your car.

Always obtain a number of quotations for major mechanical work or body repairs and tell the garage if an accident repair is to be paid for privately, as many will increase the price when an insurance company is paying. Quotations for accident repairs usually vary wildly and some garages will include the replacement of unnecessary parts. Always get a second opinion if you're quoted a high price for a repair, e.g. by simply ringing an approved dealer. High-tech systems are often replaced needlessly, often in ignorance rather than deliberately. Poor workmanship and overcharging by garages are the biggest concerns for motorists in Britain. Always instruct a garage what to do in writing and for anything other than a standard service, get a written estimate that includes labour, parts and VAT. Ask the garage to contact you (give them a phone number) and obtain approval before doing anything that isn't listed or if the cost is likely to exceed the original estimate. **Not that large official dealers in Britain typically charge around £50 an hour for servicing and you can usually save two-thirds or more by having your car serviced in Belgium or France (and enjoy a 'free' day out).**

If you need to buy spare parts, you can save 50 per cent or more by buying them from a specialist company advertising in the motoring press or in weekly magazines such as *Exchange & Mart*. Wherever you buy parts, beware of cheap supposedly branded parts, which can prove fatal (Britain is a prime target for counterfeiters as motorists often go for the cheapest parts). You should never buy secondhand tyres, many of which fail to meet legal standards and are liable to suffer blow-outs and cause serious accidents. Always make sure that your tyres are correctly inflated as they are the most crucial part of your car with regard to safety.

Check how a bill is to be paid and make sure there's no misunderstanding about the collection time and date. If the car isn't ready, the garage should supply you with a replacement car free of charge. Always obtain a bill listing all work completed, showing parts and labour costs. A garage must use reasonable care and skill when servicing your car. This includes car washes, and tyre and exhaust replacement companies, Department of Transport testers or anyone else who does work on your car. If your car is damaged in any way while it's in a garage's care, they are liable and a sign disclaiming liability isn't legal.

The motor trade business in Britain has a terrible (and generally well deserved) reputation, although admittedly only a relatively small percentage of garages are real rogues (which is no consolation if you fall victim to one of them). In checks carried out after servicing, many jobs are found not to have been done properly or indeed at all, and the percentage of complete and satisfactory services is often as low as 10 or 20 per cent. Probably every experienced motorist in Britain has had unsatisfactory service from a garage at some time or another. Women are particularly vulnerable to crooked garages and mechanics, who routinely charge women two-thirds more than men for the same work. Note that a garage is usually entitled to keep your car until you've paid the bill, even if the work was done badly, and you must pay the bill and try to obtain satisfaction afterwards.

Free legal advice can be obtained from a Consumer Advice Centre (CAC) or a Trading Standards (or Consumer Protection) Department. British motoring organisations operate a free legal advice service for members and if you have a major problem it may be worthwhile getting them to carry out an independent inspection of your car (see page 269). If a garage is a dealer, you can complain to the manufacturer or importer, although some manufacturers seem to prefer bad publicity rather than ensure that customers are satisfied. If the garage is a member of a trade association or is approved by the AA or RAC (see page 269), you can make a complaint to them.

Although you're covered by law against shoddy workmanship and overcharging, trying to obtain redress through the courts is a long and arduous business, with no guarantee of success. It's often not worth the time and effort unless the sum involved runs into hundreds or thousands of pounds. There's probably a higher percentage of 'dishonest people' in the car trade than in Parliament, which is certainly quite an achievement. Not surprisingly many motorists in Britain do their own servicing.

ROAD MAPS

Britain's roads are designated by letters that define the type of road, followed by a route number. Motorways (coloured blue on maps) have the prefix 'M' followed by a low number such as M1, M2, M3 or M25. Trunk roads link principal towns and cities, as well as taking in more remote parts of the country. They are coloured red on maps and have the prefix 'A', e.g. A1 or A2. The higher the number, the more minor the trunk road. Minor or secondary roads, many of which are prefixed with the letter 'B', link small towns and villages, and are coloured brown or yellow on maps. In Wales, town and route signs are in both English and Welsh. There are a vast number of road maps available in Britain, from local town maps to road atlases for the whole of the British Isles. The following road maps are among the best available:

- Geographers' A-Z Map Co. Ltd. produce an excellent range of street atlases, street plans, town maps, and road and county maps for all areas of Britain, many containing a comprehensive index of every street.

- The AA and RAC motoring organisations (see page 269) and the Ordnance Survey produce a variety of comprehensive maps of Britain, including the AA *Big Road Atlas Britain*. Other good LARGE scale maps (around 3mi/5km to the inch) are the *Ordnance Survey Motoring Atlas*, *Collins Road Atlas Britain* and *Philip's Motoring Atlas Britain*.

- Local town maps are often available from libraries and tourist information centres, including touring maps such as the AA county series of 'day drives'. Detailed town maps are usually available from local bookshops and newsagents.

- Good free maps are available from tourist information centres, libraries and car hire companies.

CAR HIRE

There are four multinational car hire (which is usually preferred to 'car rental') companies in Britain (Avis, Budget, Europcar and Hertz), plus a number of large independents, e.g. British Car Rental, Godfrey Davis, Kenning Car Rental, Practical and Swan National. All have offices in towns throughout the country and at most major international airports (open from around 0630 to 2300). Most major companies provide one-way hire, which means you can hire a car at one branch and leave it at another (for an extra charge). When hiring from a national company, check whether you're being quoted the national or local rate (which is cheaper). The national rate is usually charged when hiring in major cities or at airports and should be avoided unless someone else is paying. Always check what's included in the rental charge as what appears to be an expensive quote could turn out to be the cheapest.

Cars can also be rented from many garages and local car hire offices in most towns, which often charge much lower rates than the nationals. Look in local newspapers and under 'Car rentals' in the Yellow Pages. Shop around for the best buy, as the car hire business is extremely competitive. However, you should beware of cowboy hire companies who offer 'hire cars from hell'. Many cars offered by local companies, particularly in tourist areas, are unroadworthy and could put your life at risk. Be particularly careful if hiring an older car (cars from major hire companies aren't more than three years old and are usually less than one year old) as it could be in a dangerous condition. If you're offered an old car or a car with high mileage, it's probably wise to reject it (unless the company is in the business of renting cheap wrecks). If you hire a car in an unroadworthy condition, you're responsible if you're stopped by the police or cause an accident.

All national hire companies offer fly-drive deals on flights to or within Britain, which must be booked in advance. You can also hire a car from major railway stations and leave it at another station or delivery point. Providing you book 24-hours in advance, a car can be waiting to meet you at the station at any time of day or night. Cars can also be hired on the spot from some stations from Hertz and other hire companies. Note that Hertz (and other companies) charge their highest rate for fly-drive and executive connection services. Special rates are available when combined with British Rail InterCity weekend or longer trips. Rental costs vary considerably between rental companies, particularly over longer periods (weekly and monthly rates are lower). Rates are inclusive of unlimited mileage, collision damage waiver insurance, personal accident, baggage insurance and VAT. Rental cars usually mustn't be driven outside Britain unless prior arrangement is made with the rental company and continental insurance (a green card) obtained.

Rental cars from national companies can often be ordered with a portable phone, child restraints or a roof rack, for which some companies charge a fee. All rental cars from national companies are covered for roadside breakdown assistance from a British motoring organisation (see page 269). You can also hire a 4-wheel-drive car, estate, minibus, prestige luxury car or a sports car, and a choice of manual or automatic gearbox is often available. Minibuses are also for hire (e.g. from Hertz) and are accessible to wheelchairs. Performance cars can be hired from a number of specialist hire companies, although if you want to test drive a car for a few days with a view to buying one, you may get a better deal from a garage. Some companies also hire cars with hand controls for registered disabled drivers.

To hire a car in Britain you require a full British, European or international driving licence, which must have been held for a minimum of one year (or two years if aged under 23). If you hold a British licence with an endorsement for driving without due care and attention (or worse), you may be refused car hire, although an endorsement for speeding is usually permitted. You may be asked for some form of identification in addition to your driving licence. The minimum age is usually between 18 and 23, although those aged 18 to 21 must normally provide their own fully comprehensive insurance or purchase collision damage waiver (CDW) insurance at a special (high) rate. Drivers aged under 21 are usually restricted in their choice of cars and some hire companies insist on a higher minimum age (e.g. 25) for some categories of cars.

You must usually be aged 23 to 25 to hire a minibus or motor caravan (the maximum age for hiring a car may be 70 or 75). A minimum deposit of £50 to £75 (or equal to the total hire charge) is usually required if you don't pay by credit card (national car rental companies also have their own credit cards) and may be much higher if you don't take out CDW insurance. Cheques must be supported by a guarantee card. When paying by credit card, check that you aren't charged for erroneous extras or for something for which you've already paid, e.g. petrol. In fact paying by credit card usually means that you give the hire company a 'continuous authority' (or blank cheque) to debit your card account.

Note that cars can be rented in Britain through major international rental companies such as Alamo (00-1-800-327-9633), Avis (00-1-800-331-1212), Budget (00-1-800-527-0700) and Hertz (00-1-800-654-3131) by booking a car through their American offices and paying by credit card. This is a legitimate practice and can save 50 per cent or more on local hire rates. At present the car hire companies have no way of knowing where the calls were made and therefore cannot prevent this practice. Freefone (800) numbers of other US-based rental companies can be obtained from international directory enquiries, although you pay international rates when phoning from abroad.

Vans and pick-ups are available from major rental companies by the hour, half-day or day, or from smaller local companies (which once again, are cheaper). You can also hire a motor caravan, a caravan or trailer, or a minibus, from a number of companies (prices vary with the season). In addition to self-drive car hire, in many cities you can hire a car with a chauffeur for business or sightseeing. The British Tourist Authority publish an annual *Vehicle Hire* directory.

MOTORING ORGANISATIONS

There are five national motoring organisations in Britain: the Automobile Association (AA – ☎ freefone 0800-444999), Britannia Rescue (☎ freefone 0800-591563), Green Flag National Breakdown (☎ freefone 0800-001313), Mondial Assistance (☎ 0181-666 9520) and the Royal Automobile Club (RAC – freefone 0800-770099). By far the largest organisation is the AA, followed by the RAC and Green Flag. All organisations offer continental cover as an option and a sixth company, Europ Assistance (☎ 01444-411999), offers continental cover only. Other companies also offer breakdown cover through contractors. There are few essential differences between the services provided by British motoring organisations, although membership costs vary. Free gifts and discounts are usually offered to new members.

All organisations offer a range of membership levels (e.g. individual, couple and family) and different levels of service which may include roadside assistance, relay (get you home), 72-hour European breakdown cover, home start and relay plus (which provides a free replacement car for up to 48 hours). Some organisations cover the car (for any driver), while others cover the driver (in any car). Organisations charge from around £40 a year for recovery only, up to around £150 for their premium service that includes European recovery. Direct Line Rescue (☎ 0181-760 9933) recently introduced a new roadside-rescue service (using a network of 1,500 contractors), which undercuts the rates charged by motoring organisations, and some insurance companies offer membership of a motoring organisation for a low fee, e.g. £20 a year. Most organisations offer inducements to new members such as free mobile phones, free or reduced cost MOT tests, free safety checks and 50 per cent off windscreen replacements.

All motoring organisations waive the enrolment fee (if applicable) or give a discount when you pay by direct debit (from a current account) or continuous payment via a credit card. Associate membership is usually available and applies to your spouse (or partner) and dependent children under the age of 25 up to a maximum of three people. Some organisations provide personal cover for an extra charge, so that you and your spouse can drive any car. Most organisations charge an extra fee for older cars (e.g. those over seven or ten years old). Note that if you use the breakdown service a large number of times (e.g. ten) during a year, you may find that your premium is increased dramatically or you're expelled from the organisation (they prefer members who never use their services).

Although a relative newcomer compared with the AA and RAC, Green Flag National Breakdown deserves a special mention and is highly rated for its customer care, not just against other motoring organisations but against allcomers. It guarantees that all customers will be seen within one hour of reporting a problem (an average 35-minute wait is claimed) and pays a £10 penalty if it fails. Green Flag offer a continental European service for an additional £16.

Members of British motoring organisations who break down anywhere in Britain can call their organisation by phoning a 24-hour service telephone number for assistance. Keep your membership card in your car and quote your membership number when calling for help. Most organisations have reciprocal arrangements with motoring organisations in other European countries. Non-members can also get assistance, but it can be expensive (although you may be able to join on the spot and save the fee). Emergency SOS roadside telephones are provided on motorways, connected to police control rooms. Beware of having your car repaired after it's towed away by a garage 'approved' by a motoring organisation, as some are crooks and charge an arm and a leg for repairs. **Always get a quotation first and make sure it's competitive.**

Some motoring organisations will carry out an independent inspection of a car, for example prior to buying a secondhand car. It usually takes around a week to arrange an inspection, which can be carried out at your home or office. The fee depends on the organisation and the make and model of car.

PARKING

Parking in most British cities and towns is often a problem, particularly on Saturdays when everyone's doing their shopping. On-street parking is a particular problem and most roads without parking meters or bays have restricted or prohibited parking (except the M25 motorway, which is the biggest free car park in the world). Despite the fact that the average car spends 95 per cent of its life parked, half the cars in a city centre during peak hours are looking for a parking space (fascinating these statistics). In residential areas, most homes either have limited or no off-road parking, which means that when driving in residential areas you must usually weave in and out of parked cars, which often entirely block one side of the road. British companies don't usually provide employees (except directors) with parking facilities in large cities and towns, so check in advance whether parking is available at your workplace (if it isn't, it could be *very* expensive). Outside cities and towns, parking is usually available at offices and factories.

Parking Restrictions: On-road parking (waiting) restrictions in Britain are indicated by yellow lines at the edge of roads, usually accompanied by a sign indicating when parking is prohibited, e.g. 'Mon-Sat 8am-6.30pm' or 'At any time'. If no days are indicated on the sign, restrictions are in force every day including public holidays and Sundays. Yellow signs indicate a continuous waiting prohibition and also detail times when parking is illegal. Blue signs indicate limited waiting periods. Yellow lines give a guide to the restrictions in force, but the signs must always be consulted. The following road markings are in use in most towns:

Road Marking	Prohibitions
white zig-zag line or studded areas	no parking or stopping at any time (often located next to a zebra crossing)
double yellow lines	no parking most or at all times (it may be possible to park on double yellow lines during some periods, but if in doubt don't)
single yellow line	no parking for at least eight hours between 0700 and 1900 on four or more days of the week
broken yellow line	restricted parking shown by a sign

Double red lines indicate a red route, which came into operation in London in 1991 to speed up traffic. On red line routes you aren't permitted to stop between the hours of 0800 and 1900 (or as indicated by a sign) Mondays to Fridays, except for loading. Special parking bays are marked in red, where parking is strictly limited, e.g. for loading or delivering between 1000 and 1600 only. If you park illegally on a red route, your car will be towed away in double quick time.

Loading restrictions for loading and unloading goods are shown by one, two or three short yellow lines marked diagonally on the kerb and a sign. For more information consult *The Highway Code* (see page 253). In most towns there are public and private off-road car parks, indicated by a sign showing a white 'P' on a blue background. Parking in local authority car parks usually costs from around 20p for a half-hour or hour. Parking in short-term car parks may become progressively more expensive the longer you stay and can cost as much as £5 for over five hours parking. However, parking is generally cheaper (per hour) the longer you park, up to a maximum of around nine hours. It's often cheaper to drive to a convenient British Rail (BR) station, where parking costs from £1 to £3 a day and take a train into town. Weekly, monthly and annual season tickets are usually available at railway and London Underground stations and some private car parks.

Parking in public car parks and at meters may be free on Sundays and public holidays (check the notice *before* buying a ticket). In many areas there are 'park and ride' parking areas, where parking and/or public transport into the local town or city may be free (particularly at Christmas time). Some supermarkets without their own car parks offer parking refunds to customers. Many councils produce car park maps showing all local parking areas, which are available free from council offices, libraries and tourist information centres. Temporary car parks are provided in the weeks before Christmas in many towns and cities. When parking in any official parking area, ensure that you're parked within a marked bay, otherwise you can receive a parking ticket.

Multi-Storey Car Parks: The method of payment in multi-storey car parks varies. On entering most private car parks you collect a ticket from an automatic dispenser (you may need to press a button) and pay either *before* collecting your car (at a cash desk or in a machine, which may accept both coins and banknotes), or in an automatic machine at the exit (keep some coins handy). Some machines don't issue you with a ticket with which to exit the car park, and after paying you must exchange your ticket at a special kiosk for yet another ticket. If you've already paid, you insert your ticket in the slot of the exit machine (in the direction shown by the arrow on the ticket).

Other multi-storey car parks (usually operated by local councils) are pay-and-display (see below), where you must decide in advance how many hours parking you require and buy a ticket from a machine for this period. If you park in a multi-storey car park, make a note of the level and space number where you park your car (it can take a long time to find your car if you have no idea where to start looking). Note that speed humps are common in multi-storey car parks. Many private car parks offer season tickets, e.g. NCP. **Note that British car parks, particularly multi-storey car parks, are designed for toy cars and have tiny parking bays where cars must be parked at right angles – why cannot we learn from the Americans and park our cars at an angle?**

Apart from multi-storey car parks and on-street parking, the following parking is provided in most towns:

Parking meters: Where the maximum permitted parking period varies from 30 minutes to two hours. Meter-feeding is illegal. You must vacate the parking space when the meter time expires, even if it was under the maximum time allowed, and you may not move to another meter in the same group. Meters normally accept a combination of 5p to 20p coins, and are usually in use from 0700 to 1900, Mondays to Fridays, and from 0700 to 1800 on Saturdays (check meters to be certain). Meters at railway stations and airports may be in use 24-hours a day. Don't park at meters which are suspended as you can be towed away. If you remain at a meter beyond the excess charge period, you will be liable for a fixed penalty (which is usually £20) handed out by a police officer or the infamous, much reviled, traffic warden (high on every motorist's hate list). Parking meters are being phased out (hurrah!) and replaced by pay-and-display parking areas (boo!).

Pay-and-Display: Parking areas where you must buy a parking ticket from a machine and display it behind your windscreen. It may have an adhesive backing which you can peel off and use to stick the ticket the inside of your windscreen or a car window. Parking costs 20p or 30p an hour in most towns and machines usually accept all coins from 5p to £1. When you have inserted sufficient coins for the period required, press the button to receive your ticket. Pay-and-Display parking areas usually operate from 0700 to 1900, excluding Sundays and public holidays. A new pre-paid parking scheme (called Easypark) is in operation in some towns. Motorists buy a card costing from £3 to £125 (gold card), which is used to pay for parking in special machines (a bit like using a phone card). Cards are sold at post offices, shops, garages and council offices. In some towns a 'scratch and display' parking scheme has been introduced, where motorists buy vouchers and scratch off panels to show the month, day, date and time of arrival (and display the voucher in their window).

Parking Fines: The fine for illegal parking depends on where you park. There's usually a fixed penalty ticket of £20 for parking illegally on a yellow line. Parking in a dangerous position or on the zig-zag lines near a pedestrian crossing results in a higher fine, e.g. a £40 fixed penalty and three points on your driving licence (see page 241). Penalties for non-payment or overstaying your time in a permitted parking area (e.g. at a parking meter or in a Pay-and-Display area) are set by local authorities, when you will receive a yellow ticket.

In some cities you shouldn't even *think* about parking illegally on a yellow line, as your car will be towed away in the blink of an eye. You must then pay an £80 or

£100 towing fee and a fixed penalty. A car pound won't release your car until you've paid and will accept only cash or a guaranteed cheque. All car pounds charge a daily storage fee after the first 24 hours of around £10 a day. You cannot be towed away from a pay-and-display area or a parking meter (unless the parking bay is suspended).

Illegal parking is a serious problem in central London and this has led some boroughs to employ private contractors to control parking. In London and other major cities, parking permits are issued to local residents allowing them to park in reserved 'residents only' spaces. If you park there without a permit you will get a ticket. Some three million parking tickets are issued each year in London. If a car is parked in a dangerous position or is causing an obstruction, it can be removed and impounded by the police. This will result in a fee of around £80 to get it released plus a fixed penalty fine.

Clamping: In central London (and an increasing number of other cities and towns) illegal parking can result in your car being 'clamped', where a large metal device (a clamp) is clamped onto one of the wheels of your car, thus preventing you driving it away. Over 3,000 cars are clamped a week in London alone and 2,000 are towed away. To free your car from this heinous (but very effective) device, you must go to the clamping station listed on your ticket, pay an unclamping fee plus a fixed penalty fine, and return to your vehicle and await the truck to come and unclamp your car (which usually takes around four hours). If you don't remove your car within a certain period, you can be clamped a second time. In one case in London a woman's car was seized by bailiffs and sold at auction to pay a £30 fine while she was on holiday. Of the auction proceeds of £3,500 (£1,500 below its market value) she eventually received £1,700. There's a new Parking Appeals Service in London (PO Box 3333, London SW1Y, ☎ 0171-747 4700).

Cars parked at meters aren't usually clamped unless the parking bay is suspended, the meter was 'fed' with coins, or the car has stayed two hours beyond the period paid. Note also that owners of private car parks or private land can also clamp a car parked illegally and can set their own charge to remove clamps (e.g. £100 or more). It's inadvisable to park on private land, particularly where there's a 'clamping' sign, as illegal clamping is widespread throughout Britain. Many 'cowboy' clamping companies clamp and tow away cars that are legally parked and charge up to £250 a time (clampers often take money, jewellery or even clothing from victims to pay 'fines'). You will be pleased to hear that most clampers and towers enjoy their work despite the universal abuse they attract!

Whether parking restrictions exist or not, when parking on a road be careful where you park as you can be prosecuted for parking in a dangerous position and could also cause an accident. If your parked car contributes to an accident you may also have to pay damages. Take care in car parks, as accidents often occur there and may not be covered by your car insurance. Parking on pedestrian footpaths is illegal everywhere. Note that parking in towns with your hazard warning lights on makes no difference if you're parked illegally. Wherever you drive in Britain, keep a plentiful supply of coins handy for parking and pay-and-display meters.

12.
HEALTH

Britain is renowned for its National Health Service (NHS), which provides health care to all British citizens and most foreign residents. The standard of training, dedication and medical skills of British doctors and nursing staff is among the highest in the world, and British medical science is in the vanguard of many of the world's major medical advances (many pioneering operations are performed in Britain). Emergency medical services in Britain are generally excellent. Many foreigners visit Britain each year for private medical treatment and Harley Street (London) is internationally recognised as having some of the world's pre-eminent (and most expensive) specialists, encompassing every conceivable ailment. However, Britain spends only around 7 per cent of its GDP on healthcare compared with almost 10 per cent in France and Germany and over 14 per cent in the USA.

The infant mortality rate in Britain is around 6 per 1,000 births (an all-time low), while the average life expectancy is around 74 for men and 79 for women. The main causes of death are circulatory diseases (including heart attacks and strokes) and cancer. Nearly half of all British men and more than a quarter of the women who die between the ages of 45 and 55, do so as a result of heart and circulatory disease, in which Britain is a world leader. However, the total number of smokers is reducing, although it remains the greatest preventable cause of illness and death in Britain, and is responsible for over 100,000 deaths and 30 million lost working days each year. Around 30 per cent of Britons smoke, including many more women (particularly young women) than men.

Alcohol abuse is an increasing problem, although drunkenness (lager louts) is more of a social problem than a serious health problem (unlike alcoholism). According to the Mental Health Foundation, around six million people in Britain (one in ten) suffer from mental illness (including most politicians!). Stress is an increasing problem and an estimated 250 million working hours are lost annually due to stress-related absences (more people are also turning to anti-depressants to cope with life.

As you have probably already realised, the British aren't exactly the healthiest of people, a fact largely contributed to their fatty diet and generally bad eating habits, followed closely by excess alcohol, smoking and general sloth (armchair sport is much more popular than working up a sweat). Some doctors even prescribe exercise classes on the NHS for those who are overweight. The NHS organises a number of health education schemes, including campaigns to promote the dangers of heart disease, smoking, drugs and Aids. However, preventive medicine has a low priority in Britain.

Air pollution caused by sunshine and high temperatures (they do occur occasionally in Britain) is an increasing concern in Britain, not just in the cities but in rural areas, where asthmatics, bronchitis sufferers and the elderly are particularly at risk. Levels of air pollution are already well above safe health limits on hot days and in cities signs of asthma are found in some 20 per cent of children. Hay fever sufferers can obtain the daily pollen count between March and July from weather broadcasts and daily newspapers. Noise pollution is also a problem in Britain, where many people's lives are ruined by noisy neighbours (incessant noise causes chronic illnesses and drives people to commit murder and suicide). Britain has a high incidence of skin cancer due to over-exposure to the sun and the maximum exposure time for the fair-skinned is now included in TV weather forecasts on hot days.

Private clinics are common in Britain and do a profitable business in abortions and cosmetic surgery (among other things), a field in which Britain has considerable expertise (although if the number of ugly millionaires is any indication, plastic surgeons are unable to perform miracles). If your nose, ears or derrière are too big, or you would love to fill a full C cup, just nip down to your local specialist who will tuck those unwated bits out of sight (or make others more prominent) as fast as you can say £2,000. Britain also has many private health farms, where inmates pay a queen's ransom for the privilege of being locked away from temptation (e.g. alcohol, cream cakes, chocolate and sweets) for a week or two.

Residential and nursing homes are also an important part of the private health sector (although not all are private). Long-term health care is an increasing problem in Britain, where many people are forced to pay for the cost of a nursing home with their savings and homes. Local councils can no longer afford to provide free care for those who need it and the elderly may be evicted from residential care because social security payments are failing to keep up with the increasing fees. Local authority social services and voluntary organisations provide invaluable help and advice to the most vulnerable members of the community, including the elderly, disabled and children in need of care.

Health Information: For a quick and confidential answer to health problems, you could try calling one of the many helplines that have sprung up in recent years that provide recorded information on a wide variety of topics. These include the Self Helpline (☎ 0898-777444), Healthcall (☎ 0898-600600) and Healthline (☎ freefone 0800-252100). Helpline calls are charged at expensive premium telephone rates (see page 141). There are also many Internet sites where medical advice is available (one of the best British sites is healthworks.co.uk). Note that recorded information, although approved by medical experts, should never be used as a substitute for consulting your family doctor and Internet 'doctors' and medical advice must be used with extreme caution.

The Medical Advisory Service (☎ 0181-995 4448) provides a free telephone helpline from 1800 to 2200 for men (there's generally less information available to men, who are often ignorant of health matters). 'Do-it-yourself' doctors may also be interested in the British Medical Association (BMA) *Complete Family Health Encyclopaedia* (Dorling Kindersley), a comprehensive family medical book, which although expensive at around £25 (but cheaper than phoning premium telephone numbers), is highly recommended. Other useful books include *Which? Medicine, Women's Health* and *Men's Health*, all published by Which? Books, who also publish a monthly magazine, *Which? Way to Health* (see **Consumers' Associations** on page 437). The College of Health publishes a *Consumers' Guide to Health* and the Health Education Authority (Trevelyn House, 30 Great Peter Street, London SW1P 2HW, ☎ 0171-222 5300) publishes information on a wide range of health topics (a catalogue is available), many of which are available free from chemists, clinics and doctors' surgeries.

Finally, if you have any spare body parts you can no longer use, e.g. after your death, you can carry a Donor Card, available from chemists, libraries, doctors' surgeries and supermarkets. A move is afoot to reverse the current situation so that you will need to carry a card if you *don't* want to donate your organs. If the thought of donating your organs is more than you're prepared to contemplate, perhaps you're willing to donate a pint of blood twice a year. If you're over 18 and under 60 and in good health, the National Blood Service would like to hear from you (☎ 0345-711711 for information).

You can safely drink the water in Britain but wine tastes much better (and in moderation, it even does you good!).

EMERGENCIES

The action to take in a medical 'emergency' depends on the degree of urgency. If you're unsure who to call, ask the telephone operator (100) or call your local police station. They will tell you who to contact or even call the appropriate service for you. Whoever you call, always give the age of the patient and if possible specify the type of emergency. **Keep a record of the telephone numbers of your doctor, local hospitals and clinics, ambulance service, first aid, poison control, dentist and other emergency services next to your telephone.**

• In minor emergencies or for medical advice, you should phone your family doctor if you have one. Failing this you can ask the operator (100) for the telephone number of a local doctor or hospital (or consult your phone book). Some hospitals have minor injuries units, emergency units, and accident and emergency department (it's advisable to check where they are in advance and the quickest route from your home). Police stations keep a list of doctors' and chemists' private telephone numbers, in case of emergency. In some cities and regions there are private, 24-hour, doctor services making house calls, but check the cost before using them.

• Call 999 for an ambulance without a doctor in **an emergency only**. Most ambulances are equipped with cardiac, oxygen and other emergency equipment. Note that health authorities can make a charge when an ambulance is called to an emergency, although this is unlikely. The cost of a private ambulance is usually covered by a private health insurance policy. Britain doesn't have a national air ambulance service, although there are emergency helicopter services in some cities (e.g. London) and the Royal Air Force operates a rescue service in remote inland and coastal areas.

• If you're physically able, you can go to the Accident, Casualty or Emergency department of an NHS general hospital, many of which provide a 24-hour service. Check in advance which local hospitals are equipped to deal with emergencies and the quickest route from your home. This information may be of vital importance in the event of an emergency, when a delay could mean the difference between life and death. Emergency cases, irrespective of nationality and ability to pay, are *never* turned away in Britain and treatment is free for everybody (including visitors), except when hospitalisation for longer than one night is necessary (if you're a national of a country with a reciprocal health agreement with Britain treatment is free). In some cities, e.g. London, there are private walk-in clinics open around 12 hours a day, providing emergency treatment for medical and dental accidents and minor ailments.

• If you have a dental problem, phone your own dentist, or of it's out of normal surgery hours, phone your own or another dentist providing an emergency service (listed in Yellow Pages). Some dental and general hospitals provide a free emergency service. Note that a dentist isn't obliged to treat anyone, even in an emergency.

If you have a rare blood group or a medical problem which cannot easily be seen or recognised, e.g. a heart condition, diabetes, a severe allergy or epilepsy, you may be interested in **Medic-Alert**. Medic-Alert members wear an emblem on their wrists or around their necks that's internationally recognised. On the back of your emblem is engraved your medical problem, membership number and a telephone number. When you're unable to speak for yourself, doctors, police or anyone providing aid, can obtain immediate vital medical information from anywhere in the world by phoning a 24-hour emergency number. Medic-Alert is a non-profit registered charity and life membership is included in the cost of the bracelet or necklace plus an annual fee. For more information contact the Medic-Alert Foundation, 1 Bridge Wharf, 156 Caledonian Road, London N1 9UU (☎ 0171-833 3034).

NATIONAL HEALTH SERVICE (NHS)

The pride of the British welfare system is (or was) the National Health Service (NHS), established in 1948 to ensure that everyone had equal access to medical care. The NHS includes services provided by family doctors, specialists, hospitals, dentists, chemists, opticians, community health services (e.g. the district nursing and health visitor services), the ambulance service, and maternity and child health care. Originally all NHS medical treatment was free, the service being funded entirely from general taxation and National Insurance contributions.

However, as the cost of treatment and medicines have increased, part of the cost has been passed onto patients via supplementary charges. While hospital treatment, the ambulance service and consultations with doctors remain free, many patients must now pay fixed charges for prescriptions, dental treatment, sight tests and NHS glasses, although charges are usually well below the actual cost. Family doctors, called General Practitioners (GPs), still make free house calls and community health workers and district nurses visit people at home who are convalescent, bedridden or have new-born babies.

The NHS is run by Regional Health Authorities, District Health Authorities (corresponding approximately to local authority boundaries), Family Practitioner Committees and Special Health Authorities. If you want to find the name of your District Health Authority, inquire at your local library or ask a doctor's receptionist. Often health service boundaries aren't the same as the local council area, so looking in your phone book may not help. For information about how to register with an NHS family doctor (GP), see **Doctors** on page 282. The quality of service you receive from the NHS depends very much on where you live, as waiting lists for specialist appointments and hospital beds vary from area to area. Patients of fundholding GPs (see page 283) often have shorter waits, as GPs can shop around for the shortest queues.

The NHS provides free or subsidised medical treatment to all British Subjects and foreigners with the right of abode in Britain and to anyone who, at the time of treatment, has been a resident for the previous year. Exceptions to the one-year qualifying rule include EU nationals; refugees or those with 'exceptional leave to remain' in Britain; students on a course of over six months; foreign nationals coming to take up permanent residence in Britain; certain groups of sailors or off-shore workers; non-EU recipients of British war disablement pensions; overseas crown servants; British pensioners living abroad; NATO personnel stationed in Britain;

prisoners; anyone with a permit to work in Britain; and the spouse and children of the above.

Nationals of countries with reciprocal health agreements with Britain also receive free or subsidised medical treatment, including EU nationals and citizens of Anguilla, Australia, Austria, Barbados, British Virgin Islands, Bulgaria, Channel Islands, Czech Republic, Falkland Islands, Gibraltar, Hong Kong, Hungary, Iceland, Isle of Man, Malta, Montserrat, New Zealand, Norway, Poland, Romania, Russia, Slovak Republic, St. Helena, Turks and Caicos Islands, and states comprising the former Yugoslavia. Exemption from charges for nationals of the above countries is generally limited to emergency or urgent treatment (e.g. for a communicable disease) required during a visit to Britain.

Anyone who doesn't qualify under one of the above categories, must pay for all medical treatment received, although minor medical and dental emergencies may be treated free of charge, e.g. emergency treatment at a hospital 'out patients' department as a result of an accident (or patients admitted to hospital for no longer than one night). **If you aren't covered by the NHS, you should take out private health insurance** (see page 315), **as medical treatment in Britain can be very expensive with the cost of an operation and hospitalisation running into £thousands.**

The NHS Today

In the last few decades there have been sweeping NHS reforms which have included self-governing hospitals, practise and prescribing budgets for GPs, funding and contracts for hospital services, and the creation of an NHS internal market. The NHS has traditionally been a political football and some of these reforms are now being reversed by the current Labour government. The services provided by the NHS have come under increasing pressure in recent years, largely as a result of a lack of funding by central government and the increasing demands on the NHS from an ageing population.

One of the most serious problems facing the NHS is the chronic shortage of staff, particularly nurses (especially specialist trained nurses), midwives and health visitors who have been leaving the NHS at a rate of up to 50,000 a year. The main problems is low salaries (one in five nurses is forced to take a second job to survive), although poor working conditions, a lack of resources and stress also take their toll. Ironically the NHS is forced to make up the shortfall of nurses by using agency staff at a cost of over £200 million a year. A lack of doctors has meant that many hospitals and deputising services are forced to recruit an increasing number of doctors from abroad. Foreign doctors have flooded into Britain in recent years (5,500 were registered in 1997 – one-third more than the number trained in Britain), most from EU countries. Britain doesn't train sufficient doctors but also loses a lot of doctors who become disillusioned with the NHS to other countries. One-fifth of all GPs practising in Britain are from overseas, some of whom speak poor English or lack sufficient experience. The bulk of supply doctors (who fill shortages, e.g. when doctors are on holiday) are also foreign.

Lack of funds have resulted in hospital ward closures, long waiting lists for specialist appointments and hospital beds (patients are often left on trolleys in hospital corridors because no beds are available), cancelled operations, and long queues in doctors' surgeries and hospital waiting rooms. Although funding has been increasing (in real terms) for a number of years, demand is rising at an ever faster rate. Lack of resources have meant that NHS health services are having to be rationed and decided on the basis of a patient's chances of recovery or life expectancy. This means that pensioners, heavy smokers, alcoholics and those who are dangerously overweight have little chance of receiving expensive operations, such as heart surgery and transplants on the NHS. Lack of hospital resources have led to increasing waiting lists for all non-emergency operations such as hernias, gallstones, varicose veins, cataracts and replacement hips. The number of people on NHS surgery waiting lists was over 1,000,000 in 1999.

The present government is attempting to address the NHS problems by injecting extra funds and resources, although it will take many years to resolve the problems of under-staffing and eradicate the waiting lists (if it's possible). Another problem that need addressing is how to tackle the long-term needs of an ageing population. Many people believe that more resources should be channelled into preventive medicine rather than cure, in particular the promotion of regular exercise and a healthy diet.

PRIVATE HEALTH TREATMENT

Private health treatment functions both within the NHS and independently of it. Private patients can choose to pay for treatment in most NHS hospitals and all NHS consultants are permitted to treat private patients in addition to their NHS patients (some have been accused of neglecting their NHS patients for lucrative private work). In addition to specialist appointments and hospital treatment, people commonly use private health treatment to obtain second opinions, private health checks or screening and for complementary medicine. Over six million people have private health insurance of some kind in Britain and around 25 per cent of all operations are performed privately. If you need to see a GP or specialist privately, you (or your insurance company) must pay the full fee, which is usually left to the doctor's discretion. You should expect to pay around £30 or more for a routine visit to a GP.

Most patients who receive private health treatment in Britain are insured with provident associations such as BUPA and PPP, which pay for specialist and hospital treatment only, and don't include routine visits to doctors and dentists (which are covered by the NHS). The overriding reason most people have private health insurance in Britain is to circumvent the interminable NHS waiting lists for non-emergency specialist appointments and hospital treatment. Private patients are free to choose their own specialist and hospital, and are usually accommodated in a private, hotel-style room with a radio, telephone, colour TV, en suite bathroom and room service. Private health insurance is often paid by employers.

Although some health checks and scans are available on demand under the NHS or with private health insurance, many aren't (including the most expensive). They don't include a comprehensive health check-up or health screening, which can be performed at private clinics throughout Britain, costing from around £200 to £300. Complementary (or alternative) medicine is popular in Britain and is chosen by some five million patients a year, although with the exception of certain fields such as acupuncture, chiropractic, homeopathy and osteopathy, it isn't usually covered by the NHS or private health insurance in Britain.

Always make sure that a 'doctor' or medical practitioner is qualified to provide the treatment you require, as (surprisingly) anyone can call himself a doctor in

Britain. When selecting a private specialist or clinic, you should be extremely cautious and only choose someone who has been recommended by a doctor or clinic you can trust. It's sometimes advisable to obtain a second opinion, particularly if you're diagnosed as having a serious illness or require a major operation (but don't expect your doctor or specialist to approve). According to some reports, unnecessary operations are becoming increasingly common in Britain. Private patients don't have the same protection as NHS patients, although complaints about treatment that's paid for by a private health insurance policy may be taken up by your insurance company. As a last resort you can complain to the General Medical Council, providing a medical practitioner is a qualified doctor.

With the deterioration of the NHS and its ever increasing waiting lists, you're strongly advised to consider taking out private health insurance in Britain, which will ensure you receive the medical treatment you need, when you need it. Note, however, that the quality of private treatment isn't better than that provided by the NHS and you shouldn't assume that because a doctor (or any other medical practitioner) is in private practise, he's more competent than his NHS counterpart. In fact often you will see the same specialist or be treated by the same surgeon on the NHS and privately. For information about private health insurance see page 315.

DOCTORS

There are excellent family doctors, generally referred to as General Practitioners (GPs), in all areas of Britain. The best way to find a doctor, whether as an NHS or a private patient, is to ask your (healthy?) colleagues, friends or neighbours if they can recommend someone. Alternatively you can consult a list of GPs for your Health District in your Community Health Council (CHC) office or contact your local Family Health Services Authority (FHSA). FHSAs publish lists of doctors, dentists, chemists and opticians in their area, which are available at libraries, post offices, tourist information offices, police stations and Citizens Advice Bureaux. You can also look up doctors in the Medical Directory available in public reference libraries. If you're a student, some colleges have their own student health centre where you should register. GPs or family doctors are listed under 'Doctors (Medical Practitioners)' in the Yellow Pages.

Surgery hours vary, but are typically from 0830 to 1800 or 1900, Mondays to Fridays, with early closing one day a week, e.g. 1700 or 1730 on Fridays (evening surgeries may also be held on one or two evenings a week). Emergency surgeries may be held on Saturday mornings, e.g. from 0830 to 1130 or 1200. Most doctors surgeries have answering machines outside surgery hours, when a recorded message informs you of the name of the doctor on call (or deputising service) and his telephone number.

NHS Doctors: NHS doctors have a contract with their local FHSAs to look after a number of patients (average around 2,000) who make up their list. In Scotland the contract is with the Health Board and in Northern Ireland with the Central Services Agency. Doctors are paid by the NHS according to the number of NHS registered patients on their list and an NHS doctor can refuse to register you as a patient if he has no vacancies. If you're looking for an NHS doctor, you must live within a doctor's catchment area from where he's permitted to draw his patients. If you have trouble getting onto an NHS doctor's list, contact your local FHSA who have a duty to find you a doctor. If you're living in a district for less than three months or have no permanent home, you can apply to any doctor in the district to be accepted as a temporary resident for three months. After this period you must register with the doctor as a permanent patient or you may register with another doctor. An NHS doctor must give 'immediate necessary treatment' for up to 14 days to anyone without a doctor living in their area, until the patient has been accepted by a doctor as a permanent or temporary resident.

Fundholding GPs: Under the NHS reforms instituted in 1991, the government created fundholding GPs, where GPs manage their own budgets and can shop around and buy services for their patients direct from hospitals and other health service providers. Over 40 per cent of doctors are GP fundholders. Non-fundholding GPs must rely on their district health authority (DHA) for health services and cannot refer patients to hospitals of their choice. Fundholding GPs usually provide a wider range of services and their patients experience shorter waits to see specialists and for hospital beds as GPs can shop around for the shortest queues. This has created a two-tier health system with patients of non-fundholders being disadvantaged. However, because fundholding GPs tend to spend more time managing their funds, they spend less time with their patients than non-fundholding GPs. Generally you're much better off with a fundholding GP.

Group Practices: Around 80 per cent of GPs work in a partnership or group practise, around 25 per cent of whom practice in health centres, providing a range of medical and nursing services. Health centres may have facilities for immunisation, cervical smears, health education (well person clinic), family planning, speech therapy, chiropody, hearing tests, physiotherapy and remedial exercises. Many also include dental, ophthalmic, hospital out-patient and social work support. Most health centres or large surgeries have district nurses, health visitors, midwives and clinical psychologists in attendance at fixed times. Bear in mind that if your doctor is part of a partnership or group practise, when he's absent you will automatically be treated by a partner or another doctor (unless you wish to wait until your doctor returns).

Choosing a Doctor: It's advisable to enquire in advance (e.g. by asking the receptionist) whether a doctor has the 'qualifications' you require, for example:

- is he or she of the right sex?
- is he easily reached by public transport, if necessary?
- is it a group practise? This may be preferable to an individual practise, where you may be required to see a locum (replacement) doctor when your doctor is absent (in a group practise, doctors cover for each other outside surgery hours).
- does the practise run ante-natal, family planning, well woman (or well person), diabetic or other clinics?
- what are the surgery hours (Saturday and evening surgeries may be held)?
- what is the procedure for home visits?
- does the doctor practice preventive or complementary medicine?
- does the doctor prescribe contraception?
- if you're a private patient, what's the cost?

All NHS GPs must produce practise guides for all patients, that contain the names of doctors, times of surgeries and any special services that a practise provides, such as ante-natal, family planning, well woman or diabetic clinics. It's often advisable to meet a prospective doctor before deciding whether to register with him. When you have found a suitable NHS doctor who'll accept you, you must register with him by completing part A of your medical card and giving it to his receptionist. If you don't have an NHS medical card, you must complete a form provided by the GP which he will send to the local FHSA (who will send you a medical card within a few weeks of registration).

Appointments & House Calls: Note that most doctors operate an appointment system, where you must make an appointment in advance. You cannot just turn up during surgery hours and expect to be seen. If you're an urgent case (but not an emergency), your doctor will usually see you immediately, but you should still phone in advance. Note, however, that surgeries often overrun and you may have to wait well past your appointment time to see a doctor. NHS doctors make free house calls and emergency visits outside surgery hours (at their discretion), when patients are bedridden or unable to visit their surgery. In Britain a doctor is responsible for his patients 24 hours a day and when he's unavailable he must make alternative arrangements, either through his partners in a group practise, a voluntary rota between individual doctors or a commercial deputising service. When you call your GP outside normal hours he's unlikely to attend you personally at home. Most GPs use an outside medical service which exists to provide house calls and an 'after hours' service.

Changing Doctors: An NHS patient can change doctors providing he can find a new doctor who will accept him (a doctor can refuse to accept a patient or remove anyone from his list without giving a reason). Be careful what reason you give for wanting to change doctors, as doctors tend to be wary of accepting a patient who has had a 'disagreement' with a colleague. One 'legitimate' reason for changing doctors is that you wish to be treated by a doctor of the opposite sex to your present one (it's hard luck if all doctors in your area are male *or* female). Under new reforms it's easier to change doctors and you don't need to inform you old doctor and can just visit a new doctor's surgery and ask to be registered.

Your doctor is able to give advice or provide information on any aspect of health or medical after-care, including preventive medicine, blood donations, home medical equipment and special counselling. If you're an NHS patient, he should also be able to advise you about the range of medical benefits provided under the NHS, including maternity care, contraceptive help and psychiatric treatment. NHS patients must always be referred to a specialist, e.g. an eye specialist, gynaecologist or orthopaedic surgeon, by a GP.

If you would like a second opinion on any health matter, you may ask to see a specialist, although unless it's a serious matter, your doctor will probably refuse to refer you. If your doctor refuses, you won't be able to obtain a second opinion from another NHS doctor unless you change doctors. The only other alternative is to consult another doctor or specialist as a private patient. Patients who have a foreign (i.e. not British) private health insurance policy may be free to make appointments directly with specialists. **Note that in many cases where a second opinion is sought, the second doctor doesn't confirm the first doctor's diagnosis.** GPs often drop patients who ask questions from their registers and almost 100,000 are struck off each year. Most GPs don't like answering medical questions, including patients who question or refuse treatment or ask for a second opinion – you're simply supposed to do as you're told!

Complaints: If you have a complaint against your NHS GP, you should complain in the first instance to your local FHSA, usually within eight weeks of the event. If you need help to make a complaint, you can ask your Community Health Council or a Citizens Advice Bureau (CAB) for advice. In the event of serious professional misconduct, your complaint will be passed to the General Medical Council. Family doctor booklets are published by the British Medical Association (BMA) and are available from doctors' surgeries, clinics and chemists or direct from the BMA.

Medicentres: A new innovation in recent years has been the introduction of private drop-in medicentres where doctors and nurses are on hand for consultations and to perform tests, screening, health checks, vaccinations and minor treatment. Medicentre is a walk-in service designed to fit around your schedule – there's no need to be registered and you don't require an appointment. Medicentres are located in the high street, e.g. in branches of Boots the chemist, and in shopping centres. Patients pay around £36 for a consultation and package deals are available from insurers such as Norwich Union (☎ freefone 0800-056 2591). For more information ☎ 0870-600 0870 (Internet: www.medicentre.com).

DRUGS & MEDICINES

Medicines and drugs are obtained from a chemist (or pharmacy) in Britain, most of which provide free advice regarding minor ailments and suggest appropriate medicines. There are three categories of drugs and medicines in Britain: those that can be prescribed only by a doctor (via an official form called a prescription) and purchased from a chemist, medicines that can be sold only under the supervision of a pharmacist and general-sale list medicines (such as aspirin and paracetamol) that can be sold in outlets such as garages and supermarkets. Some drugs and medicines requiring a doctor's prescription in Britain are sold freely in other countries, although other drugs are freely available in Britain that are controlled in other countries (an increasing number of previously restricted drugs are now available over the counter).

At least one chemist is open in most towns during evenings and on Sundays for the emergency dispensing of medicines and drugs. In major cities at least one chemist may be open until 2400 or later every day of the week. A rota is posted on the doors of chemists and published in local newspapers and guides. If you require medicine urgently when all chemists are closed, you should contact your GP or local police station. Requests for repeat prescriptions may be accepted by your doctor by post or telephone. If you have regular repeat prescriptions, you can have a pharmacy pick up your prescription from your doctor, which can then be collected from the pharmacy. Many pharmacists use a computer to keep information about the health problems and medicines of regular customers.

Anyone living one mile from a chemist is entitled to obtain prescriptions from a dispensing doctor (who's permitted to dispense drugs and appliances). If he doesn't have them in stock, he will write a prescription (in a secret language decipherable only by doctors and pharmacists). In some rural areas, patients who live over a mile from a pharmacist are permitted to collect their drugs from their GP. Some medicines aren't recognised by the NHS, in which case your doctor will usually inform you and may offer to prescribe an alternative. If you insist on having the unrecognised medicine, you must usually pay for it yourself.

To obtain medicines prescribed by a doctor, simply take your prescription form to any chemist. Your prescription may be filled immediately if it's available off the shelf, or you may be asked to wait or come back later. NHS prescriptions for medicines are charged at a fixed rate of £5.90 (they cost just 20p in 1979!) per item, although four out of five prescriptions are free. Although the average cost of prescription drugs would be around £10 if they were bought over the counter, many drugs would cost much less than the prescription charge if they were available over the counter. It may be possible to get your GP to write a private prescription, although many doctors won't do this as they would be in breach of their terms and conditions of service with the NHS. Those with comprehensive private (e.g. foreign) health insurance may be able to reclaim the cost of prescriptions from their insurance company.

The Consumers' Association (see page 437) publish a booklet entitled *Cheaper than a prescription*, listing medicines which you can buy over the counter and prescription-only drugs costing less than a prescription (which your GP may prescribe privately). Some medicines prescribed by a doctor (e.g. certain pain killers) can be replaced by substitute medicines that can be purchased over the counter for less than the prescription charge. Boots, Britain's largest chain of chemists with over 1,300 stores, is often the cheapest place to buy non-prescription drugs (many own brand). An expected end to price-fixing on medicines will allow supermarkets to slash the price of common drugs.

Many people qualify for free prescriptions (e.g. prescriptions for hospital out-patients and day patients) including children under 16; students under 19 in full-time education; pensioners (men over 65, women over 60); expectant mothers and those who have had a baby in the last year; those with certain medical conditions, e.g. diabetes or epilepsy, or a permanent disability which prevents them getting around without help; and people on low incomes receiving state benefits. With the exception of children under 16 and pensioners, all those entitled to free prescriptions must apply for an exemption certificate or a refund.

When you're exempt you must complete and sign the declaration on the back of the prescription form. Ask your district health authority where and how to apply. Claim form AGI is available from local social security offices, hospitals, dentists and opticians. Those who aren't exempt but need frequent prescriptions can reduce the cost by purchasing a prepayment certificate 'season ticket', which covers all charges for a fixed period. Leaflet P11, *NHS prescriptions*, contains information about prescription charges and is available from your local social security office.

Most chemists also sell non-prescription medicines and drugs, toiletries, cosmetics, health foods and cleaning supplies. Some chemists, such as Boots, may have departments selling anything from records and books, to electrical and photographic equipment and kitchen appliances (in addition to those items mentioned above). Boots also sell a range of health care equipment. A health food shop sells health foods, diet foods, homeopathic medicines and eternal-life-virility-youth pills and elixirs, which are quite popular in Britain (even though their claims are usually in the realms of fantasy). Growing fears about the side-effects of drugs has led to a huge growth in complementary medicine in the last decade, although Britain is still way behind many other EU countries, particularly France and Germany.

Always use, store and dispose of unwanted medicines and poisons safely, e.g. by returning them to a pharmacist or dispensing doctor, and never leave them where children can get their hands on them.

HOSPITALS & CLINICS

Most British towns have a hospital or clinic, signposted by the international hospital sign of a white 'H' on a blue background. There are many kinds of hospitals in Britain including community hospitals, district hospitals, teaching hospitals and cottage hospitals. Major hospitals are called general hospitals and provide treatment and diagnosis for in-patients, day-patients and out-patients. Most have a maternity department, infectious diseases unit, psychiatric and geriatric facilities, rehabilitation and convalescent units, and cater for all forms of specialised treatment.

Some general hospitals are designated teaching hospitals and combine treatment with medical training and research work. In addition to general hospitals, there are specialist hospitals for children, the mentally ill and handicapped, the elderly and infirm, and for the treatment of specific complaints or illnesses. There are also dental hospitals. Only major hospitals have an accident or emergency department. Many NHS hospitals have sports injury clinics, although you must usually be referred by your GP, and some have minor injuries units. Cottage hospitals, as the name implies, are small local hospitals, often caring for the elderly and infirm. In many areas there are NHS Well Woman Clinics, where women can obtain medical check-ups and cervical smear tests, and NHS Family Planning Clinics. You can be referred to these clinics by your GP or can refer yourself. You can also refer yourself to an NHS Sexually Transmitted Diseases (STD) or VD clinic for an examination.

Since 1991, NHS hospitals have been able to opt out of local health authority control in favour of self-governing status and a grant from central government (NHS 'trust' status). In recent years NHS hospitals have been rated in performance tables, although these have been condemned by the BMA as unfair and misleading, and shouldn't be taken as anything but a rough guide. Small hospitals are generally rated higher than large city hospitals and district hospitals generally outperform specialist teaching hospitals (where there are longer waiting times, more cancelled operations and delayed appointments are more frequent) regarding patient care.

Private Hospitals & Clinics: In addition to NHS hospitals, there are private hospitals and clinics in all areas, many providing only specialist services (e.g. health checks and sports injuries) and which usually don't cater for accidents or emergencies (or anyone without private health insurance or a large bank balance). Some provident associations (e.g. BUPA and PPP, see page 315) operate their own hospitals and clinics throughout Britain. Private patients are provided with single rooms equipped with all the comforts of home, including radio, TV, telephone, en suite bathroom and room service (a visitor can usually enjoy a meal with a patient in the privacy of his room). A single room with en suite bathroom in a private hospital costs from around £200 to £300 per day. A day bed may cost from around £25 an hour or £200 per day.

If you don't have health insurance or are a visitor to Britain, you may be asked to pay a (large) deposit in advance, particularly if there's any doubt that you will survive the ordeal (most private hospitals accept credit and charge cards). Many private hospitals also provide fixed-price surgery, subject to an examination by a consultant surgeon. Some hospitals offer interest-free loans to pay hospital bills (e.g. a 10 per cent deposit with the rest payable over 12 months). This is one solution for those who cannot afford health insurance and don't want to wait. However, make sure that you aren't being overcharged as you can often have an operation cheaper elsewhere in Britain or even abroad (e.g. in France) and possibly save thousands of pounds.

According to Action for Victims of Medical Accidents (AVMA), there are higher health risks in private hospitals than in NHS hospitals, and there may be less emergency equipment and fewer experienced staff. You have almost no protection in law when you're treated at a private clinic or hospital compared with your rights as an NHS hospital patient and when things go wrong (as they occasionally do) you're usually better off in an NHS hospital.

Choice of Hospital: Except for emergencies, you may be admitted or referred to an NHS hospital or clinic for treatment only after consultation with a GP or a consultant (or from an NHS clinic such as a family planning or well woman clinic). Patients with private health insurance may be treated at the hospital of their choice, depending on their level of insurance cover. NHS patients can ask to be treated at a particular hospital or to be referred to a particular consultant, but have no right to have their request met. If your GP isn't an NHS fundholder (see page 283), you're admitted to a hospital under the control of your local health authority, unless special surgery or treatment is necessary that's unavailable locally. Patients of fundholding GPs may be admitted to any NHS hospital. In an emergency you will be treated at the nearest hospital. Children are usually admitted to a special children's general ward or a children's hospital well stocked with games, toys, books and other children.

Accommodation: NHS hospital accommodation is in wards of various sizes, e.g. 12-beds, some of which are mixed. Many NHS hospitals have private rooms (known as 'pay beds') and under NHS reforms, they're permitted to charge for extras such as a single room with a telephone, a TV or a wider choice of meals. In most NHS hospitals you choose the meals you would like the day before and provision is made for vegetarian and other diets. Some wards have dining room tables for those sufficiently mobile and most have day rooms for mobile patients. The service, facilities and standards of NHS hospitals vary considerably depending on the area, the best of which compare favourably with private hospitals (apart from a possible lack of modern conveniences). On the other hand, some NHS hospitals are dingy and depressing, and are perhaps the last place on earth you would wish to be when you're ill. However, there's some consolation to being in an NHS general ward – just think how lonely and bored those poor private patients must be, ensconced in their luxury rooms with nobody to talk to all day!

Hospital stays for the same complaint or operation vary considerably (e.g. by up to double the period) depending on the hospital and the surgeon. If possible you should choose your surgeon carefully, as some have insufficient experience or skills, particularly when it comes to using the latest techniques such as keyhole surgery. Many new treatments aren't properly evaluated for their effectiveness and unnecessary and even harmful operations aren't uncommon. Needless tests and X-rays are estimated to cost the NHS over £20 million a year. NHS hospital patients receive free medicines and appliances. Medicines given to out or day patients at a hospital are also free, but medicines prescribed to be taken at home must be paid for (in the same way as all prescriptions), unless you're entitled to free prescriptions.

Visiting Hours: Visiting hours vary depending on whether you're in a private or a general ward (no prizes for guessing which patients have the most generous visiting hours), although some NHS hospital general wards have liberal visiting hours. In a private hospital or clinic there may be no restrictions on visiting hours. Parents of children in hospital may have unrestricted visiting hours and many hospitals provide a bed for a child's parent to stay overnight (the whole family is discouraged from taking up residence).

Complaints: Hospitals usually have a specially appointed officer to deal with complaints (e.g. the hapless hospital administrator). If you don't receive satisfaction, you should contact your FHSA or the general manager of the local health authority as soon as possible. If you're an NHS patient, you can ultimately complain to the health service commissioner. Ask your Community Health Council or a Citizens Advice Bureau for advice and information.

CHILDBIRTH

Childbirth in Britain usually takes place in a hospital, where a stay of two days is usual. If you wish to have a child at home, you must find a doctor or midwife (see below) who's willing to attend you, although it's generally impossible for the birth of a first child. Some doctors are opposed to home births, particularly in cases where there could be complications (although rare) and when specialists and special facilities (e.g. incubators) may be required. You can also choose to hire a private midwife (a nurse specialising in delivering babies), who'll attend you at home throughout and after your pregnancy.

For hospital births, you can usually decide (with the help of your GP or midwife) the hospital where you wish to have your baby. You aren't required to use the hospital suggested by your GP, but should book a hospital bed as early as possible. Your GP will also refer you to an obstetrician. Find out as much as possible about local hospital methods and policies on childbirth, either directly or from friends or neighbours, before booking a bed. The policy regarding a father's attendance at a birth varies depending on the hospital. A husband doesn't have the right to be present with his wife during labour or childbirth (which is at the consultant's discretion), although some doctors expect fathers to attend. If the presence of your husband is important to you, you should check that it's permitted at the hospital where you plan to have your baby and any other rules that may be in force.

In Britain, midwives are responsible for educating and supporting women and their families during the childbearing period. Midwives can advise women before they become pregnant, in addition to providing moral, physical and emotional support throughout a pregnancy and after the birth. Your midwife may also advise on parent education and ante-natal classes for mothers. After giving birth, mothers are attended at home by their midwife for the first ten days or so, after which they see a health visitor and their GP to monitor their child's health and development.

Information: There are many organisations providing information about family planning and support in pregnancy and childbirth including the Family Planning Association, 27-35 Mortimer Street, London W1N 7RJ (☎ 0171-636 7866), the National Childbirth Trust, Alexandra House, Oldham Terrace, Acton, London W3 6NH (☎ 0181-992 8637) and Lifeline (Cae bach, 4 Pant-y-Wennol, Bodafin, Llandudno, Gwynedd LL30 3DS, ☎ 01492-543741). For general information about benefits and other help during pregnancy and when your baby is born, see social security leaflet FB8, *Babies and benefits*. An interesting book for mothers-to-be is *The New Good Birth Guide* by Sheila Kitzinger (Penguin).

DENTIST

Britain's annual consumption of over 750,000 tonnes of sweets (over 13kg per person) ensures that dentists (and sweet manufacturers) remain financially healthy, although despite the efforts of dentists to promote preventive dentistry, millions of Britons never go near a dentist (mostly out of fear) unless they are dying from toothache. Fortunately when you need help there are excellent dentists in all areas. The best way to find a good dentist, whether as an NHS or a private patient, is to ask your colleagues, friends or neighbours (particularly those with perfect teeth) if they can recommend someone. Dentists are listed under 'Dental Surgeons' in the Yellow Pages and are permitted to advertise any special services they provide such as private and NHS patients, emergency or 24-hour answering service, dental hygienist, and evening or weekend surgeries. Around 50 per cent of dentists hold an evening surgery one day a week or on Saturday mornings. There are mobile dentists in some regions.

In some areas, community dental clinics or health centres provide a dental service for children, expectant and nursing mothers, and handicapped adults. Some hospitals provide a free emergency service, e.g. on Sundays and public holidays. Dental hospitals (e.g. in London) provide a free emergency service on most days. Many family dentists in Britain are qualified to perform special treatment, e.g. periodontal work, although you must usually see a specialist. In Britain, false teeth (dentures) are made by a dental technician and prescribed and fitted by dentists. Most dental technicians carry out emergency repairs on dentures (see your Yellow Pages).

The cost of dental treatment has risen considerably in recent years and it will pay you to keep your mouth shut during dental check-ups, which are recommended every six months in Britain. However, dental care isn't particularly expensive in Britain compared with many other western countries, although fees vary considerably depending on the area and the dentist, e.g. from £10 to £35 for a check-up, from £15 to £30 for scaling and polishing, and from £20 to £35 for an X-ray and a small (amalgam) filling.

NHS Treatment: In 1990, a new NHS contract was drawn up between the NHS and the British Dental Association, which caused many dentists to leave the NHS and accept only adult private work, rather than accept the fees and conditions imposed by the NHS. Since 1992, over one million people have been de-registered as NHS patients, many opting to go private. Less than half of all dentists accept new non-exempt NHS patients. The quality of work performed under the NHS often isn't as good as that provided under private treatment, because dentists often use inferior materials due to cost restraints and have less time to treat patients (NHS dentists may treat up to 60 patients a day).

NHS patients are asked to sign a form and give their NHS number (or show a medical card) before beginning treatment. You must sign the form again when treatment has been completed to acknowledge that you have had the treatment listed. Don't sign it a second time before your course of treatment is complete. Many dentists treat both NHS and private patients and don't have a list of NHS registered patients like GPs. A dentist who accepts NHS patients may have a quota and if it's full he may offer to treat you only as a private patient. Consult your FHSA if you have trouble finding an NHS dentist. **If you want to have treatment as an NHS patient, you must make this clear to the dentist's receptionist when registering.**

You should take your NHS medical card to the dentist when you have your initial examination. Each time you visit a dentist, whether the same dentist or another one, you must re-confirm that you will be treated as an NHS patient. NHS dental patients aren't required to live within a certain catchment area and can change dentists whenever they like. Once registered as an NHS patient, a dentist cannot refuse to treat you and essential work is always completed under the NHS when clinically necessary. Patients who aren't exempt (see the list below) pay 80 per cent of the set NHS fees (up to a maximum of £300 per treatment) for 'normal' dental treatment (e.g. fillings, extractions and hygiene work), and standard bridges and dentures, according to a fixed scale of fees. There's a standard NHS charge of around £5 for a dental check-up. There's no extra charge for stopping bleeding, denture repairs, home visits or opening a surgery in an emergency (although you must pay for treatment as usual).

A list of dental charges and exemptions is published by the DSS and is available from them or your FHSA. Exemptions include children under 18 (although those aged 16 to 18 must pay for bridges, crowns or dentures); full-time students under 19; expectant mothers and those who have had a baby in the last year; and those on low incomes receiving state benefits. NHS patients who aren't under 18, or receiving unemployment or supplementary benefits, must usually pay a proportion of their dental treatment and for the whole cost of cosmetic treatment, e.g. bridges and crowns.

Dentists may ask for payment in advance and NHS dentists must receive prior permission from the Dental Estimates Board (DEB) before certain expensive work can be undertaken. Note that if you miss a dental appointment without giving 24 hours notice, your dentist may charge you a standard fee (amazing how people who never forget anything often forget dental appointments!). Of course, had you turned up on time, your dentist would probably have kept you waiting. If a dentist sees you as an emergency NHS patient outside normal surgery hours, he isn't permitted to make an extra charge. In some areas an emergency dental service is operated by the local health authority. Note that a dentist isn't obliged to treat someone who isn't a patient, even in an emergency.

Unnecessary Treatment: According to a report by the General Dentist Practitioners Association (GDPA), a number of dentists remove or fill teeth unnecessarily, a few of whom even deliberately perform unnecessary treatment ('drill for profit'!). Always try to obtain an accurate (preferably) written quotation before beginning a course of treatment, although few dentists are willing to quote an exact fee for work, and often a 'rough estimate' is only a fraction of the final bill. If you have regular check-ups and usually have little or no treatment, you should be suspicious if a (new) dentist suggests you need a lot of fillings or extractions. In this case you should obtain a second opinion before going ahead (note, however, that two dentists rarely agree on exactly the same treatment).

Complaints: If you have a complaint concerning dental treatment completed under the NHS, you should write to your local FHSA within six months of the end of the course of treatment. For complaints regarding private treatment, you must contact the General Dental Council, 37 Wimpole Street, London W1M 8DQ (☎ 0171-887 3800). The British Dental Association, 64 Wimpole Street, London W1M 8AL (☎ 0171-935 0875) provides a list of dentists in your area, but (wisely) doesn't handle complaints. A useful book is *You and Your Dentist - A Guide to Patients Rights* published by The Stationery Office and the National Consumer Council. Finally it isn't true that all dentists are sadists; many have a good (if somewhat strange) sense of humour and are fond of children and kind to animals (particularly those *without* teeth). For information about **Dental Insurance** see page 318.

OPTICIAN

As with dentists, there's no need to register with an optician. You simply go to the one of your choice, although it's advisable to ask your colleagues, friends or neighbours if they can recommend someone. Opticians are listed under 'Opticians-dispensing' or 'Opticians-ophthalmic (optometrists)' in the Yellow Pages and may advertise their services such as contact lenses or an emergency repair service. Opticians (like spectacles) come in many shapes and sizes.

Your sight can be tested only by a registered ophthalmic optician (or optometrist) or an ophthalmic medical practitioner. Most 'high street' opticians are both dispensing opticians (who make up spectacles) and ophthalmic opticians, who test eyesight, prescribe glasses and diagnose eye diseases. An eye specialist may be an ophthalmic medical practitioner (a doctor who treats eye diseases and also tests eyesight and prescribes lenses), an ophthalmologist (a senior specialist or eye surgeon) or an orthoptist (an ophthalmologist who treats children's eye problems). If you need to see an eye specialist, you must usually be referred by your GP.

The optometrist business is competitive in Britain and unless someone is highly recommended, you should shop around for the best deal. Recent years have seen a flood of 'chain store' dentists such as Vision Express (and those in Boots stores) opening in high streets and shopping centres. Prices for both spectacles and contact lenses vary considerably, so it's wise to compare costs (although make sure you're comparing like with like) before committing yourself to a large bill, particularly for contact lenses. The prices charged for most services (spectacle frames, lenses, hard and soft contact lenses) are often cheaper in Britain than elsewhere in Europe, although higher than North America.

Spectacles: The price of spectacle frames vary considerably (e.g. from around £20 to over £200 for designer frames) depending on the quality, style and origin (and the optician). The cost of spectacle lenses also vary widely (e.g. £50 to £300) depending on the strength and complexity of your prescription, and whether you choose a tint or special lenses. Most people should expect to pay between £100 and £150 for frames and lenses. Special offers are common such as 'buy a new pair of glasses and get a second pair of prescription sunglasses free'. Some opticians offer free spectacles for a child when a parent buys a new pair of glasses. Always carefully compare offer prices and consider whether you really need (or want) what's offered, e.g. will you actually use a free pair of prescription sunglasses?

Ready-made reading glasses are available from chemists (e.g. Boots) and other shops without a sight test or prescription, at a fraction of the cost of a prescription pair, e.g. £10 to £20. They are also available from opticians, but are more expensive. Wherever you buy your spectacles, take advantage of any guarantee, after-sales service or insurance arrangements for repairs or replacements. Most opticians offer insurance against accidental damage, e.g. £20 a year for lenses and £10 for frames. If you're sold defective glasses or contact lenses, you have rights under the law relating to the sale of goods.

Contact Lenses: Soft contact lenses are available in major cities from around £40 or £50, although the more usual price is £80 to £140, depending on the optician and the brand of lenses. You can insure contact lenses against loss or damage for around £25 a year. Disposable (one-day) and extended-wear (e.g. one or three months) contact lenses are widely available, although most medical experts believe extended-wear lenses should be approached with extreme caution. **Obtain advice from a doctor or eye specialist before buying them.** One-day contact lenses cost around £1 a day.

Sight Tests: If you aren't entitled to a free sight test under the NHS, you must have the test as a private patient, which usually costs between £15 and £20. Some opticians offer a special low price (or even free tests) for pensioners. Sight tests are valid for two years, although you should be aware that your eyesight can change considerably during this time. You don't need to buy your spectacles (lenses or frames) or contact lenses from the optician who tests your sight, irrespective of whether you're an NHS or private patient, and you have the right to a copy of any prescription resulting from an NHS or private sight test.

Certain people receive free sight tests under the NHS including children under 16; full-time students under 19; the registered blind or partially sighted; diagnosed diabetic or glaucoma sufferers; and people on low incomes receiving state benefits. NHS leaflet G11, *NHS sight tests and vouchers for glasses*, explains who's entitled to free sight tests and NHS vouchers for glasses, and is available from social security offices, NHS family doctors and opticians.

Laser Surgery: In the last few years, laser surgery to correct short-sighted vision has become increasingly popular in Britain. It's heavily promoted by laser surgery clinics, which are unregulated and don't need any special qualifications or registration, and costs between around £500 and £1,000 per eye. There are conflicting reports about its effectiveness, particularly for those with severe short-sighted vision who are generally considered poor candidates. Some eye specialists warn against having it done as it can cause permanent eye damage in certain cases, although it also achieves some remarkable results. **However, the long-term effects are unknown and it should be treated with caution.**

Complaints: If you have a complaint regarding your optician which you're unable to resolve, you should write to the Association of Optometrists, Consumer Complaints Service, Bridge House, 233 Blackfriars Road, London SE1 8NW, or for dispensing opticians, the Association of British Dispensing Opticians, 22 Nottingham Place, London W1M 4AT (☎ 0171-736 0088). Help the Aged (St. James's Walk, London EC1R 0BE) collect unwanted spectacles, which they distribute to the elderly in Africa and Asia.

COUNSELLING

Counselling and assistance for health and social problems is available within the NHS, and from thousands of local community groups and volunteer organisations, ranging from national associations to small local groups (including self-help groups). Local authorities provide social workers to advise and support those who need help within their community. If you need to find help locally, you can contact your local authority, local voluntary services or a Citizens Advice Bureau (see page 450) for advice. Many colleges and educational establishments provide a counselling service for students, and hospital casualty departments have a psychiatrist on call 24 hours a day. Problems for which help is available are numerous and include drug rehabilitation; alcoholism (e.g. Alcoholics Anonymous); gambling; dieting (e.g.

Weight Watchers); smoking; attempted suicide and psychiatric problems; homosexual and lesbian related problems; youth problems; battered children and women; marriage and relationship counselling (e.g. Relate); and rape.

Trained counsellors provide advice and help for sufferers of various diseases (e.g. multiple sclerosis and muscular dystrophy) and the disabled (e.g. the blind and deaf). They also help very sick and terminally ill patients (e.g. cancer, leukemia and Aids sufferers) and their families come to terms with their situation. A number of voluntary organisations and local authorities run refuges for battered wives (and their children) or maltreated children, whose conditions have become intolerable (some provide 24-hour emergency phone numbers). If you or a member of your family are the victims of a violent crime, the police will put you in touch with a local victim support scheme.

In times of need there's nearly always someone to turn to and all services are strictly confidential. In major towns, counselling may be available in your own language if you don't speak English. If you need help desperately, someone speaking your language will usually be found. The Samaritans provide a strictly confidential telephone counselling service in periods of personal crisis, for the lonely, desperate and suicidal through over 175 branches throughout Britain and Ireland (see your phone book or ask the operator for your local phone number). Children can call Childline (☎ freefone 0800-1111), which answers around 10,000 calls a day.

DRUG & ALCOHOL ABUSE

Drug abuse is a serious problem in Britain, where drug addiction has increased almost ten-fold in the last two decades and areas of some cities are being slowly turned into no-go areas by the drug trade. Despite a major campaign of education for the young, and increased vigilance by police and customs officers to reduce the supply of drugs from abroad (particularly heroin, cocaine and crack), record levels of drugs are still being imported into Britain. Soft drugs such as cannabis are treated more leniently in most areas and many people found in possession of a small amount are unlikely to be prosecuted (although it's still illegal). Many people believe that the authorities are fighting a losing battle against the drug barons and that universal prohibition has increased consumption. There have even been calls to legalise drugs, which although taken seriously by some professionals are rejected outright by the authorities.

The drug problem is also of increasing concern to those in the fight against Aids (see page 295), as the sharing of needles among drug addicts (many of whom are also homosexuals) is a major cause of the spread of Aids. Many cities operate a needle exchange scheme for drug addicts. Glue sniffing is a big problem among the young in certain areas of Britain. It's illegal to sell certain solvents (e.g. glue, lighter fuel and other solvents) to children under 18 while knowing or having reason to believe they are to be used for intoxication.

Some NHS hospitals have special drug treatment units, where treatment is usually on an out-patient basis, although in-treatment may be provided when necessary. Note that doctors in Britain have a duty to notify the authorities of any patient they consider to be addicted to a controlled drug. Many voluntary organisations provide drug advice and rehabilitation services, including residential facilities. There are dozens of voluntary groups in all areas of Britain providing counselling, advice and support for drug users and their relatives and friends (see your local phone book or

Yellow Pages). If you can afford to pay for private treatment, a number of private clinics and hospitals specialise in treating people for drug, alcohol and chemical abuse and other health problems.

Alcohol Abuse: Apart from the direct or indirect loss of life, alcohol abuse costs British industry over £1 billion a year in lost production due to absenteeism. It's estimated that some seven million Britons have a drink problem, many of whom are 'blissfully' unaware that they have a problem. The consumption of alcohol is also a serious problem among children. A National Alcohol Helpline (☎ 0171-332 0202) operates from 1800 to 2300 Mondays to Fridays, Drinkline (☎ 0345-320202) can advise those concerned about their own or someone else's drinking, and Alcoholics Anonymous has groups in all areas (see your phone book). A free guide to sensible drinking entitled *That's The Limit* is published by the Health Education Authority (see page 277).

Smoking: As in most countries, smoking contributes to a huge loss of life and working days in Britain, although the number of smokers has steadily decreased over the last 15 years, from some 45 per cent in 1975 to less than 30 per cent in 1999. However, smoking among teenagers is increasing and there have been calls to curb or ban the advertising of tobacco products, particularly ads. targeted at the young. In recent years there has been increasing concern about 'passive smoking' (where non-smokers involuntarily inhale the smoke generated by smokers), although the issue is nothing like as heated as in the USA (where anyone who smokes in a public place is liable to be summarily executed). However, smoking is banned in many public places and on most public transport. The cost of cigarettes in Britain is among the most expensive in the EU and the government collects around £10 billion in tobacco tax from the £13 billion spent annually on cigarettes and tobacco. High tobacco taxes are allegedly intended to curb consumption. Employers estimate that they get 20 per cent less work from employees who are unable to smoke in the workplace and some pay smokers less in a effort to encourage them to quit. Smoking-related illness accounts for 50 million lost working days a year and bosses are also worried about claims for passive smoking from non-smokers.

Action on Smoking and Health (ASH), 16 Fitzharding Street, London W1H 9PL (☎ 0171-244 0743), provides advice on giving up smoking and information on smoking and the rights of non-smokers. There are also non-smoking clinics and self-help groups throughout Britain to help those wishing to stop smoking. Contact your local health authority for information. Two useful free publications are *A Smoker's Guide to Giving Up* (Health Education Authority) and *Passive Smoking at Work* (Health and Safety Executive).

SEXUALLY-TRANSMITTED DISEASES

Like most western countries, Britain has its fair share of sexually-transmitted diseases, including the deadly Acquired Immune Deficiency Syndrome (Aids). The furore over Aids has died down in the past few years, which many fear may cause those most at risk to be lulled into a false sense of security. The explosion of aids predicted by many 'experts' hasn't materialised, particularly among the heterosexual population, although the number of heterosexual cases is increasing. **Aids is always fatal (over 10,000 people have died from it in the UK) and to date there's no cure.**

The spread of Aids is accelerated by the sharing of syringes by drug addicts, among whom aids is rampant (many of Britain's heroin addicts are infected with the HIV virus). In an effort to reduce syringe sharing among HIV positive drug addicts, syringe exchange centres have been set up throughout England (☎ freefone 0800-567123 for 24-hour information), and in some cities free syringe vending machines have been provided. The spread of Aids is also accelerated by prostitutes, many of whom are also drug addicts, which is an increasing international problem.

Prostitution is illegal in Britain, therefore it's impossible to effect any control over the spread of sexually-transmitted diseases by prostitutes. The best protection against Aids is for men to wear a condom, although they're not foolproof (either against Aids or pregnancy) and the only real protection is abstinence. Condoms are on sale at chemists, some supermarkets, men's hairdressers, and vending machines in public toilets in pubs and other places. They are also available free from family planning clinics.

Many hospitals have clinics for sexually transmitted diseases or you can refer yourself to a Sexually Transmitted Diseases (STD) or VD clinic. Both provide free tests, treatment and advice. All cases of Aids and HIV-positive blood tests in Britain must be reported to local health authorities (patients' names remain anonymous). If you would like to talk to someone in confidence about Aids, there are many organisations and self-help groups providing information, advice and help in all areas, including the National Aids Helpline (☎ freefone 0800-567123). Other organisations are listed in phone books. The Health Education Authority (see page 277), health authorities, councils and many organisations (including those listed above) publish free information about Aids.

BIRTHS & DEATHS

Births and deaths in Britain must be reported to your local Registrar of Births, Deaths and Marriages (look in your local phone book).

Births: In recent years the British birth rate fell to its lowest level for 150 years (1.7 children per family), despite that fact that Britain has the highest rate of teenage pregnancies in Europe. Either parent can register a birth by simply going to the registrar within six weeks of a birth and giving the child's details (no proof of birth is necessary). Both parents must report to the registrar if they aren't married, i.e. the child is illegitimate, if they both want their details to be included on the birth certificate, otherwise the mother registers the birth and only her details are listed. A birth is usually registered in the area where the baby was born, but can be done through another office. Births and deaths of foreigners in Britain may need to be reported to a consulate or embassy, for example to obtain a national birth certificate and passport for a child, or to register a death in the deceased's country of birth.

Deaths: When someone dies in Britain, a medical certificate must be completed by a doctor and taken to the registrar (see above) within five days. If someone dies suddenly, accidentally, during an operation, in unusual circumstances, or the cause of death is unknown, the doctor will notify the police and/or the coroner, who will decide whether a post-mortem is necessary to determine the cause of death. The registrar will need to know the personal details of the deceased, including his date and place of birth and death, details of a marriage (if applicable), and whether he was receiving a state pension or any welfare benefits. The registrar then issues a death certificate and the 'notification of disposal', which authorises the funeral to take place.

The death certificate must be given to a funeral director (or undertaker) to arrange the burial or cremation (or alternatively he will arrange for the body to be shipped to another country for burial). Note that if you wish to remove a body from England or Wales, permission must be obtained from a coroner at least four days prior to the date of shipment. You may wish to announce a death in a local or national newspaper, giving the date, time and place of the funeral, and your wishes regarding flowers or contributions to a charity or research. In Britain, the traditional dress for a Christian funeral is black or dark dress.

Cost: Funerals are expensive in Britain (many think they are a rip off), partly as a result of many family and small funeral businesses being gobbled up by large national and international companies, which have grabbed a large slice of the market. With some 650,000 deaths in Britain each year, it's big business and the increase in the cost of dying in the last few decades has exceeded the increase in the cost of living. In the last ten years, the cost has doubled to around £1,000. You can save money by having a body cremated rather than buried. You can pay in advance for your funeral through a variety of pay-now-die-later schemes, with price and service guaranteed, although there are no legal safeguards and the prepaid funeral trade is ripe for fraud, mismanagement and over-selling (a number of funeral plans have 'gone bust' in recent years). Pre-paid funeral schemes cost between £1,000 and £2,000 and have been taken out by some 250,000 people (although this is expected to increase ten-fold in the next few years).

As the cost of traditional burials increases, alternative burials are becoming increasingly popular (you can even take a body to a crematorium yourself). The Natural Death Centre (☎ 0181-208 2853) can provide information about cheap, green funerals. There's a shortage of burial space in Britain and graves may soon have to be recycled (as already happens in many other countries). You can also choose to be buried in your own garden, although this isn't recommended as it can reduce the value of your property by up to 50 per cent! If you want to have a body buried abroad or have someone who died abroad buried in Britain, the body will probably need to be transported by air, which can be *very* expensive.

In the event of the death of a resident of Britain, all interested parties must be notified (see **Chapter 20**). You'll need a number of copies of the death certificate, e.g. for the will, pension claims, insurance companies and financial institutions. If you need to obtain a copy of a birth, marriage or death certificate, the cheapest way is to apply to the registrar in the area where it was registered. Alternatively you can apply to the General Register Office, St. Catherine's House, 10 Kingsway, London WC2B 6JP (☎ 0171-242 0262) and pay a search fee.

Information: The DSS publish a number of booklets including *What to do after a death* (D49) and *Help when someone dies* (FB29). The Inland Revenue (taxman) publish a leaflet *What Happens When Someone Dies* (IR45). Help the Aged (see address on page 305) publish a free booklet entitled *Bereavement*. Other useful books include *What to Do When Someone Dies* by Paul Harris (Which? Books) and *Through Grief* by Elizabeth Collick (Darton, Longman and Todd). See also **Wills** on page 364.

13.

INSURANCE

In Britain you can insure practically anything from your car to your camera, the loss of your livelihood to your life. You can also insure against most eventualities, such as rain on your parade or village fete, or the possibility of twins (or sextuplets) or missing your holiday. For particularly unusual requests you may be required to obtain a quote from Lloyd's of London, the last resort for unusual insurance needs (not only within Britain, but also internationally). If you earn your livelihood courtesy of a particular part of your anatomy, e.g. your voice, legs, teeth or posterior, you can also insure it against damage or decline. Note, however, that if an insurance requirement is particularly unusual or risky, you may find premiums prohibitively high and restrictions may be placed on what you can and cannot do.

Britain is renowned as a nation of gamblers, which is reflected in the relatively low level of insurance, not only for such basic requirements as loss of income or life insurance, but also insurance for homes and their contents. After serious flooding caused £millions of damage in recent years, it was revealed that as many as half of all households in some areas had no building or home contents insurance or were under-insured. Many people tend to rely on state 'insurance' benefits, which come under the heading of 'Social Security'. These include sickness and unemployment pay, Income Support (for families on low incomes) and state pensions. Note, however, that social security usually provides for the most basic needs only and those who are reduced to relying on it often exist below the poverty line.

It isn't necessary to spend half your income insuring yourself against every eventuality from the common cold to a day off work, but it's important to be covered against any event which could precipitate a major financial disaster (like telling your boss what you think of him when you've had a few drinks too many). **As with everything to do with finance, it's important to shop around when buying insurance. It bears repeating – always shop around when buying or renewing insurance!** Simply picking up a few brochures from insurance brokers or making a few phone calls can save you a lot of money (enough to pay for this book many times over).

If you're coming to Britain from abroad, you would be wise to ensure your family has full health insurance during the period between leaving your last country of residence until you arrive in Britain. This is particularly important if you're covered by a company health insurance policy terminating on the day you leave your present employment. If possible, it's better to continue with your present health insurance policy, particularly if you have existing health problems which may not be covered by a new policy. If you aren't covered by the National Health Service (see page 279) it's important to have private health insurance.

There are just two cases in Britain when insurance for individuals is compulsory: buildings insurance if you have a mortgage (because your lender will insist on it) and third party motor insurance, which is required by law. You may also need compulsory third party and accident insurance for high-risk sports such as hang-gliding, mountaineering and parachuting. Voluntary insurance includes pensions, accident, income protection, health, home contents, personal liability, legal expenses, dental, travel, motor breakdown and life insurance.

If you want to make a claim against a third party or a third party is claiming against you, you would be wise to seek legal advice for anything other than a minor claim. Note that British law is likely to be different from that in your home country or your previous country of residence, and you should never assume that it's the same.

INSURANCE COMPANIES

Insurance is big business in Britain and there are numerous insurance companies to choose from, many providing a wide range of insurance services, while others specialise in certain fields only. You can buy insurance from many sources including traditional insurance companies selling through their own salesmen or independent brokers, direct insurance companies (selling direct to the public), banks and other financial institutions, post offices, motoring organisations, and department and chain stores. Note that policies offered by banks are generally the most expensive and don't offer the best cover. The major insurance companies have offices or agents (brokers) throughout Britain, including most large towns, many of whom will provide a free analysis of your family's insurance needs.

Brokers: If you choose a broker, you should use one who's independent and sells policies from a wide range of insurance companies. Many brokers or agents are tied to a particular insurance company and sell policies only from that company (which includes most banks and building societies). A broker should research the whole market and take into account your individual requirements, why you're investing (if applicable), the various companies' performance, what you can afford and the type of policy that's best for you. He mustn't offer you a policy because it pays him the highest commission, which incidentally you should ask him about (particularly regarding life insurance) as he's obliged to tell you. It's also worthwhile trying Internet brokers such as Screentrade (www.screentrade.co.uk) who usually provide very competitive quotes (most major insurance companies also have websites).

Direct Insurance: In recent years direct marketing and direct response insurance companies (bypassing brokers) have resulted in huge savings for consumers, particularly for car, buildings and home contents insurance. Direct marketing companies provide quotations over the phone and often you aren't even required to complete a proposal form. Compare premiums from a number of direct sales insurance companies (e.g. Direct Line, Churchill, Eagle Star Direct and The Insurance Service) with the best deals from brokers, *before* choosing a policy.

Shop Around: When buying insurance you should shop 'til you drop and then shop around some more! Premiums vary considerably (e.g. by 100 to 300 per cent), although you must ensure that you're comparing similar policies and that some important benefits haven't been omitted. The less expensive companies may be stricter when it comes to claims and may also take longer to settle claims. The general wisdom is that it's better to pay for independent insurance advice than accept 'free' advice, which is often more expensive in the long run. You should obtain a number of quotations for each insurance need and shouldn't assume that your existing insurance company is the best choice for a new insurance requirement. Buy only the insurance that you *want* and *need* and ensure that you can afford the payments (and that your cover is protected when you're sick or unemployed). Don't sign a contract until you have had time to think it over.

Claims: Although insurance companies are keen to take your money, most aren't nearly so happy to settle claims. Some insurance companies practically treat customers as criminals when they make a claim. Fraud is estimated to cost the insurance industry some £600 million a year (£200 million in motor insurance fraud alone) and staff may be trained to automatically assume that claims are fraudulent. If you need to make a claim, don't send original bills or documents to your insurance company unless it's absolutely necessary (you can always send a certified copy).

Keep a copy of all bills, documents and correspondence, and send letters by recorded or registered mail so that your insurance company cannot deny receipt.

Don't bank a cheque received in settlement of a claim if you think it's insufficient, as you may be deemed to have accepted it as full and final settlement. Don't accept the first offer made, as most insurance companies try to get away with making a low settlement (if an insurer pays what you claimed without a quibble, you probably claimed too little). When dealing with insurance companies, perseverance often pays. Insurers are increasingly refusing to pay up on the flimsiest of pretexts as they know that many people won't pursue their cases, even when they have a valid claim. Don't give up on a claim if you're sure you have a good case, but persist until you have exhausted every avenue. Some insurance companies provide a 24-hour help line for policyholders in case of emergencies.

Complaints: Regrettably you cannot insure yourself against being uninsured or sue your insurance broker for giving you bad advice. However, if you buy insurance through a registered insurance broker and discover that your insurance premiums haven't been paid or that you've been sold the wrong policy, you should be able to obtain compensation through the broker's compulsory professional indemnity insurance (insurance for insurance for insurance). This insurance pays out if, due to a broker's error, you discover you aren't insured. Members of the Association of British Insurers have similar (but not so comprehensive) cover, although you have greater protection if you buy from a registered broker or direct from an insurance company. In recent years the insurance ombudsman (see below) has received more complaints than at any time being established almost 20 years ago. Note, however, that only around a third of cases dealt with by the ombudsman end in success for policyholders.

In recent years British insurance companies (or their representatives) have plummeted in public esteem after being involved in a number of scandals and dubious practices. These include the mis-selling of pensions and annuities; levying exorbitant commissions and charges; refusing to pay out on legitimate claims by bending the rules and exploiting 'small print' loopholes (some insurance companies go to extraordinary lengths not to pay claims); 'churning' (the dubious buying and selling of policies to generate commissions); offering fraudulent advice; overcharging on buildings and other insurance; and handing over 'surplus assets' to shareholders rather than to policyholders. **Misrepresentation or even outright fraud on the part of insurance companies and agents isn't uncommon.**

Disputes: Most financial fields have their own independent arbitrator, called an ombudsman, whose job is to mediate between companies and individuals in dispute, but only when a company's internal complaints procedures have been exhausted. There are ombudsmen for disputes involving insurance companies, banks, building societies and investments. If you decide to go to arbitration with an ombudsman, his decision is usually binding on all parties. There's a maze of insurance associations, ombudsmen and regulators in Britain. The Insurance Ombudsman Bureau (IOB), Citygate One, 135 Park Street, London SE1 9EA (☎ 0171-928 7600 or 0845-600 6666) deals with most insurance complaints or will tell you who to contact. The Association of British Insurers (ABI), 51 Gresham Street, London EC2V 7HQ (☎ 0171-600 3333), publish a number of free leaflets regarding insurance matters and also handle complaints regarding policies issued by member companies. You can also ask your insurance company or broker for guidance or contact a Citizens Advice Bureau (see page 450).

INSURANCE CONTRACTS

Read all insurance contracts before signing them. If you don't understand everything, ask a friend or colleague to 'translate' it or take legal advice. If a policy has pages of legal jargon and gobbledegook in very small print, you have a right to be suspicious, particularly as it's common practice nowadays to be as brief as possible and write clearly and concisely in language which doesn't require a legal degree. In recent years many individuals have lost out under the most outrageous terms of contracts. Always check any exclusions or conditions and have them explained if you don't understand them. New EU directive on unfair terms and legal-speak in consumer contracts may curb the insurance companies discretion to increase future charges as they wish. At present, there's no requirement for insurers to notify policyholders about increases or how they affect the final pay-out (e.g. of a with-profits policy). Take care how you answer questions in an insurance proposal form, as even if you mistakenly provide false information an insurance company can refuse to pay out when you make a claim.

Long-term life insurance and pension plans are designed so that it's almost impossible to work out how much you're being charged in fees. Since 1st January 1995 insurance companies have been required to reveal to customers how much is taken from pension and insurance premiums for commission, administration and management expenses (plus providing specific illustrations of the maturity and surrender values for policies from July 1995). However, the new rules apply only to endowment policies, personal pensions, and term assurance paying out benefits after the age of 70. If you have ordinary term insurance (e.g. to cover a mortgage), permanent health insurance, critical illness cover, unit trusts, mortgage payment protection or an independent savings account (ISA), a salesman doesn't have to reveal the costs of the policy. Commission on a life policy amounts to around 20 per cent of the first year's premiums. Some direct insurers such as Virgin Direct charge no commission on premiums, which has forced others to follow suit. There's a government tax of 5 per cent on insurance premiums.

Most insurance policies run for a calendar year from the date on which you take out a policy. All insurance policy premiums should be paid punctually, as late payment can affect your benefits or a claim, although if this is so, it should be noted in your policy. **Before signing any insurance contract you should shop around and take a day or two to think it over. Never sign on the spot as you may regret it later. With some insurance contracts, e.g. life insurance and pension annuities, you have a 'cooling off' period of up to 14 days, during which you can cancel a policy without penalty.**

SOCIAL SECURITY

Social Security is the name given to the state benefits paid to residents of Britain, e.g. unemployment and sickness benefits, maternity pay, Income Support and family benefit. Social security is an 'insatiable monster' costing over £100 billion a year (payments have grown by over two-thirds in the last 15 years). Some benefits are dependent on your National Insurance contributions (see page 306), others on your circumstances, income or savings, while some have no pre-conditions. Benefit dependency has soared in recent years and the government is now trying to rein in the cost (many experts now people believe that the benefit system is unworkable and should be replaced rather than reformed). Almost one-third of the population receives some form of state benefit, including over two million people (a three-fold increase between 1982 and 1997) who receive incapacity benefit and severe disablement allowance for being unable to work (the qualifying 'test' is a farce).

It's estimated that as many as one million people don't claim the social security benefits to which they're entitled, therefore it's important to know your rights. On the other hand, many thousands of people receive social security payments in error to which they aren't entitled and many more make fraudulent claims. An estimated over five million national insurance numbers are bogus and may be used by fraudsters to claim social security benefits at a cost of up to £4 billion a year. Benefit errors are estimated to total some four million a year (most concerning Income Support) and claimants are just as likely to be overpaid as underpaid. If you're turned down for social security or receive less than you think you're entitled to, you should challenge the payment and take independent advice, e.g. from your local Citizens Advice Bureau.

It isn't necessary to be a British citizen to claim social security and some foreigners move to Britain purely to take advantage of social security payments. Social security payments can be made in cash from any post office or can be paid directly into a bank, building society or post office account. Social security benefits and National Insurance contributions are reviewed annually and increased in line with the Retail Price Index (RPI). Increases are paid from 6th April, which is the start of the tax year in Britain.

Leaflets: Leaflets are published for all social security benefits and are available from social security offices and (usually a limited number) from post offices, jobcentres and council offices. Leaflets include *Which Benefit* (FB2), which includes details of all social security benefits and lists all available leaflets, and *Social Security Benefit rates* (NI196), which lists the latest benefit rates, earnings rules and National Insurance contribution rates. Other general leaflets include *Bringing up Children?* (FB27) and the *Young People's Guide to Social Security* (FB23). All social security leaflets are available from the Leaflets Unit, PO Box 21, Stanmore, Middx. HA7 1AY.

Information: General information can be obtained from the Department of Social Security (DSS), Information Division, Alexander Fleming House, Elephant and Castle, London SE1 6BY (☎ 0171-238 0800). In addition to English, some leaflets are also available in other languages including Arabic, Bengali, Chinese, Greek, Gujarati, Hindi, Punjabi, Somali, Turkish, Urdu and Vietnamese. General information is available from any social security office (listed in phone books under 'Benefits Agency') or you can ☎ freefone 0800-666555 (in Northern Ireland ☎ freefone 0800-616757). Telephone information is also available in other languages. Information about social security can be obtained from your local Citizens Advice Bureau (CAB), Welfare Rights Office, Consumer Advice Centre or Legal Advice (or Law) Centre. Your local council may also provide a telephone advice service.

Detailed information about all social security benefits is contained in the *National Welfare Benefits Handbook* (income-related benefits) and the *Rights Guide to Non-means-tested Social Security Benefits*, both available from the Child Poverty Action Group, 1-5 Bath Street, London EC1V 9PY (☎ 0171-837 7979). *Your Rights* by Sally West is a guide to benefits for older people published by Age Concern England (1268 London Road, London SW16 4ER, ☎ 0181-679 8000) and available from most bookshops. Help the Aged (St. James's Walk, London EC1R 0BE, ☎ 0171-253 0253) publish a number of leaflets for the aged including *Can I Claim It?*.

Appeals: If you disagree with a decision regarding a claim for social security, you usually have the right of appeal (see leaflet NI246 *How to appeal*). You must appeal in writing to your local social security office or Unemployment Benefit office (if applicable), usually within three months of a decision, although some appeals must be made within 28 days, so make sure you check.

Going Abroad: With the exception of pensions, benefits are paid only to those resident in Britain, although you can leave Britain for a limited period and still qualify for certain benefits. For information see leaflets *Social Security abroad* (NI38) and *Your Social Security and pension rights in the European Union* (SA29). Leaflets SA4 to SA43 detail the social security benefits available in other countries under international agreements. Britain currently has bilateral agreements with all EEA countries plus Australia, Barbados, Bermuda, Canada, Cyprus, Israel, Jamaica, Jersey, Guernsey, Malta, Mauritius, New Zealand, the Philippines, Switzerland, Turkey, the USA, and Yugoslavia and its former republics.

Benefits

There are three main categories of social security benefits in Britain: situation-related benefits, income-related benefits and National Insurance-related benefits:

Situation-related benefits have nothing to do with your NI contributions (see page 306), income or savings, but depend entirely on your situation, e.g. whether you're a parent or the state of your health. They include benefits for parents, the disabled or chronically ill, and those injured at work. Benefits for parents include Child Benefit, One-Parent Benefit and a Guardian's Allowance. Benefits for the disabled or chronically ill are paid to a disabled person or to someone who looks after a disabled person, and include Attendance Allowance, Disability Living Allowance, Disability Working Allowance, Invalid Care Allowance and Severe Disablement Allowance. Benefits for those injured or killed at work, or those who contract a severe illness at work include Industrial Injuries Disablement Benefit, Workmen's Compensation Supplement and Industrial Injury Compensation.

Income-Related benefits depend on your income and your savings. They include Income Support, Family Credit, Housing Benefit, Council Tax Benefit and the Social Fund. If your savings are over £8,000 (£16,000 for Housing benefit or Council tax benefit), you won't be eligible for income-related benefits. If your savings are between £3,000 and £8,000, you receive a reduced benefit. Maximum benefits are paid to those whose savings are below 3,000. If you have a partner, his savings are included with yours.

National Insurance-Related benefits depend on the amount of national insurance (NI) contributions you have made (see below). They include benefits for the unemployed, expectant mothers, the sick, pensioners and widows. The Jobseeker's Allowance (formerly called 'unemployment benefit') is a weekly cash payment, payable from the first day you're unemployed for a period of up to one year (after which you can apply for Income Support). Benefits for expectant mothers include Statutory Maternity Pay and Maternity Allowance. There are a number of social security benefits for people who are sick, injured or disabled. Statutory Sick Pay (SSP) or Incapacity Benefit are paid after four days illness up to a maximum of

28 weeks. The long-term sick or disabled may be entitled to Invalidity Benefit, Invalidity Pension, Invalidity Allowance or Severe Disablement Allowance.

The state Retirement Pension is paid to all who qualify at the age of 65 for men and 60 for women (see below). In 1999/2000, the pension was £66.75 a week for a single person and £106.70 a week for a married couple, among the lowest in the EU. Following a European Court decision that it's unlawful to pay pensions to men and women at different ages, the woman's pension age has been increased to 65, although it currently depends on when she was born. For women born before 6th April 1950, the state pension age is 60. For women born after this date it's 65, although women born between 1950 and 1955 have a sliding scale of pension ages between 61 and 65. To qualify for the maximum pension a man must have worked at least 44 years and a woman (born before 6th April 1950) 39 years. Special pensions include the Over 80 Pension, War Disablement Pension and a War Widow's or Dependants Pension. Widows may be entitled to a Widow's Payment, Widowed Mother's Allowance or a Widow's Pension.

The government operates a scheme, called the State Earnings Related Pension Scheme (SERPS), whereby people can boost their state pension by paying higher NI contributions based on their earnings. Changes in pension legislation in 1988 were intended to encourage people to opt out (or 'contract out') of SERPS, which is proving too expensive for the government. The increasing pressure on the government to finance state pensions and other benefits for the aged is causing increasing concern in Britain (and most other western European countries), where the cost of pensions will soon far exceed contributions. Sweeping changes are planned to state pensions through the introduction of a new 'stakeholder' pension, that's expected to be introduced in April 2001. This will dramatically increase pensions for millions of people have no pension provision apart from the state pension. SERPS is expected to be replaced by a State Second Pension (SSP) in 2002. Changes are designed to help the lower paid who have traditionally made no private pension provisions. The basic pension is expected to continue.

NATIONAL INSURANCE

National Insurance (NI), called social security in most countries, is mandatory for most working people in Britain aged from 16 to the state pension age of 65. NI contributions entitle you to state benefits such as the Retirement Pension, Unemployment Benefit, Sickness Benefit, Maternity Allowance, Widow's Benefits and Invalidity Benefit. You qualify for these benefits only if you have already paid (or have been credited with) enough of the right class of contributions at the right time.

When you arrive in Britain, you must apply for a National Insurance number from your local Department of Social Security (DSS) office, which may take six to eight weeks to be allocated. You will receive a plastic NI Numbercard with your personal number on it, which usually remains the same all your life. You must give your NI number to your employer if you're an employee or to your local social security office if you're self-employed, so that your NI contribution record can be kept up to date.

Your contributions and those of your employer depend on your income and status, e.g. employee or self-employed. NI contributions are calculated as a percentage of your salary and are paid on earnings between £66 (lower earnings limit) and £500 a week (upper earnings limit) in the tax year 1999/2000. You don't pay NI contributions if you earn less than the lower earnings limit or on earnings above the upper earnings limit. NI rates are normally increased in April at the start of each tax year and sometimes change during the tax year (see leaflet NI196, *Social Security benefit rates*).

If you're over 65 you aren't required to pay NI contributions, whether or not you have retired from work, although if you continue to work as an employee, your employer must still pay contributions for you. Your level of NI payments depend on whether your employer's pension scheme (see page 309) is contracted in or out of SERPS. There are five classes of NI contributions:

Class 1: Is for employees earning between £66 and £500 a week. Both the employee and employer contribute and providing your NI contributions are up to date, you qualify for most state benefits. Employees contracted out of SERPS pay 8.4 per cent on the next £434 of earnings between £66 and £500 and those contracted in to SERPS pay 10 per cent. Employers contributions vary depending on an employee's earnings. Married women and widows paying the reduced rate of NI pay 3.85 per cent on earnings from £66 to £500. Your NI contribution card is stamped by your employer. If you go abroad, e.g. to work, you can continue to pay class 1 contributions voluntarily for one year, after which you can pay class 3 contributions (see below) in order to maintain your payment record and qualify for a full retirement pension.

Class 1A: Is for employers who provide their employees with a car or petrol for private use. The employer pays Class 1A contributions, not the employee.

Class 2: Is for self-employed people (men under 65, women under 60) whose profits are more than £3,590 a year. Your contribution is a flat rate of £6.55 a week which entitles you to claim all state benefits except Unemployment Benefit, compensation for industrial injuries, Statutory Sick Pay and Statutory Maternity Pay. Your contributions go towards any SERPS entitlement in your pension. If your profits are above a certain amount, you may need to pay profit-related Class 4 contributions (see below) in addition to Class 2 contributions. Payment can be made by buying NI stamps from a post office or via a direct debit from a bank, building society or post office account.

Class 3: Are voluntary contributions for anyone without a full record of NI contributions or who isn't liable to pay Class 1 or Class 2 contributions, e.g. someone working abroad or a self-employed person with low profits, or someone who stopped working voluntarily. Class 3 contributions can also be paid if you have been excluded from class 2 contributions. Class 3 allows you to make voluntary payments at a flat rate of £6.55 a week, at anytime during the six years following a break in payments (after which it's too late). By filling the gaps in your NI contributions, you can protect your retirement pension or widow's benefits. Payment can be via a lump sum in addition to those methods listed under Class 2 above.

Class 4: Payments are also for the self-employed. In addition to Class 2 contributions, you must pay a further 6 per cent of any profits between £7,310 and £25,220 a year (1998/99). Class 4 contributions are assessed and collected by the Inland Revenue, when you pay income tax on your profits. You receive tax relief of 50 per cent on these contributions.

If you aren't working for any of the reasons listed below, you receive NI credits, which means that your NI contribution record is unbroken during the non-working period:

- you're claiming Unemployment, Sickness, Maternity or Invalidity Benefit or Statutory Sick Pay;
- you're in full-time education;
- you're on an approved training course, e.g. youth training;
- you're aged 60 to 64 and not working, e.g. you retire early.

If you're at home looking after children and claiming Child Benefit, or looking after a sick, disabled or elderly person (without invalid care allowance), you may qualify for Home Responsibilities Protection. This helps you to keep your pension rights, even though you aren't paying NI contributions or receiving credits. See leaflet NP27A, *Looking after someone at home? How to protect your pension*.

Britain has a reciprocal arrangement with around 30 countries, including all EU member states, allowing social security contributions paid in one country to be taken into account under the social security schemes of another country. If you live in Britain for a short period only, you may be exempt from paying NI contributions, particularly if your home country has a bilateral agreement with Britain. To qualify you must usually have been transferred to Britain by your employer for a limited period only and must remain covered by your home country's social security scheme. Information can be obtained from the Department of Social Security, Overseas Branch, Longbenton, Newcastle-upon-Tyne NE98 1YX (☎ 06451-54811).

Note that if you retire to a country with which Britain doesn't have an agreement, you must arrange with the DSS to receive your pension abroad. Under agreements with Australia, Canada, New Zealand and Norway, the level of pension is frozen when you leave Britain and you won't receive annual increases based on the retail price index. Employees of international organisations and diplomatic missions are usually exempt from paying NI contributions.

PENSIONS

Everyone who pays National Insurance (see above) is entitled to a state retirement pension, although for most people this barely provides sufficient income to pay for their basic needs, let alone maintain their standard of living in retirement. The value of the state pension has fallen considerably in real terms in the last few decades, and many pensioners in Britain live in poverty. Most people make far too little provision for retirement and will be in for a rude shock when they retire (some 80 per cent of people don't save enough for their retirement and a spectre of poverty hangs over many in retirement). Most people should double their pension payments in order to retire on a good salary and you need to pay even more into your fund if you want to retire early at age 50 or 55 on a decent income.

Falling gilt yields (on which annuities are based) in recent years has also hit retirement incomes (as a result most insurance companies have been hit by pension guarantees made when gilt yields were high, which are costing insurers some £10 billion). In recent years an increasing number of people have been taking early retirement, either voluntarily or after having been made redundant. This means that unless you have a large private income or pots of money, it's imperative to have a company or private pension to secure your future after retirement.

Most people who have the opportunity join a company pension fund, or providing they can afford it, take out a personal pension plan (both of which are described below). You receive tax relief on all pension contributions at the highest rate paid on your earned income and can pay contributions into a personal pension fund net of income tax. The gains on investments from a pension are tax-free, but your pension on retirement is taxable as earned income. **It's worth noting that no other form of savings provides more tax breaks than pensions, e.g. free of income and capital gains tax.**

The investment fund accrued by your pension must be invested in an annuity to pay your pension in your retirement years. When you retire you have the right to shop around for the best annuity you can find from *any* insurance company. Many people fall into the trap of opting for an annuity recommended by their insurance company, which often costs them thousands or even tens of thousands of pounds. Retirees can now buy annuities at different times during their retirement up to the age of 75, when they must buy a conventional annuity. For information, consult an annuity specialist or the London-based Annuity Bureau or Annuity Direct. If you retire abroad, your British pension(s) is paid gross, but you must obtain a declaration from the foreign country's taxation authorities that you're a resident there for tax purposes and are taxed on your worldwide income there (see also **Double Taxation Agreements** on page 353).

Information: Before making any decisions regarding your pension, you should thoroughly investigate the various options available and take professional advice, e.g. from a member of the Society of Pension Consultants, St. Bartholomew's House, 92 Fleet Street, London EC4Y 1DG (☎ 0171-353 1688) or the Association of Consulting Actuaries, Watson House, London Road, Reigate, Surrey RH2 9PQ. There are many publications dedicated to pensions in Britain including *Your Pension* magazine and *The Which? Guide to Pensions* by Jonquil Love (Which? Books). However, bear in mind that pensions are the most expensive, mis-sold, misunderstood, poorly performing financial product you can buy (and the one most people need most of all)!

Company Pension Scheme

Many companies operate voluntary employee pension schemes, particularly for management and key staff, which are invariably better than a personal pension plan. An employer must contribute something to a company pension scheme and in certain cases he may pay the whole contribution, called a non-contributory scheme. Company schemes aren't universal (particularly in smaller companies) and are still considered by many employers to be a fringe benefit, like company cars and expense accounts. Since 6th April 1988, employees have been under no obligation to join an employer's pension scheme, which may be important to those with their own personal pension plan or who think they can do better somewhere else.

Company pension schemes almost always offer a better deal than you could find elsewhere, particularly if you plan to stay with a company until retirement. You should think twice before turning down the opportunity to join a company pension scheme, as your employer pays (on average) twice as much as you do into the scheme, whilst most companies pay *nothing* towards a personal pension fund. It follows that for a personal plan to provide an equal pension, it must do twice as well as a company scheme. **In short, it almost never pays to opt out of an employer's pension fund in favour of a personal pension plan.**

On average, employees pay around 5 per cent of their gross salary into a company pension fund. The typical fund member builds up retirement benefits at the rate of one-sixtieth of his final salary for each year worked. So after 40 years service, you receive two-thirds of your final salary. However, just 1 in every 100 people actually achieves this, as usually only your basic salary is used by an employer to calculate your pension, and bonuses, overtime, company cars, free insurance and other benefits aren't taken into account.

A company pension scheme is usually 'contracted out' of SERPS, which means the company has removed its pension scheme members from the State Earnings Related Pension Scheme (SERPS). Your employer's pension scheme is then responsible for providing you with a pension on retirement, which mustn't be less than the guaranteed minimum pension provided by the state. Usually your pension will be much higher than under SERPS and you (and your employer) will also pay lower NI contributions. Contracted out employees and their employers pay the normal NI contributions on earnings up to the lower earnings limit, plus a lower contribution on the part of earnings between the lower and upper earnings limits (see page 306).

Most company pensions are index-linked after retirement to offset inflation, include the option to retire early and generous treatment if you retire early through ill health. Many also include a widow's or dependant's benefit if you die before or during retirement. One of the most significant changes in recent years in company pensions, has been the possibility of transferring your pension to a new scheme when changing jobs. If you have been in a company pension scheme for less than two years, you can obtain a refund of your contributions less tax, and you may receive interest but won't receive your employer's contributions. If you have been in a company pension scheme for more than two years, you can choose to leave your pension behind (a deferred pension) and receive a reduced pension on retirement, or transfer it to another scheme. If you leave Britain permanently, your contributions will remain in the fund and you will receive a reduced pension on retirement.

Company pension schemes are usually either 'final salary' or 'money purchase' schemes. A final salary scheme is the most common type (around 90 per cent of the total, including most large or medium sized companies) and guarantees you a pension based on a percentage of your final salary. This is advantageous because salary increases usually keep pace with (or exceed) inflation and your salary may also be increased by promotions. The longer you have worked with a company, the larger will be the percentage, which is usually a maximum of two-thirds on salaries up to the maximum earnings limit of £87,600 a year. The pensionable salary ceiling is fixed by the government and is increased annually in line with the retail price index (see page 366). A money purchase scheme means that pension contributions, from both the employee and the employer, are paid into an individual fund which doesn't guarantee to pay a certain income on retirement. When you retire, your fund is used to 'buy' a pension from an insurance company. A money purchase scheme is common in small companies, but isn't portable if you change employers (i.e. you cannot transfer it to a new employer).

Employee contributions to the fund vary depending on the rules and can be up to 15 per cent of gross salary. If you pay less than 15 per cent of your gross salary into a company pension scheme, you can increase your pension by paying the difference, called Additional Voluntary Contributions (AVCs), either into the company scheme or into a separate personal pension plan (see below), called a free-standing AVC

(FSAVC) scheme. AVCs can be paid on a regular or occasional basis or as one-off payments. The main benefit of a money purchase pension scheme is that not only are all contributions tax-free, but the fund is also allowed to grow free of tax. If you take part of your pension in cash (up to 25 per cent is permitted) when you retire, that's also tax-free. A money purchase scheme must use the money saved on NI contributions as the guaranteed minimum contribution to the pension scheme.

Most company pension schemes conform to the state retirement age of 65. If you want to retire early you will usually receive a (much) lower pension, although if you take early retirement on grounds of ill health, you usually receive your full pension. Redundancy (voluntary or forced) may result in a slightly reduced pension, but voluntary early retirement may reduce your pension by half. The early retirement pension entitlement will be detailed in your company pension scheme rules. On the other hand, if you delay receipt of your company pension, e.g. for five years, your pension may increase by as much as 50 per cent.

Inland Revenue rules allow you to retire for any reason from the age of 50. If you're opting for early retirement before that age, you may need to show serious ill-health before the Inland Revenue will allow you to take advantage of tax concessions. Pensioners usually pay little tax on their pensions (a lump sum is tax-free) and the IR might think you're avoiding paying tax on your earnings if you retire at 35 (tax inspectors are a suspicious lot).

Information: Information about company pensions is available from the Company Pensions Information Centre, Old Park lane, London W1Y 3LJ. There's no Ombudsman (independent arbitrator) for employers' pension schemes. If you have a complaint you can write to the Occupational Pensions Advisory Service, 11 Belgrave Road, London SW1V 1RB (☎ 0171-233 8080).

Personal Pension Plan

If you're self-employed or don't belong to a company pension scheme (or joined a company pension scheme at a late age), you should consider a personal pension plan (PPP). Plans are available from many financial institutions including banks, building societies, insurance companies, friendly societies, unit trust companies and various other companies. In the last five years, sales of PPPs have fallen considerably due to the bad publicity generated by the mis-selling of pensions since 1988.

Under legislation introduced in 1988, thousands of employees were encouraged to opt out of company pension schemes (where employers typically contribute twice as much as employees) and buy personal pension plans (where employers rarely make any contributions at all). This has had disastrous results for millions of people who transferred out of employer schemes into PPPs, thus greatly reducing their pensions. Nobody spelt out the consequences and cost of leaving an employer's pension fund and millions of people were mis-sold personal pensions (3.5 million were sold in the first year alone). While not actively encouraging employees to leave company schemes, most employers did little or nothing to discourage their employees from opting out of their schemes, which saved employers £millions in pension premiums. **It's almost never advisable to leave an employer's pension scheme!**

Insurance companies have been forced to acknowledge that they or their representatives mis-sold over two million pensions between April 1988 and June 1994. They are now facing a vast compensation bill that could exceed £3 billion (although policyholders will have to foot most of the bill through a reduction in bonus levels). Needless to say, insurance companies are trying to wheedle out of their responsibilities and victims have waited years for compensation (most are still waiting). Tens of thousands of victims will receive no compensation at all and many could be left with virtually worthless pensions.

Although better than nothing, most independent financial advisers agree that most personal pensions offer poor value for money and many are a rip-off and under-perform most employers' schemes. There's a hefty penalty for switching your personal pension to a different company, so it pays to get it right first time. Among the companies recommended by the 'experts' are CGU, Merchant Investors, Royal & Sun Alliance, Standard Life and Winterthur Life. Note, however, that the 'best' company depends on how much you plan to invest and whether you plan to invest a monthly sum or a lump-sum (or both). You can also find a personal pension via the Internet (e.g. www.discountpensions.co.uk, who will refund the initial commission on pension funds with certain companies). Note that many companies penalise you if you take early retirement.

Charges, Costs & Commissions: When comparing plans, you must compare the true cost, particularly of endowment policies, as many companies levy very high charges which often reduce funds by up to 40 per cent. Check the pension administration and commission charges, and what percentage of your contributions are actually paid into your fund, as some pension companies have very high (extortionate) charges. A few companies have low fees and will tell you exactly what they are. Note, however, that good investment performance may more than compensate for slightly higher fees. If you belong to a group (company) personal pension plan, you should ensure that it's portable, otherwise you could lose up to half the contributions made by you and your employer on changing jobs. If you leave Britain permanently, your contributions will remain in the fund and you will receive a reduced pension on retirement.

Personal pension plans are similar to company money purchase schemes (see above) in that you pay money into your own personal fund. Contributions can be paid monthly, quarterly or annually, as agreed between you and your fund. Withdrawals can be made at any time between the age of 50 and 75, without you having to retire. On retirement, the amount accrued is used to buy an annuity from an insurance company, which will pay you a regular pension. If preferred you can also take a percentage (currently 25 per cent up to a limit of £150,000) as a tax-free cash sum, although this will reduce your pension. Note that if you wish to buy an annuity with another company, most insurers charge a fee of between 2 to 5 per cent of your entire fund!

The maximum you can contribute to a PPP on which you receive full tax relief, depends on your age at the start of the tax year, as shown below:

Age	Per Cent	Amount*
under 36	17.5	£15,330
36 to 45	20	£17,520
46 to 50	25	£21,900
51 to 55	30	£26,280
56 to 60	35	£30,660
61 or over	40	£35,040

* The amounts shown above are based on a maximum earnings limit of £87,600 a year (which is liable to change).

Types of Plans: There are three types of personal pension plans: deposit, with-profits and unit-linked. A 'deposit' plan is the safest as it grows by just having interest added to it and no risk is involved. Those with a 'with-profits' plan know from the start the minimum pension or lump-sum they will receive on retirement. In addition, bonuses are added annually and there may also be a final termination bonus. Your payments are invested in stocks and shares and the level of bonuses you receive are determined by the investment skill of your fund manager (if he's useless you had better watch out) and the state of the stock market.

Like a with-profits plan, 'unit-linked' contributions are also invested in the stock market, but your fund is linked to various investments. There's no guaranteed pension or lump sum, which depends on the performance of your fund's investments. This is the riskiest personal pension plan, but it can also be the most rewarding. Although there are no guarantees, over a number of years the value of stocks and shares usually rise at a much faster rate than inflation. One advantage of a personal pension plan that may be overlooked, is that it can be used as collateral for a personal loan at a preferential interest rate.

A personal pension plan can be used to contract out of the SERPS (see page 306) part of your national insurance contributions, which will be paid into your fund. Contracting out of (or back into) SERPS is a complicated subject on which professional advice should always be sought. For information about SERPS write to the Department of Social Security (DSS), COE Group, Newcastle-upon-Tyne, NE98 1YX, quoting your National Insurance number and the name of your PPP shown on your contribution notification document.

DIY Pensions: You can save £thousands with a DIY pension by cutting out the middleman as there's no or little commission to pay. The savings on pension payments of just £100 a month can be almost £1,000 in the first year alone. A number of companies offer execution-only services including Best Investment (☎ 0171-321 0100), Chartwell Investment Management (☎ 01225-446556), Lansdown Pensions Direct (☎ 0117-988 9880) and TQ Direct (☎ freefone 0800-056 1836).

SIPPs: In addition to a managed PPP, you can also have a self-invested personal pension (SIPP), although this is worthwhile only for those investing large sums (e.g. £50,000 or £500 a month) as the costs are high. A SIPP allows you to manage your own pension fund, investing in individual shares, investment trusts or other schemes. In the wake of the pensions mis-selling scandal, SIPPs and DIY pensions have boomed.

Information about PPPs is published in daily newspapers, financial magazines and is available via the television teletext information service. Performance tables are published regularly in pension and financial magazines showing the best-performing personal pension funds. You would be wise to consult them before joining a scheme.

ACCIDENT INSURANCE

Accident insurance, although uncommon in Britain, is available from a number of companies. It includes lump-sum pay outs in the event of death or permanent disability (e.g. £100,000 to £250,000) or hospitalisation as the result of an accident, and usually provides hospital (e.g. £50 to £125 a day) and convalescence benefits (e.g. £200 a week) after a minimum period in hospital. The cost of accident insurance is usually between £5 and £20 a month depending on the number of people insured and the cover provided. You may be able to choose higher cash payments by increasing your premium. Accident insurance can often be combined with Permanent Health Insurance (see below). Occupational accident insurance is compulsory and is paid by your employer. It covers accidents or illness at work and may also cover accidents that occur when travelling to and from work or when travelling on company business.

PERMANENT HEALTH INSURANCE

Permanent health insurance (PHI) is designed to provide you with a weekly or monthly income when you're unable to work due to sickness or injury. Most employees have three possible sources of income when they're unable to work: Statutory Sick Pay (SSP) or Occupational Sick Pay (OSP) paid by their employer and Incapacity Benefit paid by the DSS. Your right to OSP depends on your employment contract (see **Chapter 2**). Around 50 per cent of small companies with less than ten employees and some 55 per cent of all private sector firms in Britain have an OSP scheme.

OSP Schemes: An OSP scheme pays an employee's salary for a limited number of weeks only, depending on his length of service, for example:

Period of Service	No. Weeks Salary
less than 13 weeks	0
13 weeks - 2 years	8
2 years - 5 years	10
5 years - 10 years	15
10 years plus	26

PHI Policies: To ensure an adequate income when you're unable to work, you should take out a permanent health insurance (PHI) policy, also called income replacement insurance, which guarantees you a fixed amount each week (you decide how much) in the event of illness, injury or invalidity. A permanent health insurance policy (which shouldn't be confused with private health insurance, see page 315), will pay you a fixed amount each month or a percentage of your salary if you're ill for a long period or permanently disabled in an accident. This type of policy is common among the self-employed and is also provided by employers with an OSP scheme. However, only some 15 per cent of the population have PHI insurance, either on their own account or through their employer. Note that you're around 15 times more likely to be off work for six months or longer, than you are to die before the age of 65!

PHI policies typically pay up to 75 per cent of your gross annual earnings (up to maximum salary of around £50,000), although you can insure a smaller proportion of your salary to reduce the premiums. The longer you wait for the income protection insurance to pay out, the lower your monthly premium. Usually you can choose when the payments start, e.g. four weeks, three months or six months, or even one or two years after an accident or the onset of an illness. For example your company may pay your salary for up to six months of an illness or accident, in which case you can choose to defer payments from your PHI policy for this period. Some policies pay benefits for a limited period only, e.g. up to a maximum of five years, while others continue payments until you return to work or retire. **You should avoid a policy that defines disability as the inability to do any job!**

The longer the period for which you require cover, the higher your monthly premium will be. Premiums also depend on your health record, age, salary, sex, job (high or low risk) and whether you smoke. Premiums and benefits may be index-linked. The younger you are, the lower your premiums, although women tend to pay more than men on average (due to a worse claims record). Depending on your age and type of job, some insurance companies may require you to have a medical examination or will obtain a report from your family doctor. If you take out income protection insurance, policy payments are tax-free for the financial year in which you fall sick and the following year. If your employer provides the insurance, all income is taxable.

Homeowners in particular may need PHI (or mortgage protection insurance) to ensure they can continue to pay their mortgage should they become unemployed or sick for a long period. Note, however, that redundancy insurance is one of the most abused of all insurance markets. You can take out a 'mortgage protection' (see page 347) or payment care policy (usually with your lender) specifically to cover your mortgage and other regular bills (such as gas, electricity and water), if you're unemployed or off work due to an accident or sickness. You're typically covered for two years as a result of unemployment and five years in the event of a disability (sometimes you're covered until retirement or your mortgage is paid off). Benefits are usually paid out after a deferred period, e.g. 4 to 52 weeks and may extend until the age of 60 or 65 (in the event of your being unable to work due to illness or accident). A typical policy providing cover of £15,000 a year with a deferred period of 13 weeks costs around £25 a month. Note, however, that many insurance analysts believe that some policies are so expensive and so full of exclusions (many people who are sold policies are ineligible from the start!) that you may be better off without it!

It's also possible to take out an international sickness or accident policy against being unable to work due to a disability. A typical policy provides for 75 per cent of your insured income to be paid after a three-month deferment period for a maximum of three years. If incapacity continues after three years, you receive a lump sum payment.

HEALTH INSURANCE

The National Health Service (NHS) provides free or subsidised medical treatment to all British subjects with the right of abode in Britain and to anyone who, at the time of treatment, has been a resident for the previous year (there are exemptions for certain groups). For further information about the NHS see page 279. Anyone living or working in Britain who isn't eligible for treatment under the NHS should take out a private health insurance policy (also referred to as private medical insurance or PMI).

This section deals exclusively with private health insurance, which is available from non-profit provident associations (e.g. BUPA, PPP and WPA) and various other sources including general insurance companies, banks, building societies and motoring organisations. Many schemes offered by banks and other financial institutions are provided through the British United Provident Associations (BUPA) or the Private Patients Plan Ltd. (PPP), although terms, benefits and premiums usually vary. Note that permanent health insurance is another name for income protection insurance (see page 314) and shouldn't be confused with private health insurance.

The number of people with private health insurance in Britain increased from around 1.5 million in 1966 to some 6.5 million in 1998 (around 12 per cent of the population), half of whose premiums are paid by employers. The remainder are spilt between those who pay their own premiums and those who share them with their employers. Private health care is restricted mainly to the middle to upper income brackets. The best advertisement for private health insurance is the eternal NHS waiting lists for non-emergency operations. NHS waiting lists for all types of treatment (including operations) totalled over one million people in 1998. One in every five operations in Britain is performed privately.

There's no tax relief on private health insurance premiums, despite the fact that they save the NHS £billions a year. Private health insurance isn't usually intended to replace NHS treatment, but to complement it. Most health insurance policies fall into two main categories: those providing immediate private specialist or hospital treatment (e.g. BUPA, PPP and WPA) and so-called 'budget' or 'waiting-list' policies, where you're treated as a private patient when waiting lists exceed a certain period. Under waiting-list policies, if you cannot obtain an appointment with an NHS specialist or an NHS hospital admission within a certain period (e.g. six weeks), you can do so as a private patient.

Most health insurance policies have an annual limit on the amount they will pay out for each policyholder, which may be anywhere between £5,000 and £1 million. They usually include consultations with specialists; hospital accommodation and nursing; operations or other treatment (e.g. physiotherapy, radiotherapy, chemotherapy); physician's, surgeon's and anaesthetist's fees; all drugs, X-rays and dressings while in hospital; home nursing; and a daily cash allowance when hospitalised under the NHS.

You cannot take out private health care to cover or obtain treatment for an existing or previous medical condition (depending on how serious and long ago it was) and there's usually a qualifying period of around three months before you can make a claim. For example, if you need a hernia operation, for which there are currently long NHS waiting lists, you cannot obtain private health cover to jump the queue. Your only solution, other than waiting your turn under the NHS, is to have private treatment and pay for it yourself (a hernia operation costs around £2,000 and a hip replacement up to £7,000). In fact, if you have serious health problems you will need to pay extra for insurance or may be refused cover altogether.

The cost of private health insurance depends on your age and the state of your health. There are maximum age limits for taking out health insurance with some insurers, e.g. 65 for BUPA, although age limits may be higher if you're willing to accept some restrictions. Some companies have special policies for those aged over 50 or over 55. There are generally no restrictions on continuing membership, irrespective of age. Treatment of any medical condition for which you have already received medical attention or was aware existed in the five years prior to the start date of the policy, may not be covered. However, existing health problems may be covered after two years membership, when no further medical attention has been required. Some group policies do, however, include cover for existing or previous health problems. Other exclusions are listed in the policy rules.

The cost of health insurance has increased at double the rate of inflation in recent years. One of the reasons is that BUPA and PPP have a stranglehold on private healthcare in Britain (they also own many hospitals) and other companies find it difficult to gain a foothold in the market. The cost varies considerably depending on the insurance company and whether you have fully comprehensive health insurance or a 'waiting-list' policy. The cost of insurance also depends on the hospital in which you're treated (the more expensive hospitals cost around twice as much as the cheapest). Note that should you choose to have treatment outside the hospitals covered by your insurance policy (which may be severely restricted), you may have to pay the whole cost of treatment yourself!

Standard policies may offer three scales (usually designated A, B and C) of hospital treatment which may include London NHS teaching hospitals (A, high scale), provincial NHS teaching hospitals (B, medium scale) and provincial non-teaching hospitals (C, low scale). Accommodation is usually in a private room, but in some hospitals it may be in a twin or four-bedded ward. Premiums range from a few pounds a week for a budget plan offering limited benefits (e.g. HSA) up to £hundreds a month for a comprehensive policy with a major insurance company. Comprehensive top-of-the-range cover costs from £40 a month for a single person and from around £100 for a family (some companies offer lower premiums but have a compulsory annual excess of £500 or £1,000).

Always shop around and compare premiums and levels of cover from a number of insurers (over 60 plans are available from around 30 companies). Take care to find the right policy for your family, as benefits vary widely and many people waste money on policies that are useless to them. The major companies include BUPA, PPP, Norwich Union and WPA, which together have around 80 per cent of the market. Budget policies are better than nothing (particularly to bypass NHS waiting lists), but aren't usually such good value as standard policies. A no-claims discount is usually available, which means you can save up to 50 per cent on the 'standard' rate, and some companies offer discounts for non-smokers. You may also have the option of paying an excess (deductible) in order to reduce costs, e.g. the first £150 of a claim.

Premiums must usually be paid by direct debit via a bank, building society or post office account, either monthly, quarterly or annually. If you don't pay annually, there's usually an extra charge, e.g. 5 per cent. Premiums are usually reviewed annually and increased in line with (or above) inflation. Premiums usually increase with age, but won't generally be increased as the result of the number of claims you have made (unless you change insurance companies, so take care). Your policy also cannot be cancelled due to ill health. You don't usually require a medical examination to take out private health insurance, but must complete a medical questionnaire. Depending on your age and health record, your family doctor may be required to provide a medical report.

It's also possible to take out an international health insurance policy, which may be of interest to those living in Britain temporarily or those who work in different countries. Some policies offer members a range of premiums from budget to comprehensive cover. Policies offer at least two fee scales, one covering the whole world including North America and the other excluding North America. Most policies include a full refund of hospital, ambulance, home nursing (usually for a limited period), out patient, emergency dental treatment and repatriation charges. Policies include an annual overall claims limit, e.g. from £100,000 to £1,000,000 (the higher the better, particularly for North America).

Some comprehensive policies provide a fixed amount for general medical costs (including routine doctor's visits) and optional dental, optical and maternity expenses. Premiums range from around £600 to over £2,000 a year, depending on your age, level of cover and the areas covered (if North America is covered, premiums are much higher). If you don't require permanent international health insurance, you should consider a policy which provides limited or optional cover when you're abroad. Note that all bills, particularly those received for treatment outside Britain, must include precise details of treatment received. Terms such as 'Dental Treatment' or 'Consultation' are insufficient. It's also helpful if bills are written in English (although impossible in many countries).

When changing employers or leaving Britain, you should ensure that you have continuous medical insurance. For example, if you and your family are covered by a company health scheme, your insurance will probably cease after your last official day of employment. If you're leaving Britain, you must cancel a British health insurance policy in writing if you aren't a member of a company health scheme. **If you're planning to change your health insurance company, you should ensure that no important benefits are lost. When changing health insurance companies, it's advisable to inform your old insurance company if you have any outstanding bills for which they are liable.**

DENTAL INSURANCE

Dental treatment that isn't covered by the NHS isn't usually included in private health insurance policies, although it's often available as an extra, and a number of specialist dental policies are also available. Dental insurance has boomed in the '90s and has been boosted by the ever-diminishing number of dentists that accept NHS patients (less than half). Plans provided by BUPA and Denplan (a subsidiary of PPP) have an average premium of around £12.50 a month. Patients must be 'dentally fit' (so if you have 'bad' teeth, you won't be accepted) and are graded according to the condition of their teeth. Insurance doesn't usually cover expensive items such as crowns, bridges and dentures.

You can also obtain dental insurance (usually optionally) under some foreign health insurance policies or a worldwide health scheme. Emergency dental treatment and treatment required as the result of an accident may, however, be covered by a standard health insurance policy or an accident policy. If in doubt contact your health or accident insurance company. For details of dental treatment covered by the NHS, see page 290. **Note that if you have healthy teeth and rarely pay for more than an annual check-up and a visit to a hygienist, dental insurance offers poor value for money.**

LONG-TERM CARE INSURANCE

Long-term care (LTC) insurance is becoming increasingly common in Britain and will become even more important as the NHS and social security system struggle to meet the requirements of the aged. There's already a crisis in providing care for the elderly in nursing and residential homes, many of which are funded partly or wholly by local governments and charities. With the number of elderly people set to grow dramatically in the next few decades, caring for the elderly is a problem that won't go away. There's a huge discrepancy between the cost of keeping people in homes and the benefits paid by social security and many councils can no longer afford to accommodate their elderly in residential homes.

Fees for residential and nursing homes are from around £400 to £600 per week, depending on the area, or £20,000 to £30,000 a year. If you don't have insurance and need to go into a nursing home, the government will take your savings and even your home to pay for the cost (around 40,000 homes are sold each year to pay for nursing home fees). The solution is to take out long-term care insurance (also called a 'nursing home plan'), although premiums are high unless you start paying when you're relatively young, and benefits are limited to a number of years and/or a relatively small monthly payment (in relation to nursing home costs). Insurance pays for private nursing, either in your own home or in a retirement or residential home, and costs around £150 to £200 a month for someone aged 60 to 65 for a policy paying out £1,000 a month. With some policies you can pay a lump sum, e.g. £10,000, for fixed monthly cover of around £1,000. Typical policies pay out when you're unable to carry out two or three out of the five main daily activities (dressing, washing, feeding yourself, continence and getting around).

BUILDINGS INSURANCE

For most people, buying a home is the biggest financial investment they will ever make. When buying a home, you're usually responsible for insuring it before you even move in. If you take out a mortgage to buy a property, your lender will usually insist that your home (including most permanent structures on your property) has buildings insurance from the time you exchange contracts and are legally the owner. If you buy the leasehold of an apartment, your buildings insurance will be arranged by the owner of the freehold. Even when not required by a lender, you would be extremely unwise not to have buildings insurance.

Buildings insurance usually includes loss or damage caused by fire; theft; riot or malicious acts; water leakage from pipes or tanks; oil leakage from central heating systems; flood, storm and lightening; explosion or aircraft impact; vehicles or animals; earthquake, subsidence, landslip or heave; falling trees or aerials; and cover for temporary homelessness, e.g. up to £5,000. Some insurance companies also provide optional cover to include trees and shrubs damaged maliciously or by storms. Note that there may be an excess, e.g. from £25 or £50, for some claims, which is intended to deter people from making small claims. Buildings insurance should be renewed each year and insurance companies are continually updating their policies, so you must take care that a policy still provides the cover required when you receive a renewal notice.

Lenders fix the initial level of cover when you first apply for a mortgage and usually offer to arrange the insurance for you, but you're usually free to make your own arrangements. Note that if you change your buildings insurance from your lender to another insurer, you may be charged a transfer fee (e.g. £25) and an 'administration' fee to encourage you *not* to change. If you arrange your own buildings insurance, your lender will insist that the level of cover is sufficient. Most people take the easy option and arrange insurance through their mortgage lender, which is generally the most expensive option, e.g. some direct insurance companies guarantee to cut buildings insurance costs for the majority of homeowners insured through banks and building societies.

The amount for which your home must be insured isn't the current market value, but the cost of rebuilding it should it be totally destroyed. This varies depending on the type of property and the area, for example an inexpensive terraced house in the north of England could cost twice its market value to rebuild whereas a more expensive detached property in the south of England, may cost a lot less than its market value to rebuild, due to the high value of land. There's generally no deduction for wear and tear and the cost of redecoration is usually met in full. Note that buildings insurance doesn't cover structural faults that existed when you took out the policy, which is why it's important to have a full structural survey done when buying a property.

Many people pay far too much for their buildings insurance as many insurance companies have greatly over-estimated the cost of rebuilding. In many cases building costs were calculated using the Royal Institute of Chartered Surveyors (RICS) Rebuilding Costs Index rather than the correct Tender Price Index, which takes into account actual building prices. The RICS produce a table to calculate the cost of rebuilding your home, which should be used when assessing the cost. If you're in doubt, check how the rebuilding cost of your home was calculated and whether it's correct.

Most lenders provide index-linked buildings insurance, where premiums are linked to inflation and building costs (premiums are usually added to your monthly mortgage payments). It is, however, your responsibility to ensure that your level of cover is adequate, particularly if you carry out improvements or extensions which substantially increase the value of your home. All lenders provide information and free advice. If your level of cover is too low, an insurance company is within its rights to reduce the amount it pays out when a claim is made, in which case you may find you cannot afford to have your house rebuilt or repaired should disaster strike.

The cost of buildings insurance varies depending on the insurer, the type of building and the area, and is calculated per £1,000 of insurance, e.g. from £1 per £1,000 of cover per year in an inexpensive area to between £2 to £4 (or over £4 in London) in more expensive areas. Therefore insurance on a property costing £100,000 to rebuild usually costs from £100 to £400 a year. In recent years increased competition, particularly from direct insurers, has reduced premiums. Shop around as many people can reduce their premium by half (but don't believe the advertising blurb as some companies that claim to save you money actually charge more). Insurance for 'non-standard' homes such as those with thatched roofs, timber construction, holiday homes, old period properties and listed buildings is usually much higher. The highest level of cover usually includes damage to glass (e.g. windows and patio doors) and porcelain (e.g. baths, washbasins and WCs), although you may have to pay extra for accidental damage, e.g. when your son blasts a cricket ball through the patio window. Always ask your insurer what *isn't* covered and what it will cost to include it (if required).

Premiums can usually be paid monthly (although there may be an extra charge) or annually. Some home insurance policies charge an excess (e.g. £50) for each claim, while others have an excess for certain claims only, e.g. subsidence or landslip (when your house disappears into a hole in the ground or over a cliff), which is usually £1,000 or £2,000. Owners of houses vulnerable to subsidence (e.g. those built on clay) and those living in flood-prone areas are likely to pay much higher premiums.

However, it's estimated that over a million people pay too much for their insurance cover because their insurers have wrongly assumed that they are at risk from subsidence (even when your home isn't at risk from subsidence, it's difficult to find a policy that excludes it).

Many insurance companies provide emergency telephone numbers for policyholders requiring urgent advice. Should you need to make emergency repairs, e.g. to weather-proof a roof after a storm or other natural disaster, most insurance companies allow work up to a certain limit (e.g. £1,000) to be carried out without an estimate or approval from the insurance company, but check first. If you let your house (or part of it) or you intend leaving it unoccupied for a period of 30 days or longer, you must usually inform your insurance company. A booklet entitled *Buildings Insurance for Home Owners*, including a valuation table, is available from the Association of British Insurers (see address on page 302).

Buildings insurance is often combined with home contents insurance (see below), when it may be termed household insurance, although it's often cheaper to buy buildings and home contents insurance separately.

HOME-CONTENTS INSURANCE

Home contents insurance (also called house insurance) is advisable for anyone who doesn't live in an empty house. Burglary and house-breaking is a major problem in Britain (particularly in cities) and there's a burglary every minute somewhere. Although there's a lot you can do to prevent someone breaking into your home, it's often impossible or prohibitively expensive to make your home burglar-proof without turning it into a fortress. However, you can ensure you have adequate contents insurance and that your most precious possessions are locked in a safe or safety deposit box. Around one in four homes in Britain have no home contents insurance.

Types of Policy: A basic home contents policy covers your belongings against the same sort of 'natural disasters' as buildings insurance (see page 319). You can optionally insure against accidental damage and all risks. A basic contents policy doesn't usually include such items as credit cards (and their fraudulent use), cash, musical instruments, jewellery (and other valuables), antiques, paintings, sports equipment and bicycles, for which you normally need to take out extra cover. You can usually insure your property for its secondhand value (indemnity) or its full replacement value (new for old), which covers everything except clothes and linen (for which wear and tear is assessed) at the new cost price. Replacement value is the most popular form of contents insurance in Britain. In the case of replacement value, it's best to take out an index-linked policy, where the level of cover is automatically increased by a percentage or fixed amount each year.

A basic policy doesn't usually include accidental damage caused by you or members of your family to your own property (e.g. 'accidentally' putting your foot through the TV during a political party broadcast) or your home freezer contents (in the event of a breakdown or power failure). A basic policy may include replacement locks, garden contents, personal liability insurance (see below), loss of oil and metered water, and temporary accommodation. If not included, these can usually be covered optionally. Some policies include legal expenses cover (e.g. up to £50,000) for disputes with neighbours, shops, suppliers, employers and anyone who provides you with a service (e.g. a plumber or builder). Most contents policies include public liability cover up to £1 million. Items such as computers and mobile phones may need to be listed as named items on your policy, and computers and other equipment used for business aren't usually covered (or may be covered only for a prohibitive extra payment). If you have friends or lodgers in your home, their personal property won't usually be covered by your policy.

Premiums: Premiums depend largely on where you live and your insurer. All insurance companies assess the risk by location based on your postcode. **Check before buying a home as the difference between low and high-risk areas can be as much as 500 per cent!** The difference between premiums charged by companies for the same property can also vary by as much as 200 per cent. Annual premiums are usually calculated per £1,000 of cover and range from around £2 to £3 in a low-risk area to between £10 and £15 in a high-risk area. Although many homeowners in high-risk areas would be willing to forego theft insurance, insurance companies are unwilling to offer this, because premiums would be substantially reduced if theft was omitted (theft is a convenient excuse to load premiums). Your premiums will also be higher if you live in a flood-prone area.

As with buildings insurance, it's important to shop around for the lowest premiums, which vary considerably depending on the insurer (premiums have fallen in recent years due to intense competition). If you're already insured, you may find that you can save money by changing insurers, particularly if you're insured through a bank or building society, which are usually the most expensive. However, watch out for penalties when switching insurers.

Combining your home contents insurance with your buildings insurance (see page 319) can save you money, although it's often cheaper to buy separate insurance. However, it can be advantageous to have your buildings and contents insurance with the same insurer, as this avoids disputes over which company should pay for which item, as could arise if you have a fire or flood affecting both your home and its contents. Those aged over 50 or 55 (and possibly first-time homeowners) are offered discounts or special rates by some companies (e.g. Saga, who specialise in insurance for people over 50). Some companies also provide special policies for students in college accommodation or lodgings (ask an insurance broker).

Security: Most insurers offer no-claims discounts or discounts for homes with burglar alarms, high security locks, neighbourhood watch schemes and smoke detectors. In high-risk areas, good security is a condition of insurance. Beware of the small print in policies, particularly those regarding security, which insurers often use to avoid paying claims. You will forfeit all rights under your policy if you leave doors or windows open (or the keys under a mat or flower pot), particularly if you have claimed a discount due to your 'Fort Knox' security. If there are no signs of forced entry, e.g. a broken window, you may be unable to claim for a theft. You should inform your insurer of any changes that may affect your policy, e.g. a storm blows away a wall of your house (a common occurrence in recent years). If you're going to leave your house empty for a long period, e.g. a month or longer, you should inform your insurer.

Sum-insured or bedroom-rated? There are two ways to insure you possessions: 'sum-insured' (where you calculate the cover you need and the insurer works out the premium based on the cover required) and 'bedroom-rated' policies (where you pay a set premium based on the number of bedrooms). Take care that you don't under-insure your house contents (including anything rented such as a TV or video recorder) and that you periodically reassess their value and adjust your premium accordingly (half of all homeowners are thought to underestimate the value of their home contents). Your contents should include everything that isn't part of the fixtures and fittings and which you could take with you if you were moving house. If you under insure your contents, your claim may be reduced by the percentage by which you're under insured.

With a bedroom-rated policy the insurance company cannot scale down a claim because of under-insurance, however, you're usually better off calculating the value of the contents to be insured. Some companies have economy (e.g. for struggling authors), standard and deluxe rates for contents valued, for example, from £10,000 to £40,000. You can take out a special policy if you have high-value contents, which may be cheaper than a standard contents policy. However, this usually requires a valuation costing around £300 and therefore isn't worthwhile unless your home contents are worth over £50,000. **Always list all previous burglaries on the proposal form, even if nothing was stolen.**

World-wide Cover: An 'all risks' (also termed a worldwide or extra cover policy) is offered by most insurance companies as an extension to a home contents policy. With this type of policy your personal possessions (such as jewellery, watches and cameras) are covered against accidental loss or damage outside your home, anywhere in the world. Usually each item valued above a minimum sum, e.g. £250 to £1,000. must be declared in writing (it's wise to take photographs of your valuables and to keep a record of the make and serial numbers of valuable items). The cost is between £10 and £30 a year for each £1,000 covered, depending on where you live.

Claims: Some insurers provide a 24-hour emergency helpline for policyholders and emergency assistance for repairs for domestic emergencies, such as a blocked drain or electrical failure, up to a maximum limit (e.g. £200) for each claim. Take care when completing a claims form as insurers have tightened up on claims and few people receive a full settlement. Many insurers have an excess of from £25 to £75 on claims. Bear in mind that if you make a claim, you must usually wait months for it to be settled. Generally the larger the claim, the longer you have to wait for your money, although in an emergency most companies will make an interim payment. If you aren't satisfied with the amount offered, don't accept it and try to negotiate a higher figure. If you still cannot reach agreement on the amount, you can contact the insurance ombudsman for independent arbitration.

PERSONAL LIABILITY INSURANCE

Although common on the continent of Europe and in North America (where people sue each other for $millions at the drop of a hat), personal or legal liability insurance is unusual in Britain. However, home contents policies (see above) usually include personal liability insurance up to £1 million and it's usually included in a travel policy (see below). Personal liability insurance provides personal insurance for individuals and members of their families against compensation for accidental damage, injury or death caused to third parties or their property. It usually covers anything from spilling wine on your neighbour's Persian carpet (NB: if you pour white wine on a red wine stain it will disappear) to your dog or child biting someone.

HOLIDAY & TRAVEL INSURANCE

Holiday and travel insurance is recommended for all who don't wish to risk having their holiday or travel spoilt by financial problems or to arrive home broke. As you know, anything can and often does go wrong with a holiday, sometimes before you even get on the aeroplane (particularly if you *don't* have insurance). Travel insurance is available from many sources including travel agents, insurance brokers, tour operators, insurance brokers, banks, building societies, post offices, motoring organisations and railway companies. Around 85 per cent of Britons take out holiday or travel insurance.

When you pay for your travel costs with some credit cards, your family (e.g. including children under the age of 25), are provided with free travel accident insurance up to a specified amount, e.g. £150,000. **Don't rely on this insurance, as it usually covers death or serious injury only.** Special motor insurance providing added protection is available from some travel agents for anyone driving in North America, where standard motor policies for hire cars *don't* include adequate insurance. If you're motoring in Europe, you should also consider continental motor breakdown insurance (see page 269).

Level of Cover: Before taking out travel insurance, carefully consider the level of cover required and compare policies. Most policies include loss of deposit or holiday cancellation (usually limited from £2,500 to £5,000); missed flight; departure delay at both the start *and* end of a holiday (a common occurrence); delayed baggage; personal effects; lost baggage (e.g. £1,500); medical expenses (up to £2m) and accidents (including evacuation home if necessary); personal money (e.g. £250 to £500); personal liability (£1 million or £2m); legal expenses; and a tour operator going bust.

You should also insure against missing your flight due to an accident or transport breakdown, as almost 50 per cent of travel insurance claims are for cancellation (you should be covered for transport delays at the end of your holiday, e.g. the flight home). With some policies, the amount you can claim for personal belongings may be limited to around £200 per item, which will be insufficient to cover your Rolex watch or SLR auto-focus camera. If you have a worldwide home contents policy (see page 321), you will automatically be covered for the full cost of all listed items anywhere. However, note that your insurance company won't pay out if you're negligent, e.g. you leave your camera in a taxi or on a beach.

Medical Expenses: Medical expenses are an important aspect of travel insurance and it isn't advisable to rely on reciprocal health arrangements (such as provided by form E111 in European Union countries). You also shouldn't rely on travel insurance provided by charge and credit card companies, house contents policies or private medical insurance, none of which provide the necessary cover. The minimum medical insurance recommended by experts is £250,000 for Europe and £1 million for North America and the rest of the world. Personal liability should be at least £1 million for Europe and £2 million for the rest of the world. **Note that most travel and holiday insurance policies, don't provide the minimum level of cover that most people need.** Always check any exclusion clauses in contracts by obtaining a copy of the full policy document, as all relevant information *isn't* included in insurance leaflets.

Exclusions: Health or accident insurance included in travel insurance policies usually contains exclusions, e.g. dangerous sports (mountaineering, hang-gliding and scuba-diving) or even riding a motorbike. Check the small print and find out exactly what terms such as 'hazardous pursuits' include or exclude. Skiing and other winter sports should be specifically covered and *listed* in a travel insurance policy. Special winter sports policies are available, which are usually more expensive than normal holiday insurance (higher cover is required for North America than for Europe). Some holiday companies insist that you use their insurance. Skiing or winter holiday insurance costs from around £25 to £80 a week, for basically the same package of £1 million medical expenses, £1 million personal liability, £300 to £400 for skis and £1,000 personal effects.

Cost: The cost of travel insurance varies considerably, depending on your destination. Many companies have different rates for different areas, e.g. Britain, Europe, North America and worldwide (excluding North America). Premiums for British travel are around £7.50 per person for two weeks, European destinations are usually £15 to 20 for two weeks, and North America (where medical treatment costs an arm and a leg) and a few other destinations costs £35 to £50 for three weeks. The cheapest policies offer reduced cover, but may not be adequate for most people. Premiums may also be increased for those aged over 65 or 70. Generally the longer the period covered, the cheaper the daily cost, although the maximum period is usually limited, e.g. six months. With some policies an excess (e.g. £25) must be paid for each claim. Compulsory (expensive) travel insurance, which was previously included in holiday package deals, is now illegal (although many travel agents may still try to pressure you into buying expensive travel insurance).

Annual Policies: For people who travel abroad frequently, whether for business or pleasure, an annual travel policy is often an excellent idea, costing from around £100 to £250 a year for worldwide cover for an unlimited number of trips. However, always carefully check exactly what it includes (some exclude winter sports) and read the small print (some insist that travel is by air). Most annual policies don't cover you for travel in Britain and there's a maximum limit on the length of a trip of from one to six months. Some companies offer 'tailor-made' insurance for independent travellers for any period from a few days to one year.

Claims: Although travel insurance companies will gladly take your money, they aren't so keen to pay claims and you may have to persevere before they pay up. Fraudulent claims against travel insurance are common, so unless you can produce evidence to support your claim the insurers may think you're trying to cheat them. Always be persistent and make a claim irrespective of any small print, as this is often unreasonable and therefore invalid in law. **All insurance companies require you to report any loss (or any incident for which you intend to make a claim) to the local police or carriers within 24 hours and to obtain a report. Failure to do this will mean that your claim usually won't be considered.**

MOTOR BREAKDOWN INSURANCE.

Breakdown insurance for cars and motorcycles, both when travelling within Britain and in most European countries, is available from British motoring organisations (see page 269). Travel insurance for motoring holidays is also available from travel agents, banks and building societies.

CAR INSURANCE

Comprehensive or third party fire and theft (part comprehensive) car insurance is available from numerous insurance companies in Britain (see page 243). Third party motor insurance is compulsory in Britain.

14.

FINANCE

Competition for your money in Britain has never been fiercer and in addition to many British and foreign banks, financial services are provided by building societies, investment brokers, insurance companies, the post office and even large chain stores, supermarkets and service organisations. London is most important financial market in Europe and the third most important in the world after Tokyo and New York (although there are fears that it could lose its position if Britain remains outside the Euro group of countries). In 1998, Britain's gross domestic product (GDP) was US$18,950. Deductions from gross salary including income tax, social security and other benefit contributions, total an average of around 30 per cent (overall the tax burden taxes have increased in recent years when direct and indirect taxes are taken into account). However, taxes (particularly income tax) are still lower in Britain than in many other European countries. The cost of living has been steadily rising in recent years and Britain is now one of the most expensive countries in Europe in which to live and London one of the most expensive cities in the world.

Britain is a credit-financed society and companies queue up to lend you money or give you credit, although they are more circumspect than they were in the '80s when they would lend to anyone. Credit and assorted other plastic cards have largely replaced 'real' money and now account for over 75 per cent of all retail purchases (Britons owe some £16 billion on credit cards). Your financial standing in Britain is usually decided by the number of cards you have, which include credit cards, cash cards, debit cards, cheque guarantee cards, charge cards, store cards, affinity cards and mystery cards. British banks are following America's example and are trying to introduce a cash-less society, and in future to be card-less may equate to being credit-less.

Britain has one of the most unregulated financial service industries in the western world and anyone can set themselves up as an investment expert and charge whatever fees and interest they wish. Britain has been described as the financial rip-off centre of Europe and it's estimated that finance companies over-charge small investors by some £500 million a year. Personal finance is a jungle and there are plenty of predators about just waiting to get their hands on your loot. Always shop around for financial services and never sign a contract unless you know exactly what the costs and implications are. Although bankers, financiers and brokers don't like to make too fine a point of it, they aren't doing business with you because they like you, but simply to get their hands on your pile of chips. It's up to you to make sure that their share is kept to a minimum and that you receive the best possible value for your money. **When dealing with financial 'experts' bear in mind that while making mistakes is easy, fouling up completely requires professional help!**

When you arrive in Britain to take up residence or employment, make sure you have sufficient cash, travellers cheques, eurocheques, credit cards, luncheon vouchers, coffee machine tokens, silver dollars, gold sovereigns and diamonds, to last at least until your first pay day, which may be some time after your arrival. Don't, however, carry a lot of cash. During this period you will find that a credit card or two is useful. Note that among the many British eccentricities is the government's financial tax 'year', that runs from 6th April to 5th April of the following year (for reasons known only to the government).

There are numerous books and magazines published to help you manage your finances including *The Penguin Personal Financial Guide* by Alison Michell (Penguin) and the *Moneywise Family Finance Guide* (Clark Publishing). The Consumers Association (see page 437) publish a number of excellent financial books including *450 Money Questions Answered, Getting the Best Deal for Your Money, Which? Way to Save and Invest, Finance Your Future* and *How to Buy, Sell and Own Shares*. Personal finance magazines include *Personal Finance, Money Observer, What Investment* and *Moneywise*. Personal finance information (including the best loan and mortgage interest rates) is published in the financial pages of the Saturday and Sunday editions of national newspapers, and is also available via the television teletext information service. For information regarding pensions, see **Chapter 13**.

Note that the figures and information contained in this chapter are based on current law and Inland Revenue practice, which in Britain are subject to change (frequently).

BRITISH CURRENCY

As you're probably aware, the British unit of currency is the pound sterling, which has been very strong (too strong for British exporters) and stable in recent years. Due to the widespread Europhobia generated by elements of the previous Conservative government, Britain declined to join the euro (€) which was launched on 1st January 1999 in Austria, Belgium, Finland, France, Germany, Ireland, Italy, Luxembourg, the Netherlands, Portugal and Spain. Many analysts believe that remaining outside the euro group of countries will do irreparable damage to Britain's economy and London's international financial standing, although the present Labour government has expressed its intention to join in the new millennium (providing the British people approve in a referendum).

The British pound has a number of colloquial names including quid and smacker. Fiver (£5) and tenner (£10) are also commonly used. The pound is divided into 100 pence and British coins are minted in 1p and 2p (bronze); 5p, 10p, 20p and 50p (cupro-nickel); and one (nickel-brass) and two (bronze outer rim, cupro-nickel centre) pounds. The 20p and 50p coins are seven-sided; all other coins are round. Smaller, lighter coins have been introduced in recent years, although British coins are still heavier than those in many other countries. Banknotes are printed in denominations of £5, £10, £20 and £50 pounds; the higher the denomination, the larger the note (it's best to avoid £50 notes as many people seem to think they are home-made). Forgery is a problem in most western countries and there are a 'significant number' of forged £10, £20 and £50 notes in circulation, so be on your guard if someone insists on paying a large bill in cash (the £20 note is to be redesigned to thwart counterfeiters).

If you believe that banks have a licence to print money, with respect to Scottish and Northern Irish banks, you would be absolutely correct. Shopkeepers and traders don't legally need to accept notes issued by Scottish and Northern Irish banks (which include a £1 note, replaced by a coin in England and Wales, and a £100 note), even in Scotland and Northern Ireland. Scottish banknotes are naturally accepted without question in Scotland, but understandably they aren't so well received in the rest of Britain. Don't take Scottish or Northern Irish banknotes abroad as you will receive a much lower exchange rate than for Bank of England banknotes (that's if anyone will accept them at all). The Channel Islands and the Isle of Man have some local coins and notes, but the monetary system is the same as in the rest of Britain.

FOREIGN CURRENCY

Britain has no currency restrictions and you may bring in or take out as much money as you wish, in practically any currency. The major British banks will change most foreign bank notes (but not coins), but usually give a better exchange rate for travellers cheques or eurocheques than for bank notes. In addition to banks, many travel agents, hotels and shops in major cities either change or accept foreign currency, but usually at a less favourable exchange rate than banks. There are currency exchange machines at some international airports where you can change a range of foreign currencies for sterling.

Buying & Selling Currency: When buying or selling foreign currency in Britain beware of excessive charges. Apart from differences in exchange rates, which are posted by all banks and bureaux de change, there may be a significant difference in charges. Most high street banks and building societies charge 1 or 2 per cent commission with a minimum charge of £2 or £2.50 (some such as Nationwide have scrapped commission charges). All banks and building societies buy and sell foreign currency, although not all keep foreign currency and you often need to order it two or three days in advance. You can also buy and sell foreign currency at main post offices, although you need to order currency at sub post offices 24 hours in advance. Post offices charge 1 per cent commission on both currency and travellers' cheques, with a minimum fee of £2.50, and accept payment by credit card.

Exchange Rates: It pays to shop around for the best exchange rates (the worst rates are offered by high street banks), particularly if you're changing a lot of money (it's possible to barter over rates in some establishments). Most banks have a spread of up to 8 per cent between their buying and selling rates for foreign currencies. The sterling exchange rate against most European and major international currencies is listed in banks and the quality daily newspapers. **Don't change money at hotels or the ubiquitous independent 'Bureau de Change' in London and other cities unless you have no choice or money to burn, as they levy high charges or offer poor exchange rates.**

Travellers' Cheques: Travellers' cheques are widely accepted in Britain in all major currencies. The commission for cashing travellers' cheques is usually 1 per cent (you need your passport). Lost or stolen travellers' cheques can be replaced in Britain and many countries abroad (the easiest to replace are American Express). Always keep a separate record of cheque numbers. You can buy travellers' cheques commission-free from many building societies (although you may need to be an account holder), stores (e.g. Marks & Spencer) and some travel agents. Most banks charge commission of 1 per cent of the face value. Sterling travellers' cheques are accepted in most countries, although some banks in some European countries (e.g. France) refuse to change all travellers' cheques. US dollar cheques are the most widely accepted and you should always buy them when visiting the USA.

Cash Transfers: If you have money transferred to Britain by banker's draft or a letter of credit, bear in mind that it may take up to two weeks to be cleared. You can also have money sent to you by international money order (MoneyGram) via a post office, a cashier's cheque or telegraphic transfer, e.g. via Western Union (the quickest, safest and most expensive method). You usually need your passport to collect money transferred from abroad or to cash a banker's draft (or other credit note). If you're sending money abroad, it's best to send it in the local currency so that the recipient won't have to pay conversion charges. Note that some countries have foreign exchange controls limiting the amount of money that can be sent abroad. Insured mail is the only safe way to send cash, as the insured value is refunded if the money is lost or stolen.

Postal orders can be sent to Commonwealth countries and a Girobank post office transfer can be made to most countries (usually free when transferring money to a Girobank holder). Eurocheques can be sent within Europe and postcheques (Girobank customers only) to certain countries. You can also send money direct from your bank to another bank via an interbank transfer. Most banks have a minimum service charge for international transfers, which generally make it expensive, particularly for small sums. Overseas banks also take a cut, usually a percentage (e.g. 1 or 2 per cent) of the amount transferred.

One thing to bear in mind when travelling anywhere is not to rely on one source of funds only.

CREDIT RATING

Whether you're able to get credit (or how much) usually depends on your credit rating, which is becoming increasingly important in today's financial world. Most financial institutions use credit scoring and a credit reference agency report to find out whether you're credit worthy. If you're newly arrived in Britain, a lender may use an agency in your previous country of residence. If you're refused credit in Britain, you can ask why and can demand (on payment of a £1 fee) to see the credit agency's file on you (they cannot refuse), which must be supplied within 40 days. You can obtain a copy of your credit file by writing to Experian, Consumer Help Service, PO Box 8000, Nottingham NG1 5GX or Equifax, Department 1E, PO Box 3001, Glasgow G81 2DT (to be safe, check with both agencies). Individuals can also check the credit rating of a company or person with whom they're planning to do business.

In many cases, files are found to contain false information or information about unpaid debts belonging to family, friends or neighbours, or because a person shared an address with someone. If the information in your file is incorrect, you have the right to demand that an agency removes the false information or corrects it, which should be done within 28 days. You must show that information was registered in error, that your defence wasn't considered (perhaps due to being abroad at the time), or that the amount owed was paid in full within a month of a county court judgement. If an agency doesn't correct false information you can appeal to the Investigation Department, Office of the Data Protection Registrar, Springfield House, Water Lane, Wilmslow, Cheshire SK9 5AX (☎ 01625-545745). Write giving full particulars of the incorrect information and the date you sent a correction to an agency.

Banks and other financial institutions usually have a credit scoring system, based on information received from credit reference agencies. If you have a bad credit rating, it's almost impossible to obtain credit in Britain. Your credit score depends on many factors such as your age and occupation, marital status, how long you have held your current job, whether you're a home owner or not, where you live, whether you're on the electoral roll, whether you have a telephone, your credit track record and the colour of your eyes (those with green eyes have the best rating). However, if you're able to provide collateral (i.e. security such as a property), for example for a bank loan, people will fall over themselves to lend you money (particularly those who charge extortionate interest rates). Finally, if you're refused credit, try looking on the bright side: without credit you cannot run up any debts.

The Office of Fair Trading (Field House, 15/25 Browns Buildings, London EC1A 1PR, ☎ 0345-224499) publish a leaflet entitled *No Credit* and the CCN Group (Consumer Help Service, CCN Group, PO Box 40, Notts. NG7 2SS) publishes a free leaflet entitled *Helping You to Understand Your Credit File.*

BANKS

The major British banks with branches in most towns throughout Britain (termed 'high street' banks) include the National Westminster, Barclays, Lloyds TSB, Midland (now owned by the HSBC) and the Abbey National. Other major banks with branches in large towns are the Bank of Scotland, the Royal Bank of Scotland and the Co-operative Bank. There are also telephone banks (including First Direct and Girobank) that don't have branches and are 'open' 24-hours a day. For the wealthy there are many private banks (mainly portfolio management) and foreign banks abound in major cities (there are over 500 foreign banks in the City of London alone). Most banks have Internet websites and many offer online banking, although it's in its infancy with some 500,000 customers only in early 1999. In recent years there has been a flood of new-style 'banks' such as Virgin Direct, supermarkets and stores such as Marks and Spencer, who have shaken up the traditional high street banks with their innovative accounts and services.

British banks provide free banking for personal customers who remain in credit, pay interest on account balances and offer a range of financial services (although they usually *aren't* the best place to buy insurance or pensions). If you do a lot of travelling abroad, you may find the comprehensive range of services offered by the high street banks advantageous. In a small country town or village, there's usually a sub post office, but not usually a bank. Note that many services provided by British banks are also provided by Building Societies (see below).

The relationship between the major banks and their customers has deteriorated in the last decade (particularly during the recession), during which banks dramatically increased their charges to personal and business customers to recoup their losses on bad loans to developing countries. Few people in Britain have a good word to say about their banks which are widely perceived to be profit-hungry, impersonal and definitely not customer-friendly. Complaints against banks have risen dramatically in recent years. British banks have made record profits (running into £billions) in the '90s, which has served only to further annoy customers (who think their banks are ripping them off). Note that often the worst place to buy financial products is from a major high street bank, and building societies usually offer better deals.

Not surprisingly banks aren't exactly happy with their poor public image (on a par with that of used car salesmen and politicians) and most have been busy trying to improve customer relations by introducing codes of conduct and payments for mistakes or poor service. Many people could save money by changing their banks. You shouldn't allow loyalty to prevent you from switching banks as when times are hard your bank won't hesitate to withdraw your safety net (during the recession banks were directly responsible for the failure of hundreds of small businesses through arbitrarily withdrawing or refusing overdrafts and loans).

Deposit Protection: All banks, including branches and subsidiaries of foreign banks accepting sterling deposits in Britain, must be licensed by the Bank of England and contribute to the Deposit Protection Fund (DPF) which guarantees that 90 per cent of deposits up to £20,000 will be repaid if a bank goes bust. Because of the limit, it's worthwhile spreading your investments around several banks and financial institutions (see also **Building Societies** below).

Complaints: British banks are very (very) slow to rectify mistakes or to resolve disputes and rarely accept responsibility, even when clearly in the wrong. It has been estimated (based on actual proven cases) that banks routinely overcharge small business customers by hundreds of £millions a year. If your bank makes a mess of your account and causes you to lose money and spend time putting it correct, you're quite within your rights to claim financial compensation for your time and trouble in addition to any financial loss. Note, however, that banks typically stall complaints for up to six years and simply use their financial muscle to wear down customers (some banks fight every case with litigation). If you have a complaint against a British bank and have exhausted the bank's complaints' procedure, you can apply for independent arbitration to the Office of the Banking Ombudsman, 70 Grays Inn Road, London WC1X 8NB (☎ 0171-404 9944).

BUILDING SOCIETIES

Building societies date back to 1775 and were originally established to cater for people saving to buy a home. Savers saved a deposit of 5 or 10 per cent of the cost of a home with the building society, who then lent them the balance. A building society would rarely lend to anyone who wasn't a regular saver, although this changed many years ago. In 1987, the regulations governing institutions offering financial services were changed and as a result banks and building societies now compete head-on for customers. There has been a wave of mergers and take-overs in recent years, and in the past ten years the number of societies has fallen dramatically. Many building societies have converted to banks (called demutualisation) in recent years earning £millions for account holders. Many people (known as carpetbaggers) have taken advantage of pay-outs by opening accounts at a number of building societies.

Nowadays building societies offer practically all the services provided by banks, including current and savings accounts, cheque guarantee cards, cash cards, personal loans, credit cards, insurance and travel services. In an effort to woo customers away from banks, many building societies produce special brochures and 'transfer packs' (even containing pre-printed 'letters') detailing exactly how to transfer your account. Building societies don't all offer the same services, types of accounts or rates of interest (those offering the best interest rates are often the smaller societies). If you're looking for a long-term investment, the number of branches may not be of importance and members of all building societies can use cash dispensers at other building society branches via the Link system.

Complaints: If you have a complaint against a building society and have exhausted its complaints' procedure, you can apply for independent arbitration to the Office of the Building Societies' Ombudsman, Millbank Tower, Millbank, London SW1P 4XS (☎ 0171-931 0044). Deposits in British building society accounts are protected by a similar compensation scheme to banks, under which you're guaranteed to receive 90 per cent of your investment (up to a maximum of £20,000) if it goes bust.

Business Hours

Normal bank (and building society) opening hours are from 0900 or 0930 until 1530 or 1600 (some are open until 1730) Mondays to Fridays, with no shutdown over the lunch period in cities and most towns. Most branches are open late one day a week until between 1730 or 1800 (it varies depending on the bank and its location) and many open on Saturdays, e.g. from 0930 until 1230 (some are open until 1530). Most banks in Scotland and all banks in Northern Ireland close for an hour at lunchtime. Building societies are generally open from 0900 to 1700, Mondays to Fridays, and from 0900 to 1200 on Saturdays.

Bureaux de change have longer opening hours, including Saturdays and Sundays in tourist areas and large cities, but should be used in dire circumstances only (e.g. the taxi meter is running and the driver is threatening your life if you don't pay him!) due to their high commission and/or poor exchange rates. When banks are closed you can change money at post offices, which are usually open from 0900 to 1730, Mondays to Fridays, and from 0900 to 1230 on Saturdays. All banks are closed on public holidays, which in Britain are generally called bank holidays (no prize for guessing why).

Banks at major airports are open from 0630 or 0700 to 2300 or 2330, seven days a week and some airports, e.g. London's Gatwick and Heathrow airports, have 24-hour banks. Some banks at London railway stations also have extended opening hours (e.g. Victoria). Most banks, building societies and main post offices in Britain have 24-hour cash dispensers/machines (officially called Automatic Teller Machines/ATMs) at branches for cash withdrawals, deposits and checking account balances (see page 338). Cash machines also located in some supermarkets and other large stores.

Opening An Account

If you're planning to work in Britain and .will be paid monthly one of your first acts should be to open a current (or cheque) account with a bank, building society or the Girobank (post office), like over 80 per cent of the British working population. Your salary will usually be paid directly into your account by your employer (many will insist that your salary is paid into an account) and your salary statement will be either be sent to your home address or be given to you at work.

On arrival in Britain, you may need to wait up to two months for your first pay cheque. Although this is unusual, you should check with your employer, who may (if necessary) give you a salary advance. Employees who are paid weekly are often paid in cash, in which case it's up to you whether you open a bank or building society account (although it's difficult to survive without one nowadays). Many people have at least two accounts, a current account for their out-of-pocket expenses and day-to-day transactions, and a savings account for long-term savings (or money put aside for a rainy day (which is every other day in Britain). Many people have both bank and building society accounts. Before opening an account compare bank charges, interest rates (e.g. on credit cards) and other services offered by a number of banks. **If you're planning to buy a home with a mortgage, one of the best accounts is a an all-in-one account or mortgage current account** (see page 345).

To open an account, you simply go to the bank or building society of your choice and tell them you're living in Britain and wish to open an account. You will be asked for proof of identity, e.g. usually a passport or driving licence, plus proof of address in the form of a utility bill. Foreign residents may be required to provide a reference from their employer or a foreign bank. Many banks provide new account holders with a free cash card wallet, cheque book cover and statement file. After opening an account, don't forget to give the details to your employer (if you want to get paid). The facilities you should expect from a current account include a cheque book; a paying-in book; a cheque guarantee card (preferably £100 or £250); interest paid on credit balances; no charges or fees when in credit; a free cash card and lots of cash machines; a free debit card; monthly statements; an automatic authorised overdraft facility; and the availability of credit cards. Most of these are standard.

With a current account you receive a cheque book (usually containing 30 cheques) and a cash card (see page 338). A cheque guarantee card is usually provided on request and guarantees cheques up to £50, £100 or £250. Note that when using a cheque guarantee card, the card number must be written on the back of the cheque. Most businesses won't accept a cheque without a guarantee card. A cheque book usually also contains paying-in slips (at the back), with which you can make payments into your account. You also receive a separate paying-in book.

Most people pay their bills from their current account, either by standing order or by cheque. Bank statements are usually issued monthly (optionally quarterly), interest may be paid on deposits (usually quarterly) and an overdraft facility may be provided. Most banks don't levy any charges on a current account, providing you stay in credit. However, if you overdraw your account without a prior arrangement with your bank (see **Overdrafts** on page 343), you may be billed for bank charges on all transactions for the accounting period (usually three months).

Cheques: Cheques are usually crossed, which normally takes the form of two parallel lines across the face of the cheque. A crossed cheque theoretically provides additional security, because it can be paid only into a bank account and cannot be cashed by a bank. Banks don't recommend uncrossed cheques, although some will supply them. To obtain cash from a bank, write the cheque in your own name or write 'cash' alongside 'Pay' (but never send a cheque made out to cash through the post). If you make a mistake when writing a cheque, you can change it, but the correction must be initialled.

Take great care when sending cheques through the post, particularly for large amounts, as cheques are sometimes stolen and paid into someone else's account, from which the money is quickly withdrawn. This may be done by someone simply forging an 'endorsement' (signature) on the back of a cheque in the name of the payee, which makes the cheque negotiable. Banks aren't required to check the signatures on the back of cheques and in fact couldn't even if they wanted to. Crooks often steal mail from post offices and pay cheques into their own accounts. They simply use the name of the payee but their own account number and banks don't check that the payee and account number tally. This makes a mockery of the safety of cheques! Note that cheques usually take three to five days to clear (some banks make customers wait up to ten days for clearance), although some banks have scrapped the cheque-clearing period on payments and credits cheques of up to £1,000 to accounts before they have cleared.

Cheque Safeguards: There are a number of ways to safeguard your cheques, one of which is to write 'not negotiable' between the lines on a crossed cheque. This means that although the cheque can be signed on the back and handed over to someone else, you have legal rights against the person who cashes the cheque if the endorsement was forged. An additional safeguard is to add the words 'account payee only' to the crossing (in between the two parallel lines). Although this has no legal significance, it means that your bank should only credit the account of the named payee and they would be considered negligent if they credited an 'account payee only' cheque to the wrong account. For extra security, you can add both 'not negotiable' and 'account payee only' to a cheque.

Claims: If a cheque is converted, cashed, negotiated or transferred unlawfully, your bank will probably take refuge behind the law and refuse to accept any responsibility (unless you have £billions on deposit). However, if the amount or other details on a cheque are changed and your bank pays out, it cannot make you liable for the forgery. If you're a victim of fraud and believe your bank or building society was negligent, you should demand compensation. If it isn't offered you should take your case to the banking ombudsman.

Charges: All banks make a charge for 'bounced' cheques. If you accidentally go into the red for a few days and are charged bank charges for a full month or three months, a complaint to your bank manager in writing, if necessary threatening to transfer your account elsewhere, may get you a reduction (if not, you can always carry out your threat). Most banks and building societies have a long list of service charges for current accounts. Note, however, that providing you stay in credit it's still possible to avoid paying charges by shopping around. If you're thinking of changing banks (or building society), check carefully whether you will lose any important benefits such as a credit card (with a high spending limit) or a preferential loan or overdraft facility.

High-Interest Cheque Accounts: Most banks and building societies offer high-interest cheque accounts for customers who maintain a minimum balance, e.g. £1,000. These accounts offer a range of benefits including a cheap overdraft facility and a £250 cheque guarantee card. Some current accounts pay variable rates of interest depending on the account balance. Interest on high-interest accounts may be paid monthly and there's usually no transaction or monthly fees. However, if you don't need instant access to large sums of cash, you're better off with a savings account (see page 336) than a high-interest cheque account. **It's never advisable to keep a lot of cash in an account with a cash card as fraudulent withdrawals aren't unknown!**

It would appear that many people in Britain have money to throw away, as they keep quite large sums in accounts that pay no interest or minimal interest only, e.g. 0.5 per cent. Naturally banks don't go out of their way to explain to customers the most advantageous accounts for their money, or indeed even explain about account fees or charges (which helps boosts profits by £millions each year). Even modest balances in an interest-earning account can earn enough to ward off inflation. If you never overdraw on your current account and aren't being paid interest, you're making a free loan to your bank (something they most certainly *won't* do for you).

SAVINGS ACCOUNTS

All banks and building societies provide a wide range of savings accounts, also called deposit, term deposit or high-interest accounts, most of which are intended for short or medium term savings rather than long-term growth. When opening an account, the most important considerations are how much money you wish to save (which may be a lump sum or a monthly amount), how quickly you need access to it in an emergency and whether you're a taxpayer.

Before committing your money to a long-term savings account or investment, shop around, not just among banks and building societies, but also other financial institutions. Interest rates, conditions and fees vary, so take them into account. Note that banks and building societies often introduce new types of accounts paying increased rates of interest, **but they don't usually notify existing customers of this (some even forbid staff to tell customers about accounts paying higher interest).** The interest rates on obsolete accounts are criminal and are often less than 0.5 per cent on balances of £500 to £25,000 (no wonder they make large profits!). It's estimated that £billions are languishing in obsolete accounts earning derisory amounts of interest. Interest rates are forever changing in Britain (increasing or decreasing in line with the official bank lending rate) and it may not pay you to tie your money up for a long period. Note that when there's a cut in the base rate, most banks cut savings interest rates long before they cut their mortgage rates. In 1999, savings rates on instant access accounts hit their lowest levels for 125 years!

Most banks and building societies have two basic types of accounts: instant access and notice accounts. Instant access accounts, as the name implies, allow you instant access to your money. There's usually a minimum balance, although this may be as low as £100. Interest rates usually depend on the account balance, e.g. £100, £1,000, £3,000 or £10,000. With a notice account you're required to give notice before you make a withdrawal, usually between 30 and 90 days. Notice accounts pay marginally higher rates of interest. If there's any chance that you will need immediate access to your money, you should keep it in an instant access account (the extra interest on the best 90-day accounts is usually only around 0.5 to 1 per cent more than on the best instant access accounts). Interest is paid quarterly, half-yearly or yearly.

You may find a high-interest cheque account useful, as it offers all the usual facilities of a current account, plus high interest depending on the account balance (which must usually be a minimum of £1,000). There are also high-yield bonds and 'investment' accounts for large deposits, e.g. £10,000, providing you can tie your money up for a long period (at least one year). A 'monthly income' account requires you to invest a lump sum (usually over £1,000) on which you receive a high rate of interest paid monthly. Building societies also offer monthly income accounts and regular savings accounts for those who wish to save a regular amount each month. Regular savings accounts usually pay a higher rate of interest, but you may have limited access to your money, e.g. one withdrawal every six months only. Taxpayers looking for a long-term investment are usually better off investing in a tax-exempt special savings account such as an Individual Savings Account (ISA).

Interest on accounts is paid tax-free (gross) to non-taxpayers, e.g. married women who aren't working, retirees, children and non-residents. Non-taxpayers must complete a form to confirm their tax status, otherwise interest will be paid net of basic rate income tax, which can be reclaimed by non-taxpayers. A leaflet entitled *Can you stop paying tax on your bank and building society interest* (IR110) is available from tax offices. Higher rate taxpayers are required to declare their interest income on their income tax return. Savings can also be deposited in offshore bank accounts, where interest is paid gross, although if you're a British resident interest may be taxable in Britain.

The best savings interest rates are published in Saturday and Sunday newspapers such as *The Times* and *The Sunday Times*, and in financial magazines such as *Personal Finance*, *Money Observer*, *What Investment* and *Moneywise*. Information is also available via the television teletext information service. *Which?* magazine (see page 437) also offers invaluable advice and surveys.

CASH & DEBIT CARDS

One of the most important innovations in banking in the last decade or so has been the introduction of cash (or cashpoint) and debit cards, which are routinely issued to current account holders in Britain.

Cash Cards: A cash card allows you to withdraw money from cash machines (ATMs), 24 hours a day (or 0600 to 2400), seven days a week. The freedom from bank queues, banking hours and bank tellers provided by cash cards is very convenient, and you should think twice before opening an account with a bank or building society which doesn't provide cash machines locally (although most small institutions have agreements with other banks or building societies). Most people prefer to use cash machines rather than deal with a person, particularly those aged under 35.

All banks and building societies issue cash cards for account holders which can be used to withdraw up to £1,000 a day (although a maximum of £250 is more usual) from any of the participating bank's or building society's cash machines (providing you have the money in your account) or those belonging to the same network. The main networks are Visa, Plus, Cirrus and Link. All major banks have networks of over 5,000 machines. Most banks and building societies allow free withdrawals from machines belonging to the same network, although most levy a 'handling' fee (e.g. 1.5 to 2.25 per cent) for a cash withdrawal from a cash machine belonging to a bank outside their network. However, some building societies such as Nationwide don't levy these fees.

Other services offered by banks and building societies via cash machines include mini-statements (usually the last five transactions), account balances, the paying of bills (via a bank giro), deposits, transfers between accounts, cheque book and statement ordering, and the facility to change your PIN. These services are usually available only via cash machines located at branches of your own bank.

When your application for a card is approved, your card and personal identification number (PIN) are sent under separate cover (for security reasons). If you don't have a secure mail box (i.e. a private address or personal mail box), you should collect your PIN from your bank. Cards aren't usually sent by registered mail. For extra security, some banks activate cards only after customers have reported their safe arrival. **If you receive an unwanted card, cut it up and return it to your bank or building society with instructions to cancel it.** For security reasons, you should **destroy your PIN as soon as you've remembered it and should never write it down (not even coded).**

The procedure for withdrawing money from cash machines varies from bank to bank and even between machines at different branches of the same bank, but is roughly as follows:

1. Check that the machine is in service, which may be shown by an 'OPEN' sign, a light or a display on the screen. If the machine is out of service a message to this effect is usually displayed on the screen. If an machine is out of service it usually

means that it has run out of cash (common at weekends) or that the bank's computer is out of order. Sometimes a machine will be unable to dispense cash, but will allow you to do other things such as check your account balance.

2.   Insert your card as shown in the illustration on the machine. Most machines have a (usually transparent) protective cover which opens automatically. A screen message asks you to enter your PIN on the keyboard. **As a security measure, if you enter the wrong PIN three times your card will be retained by the machine and you must contact your bank for its return.** You usually need to press a 'proceed key' (usually coloured green) to continue after entering your PIN.

3.   After you've entered your PIN the display will ask you which service you require, e.g. cash withdrawal (with or without a receipt). Press the 'button' corresponding to the service required (usually indicated by arrows at the edge of the screen).

4.   If you're withdrawing cash, you must now enter the amount required (up to your card's limit) in multiples of £10, e.g. £10, £20 or £50, usually dispensed in £10 or £20 notes. Sometimes you will need to press the 'proceed key' to continue.

5.   At this point your card will be returned and your cash and receipt dispensed. Don't forget to take them all with you.

A 'cancel' or 'error' button (usually coloured red) is provided to terminate a transaction at any point. Your card will be returned and you can start again, if required. Some machines inside banks have no screen and can be used only to obtain cash. The procedure is roughly the same as outlined above, except that the amount required is entered by pressing a button, e.g. £10, £20, £30, £50, £75 or £100. Instructions are posted on the machine.

Note that although it's relatively rare, cash machines do go wrong and occasionally give the wrong amount of cash, make mistakes on receipts, and 'phantom withdrawals' can turn up on your bank statement. You should obtain a receipt for withdrawals and check them against your statement. If you have a problem with a machine, make a note of its location, the date and time, and exactly what happened. Notify your bank as soon as possible. Note, however, that you have only a slim chance of convincing your bank that their 'infallible' machine has made a mistake. The banking ombudsman investigates more complaints about cash machines than anything else. Don't keep a lot of money in an account for which you have a cash card and *never* have a cash card for a savings account with a large balance. Don't use a cash dispenser in a 'high risk' area at night as muggings occasionally occur.

If you lose your cash card, you must notify the issuing bank or building society immediately by telephone and confirm it in writing within seven days. Your liability is limited to £50, providing you aren't negligent, e.g. by writing your PIN where somebody can find it.

Debit Cards: Most cash cards are also debit cards belonging to either the 'Switch' or 'Delta' networks. Debit cards are accepted by most retailers and mail-order businesses in Britain and have largely replaced cheques. There's no limit to the amount you can pay with a debit card, providing you have the money in your account or have a pre-arranged overdraft. Debit cards have certain advantages over cheques, one of which is that they eliminate the need for cheque-guarantee limits. Many retailers, e.g. supermarkets, allow customers to obtain up to £50 in cash, known as 'cash-back', when paying a bill with a debit card. Most cash and debit cards can also be used as cheque guarantee cards and can also be used abroad, e.g. as Visa or Mastercard 'debit' cards, to obtain cash and buy goods and services. They aren't, however, credit cards and you can draw only on funds in your account. There's usually a charge for obtaining cash abroad.

CHARGE & CREDIT CARDS

The British love plastic money and Britain is one of the most credit-oriented societies in the world. However, banks love them even more as interest rates on unpaid balances are the highest in Europe (most British banks charge British cardholders much higher interest rates than they do in other European countries). British based companies offer some 1,500 different brands of plastic – enough to burst the seams of even the fattest of wallets. It has been calculated that if the over 30 million plastic cards in Britain were laid end to end, they would stretch from the doors of the Bank of England to the shores of Africa (not many people know that). British retail outlets, whatever their size, usually accept both credit and charge cards, generally referred to collectively as credit cards in Britain.

The main difference between charge and credit cards is that with a charge card you defer paying the bill for a few weeks or months, but you *must* pay the total balance outstanding when it's due (otherwise a penalty payment is payable), whereas a credit card allows you to spread your repayments over a period. Credit cards are much more popular in Britain than charge cards, both with cardholders and businesses. Both credit and charge cards may be issued as ordinary, gold and platinum cards, with different credit and benefit levels. Always sign a card as soon as you receive it. Cards can be used to purchase goods by mail or over the telephone, both in Britain and abroad, although goods should be sent only to the cardholder's address. Always check that a credit card slip is made out for the correct amount before signing it.

Charge Cards: A charge card allows you to charge the cost of goods and services to a card company and they include American Express (Amex), Diners Club, Eurocard and the Thomas Cook Corporate card. You can also obtain cash via cash machines, although the fee is high. With most charge cards there's a high spending limit or possibly none at all. Holders of charge cards pay an annual fee to the card company, e.g. Amex and Diners Club fees are £37.50, which may be waived for the first year for new customers. Diners Club also have an enrolment fee of £20. In general, charge cards are issued to high earners only (£20,000 may be the minimum) or those with a high 'net worth'.

Some charge card companies (e.g. Amex) and banks issue 'gold' and 'platinum' cards to 'high-rollers', that allow instant access to large amounts of cash, an unsecured overdraft facility of up to £10,000 at an advantageous interest rate and a cheque guarantee facility of up to £300 a day. Annual fees for gold cards are around £60 to £70. Charge card companies also issue corporate cards for businesses. Amex and Diners Club cards provide holders with a range of benefits including free travel and accident insurance (when travel costs are paid with the card); emergency legal and medical assistance; discounts on private medical insurance; the opportunity to collect dividend points (Diners Club) or 'membership miles' (Amex) when you use your card (redeemable against flights, hotel rooms, restaurant meals, car hire, goods and holidays); and a 'purchase protection' scheme providing up to 90 days free protection on most purchases against loss, theft or accidental damage. Amex also offer cardholders a 'global assist' service, which can put you in contact with an English-speaking doctor or lawyer in some countries. Many companies provide their own charge cards for customers, e.g. department and chain stores, petrol companies, British Telecom, car hire companies and airlines.

One of the major advantages of international charge cards is that if they are lost or stolen they can usually be replaced at short notice when you're travelling, e.g. within 24 hours in some countries. Apart from the on-the-spot replacement of lost cards, you will find that charge cards offer few advantages over credit cards (see below), most of which, e.g. Visa or Mastercard, are more widely accepted, both in Britain and worldwide. They are also cheaper and more convenient to use.

Credit Cards: Credit cards are issued by most financial institutions in Britain including all banks and building societies, plus a range of other businesses such as car manufacturers, newspapers and travel agents. Visa is the most widely acceptable credit card in Britain and is issued by most banks, closely followed by Access (Mastercard). Some issuers allow you choose between Access or Visa or to have both. Due to the waning popularity of charge cards, American Express introduced a credit card in 1995. Credit cards are definitely not for long-term borrowers, although if you borrow less than £1,000 and pay it off within one year, it's generally cheaper than a loan.

Costs & Interest Rates: Banks compete fiercely for credit card customers, both on interest rates and the supplementary services attached to cards. You can apply for a credit card at any bank or building society and it may not be necessary to be a customer. Most charge an annual card fee of from between £10 and £12. A number of cards can be issued for one account (a second card is usually issued free). When choosing a card, bear in mind that a free card with no annual fee may have a high interest rate (which is fine if you plan to pay off the balance each month). Interest rates vary considerably from around 10 to 20 per cent. Some banks offer lending tiers, where the higher the balance the lower the interest rate charged. The best cards are those with no annual fee and a low interest rate, usually restricted to homeowners and/or those with an excellent credit rating. The best credit and store card interest rates are published in the Saturday edition of newspapers such as *The Times* and *The Daily Telegraph*.

Benefits: You should also compare the benefits offered by card issuers, which may include cash discounts on travel bookings; holiday discounts; foreign currency ordering; helplines; air miles; discounts on new cars; points schemes; reduced hotel and car hire rates; free accident travel insurance; commission-free travellers' cheques; and free insurance on goods purchased with cards. Some cards, called affinity cards, have ties with registered charities, where a charity (or a number of charities) benefits with each new card issued and each time a card is used.

Credit Limit: The credit limit for most cardholders starts at around £1,000, although some card issuers allow you to choose your spending limit up to £5,000. Increasing your credit limit is usually a formality, providing your credit rating is good and you pay your bills on time. When changing card companies, check that you will be able to keep your previous credit limit and that you don't lose any important benefits. Many card companies allow existing cardholders to transfer their card balance when switching cards.

Cash Withdrawals: Both Access and Visa can be used to obtain cash from cash machines in Britain and abroad. You need a PIN to withdraw cash. When you use your card to obtain cash there's a handling charge and/or commission, e.g. from 1.5 to 2.25 per cent or a minimum of £1.50. There's a daily limit on cash withdrawals both in Britain and abroad, e.g. between £200 and £500. There are also hidden charges in currency conversion of from 0.5 to 2.75 per cent. Interest is usually charged on cash withdrawals from the date of the withdrawal.

Bills: Access and Visa require you to repay a minimum of £5 or 5 per cent of the balance each month, whichever is higher. If you pay off the full amount outstanding, you won't be charged interest and will receive up to seven weeks free credit. Some credit card issuers offer protection insurance which covers payments in case of sickness, accident or unemployment (check exactly what's covered), which is worth considering. Protection insurance premiums are calculated according to your account balance and are added to your card payments each month.

Legal Protection: Under the Consumer Credit Act 1974, when you pay for goods or services with plastic you have legal rights against the credit card company as well as the supplier for goods valued from £100 to £30,000 (including bankruptcy of a supplier). Most credit card users can also claim compensation from their credit card company when they buy faulty goods or services abroad (see page 435). Note, however, that not all card issuers are party to this agreement, so ask your card issuer. Claims must usually be made within 90 or 120 days. **If you have a legitimate complaint, you shouldn't pay the bill until you have received satisfaction.**

Lost or Stolen Cards: Over 5,000 credit cards are lost or stolen every day in Britain. If you lose a credit card or have it stolen, report it immediately to the police and the issuing office, and confirm the loss in writing as soon as possible. Credit card fraud costs some £200 million a year, although it could be almost eliminated by adopting cards containing the holder's photograph and using a PIN number (which must be entered via a special keypad each time a card is used), as is the case in France. Many retailers don't bother to check signatures, many of which are illegible anyway.

Insurance: You can insure all your credit, cash and cheque cards for around £10 a year with a number of credit card protection companies, e.g. Sentinel and the Card Protection Plan. If your lose any of your cards, you simply telephone a 24-hour number and the insurance company contacts your card issuers for you. When a signed credit card is lost or stolen, your liability is limited to £50 before notification and nothing after notification (providing you weren't negligent).

Foreign Cards: Many foreigners can obtain an international charge or credit card in a country other than Britain and be billed in the currency of that country (or retain existing international cards). You may, however, find it more convenient and cheaper to be billed in sterling, rather than a foreign currency, e.g. US dollars, where you must wait for the bill from outside Britain, payments may vary due to exchange rate fluctuations and bills may arrive after the 'payment due date'.

Store Cards: Most major department and chain stores issue their own account credit cards, e.g. Marks & Spencer, Debenhams and John Lewis, and some stores don't accept any credit cards but their own. Interest rates are quoted monthly and are usually *very* high, e.g. up to double what you pay with an Access or Barclaycard.

Even if you don't like plastic money and shun any form of credit, credit cards do have their uses. For example, no deposits on hire cars, no pre-paying hotel bills, safety and security, and above all, convenience. However, in the wrong hands they are a disaster and should be shunned by spendthrifts and politicians (in fact, by anyone who's reckless with money).

OVERDRAFTS

Generally if you wish to overdraw your current account you must make a prior arrangement with your bank, although an increasing number of accounts allow an automatic authorised overdraft of up to £200 or £250. Note that some banks have a standard charge for using an authorised overdraft, e.g. £12 per month even if you overdraw only by 1p. Some accounts, e.g. those for students, allow holders an overdraft of up to £1,000 at preferential interest rates or without incurring any charges. Cheque accounts for high earners (e.g. over £20,000 a year) with a minimum balance of £1,000 often offer an automatic overdraft facility, e.g. £2,500.

If you overdraw your account without a prior arrangement, you may find that your cheques bounce (i.e. they aren't paid) or that you're charged a punitive rate of interest (as much as 10 per cent above that charged for authorised overdrafts). A cheque covered by a cheque card cannot be bounced, irrespective of whether your account is overdrawn. An administrative charge (fine?) of £10 to £25 is made by most banks for unauthorised overdrafts, ostensibly for letters, interviews or other administration work. Your bank may also charge you a service charge for the month in which you were overdrawn or charge a fee for each transaction during the quarter *plus* a maintenance charge.

Unauthorised overdrafts may cost you £2.50 a day, even if you overdraw only by a small amount, plus a service charge. Note that the difference between overdraft charges (both authorised and unauthorised) levied by banks can run to £hundreds. In one notable case, a bank charged a customer an interest rate equivalent to 100,000,000 per cent on a small unauthorised overdraft! Building societies generally charge much lower fees for overdrafts, most of which charge fees for authorised overdrafts, although some charge interest only.

It's usually easier to obtain an overdraft than a loan, particularly if your need is short-term only (longer than six months and you should consider a loan). The advantage of an overdraft over a loan, is that you pay interest only when you're actually overdrawn, so although you may have a £2,000 overdraft at the end of the month, this may be cleared by your salary at the beginning of the next month (if you're well paid). Foreigners may find it easier to get an overdraft than a loan, particularly during their first year in Britain, although credit may be limited. Business overdrafts are the best value and are usually only a few percentage points above the base rate.

The interest rate for authorised overdrafts varies, so shop around. Try to ensure you're charged a low interest overdraft, as interest rates for short-term, small overdrafts can be extremely high. Overdrafts are insured free by some banks against customers being unable to pay. Note that for some people short-term borrowing is cheaper with a credit card (see page 340), for which you don't need permission and which can be repaid at any time. Overdraft interest rates are published in the Saturday editions of newspapers such as *The Times* and *The Daily Telegraph*.

LOANS

It pays to shop around when you want a loan as many borrowers pay too much interest on their loans. Interest rates for borrowers are high in Britain and vary considerably depending on the lender, the amount, the period of the loan, and most importantly, whether the loan is secured or unsecured. A secured loan is cheaper, for which you must offer collateral as a guarantee against defaulting on the repayments, e.g. a life insurance policy (75 to 90 per cent of the surrender value is usual) or a property. However, you should beware of loans where your home is used as security, as if you fail to repay it you can lose your home (if you have spare equity in a home, re-mortgaging may be the best way to raise money). If you want a loan to buy a new car, the best deals are usually provided by motor manufacturers. **If you're planning to buy a home with a mortgage, one of the best accounts is a an all-in-one account or a mortgage current account (see page 345), which allows you to borrow at the same rate as your mortgage interest rate.**

The rate of interest charged on loans in Britain is quoted as a flat rate or the Annual Percentage Rate (APR), which is the true rate of interest and includes all charges (e.g. documentation fees or maintenance charges). APR is usually just under double the flat rate. All interest rates on goods must, by law, quote the APR figure, so you're able to instantly compare rates. Most personal loans offer a fixed rate of interest throughout the term of the loan. Beware of loans with a variable rate of interest (APR var.), as the interest rate could rise and you may be unable to meet the repayments (or alternatively your loan repayments could be extended). Some loan repayments are delayed for six months, although you should be aware that low-start interest or deferred loan repayments ultimately cost you much more than ordinary loans.

Always shop around and compare APRs for personal loans from a number of financial institutions, as they vary considerably. It isn't always necessary to have an account with a bank or building society to obtain a loan from them. If you're able to offer security for a loan or can get someone to stand as a guarantor, you will usually be eligible for a lower interest rate (with an APR up to 10 per cent lower than an unsecured loan). However, you should be wary of acting as a guarantor for someone else's debts without some sort of security (or at least being prepared for the worst). Anyone providing a loan or mortgage where your home is security must state in their advertising and documentation that 'your home is at risk if you don't keep up repayments on a mortgage or other loan secured on it.'

In addition to a personal loan from a bank or building society, loans are available from a variety of sources. You may be able to get an 'ordinary' loan or a loan account from your bank (the terms of which are negotiated with your bank manager) which is usually cheaper than a personal loan. Other sources may include a credit card (usually best for short-term borrowing only), a gold card (may allow an unsecured overdraft facility of up to £10,000), a bank overdraft (although this may be expensive) or interest-free credit. Many banks have savings accounts where you deposit a set amount each month (e.g. £10 to £100) that allows you to borrow up to 20 or 30 times your monthly payment.

If you want a loan (e.g. to start a business) and don't have sufficient security, one of the places you're least likely to get it is from your friendly bank manager. Banks are awash with money but they have few people to lend to since they tightened up their lending criteria a few years ago. Business loans are generally even harder to obtain than personal loans. If there's the slightest risk involved, your bank manager will demand security in the form of property or a water-tight insurance policy (or your first born) before he commits himself. However, the fact that you tried to wrest money from your long-suffering bank manager when you were struggling, won't usually be held against you when you're rich (when he'll be only too happy to do business with you). It's a sad fact of life that when you most need money it will be hardest to come by, but when you're flourishing people will fall over themselves to lend it to you.

Borrowing from private loan companies (moneylenders), as advertised in newspapers, is expensive (very high interest rates, plus fees and commission). Use them only as an absolute last resort when all other avenues have been exhausted and the loan is a matter of life and death. Note that Britain is a loan shark's paradise and there's little control over interest rates. One a loan shark in Glasgow was found to be charging 30p in the £1 each week – an APR of 84,000,000 per cent! Extortionate deals like this are in fact illegal, although there's no legal definition of extortionate and loans with around 50 per cent APR have been judged legal. In general, the more desperate your financial situation, the more suspicious you should be of anyone who's willing to lend you money (unless it's your mum).

If you take out a loan, you can usually take out a credit protection insurance policy at the same time (sometimes included 'free'). If you're unable to pay your loan because of sickness, accident or unemployment, the insurance pays your loan instalments. If you're in doubt about the terms of a loan, you should seek independent advice from a Citizens Advice Bureau (CAB), consumer advice centre or law centre, all of which provide free advice (see page 448) concerning loans.

The best personal (unsecured) and secured (by second mortgage) loan rates are published in the Saturday editions of newspapers such as *The Times* and *The Daily Telegraph*. See also *CreditWise*, *Debt - A survival guide* and *Moneyfax* (a guide to credit and debit), all published by the Office of Fair Trading.

MORTGAGES

Mortgages (or home loans) in Britain were traditionally provided by building societies, which were created as savings banks for people saving to buy a home. They usually had a strict lending policy and were reluctant to lend money to anyone who wasn't a regular saver. Nowadays, in addition to building societies, you can obtain a home loan from high street and foreign banks, insurance companies, mortgage companies (including new direct mortgage companies), local authorities and even employers. Competition to lend you money is fierce and homebuyers in Britain have a greater variety of home loan finance available than elsewhere in Europe.

The usual home loan period is 25 years, which can be extended to 35 years. In Britain borrowers can usually obtain 90 to 95 per cent mortgages, unlike many other countries where they are usually limited to 50 or 75 per cent of a property's value (the average loan to homebuyers in France, Germany, Holland and Italy is 60 per cent of the value of a property). Hence the average age of first-time buyers in Britain is around 25, compared with the mid to late thirties in Germany and Italy. Some financial experts believe that the maximum mortgage available to first-time buyers should be 80 per cent and for second time buyers 60 per cent, which would greatly reduce negative equity (where the amount owed on the mortgage exceeds the value of a property). Lenders have been getting tougher with those in arrears in the last decade, during which some 500,000 homes have been repossessed. If you're an employee in steady employment, Britain is one of the easiest countries in the world in which to obtain a mortgage.

Mortgage Rates: In the last seven years, the cost of mortgages has fallen considerably to stand at around 7 per cent for standard variable rate mortgages in 1999 (from a peak of over 15 per cent in 1988), with most lenders offering even lower rates to first-time buyers or to induce homeowners to switch lenders. British base rates are expected to come into line with the Euro base rate (which was just 3 per cent in early 1999) during the next few years. Rates would be even lower if the difference between the rate at which lenders borrow and the rate they charge homeowners hadn't grown over the last few years (profit margins on mortgages in Britain are around double those in many other countries). Special offers includes low-start or deferred-interest mortgages, which reduce your mortgage payments for a number of years, and deferred-interest mortgages, which are primarily targeted at those who expect their salaries to rise sharply in the coming years.

In 1999 there were over 200 mortgage discounts on offer (millions of homeowners could slash their mortgage repayments by switching lenders). In 1999 mortgages had never been more competitive and in addition to low rates, many lenders were also offering cash-back for changing lenders. While most borrowers never change their lenders, some homeowners re-mortgage every two or three years after shopping around for the best deal available. However, lenders are now wise to this and many impose stiff redemption penalties for changing lenders, which often continue long after a special rate ceases.

Fixed or Variable Rate: In Britain, you can usually choose between fixed and variable rate mortgages, where the interest rate goes up and down depending on the base rate. Those who cannot afford an increase in their mortgage repayments are better off with a fixed-rate mortgage, where the interest rate is fixed for a number of years (e.g. one to five years), no matter what happens to interest rates in the meantime. The longer the fixed-rate period, the lower the interest rate offered. If interest rates go down, you may find yourself paying more than the current mortgage rate, but at least you will know exactly what you must pay each month. To judge whether a fixed-rate mortgage is worthwhile, you must estimate in which direction interest rates are heading (a difficult feat). The standard variable rate is usually 1.25 per cent above the base rate, which it tracks, and isn't the best deal. Mortgages that offer a discount on the standard variable rate for up to five years are the best deal, where your interest rate falls (or rises!) in line with the base rate, but at a discount to the standard variable rate. Building societies typically offer standard variable rate mortgages that are around half a percentage point below high street banks.

Redemption Charges: Some mortgages carry crippling redemption penalties, e.g. 5 or 6 per cent, if repaid early (some lenders have even imposed retrospective redemption penalties). A redemption charge used to be around three months interest, although this has now been increased by many lenders to as much as 12 months interest. The period during which high redemption charges are valid has been extended and is intended to lock borrowers into their lenders for longer periods. This is common when lenders offer low, fixed-interest rates for up to five years or discounts on their standard variable rates. Always read the small print. The typical cost of a re-mortgage is around £1,000 (includes lender's fee, valuation fee, solicitor's fee, local registry charge, search fee and other costs). Note, however, that many borrowers are better off changing lenders, even after paying a redemption fee. Fixed rate mortgages can carry crippling costs and early repayment costs can be staggering.

Deposit: Although it's still possible to obtain a loan for the whole cost of a property (a 100 per cent mortgage), particularly if you're a first-time buyer, many lenders require a deposit of at least 5 per cent (95 per cent mortgage) and possibly 10 or 15 per cent (85 or 90 per cent mortgage) of the cost. A sensible way of calculating your safe mortgage limit is around three times your annual income, plus an amount equal to the secondary income of a partner, if applicable (or two and a half times your joint income). For example, if a wife earns £20,000 a year and the husband £15,000, then the mortgage limit should be £75,000 (three times £20,000 plus £15,000). In the late '80s, before the housing market crashed, mortgages were available for up to six times your annual salary. Up to four people can legally share the ownership of a property, although most lenders allow a maximum of three co-owners.

In recent years lenders have tightened their lending criteria and buyers are becoming more wary, which has led to a fall in the number of people taking out mortgages. It's advisable not to rush into a mortgage, particularly if your income isn't absolutely secure. Thousands of people are denied mortgages because of bad credit ratings or uncertain income. Many lenders are also unwilling to lend to the self-employed, who usually need to produce three years accounts. Some lenders who charge *very* high interest rates target people who are considered poor risks and impose swinging penalties if borrowers fall into arrears.

MIRAS: Mortgage Interest Relief at Source (MIRAS) is allowed on mortgage interest payments at your highest rate of tax, up to a limit of £30,000. Relief was restricted to 10 per cent on the first £30,000 of a mortgage for the 1999/2000 tax year. For example if your mortgage rate is 5 per cent you pay £1,500 in interest on £30,000, on which tax relief is £150. MIRAS is to be abolished in the year 2000.

Mortgage Protection: It's advisable to take out a mortgage protection policy (which could eventually become compulsory) in case you fall ill, have an accident or are made redundant and are unable to pay your mortgage (new borrowers aren't eligible for social security to pay their mortgage interest until nine months or longer after a disability or unemployment). The cost is around £5 to £7 per month for each £100 per month of benefit required, e.g. if you want to receive a payment of £500 a month your premium will be £25 to £35 a month. Some lenders provide free mortgage protection insurance. **Note, however, that there are numerous flaws in mortgage insurance and many claims are rejected due to hidden clauses in insurance policies.** Policies are frequently mis-sold and insurers regularly bend the rules to avoid paying claims. Some experts advise that many mortgage protection policies aren't worth the paper they're printed on (payments for redundancy are fraught with problems). Get a policy checked by your legal adviser for hidden loopholes and make sure it covers what it says it does.

Types of Mortgages: Once you've calculated how much you wish to pay for a home, you must decide what kind of mortgage you want. Although there are many different mortgages on the market, all fall into three main categories: endowment, pension and repayment mortgages (plus interest-only mortgages, which are becoming more common).

Endowment Mortgage: With an endowment mortgage, you borrow a sum of money and pay interest over the length of the loan. You also take out an endowment life insurance policy, which will hopefully provide a large enough lump sum to pay off the mortgage at the end of the term, usually 25 years. Your monthly mortgage payments are made up of an interest payment and an insurance (endowment) payment. The policy also carries life insurance, which ensures that if the policyholder dies, the mortgage is paid off in full and any money left over is paid to his estate. Note that the loan and endowment are separate and you can obtain them from different sources. Take independent advice and try to find a lender with a low interest rate and an insurance company with a good track record.

Like all endowment policies, you could be left with a tax-free sum at the end of the term, after your loan has been paid off (although there are no guarantees). In recent years many endowment mortgages have been performing badly and weren't on target to repay loans let alone provide a surplus! One advantage of an endowment loan is that the life policy can be transferred when you move house. If this results in a bigger loan, you take out a new policy to cover the increase and continue to pay the premiums on earlier policies. Never allow yourself to be persuaded to surrender an existing policy simply to take out another without good reason. If you surrender your old endowment policy and take out a new policy, you stand to forfeit £thousands as a penalty.

This buying and selling of policies to generate commissions, is called 'churning' in the industry and is encouraged by some lenders. The reason endowment mortgages were so popular is that they were heavily promoted by lenders (who usually don't tell borrowers about the disadvantages or alternatives) due to the high commission on the endowment. However, endowment mortgages have plummeted in recent years and now comprise some 30 per cent of the total compared with 80 per cent in the '80s. Endowment mortgages aren't recommended for first-time buyers with limited financial resources and low salaries, who should consider a repayment mortgage which is more flexible if you have trouble meeting your repayments. Many lenders will try to persuade you not to take out a repayment mortgage (see below) and may even refuse to give you one. **A repayment mortgage is by far the best choice for most borrowers!**

If you choose an endowment mortgage, you must then choose the type of policy that suits you. A with-profits policy is the most expensive and is therefore not so popular nowadays. Bonuses are added regularly, which once paid cannot be taken away, and there's usually also a final termination bonus. Your payments are invested in a wide range of investments and the level of bonuses you receive is determined by the skills of your fund manager (and the ups and downs of the stock market). **Don't be taken in by the promise of a huge lump sum in 25 years time, which after inflation has been taken into account may not be worth much.** In recent years with-profits insurance policies have looked less attractive when compared with the alternatives.

Pension Mortgages: These are broadly similar to endowment mortgages, where monthly interest is paid on the loan. However, with a pension mortgage you pay into a pension plan, which pays off your mortgage on retirement and also pays you a pension. This is a good choice for the self-employed and for employees who aren't members of a company pension scheme, as the premiums attract tax relief at your highest tax rate and you can pay in from 17.5 to 40 per cent of your annual earnings, depending on your age (see page 308). Your money usually builds up faster in this kind of fund, although you will receive a smaller pension if most of your lump sum is used to pay off your loan.

Repayment Mortgages: These are so called because you repay the original loan and interest over the period of the mortgage, similar to most personal loans. As interest rates rise and fall, your repayments go up or down, but assuming a constant interest rate your payments would remain the same for the period of the loan. One advantage is that the term of the loan can be extended if you have trouble meeting your monthly repayments. A disadvantage of a repayment mortgage is that you don't have a life policy and you must therefore take out a 'mortgage protection' policy to insure that your loan is paid off should you die. This policy isn't expensive as it pays off the mortgage only if you die before the term of the loan is completed (and the term decreases over time). **For the majority of people, a repayment mortgage together with adequate life insurance is the best choice.**

Interest-Only mortgages are offered by an increasing number of lenders, where you take out a mortgage loan in the normal way and pay interest as usual. However, instead of agreeing to repay the loan at a fixed date in the future, the loan simply stays in existence until you (not the lender) decide to repay it, which could be anytime from six months to 60 years. Interest-only loans are good for single people with no dependants, heavily mortgaged families, those whose earnings fluctuate and people who expect to inherit money sometime in the future. It isn't necessary to have an insurance policy to repay the loan should you die, but it's advisable if others are dependent on your income. Most lenders will only lend from 50 to 75 per cent of a property's value on an interest-only mortgage. Note that a flexible payment mortgage, where you can increase or lower your payments depending on your income, are a good choice for many people as you can save a fortune in interest by paying off a mortgage earlier.

Current Account Mortgage: One of the most significant innovations for mortgage seekers in recent years has been the current account mortgage (or all-in-one account), where in effect you operate your mortgage as a current account within certain limits. With a current account mortgage you can have your salary paid into your mortgage account, which automatically reduces your mortgage debt and saves you interest until you withdraw money. You also earn the same interest rate on your savings as you pay on your mortgage and you can borrow additional money at any time at the same interest rate you pay for your mortgage. Most analysts agree that these accounts are difficult to beat and if you make full use of the account you could save tens of £thousands and pay off your borrowing as quickly or as slowly as you wish. Among the lenders offering this type of loan are Virgin One (☎ 08456-000001), First Active (☎ freefone 0800-550551) and Kleinwort Benson (☎ freefone 0800-317477).

Foreign Currency Mortgages: It's also possible to obtain a foreign currency mortgage, e.g. in euros, Swiss francs, US dollars, Deutschmarks or Japanese yen, all currencies which, with their historically low interest rates, have provided huge savings for borrowers in recent years. However, you should be cautious about taking out a foreign currency mortgage as interest rate gains can be wiped out overnight by currency swings. Most lenders such as high street banks and building societies, advise against taking out foreign currency home loans unless your paid in a foreign currency (such as euros). The lending conditions for foreign currency home loans are much stricter than for sterling loans and are generally granted only to high-rollers (those earning a minimum of £40,000 or £50,000 a year) and are usually for a minimum of £100,000 and a maximum of 60 per cent of a property's value.

Advice & Information: Whatever type of home loan you choose, shop around and take the time to investigate all the options available. One way to find the best deal is to contact an independent mortgage broker. Mortgage advice offered by lenders is often misleading and not to be trusted (surveys have found that the mis-selling of mortgages is widespread among high street lenders). The best variable, fixed-rate and discount mortgage rates are published in Saturday and Sunday newspapers such as *The Times* and *The Sunday Times*, and are also available via the television teletext service. Monthly money and mortgage magazines such as *What Mortgage* and *Mortgage Magazine* are also useful sources of information. You can also make quick comparisons on the Internet (e.g. www.moneynet.co.uk, www.moneyextra.co.uk, www.infotrade.co.uk and www.ftquicken.com).

COUNCIL TAX

The council tax replaced the reviled poll tax (or community charge) in 1993, which itself replaced property rates in 1989 in Scotland and 1990 in England and Wales. The council tax is a local tax levied by local councils on residents to pay for such things as education, police, roads, waste disposal, libraries and community services (see **Local Government** on page 447). Each council fixes its own tax rate, based on the number of residents and how much money they need to finance their services.

The amount payable depends on the value of your home, relative to others in your area, as rated by your local council (not necessarily the market value). Properties in England, Scotland and Wales (there's no council tax in Northern Ireland) are divided into the following bands:

		Property Value	
Band	**England**	**Scotland**	**Wales**
A	up to £40,000	up to £27,000	up to £30,000
B	£40,001-£52,000	£27,001-£35,000	£30,001-£39,000
C	£52,001-£68,000	£35,001-£45,000	£39,001-£51,000
D	£68,001-£88,000	£45,001-£58,000	£51,001-£66,000
E	£88,001-£120,000	£58,001-£80,000	£66,001-£90,000
F	£120,001-£160,000	£80,001-£106,000	£90,001-£120,000
G	£160,001-£320,000	£106,001-£212,000	£120,001-£240,000
H	over £320,000	over £212,000	over £240,000

The tax payable varies considerably depending on the borough or county where you live. In a rural county the council tax may range from between £400 and £500 (band A) to between £900 and £1,250 (band H). The tax includes payments for the county, borough or district council; the local police, fire and civil defence authorities; and possibly a 'special expenses' payment in certain areas. It can usually be paid by direct debit from a bank or building society account, by post with a personal cheque, in person at council offices, by credit card, or at a bank or post office. Payment can be made as a lump sum (for which a reduction may be offered) or in ten instalments a year, from April to January (12 instalments in Scotland). In recent years taxes have increased due to inadequate funding from central government and many councils have been forced to cut services to meet their budgets. Taxes increased by 5 to 10 per cent in many parts of England in 1999.

The full council tax assumes that two adults are living permanently in the dwelling. If only one adult lives in a dwelling (as their main home), the bill is reduced by 25 per cent. If a dwelling isn't a main home, e.g. it's unoccupied or is a second home, the bill is reduced by 50 per cent. Exempt dwellings include those that are unfurnished (exempt for up to six months); undergoing structural alteration or major repair (exempt for up to six months after completion); are left empty for specific reasons (e.g. the occupier is in hospital, a nursing home or prison, or is a student); or are occupied only by people under 18 years of age.

Certain people aren't counted when calculating the number of adults resident in a dwelling, e.g. full-time students and 18 and 19 year-olds who have just left school. If you or someone who lives with you has special needs arising from a disability, you may be entitled to a reduction in your council tax bill. Those receiving Income Support (see page 303) usually pay no council tax and others on low incomes have their bills reduced. You can appeal against the assessed value of your property and any errors due to exemption, benefits or discounts.

All those who are liable for council tax must register with their local council when they take up residence in a new area, and are liable to pay council tax from their first day of residence. A register is maintained by councils, containing the names and addresses of all people registered for council tax, which is open to public examination. If you don't want your name and address to appear on the register, e.g. for fear of physical violence, you can apply for anonymous registration. New arrivals in Britain must register with their local council after taking up residence in Britain or after moving house. When moving to a new county or borough, you may be entitled to a refund of a portion of your council tax.

VALUE ADDED TAX (VAT)

Value Added Tax (VAT) is payable at a standard rate of 17.5 per cent on all goods and services, with the exception of domestic fuels on which the rate is 8 per cent. The following goods and services are zero rated:

- most food (but not catering, which includes meals in restaurants, cafés, and hot take-away food and drink);

- sales and long leases of new buildings, construction of most new buildings (but not work to existing buildings);

- young children's clothing and footwear;

- books and newspapers;

- mobile homes and house boats;

- dispensing of prescriptions and the supply of many aids for handicapped people;

- the export of goods.

Certain business transactions are exempt from VAT (not the same as zero rated), on which VAT isn't applicable. Exempt supplies include most sales, leases and lettings of land and buildings; insurance; betting, gaming and lotteries; the provision of credit; certain education and training; and the services of doctors, dentists and opticians.

If you're self-employed and your annual turnover (not just profits) is more than £50,000 annually, you must be registered for VAT. A business which makes exempt supplies only cannot register for VAT, but a company making zero-rated supplies can. An individual is registered for VAT, not a business, and registration covers *all* the business activities of the registered person. The prices of some goods, e.g. computers and other business equipment, are advertised or quoted exclusive of VAT (although almost all other advertised prices are inclusive of VAT). The VAT you're charged on goods and services that you use in setting up your business can be reclaimed, subject to certain conditions.

There are stiff penalties for anyone who fails to register for VAT or who makes a false declaration. A serious wrong declaration could result in a 30 per cent penalty (even for accidental errors) plus interest being levied on all underpayments. There are also penalties for making late returns, which must be made quarterly (this may be extended to annually for traders with an annual turnover under the £50,000 threshold). If you're in any doubt as to your registration or VAT declarations (every three months), you should contact your local VAT office, the address of which is in your local phone book under 'Custom and Excise'. A range of VAT publications and leaflets are published, including *Should I be Registered for VAT* and *The VAT guide*, copies of which are sent to you when you register. All VAT publications are available on request from VAT offices. Many people believe VAT is actually short for Vague Additions to the Total (it's usually the difference between a reasonable price and too expensive).

It's the declared aim of the EU to eventually have just one universal rate of VAT for the whole union, although this will take some time (i.e. eons) to accomplish.

INCOME TAX

It's hardly surprising that the British don't always see eye to eye with the French. After all it was because of a damned Frenchman (Napoleon) that income tax was introduced in 1799 (the 'good' news is that it was introduced as a temporary measure only and may be rescinded at any time). Another Frenchman, William the Conqueror, was to blame for the introduction of the budget.

Domicile: Your liability for British taxes depends on where you're domiciled and whether you're a British resident. Your domicile is the country which you regard as your natural and permanent home, so unless you intend to live in Britain permanently you won't normally be considered to be domiciled there. A person can be resident in more than one country, but at any given time he can be domiciled in one only. From 1st January 1974 the domicile of a married women hasn't necessarily been the same as her husband's, but is decided using the same criteria as anyone capable of having an independent domicile.

To be regarded as resident in Britain for a given tax year (the tax year in Britain runs from the 5th April to the 6th April of the following year and not a calendar year), you must normally be physically present there for at least part of that year. You will always be regarded as resident in Britain with respect to income tax if you spend six months (183 days) or more there in any one year (whether in one continuous period or during a number of visits). A resident in Britain may be classified as 'resident' or 'ordinarily resident'. Ordinarily resident is broadly equivalent to being habitually resident, i.e. a person who's resident in Britain year after year is ordinarily resident there. A person may be resident but not ordinarily resident in Britain for a given tax year, e.g. he could normally live outside Britain but visit Britain for six months or more in that year. Alternatively he may be ordinarily resident in Britain, but not resident for a given tax year, e.g. he usually lives in Britain but goes abroad for a long holiday and doesn't set foot in Britain during that year. Each tax year is looked at as a whole and a person can be classified only as resident or non-resident for a particular tax year and not, for example, resident for part of the year and non-resident for the remainder.

If you're a new permanent resident in Britain (i.e. someone not ordinarily resident in Britain), you will be considered resident only from the time of your arrival (the same rule applies to anyone leaving Britain for permanent residence abroad, who becomes not ordinarily resident in Britain from the time he left). If you're classified as a resident in Britain, you will be liable to British income tax on all income arising from a source in Britain. If you're a British resident *and* domiciled in Britain, you're liable for taxation in Britain on your worldwide income, including capital gains tax. A booklet (IR20) entitled *Residents and Non-residents - Liability to tax in the United Kingdom* explains the rules outlined above.

Double Taxation Agreements: Britain has double taxation agreements with around 80 countries, which despite the name, are to prevent you paying double taxes and not to ensure that you pay twice. Under double taxation treaties, certain categories of people are exempt from paying British tax. If part of your income is taxed abroad in a country with a double taxation treaty with Britain, you won't need to pay British tax on that income. If you're a British citizen living abroad, you won't usually be liable for British tax providing your absence from Britain covers a complete tax year and you don't:

● remain in Britain for 183 days or more in any tax year;

● have accommodation available in Britain and don't make any visits to Britain no matter how short, unless you're employed full-time abroad;

● visit Britain for more than three months a year in four or more consecutive years.

Besides British taxes, you may also be liable for taxes in your home country. Citizens of most countries are exempt from paying taxes in their home country when they spend a minimum period abroad, e.g. one year. It's usually your responsibility to familiarise yourself with the latest tax procedures in your home country or country of domicile. If you're in doubt about your tax liability in your home country, contact your embassy or consulate. It's possible for some foreigners to live legally in Britain without paying British tax. To qualify you must reside in Britain for less than 183 days in a calendar year or your salary (if applicable) must be paid and taxed by your employer in another country with a 'double taxation' treaty (see above) with Britain. For information about double taxation agreements, refer to *Double Taxation Relief* (IR6), available from tax offices.

Tax Rates: Britain has three income tax rates (1999/2000). The first £1,500 of taxable income is taxed at the **lower rate** of 10 per cent. Taxable income from £1,501 to £28,000 is taxed at 23 per cent (this will be reduced to 22 per cent from April 2000), known as the **basic rate** of tax. The **higher rate** tax of 40 per cent is the highest rate of tax on earned income in Britain and is payable on taxable income above £28,000 a year. The rate of income tax payable in Britain is among the lowest in Europe. Your taxable income is your income after all allowances and deductions have been made from your gross income (from all sources).

Like everything in Britain, there's a two-tier tax system, first class for the self-employed and a second class system, called PAYE, for employees. The self-employed pay their tax in arrears (as all employees do in many European countries), whereas an employee's income tax is deducted at source weekly or monthly from his salary by his employer. Although the Inland Revenue (IR) may give individuals a hard time when it comes to paying their tax bills, British companies withhold £billions from the tax authorities each year due to disputed corporation tax bills, plus £billions more that's contested by the self-employed and those owing capital gains tax.

Tax Evasion: Tax evasion is illegal and is a criminal offence in Britain, for which you can be heavily fined or even sent to prison. Nevertheless, there's a flourishing black economy which the Inland Revenue estimate amounts to around £10 billion a year in unpaid tax on undeclared income. The IR has tightened up its ability to collect tax and catch tax dodgers in recent years and carries out investigations into tens of thousands of 'suspicious' tax returns each year (it has 12 months from the date you file a return to launch an enquiry). In most cases where taxpayers owe money, the investigation is conducted out of court with taxpayers making a full disclosure and a monetary settlement.

Tax Avoidance: Tax avoidance, i.e. legally paying as little tax as possible, if necessary by finding and exploiting loopholes in the tax laws, is a different matter altogether (from tax evasion). It's practised by most companies, wealthy individuals and self-employed people, although the opportunities for anyone paying direct or PAYE tax are strictly limited. Unfortunately there are few (legal) ways an individual paying PAYE tax can reduce his income tax bill (dying is one of them), although it's possible to appeal against your PAYE coding notice or anything connected with your tax affairs that you believe is incorrect. Whether you're self-employed or an employee, you should ensure that you don't pay any more tax than is necessary.

Accountants: If your tax affairs are complicated or you're unable to understand your own finances (like the majority of people), you should consider employing an accountant to deal with your tax affairs (most high street banks also provide a personal tax service). This probably applies to most self-employed people, but very few who are on PAYE (see page 355). However, don't just pick an accountant with a pin from the phone book, but ask your friends, colleagues or business associates if they can recommend someone. If you're self-employed, you should choose an accountant who deals with people in your line of business and who knows exactly what you can (and cannot) claim.

Substantial tax savings can be made with regard to pensions, independent taxation, and trusts to avoid capital gains and inheritance tax. Some tax avoidance schemes apply only to the very rich as the cost of using them is prohibitive to anyone else. As soon as the Inland Revenue close one loophole tax accountants find another one. Accountant's fees vary from £50 to £150 an hour, so ask in advance what the rates are (they're highest in London). Avoid 'high-power' accountants who will cost you the earth. You can reduce your accountant's fees considerably by keeping itemised records of all your business expenses (preferably on computer), rather than handing him a pile of invoices and receipts. Note, however, that a good accountant will usually save you more than he charges in fees.

Tax Changes: Changes in direct or indirect taxation are generally announced in the main Budget Statement in March each year. Changes to income tax come into effect in the following tax year (from 6th April to 5th April), although amendments can be made at any time and some tax changes don't come into effect until a year later. Taxes and allowances quoted in this section largely refer to the 1999-2000 tax year (ending on 5th April 2000).

Information: There are many books published about how to reduce your income tax bill including the Daily Mail *Income Tax Guide* and the Daily Telegraph *Guide to Income Tax*. The Consumer's Association publish an annual *Tax Saving Guide* which isn't sold by newsagents or bookshops but is 'free' to subscribers of *Which?*

magazine (see page 437), plus an annual guide entitled *Which? Way To Save Tax*. A tax guide written especially for the elderly is *Your Tax and Savings* by John Burke, available from Age Concern England. The Inland Revenue publish a huge number of leaflets on every conceivable tax subject, all of which are listed in a leaflet entitled *Catalogue of leaflets and booklets*. Copies of tax leaflets can be ordered by phone from tax offices and tax enquiry centres (TECs), which are usually open from 1000 to 1600. If you have a home or business computer, a number of tax computer programs are available such as *QuickTax* (Intuit) and *TaxCalc* (Which? Books), designed to make it easier to calculate and check your income tax payments.

Finally, never trust the tax man to take only what he should or to allow you the correct allowances and deductions. While the IR won't cheat you deliberately, it isn't uncommon for them to make mistakes. If you pay PAYE tax, make sure that your tax code is correct (see page 356) and never hesitate to dispute a tax bill with which you disagree. It's estimated that Britons pay some £5 billion in unnecessary tax each year (mostly on income) and that savers and investors waste £millions by not taking advantage of tax concessions.

Independent Taxation

Under independent taxation, spouses are allocated their own tax allowances and privacy in their dealings with the Inland Revenue. Each partner has his or her own tax bill and needn't tell the other what they earn or how much tax they pay (not that most people would dream of telling fibs about their income to their spouses). Note, however, that a couple usually need to work together to make the most of independent taxation. Prior to the introduction of independent taxation (April 1990), a wife didn't pay her own tax on savings and investments, even if a couple opted for separate taxation, and her husband was responsible for the tax bill on her investments.

Married couples can reduce their tax bill by switching savings and assets between them. If one partner isn't working it's important to put any savings in the non-working partner's name in an account or investment that pays interest gross, and which allows the interest to be offset against the tax allowance. Despite the savings to be made, many couples are slow to take advantage of tax rules. In addition to a personal allowance, married couples also receive a married couple's allowance, usually claimed by the male partner. The down side of independent taxation is the extra work involved in completing two tax returns and the extra cost if an accountant is employed. The Inland Revenue publish many leaflets about independent taxation and most banks and building societies offer free advice (alternatively you can discuss it with your accountant).

Pay As You Earn (PAYE)

Income tax is collected by the Inland Revenue (IR). All employees pay direct income tax or Pay As You Earn (PAYE) income tax, which is deducted from gross salaries at source by employers. PAYE isn't a separate tax, but simply the name given to the system of direct (income) taxation in Britain. Any additional income, whether tax is deducted at source or not, must be declared to the Inland Revenue. This may include part-time employment or income from investments or savings. PAYE tax applies to all income tax which is payable on earnings to which the scheme relates and includes tax at both the basic and higher rates.

Some employers may not deduct PAYE tax from an employee's earnings, particularly in the case of casual or part-time employees, and where the distinction between employee and self-employed is blurred. This is illegal and a hazardous practice for employers, who are responsible for deducting all their employees' income tax at source, unless a person is categorised as self-employed by the tax office. Tax on Unemployment Benefit and other social security benefits, such as Maternity Pay and Statutory Sick Pay, also comes within the PAYE scheme. The PAYE scheme is disadvantageous to many employees, who would be entitled to claim larger and more allowances if they were classified as self-employed, and would also have the benefit of paying their tax in arrears.

PAYE Tax Code

In Britain, the level of tax for those taxed under the PAYE system is denoted by a tax code. A notice of coding 'Form P2 (T)' is sent out in January or February for the next tax year starting in April, to both employers and employees (although not everyone receives one each year). When you receive a new code, your notice of coding will show how the calculations have been made. You should check that the deductions, allowances and the total are correct. You don't receive a notice every year, but your current tax code is always given on your pay or wage slip (which you get when you receive your weekly or monthly salary). Your pay slip also shows your gross pay (your salary without any deductions) to date and the amount of tax you have paid to date.

If your circumstances change you should tell the Inland Revenue. They will either send you a new income tax return to complete (see below) or simply change your tax code. You must inform the IR of any changes in your tax status, e.g. marriage, a dependant relative, divorce or separation, which entitles you to an additional allowance, or a change in your income (maybe from a part-time job) or company benefits (e.g. a company car). It's in your interest to do this, as when the Inland Revenue find out later you won't only be liable for any tax owed plus interest, but can also be fined up to 100 per cent of the amount of unpaid tax.

Your tax code is also printed on your P45, a certificate given to you when your leave your employment and which should be given to a new employer when you start a new job. Your P45 shows your PAYE code, your total earnings and how much tax you've paid since the start of the current tax year. If you're unemployed after leaving a job and are eligible to claim Jobseeker's Allowance (see page 303), you must give your P45 to the benefit office when registering for Unemployment Benefit. When you find a job, the benefit office will give you a P45 for your new employer. If you don't have a P45 when starting a job, e.g. for your first job from school or after arriving in Britain from abroad, you should ask your new employer for a P15 *Notice of coding* form. Complete this form and ask your employer to send it to the IR, who will then give you a tax code (you can send it yourself if you want to keep the information private). Your employer will also complete a P46 form (stating your salary) to notify the Inland Revenue that you're employed by him, which you will be asked to sign. If you don't have a P45 on starting a job, your employer will tax you under a special system called an emergency code. If you pay too much tax, it will be repaid by your employer in your next pay cheque as soon as he receives your PAYE tax code.

Your tax code is made up of a series of numbers (usually three) and a letter, e.g. 645H. The numbers are the total allowances minus the last digit, e.g. allowances of £6457 become code number 645. A code of 0 (zero) applies when you have two or more jobs and your allowances have already been used to calculate the code number for your main employment. Some codes don't have a number or have numbers that don't stand for allowances, e.g. BR or DO. The letter tells the Inland Revenue you tax status:

Code	Status/Meaning
BR	tax is deducted at the basic rate;
DO	tax is deducted at a higher rate;
H	you're entitled to the personal allowance for those aged under 65 plus the married couple's allowance for those under 65 or the additional personal allowance;
K	deductions from your free-of-tax pay, such as taxable state benefits, exceed your personal allowances;
L	entitlement to the basic personal allowance (for those aged under 65);
NT	no tax is to be deducted;
OT	you receive no allowances after adjustments and tax is deducted at the lower, basic and higher rates depending on your income;
P	entitlement to the personal allowance for those aged 65 to 74;
T	someone who doesn't fall within the above categories (e.g. no allowance due to other employment) or someone whose code should end in L, H, P or V, but doesn't want an employer to know his or her status;
V	someone who's entitled to the personal and married couple's allowance for those aged 65 to 74.

If you have the letter H, L, P or V after your tax number, your employer can alter your tax when allowances are changed by a budget. If you have a T code and allowances are changed by the budget, the IR will need to work out your code again and inform both you and your employer. Codes BR and D are affected only if the tax rates or bands change. The tax code is used by your employer to calculate the amount of income tax to be deducted from your salary. If it's wrong, tell the Inland Revenue. Never assume that your tax code is correct, but check it yourself or ask an accountant or tax expert to check it for you. If you have any questions about tax, contact any tax office or tax enquiry centre. Around April you should receive a form P60 showing how much tax that you have paid in the previous tax year. You should check it and keep it in a safe place as you may be asked to produce it at a later date.

There are a number of forms with which to reclaim tax or ensure you don't pay tax unnecessarily. These include a form P50 which is used to reclaim tax, for example when you return to work after a period of not working, during which you didn't claim Unemployment Benefit. A form P187 is used to reclaim tax if you have no P45 and a form R40(S) is used to reclaim tax if you think you've paid too much (for whatever reason). Students should complete a form P38(S) when they start a holiday job and think their total taxable income for the whole tax year is likely to be *less* than the basic personal allowance. This will ensure you don't pay tax on your holiday earnings or that it's refunded.

Self-Employed

One person in eight in Britain is self-employed, either as a 'sole trader' or in partnership with others. You're generally much better off if you're self-employed, as you can claim more in the way of expenses than employees (paying PAYE tax). Another advantage for the self-employed is the delay between making profits (hopefully) and paying tax on them. To be treated as self-employed, you must convince your tax office that you're genuinely self-employed and in business for yourself. The definition of self-employed is much the same as in most countries and includes:

- working freelance for a number of clients;
- supplying your own tools or equipment;
- risking your own money in a business;
- having the final say in how the business is run;
- using your home as your office;
- responsibility for meeting losses as well as taking profits;
- the freedom to hire other people on your own terms and paying them out of your own pocket;
- correcting unsatisfactory work in your own time at your own expense;
- paying your own expenses and charging an overall fee for your services.

To check whether you're entitled to be self-employed, contact your local Inland Revenue office (see also leaflet IR56 *Employed or Self-employed*). If they decide that you're self-employed, get your tax office to confirm its decision in writing. Self-employed, as used in Britain, means a 'sole trader' or someone in a partnership, and not someone with a limited company. If you have a Limited Company, you must pay Corporation Tax on your profits, and will need the services of an accountant to deal with this. If your total turnover is less than £10,000 a year, you aren't required to submit detailed accounts to your tax office, but can give the Inland Revenue 'three-line accounts' showing turnover, expenditure and profits only.

Prior to 6th April 1994, the self-employed weren't required to pay tax on their profits for their first tax year until after the end of that year, as no assessment was made until you had been in business for 12 months. However, from 6th April 1994, new self-employed persons have been taxed on what they earn in the current tax year and not their preceding year's earnings. With the introduction of self–assessment (see page 361), the self-employed (and those who receive income from letting property or who have income from savings or investments that isn't taxed at source) must pay their income tax on account, as advance payments towards their final tax bill. Payments on account are due on 1st January and 1st July each year. The second instalment in July is for the previous tax year ending in April of that year, e.g. the July 1999 payment is the second instalment of income tax for the tax year 1998/99. Usually each payment is equal to half your tax liability for the previous tax year. Any balance of tax due must be paid by 31st January 2000.

If you're self-employed, you will also pay class two National Insurance contributions (see page 306) and must also pay class four contributions at 6 per cent on profits between £7,310 and £25,220 a year (1998/99), payable at the same time as your income tax. The following list is a guide to the deductions you can make from your gross income when calculating your taxable profits:

- National Insurance contributions, accident insurance, health insurance and unemployment insurance.
- Premiums for life insurance, endowment and private pensions.
- Business expenses, e.g. car expenses (including travel to and from your place of work), outside or subsidised meals (not free meals), employment-related education and books, and accountant's fees.
- Standard allowances are permitted for many items without proof of expenditure. Personal allowances vary depending on individual circumstances, e.g. single or married, divorced or widowed, and the number of children or dependants.
- Interest charges on loans, overdrafts and leasing contracts.
- Telephone, electricity and office expenses.
- Capital allowances for equipment, e.g. computers, office equipment and car.
- Donations to recognised charities above £600 in a financial year.

You shouldn't hesitate to claim for anything that you believe is a legitimate business deduction. The IR will delete them if they don't agree, but what they will never do is allow you a deduction that you're entitled to and have forgotten to claim. The Inland Revenue publish a number of leaflets for the self-employed including *Starting in Business* (IR28). If you're self-employed, you will probably find it pays to hire an accountant to complete your tax return.

Allowances

Before you're liable for income tax, you're allowed to earn a certain amount of income tax-free. If you earn below your taxable limit, you aren't liable for tax. Everyone has a tax-free personal allowance and a married couple is entitled to an additional married couple's allowance, both of which are increased for those aged 65 and over (even more for the over 75s). Under independent taxation for married couples (see page 355), each partner is wholly responsible for his or her own tax affairs, including both income and capital gains tax. The tax-free allowances for the 1999/2000 tax year are as follows:

Personal Allowance: Every taxpayer has a personal allowance to set against his taxable income. The personal allowance is applicable to all residents in Britain who have an income from any source, e.g. salary, pension, interest on savings or dividends from investments. The personal allowance you receive depends on your age as follows:

Age	Allowance (£)
under 65	4,335
65 to 74*	5,720
75 and over*	5,980

* Pensioners whose income exceeds £16,800 a year have their age allowance reduced by £1 for every £2 of income above this level, until they are reduced to the basic personal allowance.

Married Couple's Allowance: A married couple receive the married couple's allowance in addition to their individual personal allowance outlined above. The married couple's allowance can be split between both spouses or allocated entirely to either spouse. The higher 'age allowance' is paid when either partner qualifies. The married couple's allowance depends on your age as follows:

Age	Allowance (£)
under 65	1,970
65 to 74*	5,125
75 and over*	5,195

* See note above under personal allowance table.

Initially the married couple's allowance is set against the husband's income. Although it's called the married couple's allowance, if the husband doesn't work (e.g. he's a house-husband) and the wife does, then the married couple's allowance can be claimed by her. However, if the husband receives Unemployment Benefit, a pension or any taxable income, it must be set against his allowance first. Anything left over can be transferred to his wife. In the first year of marriage, the husband receives one twelfth of the married couple's allowance for each month he's been married. You must inform your local tax office when you get married in order to claim the allowance. If two people live together as a couple without getting married, they are taxed as two single people and don't receive the married couple's allowance. If a couple is separated or divorced, they're able to claim the allowance for the tax year in which they permanently separate.

An **additional personal allowance** of £1,970 (1999/2000) can be claimed by anyone bringing up children (under the age of 16 or in full-time education) on their own, regardless of whether they are single (unmarried), divorced, separated or widowed. There's a **blind person's relief** of £1,330 for registered blind people and a **widow's bereavement allowance** of £1,970, which is paid to a widow for the year of assessment in which her husband dies and for the following year (providing she doesn't remarry before the start of the next tax year).

Income Tax Returns

If you're self-employed or a higher-rate taxpayer, you should be sent a tax return annually, although if you pay your income tax through PAYE and your tax affairs are fairly simple, you will rarely receive one. If you think you're paying too much tax, inform your tax office. Similarly, if you aren't paying tax on part of your earnings, it's up to you to inform the tax office. If you don't receive a return (or all the forms required) and need one, it's your responsibility to request it (☎ 0645-000404).

Self-Assessment: A new system called self-assessment was introduced in the 1997/98 tax year (from April 1997) and was the biggest tax reform for 50 years. Under the old system the Inland Revenue issued estimated assessments which could then be challenged by individual taxpayers (an exercise that could become 'confrontational'). Self-assessment embraces some nine million self-employed people, company directors and taxpayers with substantial investment income or complex tax affairs, who must calculate their own tax liability. In theory it's a simpler method of calculating tax, although there are hidden complexities and harsh penalties for late filing, and reservations have been expressed about the IR forcing people to become tax 'experts'. Many reports indicate that the first few years of self-assessment have been chaotic to say the least, with many people wrongly fined and over one million people sent incorrect bills.

Schedule: The self-assessment schedule for tax payment for the tax year 1998/99 is as follows:

April 1999	Self-assessment tax returns for the tax year 1998/99 are sent to taxpayers who are subject to self-assessment.
By 31ˢᵗ May 1999	P60s forms are issued providing details of your taxable pay and tax paid for tax year 1998/99. P60s apply to all employees and pensioners who receive an income from a previous employer's pension scheme or a private pension plan.
By 6ᵗʰ July 1999	P11D forms issued providing details of your taxable fringe benefits and expenses for tax year 1998/99. This applies to employees and directors earning £8,500 or more and receiving fringe benefits and/or expenses.
31ˢᵗ July 1999	Second payment on account for 1998/99 tax year is due (mostly applies to the self-employed).
30ᵗʰ September 1999	Complete and send your return (without calculation) for the tax year 1998/99 to the IR if you want them to calculate your tax bill.
31ˢᵗ January 2000	Final deadline for sending your tax return and paying any outstanding tax for 1998/99. If you make payments on account, you must make the first payment for the 1999/2000 tax year. The IR must inform you by this date if it intends to investigate your 1997/98 return.
January/February 2000	PAYE coding notices for tax year 1999/2000 sent.

Completing the Return: Under self-assessment, all taxpayers receive the same standard eight-page return which covers savings, investments, state benefits and pensions, in addition to allowances and reliefs that you wish to claim. You may receive additional forms depending on your sources of income, e.g. those in a partnership. The return is supplied with explanatory notes that are relatively easy to understand and most people can complete it without any trouble. If you need help with your tax form or are unclear about a specific point, you can call the self-assessment helpline (☎ 0645-000444) from 0800 until 2000 from Mondays to Fridays and at weekends. Always keep a copy of your tax form and anything else you send to your tax office. This will be vital if your tax form gets lost in the post or there are any queries later. **Don't forget to sign the return!** All tax records should be retained for five years from the latest date by which the tax return is to be filed.

Filing: Filing is due by 31st January after the end of the tax year, e.g. a tax return for the tax year ending 5th April 1999 must be submitted no later than 31st January 2000. You can also give your figures to the Inland Revenue and have them calculate your tax liability, although if you use this method you must submit your tax return by 30th September of the tax year in question, i.e. four months earlier than if you do the assessment yourself.

Late filing: There are heavy fines for late filing and late payers under the self-assessment scheme. If you miss the deadline for filing your tax return by a single day you must pay an automatic £100 fine (incurred by hundreds of thousands of people each year). Failure to return the tax form by the end of February means a 5 per cent surcharge is levied on the tax owed. If you send in your return after the 31st July (i.e. over six months late) you must pay a further £100 fine, and a delay of 12 months incurs a penalty of up to 100 per cent of the tax payable, plus a discretionary charge of £60 a day until your return is filed. You must also pay interest on unpaid tax bills. You can appeal against a penalty for filing a late return.

Payment on Account: If you're self-employed or receive rental or investment income without having tax deducted at source, you must pay income tax on account. Two payments must be paid on account of tax due, one by 31st January (the same day as filing your return) and the other by 31st July, each amounting to half of your liability for the previous year (excluding tax deducted at source, e.g. on PAYE income). A third balancing payment (or refund if you have over-paid) is made by the following 31st January.

Late payment: Late payment of tax incurs interest charges at a floating rate decided by the Treasury. A delay of 28 days will add a 5 per cent surcharge and a delay of six months a further 5 per cent (total 10 per cent). Interest on surcharges will be due within 30 days of their imposition. In 1999, interest was 7.5 per cent on overdue income tax, although the IR paid just 3 per cent interest if it owed you money.

CAPITAL GAINS TAX

Capital Gains Tax (CGT) is applicable whenever you sell or otherwise dispose (e.g. lease, exchange or loss) of an asset, which broadly speaking is anything you own. Anything you sell, from a second home to shares or antiques, which reap profits above £7,100 a year (1999/2000) is liable to CGT payable at your highest rate of income tax, either 10, 23 or 40 per cent (companies pay corporation tax at their normal rate). CGT liability must be included in your income tax return. It's usually payable on private motor vehicles; private homes; household goods and personal effects; SAYE contracts and National Savings certificates and bonds; premium bonds; betting winnings; most life insurance policies; government securities such as 'gilts'; and personal injury compensation.

If an asset disposed of was acquired *before* 31st March 1982, no capital gains tax is usually payable. The value of assets purchased and disposed of after this date are adjusted for the increase in the Retail Prices Index (RPI) between 31st March 1982 and the date of disposal. If the asset was acquired *after* 31st March 1992 then its cost is adjusted for the increase in the RPI between the date of acquisition and its disposal. The adjusted cost is then deducted from the net sales proceeds to arrive at the gain or loss. This calculation is termed the indexation allowance (RPI tables are provided to make calculation easy). To complicate matters further, from 6th April 1998 a new taper relief system was introduced and applies to assets purchased from this date. This works by reducing the tax payable on a gain depending on how long you have owned it. You must own a non-business asset for at least three years and a business asset for at least one year before taper relief reduces your tax bill. The percentage of capital gains payable on a non-business asset reduces to 95 per cent after three years and a maximum of 60 per cent after ten or more years.

If you have two homes, living part of the year in one and part in another, you must choose which is your main residence for capital gains tax purposes. It's best to choose the one on which you think you will make the largest profit as your main home. You should inform the tax office within two years of buying a second home (otherwise the Inland Revenue may decide which property is your main home), although you can change your mind at any time by informing your tax office. Your choice of main residence for capital gains tax purposes shouldn't affect your choice for council tax purposes (see page 350).

Under independent taxation, husbands and wives each have an annual capital gains exemption of £7,100 (total £14,200) and it isn't possible for one spouse's losses to be set against the other's gains. Capital gains tax is payable on overseas investments only when the money is brought back into Britain. The Inland Revenue publish a number of leaflets about capital gains tax. If you're liable for CGT, you should obtain advice from an accountant as you may be able to reduce your tax liability.

INHERITANCE TAX

In Britain, inheritance tax (IHT) of 40 per cent is payable on any bequests above £231,000 (1999/2000) when left to anyone other than your spouse or a registered charity (expensive business dying, unless you have lots of lovely debts and no money). The tax-free threshold is usually increased annually and is likely to be much higher when you die (but then so will the value of your estate). The best way to reduce your IHT liability is to simply give some of your money away to family or friends or to a deserving cause (such as struggling authors), so long as it doesn't adversely affect your standard of living. Your liability to inheritance tax can be avoided by judicious financial planning and transferring assets, which is one of the most effective forms of tax planning. One way to avoid IHT is with a trust or an insurance policy, which pays the tax liability (with your children or grandchildren as beneficiaries), although you must live for seven years after setting it up.

You're permitted to give away up to £3,000 a year, which can be carried over for one year. Small gifts up to £250 don't count and you can give £250 to as many people as you wish in one year (my account number is XXXXXXX). Any taxable gifts over £250 made in the previous seven years are included in your estate, although the amount of tax payable is reduced according to a sliding scale. A gift given seven years before death incurs no inheritance tax and relief of from 20 to 80 per cent is given on gifts made between three and seven years before death. Inheritance tax is payable in full on gifts made within three years of death. Tax payable on lifetime gifts (other than those that fall under the seven-year rule) is 20 per cent. You can also make a one-time gift to a non-domiciled spouse of up to £55,000.

Those liable for inheritance tax must submit an account to the IR detailing the assets they have inherited and their value within 12 months of receiving them. There's a fine of £100 for anyone who makes a late declaration and much higher fines for providing fraudulent or incorrect information.

Inheritance tax is a complicated subject and depends on whether you're domiciled in Britain (defined in Inland Revenue leaflet IHT1). Before making any gifts or transfer of property or any bequests in your will (see below), it's vital to obtain legal advice from a solicitor who specialises in inheritance tax. There are a number of useful books including *The Which? Guide to Giving and Inheriting* by Jonquil Lowe (Which? Books).

WILLS

It's an unfortunate fact of life, but you're unable to take your worldly goods with you when you take your final bow (even if you have plans to come back in a later life), so it's better to leave them to someone or something you love, rather than to the Inland Revenue or leave a mess which everyone will fight over (unless that's your intention!). Surprisingly, around two-thirds of Britons die intestate, i.e. without making a will, which means that the inflexible laws of intestacy dictate how the estate is divided. It's estimated that over £750 million in inheritance tax could be avoided if more people planned their taxes and made wills. Most married people in Britain imagine that when they die, everything they own will automatically be inherited by their partner, which isn't true.

A surviving spouse is entitled to as much as half of a house and any other property, plus between £125,000 and £200,000 of the spouse's cash, depending on whether there are any children. If you have no children, then a share of your estate passes to your parents (if they're alive) or other relatives. Under the laws of intestacy, common law spouses have no legal rights. The biggest problem of leaving no will is the delay in winding up your estate (while perhaps searching for a will), which can cause considerable hardship and distress at an already stressful time. Note that when someone dies, an estate's assets cannot be touched until inheritance tax (see above) has been paid and probate (the official proving of a will) has been granted. You usually require probate for estates worth more than £5,000, although you can exclude assets (e.g. a home) owned as 'joint tenants' from this sum.

All adults should make a will regardless of how large or small their assets. If your circumstances change dramatically, for example you get married, you must make a new will as marriage automatically revokes any existing wills under English law (similarly, divorce means that gifts in a will to an ex-spouse are invalid). Both husband and wife should make separate wills. Similarly, if you separate or are divorced, you should consider making a new will (but make sure you have only one valid will). A new bequest or a change can be made to an existing will through a document called a 'codicil'. You should check your will every few years to make sure it still fits your wishes and circumstances (your assets may also increase dramatically in value).

If you're a foreign national and don't want your estate to be subject to British law, you may be eligible to state in your will that it's to be interpreted under the law of another country. To avoid being subject to British death duty and inheritance laws, you must establish your country of domicile in another country. Domicile in Britain is defined in Inland Revenue leaflet IHT1 and information is also given in a booklet (IR20) entitled *Residents and Non-residents - Liability to tax in the United Kingdom* (see also page 352). If you don't specify in your will that the law of another country applies to your estate, then British law will apply. If your estate comes under British law, your dependants will be subject to British inheritance laws and tax. Inheritance law is slightly different in Scotland from in the rest of Britain, where part of the estate must be left to any children and where you can hand-write your own will, called a holograph, which doesn't need to be witnessed.

Many people in Britain make tax-free bequests to charities in their wills, which is why charities are so keen for you to make a will. One of the best reasons for leaving money to charity is to cut the tax man out of your will or at least reduce his share. You can even leave money tax-free to your favourite political party (providing it has more than two MPs), although most people would prefer to leave it to the devil (anyone who leaves money to a political party cannot possibly have been of sound mind, so relatives would have an excellent case for challenging a bequest).

Once you've accepted that you're mortal (the one statistic you can rely on is that 100 per cent of all human beings eventually die), you will find that making a will isn't a complicated or lengthy process. You can draw up your own will (which may be better than none), but it's advisable to obtain legal advice from a bank or solicitor who will draw up a simple will for around £50 for a single person, or up to £100 for a couple (fees vary considerably and you should shop around). Some banks will draw up wills only if they are made executors of the estate (see below) and should therefore be avoided. Note than many wills are drawn up incorrectly by solicitors and you may be better off doing it yourself!

For those who would rather do it themselves, a simple will form can be purchased from stationers for about 50p, which also provides some guidance on writing your will. Better still buy a copy of the *Make Your Will* action pack produced by the Consumers' Association (see page 437), which contains three alternative will forms. However, bear in mind that a will must be written in a tax-efficient manner and that lawyers have a field day sorting out home-made wills. You must have two witnesses (to your signature, not the contents of the will) who cannot be either beneficiaries or your spouse. If you wish you can list all your 'valuables' and who's to get what (the list can be kept separate from the will and changed without altering the will itself).

You'll also need someone to act as the executor (or personal representative) of your estate, which can be particularly costly for modest estates. Your bank, building society, solicitor (the least expensive, but far from cheap), or other professional will usually act as the executor, although this should be avoided if at all possible as the fees can be astronomical. Banks' fees are based on a percentage of the estate and work out at around £500 or more an hour! **It's best to make your beneficiaries the** executors and then they can instruct a solicitor after your death if they need legal assistance. Keep a copy of your will in a safe place (e.g. a bank) and another copy with your solicitor or the executors of your estate. You should keep information regarding bank accounts and insurance policies with your will(s), but don't forget to tell someone where they are!

There are a number of books on wills including *Wills and Probate* and *What to do when Someone Dies* (Which? Books). Many charities also produce free guides in the hope that you will leave them a bequest.

COST OF LIVING

No doubt you would like to know how far your pounds will stretch and how much money (if any) you will have left after paying your bills. Britain has a high cost of living and high rates of duty on everything from petrol to tobacco and alcohol to cars make it one of the world's most expensive places to live. British consumers pay more for food and most consumer goods that people in most other major countries. While direct taxes are relatively low, indirect taxes are high. In 1998 Britain had the highest cost of living in the world after Japan and Denmark according to figures from Employment Conditions Abroad. London is one of the world's most expensive cities with a cost of living higher than Amsterdam, Berlin, Luxembourg, Montreal, Munich, New York and Sydney.

Britain's inflation rate is based on the Retail Prices Index (RPI), which gives an indication of how prices have risen (or fallen) over the past year. The prices of around 600 'indicator' items are collected on a single day in the middle of the month (a total of around 130,000 prices are collected for the 600 items in the RPI basket). Britain's inflation rate in early 1999 was around 2.5 per cent.

However, on the plus side Britain's standard of living has soared in recent years and compared with most other European Union countries British workers take home a larger proportion of their pay after tax and social security. The gap between rich and poor in Britain is the largest since records began in 1886 and state pensioners are unable to afford basic comforts such as a healthy diet, a car and an annual holiday. There's a huge gap between the wealthy south of England and the poor north of England, Scotland and Northern Ireland, although the gap was narrowed by the recession in the early '90s. In contrast, the middle classes have never been better off than in recent years and the super rich go on spending sprees buying holiday homes, cruises, yachts, power boats, luxury cars and private aircraft.

It's difficult to calculate an average cost of living, as it depends on each individual's particular circumstances and lifestyle. What is important to most people is how much money they can save (or spend) each month. Your food bill will naturally depend on what you eat and is usually around 50 per cent higher than in the USA, and up to 25 per cent higher than in other Western European countries. Approximately £200 should be sufficient to feed two adults for a month in most areas (excluding alcohol, fillet steak and caviar). Even in the most expensive areas of Britain (i.e. London), the cost of living needn't be astronomical. If you shop wisely, compare prices and services before buying and don't live too extravagantly, you may be pleasantly surprised at how little you can live on. Note that it's also possible to save a considerable sum by shopping for alcohol and other products in France, buying your car in Europe, and shopping overseas by mail and via the Internet (see page 435).

A list of the approximate **MINIMUM** monthly major expenses for an average person or family in a typical provincial town are shown in the table below. **Note that these are necessarily 'ball park' figures only and depend on your lifestyle, extravagance or frugality and where you live in Britain (almost everyone will agree that they are either too low or too high!).** When calculating your cost of living, deduct the appropriate percentage for income tax (see page 352), National Insurance (see page 306) and pensions from your gross salary.

ITEM	Single	Couple	Couple with 2 children
MONTHLY COSTS (£)			
Housing (1)	300	400	600
Food	100	200	300
Utilities (2)	50	80	100
Leisure (3)	100	100	150
Car/travel (4)	100	125	150
Insurance (5)	25	50	50
Clothing	50	100	150
Council Tax (6)	30	40	60
TOTAL	**£755**	**£1,095**	**£1,560**

(1) Rent or mortgage on a modern apartment or semi-detached house in an 'average' provincial suburb. The amount for a single person is for a bedsit or sharing accommodation (a young man is assumed!). Other costs are for a two (couple) or three-bedroom property (couple with two children). They don't include council or other subsidised housing.

(2) Includes electricity, gas, water and telephone, plus heating bills.

(3) Includes all entertainment, sports and holiday expenses, plus TV licence, newspapers and magazines (which could of course be much higher than the figure given).

(4) Includes running costs for an average family car, plus third party insurance, road tax, petrol and servicing, but not depreciation or credit costs.

(5) Includes all 'voluntary' insurance, excluding car insurance.

(6) This is a guesstimate only, as council tax is based on a property's value.

15.

LEISURE

The tourist industry is one of Britain's largest and most profitable, employing 1.5 million people directly or indirectly and earning over £30 billion a year. Britain is one of the world's six leading tourist destinations and it receives over 20 million overseas visitors a year (almost 20 per cent from North America). The diversity of leisure opportunities in Britain is enormous and London provides more cultural activities than any other city in the world (some foreigners believe that Britain is a giant theme park). Whatever your favourite leisure pursuits, you will find them in abundance in Britain including art galleries, museums, gardens, stately homes, zoos, sports facilities and sporting events, children's entertainment, cinema, theatre, dance, music, gambling, pubs and restaurants, plus many more.

Britain is a land of many faces, ranging from picturesque country towns and villages to bustling modern cities, all exuding a sense of history to be found in few other countries in the world. People are drawn to Britain for many reasons, among which its rich traditions, quality of live entertainment (particularly in London and other cities) and comprehensive arts centres feature prominently. Nowhere provides a more varied and vibrant nightlife for the young (and young at heart) than London, which is besieged by the youth of all continents. London is also home to some of the world's best (and most expensive) hotels and restaurants.

However, don't make the mistake of visiting only London and neglecting Britain's magnificent provincial cities and countryside, where a wealth of spectacular natural beauty and historic sights await you including fishing villages, national parks, Scottish moors, castles, wild moorland and heaths, country inns, charming villages, bleak and rugged mountains, farmlands, ancient cathedrals, sandy beaches, rivers, broads and marshlands. Whether you're a country or city lover, there's something for everyone in Britain, which is a small country and no matter where you live you can regard most of it as your playground. Good road and rail connections ensure that a huge area is accessible for day excursions and practically anywhere is within reach for a weekend trip, particularly if you travel by air. The cost of air travel from Britain to most European countries is very reasonable (by European standards) and means you can also travel much further afield for a weekend.

In most cities there are magazines and newspapers devoted to entertainment, e.g. *Time Out*, *What's On* and *City Limits* in London. *Time Out* magazine also publish the *Time Out London Visitors' Guide*. Weekly, fortnightly, monthly, bimonthly and quarterly entertainment and arts programmes and magazines are available from tourist information centres in all major cities and towns. Many councils also publish maps and brochures listing local places of interest and leisure facilities. Youth organisations and centres organise a range of leisure and sports activities for youths and children during school holidays, that are often subsidised by local authorities.

Most district, borough and county councils publish free directories listing local sports clubs and facilities, arts and community centres, countryside and outdoor activities, useful contacts for the disabled and a directory of local leisure facilities. A good source of general tourist information is, *In Britain*, the official monthly magazine of the British Tourist Authority (BTA), which contains a comprehensive list of forthcoming events throughout Britain. The BTA also publish a brochure entitled *Forthcoming Events*. Other magazines of interest are *In England* and *The Scots Magazine*, plus local county magazines. Public transport companies publish leisure maps and information leaflets for travellers and many local newspapers publish entertainment and 'What's On' guides and entertainment pages.

The main aim of this chapter (and indeed the purpose of the whole book) is to provide information that isn't found in standard guide books. General tourist information is available in literally hundreds of guide books, many encompassing the whole of Britain while others concentrate on England, Scotland, Wales or Ireland, or a particular region. Among the best guides are the *Michelin Green Guide to Britain*, *Baedeker's Britain* and *Fodor's Britain* (see **Appendix B** for a list). The latest entertainment and tourist information can be obtained from the television teletext information service. Guides for the disabled are published by many local tourist boards and councils (ask at tourist information centres).

All tourists and day-trippers in Britain should take care not to become victims of rip-off tourist prices in tourist areas (particularly in central London) and at tourist attractions throughout Britain. If prices aren't displayed always ask the price before ordering or buying anything, and check the service charge and other extras in restaurants. For information about sports facilities in Britain, see **Chapter 16**.

TOURIST INFORMATION

There are Tourist Information Centres (TICs), in all major cities, towns, major railway stations, ports and airports, where staff will provide you with a wealth of information and book you a hotel room. Centres are signposted by the National 'Tourist Information' sign of a red 'i' on a white background and are often housed in public library buildings. A booklet containing a list of all centres is available from all TICs or from the British Tourist Authority (BTA), Thames Tower, Black's Road, Hammersmith, London W6 9EL (☎ 0181-846 9000, Internet: www.visitbritain. com), which also has offices in some 20 countries.

TICs have no standard opening hours although most are open from around 0930 or 1000 to 1700 or 1730, Mondays to Saturdays (when they may close an hour earlier) and on public holidays. Longer opening hours may be in operation during summer, including Sunday opening. In smaller towns and resorts, centres may close for lunch, e.g. from 1300 to 1400. Some TICs are open from Easter to September or mornings only in winter, e.g. from November to March. Many centres in rural areas are closed from 24th December to 1st January inclusive. Always phone and check opening hours in advance. An answer-phone service may give the opening hours and take messages when centres are closed. Services provided by TICs include local and regional guides and information; hotel reservations; box office for local theatre and concert halls; local and city tours; excursions; guided walks; congresses; car hire; guides and hostesses; and rail and bus information. Most centres will book you a room locally or in any other town with a TIC providing the 'Book-a-Bed-Ahead' service (a fee is charged).

In addition to local TICs, the British Travel Centre (12 Regent Street, London SW1Y 4PQ) provides an all-Britain and all-Ireland information service. Services include a full travel service; accommodation; air, bus and rail travel; car hire; sightseeing; bureau de change; theatre tickets; and London's most comprehensive British travel bookshop stocking over 1,000 different maps and travel guides. You can book a room anywhere in Britain or Ireland (☎ 0171-930 0572). Whatever you want to know about travel within Britain, the British Travel Centre will either provide you with the information directly or will give you the address of someone who can help you. They will answer telephone enquiries (excluding Sundays) and send information by mail. Opening hours are 0900 to 1830 Mondays to Fridays and

1000 to 1600 on Saturdays and Sundays. Saturday opening is extended from mid-May to September. The British Travel Centre and local TICs provide a wealth of leaflets and brochures covering all areas of Britain, many of which are published by the English, Scottish, Welsh and Northern Irish Tourist Boards (including a local *Diary of Events*) and by regional tourist boards. You may also be interested in the London Tourist Board's services (☎ 0171-932 2000 or 0171-932 2020 for accommodation bookings, Internet: www. londontown.com).

HOTELS

The quality and standard of British hotels varies considerably, from international five-star luxury hotels, castles and stately homes converted into hotels, to budget hotels, guesthouses and bed and breakfast accommodation. Don't judge the rest of Britain by the standards and rates charged in London, where demand outstrips supply, allowing even the worst establishments to charge exorbitant rates (and where the best hotels such as the Savoy and Claridges charge astronomical prices). If you're planning to stay in London, you should always book in advance and spend as much as you can afford if you want a half-decent hotel (which costs over £50 a night). If you don't need to be in the middle of town, out of town hotels (except those at Heathrow airport, which charge London rates) offer better value for money.

British hotels are among the most expensive in Europe and often offer poor service (around a quarter of all visitors to Britain are dissatisfied with their accommodation). A survey conducted by the Department of National Heritage found that British hotels were the most expensive and worst value for money in Europe. Inexpensive hotels (e.g. around £20 a night) are particularly hard to find and budget travellers must usually settle for bed and breakfast accommodation (see page 374), rather than a 'proper' hotel. Hotel rates vary considerably depending on the standard, location, season and the amenities provided. Many hotels offer special weekend rates (two nights – Friday and Saturday), particularly during off-peak periods, which usually include dinner, bed and breakfast. Some hotels provide special low rates at certain times of the year (e.g. in the autumn) for stays of five nights or longer, which include breakfast and dinner.

There are a wealth of hotel grading systems in Britain including those used by tourist boards, motoring organisations and publications. The BTA have their own 'crown' grading system (denoted by a blue and silver plaque) covering a total of around 16,000 hotels, motels, private hotels, guesthouses, inns, bed & breakfast and farmhouse accommodation throughout Britain (excluding Northern Ireland). The standards and facilities required to earn crowns are similar to the international 'star' hotel rating system. Further quality standards are denoted by the terms approved, commended, highly commended and de luxe, which when granted, appear alongside the crown classification. BTA recommended hotels are listed in a booklet entitled *BTA Recommended*, available free from TICs.

Many hotels are also rated under other classification systems including Michelin, Les Routiers, and the AA and RAC motoring organisations (see page 269). Note that the BTA, the English Tourist Board, the AA and RAC (among others), all charge establishments for the privilege of being included in their listings. Therefore the fact that a hotel isn't recommended <u>isn't</u> an indication that it didn't meet the quality criteria.

The following table can be used as a *rough* guide to prices:

Crown Rating	Price Range
listed	£20 – 40
1	£30 – 50
2	£40 – 75
3	£50 – 100
4	£75 – 150
5	£100 – 250 +

Budget hotels in London cost from £35 to £65 per person, per night, although the average price is from £70 to £150; outside London the average hotel price is from £50 to £90. The average price of a single room in a four-star hotel in London is £150 to £200. The prices quoted above are for two people sharing a double room with bath (prices in Britain are almost always quoted per room and not per person). Many hotels charge a punitive single room supplement (up to 50 per cent) for a single occupant of a double room. Always check whether the price quoted includes VAT, which at 17.5 per cent can make quite a difference. Watch out for expensive extras such as phone charges, breakfast and menu mark-ups.

During off-peak periods and at weekends you can usually haggle over room rates, particularly late at night at large hotels (which often have reduced rates), but won't usually tell you unless you ask). Bargains can also be found via the Internet (try the Hotel Reservations Network at www.180096hotel.com for London and other cities). There's usually a reduced charge for children sharing their parent's room and many hotels have family rooms. A deposit may be required when booking a room and when you have confirmed bookings you're liable to pay the full bill even if you cancel. An English cooked breakfast may be included in the cost, although an extra charge is usually made, which may be 'served' buffet style (self-service) in some hotels. It consists of fruit juice or cereal, hot main course such as grilled bacon, eggs, sausages and tomatoes ('heart attack on a plate'), toast and marmalade or jam, and coffee or tea. Most hotels with restaurants offer half-board (breakfast and evening meal) or full-board (breakfast, lunch and evening meal) at advantageous rates.

Most top class hotels provide air-conditioned rooms with tea and coffee making facilities; room service; radio and colour TV (maybe with an in-house video film service and satellite TV); en suite bathroom or shower; telephone (often direct dial); mini-bar; hair drier; and trouser press. Some hotels provide no-smoking rooms and special rooms for the disabled. Many top class hotels have a choice of restaurants and bars; provide secretarial, business and conference facilities; and have health and leisure centres with swimming pools, gymnasiums, solarium, sauna, Jacuzzi and a range of other sports facilities. Top class hotels in many cities also provide theatre booking agencies, hairdressing salons and a range of shops.

The latest trend to hit Britain is the budget hotel, which is basically a two-star format providing cheap basic accommodation at reasonable rates. These include Travelodge (☎ freefone 0800-850950) where two adults and two children can stay for a flat rate of around £30 to £40 a night (possibly less with special offers) with en suite bathroom, TV, radio and tea-making facilities. No meals (not even breakfast) are provided, but there's usually a restaurant nearby. Many hotels in Britain have special rates for senior citizens and children. Some hotels provide special weekly full-board rates, particularly those catering for overseas students. Most people should be able to find something to suit their budget and taste among the many thousands of hotels and boarding houses in Britain. Note that if you need a hotel room during an international convention or fair, or in a popular resort or city, you should book well in advance, particularly for a top class hotel. Many hotels provide special Christmas and New Year festivities' programmes with special tariffs, which include accommodation and all meals. Accommodation in London can be booked via the London Tourist Board (☎ 0171-604 2890) and paid by Access, Mastercard or Visa.

All hotels, motels, inns and guesthouses in Britain with four bedrooms or more (including self-catering accommodation) must display a notice showing their minimum and maximum overnight charges. Prices shown must include any service charge and may include VAT, although it must be indicated whether or not these are included (if VAT isn't included, it must be shown separately). If meals are provided with accommodation, it must be made clear and where prices aren't standard for all rooms then the price range can be shown.

Information: A wealth of information encompassing all standards of hotel accommodation is published by the BTA including *London Budget Hotels*, *Country Hotels, Guesthouses and Restaurants*, and *Stay at an Inn*. The English Tourist Board publish a *Where to Stay* series of guides that include *Hotels & Guesthouses* and *Farmhouses, Bed & Breakfast, Inns & Hostels*. General hotel guides include *The Good Hotel Guide* (Vermillion), *Egon Ronay's Cellnet Guide - Hotels & Restaurants*, the *AA Hotel Guide*, the *Which? Hotel Guide* and the RAC's *Hotel Guide*.

Many kinds of accommodation are also rated by tourist associations according to their accessibility for wheelchair users and others who have difficulty walking. Information and advice about accommodation for physically handicapped people is available from the Holiday Care Service, 2nd Floor, Imperial Buildings, Victoria Road, Horley, Surrey RH6 7PZ (☎ 01293-774535) or the BTA.

BED & BREAKFAST

Bed and breakfast (B&B) accommodation consists of a room in a private house, country pub, farmhouse or even a university campus, and is found throughout Britain from cities and large towns to villages and remote hamlets. B&B accommodation (sometimes referred to as a B&B hotel) is more informal than a hotel and provides a friendly place to meet the British in their own homes. Many homes providing B&B accommodation are indicated by a *Bed & Breakfast* sign outside or in the window. Guest house accommodation is similar in price and standard to B&B, but is usually available only in towns.

Although it's advisable to book in advance, especially over public holiday weekends or in London, it's usually unnecessary, particularly if you're touring and need a room for one or two nights only. If you're a smoker, you should check in advance whether smoking is permitted. If you don't book in advance you will have more freedom to go where you please, but you should bear in mind that some B&Bs have a minimum stay of two or three nights. When booking in advance, confirm your arrival time to ensure that your hosts will be at home. If you're staying for more than one night, you may be expected to vacate your room for most of the day and to leave by 1200 (or earlier) on your last day.

Like hotel accommodation, B&B standards vary greatly from a basic single room sharing a bathroom to a luxury double room with *en suite* bathroom (possibly in a stately home). Many B&Bs are graded by regional tourist boards using the BTA crown classification system used to grade hotels (see page 372). Room rates range from around £15 to £40 per person, per night outside London, to £20 to £50 in London. More expensive B&B accommodation, e.g. £50 or more per night, is available in luxury homes throughout Britain. B&B accommodation is the cheapest form of accommodation for tourists or travellers who don't want to stay in one place for more than a few days. If you require temporary accommodation for a week or longer there may be a reduced rate. The cheapest rooms don't contain a television and may not include towels, which are usually included for a small fee. Many B&B hotels provide tea and coffee-making facilities in all rooms. Note that B&B establishments and cheap hotels aren't usually very warm in winter. As the name suggests, bed and breakfast always includes breakfast (usually a full cooked English breakfast). Many B&Bs also provide an optional evening meal (dinner) for a reasonable price, which must usually be ordered in advance. Some B&Bs won't accept children and many don't cater for the disabled.

The BTA publish a booklet *Stay with a British Family*, listing agencies and individuals offering 'home-stay' accommodation. These are similar to B&Bs except that with home-stay accommodation you're treated more like a guest of the family and may be invited to partake in family activities. Most families also offer a reasonably-priced evening meal. Farmhouse B&Bs are an interesting alternative for those who want a change from towns. Guesthouses are found mainly in seaside towns and other tourist centres and are similar to B&Bs. They usually cater more for tourists wishing to stay for a week or two rather than a few nights. Rates range from around £20 to £30 per person per night outside London and usually include half-board.

Tourist information centres provide a wide range of brochures, guides and books containing information about bed and breakfast accommodation throughout Britain, including a series of B&B touring maps. The most comprehensive guide to B&Bs in Britain is *The Good Bed & Breakfast Guide* by Elsie Dillard & Susan Causin (Which? Books), listing over 1,000 B&Bs. There are numerous other B&B guides including *The Best Bed & Breakfast in the World*, *The Best Bed and Breakfast - England, Scotland and Wales* (UKHM Publishing), the *AA Bed & Breakfast Guide*, Alastair Sawday's *Special Places to Stay in Britain* and *Wolsey Lodges*. B&B accommodation can be booked through a number of agencies including Bed & Breakfast (GB), 94-96 Bell Street, Henley-on-Thames, Oxon RG9 1XS (☎ 01491-578803, e-mail: bookings@bedbreak.demon.co.uk), Wolsey Lodges Ltd., 9 Market Place, Hadley, Ipswich, Suffolk IP7 5DL (☎ 01473-827500) and London Homestead Services, Coombe Wood Road, Kingston-upon-Thames, Surrey KT2 7JY (☎ 0181-949 4455). See also the books listed under **Hotels** on page 372.

SELF-CATERING

Self-catering cottages, bungalows, apartments (flats), houseboats, houses, chalets and mobile holiday homes, are available for rent in most cities and holiday areas. An apartment is often a good choice for a family as it's much cheaper than a hotel room (particularly in London), provides more privacy and freedom, and allows you to prepare your own meals as and when you please. Standards, while generally high are variable, and paying a high price doesn't always guarantee a well furnished or well appointed apartment (most look wonderful in a brochure). Many self-catering establishments are graded by regional tourist boards using the BTA crown classification system used to grade hotels (see page 372) or a similar 'key' system.

Studios (bed-sitters) are available in London from around £150 per week or £30 per night, per person. The cost of an apartment in London for four people ranges from around £500 to £2,000 per week. There's no low season and rates are usually the same throughout the year (in the rest of Britain rates usually vary depending on the season). In London and other cities, student hostels are available in some areas from around £10 a night in shared dormitories with cooking facilities. Rooms are also available in private homes with cooking facilities, that are either provided in the room or in a shared kitchen.

The weekly rent of a country cottage varies considerably from around £200 to £1,000 per week for four people, depending on its location, size, amenities and the season. If you want to try something different you can hire a canal-boat or choose a hotel-boat, where all you need to do is sit back and enjoy the passing scenery along some of Britain's 3,220km (2,000mi) of canals. No previous boating experience is necessary to hire a boat in Britain (or to enjoy the canal-side pubs). The cost of hire varies from around £250 to £750 per week for four people, depending on the size and class of boat and the season. For information about holiday hire boats, contact British Waterways, Melbury House, Melbury Terrace, London NW1 6JX (☎ 0171-262 6711).

Before booking any self-catering accommodation you should check the holiday changeover dates and times; what's included in the rent (e.g. cleaning, linen); whether cots or high chairs are provided or pets are allowed; if a garden or parking is provided; and access to public transport (if necessary). Self-catering accommodation in Britain is usually let on a weekly basis from Saturday to Saturday, often for a minimum of one or two weeks.

Many brochures and booklets are available from the BTA and Tourist Information Centres, including *Apartments in London and Britain: Holiday Homes* and *Apartments in London*, both of which list a variety of letting agencies, apartment rentals and serviced blocks of apartments. The English Tourist Board (ETB) publish *Self-Catering Holiday Homes* containing hundreds of cottages, bungalows, apartments, houseboats, houses and chalets, that are graded according to a 'key' rating system (similar to the 'crown' rating system for hotels), based on the facilities and equipment provided.

Books for self-caterers include the AA's *Holiday Homes, Cottages and Apartments Self-Catering in Britain*, *The Good Holiday Cottage Guide* and *English Country Cottages*. The National Trust (see page 379) can also provide you with a list of holiday homes and cottages for rent throughout Britain. Cottages and other self-catering accommodation is advertised in magazines and national newspapers such as *The Sunday Times*, *The Observer* and *Dalton's Weekly*.

YOUTH HOSTELS

For those travelling on a tight budget one way to stretch limited financial resources is to stay in a youth hostel, which in Britain may vary from a castle to a cottage, a hunting lodge to a stately home. There are over 400 youth hostels in Britain, including around 80 in Scotland run by the Scottish Youth Hostel Association

(SYHA), many of which open all year round. Membership is open to all, although the minimum age of children accompanied by an adult is five or 14 when unaccompanied. Children aged between 5 and 15 are given free membership when their parents (or single parent) are members.

Youth hostels provide separate dormitories (8 to 16 beds) for males and females. Duvets (or blankets), pillows and a short sleeping bag. Many youth hostels have small dormitories (four to six beds) that can be used by families and some have a self-contained family annex or special family rooms (with their own kitchen, living room and bathroom), where you can come and go at any time of the day. Family or group accommodation must be booked in advance by phoning before 1000 or after 1700. It isn't necessary for singles to book in advance, but it's often advisable to avoid disappointment. Most hostels also provide hot showers, central heating, continental quilts (duvets), laundry facilities, and small stores selling souvenirs and foodstuffs. Most hostels are closed during the day from 1000 to 1700 (except for family units) and close for the night at 2300. Guests are required to remain quiet until 0700 and alcohol isn't permitted on the premises. You're expected to help with simple chores, such as sweeping the floor and washing up.

Self-catering kitchens are provided at all permanent youth hostels and many hostels also provide a cheap restaurant (full breakfast £3.10, packed lunch £3.50 and an evening meal for £4.60). Overnight rates in England and Wales vary depending on the particular hostel, which are graded on a scale from 1 to 9 (9 is London). Prices range from £5 to £10 per night for under 18s and from £7 to £12 per night for adults. Rates are sometimes higher in July and August. Hostels in Scotland are graded from one to three and rates are similar to those in England and Wales.

All guests must be members of their national Youth Hostelling Association or an association affiliated to the International Youth Hostel Federation (IYHF). Individual membership of the YHA costs £5.50 a year for youths (under 18), £11 for adults, £22 for families (includes both parents and all children under 18) and £11 for a one-parent family (life membership costs £150). Membership fees of the SYHA (Scotland) and the YHFNI (Northern Ireland) are slightly less than for the YHA. Both the YHA and SYHA organise a wide variety of action and adventure holidays from a few days to a few weeks, where you can participate in a variety of sports and pastimes including adventure sports such as abseiling, rock-climbing or parachuting. Local YHA groups organise regular social evenings and weekend activities.

For further information about youth hostels in England and Wales, contact the YHA National Office, Trevelyan House, 8 St. Stephen's Hill, St. Albans, Herts. AL1 2DY (☎ 01727-855215). For information about Scottish youth hostels, contact the Scottish Youth Hostel Association, 7 Glebe Crescent, Stirling FK8 2JA (☎ 01786-451181). The Youth Hostelling Association of Northern Ireland is at 56 Bradbury Place, Belfast BT7 1RU (☎ 01232-324733). All YHAs publish handbooks and accommodation guides, and excellent maps (usually free) showing hostel locations, opening dates and facilities. A *YHA Accommodation Guide* is available from bookshops. The YHA publishes a quarterly member's magazine. If you're interested in international youth hostelling staying at some of the 6,000 youth hostels around the world, contact YHA Travel, 14 Southampton Street, London WC2E 7HY (☎ 0171-836 8541), who provide information, tickets and reservations.

CARAVANS & CAMPING

Britain has around 3,500 licensed caravan (trailer), chalet and camping parks, many of which are graded under a quality (Q) scheme operated by the British Holiday and Home Parks Association and the National Caravan Council, using a system of one (acceptable) to five (excellent) ticks (or in Scotland the Thistle Commendation Scheme). Gradings are similar to the 'crown' rating system for hotels, but are mainly based on quality and not necessarily the facilities provided. The best caravan parks in England and Wales have also been given a 'Rose Award'. In addition to the main caravan parks, the Camping and Caravanning Club (see address below) and other associations have over 6,000 certificated locations, that are generally small and secluded camps often located in the grounds of a house or farm.

The cost of parking a touring caravan is from around £5 to £10 a night or from around £5 to £7.50 for motor caravans, depending on their length and the particular caravan park. The cost of pitching a tent at a camping site is usually from £4 to £7 a night, again depending on the tent size and the site. Many caravan parks also have static caravans that can be hired for £75 to £250 a week, depending on the size, amenities and number of berths required. In addition to buying your own caravan, which costs anything from £5,000 to £20,000 depending on its size (e.g. two to six-berths), build quality and fittings, you can also hire touring caravans in all areas.

Whether you own or hire a caravan, ensure that it's roadworthy as over half are found to have faults in police spot checks. Campers must have an FICC international camping carnet which covers them for £100,000 against third party risks. It can be purchased from British motoring organisations for around £5 (you need your passport) and there's also an order form in the free AA booklet *Guide to Motoring Abroad*. It's also available from camping and caravanning organisations. Permission is required to park or camp on private property or anywhere outside official caravan and camping parks.

The AA publish *Camping & Caravanning in Britain* and the RAC publish the *RAC Camping and Caravanning Guide* to Britain and Ireland. The English Tourist Board *Where to Stay* series of guides includes *Camping & Caravan Parks*, listing over 700 parks throughout Britain. The ETB also publish *Caravan Holiday-Home Parks*, listing many parks with a wide range of facilities and amusements, most of which provide caravan pitches for touring caravans. The BTA publish *Touring Caravan and Camping* guides for some regions. Many magazines for caravanners, motor caravanners and campers are published in Britain, including *Practical Caravan* and *Camping & Walking*.

There are various organisations for caravanners and motor caravanners in Britain including the Camping and Caravanning Club, Greenfields House, Westwood Way, Coventry CV4 8JH (☎ 01203-694995), The Motor Caravanners' Club Ltd., 9 Pembury Road, Bexley Heath, Kent DA7 5LW and the National Caravan Council Ltd., Catherine House, Victoria Road, Aldershot, Hampshire GU11 1SS (☎ 01252-318251).

MUSEUMS & ART GALLERIES

Britain has numerous museums and art galleries, including some of the most important collections to be found anywhere in the world (the British have been looting and pillaging for centuries to fill their museums and galleries). London is home to Britain's most celebrated collections, admission to many of which is free (a great British tradition). Although some national museums introduced entrance fees in the last decade, most will gradually return to being free (children in 1999, pensioners in 2000 and everyone in 2001).

Other London museums and art galleries charge an admission fee of £2 to £5 (average around £4.50 for adults) and £1 to £2.50 for children (usually under the age of 16); students often receive a reduction on production of a student identity card. Some museums and art galleries offer free admission one day a week. Admission is free to all commercial art galleries. Museum fans can buy a three or seven-day pass for 13 museums and galleries in London (called a 'white card'), costing around £15 for three days or £25 for seven days. To make it pay you must visit at least four museums in three days or six in seven days. Some museums offer annual family season tickets. Leading museums and galleries are open seven days a week (including most public holidays) from around 1000 to 1700 or 1800 Mondays to Saturdays and 1400 or 1430 to 1800 on Sundays. Opening times vary, so check in advance, particularly when planning to visit the smaller London and provincial museums and galleries, some of which open a few days a week only. Many museums and galleries provide reductions for the disabled and some have special access or provide wheelchairs.

In addition to the renowned national collections in London and other major cities, there are also many excellent smaller museums, art galleries and stately home collections throughout Britain, many of which are well worth a visit. Most district, borough and county councils publish free directories of arts clubs and associations in their area, and local arts councils in many areas provide information about local activities. Art lovers may be interested in *The Times Museum & Gallery Guide* (Spero).

GARDENS, STATELY HOMES, PARKS & ZOOS

Lists of gardens, stately homes, theme parks, zoological gardens, botanical gardens, nature parks and national parks are available from the BTA or any good guide book. All tourist information centres provide information about local attractions. Touring by car is often the best way to see Britain's castles, historic houses, stately homes, gardens, monuments and ruins. Most are open throughout the year, although many have reduced opening hours from October to March.

The National Trust (NT) is a privately funded charitable organisation that looks after over 250 historic buildings in England, Wales and Northern Ireland, plus many gardens and landscaped parks, prehistoric and Roman sites, farms, villages and hamlets. You can become a member for £29 a year for an individual (under 25 years £14.50) or £56 a year for a family (including all children aged under 18), which provides free access to all NT buildings and sites. Life membership is also available for £700 (member plus one guest). The NT publish a free *Family Handbook* packed with ideas for family day trips and has over 160 local associations and centres throughout Britain organising a range of activities. For further information write to the National Trust, Membership Department, Freepost MB1438, Bromley, Kent BR1 3XL (☎ 0181-315 1111) or you can join at any National Trust property and have your entrance fee refunded. There's also a National Trust for Scotland (5 Charlotte Square, Edinburgh EH2 4DU, ☎ 0131-226 5922).

You can join English Heritage (adults £26 a year) which provides free admission to over 350 English Heritage properties, a property guide book, maps, a diary of events, quarterly magazine and free entry to special events. For information contact English Heritage, Membership Department, PO Box 1BB, London W1A 1BB (☎ 0171-973 3434, Internet: www.english-heritage.org.uk). If you're a keen horticulturist, you may be interested in joining the Royal Horticultural Society (Membership Department, 80 Vincent Square, London SW1P 2PE, ☎ 0171-821 3000), which entitles you to free entry to many beautiful gardens throughout Britain and a range of other benefits.

Britain has a number of internationally acclaimed zoos, including London and Whipsnade (50km/30mi north of London). There are many other outstanding zoos throughout Britain (e.g. Bristol, Chester, Edinburgh, Glasgow and Manchester) plus a number of Safari parks (e.g. Longleat) where animals roam free (so keep your car windows closed). Many zoos are open almost every day of the year (some close only on Christmas day) and admission is from around £5 (children from around £2).

Britain's almost 100 theme parks are very popular (around 100 million visitors annually) and are an excellent place for a special (i.e. expensive) day out for thechildren. The most popular include Blackpool Pleasure Beach, Alton Towers (Staffordshire), Pleasureland (Southport), Thorpe Park (Surrey), Chessington World of Adventures (Surrey), Fantasy Island (Lincolnshire) and Legoland (Windsor, Berkshire).

CINEMAS

There has been a cinema renaissance in the last two decades, following a decline in the '60s and '70s when many cinemas were turned into shops, bingo halls and even places of worship. Today the remaining 1,500 cinemas are thriving and attendances have doubled in the last ten years. The mainstream cinema scene is dominated by the major chains such as MGM and Odeon. In the last decade many multiplex cinemas have been built (often in new out-of-town, leisure and shopping complexes) each with ten or more screens. New centres have extra-wide comfortable seats with ample leg-room, dolby stereo or THX surround sound, air-conditioned (usually non-smoking) auditoriums, free parking, and many also have cafés, restaurants, bars and games rooms.

London has numerous cinemas (100 in the 'West End' alone) showing not only the latest first-run films, but a huge variety of classics and foreign-language films, that are usually screened with their original soundtracks and subtitles. Note, however, that many London cinemas have small screens, having been sub-divided into multiplex cinemas. Ticket prices range from £1 or £2 for children's matinees in provincial cinemas up to around £10 (average £6 to £9) for first-run films in London's West End. Most cinemas offer reductions (usually half price or less) for children (where applicable) and pensioners, although you should check in advance as some reductions apply to certain performances only. Many cinemas have a reduced price day, usually Mondays, when admittance for afternoon shows is reduced (discounts may be available on any afternoon). Many cinemas have special facilities for the disabled.

All films on general release in Britain are giving a film certificate classification by the British Board of Film Censors (shown below) which denotes any age restrictions:

Classification	Age Restrictions
U	no restrictions;
PG	parental guidance advised (not mandatory);
12	no-one under age 12 admitted;
15	no-one under age 15 admitted;
18	no-one under age 18 admitted.

Children (or adults) who look younger than their years may be asked for proof of their age, e.g. a school identity card, student card or driving licence, for admittance to age-restricted performances. Most cinemas accept telephone bookings (major credit cards accepted) and tickets can usually be purchased in advance. There may be an additional fee when booking by credit card, e.g. 50p to £1 a ticket. Tickets may, however, be sold only on the day of the performance. Booked seats are usually held until 30 minutes before a performance begins.

There are private film clubs in the major cities and local film societies in all areas. A number of magazines for film buffs are published in Britain. In London, *City Limits*, *Time Out* and *What's On* provide comprehensive film reviews and a list of all London cinema programmes and performance times. Both national (usually London programmes) and local papers publish cinema programmes and most also review the latest films.

THEATRE, OPERA & BALLET

Britain is world renowned for the quality, quantity and variety of its theatre, opera and ballet companies. London has the most vibrant theatre in the world and has over 150 commercial and subsidised theatres (50 in the West End) producing up to 25 new productions every week. Major theatres include the Royal National Theatre (South Bank), the Royal Shakespeare Company (Barbican Centre), the Royal Opera House (Covent Garden), the Royal Court, and the English National Opera (Coliseum). Theatre entertainment includes modern drama; classical plays; comedy; modern and traditional musicals; revue and variety; children's shows and pantomime; opera and operetta; and ballet and dance. The theatre is widely patronised throughout the country and is one of the delights of living in Britain, particularly if you live within easy reach of London.

The arts in Britain are subsidised by the Arts Council, but its budget has been cut in recent years leaving many theatres and opera houses in deep financial trouble. However, there's a new fairy godmother in the shape of the National Lottery fund (see page 386), which made a large grant to building the new £214 million Royal Opera House scheduled to open in December 1999. The Arts Council funds a repertory company touring programme that ensures that the arts reach areas without permanent theatres. Excellent theatre and musical entertainment isn't confined to London and many provincial towns have acclaimed theatres, concert halls and arts centres attracting international stars (and charge only a fraction of London's West End prices). Fringe theatre in London is both lively and extensive, and provides an excellent training ground for new playwrights and companies. Many London and provincial theatres support youth theatres (e.g. 14 to 21) and people of all ages who see themselves as budding Lawrence Oliviers or Katherine Hepburns can audition for local amateur dramatic societies. The cost of tickets for most London musicals and plays range from around £5 to £35 and from £5 to £25 for provincial theatres.

Opera (along with ballet) is largely a middle and upper class entertainment in Britain, patronised by some 6 per cent of the population only. Rural opera is thriving and many outdoor performances are staged in summer, organised by English Heritage. Tickets at the Royal Opera House, Covent Garden, range from around £10 (restricted view) to £250, depending on the performance and the part of the theatre. Prices for boxes (four seats) range from around £200 to over £500 for most performances. At the other end of the scale there are bargain 'slip' seats with a restricted view from £2 and standing places are also usually available from around £10. Provincial ballet and opera tickets, e.g. for the English National Ballet or the Glyndebourne Touring Opera, range in price from around £5 to £30. England, Scotland and Wales each has its own national opera company. In addition to classical ballet, dance companies and troupes are popular and numerous throughout Britain, and include everything from classical dance to mime, contemporary dance to an abundance of traditional dance from all corners of the globe. Dance is usually inexpensive and sometimes surprisingly cheap.

Tickets for ballet, opera and musicals are in heavy demand, so you should apply well in advance. Many London musicals are solidly booked for months in advance, with many tickets being purchased by overseas tour operators providing theatre package tours. British ticket agencies also have agents in many countries, where tickets can be purchased locally. Most theatres accept credit card telephone bookings. Non-credit card telephone bookings are usually held for a number of days (e.g. three) unless booked on the day of the performance, when they are kept until around an hour before the performance is due to commence. Tickets can also be booked by post with payment by cheque or credit card (many theatres ask for a first class stamped addressed envelope). Tickets can also be booked and paid for in person at theatre booking offices.

Group discounts are usually available for groups (size varies) and school parties. Concessions (reduced price tickets) are often available for families, senior citizens (60+), youths (age varies from under 18 to 14-30 year-olds), students and the unemployed (students must show student identification and the unemployed a form UB40). Note that concession tickets may be standby tickets only, which are sold a few hours before a performance. Some theatres sell all unsold seats at reduced prices on performance days or a few hours before a performance, e.g. the Royal National Theatre.

When buying tickets for any event, whether theatre, cinema, opera or a concert, it's advisable to purchase them direct from the venue. If you're in London and wish to buy tickets for a West End show, it's usually convenient to buy tickets in person from a theatre box office, most of which are open from around 1000 daily on performance days. Tickets can also be purchased from most box offices by mail, simply by writing and requesting tickets for a particular performance (give alternatives if possible) and enclosing a cheque. However, it's advisable to telephone in advance and make a reservation. Tickets must be collected in person or payment sent, usually within three days. Telephone credit card bookings can also be made, usually by telephoning a special number. You can make a subscription to a season of performances at many theatres and obtain a large discount, e.g. 30 to 40 per cent.

Tickets can also be purchased from ticket agencies, who charge a booking fee of from 15 to 25 per cent of the face value of the ticket (similar to ticket touts). Before buying tickets from any source other than directly from a theatre, you should check the official box office price first (printed on the ticket) so that you know exactly how much commission you're being asked to pay. Most ticket agencies don't actually have any tickets, but simply ring the box office, which you can do yourself. If you desperately want to see a show and cannot wait, you may be able to buy tickets from ticket touts, although you may be asked two or three times a ticket's face value.

Always check performance times with the box office or in a daily or local newspaper or entertainment magazine. If you're late for a live performance, you may have to wait until the interval before being permitted to take your seat, although it may be possible to watch the show on a TV monitor. There are usually daily evening performances from Mondays to Saturdays and often a matinee performance on one weekday, usually Wednesdays or Thursdays, and Saturdays. There are no performances on Sundays (even actors and actresses are entitled to a day off!).

Most theatres have a number of spaces for wheelchairs, induction loops for the hard of hearing, and toilets for wheelchair users (mention when booking). Some theatres produce braille programmes and brochures and most allow entrance to guide dogs for the blind. Most theatres, both London and provincial, have restaurants and bars, and some London and most provincial theatres have private or public car parks nearby. If you wish to have a drink or a cup of coffee during the interval, it's best to order it in advance before the show starts and avoid the crush. Note that many of the points mentioned above concerning theatre facilities and tickets, also apply to concert halls and concert tickets (see below).

Free programmes for London and provincial theatres are available from tourist information centres, including the *London Theatre Guide* published bi-weekly (also available on subscription from LTG Subscriptions, SOLT, Bedford Chambers, The Piazza, Covent Garden, London WC2E 8HQ). Most British newspapers contain reviews of London and provincial shows, particularly broadsheet daily and Sunday newspapers which have their own theatre critics. London's entertainment magazines such as *What's On* (mainstream, conservative) and *Time Out* (progressive, more for the younger reader) and *City Limits* (similar to *What's On*), carry comprehensive reviews and details of all London's shows.

Keen theatregoers can join the Theatregoers' Club of Great Britain (TCGB), Harling, Great Suffolk Street, London SE1 0BS (☎ 0171-450 4040), which has branches in around 25 counties. The TCGB organises trips to both regional and West End theatres in luxury coaches, which spare you the frustrations of driving and parking (or using public transport). Individual membership costs around £25 a year. If you're aged between 14 and 29, you may be interested in the Stage Pass (Stage Pass, Youth & Music, 28 Charing Cross Road, London WC2H 0DB, ☎ 0171-379 6722), a national discount ticket scheme offering discounts of up to 70 per cent on tickets for Britain's leading arts companies and venues.

CONCERTS

Classical concerts, music festivals and solo concerts are staged regularly throughout Britain by British and international musicians and performers. There are many celebrated international music festivals including orchestral, choral, opera, jazz, folk and rock. London is unrivalled in its concentration and variety of music venues and is the music capital of the world. London has four major orchestras, the London Symphony Orchestra (LSO), the London Philharmonic, the Royal Philharmonic and the Philharmonia. Acclaimed provincial symphony orchestras include Birmingham, Manchester, Bournemouth and the BBC National Orchestra. One of the most famous classical music seasons is the Proms (promenade concerts), performed at the Royal Albert Hall, culminating in the celebrated 'Last Night of the Proms' concert.

Most major cathedrals take part in a summer festival of music performed by the London Festival Orchestra. Provincial professional and amateur orchestras and ensembles perform both individual and subscription series of concerts, tickets for which are reasonably priced. Subscription or season tickets are usually available for a whole season of classical performances or a selection, when interest-free payment can sometimes be made by direct debit and spread over a period, e.g. six months. In summer, free open-air concerts are staged in public parks by orchestras and bands throughout the country.

Local music societies or music clubs regularly organise concerts and recitals, where members (or 'friends') receive priority bookings; reduced seat prices; savings on meals, holidays and special events; free mailing list; and even participation in programme planning. Tickets usually range from around £5 to £10. You can become a member or friend of a music society, orchestra or theatre for as little as £5 or £10 a year. Free lunchtime organ and choral concerts are performed in cathedrals and churches throughout the year, and free outdoor concerts are staged in summer (a collection is usually made to help meet expenses). The BTA publish a booklet entitled *Singing in Cathedrals*, which contains a complete list of choral services throughout Britain. Look for announcements in your local newspapers or enquire at your local tourist information centre.

In addition to classical and choral music, just about every other kind of music is performed regularly somewhere in Britain, including brass and steel bands, country & western, easy listening, folk, heavy metal, hip hop, house, jazz, indie, medieval, raga, reggae, rock, rhythm & blues and soul to name just a selection. Fans of certain kinds of music, e.g. folk or jazz, will find there are clubs in most cities, usually with low membership fees. Britain is a world leader in the popular music industry, where London is again the centre of attraction, with more 'gigs' in one night than most provincial cities stage in a week, ranging from pub entertainment to mega rock stars who fill Wembley stadium. Tickets cost from £5 to £50 depending on who's performing and the venue.

Many local venues offer discounts for students and usually have increased ticket prices on Fridays and Saturdays. Concert ticket prices in Britain are generally lower than in many other western countries, although the prices for 'Superstars' (e.g. Pavarotti, Barbara Streisand, Madonna and the Rolling Stones) can be astronomical. There are also a wide range of amateur musical groups including orchestras, military bands, choral societies and even barbershop singers, most of which are constantly on the lookout for new talent. Free music is also provided by an army of buskers, many of whom are excellent (and most of whom are illegal).

There are many newspapers and magazines in Britain dedicated to the popular music industry including *Melody Maker* and the *New Musical Express*. The London entertainment magazines *Time Out*, *What's On* and *City Limits* provide comprehensive music reviews and a list of all concerts in the London area. Free music newspapers and magazines are also available in some areas. Information about provincial concerts is available from local tourist information centres, libraries and the British Tourist Authority. Concertline (0898-600377) provides 24-hour recorded information on concerts, ticket availability, prices and venue information. Note that many of the points listed under **Theatre, Opera & Ballet** on page 381 concerning theatre facilities and tickets also apply to concert halls and concert tickets.

SOCIAL CLUBS

There are numerous social clubs and organisations in Britain catering for both foreigners and Britons including Ambassador clubs, American Women's and Men's Clubs, Anglo-British clubs, Business Clubs, Church clubs and groups, Conservative clubs, the Freemasons, International Men's and Women's clubs, Kiwani Clubs, Labour clubs, Lion and Lioness Clubs, RAOB clubs, Rotary Clubs, Round Table clubs, ex-Servicemen's clubs, Sports clubs, Women's clubs and Working Men's clubs. There are also many famous and exclusive men's clubs in London and other cities, where men go to escape from their wives (women also have their own exclusive clubs).

Expatriates from many countries have their own clubs and organisations in major cities and many counties; ask at your embassy or consulate in Britain for information. Many local clubs organise activities and pastimes such as chess, bridge whist, art, music, sports activities, outings, theatre, cinema and local history. If you want to integrate into your local community or British society in general, one of the best ways is to join a local social club (even better join a number). In major cities there are singles clubs, some of which operate nationally and organise a comprehensive range of activities on every day of the week. At the other end of the scale, if you're retired, you may find your local council publishes a programme of recreational activities for the retired in your area. Most councils publish a calendar of local sports and social events (some publish booklets listing activities for women only), and most libraries have information centres where information about local groups and associations is available.

DISCOTHEQUES & NIGHTCLUBS

There are discotheques and night-clubs in all major British towns and cities. The entrance fee for discos is usually between £2 and £5, which sometimes includes a 'free' drink (drinks are usually expensive). Most towns and cities have jazz and night clubs, bars, cabarets and discotheques, many open until 0200 or 0400. Admission may be cheaper if you arrive early (before the real 'action' starts). London has one of the most cosmopolitan nightlife scenes to be found anywhere, with venues to suit every taste in music, fashion and atmosphere. There's also a huge variety of gay clubs in London. Information is available from the flourishing free gay press such as *Pink Paper* and *Capital Gay*, available in bars and cafés.

It's common to include a membership fee (which may provide only temporary membership) in the admission price, although membership sometimes requires being sponsored by at least two members and waiting a few days until it becomes valid. Admission to clubs usually costs anything from £3 to £10. Some private clubs will admit visitors accompanied by a member. The dress code is usually smart casual, which excludes jeans, leather, T-shirts and trainers, although in some establishments this may represent the perfect 'costume' (fashion usually dictates, depending on the venue). Some up-market discos and dance clubs allow admission only to couples. Note that only clubs with a music or dancing licence can sell alcohol after 2300 (the end of pub licensing hours). All-night clubbing was legalised in 1990, but around 0300 alcohol gives way to fruit juices.

Alternative cabaret or new comedy provides cheap and exciting entertainment and is popular in London (which has more comedy clubs than any other city in the world) and some provincial cities. Acts include impressionists, mime artists, acappela singing groups, performing poets, jugglers, magicians, comic stunt-men, fire-eaters, bands and other musical acts, double acts, sketch teams and a huge variety of other 'oddballs', who compete nightly for the limelight. Admission is usually around £3 to £5 and there's often a reduction for students.

GAMBLING

Gambling is one of the Britain's favourite pastimes (sometimes it's an occupation) and includes horse and greyhound racing; football pools; sweepstakes; the national lottery; bingo halls; casinos; slot machine (or 'amusement') arcades; card games; TV game shows; raffles; competitions (e.g. in newspapers and magazines); betting on the results of general elections, public appointments, football matches and other sports events; and forecasting the names of royal babies and major ships (etc.). In Britain you can bet on almost anything, although one bookmaker refused to quote on the date of the end of the world (the punter wanted to pay with a post-dated cheque!).

The National Lottery: was launched on 19th November 1994 and is operated by Camelot who 'earn' over £1 million a week (a licence to print money if ever there was one). It's Britain's answer to the state lotteries staged by all European countries and most US states (the last national lottery in Britain in 1826 was suspended when the operator absconded with the winnings) and has been a tremendous success. Tickets cost £1 each and jackpots can be up to £20 million or more when it's rolled over for a few weeks (when no-one has chosen the six main numbers in the draw, the jackpot is rolled over to the next week, thus allowing a bigger jackpot to build up). Your chances of landing the jackpot is 14 million to one against (you have a much greater chance of getting struck dead by lightning tomorrow), although this doesn't prevent some 65 per cent of Britons playing the lottery regularly.

You must be aged 16 or over to play (although many younger children buy tickets). Tickets can be purchased from corner shops, newsagents, supermarkets, petrol stations and post offices, shown by the national lottery symbol of a smiling hand with crossed fingers. Tickets must be purchased by 1930 on Saturdays to be included in the Saturday draw. All you need do is choose six numbers between 1 and 49 (you need three out of six to win a prize). Don't lose your ticket as it's the only proof that you're a winner. The winning numbers are drawn on Saturday evenings and shown live on BBC television. Winning numbers are broadcast on radio and television, published in national newspapers and displayed by national lottery retailers. Prizes must be claimed within 180 days after the winning draw. Don't be fooled by unofficial overseas agents for the National Lottery (e.g. in Holland) who charge around £4.50 for each £1 ticket! If you wish to subscribe from abroad you can buy a subscription ticket for six months or one year direct from the organisers (PO Box 287, Watford, Herts. WD1 8TT, Internet: national-lottery.co.uk).

The lottery was ostensibly created to provide money for 'good causes' including sports, the arts, the National Lottery Charities Board, the National Heritage Memorial Fund and the Millennium Fund (which has been set up to celebrate the year 2000). Of the proceeds, 28 per cent of turnover goes to 'good causes' and another 12 per cent to the government in tax. Donations to charities have fallen considerably since the lottery began and many face serious cash shortfalls in the next few years (most charities have been forced to abandon their own lotteries). Scratch cards with instant prizes of up to £50,000 were introduced in spring 1995, which have been likened to fruit machines and are highly addictive, and a second weekly draw (on Wednesday evenings) was introduced in recent years. Lottery addicts have swamped Gamblers Anonymous since its inception. Disputes over prize money have caused marriages and families to break up, and friends to fall out (one man even shot himself after failing to buy a ticket that would have won him the jackpot prize).

Betting Shops: There are turf accountants (usually called betting shops or bookies) in just about every town in Britain (over 10,000), which were legalised in the '60s to allow off-course betting on horse and greyhound races. Betting shop turnover has been one of the few growth areas in recent years, when turnover increased at over double the rate of inflation (in times of financial crisis many Britons turn to gambling for relief). However, betting shops and all other forms of gambling have been hard hit by the National Lottery. You can also bet on horse and greyhound races by post or phone. On course tote betting is also popular. A racing results service is provided on the teletext information service on ITV4.

Football Pools: Until the National Lottery was launched, the football pools were Britain's biggest weekly 'lottery' (£900 million turnover) and participants can win huge cash prizes by forecasting (i.e. guessing) the results of soccer matches. The treble chance is the most popular bet, where punters guess which matches will be score draws (matches which end in a draw where each team scores at least one goal) and prizes can run to around £2m. Many millions of people, both within Britain and around the world, have a weekly flutter on the pools. If you don't want to fill out a coupon every week, you can have a standing order using the same numbers each week.

Casinos: London is one of the world's most celebrated gambling centres among the seriously rich and it comes as no surprise to discover that it's home to over 20 of Britain's some 120 casinos (only France has more in Europe). London's casinos have a turnover of over £2 billion a year. Provincial casinos, where gamblers generally play more often, albeit for smaller stakes, have a much smaller turnover than London's casinos. Note that casino staff are prohibited by law from taking tips, so if you give a tip it will either end up in the pockets of the management or will be returned. One drawback to gambling in London is the '48-hour rule' that prevents anybody gambling in a casino until 48 hours after they have become a member. London casinos operate under some of the strictest rules in the world, which are criticised as archaic in the computer age with computer gambling (via credit card) on the Internet available 24-hours a day (although how you can guarantee getting your winnings is another matter).

Premium Bonds aren't an investment as no interest is paid. They are similar to a ticket in a lottery, except that you cannot lose your original investment and can cash in your bonds any time at face value. The 'possible' premium is in a monthly draw (made by 'Ernie' the premium bonds computer), which offers monthly prizes ranging from £50 to £1 million (around 250,000 prizes totalling up to £20 million a month). You need to invest a minimum of £100 at any time and purchases must be in multiples of £10 (e.g. £110, £120, etc.) and the maximum holding is £20,000. Bonds can be purchased at any post office or by post and are entered into the next draw after purchase. Results are announced in the national press and are available at main post offices (including a list of unclaimed prizes).

Other forms of popular gambling are bingo (casinos for housewives, where around 5 million have a weekly flutter in 1,000 commercial bingo clubs), slot-machine arcades (the poor man's Las Vegas) and sweepstakes (the most popular of which is the Irish Sweepstake). If you have a gambling problem, Gamblers Anonymous (☎ 0171-384 3040) may be able to help (but unfortunately they cannot provide you with a stake).

PUBS

Britain is noted for it pubs (an abbreviation of public houses), which are a British tradition going back to Roman and Saxon times (drunkenness isn't a new phenomenon in Britain – the British have been sots for millennia), when their forerunners were established to meet the needs of the traveller. A pub is one of the most welcoming places in Britain (particularly on a freezing winter's night when many have inviting open log fires) and they represent the heart of local communities. It's interesting to note that despite Britain's reputation as a nation of drunks, Britain has more teetotallers (those 'boring' people who don't drink alcohol) than any other European country. However, the purveyors of alcohol will be pleased to note that despite heavy marketing, the British drink an average of only five litres of mineral water per head annually compared to the European average of almost 50.

There's a total of around 60,000 inns and pubs in Britain, and every town and village has at least one or two (sometimes they outnumber the houses), although many rural pubs have closed in the last few years. A pub is the local meeting place for both business and pleasure, and if you arrange to meet a stranger anywhere in Britain it will invariably be at a pub (even in an unfamiliar town you can always find a pub). However, in recent years they have been under increasing pressure, with margins on beer cut to the bone and falling sales (beer consumption is at its lowest for 20 years), and few pubs could survive without serving food.

There are excellent pubs in most cities, towns and country areas, many occupying beautifully restored historic buildings. In many areas pubs have fascinating names which often date back hundreds of years, although theme pubs are popular in cities and may change their theme and name every few months. Most traditional pubs have two bars: a 'posh' bar called a 'lounge', 'saloon' or 'private' bar, and a public bar for the riff-raff and those in dirty working clothes (who aren't usually allowed into lounge bars). The public bar is usually where the darts board, slot machines and other games are to be found. Many modern pubs have only a single large lounge bar. Some pubs have a jukebox and pubs with a young clientele often play continuous loud pop music (which can be a nightmare) or have discotheques and live rock bands on a number of nights each week (places to avoid if you want a quiet drink). Karaoke is popular in many pubs, where frustrated would-be pop stars get up on stage and perform their favourite songs (taped backing music and words are provided).

Most pubs provide reasonably priced hot and cold food at lunchtimes (usually self-service from the bar) and some have excellent *à la carte* restaurants in the evenings. An increasing number of pubs serve decent wines and imaginative meals with change from £10 (but, alas, still far too few). Note, however, that the quality of food is extremely variable, so ask around. Country pubs usually offer the best value for money. Pub restaurants operate in the same way as any restaurant and credit cards are usually accepted. Many pubs also provide accommodation, traditionally called inns, although nowadays they are usually referred to as hotels or pub hotels. Many pubs also have an off-licence, which is a small room from which they sell alcohol for consumption off the premises (off-licences are shops that sell alcohol and which are governed by special licensing hours).

British pubs serve a multitude of beers and alcoholic beverages, from continental lagers to traditional British ales, with a total of over 1,000 brands. In the last few decades there has been a revival in traditional British ales or 'real ale', which is brewed from fresh barley, hops and oats. The British produce the widest range of beers in the world including many draught beers (on tap) drawn from casks or kegs, such as the ever popular bitter, stout (e.g. Guinness), mild and a wide variety of continental lagers (many brewed in Britain under licence). In addition to draught beers, a wide variety of bottled and canned beers are also available, including brown ale (Newcastle is the most famous brand name), pale ale, light ale, stout (e.g. Mackeson) and many more.

Note that although Britain pays lip service to the metric system, beer is still sold in pints (568ml) and not litres (a small beer is half a pint). Wine is sold by the glass (there's no law regarding the quantity) and spirits by one-sixth of a gill (24ml) in England and Wales (in Scotland and Northern Ireland they are larger). One big difference between Britain and other countries is that in Britain you always order drinks and bar food at the bar and pay in cash when you order. You cannot 'run a tab' and pay when you leave (or when you fall off your chair), as is common on the continent. Receipts aren't usually given unless you ask for one (which would be considered very unusual in any other establishment).

Most British pubs are owned by breweries and therefore sell beer produced only by their owners. If you want a pub with a wide selection of the best beers, choose a freehouse, which is a pub with no brewery ties and therefore free to sell whatever beer it chooses (which usually means the pick of the most popular brands). Most pubs sell an average of around 20 different draught and bottled beers. A large variety of spirits, liquers, cocktails and a (usually small) selection of wines is also available. Pubs also sell a wide range of non-alcoholic drinks.

The licensing laws governing the opening hours of pubs vary throughout Britain. Since 1988 pubs in England and Wales have been governed by more relaxed licensing laws (although they are still the most archaic in the EU), under which they can open from 1100 to 2300, Mondays to Saturdays, and from 1200 to 2230 on Sundays (Sunday afternoon opening was permitted in England only in 1995). In Scotland, pubs open from 1100 to 2300, Mondays to Saturdays, and from 1230 to 2300 on Sundays. In Northern Ireland, licensing hours are from 1130 to 2300 on weekdays and Saturdays, and from 1230 to 1430 and 1900 to 2200 on Sundays.

On public holidays such as Christmas Day, Boxing Day and New Year's Eve, pubs are usually granted an extended licence until 2400 or 0100. After 2300 you can normally legally drink only in establishments that serve food with drinks, thus ensuring that you become obese in addition to an alcoholic (legally a 'meal' is the amount of food which will satisfy your appetite for two hours). In some areas of Wales and some Scottish islands, pubs are closed on Sundays. Bars in restaurants, hotels and other buildings, are generally governed by the same licensing laws as pubs, except when a special license has been granted. Pub landlords have the right to refuse to admit or serve a customer and cannot by law serve anyone who's drunk.

Many traditional games are played in pubs, including darts, bar billiards, pool (9-ball), skittles (nine pins), dominoes, cards, and pin ball and other machines. Note that you aren't permitted to play games for money, as gambling is illegal in pubs. The legal age for buying and consuming alcohol in a pub is 18, although children over 14 are admitted at the discretion of the landlord and can consume non-alcoholic drinks. If a pub has a restaurant or dining room, beer, wine or cider may be purchased for consumption with a meal, by those aged over 16 and under 18. Children under 14 are admitted to beer gardens, family rooms, pub restaurants and an increasing number of pub lounges. Pubs can apply for a 'children's certificate' until 2100 or 2130 to allow children to join their parents in the bar for a meal.

The law with regard to driving and drinking is strict in Britain (see page 259) and the police are particularly active over Christmas and the New Year. If you have more than a couple of drinks you would be well advised to hitch a ride with a sober friend or use public transport. Most pubs sell a variety of low-alcohol beers and wines and a wide choice of non-alcoholic drinks (most pubs also serve coffee). Wine bars can be found in most cities and towns and have become increasingly popular in recent years, particularly with yuppies, young trendies and wine snobs. Most wine bars serve food, when the atmosphere usually resembles that of a trendy restaurant, rather than a pub.

Books of interest to those who like to eat before getting drunk and rolling into bed, are Egon Ronay's *Guide to Pubs & Inns* and *Guide to Bars, Bistros & Cafés, Good Food in Pubs & Bars* and the BTA's *Stay at an Inn*. Also interesting and informative are BTA's regional booklets entitled *Pubs for Everyone*. No serious beer drinker should be without the CAMRA *Good Beer Guide* edited by Jeff Evans and the *The Good Pub Guide* (Ebury Press), edited by Alisdair Aird, which contains details of over 5,000 pubs (a L-O-N-G pub crawl), including the type of food served and its quality and price, atmosphere, service, facilities for children and much more. *Time Out* publish the *Guide to Drinking Places in London*.

RESTAURANTS & CAFÉS

The variety and standard of restaurants in Britain varies widely, probably more than anywhere else in the world. Most foreigners are familiar with the infamous (and previously well-deserved) image of a Britain full of 'greasy spoon' (specialising in fried food and overcooked vegetables) establishments, which are still common in major cities and tourist areas. However, those who believe that a period spent in Britain means bringing your own food supply or facing starvation or death by food poisoning, are in for a pleasant surprise. True, there a large number of thriving restaurants, cafés and fast food establishments, whose fare would, in more discriminating countries, be condemned as unfit for human consumption.

However, there has been a revolution in Britain in the last decade or so and there's now a plethora of excellent restaurants offering a quality and variety of culinary delights hardly bettered anywhere in the world. In fact, top class restaurants are invariably excellent and sometimes outstanding. You need only to open the pages of the latest Egon Ronay or Michelin red guides to realise that British food doesn't always live up (or down) to its dreadful reputation. On the negative side, prices for good food are often astronomical (wine is also *very* expensive) and even modest food can be costly.

Although synonymous with junk food, 'fast' or 'take-away' (take out) food can be very good, as evidenced by the increasing quality and amazing variety of fast food establishments around Britain. Most 'take-away' food establishments accept telephone orders and an increasing number make home deliveries (e.g. pizzas). Most Chinese and Indian restaurants provide a take-away service, but usually no deliveries (and there may be no reduction for a take-away meal, although you will save on VAT). Many other restaurants also provide a take-away and free delivery service. One traditional British take-away meal is fried fish and chips, purchased from a fish and chip shop. Unfortunately the quality is variable (i.e. often terrible) and you usually need to go out of your way to find a good fish and chip shop, although it's well worth the effort. Self-service restaurants and cafés are also fairly common in towns, many of which should be avoided like the plague (although they are inexpensive, the food can be terrible and the coffee's even worse). A new innovation in recent year throughout Britain has been cyber cafés, where you can access the Internet, and American-style coffee shops such as Starbucks and the Seattle Coffee Co. Note that some fast food and 'cheap' restaurants in tourist areas are a rip-off, particularly in London, and motorway service stations have a well-earned reputation for everything that's worst about British food (although standards are improving).

Often the best bet for those wishing to eat well and cheaply are British pubs (pub grub or bar food, usually served at lunchtime only, e.g. 1200 to 1400) and ethnic restaurants, particularly Chinese, Indian and Italian, where the standard of food, although variable is usually high and a meal costs an average of £10 to £15 a head (without wine). A medium-priced restaurant will set you back around £20 to £30 a head. Some restaurants, particularly those in hotels, provide separate vegetarian and diabetic menus (some even provide healthy low-fat meals). Jewish Kosher restaurants are also fairly common in major cities and towns. In some areas there are restaurant clubs, where two people can eat for the price of one. Ask at local restaurants if there's a club in your area.

London is one of the great eating capitals of the world, rivalling Paris and New York for quality and ethnic variety (although it doesn't offer nearly as good value). For anyone living in London, the *Time Out Guide to Eating Out in London* is a must, listing over 1,300 restaurants, cafés and bars. However, Britain has a lot to learn from the rest of the EU with regard to quality and value-for-money food. When you do find good food, it's often outrageously expensive (it's far cheaper to eat out in France, Italy, Portugal or Spain). Paying £50 to £75 (or more) a head for a meal isn't unusual if you want the very best, although many people think the prices charged by many top restaurants are unjustified.

Most restaurants are licensed to serve alcohol with meals, although they aren't permitted to sell alcohol without providing food. The cost of wine can also be astronomical, with a mark-up of 200 per cent plus VAT. Many restaurants charge up to three times the shop price for branded wine or offer cheap plonk in make-believe, own-label bottles or in carafes (restaurant wines are usually as obscure as possible so customers won't realise the mark-up they're paying). Champagne is the biggest rip-off of all, where customers are charged £50 or £60 (or £10 a glass) for the privilege of drinking it in a restaurant. Unfortunately 'bring your own grog' (BYOG) restaurants are almost unheard of in Britain (where are all the enterprising Aussies?).

Many restaurants offer 'tourist' or set-price menus at lunch time (usually from 1200 to 1400), which include a choice of meals maybe with soup and sometimes a dessert, from around £5 or £10. Lunch in a pub is usually served from 1200 to 1400 and dinner from 1900 to 2130. Some restaurants offer half-portions for children or have a children's menu. McDonalds (the American chain of hamburger restaurants) have branches in most towns and they and others organise special events and children's parties. Children of all ages are usually admitted to licensed restaurants, although few restaurants cater particularly for children (without their own credit cards). Note that cafés in Britain, unlike those in most continent countries, aren't licensed to sell alcohol.

Many department stores have good value-for-money restaurants that often provide breakfast and lunch menus. Cheap meals are also provided by the YWCA and YMCA, YHA, community centres, and sports and leisure centres. It's advisable to make a reservation for the more expensive or more popular restaurants, particularly during lunch times, on Friday and Saturday evenings and at anytime for parties of four or more people. Most restaurants close on one or two days a week (opening times are usually posted outside). Restaurants can serve alcohol outside normal licensing hours providing it's served with food, which means that many restaurants get particularly busy after 2300 when the drunks are thrown out of the pubs (it's amazing the number of people who eat dinner in the early hours of the morning). Many restaurants are open until the early hours, particularly in London and other major cities, where you can eat until 0300 or later.

All restaurants and cafés in Britain are obliged by law to display their tariffs where customers can see them before entering. If an establishment has an extensive à la carte menu, the prices of a representative selection of food and drink currently available must be displayed, in addition to the table d'hôte menu, if offered. All charges for service and any minimum charge or cover charge must also be clearly stated and prices shown must be inclusive of VAT. If a restaurant attempts to include any charges that aren't listed on the menu (which is a common practice in tourist areas), you should refuse to pay.

If you have a complaint regarding anything stated (or not stated) in a menu, or there's a big difference between what's stated and what you're served or charged, you can make a complaint to your local Trading Standards Officer. Your best bet is to reach a compromise with the manager or owner and negotiate a reduction to cover your complaint. You can legally refuse to pay for anything which is inedible and insist on leaving, but should leave your name and address (and show proof of identity). If you do this, the management cannot prevent you leaving or call the police as you've committed no offence.

Many restaurants and hotel bills include a service charge (around 10 per cent), designed to reduce tipping (and increase profits). Most British people still feel obliged to leave a tip of around 10 to 15 per cent, a practice which is encouraged or even expected in many establishments (most employees would find it difficult to survive on their meagre salaries without tips). See also **Tipping** on page 462.

There are many excellent restaurant guides published in Britain. Note, however, that most food guides (like most hotel guides) charge restaurants for entry including Les Routiers, the English Tourist Board, the AA and the RAC, which has lead people to question their impartiality. Even motorway service stations (renowned for their awful food) are included in Les Routiers! Among those that don't charge for inclusion are the Michelin red guide, the Good Pub Guide (Vermillion), the Good Food Guide (Which? Books) and the Which? Guide to Country Pubs.

LIBRARIES

Britain has one of the best public library services in the world (although it has suffered in the last decade as local authorities have been forced to economise and reduce their library budgets) and there are public libraries in all cities and most towns in Britain. Residents in rural areas without a local library are often provided with a mobile library service. Public libraries in Britain are run by county councils and around a third of residents are registered users (hopefully the rest are book *buyers*). Anyone who lives, works or studies in Britain, can join their local library free of charge, on production of proof of identity (e.g. an NHS medical card or driving licence) and their current address, although children under 15 or 16 must usually be sponsored by a parent or guardian. Library members can borrow books from any library within their county, which also provides details and schedules regarding mobile library services. When you join a library, you're usually given a computer membership card with which you can borrow up to eight to ten books (some libraries allow less) at a time, for a period of three or four weeks.

At the end of the loan period you may renew the loan (in person or by telephone or post) of a book for a further three or four weeks, providing nobody else has reserved it. If books aren't returned by the due date (stamped in the front of the book), you must pay a small fine. There may be no fines or reduced fines for children and there are usually no fines for pensioners or borrowers aged 70 or over (although some councils have ended these concessions). Occasionally libraries have a moratorium on fines on overdue books, so that lenders can return them without paying fines.

Library opening times vary considerably but are usually around 0930 or 1000 to 1730 or 1800. There may be late opening (e.g. until 1900 or 2000) on a few days a week and earlier closing on one or two days (e.g. 1600 or 1700) and a half-day on Wednesday (or another day) when they close at 1300. Some libraries may close on one or more days a week (e.g. Mondays or Wednesdays) and all are open on Saturdays, e.g. 0930 to 1600. Libraries may have much reduced opening hours in some towns (or even be closed) as a result of cutbacks in council budgets. Many libraries have microfiche catalogues which can be used by borrowers to locate any book held in stock by the county library service. Books can be requested from other libraries within the county, for which a fee is usually charged. Many library services also provide special catalogues of books for particular groups, e.g. the retired.

In addition to lending libraries, local libraries also have reference sections where you will find encyclopaedias, dictionaries, trade directories, Stationery Office publications, atlases and maps, educational books, phone books, and any number other reference works and catalogues. Libraries are the best source of local and general information on almost any subject. Many have computerised catalogues available to the public and computers that can be hired by the half-hour (some have Internet access). All main or central libraries also have copies of local and national newspapers and magazines, which can usually be found in the reading room. Most libraries carry stocks of books in large type for those with poor eyesight and many also provide free 'talking books' (on cassette) for the blind and partially-sighted readers.

16.

SPORTS

Sports facilities are generally excellent throughout Britain, whether you're a novice or an experienced competitor. Among the most popular sports are soccer (football), rugby (union and league rules), cricket, athletics, fishing, snooker, golf, walking, cycling, squash, badminton, tennis, swimming and skiing. Most water (sailing, windsurfing, water-skiing, canoeing, yachting) and aerial sports (hang-gliding, parachuting, ballooning, gliding, light aircraft flying) are also popular. Among the most popular spectator sports are soccer, rugby, cricket, horse racing, snooker and motor racing (many of which were invented in Britain).

The leisure industry in Britain is big business and new sports facilities and complexes including golf clubs, yacht marinas, indoor tennis clubs, dry-slope ski centres, health and fitness clubs, and country clubs are sprouting in all areas. They are all part of a huge growth market which is expected to gain even greater momentum in the next millennium, as more people retire early and have more time for leisure and sport. Many sports owe their popularity (and fortunes) to TV and the increased TV coverage (and competition for TV rights) generated by the proliferation of cable and satellite TV stations. Both professional and amateur sports have also benefited hugely in recent years from the increase in the commercial sponsorship of individual events, teams, and league and cup competitions.

The vast majority of sports facilities in Britain are 'pay-as-you-play', which means you don't need to join a club or enrol in a course to use them, although there are also many private clubs where you pay an annual membership fee. Participation in most sports is inexpensive and most towns have a community sports or leisure centre financed and run by the local council. District, borough and county councils publish free directories of clubs in their area and regional sports councils provide information about local activities. Most higher educational establishments and many large companies provide extensive sports facilities for students or employees, usually for a nominal fee, and most state schools have extensive sports facilities (which may be open to the public during evenings, weekends and holiday periods). Some organisations such as the YMCA and YWCA allow members to use their sports facilities at any time, on payment of a weekly, monthly or annual fee, and many clubs have cheap rates for students and youths (e.g. under 18s).

In contrast to the extensive and often excellent sports facilities for competitors in Britain, facilities for spectators often leave much to be desired. Until a few years ago most soccer stadiums were fairly primitive (unless you had a private box) and the vast majority of spectators were expected to stand on the 'terraces', with no protection from the cold and rain. However, following a number of tragedies soccer clubs have (for safety reasons) converted to all-seat stadia, many of which are among the best in Europe.

Despite the excellent sports facilities in Britain and the fact that over 25 million people over the age of 13 regularly participate in sport and exercise, around half the population takes no regular exercise (apart from strolling to the local pub and staggering back). Participation in many sports is the reserve of an elite group with the rest relegated to the role of spectators (or TV couch potatoes). Sports participation for the young isn't helped by the government, which spent years trying to reduce the amount of time devoted to sport in state schools. However, a new government initiative to increase sport in schools was launched in 1995 and a British Academy of Sport is to be built in the Midlands at a cost of some £100m.

Perhaps the inert majority have been listening to the statisticians, who estimate that you're 5 to 17 times more likely to drop dead playing sport than reading a book, although if you exercise regularly you're actually 20 times less likely to drop dead at any time. Sports injuries are estimated to cost the economy some 8 million lost working days a year costing over £400m, most occurring in rugby, soccer, hockey, cricket and martial arts. If you injure yourself there are sports injury clinics in most towns and sports physiotherapists in most sports and leisure centres. Note that in addition to sports with an obvious element of danger (such as most aerial sports and mountaineering), many other sports (including most winter sports, power boat racing, water-ski jumping, show-jumping and pot-holing) may not be covered by your health, accident or life insurance policies. Always check in advance and take out special insurance where necessary.

Sports results are given on the television teletext information service and published widely in daily newspapers. The Sunday broadsheet newspapers provide comprehensive cover and a nation-wide results service (particularly for soccer and rugby). Numerous magazines are published in Britain for all sports, from Angling to Yachting, most of which are available (or can be ordered) from any newsagent. For information about sports facilities in Britain contact Sports England, 16 Upper Woburn Place, London WC1H 0QP (☎ 0171-273 1500), which promotes participation in sport and physical recreation in England. The Central Council of Physical Recreation (CCPR), Francis House, Francis Street, London SW1P 1DE (☎ 0171-828 3163) is the national association of governing bodies of sport and recreation in Britain. The names and addresses of sports associations and federations can be obtained from the Sports England or the CCPR.

SPORTS & LEISURE CENTRES

Most towns have a community sports or leisure centre (also called recreation centres), usually run and financed by the local council. Some cities and towns also have modern commercial sports centres, which although they are more expensive than municipal centres, offer unrivalled sports facilities (and some charge no membership or entrance fees). A huge range of sports and activities are catered for including badminton, basketball, netball, swimming and diving, squash, indoor soccer (five-a-side), roller-skating, BMX bikes, gymnastics, yoga, weight training, table tennis, tennis, racquetball, aerobics, cricket, climbing, canoeing (in the swimming pool), archery, bowls, hockey, trampolining, martial arts and snooker. Councils publish a wealth of information about local sports and leisure centres.

Some centres have ice rinks and dry-slope skiing facilities, while most have one or more (e.g. main and learning) indoor swimming pools, squash courts (usually around six), badminton courts, sports halls (which are available for hire), general activity and fitness rooms, and a games room. Note that non-marking sports shoes with light-coloured soles should be worn for all indoor activities. Many sports centres have a health and beauty salon, that may contain a sauna, Turkish bath (or steam room), Jacuzzi, solarium, spa bath, massage and a beauty treatment room.

Centres usually provide meeting and assembly rooms, nursery facilities, a sports shop (usually with a racket re-stringing service), a reasonably priced restaurant or café, and a licensed bar. All centres provide parking, which is often free. In addition to sports activities, some centres (usually called recreation centres) also organise a range of non-sporting leisure activities, e.g. art, bingo, bridge, chess, dancing, music, photography, scrabble and whist.

Sports and leisure centres are usually open seven days a week from around 0900 to 2300, although some smaller centres use school sports facilities and are available only from early evening (e.g. 1700) Mondays to Fridays and at weekends. Note that many centres close on public holidays and over the Christmas and New Year period, when leaflets listing opening hours are provided. Membership may be necessary, for which there's usually a nominal fee of a few pounds a year, although this may only be required to book courts or equipment (usually one or two weeks in advance). Non-members may need to pay in advance when booking facilities (notice of cancellation is usually 24 or 48 hours).

In some centres, particularly in London and other major cities, annual membership costs from £10 to £50 a year and may be higher for non-residents. Season tickets, block bookings and subscriptions are usually available for some facilities. Most centres charge spectators an entrance fee of around 25p and all have reduced rates for children (or juniors), which are about half or two-thirds of adult rates, and off-peak rates during the day (usually before 1700) for most facilities. Some commercial sports centres offer a day pass (e.g. £7 for adults, £5 for children) that allows you to sample as many sports or health sessions as you wish (e.g. between 0700 and 1700). Many centres organise sports sessions or senior sports clubs for the middle-aged (50+) at reduced rates and some organise women-only activities. Membership and hire fees may be reduced for youths (e.g. under 18s), senior citizens, the handicapped and the unemployed.

All sports and leisure centres run clubs and have club nights for a variety of sports, and also organise leagues, tournaments, ladders, knockout competitions and special events. Membership of a club may reduce court fees and entitle members to free participation on club nights (or for a nominal fee). Most centres run fitness training and sports courses throughout the year (junior and adult), and also offer individual and group coaching. Equipment can be hired for a number of sports including squash and badminton rackets and table tennis bats.

Holiday sports sessions and play-schemes are held during school holidays (e.g. summer) and at weekends, and most centres organise special sports and games parties for children on request. All centres have changing rooms and showers. Note that theft from changing rooms isn't uncommon and you should take ALL your belongings and clothes with you or lock them in a storage locker. Most centres allow the use of storage lockers free of charge, usually on payment of a returnable deposit.

SOCCER

Soccer (or Association Football as it's officially called) is Britain's national sport and its most popular spectator sport. All major British cities have either a professional or semi-professional soccer team and most towns and villages have a number of amateur soccer clubs (a total of over 40,000) catering for all ages and standards. Most professional clubs and leagues are sponsored and professional players wear the name of their sponsor on their shirts. The league season in Britain runs from August to May and there's no mid-season winter break, as in many other European countries, although many clubs would like one (British soccer players are *real* men and play in all weather conditions).

The vast majority of matches are played on Saturdays, although some clubs play regularly on Friday evenings and there are Sunday afternoon and Monday evening Premiership matches most weeks that are televised live (on BskyB). In addition to weekend matches, many clubs also play during the week (usually on Tuesdays or Wednesdays). It isn't usually necessary to buy a ticket in advance for most matches, although most Premiership matches, local derbies (matches between neighbouring clubs) and cup matches are all-ticket, when tickets must be purchased in advance.

In England, the Nationwide League is the world's oldest league competition (instituted in 1888) and consists of three divisions with a total of 72 clubs (24 in each division). However, the top teams split away from the league prior to the 1992/93 season to form the FA Carling Premiership, which includes Britain's top 20 clubs, although there's still promotion to and from the Nationwide Division One each season. The Premiership has created a huge gulf between the top Premiership clubs and those in the lower leagues. Relegation from the Premiership can cost a club over £5 million in lost revenue from TV, sponsorship, advertising and ticket sales (and precipitate the loss of a club's best players). In Scotland, a Premier division was established in 1975/76 to improve competition and increase gate receipts by restricting the league to the top ten clubs, who play each other four times a season (a total of 36 matches).

The cost of tickets in England has risen at double the rate of inflation in recent years to fund expensive new all-seat stadiums and they now average over £20 for Premiership games. Season tickets are even more expensive and English soccer fans pay up to four times more than their continental counterparts, e.g. Chelsea charge from £360 to £1,025. However, despite the high price of tickets, many premier league clubs sell out every home game, although the top clubs are pricing traditional working class fans out of the game. Football in England (and to a lesser extent Scotland) is now BIG business, highlighted by the failed £633 million takeover of Manchester United by BSkyB.

Thanks to the millions pumped into soccer by sponsors and TV companies in recent years, top British clubs can now (almost) compete with the richest Italian and Spanish clubs for the best foreign players. British football has been revitalised in recent years by the introduction of foreign players, although this is having a detrimental affect on the development of up and coming home-grown stars (some Premiership teams regularly field only one or two English players). It's often cheaper to buy top-class players abroad than in Britain and many clubs have resorted to buying foreign players as prices in Britain have skyrocketed with players costing £5 to £10 million commonplace. This has also put huge pressure on clubs' wage bills and salaries have gone through the roof since the Bosman ruling removed transfer fees for players at the end of their contracts. Many clubs (often without huge resources) spend tens of millions of pounds on wages in an attempt to remain in the Premiership. Premiership salaries are typically £10,000 to £20,000 a week and many star players receive up to double this.

England has a number of other semi-professional leagues, including the Vauxhall Conference League, from which teams can be elected to the English Football League division three. The Scottish League has three divisions, each with ten clubs. Northern Ireland has the semi-professional Irish League and Wales the amateur Welsh League (although two Welsh teams, Cardiff and Wrexham, play professional football in the English Football League).

In addition to national league football, Britain also has a number of national cup competitions. In England the main knockout competition is the FA Cup, instituted in 1871 and open to amateur clubs, the final of which is played at Wembley and watched by a worldwide TV audience of millions. Cup final tickets cost from £20 to

£100 and usually go for around £1,000 or more a pair on the black market. Other national cup competitions in England are the League Cup, in which all league clubs take part, and various other competitions for professional teams in the lower divisions of the Nationwide Football League.

The FA Charity Shield match is played at Wembley between the English Football League champions and the FA Cup winners on the Saturday before the start of the English football season. In Scotland teams compete for the Scottish FA Cup and the Scottish League Cup, which opens the Scottish football season. There are also cup competitions in Northern Ireland and Wales (which is almost always won by Cardiff or Wrexham). British clubs also participate in European cup competitions including the Champions League (for national league winners and other top–placed teams) and the EUFA Cup for top-placed teams that don't qualify for the Champions League and domestic cup winners.

The English football league is among the most competitive in the world and even matches between teams from the top and bottom of divisions are usually keenly contested. English teams have had considerable success in Europe over the last few decades, despite the fact that top English clubs usually play many more matches than clubs in most other European countries (although league matches were reduced in 1995). The points scoring system in the English league differs from that in most countries, three points being awarded for a win (instead of two) in order to discourage negative defensive football at away matches (it works). However, other countries have adopted this points system in recent years.

A number of controversial changes have been made to the rules in the last few years, including frequent changes to what constitutes a foul tackle. Although generally of a high standard, many referees seem to play by their own rules and some appear bent on ruining the sport by booking (yellow card) and sending off (red card) players for trivial offences. British referees are generally much harsher than those in other European countries. The latest 'fashion' is booking players who appear to 'take a dive' in the penalty area – if it happened in Italy or Spain there would be nobody except the goalkeepers on the field after ten minutes!

RUGBY

There are two separate codes of rugby (or rugby football) in Britain, rugby union and rugby league. The main difference between the codes is that rugby union (which has always been strictly amateur) plays with teams of 15 players and rugby league, which is played by both amateurs and professionals, has 13 players to a team (two less to pay). However, after a momentous decision by the International Rugby Football Board in 1995, Rugby Union is now a professional sport. This was brought about mainly because rugby union was in danger of losing its best players to new rival professional organisations (and to Rugby League) and the fact that many countries (Britain excepted) have been paying their top union stars for years.

Union is played in all regions of Britain and has a wider following than rugby league, with the top clubs in England playing in the Allied Dunbar Premiership (14 teams). Club rugby has been losing its appeal in recent years and has lurched from crisis to crisis amid falling attendances and a looming funding crisis. England, Scotland, Wales and Ireland compete each year for the rugby union Triple Crown. The home nations also compete with France (and Italy in the 1999/2000 season) for the Grand Slam, which is won by the team who wins all their matches. The annual

England versus Scotland fixture is contested for the Calcutta Cup. Rugby Union is also played internationally at the highest level by Australia (the Wallabies), New Zealand (the All Blacks) and South Africa (the Springboks) and at a lower level by many other nations (such as Argentina, Fiji and Western Samoa). The Courage Clubs Championship is the national rugby union club competition and consists of five divisions of 13 teams, with most matches being played on Saturdays.

Rugby league is played professionally in Britain, mainly by teams in the north of England who compete in the Super League and the Rugby League Challenge Cup, the final of which is played at Wembley stadium in London. There are also many amateur rugby league teams for players of all ages, including a number of teams in the London area. Rugby league is played internationally by Great Britain, Australia, New Zealand, France and Papua New Guinea. Most towns, schools and universities have rugby teams competing in local league and cup competitions, in one or both rugby codes.

CRICKET

Cricket is a peculiarly English sport which usually takes foreigners some time to understand (many British also don't understand the finer points, including your author). If you don't know the difference between a stump and a bail, or an over and a wicket, you may as well skip this bit, as any attempt to explain would take around 100 pages and almost certainly end in failure. The first-class cricket season in England runs from April to September, when the main competition is for the Brittanic Assurance County Championship, competed for by 18 county teams. Matches are played over four days, many of which are drawn, due to the vagaries of English weather. In addition to the County Championship, county teams also compete in the AXA Equity & Law Sunday League, where limited-over matches are played in one day.

Counties also compete in two, one-day knockout competitions: the National Westminster Bank Trophy and the Benson and Hedges Cup (the final of which is played at Lord's, the home of English cricket). In addition to the first-class County Championship, there's also a Minor Counties Championship (Eastern and Western Divisions) and a Second XI Championship. There are also a multitude of senior leagues, local village teams, school teams, university teams, pub teams and women's teams, who compete regularly at all levels throughout England. Scotland and Ireland also have cricket teams, although they (wisely) don't take the game seriously. There's also an England ladies cricket team (who have a hard job getting anyone to take them seriously) and the game is played at all levels by women and girls throughout Britain. For those who wish to play with a straighter bat or brush up on their googly technique, there are cricket schools and coaching courses in many areas.

Cricket is also played at international level (called test matches) by a number of Commonwealth countries including Australia, India, New Zealand, Pakistan, South Africa, Sri Lanka, the West Indies and Zimbabwe. During the English cricket season the England cricket team is usually engaged (i.e. getting beat) in one or two minor series of international matches (three tests) or a major series (five or six tests). If you think four days (county matches) is a long time for a single match to last, a test match lasts five days, usually with a rest day after two or three days play. One-day internationals are also played. The England cricket team also conducts overseas tours during the English winter, when they play a series of test matches. The old enemy (in cricketing terms) is the Aussies (Australians), with whom England compete every few years for the Ashes (not human, but from an old cricket bail). A world cup knockout competition also takes place every four or five years. For an introduction to the delights of cricket for foreigners, see **Chapter 19**.

SNOOKER & BILLIARDS

Snooker is a highly popular sport in Britain and most large towns boast at least one snooker or billiards club and many hotels, bars and sports clubs also have snooker tables. Snooker clubs, most with bars and many also with restaurants, often open from around 1000 to 2400 daily. In the last few decades the popularity of snooker has increased tremendously, due mainly to the success of televised championships. These have transformed what was once a minority sport with a seedy image into a successful national sport with a huge following (it's estimated that around eight million people play the game in Britain). Professional competitions are now held throughout the world and the top players are millionaire celebrities. It's also played increasingly by women (who also play professionally), who make up a large part of TV audiences.

Billiards is waning in popularity in Britain, although it still enjoys considerable popularity throughout the world. American pool is also played quite widely in Britain, although it's very much the poor cousin of snooker and to a lesser extent billiards. A game called 8-ball is commonly played in pubs, where teams compete in local leagues, and bar billiards is also popular.

MOTORSPORTS

Motor racing has a huge following in Britain and embraces everything from Formula One grand prix racing to stock car racing. Among the many classes of motor racing in Britain are Formula One, Two and Three; Formula 3000; sports car; rallying; Formula Ford; hill-climbing; historic sports cars; special one-make series (such as TVR, Renault 5, Maxda MX-5 and Honda CRX to name but a few); autocross; go karts; and bantam racing for the kids. The most famous motor racing venues in Britain are Brands Hatch and Silverstone, host to the British Grand Prix, which is part of the World Motor Racing Championship. The British Grand Prix is one of Britain's most expensive sporting events, with tickets costing from £60 to £125. Regular race meetings are also held at Caldwell Park, Castle Combe, Donington Park, Oulton Park, Snetterton and Thruxton Park. National hot rods, saloon stock cars and banger racing are also popular among the young (which some practice on Britain's public roads) and meetings are held on most Saturdays during the main season, which runs from April to October at stadiums throughout Britain.

Motorcycle racing is also popular in Britain and includes grand prix racing at 125cc, 250cc, 350cc, 500cc and superbikes over 1,000cc. The most famous (or infamous) circuit in Britain is the Isle of Man Tourist Trophy circuit, which because it's a road circuit lacks the safety aspects (and fast-acting emergency services) of purpose built circuits, that has led to the deaths of many riders in recent years. Other forms of motorcycling with a large following in Britain are side-car racing, speedway, scrambling and moto-cross. Speedway is held at stadiums around Britain from March to August. There are a number of magazines dedicated to motorsports in Britain.

SKIING

Skiing is a popular sport with the British, despite the fact that there are only a few ski resorts in the British Isles (in Scotland), which are hardly sufficient to cater for the around two million British skiers. Scottish ski centres include Aonach Mor, Cairngorms (Aviemore), Glencoe, Glenshee and Lecht. However, for most British skiers, skiing in Scotland is of little interest and isn't a viable alternative to a skiing holiday in the Alps or North America. In comparison with the Alps, Scotland suffers from a lack of atmosphere, and skiing conditions early in the season are unpredictable, with storms and strong winds often causing lifts to be closed and badly affecting snow conditions. The best time to ski in Scotland is generally late in the season, from March to May.

The British, however, have made up for the lack of snow (and mountains) with dry-slope skiing, of which there are around 150 centres in Britain (more than in any other country), catering for over 350,000 skiers a year. In addition to being an excellent training ground for the 'real thing', dry-slope skiing has become a popular sport in its own right. Most centres have a ski racing team and dry-slope races are held regularly throughout the year. Learning to ski on a dry-slope can save you both time and money when you arrive in a winter resort, and also helps experienced skiers find their ski-legs before arriving in a winter resort. A dry-slope consists of around 2,000 square metres of ski matting, usually with separate areas for beginners and advanced skiers. The maximum descent of 'pistes' is around 500 metres, although most are 200 to 300 metres. Poma or button ski tows (or even a chair lift) are usually provided and floodlights are provided for evening skiing in the winter. Most centres are council run or commercial ventures, although a few have been built by enthusiasts themselves.

You should use your own ski boots (they can also be hired) and wear old clothes, as the matting can damage expensive ski suits. Gloves are usually compulsory. Don't use good skis as they don't take kindly to the artificial surface and make sure that the bindings of hired skis are adjusted to your weight and ability. Equipment hire is usually included in the hourly rate, which varies considerably. Many centres offer weekly and season tickets which are usually good value for money. It's best to ski at quiet times, as centres can get extremely crowded at weekends, particularly towards Christmas when everyone is keen to get in a bit of practice before heading off to the Alps. Tuition is provided at all levels for both adults and children, although off-piste skiing isn't catered for! A six-hour course costs from around £25 to £50, depending on the centre. Skiing can also be practised indoors in Britain on a new type of artificial snow, which really feels like the real thing. Skiers at a loose end in the summer might also like to try grass skiing, which is quite popular in Britain.

If you're looking for a book about learning or improving your skiing, the Sunday Times book *We Learned to Ski* (Collins) is an excellent choice for all standards. A number of ski magazines are published in Britain. The Daily Mail International Ski Show is held at Earls Court in November, where all the latest equipment and clothing is on display (which manufacturers would like you to replace annually at least).

CYCLING

Cycling isn't very popular in Britain compared with the continent and only around 1 per cent of journeys are made by bicycle in Britain compared to an average of 15 per cent in Europe. However, although cycling isn't particularly popular in Britain, over 1.5 million cycles are sold each year (over a third bought to replace stolen machines!), which adds up to an awful lot of cyclists. Most people in Britain buy cycles for shopping or getting around towns, rather than cycling purely for pleasure, exercise or sport (e.g. touring or racing). Competitive cycling includes road and track racing, cycle speedway, time-trialling, cross-country racing, touring, bicycle polo and bicycle moto-cross.

A wide range of cycles are available to suit all pockets and needs, ranging from a basic shopping bike costing around £75 to a professional racing bike costing £thousands. In between these extremes are commuter or town bikes, touring bikes, mountain bikes, BMX bikes, tricycles, tandems and bicycles with folding frames. Before buying a bike, carefully consider your needs both now and in the future, obtain expert advice (e.g. from a specialist cycle store) and shop around for the best deal. Make sure you purchase a bike with the correct frame size. Mountain bikes have become increasingly popular in recent years and cost from around £100 up to £4,000 (expect to pay around £200 to £300 for an adequate bike).

Bicycles can also be hired by the day or week from cycle shops in cities and tourist areas; costs vary considerably but are usually from around £3 to £10 a day depending on the type of bike (town, touring or mountain) and the area. Tandems, tricycles and folding bikes can also be hired in some areas. There may be lower rates for children and for weekly rental. Ask at local tourist information centres or check the local Yellow Pages. Make sure a hired bicycle is insured against theft or damage.

Apart from cycling to work or into town, cycling is an excellent way to explore the countryside at your leisure and get some fresh air and exercise at the same time. Note, however, that fresh air is in short supply in Britain's polluted cities, where many cyclists wear face-masks as protection against traffic pollution (although, according to medical experts, they offer little or no protection against carbon monoxide). The increasing popularity of cycling in recent years has led to an increase in the number of accidents with motor vehicles. It's important never to underestimate the dangers of cycling (particularly for children) on Britain's overcrowded roads, as many cyclists are killed and injured each year. British motorists don't respect cyclists as much as they do in most continental countries and cyclists in Britain are ten times more likely to be involved in an accident than those in (for example) Denmark. Helmets are essential attire, particularly for children, as is reflective clothing and bright (preferably flashing) lights at night.

There are few off-road cycle paths in Britain, although a decision was made in 1995 to build a national network of 8,000km (5,000mi) of dedicated cycling paths at a cost of £42.5m, to be partly funded with by the National Lottery 'Millennium Fund'. Radical measures have been put forward to promote cycling in an effort to reduce traffic congestion and pollution on Britain's roads. Some towns and cities plan to solve (or ease) their traffic problems by introducing cycle priority routes, including traffic light priority, lock-up parking and even changing rooms for wet cyclists.

If you're interested in joining a cycling club your local library should have information about local clubs or you can contact the British Cycling Federation, 36 Rockingham Road, Kettering, Northants NN16 8HG (☎ 01536-412211). Keen cyclists may be interested in joining the Cyclists Touring Club (CTC), Cotterell House, 69 Meadrow, Godalming, Surrey GU7 3HS (☎ 014868-7217), which is Britain's national cyclists association with over 200 local groups throughout Britain.

The CTC actively campaign for the rights and safety of cyclists on the road and publish an excellent free booklet, *Positive Cycling*. Membership includes free third party insurance, legal aid, technical advice, touring information and a bimonthly magazine. The CTC also operates a bicycle insurance scheme.

A handbook is published for young cyclists entitled *Keep on the Safe Side* (The Stationery Office) and an interesting book for those who live in the London area is *On Your Bike*, published by the London Cycling Campaign, Tress House, 3 Stamford Street, London SE1 (☎ 0171-928 7220). Other useful books include *Richard's New Bicycle Book* by Richard Ballantine (Pan), which is a guide to choosing and using a bicycle and *The Penguin Book of the Bike* (Penguin). Ordnance Survey publish a series of excellent *Cycle Tours*. Local cycling guides and maps are published by councils, conservation and cycling groups in many areas, who also publish safety booklets and brochures for children. Around 15 magazines are published for cyclists in Britain.

HIKING

Whether you call it walking, rambling, hiking or orienteering, getting from A to B for fun and pleasure (as opposed to not being able to afford a bus or train ticket) is extremely popular in Britain and is the most common form of exercise (what's more it's free!). In England and Wales there's a total network of over 217,000km (135,000mi) of public footpaths, bridleways (a path fit for riders but not vehicles) and byways, which is more than in any other country in the world. Many paths have been joined together to form continuous well marked, long-distance routes or national trails, as they are known in England and Wales. In Scotland the law differs, although walkers there generally have an absolute right of access to uncultivated land, unless there's proven danger to walkers or wildlife.

Public rights of way grew up as part of the ancient communications system in use long before any form of transport was invented, and landowners must, by law, give walkers the right of passage across their land. Which is fine in theory. Recent campaigns by walkers have led to clashes with landowners and farmers, some of whom will go to any lengths to deny walkers access to their land. The government has reluctantly decided that the Country Landowners Association and its 50,000 members (who are estimated to own over half of the countryside in England and Wales) will never allow access to their land voluntarily. Legislation will now be introduced to open up millions of acres of countryside to hikers under a new 'right to roam' law.

In addition to the thousands of miles of public footpaths, there are 11 national parks in England and Wales which were established to protect Britain's finest landscapes from rabid developers (who see every plot of land as a potential dumping ground for an unsightly apartment block) and provide people with the opportunity to use and enjoy the open countryside. The land within the national parks remains largely in private ownership and visitors should walk only where access is permitted and should respect the life and work of those who live there. There are no national parks in Scotland (the whole of which is practically a national park), which has 40 national scenic areas and offers some of the most beautiful and unspoilt walking country in Europe.

Hiking paths are signposted (or waymarked as it's called in 'hiking talk') by signs showing the destination and sometimes the distance. In England and Wales national trails are waymarked with an acorn symbol. In Scotland long-distance footpaths are waymarked by a thistle symbol. The footpaths and rights of way in Britain are often poorly signposted (signposts are often deliberately destroyed by landowners) and away from national trails part of your time may be spent searching for the path. When following a path you should look out for waymarks and use a map (see below). In England and Wales, paths are often signposted where they join roads, but many footpaths or tracks may be indicated only by arrows (yellow for footpaths, blue for bridleways and red for byways) or by special markers if the path is used as a recreational route. A map is essential when using trails without waymarks.

Orienteering is popular in Britain and is a combination of hiking and a treasure hunt or competitive navigation on foot. It isn't necessary to be super fit and the only equipment that's required (in addition to suitable walking attire) is a special detailed map and a compass. For information contact the British Orienteering Federation, Riversdale, Dale Road North, Darley Dale, Matlock, Derbyshire DE4 2HX (☎ 01629-734042). If you're interested in joining a walking club contact the Ramblers Association, 1-5 Wandsworth Road, London SW8 2XX (☎ 0171-582 6878), which promotes rambling, protects rights of way, campaigns for access to open country and defends the beauty of the countryside. It has over 300 local groups throughout Britain and members receive a quarterly magazine, a yearbook, equipment discounts, free membership of their local ramblers group and the opportunity to participate in numerous walks guided by experienced leaders.

General information about walking in Britain is provided in a BTA leaflet entitled *Walking in Britain*, which also contains a list of companies who organise guided walking holidays. An excellent book for keen walkers is *The Good Walks Guide* by Tim Locke (Which? Books). In many towns and country areas, guided local walks are conducted throughout the year (which may be part of a comprehensive programme of walks), ranging from sightseeing tours of towns to walks around local beauty spots, for which there may be a small fee. Walks are usually graded, e.g. easy, moderate or strenuous, and dogs can usually be taken unless otherwise stated. Ask for information at tourist information centres or local libraries.

MOUNTAINEERING, ROCK-CLIMBING & CAVING

Those who find walking a bit tame might like to try abseiling, rock-climbing, mountaineering, caving or pot-holing (subterranean mountaineering). They are also an ideal training ground for social climbers and yuppies who are willing to risk life and limb to get to the top. Britain has a distinguished record in international mountain climbing and few mountains in the world haven't been climbed at some time by British mountaineers, often for the first time. If you're an inexperienced climber you would be well advised to join a climbing club (over 300 are affiliated to the British Mountaineering Council) before heading for the hills. There are climbing schools in all the main climbing areas of Britain and many local clubs have special indoor training apparatus (e.g. a climbing wall) for aspiring mountaineers. Some sports and leisure centres also provide facilities for climbing training.

Note that a number of climbers, cavers and pot-holers are killed each year in Britain (mostly in Scotland), many of whom are inexperienced and reckless. Many more owe their survival to rescuers who risk their own lives to rescue them. **It's extremely foolish, not to mention highly dangerous, to venture off into the hills** (or holes) without an experienced guide, proper preparation, excellent physical condition, sufficient training and the appropriate equipment.

Mountain, fell or hill-walking shouldn't be confused with 'ordinary' hiking (see page 405), as it's generally done at much higher altitudes and in more difficult terrain, and should be attempted only with a qualified leader. It can be dangerous for the untrained or inexperienced and should be approached with much the same degree of caution and preparation as climbing. The Royal Air Force provides a helicopter rescue service for those who get lost or stuck on mountains. A good map is vital for those who venture into remote areas. Ordnance Survey maps, available in both 1:25 and 1:50 sizes, are highly recommended and are available from bookshops, newsagents and leisure shops.

Many adventure holiday companies provide tailor-made holidays for climbers or cavers including equipment, tuition, transport and accommodation. For information ask the BTA or tourist information centres. There are a number of climbing magazines in Britain, including *Climber and Hillwalker*. For information about climbing in Britain contact the British Mountaineering Council, Crawford House, Precinct Centre, Booth Street, East Manchester M13 9RZ (☎ 0161-273 5835).

RACQUET SPORTS

There are excellent facilities in Britain for most racquet sports, particularly badminton, squash, racquetball and tennis. There are two main types of racquet sport centres in Britain: public sports and leisure centres (see page 397), and private clubs. Many sports and leisure centres have around six squash (also used for racquetball) and six badminton courts. Some centres have indoor tennis courts, although these aren't usually permanently available as halls are used for other sports. There are also private clubs for most racquet sports, particularly squash and tennis. Court fees are reasonable although annual membership fees may be high. Some private clubs are highly exclusive and it's difficult to join unless you have excellent connections, pots of money or are very famous. If you're an advanced player, you may find the level of competition is higher at private clubs than at community sports and leisure centres. Racquet sport leagues and competitions are also organised by many companies and schools, some of which have their own courts.

Tennis: Despite the popularity of tennis as a spectator sport in Britain (particularly Wimbledon), actually *playing* tennis isn't so popular, largely because it isn't much fun playing in the cold and rain. Indoor tennis courts are relatively scarce and prohibitively expensive, and are a necessity in the depths of a British winter. More indoor courts are, however, being built all the time. The cost of hiring an indoor tennis court at a sports centre (if possible) is from £10 to £15 an hour, depending on the time of day (short tennis on a reduced size court can also be played in some sports centres). Most local councils and some private sports centres provide a number of outdoor hard and grass courts (clay courts aren't common in Britain), which can be hired for £2 to £4 an hour (adults) or from around £1 or £2 an hour for under 16s. Some centres have outdoor courts with artificial surfaces which can be used in all weathers and some parks and most sports centres have floodlit outdoor courts. There may be a nominal membership fee of around £5 to use some municipal courts.

If you're a serious tennis player you may be interested in joining a private club. Costs vary but can be high, e.g. a £150 enrolment fee plus a £250 annual subscription (or a monthly fee of around £25) for single membership of an exclusive tennis club, with both indoor and outdoor courts. Many private clubs also have gymnasiums and swimming pools, that can be used by members for an increased enrolment and annual fee. Special rates are usually available for couples and families. Sports centres and private clubs usually have coaches available for both private and group lessons. National, county and local tennis competitions are held at all levels for both sexes.

Squash: Squash (or more correctly squash rackets) is the most popular racquet sport in Britain (and the second largest participant sport after fishing) and there's an abundance of courts in sports centres and private squash clubs in all areas. There are around 9,000 squash courts in Britain accommodating some three million players. The standard is high and although it's many years since Britain had a world champion, the average club standard is among the highest in the world. Private squash clubs usually cater exclusively for squash, and clubs combining squash and tennis (or other sports) are rare. Many private squash clubs have a resident coach, providing both individual and group lessons.

The cost of hiring a court in a sports centre is from around £4 to £5 for a 40 or 45 minute session or £6 to £7.50 an hour. Off-peak (before 1700) fees may be around £3 or £4 for 45 minutes (students and the unemployed are entitled to use council facilities for half price during off-peak hours in some areas). Annual membership of a private squash club varies from about £50 to £100 a year; off-peak, family and junior membership may also be available. Court fees are usually about the same or a little lower than for municipal courts, although there may be an extra charge for guests. Racquetball, the American version of squash, is played in Britain on a squash court and racquets and balls can be hired from most squash clubs.

Squash is an energetic sport and you should think twice about taking it up in middle age, particularly if you're unfit, have high blood pressure or a heart or respiratory problem. Around 50 per cent of all sports deaths in Britain occur on squash courts! Players of any age should get fit to play squash and shouldn't play squash to become fit. Doctors recommend that players don't take a sauna after a squash game, which can be dangerous as it increases the heart rate and body temperature. Tennis or badminton are a better choice for the middle aged, as they aren't as frenetic as squash and encourage oxygen to enter the body (although singles badminton can be a hard slog). Badminton is an extremely popular sport in Britain with an estimated 2.5 million players and is more popular than tennis. Most badminton facilities are provided by public sports and community centres and private clubs are rare. The cost of hiring a badminton court in a sports centre is around £5 or £6 an hour or around £3 an hour at off-peak times.

Court costs for all racket sports are usually cheaper before 1700 and after 1700 at weekends, although lunch-time periods may be charged at peak rates for some sports, e.g. squash. Courts in public sports and leisure centres can be booked up to two weeks in advance, while private clubs may allow bookings to be made further in advance. You must usually cancel a booked court 24 or 48 hours in advance, otherwise you must pay for it if it isn't re-booked. Rackets, shoes and towels can usually be hired (or purchased) from both public sports centres and private clubs. Most sports centres and private clubs organise internal leagues, ladders and knockout competitions, and also participate in local and national league and cup competitions.

Table Tennis: Finally a few words for table tennis fans (which is almost a racquet sport). Table tennis is popular in Britain and is played both as a serious competitive sport and as a pastime in social and youth clubs. Most sports centres have a number of table tennis tables for hire at around £2 an hour and bats can be hired for a small fee. If you want to play seriously there are clubs in most areas. Costs vary, but it's an inexpensive sport with little equipment necessary.

Many private sports clubs hold residential coaching holidays throughout the year. The BTA publish a leaflet about residential badminton, squash, table tennis and tennis holidays in Britain, and information can also be obtained from travel agents and tourist information centres. To find the racquet clubs in your local area look in the Yellow Pages, enquire at your local library or contact the appropriate national association.

SWIMMING

There are public heated indoor and outdoor swimming pools in most towns in Britain, many located in leisure and sports centres (see page 397). You can also swim at numerous beaches, but should note that only some 100 British beaches are given the blessing of the Marine Conservation Society (listed in the *Reader's Digest Good Beach Guide* which includes surveys of over 700 beaches). There has been much improvement in recent years and around 400 beaches pass the European Union mandatory standards each year, although around 50 are still officially polluted (often by sewage). There are no-smoking beaches in some resorts!

The temperature of indoor pools is generally maintained at 23 to 30°C (74 to 80°F). Many centres have both a main pool and a teaching pool, often with a waterslide (jet slide, water chute), flumes, wave machine, whirlpool or waterfall – great fun for kids, both young and old (i.e. adults). Some centres provide diving boards at certain times and paddling pools for toddlers. Many pools also have sunbeds, saunas, solariums and Jacuzzis. Separate sessions are arranged for various groups and ages, including early morning swimming, lane swimming, diving, senior citizens, mums & babies, over 25's, school holidays, off-peak sessions and aqua-aerobics. Aqua-natal sessions for expectant or post-natal mothers are also organised at some sports centres.

Pools are usually very busy at weekends and on public holidays and it's best to go during the week if you can. If you're going along for a general swim, check in advance whether the pool has been booked for a special session. The cost is usually from £1.50 to £2.50 for adults and £1 to £1.50 for juniors under 16 and senior citizens. There are usually reduced rates for family groups. Most centres provide annual season tickets, e.g. £75 to £100 a year, allowing you to swim at any time. Often swimming season tickets can be combined with another sport, e.g. squash. Some swimming sessions are reserved for members of a leisure or sports centre and some public pools provide closed weekly sessions for naturists and those who cannot afford bathing costumes.

Before entrusting your children to the care of some swimming pools, you should check the safety standards, as they vary considerably and some are unsafe (public pools must have adequate lifeguard cover). This also applies to beaches, many of which fail to meet basic safety standards due to a lack of emergency equipment, lifeguards and warning flags. Most sports and leisure centres provide swimming lessons (all levels from beginner to fish) and run 'improver' and life-saving courses. Swimming courses for children are usually held during term times or at weekends.

WATERSPORTS

All watersports including sailing, windsurfing, water-skiing, rowing, power-boating, canoeing, surfing and subaquatic sports are popular in Britain, which is hardly surprising considering it's surrounded by water and has hundreds of inland lakes and rivers where watersports can be enjoyed. Boats and equipment can be hired at coastal resorts, lakes and rivers, and instruction is available for most watersports in holiday areas. Jet skis and surf skis can also be hired in an increasing number of resorts.

There are around 500 rowing clubs in Britain and over 300 rowing regattas, the most famous of which is the Henley Regatta. The University Boat Race (inaugurated in 1836), between eight-oared crews from Cambridge and Oxford universities at Easter is the most famous rowing race in the world (it's shown live on TV). Canoeing for children is sometimes taught in indoor swimming pools in winter. Budding canoeists must be able to swim 50 metres before being admitted to a canoe club and the wearing of life jackets is compulsory.

Wetsuits are almost mandatory for surfing, windsurfing, water-skiing and subaquatic sports even during the summer months (the water is freezing in and around Britain at almost any time of the year) and can be hired in some areas. Surfing is popular in Britain and is centred around Newquay in Cornwall, which has staged a number of world-class events. Note, however, that pollution is one of the biggest problems for watersports (such as surfing) enthusiasts off Britain's coastline, and ear infections and stomach complaints are common among surfers. Scuba diving is another popular sport in Britain. Participants must pass a medical examination and undergo an approved training course to obtain the PADI open water diving certificate. Courses are run at many swimming pools and cost around £300. Note that equipment can cost hundreds or even thousands of pounds, although secondhand equipment is available. The season runs from April to September, with the best areas in the British Isles including Cornwall and the Scilly Isles.

Sailing has always been popular in Britain, which has a history of producing famous sailors, from Sir Francis Drake to Sir Francis Chichester. There are sailing clubs (around 1,500) and schools in all areas of Britain, and boats of all shapes and sizes can be hired from ocean-going racing yachts to dinghies (if you don't like water, there are land yachts). In recent years there has been a marina boom in the south-east and if you're a sailing enthusiast it's possible to purchase a home where you can moor your yacht outside your front door. Note that many inland lakes have a maximum speed limit of 16kph (10mph). There has been a huge increase in stolen boats and equipment in the last few years (outboard motors, navigational and other electronic equipment are the most popular targets). Ensure you have good security and adequate insurance for your boat. The BTA publish a leaflet about residential watersport holidays in Britain, which include canoeing, power-boating, rafting, sailing, surfing, water-skiing and windsurfing. A large number of magazines (over 20) in Britain are dedicated to boating and yachting plus over ten more about assorted wtersports.

No experience, tests, safety training or equipment is required to take to the waters in and around Britain, and many people needlessly risk their lives and carry no safety equipment such as flares, life jackets or radios. Don't get caught unprepared and be sure to observe all warning signs on waterways.

AERIAL SPORTS

Most aerial sports have a wide following in Britain, particularly gliding, hang-gliding, paragliding, hot-air ballooning and microlighting. The main thing most aerial sports enthusiasts have in common is madness and money, both of which are essential in liberal doses in order to fulfil man's ultimate ambition. Hang-gliding has become increasingly popular in Britain in recent years and there are hang-gliding schools in all regions. Paragliding or parascending, is the cheapest and easiest way to fly, and entails 'simply' jumping off a steep mountain slope with a parachute or being tow-launched by a vehicle or a boat. When you've gained enough height, you release the tow and float off on your own (or come crashing back to earth). Although generally safer than hang-gliding, paragliding can be dangerous or even lethal in the wrong hands. Paragliders must complete an approved course of instruction lasting around four days, after which (if you survive) you receive an F1 'licence' that allows you to purchase a paraglider and fly when supervised by an experienced pilot. Paragliding equipment costs from around £500 secondhand to £2,000 new.

Hot-air ballooning has a small but dedicated band of followers in Britain, the most famous of whom is Richard Branson (the owner of the Virgin group of companies). Participation is generally limited to the wealthy due to the high cost of a balloon, although the sport has never enjoyed greater popularity. To buy a balloon costs anything from £10,000 to £50,000, plus £100 an hour to fly it and over £1,000 annual insurance (it's the only form of transport more expensive and less reliable than Britain's railways). Lawyers and politicians usually get a reduction for supplying their own hot air. A flight in a balloon costs around £100 and is a marvellous experience, although there's no guarantee of distance or duration and flights are dependent on wind conditions and the skill of your pilot (not to mention a safe landing).

Aircraft and gliders (sailplanes) can be hired with or without an instructor (providing you have a pilot's licence) from most small airfields in Britain. A new plane can cost anything from £40,000 to £100,000, although shared ownership schemes are bringing the joys of flying to a much wider audience. There are many gliding clubs in Britain and parachuting and free-fall parachuting (sky-diving) flights can be made from most private airfields. The latest American craze to have taken off (literally) in Britain is the microlight (or ultralight), a low-flying go-cart with a hang glider on top and a motorised tricycle below. Microlights are designed to carry a maximum of two people and can be stored in a garage. Most machines are strong and safe, and the sport has a good safety record. It's one of the cheapest and most enjoyable ways of experiencing real flying, costing from around £3,500 for a secondhand machine up to £25,000 for a new top-of-the-range craft. Fliers require a private pilot's licence that costs around £500 in tuition fees and normally takes up to three months and 40 hours instruction to obtain.

Note that most aerial sports or private aviation are specifically excluded from many insurance policies, including, for example, health insurance and mortgage life insurance policies. Before taking up any aerial sport, you should ensure you have adequate health and accident insurance, that you have sufficient life insurance and that your affairs are in order. Why not take up fishing instead? A nice, sensible, SAFE sport (not that the fish would agree).

FISHING

Fishing (or angling) facilities in Britain are superb and fishing is the biggest participant sport in the country, with around four million participants (the numbers are rising by 20 per cent each decade). There are a huge variety of well-stocked waters and some of the best salmon and trout (brown, sea and rainbow) fishing in the world. In addition to the many rivers and lakes (or lochs in Scotland), trout fishing is possible at over 160 reservoirs. Scotland is world-famous for its salmon fishing (and its scotch).

There are three types of fishing in Britain: sea, game and coarse fishing. Sea fishing is simply fishing in the open sea, while game fishing takes place at specially constructed fisheries stocked with trout or salmon. Coarse fishing is the most popular form of fishing and is common in designated rivers or man-made waters for many species of fish including bream, carp, perch, pike and tench. Coarse fishermen use live bait such as maggots and worms, and none of the fish caught are killed but are returned to the water. The close season, which is the period when fishing isn't permitted, varies for different species of fish and between the various River Authorities who are responsible for recreational fishing. **Always check when the close season is before fishing anywhere in Britain.**

In England and Wales you must obtain a fishing permit (called a rod licence), which usually costs around £10 a year or season and is issued by the National Rivers Authority of the area where you plan to fish. Licences are obtainable from fishing tackle suppliers, hotels and post offices in most areas. Once you have obtained a rod licence you must obtain permission to fish from the owner of the water, which usually entails paying a membership fee or buying a ticket (a day permit costs around £2 a day in some areas). In some ponds or lakes, fishing may be free. Deep-sea and coastal fishing are free, apart from sea trout and salmon fishing, which is by licence only. For information on river fishing, contact the information officer of the appropriate National Rivers Authority. In some areas, 24-hour recorded telephone information is provided about fishing conditions and river levels, and fishing platforms are provided for disabled anglers. Ask at tourist information centres for information.

Rod licences aren't required in Scotland, although written permission must be obtained from the water's owner to fish for salmon or sea trout or to fish in freshwater for other fish. Each district in Scotland has its own close season for salmon fishing, which is generally from the end of August to the end of February. Information regarding permits can be obtained from local tourist information centres. In Northern Ireland, a licence is required for each rod for game fishing, which is issued by the Foyle Fisheries Commission or the Fisheries Conservancy Board, depending on the area. Permission to fish is also required from the owner of the water, usually through short term membership or by buying a ticket.

When sea fishing from the shore (e.g. from rocks) be careful where you position yourself, as in some areas it's possible to be swept out to sea and drowned. Note that you should be wary of eating fish caught in some of Britain's rivers, as the level of pollution could be harmful to your health, to say nothing of what it does to the poor fish – if they could talk they might plead with you not to throw them back! However, many estuaries and rivers have been cleaned up in recent years and wildlife is returning, some of which hasn't been seen for decades.

The BTA publish an annual booklet, *Game Fishing Holidays*, containing an introduction to game fishing in Britain, a list of hotels and inns with private fishing, fisheries and fishing holiday organisers. No less than 25 monthly or bimonthly magazines for anglers are published in Britain.

GOLF

There are around three million golfers and 2,000 courses, including private and practice courses, in Britain. Golf was Britain's fastest-growing sport in the '80s, although it was over-developed and many golf courses built in the last decade or so (around 600) are struggling to survive and many are on the market far below the cost price. Scotland, where golf originated in the 15th century, has many of Britain's most beautiful courses (including links courses) and no less than seven world-famous championship courses. In Britain there are public (municipal) and private courses, and although golf is a relatively expensive sport, you don't have to be a millionaire to play (unless you spend all day at the 19th hole). No membership is required to play on a public golf course, although it's advisable to book in advance. Note that in some areas there are no or few public courses and private clubs may allow visitors to play during weekdays only, providing they're members of a club and can produce a handicap certificate.

It isn't necessary to purchase a set of clubs as they can be hired for around £5 for 18 holes. Second-hand beginner's sets of clubs can be purchased for as little as £50 or from around £100 new, while full new sets start at around £200. It isn't necessary to buy all the latest golf clothes emblazoned with famous names (which simply serve to make you look even more of a twit if you cannot play). Green fees (the cost of a round) are reasonable at most public golf clubs, averaging around £5 to £8 per round (18 holes), although fees at top private courses are from between £25 and £45 (£35 to £55 a day). Fees are usually increased by around 20 to 25 per cent at weekends and on public holidays. There are reduced green fees for 9-hole courses and many municipal courses have reduced fees for juniors (e.g. under 18s). Fees may be reduced in winter.

The top private golf clubs are often difficult and expensive to join, and there's sometimes huge snob appeal attached to belonging to a fashionable club, which won't usually allow the peasants to join (except perhaps as caddies or if they have a low handicap) even if they win £millions on the National Lottery. However, membership at most clubs is available from around £500 to £3,000 a year. Private clubs usually have strict dress rules and don't allow jeans or t-shirts on the course (players are also requested to observe golf etiquette and not to strike their opponents or dig holes in the greens). Many private golf clubs are part of a larger country club or hotel sports complex, where facilities may include a luxury hotel, restaurant, bar, tennis, squash, swimming pool, snooker and clay pigeon shooting.

Many golf clubs have golf nets and covered driving ranges, and most also have professionals (instructors) to help reduce your number of lost balls (beware of courses with lots of water, which have a voracious appetite for golf balls). Driving ranges are also provided in most areas with all-weather floodlit bays, practice bunkers and putting greens. The big advantage of a driving range (apart from the reasonable cost of around £2 for a basket of 50 balls) is that you don't need to go and find your balls in the undergrowth or buy new ones when they land in the water.

Crazy golf, approach golf, pitch and putt, and putting greens (e.g. in public parks) are available in most areas for those who set their sights a little lower than winning The Open. The BTA publish an annual booklet, *Golfing Holidays*, containing a list of golf events in Britain, hotels and inns with golf, and golf holiday organisers. Many golf books are published including the *Golf Yearbook*, which contains a list of public courses, the AA/Gore-Tex *Guide to Golf Courses in Britain*, which contains details of over 1,600 golf courses, the *Benson & Hedges Golf Year* (Partridge Press), which contains a complete list of all golf clubs in Britain and Ireland, and the Sunday Telegraph *Golf Guide to Britain and Ireland*.

GYMNASIUMS & HEALTH CLUBS

There are gymnasiums and health and fitness clubs in most towns in Britain, where sadists are employed and masochists go to torture themselves. Working out is becoming increasingly popular and many companies provide health and leisure centres or pay for corporate membership for staff. In addition to many private clubs, most public sports and leisure centres have tonnes of expensive bone-jarring, muscle-wrenching apparatus, designed either to get you into shape or kill you in the attempt. Middle-aged 'fatties' shouldn't attempt to get fit in five minutes (after all it took years of dedicated sloth and over-eating to put on all that weight), as overexertion can result in serious sports injuries. A good gymnasium or health club will ensure this doesn't happen and will carry out a physical assessment including a blood pressure test, fat distribution measurements and heart rate checks. In your rush to become one of the body beautiful it pays to take the long route and give the intensive care unit (or mortuary) a wide berth.

Most sports and leisure centres (see page 397) have a health & fitness club or circuit training and exercise rooms, where supervised weight training sessions are held (both single sex and mixed). Non-supervised users may require a special card to show that they are competent users (that body-destroying equipment is no joke). Membership of a public club isn't usually necessary, although membership may confer preferential booking facilities and the free use of equipment at certain times. Some sports and leisure centres charge an annual membership fee of around £50 (e.g. in London). Peak use of the fitness room is around £4 an hour or per session on a casual basis and there's often a lower charge during off-peak times (usually 0900 to 1700, Mondays to Fridays).

Charges can often be reduced by purchasing a book of tickets (e.g. ten sessions). Many sports and leisure centres also provide a huge variety of exercise classes including t'ai chi, high impact (energetic) and low impact (gentle) aerobics classes (e.g. callanetics), yoga, aqua-aerobics (in the swimming pool) and various dance routines. Some centres hold dance and exercise classes for all ages and levels of fitness (from beginners to superpersons), both during the daytime (including weekends) and evenings. Always check the class standard before enrolling.

Private health and fitness clubs are popping up overnight in all areas in what is a huge growth market. The cost of membership of a private club varies considerably, depending on the area, the facilities provided and the local competition. It's generally around £300 a year for a single person, although this can be reduced by up to a third by taking advantage of off-peak reductions (usually before 1700, Mondays to Fridays). Casual attendance (if permitted) usually costs between £5 and £10 a session. Some clubs offer reduced rates for husband and wife or family membership.

Clubs are usually open seven days a week from 0700 or 0800 until around 2200. On Saturdays and Sundays some clubs may be open from around 0900 to 1300 only.

All clubs provide a free trial and assessment and produce personal training programmes for members. Many private health and fitness clubs organise aerobics and keep-fit classes and have a sauna, solarium, Jacuzzi, steam bath, and provide massage and aromatherapy. Many top class hotels have health clubs and swimming pools that are usually open to the general public, although access to facilities may be restricted only to residents at certain times.

MISCELLANEOUS SPORTS

The following are a selection of other popular sports in Britain, which are either served by private clubs with their own facilities or use the facilities provided at public sports and leisure centres. For the addresses and telephone numbers of national sports associations contact the Sports England or the Central Council of Physical Recreation (see page 397).

Archery: Still a popular sport in Britain, many years after the British army were issued with more lethal weapons. Britain is still searching for a modern Robin Hood who can win an elusive Olympic gold medal. Crossbow shooting is also practised in some clubs.

Athletics: Most towns and villages have local athletics clubs and organise local competitions and sports days. Competitive running has a strong following in Britain and jogging is also popular. Races are organised throughout the year in all areas, from fun runs of a few miles up to half and full marathons. All finishers in important races are awarded commemorative medals. Britain has a distinguished international record in athletics, particularly in middle-distance running. Top athletes can now earn hundreds of thousands of pounds a year.

Basketball: A sport specially created for giants (Black American giants in particular), which is becoming increasingly popular in Britain (there are over 1,000 clubs). Basketball doesn't have a strong following as a professional sport in Britain, although the top teams participate in the European Clubs' Championship.

Bowls: A sport which has its origins in the 13th century and which numbers Sir Francis Drake among its past enthusiasts. Once regarded mainly as a pastime for the elderly and retired, bowls is becoming increasingly popular with people of all ages, particularly the young (who are ruining the game's image). In addition to outdoor greens, often provided in local council parks, there are also many private and indoor bowling clubs, including facilities in some sports and leisure centres. Bowls isn't to be confused with ten-pin bowling (see below).

Boxing: Legalised punch-ups for violent types. Popular throughout the country, particularly as a spectator 'sport' (many people enjoy watching a good fight, as long as they're out of h/arms reach). Most towns have a boxing club and gymnasiums for budding professionals are common in the main cities. Britain has produced a stream of world champions over the years.

Bungee Jumping: If your idea of fun is jumping 200 feet or more from a platform or bridge with an elastic rope attached to your body to prevent you merging with the landscape, then bungee jumping may be just what you're looking for. A strictly regulated sport which is actually very safe.

Croquet: Britain's answer to American football, except that all bodily contact is strictly forbidden (even tripping opponents with your mallet is frowned upon). An extremely genteel sport which is mandatory at English garden parties and unlikely ever to catch on among football hooligans.

Darts: Not actually a sport, but an excuse to get drunk (have you ever seen anyone playing darts in a milk bar?). Around five million people play darts (colloquially called 'arrows') regularly in Britain (which has a monopoly on the world championship), usually in pubs, most of which have teams playing in local leagues.

Fencing: A sport which has lost a lot of its popularity since the invention of the gun, although a hard core of enthusiast swordsmen are holding out in a small number of clubs.

Frisbee: Believe it or not, throwing plastic discs around has actually developed into a competitive 'sport', with national and local league and cup competitions.

Gymnastics: Another popular sport in Britain and most schools and sports centres have 'gym' clubs. Participation in sports centres costs from £1 to £3 a session.

Hockey: Hockey is a very old sport in Britain and has gained wider appeal since Britain won the Olympic gold medal in Seoul in 1988, although it still faces an uphill battle to woo youngsters away from soccer, rugby and cricket. Equally popular among both sexes.

Horse & Greyhound Racing: Horse racing is popular in Britain, although not because the British are a nation of equestrians or horse lovers, but inveterate gamblers. Horse racing is known as the sport of kings and you certainly need a king's ransom to buy and keep a horse in training during the racing season. An extensive programme of events is organised throughout the year consisting of national hunt racing (steeplechasing and hurdles races) from August to April and flat racing from March to October.

Horse Riding: Equestrianism (or horse riding to those who cannot spell 'ekwestranissem') is popular in Britain and needn't be expensive unless you wish to own your own horse. There are around 2,500 riding schools in Britain, although many have closed in recent years due to falling interest and increasing costs. It's important to wear a helmet (and a back protector when riding cross-country courses) as people are killed and paralysed in riding accidents every year. Britain has a proud tradition of horse breeding and horsemanship and is one of the world's leading show jumping nations.

Lacrosse: Similar to hockey and although thought of as strictly a women's game (whose training ground is the playing fields of Britain's most exclusive private girls' schools), lacrosse is played by both men and women in Britain.

Martial Arts: For those brought up on a diet of Bruce Lee, unarmed (?) combat such as Aikido, Judo, Karate, Kung Fu, Kushido, Taekwon-Do and T'ai Chi Ch'uan, are taught and practised in many sports and leisure centres and private clubs. Judo is the most popular martial art in Britain and a sport in which Britain has had considerable international success.

Polo: Minority sport for princes and Australian millionaires. Similar to croquet on horseback, where players attempt to hit a ball into a goal while riding at speeds of up to 40mph. If you fall off your horse you look a right Charlie and can also break something. Played both indoors and outdoors. A modern variation for commoners is bicycle polo – the sport of princes from the seat of a pushbike.

Rollerskating, Rollerblading, Skateboarding and BMX: Rinks and specially designed circuits are provided in many towns for skateboarding and BMX cycles (acrobatics on a bicycle). Children can start around seven but participants of all ages should be protected against falls with crash helmets and elbow and knee pads. It's difficult to hire equipment as it's too easily stolen, although BMX bikes can usually be hired. The cost of using purpose-built facilities is around £2 or £3 (including the hire of a bike) or around £1 if you provide your own bike.

Rollerskating rinks are available in many areas, sometimes using local sports and leisure centres. Skates can be hired and coaching is usually available. Many centres organise roller-discos for teenagers. The latest craze is rollerblading using skates where the wheels are set in a line. It's one of the fastest-growing sports in Britain, although its practice has been curbed on public paths due to the risks to cyclists and pedestrians (some of whom have been killed in collisions). Keen rollerskaters and rollerbladers often play roller hockey.

Rounders: The forerunner to baseball, which is usually played in Britain by females (who prefer to wear skirts rather than pyjamas) and with a little less razzmatazz.

Shooting: Shooting clubs members of which confine their shooting almost exclusively to private shooting ranges, are popular in Britain. Clubs have strict rules regarding the handling and storage of firearms, which the general public aren't usually permitted to store at home without a special licence. In addition to range shooting, Britain is famous for its field 'sports' (such as fox-hunting and hare-coursing, which could be banned by the time you read this), game shooting (using a shotgun) and deer stalking (using a rifle). Clay pigeon shooting is also popular among the well-heeled and Olympians and costs around £200 a day.

Tenpin bowling: There are tenpin bowling centres in all major British cities (over 100 with up to 48 lanes). After a decline in the '70s, tenpin has made a comeback and is one of Britain's fastest growing sports with new centres planned throughout Britain. A game costs around £2 for adults (but may be dearer in the evening), £1.50 for under 16s and 50p for shoe hire. Most centres are open from around 1000 to 2400 or later. There are tenpin bowling leagues and clubs in all areas and many companies have teams. Many centres have a restaurant, licensed bar, snack bar, nursery facilities, amusement machines and pool tables.

Trampolining: Popular sport among high fliers and gymnasts with a large number of clubs (both junior and senior) around Britain, where courses are organised for all ages.

Volleyball: A really fun game for all the family, deserving much wider popularity. It's often played on beaches (beach volleyball).

Weightlifting: There are weightlifting clubs in most large towns in Britain, many using the facilities of a local sports or leisure centres or a health and fitness club.

Wrestling: This refers to the real sport of wrestling (as practised in the Olympics) rather than the cabaret stuff shown on TV or what you do in bed with your partner. However, when it comes to mass popularity, showbiz wrestling is streets ahead.

Other Sports: Many foreign sports and pastimes have a group of expatriate fanatics in Britain including American football, baseball, boccia, boules (and pétanque), Gaelic sports (hurling, Gaelic football), handball and softball. For information enquire at council offices, libraries, tourist information centres, expatriate social clubs, and embassies and consulates.

17.

SHOPPING

The choice, quality and variety of goods on sale in British shops is excellent, particularly in London, which is one of the great shopping cities of the world. Not only is Britain in the words of Napoleon, 'a nation of shopkeepers', but it's a country of compulsive shoppers, which is the number one 'leisure' activity (after watching TV). In Britain you often hear references made to the 'High Street' (e.g. high street stores and high street banks), which isn't usually a reference to the name of a street (although many towns *do* have a High Street), but a collective term for any business commonly found in most towns. Shops in most towns and cities vary from huge department stores, selling just about everything (e.g. Harrods and Selfridges in London), to small high-class specialist shops in Georgian or Victorian style arcades. The traditional high street has a number of small shops usually including a butcher, baker, greengrocer, grocer or general store, newsagents, chemist (pharmacy), bank, post office and the inevitable pub (or two).

In larger towns, shops may include a fishmonger (fresh fish shop), ironmonger (hardware, household wares), launderette (laundromat), off-licence (alcoholic beverages), turf accountant (betting shop), fried fish and chip shop, dry cleaners, hairdresser, bookshop, health food shop, ladies' and men's fashions, shoe shop, take-away restaurants, banks and and building societies. Many larger towns also have one or more supermarkets and department stores and most country towns have a market on at least one day a week. In most towns (outside the main shopping centre) there are 'corner shops', which are general stores or mini-supermarkets selling a wide range of food and household products. Prices in small village and town shops are necessarily higher than in supermarkets, although many have a reasonably priced Happy Shopper, Spar or VG store.

There's generally no bargaining or bartering in Britain, although if you intend to spend a lot of money or buy something expensive (e.g. hi-fi, TV, computer or furniture) you should shop around and shouldn't be shy about asking for a discount (except in most department stores, chain stores and supermarkets, where prices are usually fixed). The poor trading climate in recent years has forced many shops to haggle over prices and it's possible to pick up some excellent bargains, particularly when paying cash. Many shops will also meet any genuine advertised price.

VAT (see page 351) at 17.5 per cent is usually included in the price of most goods with the exception of food, books and children's clothes, and the advertised price is usually the price you pay (there are no hidden extras). Some items such as computers and electronic goods may be advertised exclusive of VAT, as these items are often purchased by businesses that can reclaim VAT. Always shop around before buying, and when comparing prices remember to add VAT if it isn't included. Note that the chain store Dixons has a stranglehold on the home electronics trade (they also own Curry's and PC World) and charge high prices (the company has even been criticised by manufacturers for overcharging). It's cheaper to buy a computer from a direct-marketing company such as Compaq, Dell or Gateway. PCs cost up to a third more in Britain than in the USA and even many European buyers can buy computers for up to 40 per cent less than in Britain. When comparing prices make sure that you're comparing similar goods or services, as it's easy to 'save' money by purchasing inferior products.

Most shops accept major credit cards, although in some stores they accept debit cards only or their own account cards. To ensure that customers continue digging into their pockets, many major retailers offer instant credit (e.g. over 12 or 24 months, which may be interest-free) of up to £2,000 on a range of goods, such as home appliances, electrical and electronic equipment, and furniture. Always shop around for the best deal and compare the APR charged (see page 343) if you don't receive interest-free credit (but beware as some interest-free deals are anything but and designed to con you into paying interest). Note that when buying electronic and electrical products, you may be offered an expensive extended warranty deal, which is a rip-off and a waste of money.

Most shops hold sales at various times of the year, the largest of which are held in January and July, when bargains abound, particularly in the main cities (many newspapers publish sales' guides). Sales are also held in spring and autumn (most shops will hold a sale at the drop of a hat). Some stores seem to have a permanent sale, although retailers aren't permitted to advertise goods as reduced when they have never been advertised or sold at the fanciful advertised price. Goods may, however, have been advertised at a higher price for a short time simply to get around the law. Beware of bogus bargains.

In addition to sales, you can also shop at hundreds of factory shops around Britain, where prices are much lower than at retailers, particularly if products are flawed in some way (called 'seconds'). Ask your friends and neighbours if there are any factory shops in your area and look out for them on your travels. Factory malls (another American import) have sprung up in recent years, many specialising in fashion 'seconds' and end-of-line goods from top names such as Aquascutum, Jaeger and Ralph Lauren. Prices are typically at least 30 per cent below normal retail prices. For information see *The Factory Shop Guide* by Gill Cutress and Rolf Stricker.

Most retailers offer club or loyalty cards offering a discount (typically 10 per cent) to cardholders. Some retailers participate in an Air Miles scheme, while others have clubs or belong to a discount card scheme offering members discounts. Coupons in national and local newspapers and leaflets also provide discounts. In many towns there are shops run by charitable organisations, e.g. Oxfam, Helping Hand, Imperial Cancer Research and Sue Ryder, selling both new and secondhand items (a great place to find bargains).

Shopping guides are available in many areas from tourist information centres. Comprehensive guides for those who live in the London area include the *Time Out Guide to Shopping & Services in London*, listing over 2,000 shops, and *The Serious Shoppers Guide to London* by Beth Reiber (Prentice Hall Press). Stable Publishing (☎ 01476-870870) publish a series of Alternative Shopping Guides for various regions. The *Which? Buying Guide* contains a rundown on the best buys featured in the monthly *Which?* magazine (see **Consumers' Association** on page 437) and is highly recommended. Many stores, particularly department and chain stores, provide free catalogues at Christmas and other times of the year. If you're looking for a particular item or anything unusual, you will find that the Yellow Pages (see page 152) will save you a lot of time and trouble (and shoe leather).

If you have any questions about your rights as a consumer, contact your local trading standards or consumer protection department, consumer advice centre or Citizens Advice Bureau. Most retailers, particularly department and chain stores, will exchange goods or give a refund without question (although the British rarely complain or return goods), but smaller stores aren't so enthusiastic. Another invaluable book is *Fair Deal* (Stationery Office), which is a guide to shoppers' rights and family budgeting published by the Office of Fair Trading.

Britain officially converted to metrication on 1st October 1995 and all retailers must now price goods in kilogrammes, litres and metres, despite the fact that many

Britons haven't got a clue whether a pound (454 grammes) weighs more or less than a kilogramme (1,000 grammes). However, British measures such as pounds, pints and feet can be used alongside metrication and many stores display conversion tables. For those who aren't used to buying goods with British measures and sizes, a list of comparative weights and measures are included in **Appendix C**.

COMPETITION

There has been numerous price-fixing allegations and revelations in Britain in recent years encompassing a wide range of products such as computer games and equipment, electrical goods, branded foods, watches, cameras, designer clothing, sports shoes, furniture, CDs, cars (and parts and servicing), perfumes and sports equipment. Britons also get ripped off when buying services such as pensions, banking, pensions, insurance and savings products. In recent years there has been a high profile media campaign led by *The Sunday Times* and other national newspapers against 'rip-off' Britain. The government's competition policy has been called a joke and lame industry watchdogs have been lambasted as a waste of time. A combination of high taxes, corporate greed, invisible price cartels and the apathy of consumers (plus less competition as a result of take-overs and mergers) all combine to ensure that British consumers receive among the worst deal in Europe. However, where there's genuine competition, such as telephone services and air fares, costs in Britain are among the lowest in Europe.

Illegal price-fixing is widespread and largely responsible for the increasing cost of living in recent years (retail price maintenance is legal only for certain over-the-counter medicines, which is expected to end soon). The price of many branded goods are identical or vary by a tiny fraction (typically from 1p to £1, depending on the item's price) between retailers the length and breadth of the country. Anyone who attempts to discount goods soon finds he's blacklisted and unable to obtain further supplies. Price fixing by manufacturers, who insist that retailers stick to recommended prices, is almost impossible to prevent and the manufacturers know it. Discount stores have difficulty buying goods from manufacturers and suppliers, who usually refuse to supply them on some pretext or other (a problem faced by foreign, low-cost supermarkets in recent years).

Cargo and Costco discount warehouses (the latest wave of American consumerism to hit Britain) and others can offer discounts because they buy many goods on the 'grey' market (not directly from manufacturers or official suppliers). In a effort to by-pass manufacturers some supermarkets obtained designer goods (such as Nike, Levi and Calvin Klein) on the international 'grey' market, but were later forbidden to sell them by the European Court of Justice. However, designer companies are to be stripped of their right to prevent cheap imports into EU countries after evidence that EU consumers are being forced to pay inflated prices.

If you *really* want to save money, do your shopping in France or the USA (see **Shopping Abroad** on page 435) or shop by mail-order or via the Internet (see page 434). Prices in other European countries are as much as 30 per cent lower over a wide range of goods and in the USA you can save 50 per cent or more. For example, when buying a luxury watch you could fly to Zurich, stay in a five-star hotel for the weekend and still save money (profits are up to 100 per cent on manufacturers recommended prices) and you could pay for your flight to the USA when buying an SLR camera. On the other hand, you could buy via the Internet (see page 434) and save hundreds or even thousands of pounds. See also **Buying A New Car Abroad** on page 236.

SHOPPING HOURS

Shopping hours in Britain are usually from around 0900 or 0930 to 1730 or 1800, Mondays to Saturdays. New Sunday shopping laws were introduced in 1995 in England and Wales allowing large stores to open for six hours on Sundays, although most smaller shops aren't affected. However, Sunday shopping has become very popular in the last few years and most shops open in large towns and are very busy. Most large stores and supermarkets also open on public holidays. In smaller towns, shops and businesses may close for lunch (usually 1200 to 1300). Most towns have late night shopping until around 2000 one evening a week, e.g. Wednesdays, Thursdays or Fridays. Shops also stay open later in the weeks before Christmas. Most shopping in Britain is done on Saturdays and Sundays, which are best avoided if you can shop during the week.

Small privately owned grocery stores and supermarkets in cities, towns and sometimes even villages, are often open until between 2000 and 2200 and also at weekends, which is usually the only way they can make a living and compete with supermarkets. There are even 24-hour convenience stores in some towns. Many supermarkets and superstores open from 0800 until 2000 from Mondays to Saturdays and 1000 to 1600 (or 1100 to 1700) on Sundays. Over the Christmas and New Year period, all shops are closed on Christmas Day (25th December) and many on New Year's Day (1st January). However, an increasing number of stores open on Boxing Day (26th December), when many start their 'new year' sales.

SHOPPING CENTRES & MARKETS

In the last decade or so numerous vast, out-of-town, indoor shopping centres (malls) have sprung up throughout Britain, where it's possible to do all your weekly shopping under one roof (nirvana or shopping hell, depending on your viewpoint). Centres usually contain a huge selection of shops including all the most famous high street names. Among the most popular shopping centres are Merry Hill in the Midlands, Lakeside in the south-east, Meadowhill in Yorkshire, and the MetroCentre in the north-east, which draw shoppers from up to 80km (50mi) around and shopping excursions from up to 329km (200mi) away. More recent developments include the Trafford Centre in Manchester (1.4 million ft² of shopping and leisure space) with 280 shops and Bluewater (www.bluewater-web.co.uk) in north Kent, Europe's largest, newest and classiest indoor shopping centre which opened in 1999 (it contains three 'malls' covering 1.5million ft² and has 13,000 perking spaces). Over 25 per cent of retail sales are now made in out-of-town shopping centres. There has also been a proliferation of out-of-town supermarket superstores (there are now over 1,000), similar in size to continental hypermarkets, and often selling everything from food to clothes, home furnishings to electrical goods (see **Food & Supermarkets** below).

The main attractions of shopping centres are one-stop shopping, protection from the British climate and free parking, which usually means you can simply wheel your trolley full of purchases to your car. The largest shopping centres incorporate a wide range of leisure attractions, including multiplex cinemas, ten-pin bowling centres, games' arcades, children's play areas, and a number of restaurants and bars. Like American malls, most centres aren't designed for those without cars, although many have special bus services from nearby towns. Most towns and cities also have covered shopping centres, although parking is often expensive and difficult in city and town centres, particularly on Saturdays, and parking areas may be located some distance from stores. In some cities there are park-and-ride facilities for shoppers.

There has been an uneven battle raging between high streets and out-of-town shopping centres for many years, which towns have been losing hands down, although some are belatedly fighting back. Out-of-town shopping centres have had a huge social impact on towns and the decline of small shopkeepers, which is an increasing problem in all western European countries and has led some countries to introduce restrictions on new out-of-town centres. In the last few years political opinion has also turned against out-of-town shopping centres in Britain, which have turned many towns into ghost towns, and as a result it's becoming increasingly difficult to obtain planning permission.

Markets: Most small towns have markets on one or two days a week (Wednesdays and Saturdays are most popular) and in major cities and towns there may be a market (or a number) on most days of the week. Markets are cheap, colourful and interesting, and are often a good place for shrewd shoppers, although you sometimes have to be careful what you buy (beware of fakes). Items for sale include fruit and vegetables (good place to buy at the end of the day), general food, clothes, handicrafts, household goods and secondhand (flea markets) goods (e.g. clothes, books, records, antiques and miscellaneous bric-a-brac). Farmers' markets, where farmers and other producers sell direct to the public, are becoming increasingly popular in many towns. Some towns have permanent covered or indoor market places, where markets are held from Mondays to Saturdays and in some areas there are huge and popular outdoor Sunday markets (e.g. Petticoat Lane in London). Check with your local library, council or tourist information centre for information.

FOOD & SUPERMARKETS

The quality and variety of food in British supermarkets (which sell over 75 per cent of Britain's food) has increased in leaps and bounds in the last few decades, and is now among the best in the world. They excel in all important areas including freshness, efficiency of supply, hygiene, quality standards, safety, convenience, variety (from around the world), and the ambience of the shopping environment, which is designed to maximise the temptation and impulse to buy and relieve you of your hard-earned cash. The major supermarkets have branched out into other fields such as banking and financial services in recent years.

British supermarkets are also among the most expensive in the world and British shoppers pay up to 40 per cent more for their food than those in many other western European countries and North America (of the major countries only Scandinavia, Switzerland and Japan have higher food prices). The EU Common Agricultural Policy (CAP) also helps push up the cost of food in EU countries. British supermarkets have huge mark-ups on many foods (up to 60 per cent) and have been accused of profiteering in recent years, which has resulted in an investigation by the Office of Fair Trading. Savings (e.g. by bulk buying or when commodity prices fall) are rarely, if ever, passed onto the consumer. For example meat prices bear no relation to the price paid to producers; in 1998 supermarkets were charging around

£1 for a single lamb chop while farmers received just 25p for a whole lamb! Not surprisingly, British supermarkets are the most profitable in the world.

The major supermarket chains in Britain (not all are national) include Asda, Co-op, Iceland, Kwik Save, Morrisons, Safeway, Sainsbury's, Somerfield, Tesco and Waitrose. Some department and chain stores are also famous for their food halls, including Harrods, Selfridges and Fortnum and Mason in London, and Marks and Spencer (the clothing chain store). Marks and Spencer offer a smaller range of foods than a supermarket but are renowned for their high quality, particularly their excellent range of convenience (prepared) meals in which they were pioneers (supermarkets were quick to copy them).

Superstores: The largest supermarket chains such as Asda, Sainsbury's, Safeway and Tesco have built over 1,000 huge, out-of-town superstores in the last decade, which offer much more than the traditional supermarket and a range of shops-within-a-shop. These often include a newsagent, florist, delicatessen, cheese counter, bakery, fishmonger, chemists, butchers and market-style stalls. Superstores are also providing competition for department stores, not least because their lower overheads and higher purchasing power allows them to offer lower prices. Their size also allows them to stock a wider range of goods. Most superstores provide store plans, so that you don't need to spend a week looking for the butter or tea (unfortunately they don't help you find lost children). If possible you should avoid shopping after 1800, particularly on Friday evenings and at any time on Saturdays (Monday mornings should also be avoided as the stocks of many items run out during the weekend stampede).

Quality & Choice: Whatever you may have heard about the British junk food diet, it can hardly be laid at the door of the supermarkets, whose variety and quality of fresh food is as good as or better than that available in most continental supermarkets (although more people abroad shop in street markets). However, many supermarket prepared and fast foods provide little or no nutritional value, and in some cases you would be better off eating the packaging! Although supermarkets produce an increasing amount of convenience and prepared foods, they also offer a wide range of wholesome fare produced using traditional (i.e. old-fashioned) methods.

Many foreign foods can be found in local supermarkets if you look hard enough, but don't overlook the many delicious local foods on offer. Most supermarkets have a separate delicatessen and major cities have a variety of delicatessens and imported food shops. Supermarkets are usually good for fresh fruit and vegetables, due to the high turnover of stock (although fresh produce isn't always fresh and may have been stored for up to a year in special 'bunkers' to prevent it rotting). Many supermarkets bake their own bread on the premises and most have fresh fish, meat and dairy counters. Although most supermarkets offer a wide range of frozen products, most large towns also have a freezer shop (e.g. Iceland) which generally offers a wider choice and lower prices if you buy in bulk. Note that in most areas of Britain, a local dairy 'milkman' delivers milk and other dairy produce, and often provides a wide range of other foods, although they must usually be ordered in advance. Ask your neighbours for information or contact local dairies.

Prices: There has been a supermarket price war in the last few years as the major chains tried to maintain (or increase) their share of the £90 billion a year grocery market. In 1998 many supermarkets slashed 25 per cent off the price of hundreds of own-brand products, including loss-leaders such as a 7p loaf of bread. Most savings can be made on own-brand goods and wine and spirits. Note than many manufacturers have been shrinking the size of popular brands to hide price increases (the packaging may remain the same while the contents are reduced by up to 10 per cent). Always note the price charged for special offers and check it against the offer price, as mistakes are common. Among the cheapest supermarkets are Asda and Tesco. In recent years supermarkets introduced loyalty card schemes to reward frequent customers, although the savings amount to around 1 per cent and you're better off shopping around for the lowest prices. Cards have become more popular than credit cards, with over 50 per cent of shoppers having one or more. Most supermarkets accept personal cheques (with a cheque card), debit cards and credit cards. If you have a few items only (usually around ten) or one small basket *and* are paying by cash, you can use an express check-out (of which there are usually too few).

Labelling: The latest supermarket battle is being fought over who provides the 'greenest' products, i.e. organically produced food, environment friendly products, and food and other products which don't contain potentially harmful ingredients, e.g. preservatives. Note that you usually pay a premium for anything labelled 'low fat', 'free-range' or 'low calorie', many of which are bogus. Many manufacturers make unsubstantiated and wild claims for their products (particularly 'health' foods and environmentally-friendly 'green' products), that are deliberately misleading and often illegal. Until the standards and control of labelling is improved, you would be wise to treat most health, diet and eco-friendly labels with scepticism. Many processed foods contain high salt and sugar levels (even in 'low-fat' foods). There was a fierce debate about genetically modified (GM) food in 1998, labelled Frankenstein food in Britain, and as a result of public fears many supermarkets have refused to use GM products in its own-label products. Irradiated food (irradiation use to kill germs and extend the shelf-life of foods) is also causing concern.

Alcohol: Almost all large supermarkets have a wide selection of wine (including own label) and other alcoholic drinks, although you should shop around as wine prices and choice vary considerably. Wine is expensive in Britain and is usually at least twice as expensive (for equal quality) as on the continent. Don't always go for wines with fancy names or reputations, but experiment with some of the cheaper plonk priced from £2.50 to £4, which is often good value for money. Many wine merchants make free home deliveries. However, the best place to buy wine and spirits isn't in Britain, but on a day trip to France (see **Shopping Abroad** on page 435). You can also buy wine via the Internet (e.g. www.chateauonline.co.uk) and save up to 30 per cent on UK prices. All wine buffs should have a copy of *Superplonk* by Malcolm Gluck (Faber), which is a guide to supermarket wine listing over 800 best buys.

Miscellaneous: Many supermarkets provide free 'exploding' plastic carrier bags and free boxes, and some have staff to help you pack your purchases, although you may need to ask. If you want a heavy-duty carrier bag there's usually a small fee. All supermarkets provide trolleys for your goods, which shouldn't be removed from supermarkets or their immediate surrounds, e.g. car parks. Most don't require a deposit. Most supermarkets allow customers to order their groceries by phone, fax or via the Internet (see page 434), which can then be collected from a store or delivered to your home (which may be free, e.g. when you spend over £50). Many supermarkets provide recycling collection sites at stores where you can take your old bottles, paper and cans. If you're having a party, large supermarkets provide a party service and provide a variety of prepared cold food trays plus drinks, snacks, party-ware, gifts and prizes, sandwiches and sweets. Some supermarkets provide glasses on free loan (or for a nominal fee) if you buy a large quantity of alcohol from them. Most supermarkets have a notice board where details of items for sale or services can be posted free of charge (cards are usually provided).

DEPARTMENT & CHAIN STORES

Britain has many excellent department (or departmental) and chain stores. A department store is a large shop, usually on several floors, which sells almost everything, and sometimes includes a food hall. Each floor may be dedicated to a particular type of goods, such as ladies' or men's fashions or furniture and furnishings. Department stores usually have restaurants or cafeterias, telephones and toilets (although you may need to pay to use a toilet in some stores). The major department store chains include the Army & Navy, Debenhams, House of Fraser (the owner of Harrods), British Home Stores and John Lewis. John Lewis (owned wholly by its staff) is the father of all chain stores and has a reputation for fair-trading and value for money (note that its stores are closed on Mondays). Among the many London department stores are the world-famous Harrods and Selfridges, two of the largest department stores in the world. Note that the floor at street level is designated the ground floor (not the 1st floor) in Britain and that the floor above the ground floor is the 1st floor; the floor below the ground floor is usually called the basement.

A chain store is a store with a number of branches, usually in different towns, e.g. Woolworth. There are dozens of chains stores in Britain, selling everything from electrical and electronic goods to books and clothes. One of the most acclaimed chain stores in Britain is Marks and Spencer, which is famous for its British-made clothes, home furnishings and excellent food halls. Marks and Spencer goods are usually of high quality (although questioned in recent years) and they have a reputation for exchanging anything without question, which many other stores have followed.

A new innovation in the last decade or so has been catalogue stores (e.g. Argos and Index), where customers select their purchases from catalogues. Among the reasons for their popularity are their wide range of goods, which is similar to a department store, competitive pricing, and a policy that allows you to return anything unconditionally within a limited period for any reason (so you can test something in the comfort of your home and take it back if you don't like it!).

Most department and chain stores provide customer accounts (e.g. Debenhams, House of Fraser, Marks and Spencer) and allow the account balance to be repaid over a period of time, although this isn't wise as the APR (see page 343) is usually very high. However, some stores offer up to eight weeks free credit, e.g. Marks and Spencer (which has a high APR), which is worth taking advantage of. Account customers can often take advantage of special offers and discounts and some stores provide special shopping evenings. Many department and chain stores sell gift vouchers that can be redeemed for goods at any branch.

Department stores (and many smaller shops) provide a gift wrapping service, particularly at Christmas time, and will deliver goods locally or send them by post, both within Britain and worldwide. Some stores have a 'Mister Minit' department where shoe repairs, key cutting and engraving is done on the spot while you wait.

CLOTHES

The clothing industry is extremely competitive in Britain and London is one of the world's leading fashion centres, particularly for the young. What London lacks in couture fashion houses it more than makes up for by the sheer variety, energy, innovation and vitality of its fashion scene. London is renowned for its fashion schools such as St. Martin's and the Royal College of Art, which produce a continuous stream of excellent young designers. Clothes shops in Britain offer a wide range of attire, from traditional made-to-measure clothing to the latest ready-to-wear fashions, with prices ranging from a few pounds to a few thousand. Top quality and exclusive (i.e. expensive) ladies' and men's fashion shops (many chains sell both ladies' and men's clothes) include Aquascutum, Burberry's, Gucci, Jaeger, Liberty and Yves St. Laurent.

More middle of the road (both price and quality) ladies' fashions can be found at Army & Navy, Benetton, Country Casuals, Dorothy Perkins, Etam, DH Evans, The Gap, Hennes (H&M), House of Fraser, Laura Ashley, Monsoon, Next, Miss Selfridge, Principles, Richards and Wallis. Miss Selfridge, River Island and Top Shop cater primarily for teenagers and those in their 20s to 30s. Clothes for the less wealthy shopper can be found at British Homes Stores, C & A and Debenhams. Marks and Spencer (M&S) clothes are generally more expensive than those sold by other large 'own brand' chain stores (in 1999 they declared that they may also stock British designer clothes), although they are usually of good quality and have a reputation for durability. M&S have become more adventurous in recent years, but cater mostly for the conservative, older buyer, rather than young trend-setters.

Top quality men's clothing stores include Cecil Gee, Austin Reed, Harrods and Selfridges (in London), Horne Brothers, Moss Bros. and Dunn & Co. For the young man about town, there's a wide range of fashion stores including Burtons, Ciro Cittero, The Gap, Next for Men, Principles for Men, River Island and Top Man. In addition to department and chain stores, all towns and cities have a profusion of independent stores covering the whole fashion spectrum and all price brackets. Markets are often a good place to shop for cheap clothes and mail-order fashion offers (e.g. in Saturday and Sunday newspaper magazines) usually provide good value for money. Some clothes shops don't have changing rooms, but will allow you to return anything which doesn't fit (see **Appendix C** for a comparison of British, continental and USA sizes).

Clothes in Britain are generally of good quality, particularly those from famous English manufacturers (e.g. Aquascutum, Burberry's, Jaeger and Liberty), who produce classic styles and traditional clothes that are made to last (and outlast ever changing fashions). A large proportion of the cheaper fashion clothes are made abroad (e.g. in the Far East) as it's simply too expensive for most manufacturers to produce them in Britain. Although the quality of some foreign-made clothes may occasionally be suspect, you usually get what you pay for. Most shops provide a tailoring or alteration service (for a small fee) and many stores also provide a made-to-measure tailoring service.

The most renowned men's tailors are to be found in London's Saville Row. London's Jermyn Street is famous for hand-made shirts and Bond Street is one of the most fashionable shopping streets for ladies fashion in Europe. Unless you're wealthy, beware of shops that don't price their window displays (as when buying a Rolls-Royce, if you need to ask the price you cannot afford it!). There are ladies' and men's clothes hire shops in many towns, where you can hire anything from a ball-gown to a wedding dress, a morning suit to evening dress. When clothes have been fitted with a security tag, check that it hasn't left a small hole, which could lead to a much larger hole later (in which case you would be entitled to exchange them or claim a refund).

Many clothes stores sell shoes and there's also a wide variety of specialist shoe stores in Britain. These range from the top quality (and price) Russell & Bromley, Ravel Chaussures, Bally and Charles Jourdan chains, to the more affordable Dolcis, Barrats, K Shoes, Milwards and Saxone. Like good quality English clothes, English shoes (famous makers include Crockett & Jones, Church's and Grenson) are made to last, although few manufacturers remain. Two other famous English brand names are Clarks and Startrite, both of which make excellent children's shoes in a wide range of fittings.

There are also sportswear shoe shops in most towns specialising in sports shoes, leisure shoes and trainers, which are particularly fashionable among the young. Shoe repair shops can be found in all towns and many department stores and high streets have a Mister Minit shop, where repairs are carried out while you wait. Note, however, that the quality of repairs from an established family cobbler may be superior to that of an 'instant' repair shop.

NEWSPAPERS & BOOKS

The British are a nation of inveterate newspaper readers. When city and regional newspapers are included, there are around 135 daily and Sunday newspapers, over 2,000 weekly free or paid-for newspapers and over 7,000 other periodicals published in Britain. On most weekdays the British buy some 15 million national newspapers and over five million regional morning and evening newspapers, more than any other country in the world. There's no tax on newspapers, magazines or books in Britain.

Most major newspapers traditionally support the Conservative party, although this has changed somewhat in recent years with the election of a Labour government (fickle lot, newspaper owners). Daily and Sunday newspapers range from the broadsheet 'quality' newspapers (those that are difficult to read in confined spaces) for serious readers and the popular tabloids for those who just like to look at pictures (including those of half-naked ladies). The broadsheet daily newspapers include (roughly in order of average sales, highest first), the *Daily Telegraph*, the *Times*, the *Guardian*, the *Independent* (not politically aligned) and the *Financial Times*. The popular tabloid daily press (also referred to as the 'gutter' press for their cheap sensationalist exposés) includes the *Sun*, the *Daily Mirror*, the *Daily Mail*, the *Daily Express*, the *Star*, the *Daily Record* and *Today* (the *Daily Mirror* isn't sold in Scotland, where it's replaced by its stablemate, the *Daily Record*).

On Sunday the broadsheet newspapers are the *Sunday Times*, the *Sunday Telegraph*, the *Observer* and the *Independent on Sunday*, which are good sources of advertisements for quality cars, executive appointments, property (both in Britain and abroad), entertainment, travel and holidays. The popular Sunday tabloids are the *News of the World*, the *Sunday Mirror*, the *People*, the *Mail on Sunday*, the *Sunday Express* and the *Sunday Sport* (which is a 'fictional' newspaper). Most Sunday and many daily newspapers include a colour magazine (usually with the Saturday edition), some of which have earned a reputation for quality journalism in their own right, e.g. *The Sunday Times* colour magazine. Other Sunday newspapers include *The*

Scotsman and *Glasgow Herald*, available in London and other English cities for homesick Scots. There are regional daily and evening newspapers in most areas and most major cities. Free weekly newspapers are published throughout Britain and are delivered free to homes.

If you prefer to have your newspapers and magazines delivered to your doorstep, most newsagents will deliver them for a small fee (e.g. £1 a week). You can usually take out a subscription to your favourite magazines, which is cheaper than buying them at retail price from newsagents. Note, however, that new magazines come and go with amazing frequency and have a tendency to go bust just after you have taken out a subscription! In London and other large cities, newspapers are sold from kiosks or simply from the pavement, particularly Sunday newspapers. A selection of European, American and other foreign newspapers and magazines are sold at newsagents and news kiosks in most cities and towns. The *International Herald Tribune*, *Wall Street Journal Europe*, *USA Today* and the *European Financial Times* are widely available on the day of publication, Mondays to Saturdays. European editions of *Newsweek* and *Time* magazines are sold by most newsagents. Many foreign newspapers and magazines can be purchased on subscription at a large saving over newsagent prices (if you're willing to wait a few days for delivery). A vast number of magazines are sold in Britain, including many popular European and North American titles.

Books: There are excellent book shops in all towns in Britain (hopefully all selling this book) and in addition to a branch of WH Smith (who alone account for around 20 per cent of British book sales), most larger towns and cities also have a branch of one of the major specialist book store chains which include Dillons, Blackwell, Waterstone's, Hatchards, Sherratt & Hughes, Fagin's and Hammick's. John Menzies and Martin, both large newsagent chains, also sell books (mostly novels). Many department stores also have book departments, although the range of books may be limited. In large towns and cities a number of bookshops are open until around 2000 or later each evening.

As you would expect, London has a multitude of bookshops, including the world-famous Foyles (utter chaos, but good for browsing), and many specialist bookshops such as art and design, women, ethnic interests, science fiction, sport, law, medicine, travel, politics, economics and foreign language books. In many towns there are 'remainder' or cut-price bookshops, where remaindered books that have been sold off by publishers can be bought at discount prices. In London and many other cities and towns, there are secondhand bookshops (as featured in the film *84 Charing Cross Road*) for collectors and bargain hunters. Many large bookshops in London and other cities keep a selection of foreign-language books.

Although books may not be particularly cheap in Britain, they are cheaper than in many countries (particularly textbooks). Students can also save money by buying secondhand textbooks from other students or from cut-price or secondhand bookshops. The price of books was traditionally fixed under the Net Book Agreement (NBA), which was scrapped in 1997. Books (or at least best-sellers) are now widely discounted (although not nearly as much as in the USA) and are even sold in supermarkets. The biggest challenge to traditional book shops is expected to come from Internet booksellers (such as www.amazon.co.uk), who have proliferated in recent years and discount most books. There are also many mail-order book clubs in Britain (see page 429), most of which provide bargain introductory offers and offer books at discounted prices. Some book clubs offer a wide range of general books, while others stick to a particular subject, e.g. photography or computers (many clubs advertise in newspapers and magazines, particularly free Sunday newspaper magazines). The largest book club is Book Club Associates (BCA) with over 1.5 million members, which offers discounts of from 25 to 50 per cent and has shops in some towns.

Book tokens are a popular present for people of all ages and are sold and accepted by most bookshops. Many organisations and clubs run their own libraries or book exchanges and public libraries usually have an excellent selection of books (see page 393).

FURNITURE

Furniture is usually good value for money in Britain and top quality furniture is often cheaper than in many other European countries. There's a huge choice of both modern and contemporary designs in every price range, although as with most things, you generally get what you pay for. Exclusive modern designs from Italy, Denmark and many other countries are available (usually with matching exclusive prices), although imports also include reasonably priced quality leather suites and a wide range of cane furniture from the Far East. Among the largest furniture chain stores in Britain are Courts, Perrings, Heal's and Trends, all of which offer a wide range of top quality British furniture from manufacturers such as Ercol, G-Plan, Parker Knoll and Topley.

Oak is the most common wood used for traditional British quality furniture and pine is also popular, which can be bought stained or unstained. Note that when ordering furniture you may need to wait weeks or months for delivery, so you should try to find a store which has what you want in stock or which will give you a guaranteed delivery date (after which you can cancel and receive a full refund). A number of manufacturers sell directly to the public, although you shouldn't assume that this will result in huge savings, and should compare prices and quality before buying. There are also stores specialising in beds, leather, reproduction and antique furniture, and many companies manufacture and install fitted bedrooms and kitchens. Note that fitted kitchens are an extremely competitive business in Britain and you should be wary of cowboy companies who are specialists in shoddy workmanship.

If you want reasonably priced, good quality, modern furniture, there are a number of companies selling furniture for home assembly (which helps keep down prices), e.g. MFI, Habitat and Ikea (Sweden), the latter being the world's only global furniture chain. Assembly instructions are generally easy to follow (although some people think Rubik's cube is easier) and some companies print instructions in a number of languages (Double Dutch is the favourite).

All large furniture retailers publish catalogues, that are generally distributed free of charge. Some stores offer you £50 or £100 for your old suite, when you buy a new one from them. However, this may not be much of a bargain (particularly if your suite is worth more than the amount offered) and you should shop around for the best price and quality available. Furniture and home furnishings are very competitive businesses in Britain and you can often reduce the price by some judicious haggling, particularly if you're spending a large amount. Another way to save money is to wait for the sales to come round. If you cannot wait and don't want to (or cannot afford) to pay cash, look for an interest-free credit deal. Check the advertisements in local newspapers and national home and design magazines such as *House & Garden*, *Country Homes & Interiors* and *Ideal Home*.

HOUSEHOLD APPLIANCES

Large household appliances such as cookers and refrigerators are usually provided in rented accommodation and may also be fitted in new homes. Many homeowners include fitted kitchen appliances such as a cooker, refrigerator, dishwasher and washing machine when selling their house or apartment, although you may need to pay for them separately. If you wish to bring large appliances with you, such as a refrigerator, washing machine or dishwasher, note that the standard British unit width isn't the same as in other countries. Check the size and the latest British safety regulations before shipping these items to Britain or buying them abroad, as they may need expensive modifications. There's a wide range of household appliances in Britain, from both British and foreign manufacturers, and some stores (e.g. Harrods in London) also sell American refrigerators, in which you can store a year's supply of dairy products for a family of 14 (and a few pets). Note that some appliances such as refrigerators cost twice as much to run as others.

If you already own small household appliances, it's worthwhile bringing them to Britain as usually all that's required is a change of plug, but check first. If you're coming from a country with a 110/115V electricity supply (e.g. the USA) then you will need a lot of expensive transformers (see page 108). Don't bring a television to Britain from the continent or the USA as it won't work (see page 159). Smaller appliances such as vacuum cleaners, grills, toasters and electric irons aren't expensive in Britain and are usually of excellent quality. If you want to buy a ceramic or halogen hob, bear in mind that it may be necessary to replace all your saucepans. Before buying household appliances, whether large or small, check the test reports and surveys in *Which?* magazine (see page 437) at your local library.

Stores such as Comet, Power Warehouse and warehouse clubs such as Costco and Cargo offer among the best prices for household goods. Consumers Association (see page 437) members can buy household goods at low prices from Value Direct (☎ 01295-755015, Internet: www.value-direct.co.uk/wol), who claim to offer the lowest prices in Britain and back it with a guarantee. You should also try Home Electrical Direct (www.hed.co.uk). A one-year guarantee is normally provided, which can usually be extended by a further two or four years. However, although extended warranties may provide additional peace of mind, they are a usually a waste of money and should be avoided. If you need kitchen measuring equipment and cannot cope with decimal measures, you will have to bring your own measuring scales, jugs, cups (US and British recipe cups aren't the same size) and thermometers (see also **Appendix C**). Note also that British pillows and duvets aren't the same size or shape as in many other countries.

SECONDHAND BARGAINS

There's a lively secondhand market in Britain for almost everything, from antiques to motor cars, computers to photographic equipment (the British spend around £5 billion a year on secondhand goods). You name it and somebody will be selling it secondhand. With such a large secondhand market there are often bargains to be found, particularly if you're quick off the mark. Many towns have a local secondhand or junk store and many also have an Oxfam, Imperial Cancer Research or Sue Ryder shop, which sells new and secondhand articles for charity (where most of your money goes to help those in need). There are a number of national and regional weekly newspapers devoted to bargain hunters including *Exchange & Mart, Dalton's Weekly* (both are national and include ads. for just about everything) and *Loot* (a London daily newspaper published in various editions for different areas – ads. are free to non-traders).

There are also many special newspapers and magazines dedicated to secondhand cars. If you're looking for a particular item, such as a camera, boat or motorcycle, you may be better off looking through the small ads. in specialist magazines for these items, rather than in more general newspapers or magazines. The classified ads. in local newspapers are also a good source of bargains, particularly for furniture and household appliances. Shopping centre and newsagent bulletin boards and company notice boards may also prove fruitful. Expatriate club newsletters are a good source of household items, which are often sold cheaply by those returning home.

Another place to pick up a bargain is at an auction, although it helps to have specialist knowledge about what you're buying (you will probably be competing with experts). Auctions are held in Britain throughout the year for everything from antiques and paintings, to motorcars and property. Britain has some of the most famous auction houses in the world including Sotheby's, Christies and Philips, all of which hold local antique valuation and auction receiving days throughout Britain. Local auctions are widely advertised in newspapers and through leaflets.

There are antique shops in most towns and antique street markets (e.g. Portobello Road and Camden Passage in London) and fairs are held regularly in many cities. For information about local markets, inquire at your local tourist information centre or library. Car boot (trunk) sales are popular in all parts of Britain, where people sell practically anything from the boots of their cars, and are the best place to find real bargains (they are also a good place to buy loads of absolute junk without any consumer protection), although you must arrive early. Sales may be advertised in local newspapers and signposted on local roads, and are usually held on Sundays.

HOME SHOPPING

Shopping by mail-order and phone has always been popular in Britain and shopping via the Internet is expected to take off in a big way in the next few years. Catalogue and TV shopping by mail, phone and the Internet is big business in Britain and is worth over £7 billion a year. Direct retailing by companies (cutting out the middleman) is becoming more widespread, particularly for computers and office equipment, and services such as insurance. Electronic shopping is expected to dominate retailing in future, whether in-store or from home, and TV shopping is becoming increasingly popular (products sold through infomercials are a huge success).

Mail-Order Catalogues: There are many companies in Britain selling exclusively by mail-order. Customers are provided with a (usually free) colour catalogue and can often also act as agents and collect orders from other customers on which they receive a commission. The major mail-order catalogues contain almost everything you would expect to find in a department store, although your choice is more limited and prices may be higher. The main attraction is that goods are bought on approval and can usually be paid for over a period at no extra cost. The cost of postage is usually paid by the mail-order company, although you may be required to pay postage when returning goods.

Among the major mail-order companies are Empire Stores, Freemans, Grattans, JD Williams, Kays and Littlewoods (Littlewoods also publish other catalogues such as Index Extra and Peter Craig – which contains the same goods as Index Extra but costing up to 30 per cent more!). Newcomers include direct-selling clothes manufacturers such as Cotton Traders, Damart, Hawkshead, Lands' End, Le Redoute, the Next Directory and Racing Green. Most mail-order companies also accept orders from overseas customers, although there's usually a charge for a catalogue (e.g. £5). Note, however, that the quality of own brand goods, particularly clothes, is sometimes poor, and some companies are difficult to contact and slow to send goods or refunds.

Some major stores also publish mail-order catalogues and send goods anywhere in the world, e.g. Fortnum & Masons, Habitat, Harrods and Selfridges (London). Many high street stores are moving into the mail-order business (e.g. Marks & Spencer). Most major supermarkets and food retailers accept orders by phone, fax or via the Internet including Iceland, Safeway, Sainbury's, Somerfield and Tesco. Most stores provide account facilities and accept payment by international credit and charge cards. Many charities, institutions and organisations, e.g. Amnesty International, the British Heart Foundation, the National Trust, the Natural History Museum, Oxfam, Save the Children, the Science Museum and the World Wildlife Fund also publish mail-order catalogues. The added 'bonus' for buyers is that in addition to buying beautiful, exclusive and often unusual hand-made items from around the world, you can also often contribute to a good cause.

Mail-Order Clubs: A number of companies operate mail-order clubs for books, CDs (or cassettes), computer software and video cassettes, where new members are offered a number of items at a nominal introductory price (e.g. £1 each) or pay for one of five or seven items, in return for an agreement to purchase a further number of items (usually three to six) at full price during the following one or two years. There's no catch, although there may be a restricted choice and if you want to resign before you have fulfilled your side of the bargain, you're usually required to repay the savings made on the introductory offer.

Before committing yourself to buying anything by mail, make sure you know what you're signing and don't send cash through the post or pay for anything in advance, unless absolutely necessary. It's foolish to send advance payment by post in response to an ad (or to anyone) unless you're sure that the company is reputable and offers a cast-iron money-back guarantee. Customers who buy goods or services in response to advertisements in reputable publications are usually covered by the Mail Order Protection Scheme (MOPS), 16 Tooks Court, London EC4A 1LB (☎ 0171-269 0520), which provides a money back guarantee. Check in advance that a periodical is covered, which may be shown by a MOPS logo. If purchases aren't covered by a guarantee, you may find it extremely difficult to obtain any redress. When you purchase goods by mail, you're usually protected by the Sale of Goods Act and by the codes of practice operating in the mail-order business. A leaflet published by the Office of Fair Trading entitled *Buying by post*, explains the pitfalls to be avoided when shopping by mail and what to do if things go wrong.

Internet Shopping: Shopping via the Internet is the fastest-growing form of retailing and although it's still in its infancy, UK sales are forecast to be over £3 billion a year by 2003. Shopping on the Internet is *very* secure (secure servers, with addresses beginning https:// rather than http://, are almost impossible to crack) and in most cases safer than shopping by phone or mail-order. There are literally thousands of shopping sites on the Internet including Taxi (www.mytaxi.co.uk), which contains the Internet · addresses of 2,500 worldwide retail and information sites, www.enterprisecity.co.uk, www.iwanttoshop.com, www.shopguide.co.uk. and www.virgin.net (which has a good directory of British shopping sites). One company called Priceline (www.priceline.com) even allows you to name your own price when buying such things as airline tickets, hotel rooms, cars and mortgages (if Priceline can find a company willing to accept the offer it's passed on).

With Internet shopping the world is literally your oyster and savings can be made on a wide range of goods including CDs, clothes, sports equipment, electronic gadgets, jewellery, books, CDs, wine and computer software, and services such as insurance, pensions and mortgages. Huge savings can also be made on holidays and travel. Small high-price, high-tech items (e.g. cameras, watches and portable and hand-held computers) can usually be purchased cheaper somewhere in Europe or (particularly) in the USA (for cameras try www.normancamera.com), with delivery by courier within as little as three days.

Buying Overseas: When buying goods overseas ensure that you're dealing with a bona fide company and that the goods will work in Britain (if applicable). If possible, *always* pay by credit card when buying by mail-order or over the Internet, as when you buy goods costing between £100 and £30,000 the credit card issuer is jointly liable with the supplier. Note, however, that many card companies claim that the law doesn't cover overseas purchases, although many issuers will consider claims up to the value of the goods purchased (and they *could* also be liable in law for consequential loss). When you buy expensive goods abroad, always have them insured for their full value.

VAT & Duty: When buying overseas, take into account shipping costs, duty and VAT. There's no duty or tax on goods purchased within the European Union or on goods from most other countries worth £18 or less (or £36 if a gift). Don't buy alcohol or cigarettes abroad as the duty is usually too high to make it pay. When VAT or duty is payable on a parcel, the payment is usually collected by the post office or courier company on delivery.

SHOPPING ABROAD

Shopping abroad for most British people consists of a day trip to Calais or Boulogne, and a visit to a French hypermarket (similar to a British superstore). Considerable savings can be made on a wide variety of goods including food (e.g. cheese, ground coffee, chocolate, cooked meats and paté), alcohol (beer, wine and spirits), toys, houseware (e.g. hardware, glassware and kitchenware) and clothing (if you take your car you can also save on servicing). Don't forget your passports or identity cards, car papers, foreign currency and credit cards. Many French stores accept sterling, but usually give you a worse exchange rate than a bank. It's usually best to use a credit card when shopping abroad and on board ferries, as you receive a better exchange rate (and can delay payment). Note that in towns much frequented by British shoppers and tourists, the price of some goods may be slightly higher than in inland towns.

From 1st January 1993, there have been no cross-border shopping restrictions within the European Union for goods purchased duty and tax paid, providing all goods are for personal consumption or use and not for resale. Although there are no restrictions, there are 'indicative levels' for certain items, above which goods may be classified as commercial quantities. For example, persons entering Britain aged 17 or over may import the following amounts of alcohol and tobacco without question:

- 10 litres of spirits (over 22° proof);
- 20 litres of fortified wine such as port or sherry (under 22° proof);
- 90 litres of wine (or 120 x 0.75 litre bottles/10 cases) of which a maximum of 60 litres may be sparkling wine;
- 110 litres of beer;
- 800 cigarettes, 400 cigarillos, 200 cigars and 1 kg of smoking tobacco.

There's no limit on perfume or toilet water. If you exceed the above amounts you may need to convince the customs authorities that you aren't planning to sell the goods. There are huge fines for anyone who sells duty-paid alcohol and tobacco, which is classed as smuggling. Hand-rolling tobacco is one of the smugglers' favourites, as it costs around five times as much in Britain as in France. Beer is also popular and costs less than a third of the British price in France.

The vast cross-Channel shopping business is made possible by cheap off-season ferry trips costing as little as £10 return for a car and £1 for foot passengers! Most special offers are available during off-peak periods only and are usually offered via coupons provided in daily newspapers. Cross-Channel shopping has led to a number of British companies opening outlets in Calais including Sainsbury's, Tesco, Victoria Wine and The Wine Society. If you don't fancy a trip to France, you can buy wine direct from vineyards and breweries in Austria, France, Germany, Italy and Spain (and beer direct from Belgium) via intermediaries such as Classic Wines & Beers, Crossways, Mount Pleasant, Wareham, Dorset BH20 4HG (☎ 01929-553912), which is legal. Savings of up to 40 or 50 per cent can be made on British high street prices.

Alcohol and tobacco are favourite tax targets of the Chancellor of the Exchequer in Britain, although if too many people hit the Calais trail he may be forced to rethink his taxation policies. The estimated revenue loss to the British government of cross-Channel shopping for alcohol and tobacco is over £400 millon (over £1 billion at retail cost). Cross-Channel shopping has also had a huge impact on pubs and off-licences in the south-east of England (over 150 million litres of wine are personally imported into Britain each year).

See also **Buying A New Car Abroad** on page 236.

DUTY-FREE ALLOWANCES

Duty-free shopping within the EU is set to end on the 30th June 1999, although it will still be available when travelling further afield. Although many people will miss their duty-free booze, many so-called duty-free 'bargains' are up to one-third cheaper in British shops including some alcohol, perfumes, cameras and clothes. Duty-free allowances are the same whether or not passengers are travelling within the EU or from a country outside the EU. Note that Eurotunnel doesn't sell duty-free goods on its trains, but has duty-free shops at its terminals in Folkestone and Calais. For each journey between EU member states travellers aged 17 or over are entitled to import the following goods purchased duty-free:

- two litres of still table wine;
- one litre of alcohol over 22° volume or 38.8 per cent proof (e.g. spirits and strong liquors) **OR** two litres not over 22° volume (e.g. low strength liquors or fortified or sparkling wines);
- 200 cigarettes **OR** 100 cigarillos **OR** 50 cigars **OR** 250 grammes of tobacco;
- 60cc/ml (50gr or 2fl oz) of perfume;
- 250cc/ml (8fl oz) of toilet water;
- other goods (including gifts, souvenirs, beer and cider) to the value of £75.

Duty-free allowances apply on both outward and return journeys, even if both are made on the same day, and the combined total (i.e. double the above limits) can be imported into your 'home' country. Since 1993 duty-free sales have been 'vendor-controlled', meaning that vendors are responsible for ensuring that the amount of duty-free goods sold to individuals doesn't exceed their entitlement. Duty-free goods purchased on board ships and ferries are noted on boarding cards, which must be presented with each purchase.

THE CONSUMERS' ASSOCIATION

The Consumers' Association is the most acclaimed and respected independent consumer organisation in Britain, with around a million members. It publishes an excellent monthly magazine (available on subscription only) entitled *Which*?, containing priceless information about a wide range of goods and services (just about everything is tested at some time or other). All goods and services are tested independently by the Consumers' Association including financial services (e.g. insurance, banking, pensions and investment); cars; leisure; food and health; household and domestic appliances; and items of public interest. Dangerous products are highlighted, best buys are recommended and most importantly, you're told how to obtain your legal rights when things go wrong.

It's indispensable to everyone who's interested in obtaining value for money and their rights as consumers. Fortunately for the many companies which provide poor value for money, shoddy goods and indifferent or terrible service (in particular *after* sales service), the vast majority of people prefer to throw their money away. A subscription to *Which*? costs around £60 a year, which although it may appear expensive, is excellent value for money considering the savings to be made in both time and money (not to mention peace of mind). Advertisements and leaflets appear regularly in magazines, e.g. Sunday newspaper magazines offering a free three or four-month trial period. *Which?* magazines and books can also be found in the reference sections of most public libraries.

The Consumers' Association also publishes a number of other consumer magazines including *Gardening Which?*, *Holiday Which?* and *Health Which?*. They also publish a wide range of books on subjects ranging from *Starting Your Own Business* to *Plan Your Retirement*, many of which are mentioned in this book. All Which? books are available by post from Which? Ltd, Castlemead, Gascoyne Way, Hertford SG14 1LH (☎ 01992-822800, Internet: www.which.net).

18.

ODDS & ENDS

This chapter contains miscellaneous information. Although all topics aren't of vital importance, most are of general interest to anyone living or working in Britain, including everything you ever wanted to know (but were afraid to ask) about tipping and toilets.

BRITISH CITIZENSHIP

With the exception of someone born to a foreign diplomat, anyone born in Britain before 1983 automatically qualifies for British citizenship. A person born abroad before 1983 whose father was born or adopted in Britain (or had become a British citizen in Britain) and who was married to their mother, is automatically a British citizen through descent from his father. A person born in Britain after 1982 becomes a British citizen automatically only if either parent was a British citizen or a permanent resident (settled) at the time of their birth. Anyone born after 1982 with a parent who was born or adopted in Britain (or who had become a British citizen in Britain) is automatically a British citizen by descent from either parent. If the parents were not married at the time of birth, the mother's status is relevant.

Anyone over 18 can apply to become a British citizen (called 'naturalisation'). To qualify you must have been permitted to live as a permanent resident in Britain for a minimum of one year; have lived in Britain (legally) for a total of at least five years without being absent from the country for more than 450 days and with no more than 90 days absence in the year prior to the application; plan to continue living in Britain, e.g. you cannot apply for British citizenship in order to qualify to live elsewhere in the EU; have sufficient knowledge of the English, Welsh or Scottish (Gaelic) language; be of good character, e.g. no criminal record; and pay a fee. Parents of non-British children who qualify under the above rules, can apply on their behalf (called 'registration') for which there's a reduced fee.

Anyone over 18 and married to a British citizen can apply for naturalisation providing he's permitted to live in Britain as a permanent resident and has lived in Britain legally for a total of at least three years, without being absent from the country for more than 270 days, and not more than 90 days absence in the year prior to the application. He must also plan to continue living in Britain, be of good character and pay a fee. It takes an average of over two years to become a naturalised British citizen and the Home Office has been criticised for its incompetence and inefficiency over nationality procedures (or could it be part of a master plan to discourage applicants?).

There are often delays in issuing passports and you should apply in person if you need a passport quickly. Current processing times are given in recorded messages, the phone numbers of which are provided on application forms. Application forms are available from main post offices and should be sent by post to your local passport office (listed on the form). Enclose with the completed form the fee, any relevant documents (such as your birth certificate), two passport-size photographs and your old passport (if applicable). An application form for a British passport must be signed by a person of professional standing in the community who knows you well, e.g. a doctor, member of parliament or a justice of the peace. Your family doctor may charge you around £5 to complete a passport form.

Note that from 1st January 1996, British visitor's passports and British excursion documents have no longer been valid. For further information, contact the immigration and Nationality Directorate (IND), Block C, Whitgift Centre, Croydon

CR9 2AR (procedures (☎ 0870-606 7766, Internet: www.homeoffice.gov.uk/ind/hpg. htm).

CLIMATE

Britain has a generally mild and temperate climate, although it's extremely changeable and usually damp at any time of year. Because of the prevailing south-westerly winds, the weather is variable and is affected mainly by depressions moving eastwards across the Atlantic Ocean (which make British weather reports depressing). This maritime influence means that the west of the country tends to have wetter, but also milder weather than the east. The amount of rainfall also increases with altitude and the 'mountainous' areas of the north and west have more rain (1,600mm or 60 inches annually) than the lowlands of the south and east, where the average is 800mm or 30 inches. Rain is fairly evenly distributed throughout the year (i.e. it rains most of the time) in all areas, but the driest months are usually March to June and the wettest September to January. For many, spring is the most pleasant time of year, although early spring is often very wet, particularly in Scotland.

In winter, temperatures are higher in the south and west than in the east, and winters are often harsh in Scotland and on high ground in Wales and northern England, where snow is usual. December and February are traditionally the severest months, when it's often cold, wet and windy. When it snows the whole country comes to a grinding halt (except for the kids, who love it) and people complain that the authorities were unprepared. Although temperatures drop below freezing in winter, particularly at night, it's rarely below freezing during the day, although the average temperature is a cold 4°C (39°F).

The most unpleasant features of British winters are freezing fog and black ice, both of which make driving hazardous. The 'pea-soup' fog which was usually the result of smog and pollution, and which many foreigners still associate with Britain, is generally a thing of the past. The warmest areas in summer are the south and inland areas, where temperatures are often around 26°C (75°F) and occasionally rise above 30°C (86°F), although the average temperature is 15°C to 18°C (60°F to 65°F). Fine autumn weather is often preceded by early morning fog, which may last until midday. Early autumn is often mild, particularly in Scotland. Average daily temperatures are: winter 4°C (39°F), spring 9°C (48°F), summer 16°C (61°F) and autumn 10°C (50°F).

The most depressing thing about British weather (at almost any time of year) is the frequent drizzle (light rain) and the almost permanent grey skies. Roughly translated into layman's terms British weather is terrible (if it was fine day after boring day, whatever would the British people find to talk about?). British winter weather has given rise to a condition known as seasonal affective disorder (SAD), which is brought on by the dark, depressing days of winter and causes lethargy, fatigue and low spirits. However, there's *some* good news. British winters are becoming milder and in recent years winters have been nothing like as severe as in earlier decades, although whether this is a permanent change is unclear.

In fact, British weather is becoming warmer all round, with recent years experiencing some of the driest summers since records began in 1659. To add a little spice to the usual diet of cold and rain, in the last decade Britain has been afflicted with gales and torrential rain (including the infamous storms of 1987 and 1990), which have caused severe damage and flooding in many areas. Tornadoes do occur in

Britain, but are extremely rare. There's much debate among weather experts and scientists as to whether the climatic changes (not just in Britain, but worldwide) are a result of global warming or just a temporary change. If present trends continue, some scientists predict that temperatures will increase considerably in the next century and the south-west region could become frost-free).

Weather forecasts in Britain appear designed to be deliberately evasive, as if the meteorologists are continually hedging their bets (perhaps weather reports are written by politicians), therefore most forecasts include both scattered showers and sunny periods at the very least. In fact meteorologists are the only people who are paid for being wrong most of the time (except for politicians, who are wrong *all* the time). Meteorologists usually find it particularly difficult to forecast abrupt changes or extremes of weather (which are common in Britain). A new style of weather report in recent years introduced percentage forecasting, such as a 70 per cent chance of rain, a 50 per cent likelihood of frost overnight and a 10 per cent probability of sunny periods (and a 100 per cent chance that it'll all be wrong!). The Meteorological Office sells its long-term weather predictions to industry, agriculture and tourism, who if they have any sense insist on a guarantee (the Met Office has been accused of fiddling its success-rate figures).

The weather forecast is available by telephone from Weathercall, which divides Britain into 27 areas, each of which has a separate (0891) telephone number. To obtain a free Weathercall card, phone 0171-236 3500. Similar services are provided by Weatherwatch (provided by the Automobile Association, ☎ 01256-493747 for a directory) and WeatherCheck (☎ 09001-333111). The weather forecast is also available via the television teletext services, in daily newspapers, on the Internet, and on TV (usually after the news) and radio broadcasts. Warnings of dangerous weather conditions affecting motoring, e.g. fog and ice, are broadcast regularly on all BBC national and local radio stations.

The most detailed weather forecasts are broadcast on BBC Radio 2 and BBC Radio 4 (which also broadcasts weather forecasts for shipping). Many newspapers also include temperatures and the weather outlook in European and world capitals, European holiday centres, and in winter, the weather and snow conditions in major ski resorts. During early summer, when pollens are released in large quantities, the pollen count is given on radio and TV weather forecasts and in daily newspapers. In summer, the maximum exposure time for the fair-skinned is included in TV weather forecasts on hot days. If you suffer from insomnia, *The Story of Weather* by Bill Giles (Stationery Office) should provide an instant cure.

CRIME

According to official statistics the number of crimes (apart from violent crimes) being committed have reduced in recent years. However, sceptics believe that people are simply reporting less crime because they consider it a waste of time (the clear-up rate or number of crimes solved is below 20 per cent in most areas). In the last decade there has been an upsurge in car joy-riding (where cars are stolen by kids for 'fun'), muggings, pick-pocketing, car crime, house-breaking and burglary, robbery, fraud, rape and school crime. The number of violent crimes are also increasing, although they are still relatively low compared with many other countries. There are around 500 murders a year in Britain, where you're more likely to choke to death on your food than you are to meet a violent death.

Nevertheless, violent crime has reached shocking proportions in some cities and it's becoming more common among children. The levels of street crime (where men under 30 are most at risk) are far higher than official figures suggest and the actual number of crimes is reckoned to be around four times the number recorded by the police. However, muggings and crimes of violence are still rare in most towns, where you can safely walk almost anywhere day or night. Many crimes are drug-related and are due to the huge increase in drugs flooding into Britain in recent years. The use of hard drugs (particularly cocaine and crack) is a major problem in most British cities, where gangs increasingly use guns to settle their differences. Violent crime and assaults are increasing and the police warn people (particularly young women) against tempting fate by walking alone in dark and deserted areas late at night. The increasing rate of assaults on female students has prompted many universities to issue them with rape (screech) alarms.

For many people in Britain, crime is their number one concern and in some areas people are afraid to leave the relative safety of their homes at any time of day or night. The increase in crime in many areas is attributed by psychologists to poverty, the breakdown of traditional family life, the loss of community and social values in society, and a growing lack of parental responsibility and skills. The failure to deal with juvenile crime is the biggest threat facing Britain and many children are out of control by the age of ten or even younger. Riots occasionally occur and are often sparked by a breakdown in relations between police and youths.

Crimes against property are escalating, particularly burglary and housebreaking, car thefts and thefts from vehicles. The number of cars stolen in Britain is the highest (per capita) in Western Europe and burglary is also the highest in Europe. If you work or live in a major city and park your car there, you have a one in four chance of having it stolen or broken into. In London (where around 20 per cent of all crime takes place) professional thieves even steal antique paving stones, railings and antique doors and door casings. Fraud or so-called 'white-collar' crime (which includes credit card fraud, income tax evasion and VAT fraud), costs £billions a year and accounts for larger sums than the total of all other robberies, burglaries and thefts.

The authorities' response to the crime wave sweeping Britain has been to 'get tough' with offenders and sentence an increasing number of people to prison terms, particularly women. British courts are increasingly imprisoning people for petty crimes, e.g. minor motoring offences and non-payment of TV licences and council tax. Justice is weighed heavily against women, who are often treated much more harshly than men for the same crimes. The routine imprisonment of women for petty offences has created a crisis in women's prisons, where the number of prisoners has increased by 30 per cent over the last few years. Another anomaly causing concern is the disproportionate percentage of black prisoners, which has led to accusations of racial bias in the courts. Britain sends more people to prison for more offences and sentences more people to life imprisonment than in the whole of the rest of Western Europe.

Although the foregoing catalogue of crime may paint a depressing picture of Britain, it's a relatively safe place to live. In comparison with many other countries, including most other European countries, Britain's crime rate isn't high and the incidence of violent crime is low. If you take care of your property and take precautions against crime (including avoiding potential high crime areas), your chances of becoming a victim are small. Note that the rate of crime in Britain varies considerably from area to area and anyone coming to live in Britain should avoid high crime areas if at all possible.

Information: Police forces, central government, local authorities and security companies all publish information and provide advice on crime prevention. All police forces have a local crime prevention officer whose job is to provide free advice to individuals, homeowners and businesses. Most police forces publish comprehensive police *Crime Prevention Manuals*. The Central Office of Information and the Home Office also publish numerous brochures and booklets about crime prevention including *Your Practical Guide to Crime Prevention*, available from police stations, libraries and council offices. See also **Car Theft** on page 260, **Legal & General Advice** on page 448 and **Police** on page 457.

GEOGRAPHY

The title of this book may cause some confusion, particularly as there are occasional references to the United Kingdom, England, Scotland, Wales, Ireland and Northern Ireland. The term Britain, as used in this book, comprises Great Britain (the island which includes England, Wales and Scotland) and Northern Ireland, the full name of which is the 'United Kingdom (UK) of Great Britain and Northern Ireland'. The British Isles is the geographical term for the group of islands, which includes Great Britain, Ireland and many smaller islands surrounding Britain.

Britain covers an area of 242,432km² (93,600mi²) and is about the same size as New Zealand or Uganda and half the size of France. It's some 1,000km (600mi) from the south coast to the northernmost point of Scotland and under 500km (around 300mi) across in the widest part. Nowhere in Britain is more than 120km (75mi) from the sea and the coastline, which is strikingly varied and one of the most beautiful in the world. Britain has a varied landscape and most of England is fairly flat and low lying (particularly East Anglia), with the exception of the north and south-west, while much of Scotland and Wales is mountainous. If the most dire predictions of global warming become a reality, many regions of Britain will be flooded as the sea level rises. The highest mountains are Ben Nevis in Scotland at 1,343m (4,406ft) and Snowdon in Wales at 1,085m (3,560ft). The country can roughly be divided into a highland region in the north and west, and a lowland region in the east, approximately delimited by the mouths of the River Exe (Exeter) in the south-west and the River Tees (Teeside) in the north-east. Britain has around 1,931km² (1,200mi²) of inland waters, the most famous and largest area being the Lake District in the north-west of England.

GOVERNMENT

Britain is a constitutional monarchy, under which the country is governed by ministers of the crown in the name of the Sovereign (Queen Elizabeth II), who's head of both the state and the government. Nowadays the monarchy has no real power and its duties are restricted to ceremonial and advisory only, although there are certain acts of government that require the participation of the Sovereign, such as the opening and dissolving of parliament and giving royal assent to bills. Parliament is the ultimate law-making authority in Britain (although the Channel Islands and the Isle of Man make their own laws on island affairs) and consists of two houses or chambers, the House of Commons and the House of Lords, which together make up the Houses of Parliament.

Parliament sits in the Palace of Westminster (monarchs lived there until the 16th century) in London, which was built in the 19th century after the previous building was destroyed by fire, and whose clock, Big Ben (actually the name of the large bell), is London's most famous landmark. Britain's democratic traditions date from 1265 (when King Henry III was forced to acknowledge the first Parliament) and Westminster, which is often referred to as the mother of Parliaments, is the model for many democracies around the world.

The House of Commons is the assembly chamber for the 651 Members of Parliament (MPs) who are commoners (i.e. not Lords or titled persons) elected by the people of Britain in a general election, that must be held every five years if parliament isn't dissolved earlier. Each MP represents an area called a constituency, of which there are 523 in England, 72 in Scotland, 38 in Wales and 17 in Northern Ireland. If an MP resigns, retires or dies during the term of a government, a by-election is held to choose a new MP. Any British subject or citizen of the Irish Republic over the age of 21 can stand for election as an MP in Britain, with the exception of disqualified persons, i.e., undischarged bankrupts, those sentenced to more than one year's imprisonment, most clergy, members of the armed forces and holders of certain public offices. (Contrary to popular belief insanity isn't a requirement for office and lunatics are disbarred from standing for Parliament.) To try to deter 'jokers' or no-hopers from standing for election, each candidate must make a deposit of £500 with the returning officer, which is forfeited if he receives less than 5 per cent of the vote. There's a limit on the amount a candidate can spend on a general election campaign, depending on the number of registered voters in a constituency (in stark contrast to the USA, where it's £billions).

All British and Commonwealth citizens and citizens of the Republic of Ireland over the age of 18 and resident in Britain can vote in parliamentary elections, providing they are registered voters. To be eligible to vote your name must appear in a register of electors maintained and updated annually in autumn by councils (the real purpose of which now has nothing to do with voting rights, but everything to do with collecting the council tax). If you fail to register, you're liable to a maximum fine of £400. Voting isn't compulsory and there's no penalty for not voting (but don't complain about the government if you don't vote). Between 70 and 80 per cent of people usually vote in general elections. British citizens who have been living abroad for less than 20 years also have the right to vote in parliamentary elections (but not local government elections). Anyone who's a registered voter and who's away from his constituency during parliamentary, European or local government elections, can vote by post or appoint a proxy to vote on his behalf.

The Government of the day is formed by the political party that wins the largest number of seats at a general election. If no party has a clear majority, i.e. 326 seats, then a coalition government may be formed between a number of parties which gives them an overall majority. This is extremely rare in Britain as unlike other countries in Western Europe, Britain doesn't have a system of proportional representation. The candidate in each constituency who polls the most votes is declared the winner ('first past the post'). All votes cast for other candidates aren't counted, which means that a party such as the Liberal Democrats (the third force in British politics) often receives millions of votes and ends up with just a few seats. Many people believe this system is outdated and undemocratic (particularly the Liberal Democrats), although it's difficult to see the major parties changing the system voluntarily (although Labour is investigating electorial reform). MPs hold weekly or fortnightly surgeries in their constituencies, when constituents can visit them and discuss their problems. Constituents can also write to their MP and telephone or visit him at the House of Commons (although he'll probably be having a late lunch, a round of golf or be on holiday).

The head of the government is the Prime Minister, who's the leader of the party with the majority of seats (or the leader of the major party in a coalition) and who chooses an inner cabinet of around 20 ministers. In addition to the cabinet, the government also appoints some 80 junior ministers, of which there may be two to five in each ministry. Every few years (or months if cabinet members resign suddenly) a game of musical ministries takes place, in which the Prime Minister's toadies get promoted and the 'wets' (those who are lukewarm about the PM's policies) are consigned to the back benches. The Leader of the Opposition, who's the head of the largest defeated party (and not part of a government coalition), appoints a shadow cabinet of shadow ministers, whose job is to respond to government ministers in Parliament and to act as the party's spokespersons. MPs who are members of the cabinet or shadow cabinet sit on the front benches (on opposite sides) in the House of Commons. All other MPs are known as back-benchers.

The House of Commons is presided over by the Speaker, who's the spokesman and president of the chamber and who controls proceedings (or attempts to). The Speaker is an MP of either party who's elected by the House at the start of each parliament or when the previous speaker retires or dies. He neither speaks in debates nor votes on a bill except when voting is equal (when he has the deciding vote). The Speaker has an apartment in the Palace of Westminster.

The highlight of the week in the House of Commons is question time, during which MPs can question Ministers (and which often becomes heated when the PM and the leader of the opposition trade insults). The proceedings of both houses are public (except for rare occasions involving national security) and both houses have a public gallery. Television was introduced into Parliament in 1989 for a trial period, although strict rules apply which are designed to hide the fact that the chambers are often almost empty and of the few MPs present, 99 per cent are asleep. Equity, the actors union, has refused to accept MPs as members, due to excessive histrionics, over-acting and insanity.

There are three main national parties in Britain the Conservatives or Tories, Labour (or New Labour as it prefers to be called) and the Liberal Democrats (or whatever their current name is). There are a few other smaller parties, most of which contest seats in particular regions or constituencies only. These include the Scottish Nationalist Party (SNP), the Ulster Unionist Party and the Democratic Unionist Party (Northern Ireland), Plaid Cymru (Welsh nationalists), the Green Party and the Communist Party. The Social Democratic Party (SDP), which was formed by a breakaway group of four disillusioned Labour MPs in 1981, became a major third force in British politics in the '80s, but after a series of election setbacks was officially disbanded in June 1990.

Britain is plagued by its predominantly two-party system, with its extremes of left (Labour) and right (Conservatives) and very little in between. The Conservatives are the party of big business, from which they receive the vast majority of their finances, and are loathe to do anything to interfere with its profitable operation (which leads to accusations that they allow their paymasters to flaunt the law with regard to pollution, monopolies, price maintenance and tax loopholes). The Labour party is the party of the workers and receives most of its funds from the trade unions, and has traditionally been in favour of public ownership of businesses (nationalisation), although this is no longer official policy. After over 18 years in the political wilderness (on the opposition benches), Labour finally won a general election in 1997 and in 1999 it still enjoyed strong public approval for its policies.

The House of Lords is referred to as the 'Other Place' in the House of Commons and is the geriatric ward of the constitution, where retired MPs and blue-blooded landowners spend their days in retirement. The Lords consist of the Lords Spiritual (archbishops and bishops) and Temporal, which includes all hereditary peers and peeresses who haven't disclaimed their peerages (around two-thirds of the total), life peers and peeresses, and lords of appeal (the other third), nominally a total of around 1,200 members (although the average attendance is around 300). Until the beginning of the 20th century, the House of Lords had extensive powers and could veto any bill submitted to it by the House of Commons. It remains the highest court of appeal in Britain, with the exception of criminal cases in Scotland. Members of the House of Lords are unpaid, although they receive travelling and other expenses when on parliamentary business within Britain. The House of Lords is presided over by the Lord Chancellor, who's the ex-officio Speaker of the House. The House of Lords has long been considered an anachronism in Britain and is to abolished and replaced by an elected second house (similar to the US House of Representatives).

Devolution: One of the declared aims of the Labour government that came to power in 1997 was to devolve certain powers from Westminster to Scotland and Wales, and possibly also establish regional governments within England (Northern Ireland already has its own Parliament). The establishment of a Scottish parliament was well-advanced when this book went to press with voting due to take place in May 1999 (Labour were expected to secure an overall majority over the other parties). Their main rival is the Scottish Nationalist Party (SNP), whose declared aim is to make Scotland an independent country outside the United Kingdom. Labour hopes that by offering Scotland and Wales a measure of autonomy will reduce the support for independence parties.

Local Government: The administration of local affairs in Britain is performed by local government or local authorities. In most areas of England and Wales, services are divided between two authorities, a district council and a county council. In large cities, services are usually provided by a single authority, e.g. a borough council in London and a metropolitan district or city council elsewhere. London is divided into 32 boroughs and the Corporation of the City of London. In Scotland, services are usually divided between district, regional or island councils, and in Northern Ireland between district councils, area boards and central government. England and Wales is divided into 53 counties (see map on page 496) which are subdivided into 369 districts. All districts and 47 of the (non-metropolitan) counties have locally elected councils with separate functions. In Scotland there are nine regions that are divided into 52 districts, each with its own area council.

County & Borough Councils: County and borough councils (or regional councils in Scotland) provide the main local government services that require planning and administration over wide areas, or that require substantial resources. These include the police, education, fire service, libraries and museums, public transport subsidies, traffic regulation, magistrates courts, probation service, waste disposal, highways and road safety, trading standards, personal social services and strategic planning. Other essential services include area health authorities, which are funded directly from central government.

Local Councils: District councils are responsible for local services which usually include local planning, industrial development, building regulations, environmental health, public housing, council tax collection, street cleaning, refuse collection, car parks and leisure facilities. There are also parish councils, which although they have no specific duties may have certain responsibilities such as cemeteries and crematoria, recreation, local planning consultations, public conveniences, allotments, footpaths, village halls and any other function delegated by county or district councils.

County councils, London borough councils and around two-thirds of non-metropolitan district councils, hold elections every four years. The remaining districts, including metropolitan districts, are elected in each of the three years in between county council elections. All local government councils are organised along party political lines, although some councillors are independent. All councils elect a chairman, who in boroughs or cities has the ceremonial title of mayor (or Lord Mayor in the City of London and other large cities). The turnout in local government elections is usually much lower than for parliamentary elections (around 30 per cent). Voting qualifications are broadly the same as for parliamentary elections. Councillors are unpaid, although they can claim an allowance for attending council meetings and travel and subsistence allowances. Local authority finances come from a variety of sources that include around 25 per cent from the council tax (see page 350), a further 25 per cent comes from the uniform business rate and the remainder from central government. Over 2 million people are employed by local authorities in Britain.

LEGAL SYSTEM

England and Wales, Scotland and Northern Ireland all have their own separate legal systems and law courts, and although there are a lot of similarities, there are also considerable differences. In Northern Ireland, procedure closely follows that of England and Wales, but Scottish law differs in many respects and is based on a different legal tradition from English law. Differences include the buying and selling of real property, consumer rights, inheritance and the rights of young people. Note, however, that much modern legislation applies throughout Britain and there's a common distinction between criminal law (acts harmful to the community) and civil law (disputes between individuals) in all regions. Under the British legal system, on which many other countries have based their legal systems, you're innocent until proven guilty (although you may sometimes get the impression everybody isn't aware of this).

In Britain, less serious cases are dealt with by a **Magistrates Court** (a 'peoples' court), that handles both civil and criminal cases. A magistrates court normally consists of three lay magistrates, known as justices of the peace (JPs), who are advised on points of law and procedure by a legally qualified clerk or assistant. Cases involving children under 17 are heard in **Juvenile Courts**. Minor civil claims such as small debts, are heard in a **County Court**, of which there are around 300 in England and Wales. A person convicted by a magistrates court has the right of appeal to a **Crown Court** (criminal cases) against the sentence imposed (if he pleaded guilty) or the conviction if he pleaded not guilty, or to a **High Court** in a civil case. Civil cases may be dealt with by a **Queen's Bench, Family division** or **Chancery division**, depending on the subject matter.

More serious criminal offences, such as murder, manslaughter, rape and robbery with violence, are tried by a crown court before a judge and a jury of 12 people (15 in Scotland), or in a civil case, a high court. Every local or parliamentary elector between the age of 18 and 65 who has been resident in Britain for at least five years since the age of 13, can be called on to serve on a jury unless ineligible or disqualified (for a variety of reasons). If you're found guilty in a crown court or a high court, you have the right of further appeal against conviction or sentence to a **Court of Appeal, criminal or civil division**, depending on the case. Note that all courts have a huge backlog of cases waiting to be heard.

In both criminal and civil cases involving a point of general public importance, you may be given leave to appeal to the **House of Lords** (see page 447), the highest and final court of appeal in Britain. In cases involving or conflicting with EU regulations or the European Convention on Human Rights, you can appeal to the European Court (Luxembourg) or the European Court of Human Rights (Strasbourg), although they cannot enforce fines or impose their rulings on member states, and are often seen as something of a 'white elephant'. Note that only one in four appeals in any court are successful and that often the only winners are the lawyers.

In Britain, it isn't always necessary to have legal representation in court, particularly in a small claims court (see below), although in a serious case only a foolish person (or someone who's legally competent) would attempt to defend himself. A **solicitor** is a qualified lawyer who usually defends cases in lower courts, such as magistrate's and county courts, although with the introduction of the Court and Legal Services Bill in 1990, solicitor advocates can now practise in higher courts. A **barrister** (or advocate) is a solicitor who has been 'called to the bar', which prior to 1990 was necessary in order to practise in higher courts. A **Queen's Council (QC)** is a barrister who has been appointed by the Lord Chancellor. He's the most experienced and expensive of all legal advisors and generally acts only for the very rich and the crown. Barristers (and QCs in particular) earn around £1,000,000 an hour and professionally are above the law (it's impossible to sue a barrister who makes a mess of your case as he's immune from negligence claims).

Magistrates Courts: Magistrates are usually unpaid local volunteers, chosen for their character and judgement, and they aren't usually legal professionals. Sentences in magistrates courts often vary considerably for the same offences and magistrates have considerable discretion in the fines they impose for certain offences, such as motoring offences. Moves are afoot to make sentencing more consistent and to match fines to a defendant's ability to pay (one London prostitute complained "How can I pay my fines, when every time I go to the West End to earn some money I get arrested?"). There is a chronic shortage of magistrates in some areas, particularly in blue-collar areas. A defendant in a magistrates court can sometimes opt for a crown court trial by jury.

Cost: The high cost of legal representation often ensures that unless you qualify for legal aid, you're unable to pursue justice, which leads to the accusation that 'real' justice is available only to the rich. Solicitors' fees have soared in recent years and leading solicitors charge clients hundred of pounds an hour, with top barristers (silks) charging £650 an hour to prepare a case and £3,000 a day in court and earning over £1 million a year. Cases of overcharging and fraud are commonplace. The civil justice system is geared to enriching lawyers rather than serving justice and many observers believe that legal costs are a cancer eating at the heart of justice. When forced to go to court, an increasing number of people handle their own cases, called do-it-yourself litigants, usually concerning bankruptcy, divorce and disputes involving custody of children. However, many have no idea how to present their cases adequately and are courting disaster.

As a general rule you should never go to court unless you're forced to, as a dispute over a small sum can cost you many, many times more than anything you're likely to gain. Even a relatively straightforward case such as a divorce can cost an arm and a leg. If you decide to obtain advice from a solicitor, check in advance what it will cost, as seeing a solicitor is often akin to signing a blank cheque. There are plans to deliver cheap and fast justice through a fast-track courts system in order to remedy the huge problems of cost, delay, complexity and inequality in the civil justice system (although it will probably be scotched by the lawyers).

Free Legal Advice: There are many organisations in Britain that provide free legal advice and general information on a vast range of subjects. Before taking the often expensive step of obtaining legal advice from a solicitor, you should contact one of the organisations listed below, all of which provide free or low-cost advice to everyone, irrespective of nationality or how long you've been in Britain. British people aren't usually in the habit of suing each other at the drop of a hat and whenever possible it's better to seek other avenues of redress rather than pursue someone through the courts. Many companies have internal complaints procedures and most professions and trades have independent arbitration schemes and ombudsmen (independent arbitrators). Only when these fail, should you consider taking legal action, providing of course you have a good case and the necessary financial resources. Often the threat of legal action or issuing a summons is sufficient to force someone to concede, particularly if you have a strong case.

Wherever you obtain legal advice, whether from a CAB, a law centre or a solicitor, if it's a civil matter involving a lot of money or a criminal matter where your liberty is at stake, you should obtain a second opinion. If you're given and follow bad advice (particularly free advice) there may be no redress later. If you're in doubt about your rights or obligations, check with a solicitor or lawyer before signing anything. Contracts are usually drawn up by solicitors and some may deliberately contain a number of traps in the small print designed specifically to rob you (legally of course) of your rights. The National Consumer Council would like to outlaw 'gobbledegook' in contracts. If in doubt ask a CAB or law centre for help in interpreting contracts and legal documents.

Legal advice is also available by phone from **Lawline**, which is approved and endorsed by the Law Society. Lawline provides information on a wide range of legal, domestic and consumer matters using the ubiquitous (and expensive) 0898 phone numbers, which although no substitute for personal advice from a solicitor is at lot cheaper (☎ 0898-600600 for a free Lawline directory). There are also many useful books published including *350 Legal Problems Solved* (Which? Books).

Citizens Advice Bureau (CAB): The CAB was founded in 1939 to provide an emergency service during the war. It's an independent organisation which provides free confidential information and advice on almost any kind of problem or subject. These include social security; consumer and debt; housing; family and personal; employment; justice; local information; health; immigration and nationality; and taxes. There are over 1,200 CAB offices in England, Wales and Northern Ireland (in Scotland there's a separate Citizens Advice Scotland service with 61 offices). If you would like to know more about the CAB contact the National Association of Citizens Advice Bureaux, Myddelton House, 115-123 Pentonville Road, London N1 9LZ (☎ 0171-833 2181).

Small Claims Court: If you have a claim of up to £5,000 (with a few exceptions), you can use the simplified small claims procedure. Under the small claims system you take out the summons yourself and do your own prosecuting. No costs are awarded to either side as no lawyers are required, similar to private arbitration (note that if you do use a lawyer in a small claims court, it can cost you £thousands in legal fees). The fee for taking out a county court summons varies depending on the size of your claim from around £12 to £65, but if you win your fees are paid by the other party. A free booklet (form EX50) is available from your local county court entitled *Small claims in the county court*, which explains how to sue and defend actions without a solicitor.

Ombudsmen: are industry watchdogs appointed by the government, and are completely independent arbitrators who mediate in disputes between companies (or government departments) and individuals. Usually complaints can be referred to an ombudsman only after all other complaints' procedures have been exhausted. For further information ask at your local CAB or law centre.

MARRIAGE & DIVORCE

In 1995, the law regarding where a marriage can take place was changed and in addition to a church or registry office (civil ceremony), you can now get married anywhere that's approved by the local authorities including boats, stately homes, castles, hotels, restaurants, zoos and sports venues. The bride and groom must be at least 18-years-old or 16 if they have parental consent (which also applies to foreigners who get married in Britain).

Foreigners living in Britain who are married or divorced (or widowed) should have a valid marriage licence, divorce papers, or death certificate, which is usually necessary to confirm their marital status with the authorities, e.g. to receive certain legal or social benefits. A blood test isn't required to get married in Britain. Marriage according to the rites of the Church of England can be by banns, by licence (common or special) or under a superintendent registrar's certificate. If you get married in a church, place of worship or anywhere else that isn't licensed to register marriages, a civil wedding service must take place before or after the religious ceremony (in order to be legally married under British law).

The average church marriage in Britain costs around £8,000. The alternative is to be married in a registry office or another venue licensed to stage civil weddings under a superintendent registrar's certificate, which is much simpler and cheaper than a church wedding (and without the religious significance). To be married in a registry office, either the bride or groom must live within its official area. You can be married under a **certificate** (without licence) or a **licence**. A **certificate** is for those who don't want to have a church ceremony, but perhaps wish to invite a lot of guests and have a wedding reception. Each partner must show his or her birth certificate and pay the fee to the local registry office (if you've been married before, you must produce a decree absolute or a death certificate) at least 21 days but not more than three months before the date on which you wish to be married (book early if you want to be married on a Saturday).

A **licence** is for those who wish to be married quickly and who want the minimum amount of fuss and ceremony. To be married under a licence you and your partner must take your documents (and the fee) to the registry office at least one day prior to the day on which you wish to be married. Both partners must have been living in the registry office area for at least 15 days. On the wedding day you must have two witnesses (anyone will do). A ring isn't required for a registry wedding, although most couples use one. The ceremony lasts around ten minutes after which you both sign the register (when it's too late to change your mind). Note that 'marriages of convenience', where a foreigner marries a British subject in order to remain in Britain, are illegal and subject to intense scrutiny by the Home Office.

Divorce is the name given to the legal termination of a marriage. To be divorced a couple must have been married for at least one year. Under British law it's unnecessary to prove that one marriage partner has committed an act which gives grounds for divorce (thus depriving private detectives of much lucrative work), but a marriage must have broken down beyond repair. To prove a marriage has 'irretrievably broken down' (in legal terminology) and obtain a divorce, a couple must fulfil certain legal requirements such as living apart for two years when both partners want a divorce (or five years when only one partner wants a divorce). There are many other grounds for divorce such as desertion, the behaviour of one partner in such a way that the couple cannot live together (e.g. loud snoring or cold feet), and adultery.

If possible it's best to deal with a divorce yourself as involving solicitors is very expensive and messy. However, if you *must* involve a lawyer, be sure to engage a good divorce lawyer, particularly if the divorce will be contested and there's a lot of property and the legal custody of children at stake. Note that shared or joint custody of children isn't common in Britain. A new pilot project aims to help couples work out future arrangements for children, money and property over a one-year waiting period before a divorce goes through. The scheme is intended to offer low-cost mediation in financial disputes without the need for expensive lawyer's fees. A couple can also obtain an 'undefended divorce' (a free booklet is available from county courts) and dispense with lawyers (hurrah!), for example when there are no children and neither partner is claiming maintenance.

When a divorce is granted the court issues a decree nisi and an application for a decree absolute (which makes the divorce final) can be made six weeks later and is usually a formality. Both partners receive a divorce certificate from the county court or divorce registry that proves the divorce and which is necessary if you wish to remarry. Britain is top of the European divorce league and over 40 per cent of marriages end in divorce. A new law to be introduced in 1992 created a 'child support agency' and forced absent parents to pay child maintenance, often by making deductions directly from salary or social security payments. There are many organisations in Britain providing marriage counselling (e.g. Relate) and advice for couples contemplating divorce. Many books are published about divorce including *The Which? Guide to Divorce* by Helen Garlick (Which? Books) and, for do-it-yourself couples, the *Eagle Legal Divorce Pack*.

MILITARY SERVICE

There's no conscription (draft) in Britain where all members of the armed forces are volunteers. Engagements for non-commissioned ranks are from three to 22 years and, subject to a minimum period of from three to nine years, servicemen may quit the service at any time providing they give 12 or 18 months notice. Discharge is also permitted for compassionate reasons, grounds of conscience (conscientious objection) or purchase. Reservists are also entitled to register as conscientious objectors if called up for military service. Short, medium and long-term commissions (as officers) are based on educational and personal qualifications, and all services have a range of educational sponsorship schemes.

Conscription was abolished during the '60s and there's little likelihood of it being introduced short of a major war. Britain is unique in Europe in having no national service and maintains that professional armed services are better equipped to cope in times of crisis. In addition to its full-time military services, Britain has a regular reserve force totalling over 200,000 and volunteer reserve and auxiliary forces of around 100,000 (who train at weekends and for a few weeks each year). Britain is one of the main contributors to NATO and spends around £20 billion on defence and a higher proportion of its GDP than all NATO countries except the USA. Britain has reduced its armed forces in the last few years as part of the so called 'peace dividend' resulting from the thaw in east-west relations.

THE MONARCHY

The British royal family is the longest reigning monarchy in the world and certainly the most famous. Its continuity, apart from the period from 1649 to 1660, remains unbroken for a thousand years. The head of the royal family is the Monarch or Sovereign, Her Majesty (HM) Queen Elizabeth II, who's married to His Royal Highness (HRH) the Duke of Edinburgh, Prince Philip (who's the son of Princess Andrew of Greece). The Monarch is head of state and head of the British Commonwealth, although these are ceremonial titles wielding no real power. Britain is governed by HM Government in the name of the Queen.

The Queen and Prince Philip have four children. Prince Charles (the Prince of Wales), who's the heir to the throne (and unmarried after being divorced from the late Diana, Princess of Wales); Princess Anne (the Princess Royal); Prince Andrew (the Duke of York, divorced from Sarah Ferguson, the Duchess of York); and Prince Edward (who's to be married in 1999). Most members of the Royal Family are popular with the public (their subjects), particularly Queen Elizabeth the Queen Mother, now in her 90s, and despite her great age, still active. The Queen's sister, Princess Margaret is divorced from her husband the Earl of Snowdon (formerly Anthony Armstrong-Jones) and has two children. The Royal Family includes many other major and minor royals, many of whom are descended from King George V's other children, Henry (the 1st Duke of Gloucester), George (the 1st Duke of Kent) and Mary.

Many members of the royal family work tirelessly for charities, in particular the Princess Royal, who travels the world in her work as patron of the United Nation's Save the Children Fund. The Prince of Wales has earned a reputation as the defender of Britain's architectural heritage (when not falling off horses) and a champion of aesthetically pleasing buildings, with both a TV programme and a book to his credit (although what many architects think about Charles' pronouncements are unprintable). He has also initiated a number of projects to help Britain's youth (e.g. the Prince's Youth Business Trust) and regenerate the rundown inner cities.

The most important functions of the Queen are ceremonial and include the state opening of Parliament; giving Royal Assent to bills; the reception of diplomats; entertaining foreign dignitaries; conferring peerages, knighthoods and other honours; the appointment of important office holders; chairing meetings of the Privy Council; and sorting out family squabbles. She also attends numerous artistic, industrial, scientific and charitable events of both national and local interest (the Queen and other members of the royal family are patrons or honorary heads of many leading charities and organisations in Britain). The Sovereign's official birthday is celebrated in June with the Trooping of the Colour ceremony on Horse Guards Parade. Each year the Queen and other members of the royal family visit many areas of Britain and undertake state visits and royal tours of foreign and Commonwealth countries.

Around 85 per cent of the cost of the royal family's official duties is met by public departments, including the upkeep of royal palaces, the Queen's flight and the royal train. The Queen's public expenditure on staff and the expenses incurred in carrying out her official duties is financed from the Civil List, which is approved by Parliament. Annual allowances are made in the Civil List to other members of the royal family, with the exception of the Prince of Wales, who as the Duke of Cornwall receives the net revenue of the estate of the Duchy of Cornwall. The Queen is estimated to be the richest person in Britain, although a lot of the property attributed to her actually belongs to the state.

The antics of the British royal family are the longest-running soap opera in the world and hundreds of column inches of newsprint are devoted to their affairs, both in Britain by the tabloids (or popular press, who delight in printing sensational stories about royalty and anyone famous) and abroad (e.g. France, Germany and Italy), where interest in the British royal family is almost as intense as it is in Britain.

PETS

Britain is generally regarded abroad as a nation of animal lovers and has some 14 million pet owners (including seven million dog owners). This is attested to by the number of bequests received by the Royal Society for the Prevention of Cruelty to Animals (RSPCA), which far exceed the amount left to the Royal Society for the Prevention of Cruelty to Children (RSPCC). The British are almost uniquely sentimental about animals, even those reared for food, and protests over the exports of calves for veal (which are raised in small crates) and other livestock has caused headline news in recent years. Britons are also prominent in international animal protection organisations that attempt to ban cruel sports and practices in which animals are mistreated (such as bullfighting).

Quarantine: Britain has the toughest quarantine regulations in the world in order to guard against the importation of rabies and other animal diseases (we have enough problems with 'mad cow disease' and crazy politicians). Britain has been virtually free of rabies for over 60 years. All mammals other than specific breeds of horses and livestock must spend a period of six months in quarantine in an approved kennel to ensure they are free of rabies and Newcastle disease. Rabies is a serious hazard throughout the world, including many parts of Europe. You can catch this disease if you're bitten, scratched or even licked by an infected dog, cat, fox, monkey, bat or other animal.

Quarantine in Britain applies to all cats and dogs, including guide dogs for the blind. If you're coming to Britain for a limited period only, it may not be worth the trouble and expense of bringing your pet and you may prefer to leave it with friends or relatives during your stay. Before deciding to import an animal, contact the Ministry of Agriculture, Fisheries and Food, Hook Rise South, Tolworth, Surbiton, Surrey KT6 7NF (☎ 0181-330 8174) for the latest regulations, application forms, and a list of approved quarantine kennels and catteries (the ministry also publishes a number of free brochures about rabies). Applications for the importation of dogs, cats and other mammals, should be made at least eight weeks prior to the proposed date of importation. To obtain a licence to import your pet, you must have a confirmed booking at an approved kennel (it's possible to change kennels after arrival), enlist the services of an authorised carrying agent (who will transport your pet from the port to the quarantine kennels), and your pet must arrive at an approved port or airport. Animals must be transported in approved containers, available from air transport companies and pet shops, and must be shipped within six months of the date specified by the licence.

The cost of quarantine for six months is from £75 to £150 a month for a dog, depending on its size (and what it eats) and about £50 a month for a cat. You must also pay for any vaccinations and veterinary costs incurred during your pet's quarantine period. You're permitted, in fact encouraged, to visit your pet in quarantine, but won't be able to take it out for exercise. There are different regulations for some animals, birds for example, serve a shorter quarantine time than animals, until it's established that there's no danger of psittacosis. Pet rabbits must be inoculated against rabies and cannot be imported from the USA. There's no quarantine for cold-blooded animals such as fish and reptiles. Around 5,000 dogs and 3,000 cats are quarantined each year in Britain.

New Regulations: A new system will replace quarantine in 1999 or 2000, under which animals must be microchipped and have a 'passport' listing their vaccinations. It will be restricted to animals imported from rabies-free countries and countries where rabies is under control (e.g. Western Europe and possibly North America), but the current quarantine law will remain in place for pets coming from Eastern Europe, Africa, Asia and South America. The new regulations are expected to initially cost per owners £150 a year plus £60 a year for follow-up vaccinations and around £20 for a border check.

An import licence and a veterinary examination is required for some domestic animals, e.g. horses, of which only certain breeds are kept in quarantine. Dangerous animals (e.g. poisonous snakes, man-eating tigers and teddy-bears) require a special import licence. You require a licence from your local council to keep a poisonous snake or other dangerous wild animal, which must be properly caged with an adequate exercise area, and must pose no risk to public health and safety. **It's a criminal offence to attempt to smuggle an animal into Britain and it's almost always discovered.** Illegally imported animals are either exported immediately or destroyed and the owners are always prosecuted. Owners face (and invariably receive) a heavy fine of up to £1,000 or an unlimited fine and up to a year's imprisonment for deliberate offences. There's no VAT or duty on animals brought into Britain as part of your 'personal belongings', although if you import an animal after your arrival VAT and duty may need to be paid on its value.

If you don't have a friend or relative who will look after your dog or cat while you're on holiday, you will need to board it in a kennel or cattery. If you leave a pet with a friend, always provide full instructions regarding diet, exercise and vets. Ask your friends, neighbours or colleagues if they can recommend somewhere (if they cannot help you, ask your vet). It's important not to take pot luck, as standards vary from excellent to poor. If a kennel or cattery isn't highly recommended, check it personally before boarding your pet and ask what services are charged as extras such as grooming and medicine. Any veterinary fees incurred while boarding are charged to the owner. If you plan to leave your pet at a kennel or cattery, book well in advance, particularly for school holiday periods. Dogs left at kennels may need to be vaccinated against certain diseases, although the requirements vary depending on the kennel.

You can take your dog or cat to a veterinary surgeon (vet) for a course of vaccinations and boosters or spaying and neutering for kittens, the cost of which varies greatly depending on the region and the particular vet. It isn't mandatory to have your dog (or any pet) vaccinated against any disease in Britain, although most dog owners have dogs vaccinated against a number of diseases including distemper, hepatitis, per bo virus and leptospirosis. After the initial primary vaccinations (fee around £20), annual boosters are necessary. You will receive a 'record of primary and booster vaccination' from your vet.

Shop around and compare fees and always agree a fee in advance. Note that there's a big differences in vets' fees in different parts of the country (London is the most expensive). A list of local vets can be obtained from the Royal College of Veterinary Surgeons, 62-64 Horeseferry Road, London SW1P 2AF (☎ 0171-222 2001) or the British Veterinary Association (BVA), 7 Mansfield Street, London W1M 0AT (☎ 0171-636 6541), who provide a series of booklets on pet care. If you cannot afford a vet's fees, the People's Dispensary for Sick Animals (☎ 01952-290999) may provide free treatment.

The RSPCA (The Causeway, Horsham, West Sussex RH12 1HG, ☎ 01403-264181) is the main organisation for animal protection and welfare in Britain, and operates a number of animal clinics and welfare centres. Many Britons are also concerned about the survival of wild animals and there's even a British Hedgehog Protection Society (BHPS), although they have yet to teach them how to cross roads safely. The work of the RSPCA is complemented by the National Canine Defence League (NCDL), a national charity devoted to the welfare of dogs, which takes in lost, abandoned and abused dogs, and turns them into healthy, well-adjusted pets. No healthy dog is ever destroyed by the NCDL (1 Pratt Mews, London NW1 0AD, ☎ 0171-388 0137). There are over 40 animal shelters in Britain including those run by the Cats Protection League, The Dogs Home (Battersea), the NCDL, the RSPCA and the Wood Green Animal Shelters.

After a series of vicious attacks on children the British government introduced a controversial ban on the ownership of certain breeds of dog bred for fighting. These include pit bull terriers, Japanese tosas, dogo argentinos and fila brazilieros, all of which can no longer be imported or bred in Britain (males must be neutered), and must be registered and muzzled in public. If the law is broken a dog can be destroyed and if it attacks anyone you will be liable to a fine (and your dog may also be destroyed). Keep dogs under control near livestock as you can be fined up to £400 if it kills or injures livestock (in addition to compensation) and a farmer can legally shoot a dog that molests livestock.

There isn't a dog registration or licence scheme in England, Wales or Scotland, which was abandoned some years ago. In Northern Ireland a dog licence must be obtained from your local district council office for a dog aged over six months old. Attempts to introduce a dog registration scheme have been defeated by the government, much to the dismay of veterinary surgeons and the RSPCA, who have mounted a campaign to reintroduce dog registration (which has the support of the vast majority of people).

POLICE

Britain doesn't have a national police force but 52 regional police forces (43 in England and Wales, eight in Scotland and one in Northern Ireland), each responsible for a county (or a region in Scotland) or a metropolitan area such as London. There are no special uniformed police in Britain, such as traffic or tourist police, all routine duties being performed by all police forces.

Police in England, Scotland and Wales, are among the few police forces in the world that don't carry firearms (their only weapon is a truncheon, which is a cosh to bash baddies on the head), although in recent years an increasing number of police have been armed for special services such as the prevention of terrorism and when dealing with armed suspects. This is a controversial issue as a number of innocent people have been shot dead by police marksmen in recent years. Some police forces have also been issued with new telescopic truncheons that can cause severe injuries and pepper sprays that in extreme cases can cause blinding. After the deaths of a number of police officers on duty in recent years, there has been an intense debate among the police concerning the carrying of arms. However, around 80 per cent of police officers are against arms and many would leave the force rather than carry a gun. In Northern Ireland, the police (Royal Ulster Constabulary) are armed as a result of the emergency situation in combating the Irish Republican Army (IRA) in the last few decades.

The uniform worn by police forces is generally the same throughout Britain and male bobbies (police officers) on the beat in England and Wales wear the famous British police helmet. Other police officers wear a flat cap with a chequered black and white band. Although Scotland has a different legal system, your rights regarding the police are roughly the same as in the rest of Britain. In addition to full-time police officers, each force has a part-time attachment of unpaid volunteer special constables. Traffic wardens are responsible for traffic and parking and come under the control of the local police force. The police are referred to by a variety of names including cop(per)s, the fuzz, rozzors, the bill, peelers (after Sir Robert Peel, the founder of the London police force), bobbies, flatfoot, bluebottles and various other (unprintable) names.

The British policeman used to be the most respected in the world, not least by the British people. However, in recent years they have had a bad press in England and Wales and their reputation has been badly tarnished. According to a number of surveys, many people have lost faith in the integrity and efficiency of their police force. Many people are unhappy about the police response when they ring 999 or phone their local police station and over half the victims of crime are dissatisfied with the police response. There has been an increase in the number of cases of complaints against the police, many concerning prejudice, harassment, and even brutal and violent treatment. Even more worrying, a public inquiry into the handling of the murder investigation of a black teenager (Steven Lawrence) found that racism was rife in the Metropolitan Police force. There are very few black and Asian officers in Britain (and the relative few there are are often subject to extreme racial abuse and prejudice from their white colleagues).

The police in England and Wales have consistently refused to allow independent investigations of complaints, which means that successful complaints against the police are extremely rare. Most people don't even bother to complain as they consider it a waste of time. The Police Complaints' Authority (PCA) claims to be independent, yet investigations into complaints against police are carried out by police officers. If you're seeking compensation against the police in England or Wales, you must usually seek redress in a county court, as the PCA cannot ensure that you receive compensation. The level of compensation paid by the police to the victims of illegal arrest and police brutality is increasing, often as a result of civil actions for damages. To make a complaint against a police officer, you can either write to the Chief Constable of the force involved, go to any police station or write directly to the Police Complaints Authority (PCA), 10 Great George Street, London SW1P 3AE (☎ 0171-213 5392). In Scotland, complaints against the police involving criminal conduct are investigated by independent public prosecutors, and in Northern Ireland complaints involving death or serious injury are supervised by the Independent Commission for Police Complaints.

A spate of well-publicised cases in the last decade or so have included framed defendants, planting or withholding of evidence, confessions extracted under duress, corruption, incompetence, police assaults, racism and discrimination, all of which have reduced public confidence. As a result the police are finding it harder to secure convictions against guilty criminals when the prosecution case relies mainly on uncorroborated police evidence or confessions, and many cases are thrown out by juries. In England and Wales, it's possible to convict someone solely on the strength of their own confession (but not Scotland), such as happened in a number of cases involving 'IRA terrorists'. A number of infamous cases in which alleged IRA terrorists were jailed for planting bombs were overturned on appeal (after many appeals) when their convictions were judged to be unsafe.

If the foregoing catalogue of complaints has given the impression of an incompetent, prejudiced and dishonest police force, it would be quite wrong. Britain still has one of the best police forces in the world and the vast majority of people rate the police performance as good or very good. What is evident is that the actions of a small minority of officers are increasingly bringing the whole force into disrepute. Unlike some countries, the British public expects its police to be above reproach and although it may seem old-fashioned in the '90s, are unwilling to accept anything less than absolute honesty, impartiality and efficiency from their police officers.

POPULATION

The population of Britain is around 58 million (compared with 38.2 million in 1901), the 17th largest in the world, inhabiting an area of 242,432km² (around 93,600mi²). The population is expected to grow to around 60 million by the year 2001. England is the most populous part of Britain, which with 47 million inhabitants has a density of 366 people per km² (948 per mi²), while Scotland with a total of around five million people, has a density of 66 people per km² (171 per mi²). Greater London has a density of 4,288 people per km² (11,105 per mi²). Northern Ireland has a population of around 1.5 million with a density of 112 people per km² (290 per mi²) and Wales 138 per km² (357 per mi²). Overall the population density of Britain is around 236 people per km² (611 per mi²), which is about the same as Germany and almost 2.5 times that of France.

The central belt, which stretches across England from London to North Yorkshire, contains around half of Britain's population. Outside this area there are a few high-density areas which include Bristol, the south coast, and Tyne and Tees in England; south-east Wales; and Clydeside in Scotland. Some 90 per cent of Britain's population live in urban areas, half of whom inhabit cities of over 500,000. In the last decade there has been a movement of people away from London and the south-east (which contains around 17.5 million people or around 30 per cent of Britain's population), to East Anglia, Wales, the north of England and Scotland.

RELIGION

Britain has a tradition of religious tolerance and every resident has total freedom of religion without hindrance by the state or community. The British, with a few notable exceptions, aren't particularly pious (church attendance has been declining for years), which perhaps explains their traditional tolerance towards the faiths of others. However, discrimination does raise its ugly head occasionally and both Jews and Muslims have been the targets of bigots in recent years (England is credited with having invented anti-semitism in the 12th century). Britain has few of the fire-eating bible-thumping Evangelists to be found in North America and religious programmes on television are mainly confined to a few televised church services on Sunday, none of which make pleas for pots of money to pay for your salvation (or the preacher's high life).

The vast majority of the world's religious and philosophical movements have religious centres or meeting places in London and other major cities. Over 50 per cent of the British population is theoretically of the Anglican Church or the Church of England (or its counterparts), of which the Queen is the head and the religious leader is the Archbishop of Canterbury, who's the 'Primate of all England' (the Archbishop of York is the 'Primate of England'). The Church of England was founded by St. Augustine in AD 597 and became the established church of the land in the 16th century after the reformation. Around 10 per cent or some 5 million of the population of Britain is Roman Catholic.

Other Christian groups or 'free churches' in Britain include various Presbyterian denominations, Congregational Churches, Evangelicals, Methodists, Baptists, Pentecostals, United Reformed and the Salvation Army, all of which admit both men and women to the ministry. The Church of Scotland is Presbyterian, which is more puritanical than the Church of England. Scotland also has a substantial number of Roman Catholics. The Methodists have a strong following in Wales. In Northern Ireland, 65 per cent of the population is Protestant and 35 per cent Roman Catholic.

Britain also has around 1.5 million Muslims, 500,000 Sikhs and around 300,000 Hindus, most originating from the Indian subcontinent, and around 400,000 Jews, the second largest number of any European country. Other religions represented in Britain include the Baha'i Faith, Buddhism, Christian Scientists, Humanists, Jehovah's Witnesses, Mormons, Quakers, Seventh-day Adventists, Spiritualists, Sufis, Theosophists and Unitarians, to name but a few.

British churches include some of the oldest and most magnificent buildings in the world, particularly the great cathedrals, many dating from the 11th or 12th century. You don't need to be religious to enjoy the splendid architecture and grandeur of these buildings, although many are in a state of disrepair. The church receives no public funds and relies on public contributions for the upkeep and restoration of its buildings (so please give generously when visiting them). Most cathedrals have gift shops and many also have a tea room or restaurant, where profits go towards the cathedral's upkeep. Some cathedrals have introduced an entrance fee in recent years.

Cathedrals provide free organ and choral recitals throughout the year, and many also take part in a series of concerts performed by the London Festival Orchestra. Contact your local library or tourist information centre for church information and service times or phone for information (look under 'Places of worship' in the Yellow Pages). British state schools teach religious education as part of the curriculum, when classes comprising more than simple bible study are segregated by denomination. Parents can, however, request permission for their children not to attend religious education classes.

SOCIAL CUSTOMS

All countries have their own particular social customs and Britain is no exception. As with most things in Britain, social customs, behaviour and rules are based on class, but unless you move in very distinguished circles you won't have to worry too much about them. However, good manners, politeness and consideration for others, are considered important in Britain. The British are generally informal in their relationships and won't be too put out if you break the social rules, providing your behaviour isn't too outrageous. On the other hand, in some circles, eccentricity is much prized and you may be invited to some social functions only if you act outrageously (but make sure you don't confuse the Vicar's tea party with the local wife-swapping club). As a foreigner you may be forgiven if you accidentally insult your host, but you may not be invited again. The following are a few British social customs:

- When introduced to someone you generally follow the cue of the person performing the introduction, i.e. if someone is introduced as Tom you can usually call him Tom, however, if someone is introduced as Lord Montague Downton-Cuddlethorpe, it might not be wise to address him as 'Cuddles' (unless he asks you to). Most people will usually say 'Please call me Tom', after a short time (unless his name happens to be Montague). After you have been introduced to someone, you usually say something like, 'How do you do?', 'Pleased to meet you' or 'My pleasure' and shake hands. When saying goodbye, it isn't customary in Britain to shake hands again, although some people do it. In formal circles gentlemen may be expected to bow and kiss the back of a lady's hand, while in informal gatherings strangers are more inclined to limply shake hands. Among friends, it's becoming more common for men to kiss ladies on the cheek (or once on either cheek). Men don't usually kiss or embrace each other in Britain (unless they are gay).

- If you're invited to dinner, it's customary to take a small present of flowers, a plant, chocolates or a bottle of wine. Flowers can be tricky, as to some people, carnations mean bad luck, chrysanthemums are for cemeteries and roses signify love. Maybe you should stick to plastic, silk or dried flowers, or a nice bunch of weeds. Wine can also be a problem, particularly if you're a miser and bring a bottle of cheap Italian plonk and your hosts are wine connoisseurs (they almost certainly won't invite you again). It's customary to serve wine brought by guests at the meal, although don't expect your hosts to serve your cheap Italian red stuff (particularly if they're serving fish). If you stay with someone as a guest for a few days, it's customary to give your host or hostess a small gift when you leave.

● When planning a party, it's polite to notify your neighbours (and perhaps invite them if they're particularly attractive).

● When going anywhere that may be remotely formal (or particularly informal), it's wise to ask in advance what you're expected to wear. Usually when dress is formal, such as evening dress or dinner jacket, it's stated in the invitation and you will be unlikely to be admitted if you turn up in the wrong attire. If you're invited to a wedding, enquire about the dress, unless you want to stick out like a sore thumb. In Britain black or dark dress is almost always worn at funerals.

● Guests are normally expected to be punctual with the exception of certain society parties when late arrival is *de rigueur* (unless you arrive after the celebrity guest) and at weddings (when the bride is often late). Dinner invitations are often phrased as 8pm for 8.30pm, which means arrive at 2000 for drinks and dinner will be served (usually promptly) at 2030. Anyone who arrives very late for dinner (unless his house has burnt down) or horror of horrors, doesn't turn up at all (when death is a good excuse), should expect to be excluded from future guest lists. If you're confused by a multitude of knives, forks and spoons, don't panic but just copy what your neighbour is doing. If he's another ignorant foreigner, you will at least have some company in the social wilderness, to which you will both be consigned (the rule is to start at the outside and work in).

● It isn't necessary to supply workmen, e.g. someone who's working at your home with endless cups of tea and biscuits, although a cup of tea or coffee is appreciated and it may help speed their efforts and discourage them from leaving a mess (but whatever you do, *don't* serve them alcohol).

● If you move in formal circles, such as the diplomatic corps, British government or the higher echelons of the City of London, you had better bone up on etiquette before arriving in Britain. Obtain a copy of Debrett's *Etiquette and Modern Manners* edited by Elsie Burch Donald (Pan), in order to learn the customary traditions, and Debrett's *Correct Form*, which explains the correct form of address, both in speech and writing. If you address the Queen as 'Liz', pass the port or snuff to your right, or start a letter to the Archbishop of Canterbury as 'Dear Archy', you could create a nasty diplomatic incident or at the very least be banned from the croquet club.

TIME DIFFERENCE

Britain is on Greenwich Mean Time (GMT), which is extended by one hour in winter for daylight saving. The change to British Summer Time (BST) is made in the spring (usually at the end of March) when people put their clocks forward one hour. In autumn (2400 on the fourth Sunday in October) clocks are put back one hour for winter time. Time changes are announced in local newspapers and on radio and TV. The time is given on the telephone 'speaking clock' service number and on televisions with teletext services (most remote controls have a 'time' button). When making international telephone calls or travelling long distance by air, check the local time difference, which is shown in the International Dialling section of phone books.

The time difference between Britain (when it's 1200 GMT) and some major international cities is shown below:

LONDON	CAPE TOWN	BOMBAY	TOKYO	LOS ANGELES	NEW YORK
1200	1400	1730	2100	0400	0700

In recent years there has been talk about bringing British time into line with continental Europe, of which the majority of people (some 95 per cent) in England, Wales and Northern Ireland approve (in Scotland around 85 per cent take the opposite view, as they would have even darker mornings).

Naturally there are two sides to every argument, and although the continentals gain an hour of light at the end of the day, they also have an extra hour of darkness in the morning (the further north you live, the later the sun rises). However, research has shown that twice as many road accidents occur when people travel home in the dark, as when they set out in the dark in the morning. The Royal Society for the Prevention of Accidents estimates that if we had BST permanently, road casualties would be dramatically reduced. It's hardly surprising that Britain isn't on Central European Time, seeing as Britain is out of step with Europe on most other things.

TIPPING

Whether you tip or not is a personal choice and may depend on whether you think you've had exceptional service or have received good value for money. The situation with regard to tipping in Britain is anything but clear and can often be embarrassing. In Britain tipping is customary in restaurants (when service isn't included) and when using taxis, when a tip of around 10 to 15 per cent is normal (the fare is usually rounded up to the nearest £). The tipping of hotel staff (e.g. hotel chambermaids) and porters is more discretionary, although most people tip hotel and other porters 50p to £1 per suitcase, or about the same to a doorman who gets you a taxi (the BTA recommend a tip of 10 to 15 per cent for hotel staff when service isn't included in the price). Tipping in hotels depend whether you're staying at Claridges or some back street hovel. Tipping hairdressers (£1 or £2 or 10 per cent of the bill, depending on the service), cloakroom attendants and garage staff (who clean your car's windscreen, or check its oil or tyre pressures) is fairly common.

Most Britons are anti-tipping (but usually too timid not to leave a tip) and would like to see it abolished and replaced with a universal service charge. Many restaurant owners exploit the situation and intentionally pay low wages on the expectation that employees will supplement their wages with tips. If you don't tip a waiter he may not starve (unless the restaurant's food is particularly bad), but he may struggle to survive on his meagre salary. Many bills have 'service not included' printed on them, which is an open invitation for you to leave a tip. Even when service is included in the bill, this doesn't mean that the percentage added for service goes to the staff, although 'service included' deters most people from leaving a tip.

Don't be shy about asking whether service is included (which should be shown on the menu). Restaurant tips can be included in cheque or credit card payments or given as cash. The total on credit card counterfoils is often left blank, even when service was included in the price, to encourage you to leave a tip; don't forget to fill in the total before signing it (if you don't leave a tip and the waiter tips the soup in your lap on your return, you will know why). It isn't customary to tip a barman in a pub, although you can offer to buy him a drink if you've been propping up the bar for a few hours. It is, however, customary to tip in bars and hotels when drinks are served at a table.

TOILETS

Although public toilets in Britain are usually free and are better than many found on the continent (e.g. in France), the general standard is pretty awful and many are considered no-go areas, even for the most desperate person. The most sanitary (even luxurious) toilets are found in hotels, restaurants and department stores, and are for customers only. Toilets in public offices, museums and galleries are also usually clean; railway stations, bus stations, airports, multi-storey car parks and petrol stations usually have reasonably clean toilets; while pub toilets vary from bad to excellent.

There's a charge of 10p to use toilets at London's mainline rail stations and in some department stores. Entrance is either through a turnstile or via a coin machine on the door. A change machine isn't usually provided and naturally the attendant will be absent when you're desperate and lack a 10p coin. Toilets provided by local councils are located in towns, parks, car parks and on beaches, and are generally among the worst anywhere. Many should be visited only when you're wearing a gas mask (the financial squeeze on local authorities in recent years has also meant the closure of many public toilets). Some public toilets require payment of 5p or 10p to use a WC. Many men's toilets in pubs have contraceptive machines (make sure you use the correct toilet as the stylish male and female signs are often difficult to differentiate).

One of the most surprising things about toilets (or bathrooms) in Britain is the variety of names they have, which include toilets, public conveniences, ladies or gents (room), WC (water closet), loo, bog, crapper (after Thomas Crapper who invented the WC in the 1880s), dunny (Aus.), lavatory (lav), thunder box and smallest room (many foreigners believe British culture is based on the toilet). People in Britain don't usually use the American terms powder room, wash room or bathroom when referring to a toilet. WCs are fitted with a variety of flushing methods, including chains to pull, buttons to push (located on the WC or on the wall), knobs to pull and foot buttons to tread on. Some even flush automatically. Men's urinals may also have a knob to be pushed, pulled or trodden on (which many people neglect to do), although most are automatic.

Toilets are fitted with a variety of hand-washing facilities (or none at all) which include wash basins with knobs you hold down to obtain water, which may be cold. There may be a bar of soap, although soap is usually provided in liquid or powder form from a dispenser. Hand-drying facilities include disposable paper towels, roll linen towels and hot air dryers, which may operate manually via a button or automatically (and which always stop just before your hands are dry). Often public toilets provide no soap or hand-drying facilities and may even have no running water or toilet paper. An increasing number of department stores, large supermarkets, large chemists, Mothercare shops, chemists (such as Boots), restaurants, pubs and public toilets for motorists provide nappy changing facilities or facilities for nursing mothers (breast-feeding isn't usually performed in public in Britain). Many shopping centres have special toilets for the disabled, as do airports and major railway stations. However, most public toilets for motorists aren't accessible to disabled drivers.

19.

THE BRITISH

Who are the British? What are they like? Let's take a candid and totally prejudiced look at the British people, **tongue firmly in cheek**, and hope they forgive my flippancy or that they don't read this bit (which is why it's hidden away at the back of the book).

The typical Briton is introspective, patriotic, insular, xenophobic, brave, small-minded, polite, insecure, arrogant, a compulsive gambler, humorous, reserved, conservative, reticent, hypocritical, a racist, boring, a royalist, condescending, depressed, a keen gardener, semi-literate, hard-working, unambitious, ironic, passionless, cosmopolitan, a whinger, hard-headed, liberal, a traditionalist, a couch potato, obsequious, a masochist, complacent, homely, pragmatic, cynical, decent, melancholic, unhealthy, a poor cook, pompous, eccentric, inebriated, proud, self-deprecating, tolerant, inhibited, a perpetual shopper, conceited, courageous, idiosyncratic, mean (a bad tipper), courteous, jingoistic, stuffy, well-mannered, pessimistic, disciplined, an habitual queuer, stoic, modest, gloomy, shy, serious, apathetic, honest, whimpish, fair, snobbish, friendly, quaint, decadent, civilised, dogmatic, scruffy, prejudiced, class conscious and a soccer hooligan.

If the above list contains a few contradictions, it's because there's no such thing as a typical Briton and very few people conform to the standard British stereotype (whatever that is). Apart from the multifarious differences in character between the people from different parts of England (particularly between those from the north and the south), the population of Britain encompasses a disparate mixture of Scots, Welsh, Irish and assorted ethnic groups originating from throughout the British Commonwealth, plus miscellaneous foreigners from all corners of the globe who have chosen to make Britain their home (London is the most ethnically diverse city in the world).

One of the things which initially confuses foreigners living in Britain is its class system, which is a curious British affectation. Entry to the upper class echelons is rooted in birthright and ill-bred upstarts with pots of 'new' money (particularly foreigners with unpronounceable names), find they are unable to buy entry to the most exclusive clubs and homes of England (unless they're *seriously* rich). Many Britons are obsessed with class and for some maintaining or improving their position on the social ladder is a full-time occupation (the ultimate aim being to acquire a knighthood or peerage). The rest of us pretend we're a 'better' class than we actually are, with the exception of a few politicians who are busy trying to live down their privileged past (in order to court popularity with the underprivileged masses).

At the top of the heap there's the upper class (the 'blue-bloods' or aristocracy) crowned by the British Royal Family, followed at a respectable distance by the middle class (which is subdivided into upper middle class, middle middle class, and lower middle class), the working class or lower class, and two entirely new categories that are the inevitable legacy of the unbridled market economy of the last few decades: the underclass and the beggar class. In Britain, people were traditionally officially classified according to their occupations under classes A to E. However, due to the burgeoning middle class in the last few decades (we are all middle class now) the government has introduced no less than 17 new classes (including a meritocratic super class of top professionals and managers earning zillions a year). Class is of course, wholly unimportant in Britain, providing you attended public school, speak with the right accent and have pots of inherited money.

Britain has been uncharitably described (with a hint of truth) as a society based on privilege, inherited wealth and contacts, dominated by spivs, snobs and vandals. On taking office in 1990, Prime Minister John Major declared that he intended to create a classless society, which must have sent a shudder through Conservative clubs up and down the land. Surely he didn't mean he was going to abolish the anachronistic House of Lords, the monarchy and the honours system, ban private schools and hospitals, prohibit first class transport, forbid double-barrelled names and turn all the country mansions into NHS hospitals?

Class is also what divides the bosses from the workers in Britain and the class struggle is at the root of many industrial disputes. A blue-collar (manual) worker must never accept a position that will elevate him to the ranks of the lower middle class (a white-collar job), otherwise his work mates will no longer speak to him and he'll be banned from the local working men's club (as a consolation he may be accepted as a member at the Conservative club). Similarly, middle-class management must never concede an inch to the workers and most importantly, must never have direct discussions with them about anything, particularly pay rises or a reduction in working hours.

One thing that would probably cause a strike in any country is British food, particularly in most company canteens and restaurants, where everything is served with chips or ice-cream. Of course, British food isn't *always* as bad as it's painted by foreigners (what can people who eat anything that crawls, jumps, swims or flies, possibly know about *real* food?). While it's true that British food is often bland, may look terrible and can make you sick, for most people it's just a matter of getting used to it (what's wrong with a diet of brown sauce, chips, biscuits and tea anyway?). After all, it's usually necessary to become acclimatised to the food in most foreign countries.

However, it's difficult not to have some sympathy with foreigners who think that many British 'restaurants' should post health warnings and be equipped with an emergency medical centre (there's nothing wrong with British food that a good stomach pump cannot cure). It may come as a surprise to many foreigners to learn that British bookshops are bursting with cookery books and they *aren't* full of blank pages or all written by foreigners. Britain also has many popular television cookery programmes that usually feature eccentric chefs and scrumptious looking food (could it be plastic or imported?). The British can console themselves with the knowledge that they (or some of them) at least know how to behave *at* the table, even if they don't have much idea what to serve *on* it.

To compensate for their deficiencies in the kitchen, the British are famous for their love of wine (or anything alcoholic) and are among the world's foremost (self-appointed) experts on the character and qualities of good wine, although they're often better talkers than drinkers. In Britain a wine may be described as having intense aromas and flavours (that whoosh up your nose) of berries, bramble-jelly or morello cherries, peppery spices, mint, toffee and a hint of honey (when not tasting of dirty socks, rotten eggs, unwashed feet, horse manure, hamster cages or a sumo wrestler's thighs). The secret of dining in Britain is to drink a lot, as when you're drunk most food tastes okay. It may come as a surprise to many foreigners to discover that the British even make their own wine (not that home-made stuff made from elderberries and other strange fruit, but real commercially-produced wine made from grapes!) and although it isn't exactly causing panic among continental wine producers, some of it's almost palatable. Contrary to popular belief, the British aren't *all* drunks and are languishing in a lowly 20th position in the alcohol consumption league among the world's top 30 developed countries (although Britain's lager louts are doing their best to remedy this stain on the national character).

The British do at least know how to make a good cuppa (tea) and don't believe in polluting it with lemon or herbs (just milk and sugar). The British recipe for any national disaster, whether it's a cricket thrashing at the hands of the Aussies or a power cut during Coronation Street, is to make a 'nice cup of tea'. Tea is drunk at almost any time (around 100 million cups a day), not just in the morning or for 'afternoon tea'. Many Britons drink tea in the same quantities as other Europeans drink mineral water or wine. Unfortunately coffee is a different matter altogether and although the British have been drinking it since the 16ᵗʰ century (long before tea), they have yet to master the art of brewing a half decent pot, which just goes to show that practice *doesn't* always make perfect. The British don't do anything by halves and their coffee, almost always instant, is easily the worst in the world (it would help if they actually **added some coffee**).

You may sometimes get the impression that the British are an unfriendly lot, as your neighbours won't always say hello and probably won't drop by or invite you to their home for a cup of tea (if they offer coffee, invent an urgent appointment!). As an outsider it may be left to you to make the first move, although if you drop by uninvited your neighbours may think that you're being pushy and just trying to sneek a look at their furniture. Northerners are generally friendly and warm-hearted, particularly when compared with the detached and aloof southerners who won't usually give you the time of day. If your southern neighbour does condescend to speak to you, he's likely to greet you with the ritual "How are you?" This doesn't of course mean "How are you feeling mentally, physically or spiritually", but simply "Hello". The questioner usually couldn't care less whether you're fighting fit or on your death bed. The ritual answer is (even if you've just had a heart and lung transplant) "Fine, thank you – how are you?"

If you wish to start a conversation with your neighbour (or anyone), a remark such as "nice weather" will usually elicit a response (particularly if it's raining cats and dogs). The weather is a hallowed topic in Britain and it's the duty of every upstanding citizen to make daily weather predictions due to the awful hash made of it by the meteorologists (if the official forecast is for fine weather, batten down the hatches). But seriously, British weather forecasting is a highly scientific art, seaweed being used only in the direst of emergencies when the atmospheric conditions that create the weather stubbornly refuse to co-operate with the expert's guesses (or when the satellite packs up). Britain has rather a lot of weather and there's often rain, gales, fog, snow and a heat-wave in the same day (although the weather is always described as 'nice' or 'not very nice'). When it snows in Britain, everyone and everything is paralysed and people start predicting the end of civilisation (as we know it).

The British stick steadfastly to their Fahrenheit temperature measures and many people haven't a clue whether 20°C is boiling hot, lukewarm or bloody freezing. The seasons are a mite erratic in Britain, but as a rough guide winter lasts for around 11 months, with a break of a couple of weeks for both spring and autumn, and (in a good year) a couple of days for summer. There is, however, no truth in the rumour that *all* the world's bad weather originates in the British Isles (some of it **must** come from somewhere else!). The British will do anything to escape for a few weeks to sunnier climes (whatever do they find to talk about on holiday when the sky is boringly blue each day?), even going so far as to spend days in an airport lounge for the dubious pleasure of a few weeks in a half-built hotel, bathing in polluted seas and getting sick on foreign food. The fact that no people anywhere have shown such a consistent desire to emigrate as the British may have more than a little to do with the climate.

It's a common misconception among many foreigners that the British all speak English. There are numerous accents and dialects in Britain, half of which are so thick that you could be forgiven for thinking that people are conversing in an ancient secret language (like politicians). A Briton's accent and choice of words is usually a dead give-away as to his upbringing. For example you can safely bet that someone who says, "One feels that one has a certain obligation to one's social peers to attend Royal Ascot, even though one doesn't really care for horse racing oneself", isn't from London's East End. One-third of the British use such long words that most of us cannot even pronounce them (let alone understand them) and some 25 per cent are immigrants who speak only Hindi, Welsh, Bengali, Irish, Gaelic, Chinese, American, Gujarati, Arabic, Punjabi, Swahili, Urdu, Italian, Turkish, Spanish, Esperanto, Yiddish or Polish.

The rest are tourists, who usually speak the best English of all, but unfortunately don't remain in one place long enough to hold a conversation with anyone. Some foreigners actually pay real money to come to England *to learn English*, which is part of a grand plot to get them to teach us how to talk proper at their expense. If you're a foreigner and speak good English, you can of course always practice with other foreigners who you'll understand you perfectly. If you have a few problems writing English and tend to get all the words mixed up (to say nothing of the damned spelling), fear not; you'll be in excellent company as many British are barely literate (the average Briton's vocabulary is around 1,000 words or 100 for *Sun* readers). The best compliment a foreigner can receive from a native is that his English is rather unusual or unorthodox, as he'll then blend in with the rest of us and won't be taken for an alien (if you speak perfect English you'll be instantly exposed as a foreigner).

Many Britons are prejudiced against all foreigners and the English are also prejudiced against English from other regions, Irish, Scots, Welsh, Yanks, Europeans, most other foreigners and anyone who speaks with a different (i.e. lower class) accent. However, don't be concerned, as British racism always refers to 'the others' and present company is usually excepted. The British, in common with most other races, don't have a lot of time for foreigners, particularly rich tourists and foreigners who buy up all the best property, *who should all stay at home*. Most Britons' image of foreigners is gleaned from the stereotypes portrayed on television. For example every Briton knows that *all* Americans are millionaires with flash cars, murderers or policemen (or all three), drive like maniacs at a zillion miles an hour and make love with their clothes on in full makeup. However, it's the Germans and Japanese who, despite providing us with reliable cars and other things that work, remain the baddest of baddies and are still portrayed as 'the enemy' in weekly TV reruns of World War II.

The British are masters of the understatement and rarely rave about anything. If they're excited about something they sometimes enthuse "that's nice" and on the rare occasion when they're deliriously happy, they've been known to exclaim "I say, that's rather good". On the other hand, if something disastrous happens (like their house burns down) it might be termed "a spot of bother". The end of the world will probably be pronounced "unfortunate" or, if there was something particularly good on TV that evening, it may even be greeted as "a jolly bad show" (the ultimate tragedy). The true character of the British is, however, revealed when they are at play, particularly when they're engaged in sport.

Britain is sports mad (although most people confine their interest to spectating or gambling rather than taking part) and the British, or at least the English, are famous for their sense of fair play and playing by the rules – cheating is considered terribly bad form. Soccer is Britain's national sport and if we hadn't taught all the other nations to play we might even be world champions (whatever you do don't remind the British who won the World Cup in 1998).

However, the real character and true sporting traditions of the English (other Brits have better things to do) are embodied in the game of cricket, a study of which provides a valuable insight into these strange islanders (and their attitude towards tea parties, religion, sex and foreigners). Foreigners may at first have a spot of bother understanding what cricket is all about (although it's far easier to understand than British politics), but after a few decades most get the hang of it (unlike British politics which remain a complete mystery). The first thing you need to understand is that cricket is a game for gentlemen, embodying the great British traditions of fair play, honour and sportsmanship (except when played by foreigners, who haven't the remotest concept of these things).

It's tempting (although fairly pointless) to make comparisons between cricket and a minority sport played in the USA, called baseball (the nearest equivalent in Britain is rounders, a sissy game played by girls). Imagine if you can, a baseball match that lasts five days with interminable breaks for breakfast, drinks, rain, streakers (naked runners), lunch, injuries, stray dogs, more rain, rest days, more drinks, tea, bad light, dinner, supper, and even more rain, and always ends in a draw (if not abandoned due to rain) – and you'll have a rough idea what it's all about. Despite the length of a cricket match, which varies from one to five days, it's an enthralling and thrilling sport. On the rare occasions when things get just a teensy bit boring, there's always something exciting to liven things up such as a newspaper blowing across the pitch, a stray dog or pigeon on the field, or on a good day, a streaker. The commentators do a sterling job and keep the audience spellbound with the most amazing and fascinating statistics and anecdotes about cricket's legendary heroes. Gripping stuff! (Some 85 per cent of Americans think that heaven has a baseball park – won't they be disappointed when they discover it's a cricket pitch!)

The rules of cricket are a little complicated (Einstein's theory of relativity is much easier to understand), so I won't bore you by trying to explain them in detail (fascinating though they are). A cricket team consists of 11 players and a 12th man who has the most important job of all – carrying the drinks tray. He's also sometimes called on to play when one of his team-mates collapses from frostbite or is overcome by excitement. Like baseball, one team bats and the other team attempts to get them out (or committed to hospital) by hurling a ball at the batsman's head. The team in the field (not batting) stands around in set positions with peculiar names such as gulley, slips, short leg, square leg, long leg, peg leg, cover point, third man (they made a film about him), mid-off, mid-on and oddest of all – silly mid-off and silly mid-on. The last two should really be named 'raving loony mid-off' and 'stark staring bonkers' mid-on. Only someone who's a few pence short of a pound stands directly in front of a batsman as he's about to hit a very hard ball in your direction at around 100mph (160kph).

When the bowler strikes the wicket or the batsman with the ball everyone shouts in unison "Howzat" (very loudly, because the umpire is usually asleep, hard of hearing, short-sighted or all three). Cricketers play in a white uniform (like inmates in a sanatorium) and the only colourful things about the game are the ball (red) and the language used by the batsman (blue) when he's hit by the ball or when the umpire gives him out leg before wicket (lbw) to a ball that didn't touch him, and in any case was a million miles away from the wicket. One of the unwritten rules of cricket is that the players (gentlemen) never argue with the umpire, no matter how shortsighted, biased and totally ignorant of the rules the idiot is.

The Aussies (Australians), whom everyone knows have no respect for tradition (and couldn't give a XXXX for anything that doesn't emanate from a tinny or a barrel), have attempted to brighten up the game's image by dressing up like clowns for one day matches (yet another sacrilege to the old school). One of the worst mistakes the English ever made was to teach foreigners how to play cricket (or any other sport), as the ungrateful blighters get a sadistic delight in rubbing their mentors' noses in the dirt. One of the problems with foreigners is that they have no concept of how a gentlemen should behave and fail to realise that the real purpose of sport is taking part and **nothing at all to do with winning**. Gallant losers are feted as heroes in Britain and heroic defeats against overwhelming odds are infinitely preferable to easy (hollow) victories.

The British have a passion for queuing (lining up) and appear to outsiders to have endless patience (as you would expect from a nation that can endure a five-day cricket match). The British queue everywhere for everything, including football tickets, sales (when people queue for days or weeks), buses, trains, aircraft, fast food (or slow food if there's a long queue), post offices, government offices, hospital beds, concerts, cafeterias, doctor's and dentist's waiting rooms, groceries (supermarkets), theatre tickets, banks and payphones. The other form of queue popular in Britain is the traffic jam. Many motorists spend their weekdays bumper to bumper driving round and round the M25 motorway (or 'magic roundabout'), which is circular to make it easier to get back to where you started. At weekends motorists often get withdrawal symptoms and go for a drive with the family, friends, relatives and the dog, in search of a traffic jam, usually to be found anywhere near coastal areas from spring to autumn, particularly over public holiday weekends.

Queuing isn't always a necessity in Britain, but simply a herd instinct that compels people to huddle together (in winter it helps to keep warm), except of course when travelling by public transport, when the rules are somewhat different. On public transport you must never sit next to anyone when an empty seat is available and you must spread yourself and your belongings over two or three seats and never move for anyone (the best way is to feign sleep with a belligerent expression on your face – most people wouldn't dare disturb you). You must avoid looking at your fellow passengers at all costs (in case a stranger smiles at you), usually achieved by staring fixedly at the back of a newspaper or out of the window. Whatever you do don't open a window and let in any nasty fresh air, which will cause a riot.

There's not a word of truth in the rumour that British men are lousy lovers (or all gay), which is a cheap lie put about by sex mad Latinos so that they can keep all the women for themselves. Slanderous foreign propagandists have calculated that the British make love an average of twice a month. To add insult to injury they also estimate this is more often than we bathe (which is a damn insult as the average Briton washes at least once a week). If you find a foreigner under your bed or in your bath don't be alarmed, he'll only be conducting a sex survey for *Paris Match* or *Der Spiegel*.

Although, perhaps not the most romantic of lovers (but *much* better than those unctuous Italians, who are all talk and no trousers and have the lowest birth-rate in

Europe), the British know what it's for and don't need a ruler to measure their manhood (neither do we *all* get our kicks flashing, mooning or being whipped by women in leather underwear). Judging by the illegitimate birth rate (around 25 per cent of all births), many Britons don't wait until they're married to find out what sex is all about either. 'No Sex Please We're British' is simply a challenge to women who have had their fill of Latinos with short fat hairy legs (how does a woman make love to someone who only comes up to her kneecaps anyway?). Sex is definitely not simply a person's gender in Britain and most people take more than a hot-water bottle to bed with them.

British women are among the most emancipated in the world, not that the weaker sex (men) gave in graciously, and have universal suffrage and are allowed to vote and drive cars. Nevertheless, it's difficult if not impossible for women to claw their way to the top of most professions or into boardrooms, which remain bastions of male chauvinism (although if you're 'man' enough it can be done). Of course no self-respecting man would allow himself to be dominated by a mere woman, unless of course he's a wimp and she's a handbag-wielding, belligerent battler. If British (male) politicians learnt nothing else during the Thatcher years, it was the utter havoc a woman can wreak in the boardroom.

The main problem with the British economy (apart from the ineptitude of British politicians) is that many Britons lack ambition. They certainly want 'loadsamoney', but would rather do almost anything than work for it (contrary to the popularly held misconception that 'hard work never did anyone any harm', the British know only too well that it's fatal). The British are reluctant entrepreneurs and many succeed in their own business only when forced into it, e.g. as a consequence of telling the boss what a ****** he is at the office party. Most people prefer to try their luck at gambling (rather than work) and will bet on almost anything including the national lottery, football pools, horse and greyhound racing, bingo, casinos, names of royal babies or ships, public appointments, election results and who the PM will sack next (or who will resign) – you name it and someone will make a book on it (one of the reasons that gambling is so popular is that gambling debts are unenforceable in law). However, the attitude to gambling is changing. Nowadays someone who wins a fortune on the lottery is unlikely to declare that it won't change his life and that he'll be keeping his job as a £50 a week farm labourer (instead he'll buy a villa in Spain, a yacht and a Ferrari). If the British injected as much energy into work and business as they do into gambling, they might even be able to compete with the Germans and Japanese.

Britain's electoral system is of course unique (nobody would be daft enough to copy it) and elections are decided by the first horse (or ass) past the post. This means that the party in power rarely has more than around 40 per cent of the total vote and minority parties can poll 25 per cent of the vote and end up with only a handful of seats. Of course nobody in Britain actually votes *for* a political party, particularly the one that wins the election (or at least nobody will admit it). Most are registering a protest vote or voting for the party they hope will do the least damage. Despite their singular lack of success, the minority parties battle manfully (and womanly) on and include such defenders of democracy as the 'Monster Raving Loony Party' (the only British political party with an honest name). Surprisingly few women are MPs, which proves conclusively that they are more intelligent than men and have better things to do with their lives than hurl insults at each other (politicians are the only children who immature with age). The calibre of British politicians may have something to do with the fact that politicking is the only job that doesn't require any qualifications, training or brains (the perfect job for someone who thinks he knows everything and knows *** all!).

Nonetheless, as with most charlatans and confidence tricksters, there's honour among politicians who rarely stab each other in the back (when someone is looking). Although British politicians seldom tell the truth and government statistics are all but meaningless due to the myriad ways of calculating and distorting them, politicians never in fact tell porkies (lies). A politician can only accuse another honourable member of being economical with the truth, but never of lying (in Britain, as in most countries, there are liars, damn liars and politicians). One of the favourite pastimes of British politicians (when not playing golf or holidaying in exotic places at the taxpayers' expense) is sitting on committees, which after weeks of intense discussions and committee meetings (standing, select, joint, sitting, party, etc.), produce volumes of recommendations. So as not to waste any more time and taxpayers' money these are promptly filed in the garbage bin and forgotten about. British politics are totally incomprehensible and deadly boring to all foreigners (and almost everyone else).

Some people (usually foreigners) think that the British are out of step with their 'partners' in the European Union. Of course as any Briton will tell you, the only reason we don't always see eye to eye with the damn foreigners (who make up the insignificant part of the EU) is that they refuse to listen to us and do as we tell them (whatever happened to the good 'ol days when Johnny Foreigner knew his place). It must be obvious to everyone that we know best; just look at our economy, modern infrastructure, culinary traditions, public services, cricket team, our . . er . . um . . . of course having a strong economy and things that work isn't everything.

The notion that Britain doesn't always know best is ridiculous and if there's to be a united Europe, those foreign bounders had better mend their ways (we didn't fight two world wars so that Jerry could tell us what to do!). They can start by adopting British time, driving on the left, making English their national language, anglicising their ridiculous names and moving the EU headquarters and parliament to London – which every civilised person knows is the centre of the universe. **Perhaps then we would all get on much better!** If they don't agree we can always fill in our end of the Channel Tunnel and refuse to answer the telephone. Many Britons firmly believe that Britain is still a world power, when in reality it doesn't have a lot of influence in the modern world. This 'little England' attitude is propagated by Tory Euro-sceptics who will do anything they can to throw a spanner in the Euro-works. To most Britons, Europe is a place full of foreigners where the sun shines when they go on holiday and most are unaware or choose to ignore the fact that Britain is actually part of it (at least geographically).

The secret of life in Britain is to maintain a sense of humour (and carry a big umbrella). Most Brits have a lively sense of humour and a keen sense of the ridiculous, which helps make life in Britain bearable (the worst insult is to accuse someone of having no sense of humour). One of the things that endears the British most to foreigners is their ability to poke fun at themselves (the British don't take themselves too seriously) and everyone else, as typified in TV programmes such as Monty Python and Spitting Images. Nothing escapes the barbs of the satirists, from the Pope to the Prime Minister, the President of the United States to the Royal Family, everyone is lampooned with equal affection.

It's often difficult for foreigners to understand British humour or to recognise when someone is being serious or joking, although the subject at hand usually offers a clue. Generally the more earnest or solemn the topic, the more likely they are to be joking. Amazingly some foreigners think that the British have no sense of humour (usually Americans who don't understand our subtle way with words and cannot understand *real* English anyway). Many foreigners believe the British are at least a little eccentric and at their worst, stark staring bonkers.

Enough of this flippancy – now for the serious bit!

Britain has its fair share of problems and is still failing (by its <u>own</u> criteria) in many vital areas, including education, health and industry (apart from those that we've sold to foreigners). However, we are still world leaders in pageantry and football hooliganism. Major concerns include rising crime (particularly juvenile and violent crime), deteriorating state education, a flourishing drugs culture, the failing health service, inequality (the growing gulf between rich and poor), a pensions crisis, pollution, poor public transport, homelessness, overcrowded roads, urban blight and a burgeoning underclass. The worst crisis is among Britain's young working class males, where unemployment is rife and among whom the suicide rate has risen by some two-thirds in the last decade. Perhaps the most serious decline in British life is the loss of social cohesion and sense of community and the breakdown of the family unit. Some 40 per cent of marriages end in divorce and over a quarter of all births are illegitimate, which has resulted in one family in three having only one parent.

However, don't despair. Not everything in Britain is depressing and the quality of life is considered by many foreigners to be excellent and among the best in the world (despite the results of some surveys). In the last decade, Britain has become a more entrepreneurial, risk-taking society that's less dependent on the state. It has also become a more European nation, less afraid of European bogeymen and domination by foreigners (although the euro will still be a hard sell). Most Britons are better off today than they have ever been and have become more optimistic about their future in the last few years, which coincided with the election of a dynamic and up-beat Labour government (that replaced the corrupt and discredited Tories in 1997). In recent years the government has been making far-reaching, top-down reforms that will radically change Britain (hopefully for the better) in the 21st century. The political spin doctors have also been busy re-branding New Britain as cool Britannia, with its flourishing restaurants, fashion, music, night-life and style, all fields in which Britain can hold its own with the world's best.

The British enjoy superb entertainment, leisure, sports and cultural facilities, which for their sheer variety, accessibility and reasonable cost are among the best in the world. The quality and huge choice of goods in British shops is superb and why many people travel from far and wide simply to shop in Britain. British television has no equals, national and local radio is excellent, and the country has an unrivalled choice of quality newspapers, magazines and literature. Britain is a caring society, highlighted by the abundance of charitable and voluntary organisations, unparalleled in any other country, all of which do invaluable work (both nationally and internationally). Britain remains a centre of scientific excellence and only American scientists have won more Nobel prizes. It's also one of the least corrupt and most civilised countries in the world.

The British have more freedom from government interference than the people of most countries, to do, say and act any way they like, which most people take for granted. Britain is still a great civilised power (if a little frayed at the edges) and a positive influence in the world, and London remains the centre of the English-speaking world. Whatever else it may be, life in Britain is invariably spiritually, mentally and intellectually stimulating and never dull. Although foreigners may occasionally complain about Britain and the British weather, most feel they are privileged to live there and wouldn't dream of leaving.

Last, but certainly not least, there are the British people, who although they can be infuriating at times, will charm and delight you with their sense of humour and idiosyncrasies. When your patience with Britain and the British is stretched to breaking point, simply take yourself off to the nearest pub and order a pint of ale or a large gin and tonic: Britain looks an even nicer place through the bottom of a (rose-tinted) glass and with a bit of luck you won't even notice that it's still raining.

20.

MOVING HOUSE OR LEAVING BRITAIN

When moving house or leaving Britain there are many things to be considered and a 'million' people to be informed. The checklists contained in this chapter are designed to make the task easier and hopefully help prevent an ulcer or a nervous breakdown (providing of course you don't leave everything to the last minute). Note that only divorce or a bereavement cause more stress than moving house! See also **Relocation Consultants** on page 98.

MOVING HOUSE

When moving house within Britain the following items should be considered:

* If you live in rented accommodation you must give your landlord notice (the period will depend on your contract). You may need to remain until a minimum period has elapsed, e.g. six months for an assured shorthold tenancy. If you don't give your landlord sufficient notice, you will be required to pay rent until the end of your contract or for the full notice period. This will also apply if you have a separate contract for a garage or other rented property (e.g. a holiday home).

* Inform the following:

  – Your employer.

  – If moving to a new district or borough council area, you must inform your present council when you move and re-register in your new council area after arrival. When moving to a new county or borough you may be entitled to a refund of a portion of your council tax.

  – If you're registered with the police (see page 92), you must inform them of your new address or re-register at the nearest police station in your new area.

  – The electricity, gas and water companies.

  – Inform your telephone company if you have a telephone (see **Moving or Leaving Britain** on page 153).

  – Your insurance companies (for example health, car, home contents and private pension); banks, building societies, post office (e.g. savings or Giro account), stockbroker and other financial institutions; credit card, charge card and hire purchase companies; solicitor and accountant; and local businesses where you have accounts.

  – Your family doctor, dentist and other health practitioners. Health records should be transferred to your new doctor and dentist, if applicable.

  – Your children's (and your) schools. If applicable, arrange for schooling in your new area. Try to give a term's notice and obtain a copy of any relevant school reports or records from your children's current schools.

  – All regular correspondents, subscriptions, social and sports clubs, professional and trade journals, and friends and relatives. Give or send them your new address and telephone number. Arrange to have your mail redirected by the post office (see **Change of Address** on page 130).

  – If you have a British driving licence or a British registered car, inform the Vehicle License Registration Office (see page 232) as soon as possible after moving.

- Your local consulate or embassy if you're registered with them (see page 93).
- Return any library books or anything borrowed.
- Arrange removal of your furniture and belongings by booking a removal company well in advance. If you have only a few items of furniture to move, you may prefer to do your own move, in which case you may need to hire a van.
- Arrange for a cleaning company and/or decorating company for rented accommodation, if necessary.
- If renting, contact your landlord or the letting agency to have your deposit returned (with interest, if applicable).
- Cancel the milk and newspaper deliveries.
- Ask yourself (again): 'Is it really worth all this trouble?'

LEAVING BRITAIN

Before leaving Britain permanently or for an indefinite period, the following items should be considered *in addition* to those listed above under **Moving House**:

- Give notice to your employer, if applicable.
- Check that your own and your family's passports are valid.
- Check whether any special requirements (e.g. visas, permits or inoculations) are necessary for entry into your country of destination by contacting the local embassy or consulate in Britain. An exit permit or visa isn't required to leave Britain.
- Book a removal company well in advance. International removal companies usually provide a wealth of information and may also be able to advise on various matters concerning your relocation. Find out the exact procedure for shipping your belongings to your country of destination from the local embassy or consulate in Britain of the country to which you're moving (don't rely entirely on your shipping company). Special forms may need to be completed before arrival.
- You may qualify for a rebate on your tax (see page 352) and national insurance contributions (see page 306). If you're leaving Britain permanently and have been a member of a company pension scheme (or have a personal pension plan), your contributions will remain in the fund and you will receive a reduced pension on retirement (see page 309). Contact your company personnel office, local tax office, or pension company for information.
- Arrange to sell anything you aren't taking with you (e.g. house, car and furniture) and to ship your belongings. If you have been living in Britain for less than a year, you're required to export all personal effects, including furniture and vehicles, that were imported tax and duty-free.
- If you have a British registered car which you're permanently exporting, you should complete a 'permanent export certificate' (available from a VRO) and register the vehicle in your new country of residence on arrival (as necessary).
- Depending on your destination, your pets may require special inoculations or may be required to go into quarantine for a period (see page 454).

- Contact your telephone company well in advance, particularly if you need to get a deposit reimbursed (see page 153).

- Arrange health, travel and other insurance as necessary (see **Chapter 13**).

- Depending on your destination, arrange health and dental check-ups for your family before leaving Britain. Obtain a copy of all health and dental records and a statement from your health insurance company stating your present level of cover.

- Terminate any British loan, lease or hire purchase contracts and pay all outstanding bills (allow plenty of time as some companies may be slow to respond).

- Check whether you're entitled to a rebate on your road tax, car and other insurance. Obtain a letter from your British motor insurance company stating your number of years no-claims discount.

- Sell your house, apartment or other property, or arrange to let it through a friend or a letting agency (see **Chapter 5**). If you own more than one property in Britain, you must pay capital gains on any profits from the sale of a second home above a certain amount (see page 362).

- Check whether you need an international driving licence or a translation of your British or foreign driving licence for your country of destination or any countries you will pass through.

- Give friends and business associates in Britain a temporary address and telephone number where you can be contacted abroad.

- If you will be travelling or living abroad for an extended period, you may wish to give someone 'powers of attorney' over your financial affairs in Britain so that they can act for you in your absence. This can be for a fixed period or open-ended and can be for a specific purpose only. **You should take legal advice before doing this.**

- If travelling by air, allow plenty of time to get to the airport (see page 223), register your luggage and to clear security and immigration.

- Buy a copy of *Living and Working in* ******** before leaving Britain. If we haven't written it yet, drop us a line and we'll start on it right away!

Have a safe journey.

APPENDICES

APPENDIX A: USEFUL ADDRESSES

London Embassies and Consulates

A selection of foreign embassies and High Commissions (Commonwealth countries) in London are listed below. Many countries also have consulates in other cities (e.g. Belfast, Birmingham, Cardiff, Edinburgh, Glasgow and Manchester), which are listed in phone books. All London embassies are listed in *The London Diplomatic List* (The Stationery Office).

Argentina: 65 Brook Street, London W1M 5LD (☎ 0171-486 7073).

Australia: Australia House, Strand, London WC2B 4LA (☎ 0171-379 4334).

Austria: 18 Belgrave Mews West, London SW1X 8HU (☎ 0171-235 3731).

Bahamas: 10 Chesterfield Street, London W1X 8AH (☎ 0171-408 4488).

Bangladesh: 28 Queen's Gate, London SW7 5JA (☎ 0171-584 0081).

Barbados: 1 Great Russell Street, WC1B 3JY (☎ 0171-631 4975).

Belgium: 103-105 Eaton Square, London SW1W 9AB (☎ 0171-470 3700).

Belize: 22 Harcourt House, 19 Cavendish Square, London W1M 9AD (☎ 0171-499 9728).

Bolivia: 106 Eaton Square, London SW1W 9AD (☎ 0171- 235 4248).

Bosnia & Herzegovina: 4th Floor, Morley House, 320 Regent Street, London W1R 5AB (☎ 0171-255 3758).

Brazil: 32 Green Street, Mayfair, London W1Y 4AT (☎ 0171-499 0877).

Brunei: 19/20 Belgrave Square, London SW1X 8PG (☎ 0171-581 0521).

Bulgaria: 186-188 Queen's Gate, London SW7 5HL (☎ 0171-584 9400).

Cameroon: 84 Holland Park, London W11 3SB (☎ 0171-727 0771).

Canada: Macdonald House, 1 Grosvenor Square, London W1X 0AB (☎ 0171-258 6600).

Chile: 12 Devonshire Street, London W1N 2DS (☎ 0171-580 6392).

China: 49-51 Portland Place, London W1N 4JL (☎ 0171-636 9375).

Colombia: Flat 3a, 3 Hans Crescent, London SW1X 0LN (☎ 0171-589 9177).

Croatia: 21 Conway Street, London W1P 5HL (☎ 0171-387 2022).

Cuba: 167 High Holborn, London WC1 6PA (☎ 0171-240 2488).

Cyprus: 93 Park Street, London W1Y 4ET (☎ 0171-499 8272).

Czech Republic: 26-30 Kensington Palace Gardens, London W8 4QY (☎ 0171-243-1115).

Denmark: 55 Sloane Street, London SW1X 9SR (☎ 0171-333 0200).

Dominica: 1 Collingham Gardens, South Kensington, London SW5 0HW (☎ 0171-370 5194).

Ecuador: Flat 3b, Hans Crescent, Knightsbridge, London SW1X 0LS (☎ 0171-584 2648).

Egypt: 12 Curzon Street, London W1Y 7FJ (☎ 0171-499 2401).

El Salvador: Tennyson House, 159 Great Portland Street, London W1N 5FD (☎ 0171-436 8282).

Fiji: 34 Hyde Park Gate, London SW7 5DN (☎ 0171-584 3661).

Finland: 32 Chesham Place, London SW1X 8HW (☎ 0171-838 6200).

France: 58 Knightsbridge, London SW1X 7JT (☎ 0171-201 1000).

The Gambia: 57 Kensington Court, Kensington, London W8 5DG (☎ 0171-937 9095).

Germany: 23 Belgrave Square, 1 Chesham Place, London SW1X 8PZ (☎ 0171-824 1300).

Ghana: 13 Belgrave Square, London SW1X 8PN (☎ 0171-235 4142).

Greece: 1A Holland Park, London W11 3TP (☎ 0171-229 3850).

Grenada: 1 Collingham Gardens, Earls Court, London SW5 0HW (☎ 0171-373 7809).

Guatemala: 13 Fawcett Street, London SW10 9HN (☎ 0171-351 3042).

Guyana: 3 Palace Court, Bayswater Road, London W2 4LP (☎ 0171-229 7684).

Holy See: Apostolic Nunciature, 54 Parkside, London SW19 5NF (☎ 0181-946 1410).

Honduras: 115 Gloucester Place, London W1H 3PJ (☎ 0171-486 4880).

Hungary: 35 Eaton Place, London SW1X 8BY (☎ 0171-235 5218).

Iceland: 1 Eaton Terrace, London SW1W 8EY (☎ 0171-590 1100).

India: India House, Aldwych, London WC2B 4NA (☎ 0171-836 8484).

Indonesia: 38 Grosvenor Square, London W1X 9AD (☎ 0171-499 7661).

Iran: 16 Prince's Gate, London SW7 1PT (☎ 0171-225 3000).

Ireland: 17 Grosvenor Place, London SW1X 7HR (☎ 0171-235 2171).

Israel: 2 Palace Green, Kensington, London W8 4QB (☎ 0171-957 9500).

Italy: 14 Three Kings Yard, Davies Street, London W1Y 2EH (☎ 0171-312 2200).

Jamaica: 1-2 Prince Consort Road, London SW7 2BZ (☎ 0171-823 9911).

Japan: 101-104 Piccadilly, London W1V 9FN (☎ 0171-465 6500).

Jordan: 6 Upper Phillimore Gardens, Kensington, London W8 7HB (☎ 0171-937 3685).

Kenya: 45 Portland Place, London W1N 4AS (☎ 0171-636 2371).

Korea: 60 Buckingham Gate, London SW1E 6AJ (☎ 0171-227 5500).

Kuwait: 2 Albert Gate, London SW1X 7JU (☎ 0171-590 3400).

Lebanon: 21 Kensington Palace Gardens, London W8 4QM (☎ 0171-229 7265).

Lesotho: 7 Chesham Place, Belgravia, London SW1 8HN (☎ 0171-235 5686).

Luxembourg: 27 Wilton Crescent, London SW1X 8SD (☎ 0171-235 6961).

Malawi: 33 Grosvenor Street, London W1X 0DE (☎ 0171-491 4172).

Malaysia: 45 Belgrave Square, London SW1X 8QT (☎ 0171-235 8033).

Malta: Malta House, 36-38 Piccadilly, London W1V 0PQ (☎ 0171-292 4800).

Mauritius: 32/33 Elvaston Place, London SW7 5NW (☎ 0171-581 0294).

Mexico: 42 Hertford Street, Mayfair, London W1Y 7TF (☎ 0171-499 8586).

Morocco: 49 Queen's Gate Gardens, London SW7 5NE (☎ 0171-581 5001).

Mozambique: 21 Fitzroy Square, London W1P 5HJ (☎ 0171-383 3800).

Namibia: 6 Chandos Street, London W1M 0LQ (☎ 0171-636 6244).

Nepal: 12a Kensington Palace Gardens, London W8 4QU (☎ 0171-229 1594).

Netherlands: 38 Hyde Park Gate, London SW7 5DP (☎ 0171-590 3200).

New Zealand: New Zealand House, Haymarket, London SW1Y 4TQ (☎ 0171-930 8422).

Nigeria: Nigeria House, 9 Northumberland Avenue, London WC2 5BX (☎ 0171-839 1244).

Norway: 25 Belgrave Square, London SW1X 8QD (☎ 0171-591 5500).

Oman: 167 Queen's Gate, London SW7 5HE (☎ 0171-225 0001).

Pakistan: 35-36 Lowndes Square, London SW1X 9JN (☎ 0171-664 9200).

Papua New Guinea: 3rd Floor, 14 Waterloo Place, London SW1R 4AR (☎ 0171-930 0922).

Paraguay: Braemar Lodge, Cornwall Gardens, London SW7 4AQ (☎ 0171-937 1253).

Peru: 52 Sloane Street, London SW1X 9SP (☎ 0171-235 1917).

Philippines: 9a Palace Green, London W8 4QE (☎ 0171-937 1600).

Poland: 47 Portland Place, London W1N 3AG (☎ 0171-580 4324).

Portugal: 11 Belgrave Square, London SW1X 8PP (☎ 0171-235 5331).

Qatar: 1 South Audley Street, London W1Y 5DQ (☎ 0171-493 2200).

Romania: Arundel House, 4 Palace Green, London W8 4QD (☎ 0171-937 9666).

Russia: 13 Kensington Palace Gardens, London W8 4QX (☎ 0171-229 2666).

Saudi Arabia: 30 Charles Street, Mayfair, London W1X 7PM (☎ 0171-917 3000).

Sierra Leone: 33 Portland Place, London W1N 3AG (☎ 0171-636 6483).

Singapore: 9 Wilton Crescent, London SW1X 8RW (☎ 0171-235 8315).

Slovak Republic: 25 Kensington Palace Gardens, London W8 4QY (☎ 0171-243 0803).

Slovenia: 11-15 Wigmore Street, London W1H 9LA (☎ 0171-495 7775).

South Africa: South Africa House, Trafalgar Square, London WC2N 5DP (☎ 0171-451 7299).

Spain: 39 Chesham Place, London SW1X 8SB (☎ 0171-235 5555).

Sri Lanka: 13 Hyde Park Gardens, London W2 2LU (☎ 0171-262 1841).

Swaziland: 20 Buckingham Gate, London SW1E 6LB (☎ 0171-630 6611).

Sweden: 11 Montagu Place, London W1H 2AL (☎ 0171-917 6400).

Switzerland: 16-18 Montagu Place, London W1H 2BQ (☎ 0171-616 6000).

Syria: 8 Belgrave Square, London SW1X 8PH (☎ 0171-245 9012).

Tanzania: 43 Hertford Street, London W1Y 8DB (☎ 0171-499 8951).

Thailand: 29-30 Queen's Gate, London SW7 5JB (☎ 0171-589 2944).

Tonga: 36 Molyneaux Street, London W1H 6AB (☎ 0171-724 5828).

Trinidad and Tobago: 42 Belgrave Square, London SW1X 8NT (☎ 0171-245 9351).

Turkey: 43 Belgrave Square, London SW1X 8PA (☎ 0171-393 0202).

Uganda: Uganda House, 58-59 Trafalgar Square, London WC2N 5DX (☎ 0171-839 5783).

Ukraine: 60 Holland Park, London W11 3SJ (☎ 0171-727 6312).

United Arab Emirates: 30 Prince's Gate, London SW7 1PT (☎ 0171-581 1281).
United States of America: 24 Grosvenor Square, London W1A 1AE (☎ 0171-499 9000).
Uruguay: 2nd Floor, 140 Brompton Road, London SW3 1HY (☎ 0171-584 8192).
Venezuela: 1 Cromwell Road, London SW7 2HW (☎ 0171-584 4206).
Yugoslavia: 5 Lexham Gardens, London W8 5JJ (☎ 0171-370 6105).
Zaire: 26 Chesham Place, London SW1X 8HH (☎ 0171-235 6137).
Zambia: 2 Palace Gate, Kensington, London W8 5NG (☎ 0171-589 6655).
Zimbabwe: Zimbabwe House, 429 Strand, London WC2R 0SA (☎ 0171-836 7755).

Government Departments

Department of Culture, Media & Sport, 2-4 Cockspur Street, London SW1Y 5DH (☎ 0171-211 6200).
Department for Education & Employment, Sanctuary Buildings, Great Smith Street, London SW1P 3BT (☎ 0171-925 9000).
Department of the Environment, Transport and the Regions, Eland House, Bressenden Place, London SW1E 5DU (☎ 0171-890 3333).
Department of Health, Richmond House, 79 Whitehall, London SW1A 2NS (☎ 0171-210 3000).
Department for International Development, 94 Victoria Street, London SW1E 5JL (☎ 0171-917 7000).
Department of Social Security, Richmond House, 79 Whitehall, London SW1A 2NS (☎ 0171-238 0800).
Department of Trade and Industry, 1-19 Victoria Street, London SW1H 0ET (☎ 0171-215 5000).
Foreign & Commonwealth Office, King Charles Street, London SW1A 2AH (☎ 0171-270 1500).
Home Office, 50 Queen Anne's Gate, London SW1H 9AT (☎ 0171-273 4000).
Ministry of Agriculture, Fisheries and Food, 3-8 Whitehall Place, London SW1A 2HH (☎ 0171-270 3000).
Ministry of Defence, Main Building, Whitehall, London SW1A 2HB (☎ 0171-218 9000).
Northern Ireland Office, Stormont Castle, Belfast BT4 3ST (☎ 01232-520700).
Scottish Office, St. Andrew's House, Edinburgh EH1 3DG (☎ 0131-244 1111).
Welsh Office, Cathays Park, Cardiff CF1 3NQ (☎ 01222-825111).

Tourist Information

British Tourist Authority (BTA), Thames Tower, Black's Road, Hammersmith, London W6 9EL (☎ 0181-846 9000).
British Travel Centre, 12 Regent Street, London SW1Y 4PQ (☎ 0171-730 3400).
English Tourist Board, Thames Tower, Black's Road, Hammersmith, London W6 9EL (☎ 0181-846 9000).

Irish Tourist Board, 150 New Bond Street, London W1Y 0AQ (☎ 0171-493 3201).

Scottish Tourist Board, 23 Revelstone Terrace, Edinburgh EH4 3EU (☎ 0131-557 1700).

Welsh Tourist Board, Brunel House, 2 Fitzalan Road, Cardiff CF2 1UY (☎ 01222-227281).

Travel

Association of British Travel Agents, 55-57 Newman Street, London W1P 4AH (☎ 0171-637 2444).

British Airport Authority, Corporate Office, Gatwick Airport, West Sussex RH6 0HZ (☎ 01293-517755).

British Airways, Head Office, Speedbird House, PO Box 10, Heathrow Airport, Hounslow, Middx. TW6 2JA (☎ 0181-897 4000).

British Midland, Donington Hall, Castle Donington, Derby DE7 2SB (☎ 0171-589 5599).

London Transport, 55 Broadway, London SW1H 0BD (☎ 0171-222 5600).

National Express, 13 Regent Street, London SW1 9TP (☎ 0171-824 8461).

P&O, 77-91 New Oxford Street, London WC1A 1PP (☎ 0171-831 1234).

Miscellaneous

Automobile Association (AA), Fanum House, PO Box 50, Basingstoke, Hampshire RG21 2EA (☎ 01256-20123).

British Council, 10 Spring Gardens, London SW1A 2BN (☎ 0171-930 8466).

British Broadcasting Corporation (BBC), Broadcasting House, Portland Place, London W1A 1AA (☎ 0171-580 4468).

BBC Television Centre, Wood Lane, London W12 7RJ (☎ 0171-743 8000).

British Telecom, 81 Newgate Street, London EC1A 7AJ (☎ Freefone 2466 or 0171-356 6666).

Central Office of Information, Hercules Road, London SE1 7DU (☎ 0171-928 2345).

Confederation of British Industry (CBI), Centre Point, 103 New Oxford Street, London WC1A 1DU (☎ 0171-379 7400).

Consumers' Association, Castlemead, Gascoyne Way, Hertford SG14 1LH (☎ 01992-587773).

Driver and Vehicle Licensing Centre (DVLC), Swansea SA99 1AR (☎ 01792-822800).

Good Housekeeping Institute, National Magazine House, 72 Broadwick Street, London W1V 2BP (☎ 0171-439 5000).

HM Customs and Excise, New King's Beam House, 22 Upper Ground, London SE1 9PJ (☎ 0171-620 1313).

Inland Revenue, Somerset House, Strand, London WC2R 1LB (☎ 0171-438 6622).

The Stationery Office Ltd., National Publishing, 51 Nine Elms Lane, Vauxhall, London SW8 5DR (☎ 071-873 0011, Internet: www.the-stationery-office.co.uk).

National Association of Citizens Advice Bureaux, Myddelton House, 115-123 Pentonville Road, London N1 9LZ (☎ 0171-833 2181).

National Consumer Council, 20 Grosvenor Gardens, London SW1 0DH (☎ 0171-730 3469).

National Federation of Women's Institutes, 39 Eccleston Street, London SW1W 9NT (☎ 0171-730 7212).

Office of Fair Trading, Field House, 15-25 Bream's Building, London EC4A 1PR (☎ 0171-242 2858).

Office for National Statistics, 1 Drummond Gate, London SW1V 2QQ (☎ 0171-233 9233).

Public Record Office, Ruskin Avenue, Kew, Richmond, Surrey TW9 4OU (☎ 0181-876 3444).

Royal Automobile Club (RAC), RAC House, Lansdowne Road, East Croydon, Surrey CR9 2JA (☎ 0181-686 2525).

APPENDIX B: FURTHER READING

There are many useful reference books for anyone seeking general information about Britain and the British including *Whitaker's Almanack* (The Stationery Office). Published annually since 1868, *Whitaker's Almanack* contains a wealth of information about the British government, finances, population, commerce and general statistics of the nations of the world. Another comprehensive publication is *Enquire Within Upon Everything* by Moyra Bremner (Century), first published in 1856, and containing information on a multitude of subjects from social behaviour to organisations. Newcomers to Britain may also be interested in *Britain* (The Stationery Office), an annual reference book describing many features of life in Britain, including the workings of the government and other major institutions.

In the list below, the publication title is followed by author's name and the publisher (in brackets). All books prefixed with an asterisk (*) are recommended by the author.

Tourist Guides

*Baedeker's AA Britain (Baedeker/AA)
*Berlitz Country Guide to Britain (Macmillan)
Birnbaum's Great Britain (Houghton Mifflin)
*Blue Guide England, Ian Ousby (A & C Black)
*Blue Guide Ireland, Ian Robertson (A & C Black)
*Britain Travel Survival Kit (Lonely Planet)
Britain at its Best, Robert S. Kane (Passport Books)
*The Complete Guide to London (Nicholson)
Days Out in Britain & Ireland (AA Publishing)
Eyewitness Travel Guide London (Dorling Kindersley)
*Explorer Britain (AA Publishing)
*Fodor's Great Britain, E. Fodor (Hodder & Stoughton)
Frommer's Dollarwise Guide to Britain
*The Good Walks Guide (Which? Books)
*The Good Weekend Guide (Vermillion)
Great Britain (Insight Guides)
Great Britain and Ireland (Phaidon Press)
Hatchette Guide to Great Britain (Hatchette)
*Let's Go: Britain & Ireland (Pan)
*Let's Go: London (Pan)
*Michelin Green Guide to Britain (Michelin)
*Reader's Digest Touring Guide to Britain (Reader's Digest)
*Rough Guide England (The Rough Guides)
*Travel Britain (Heritage)
*Weekend Breaks in Britain (Which? Books)
*Welcome to Britain (Collins)

General

*A-Z London Guide (Geographers' A-Z Map Co. Ltd.)

Best Behaviour, Mary Killen (Century)

*Britain (The Stationery Office)

*Britain in Figures (The Economist)

*A Class Act: The Myth of Britain's Classless Society, Andrew Adonis and Stephen Pollard (Hamilton)

*Daily Mail Year Book (Chapmans)

*Debrett's Etiquette and Modern manners, edited by Elsie Burch Donald (Pan)

Discover Britain, Christine Lindop and Dominic Fisher (Cambridge University Press)

*The English, Jeremy Paxman (Michael Joseph)

*Enquire Within Upon Everything, Moyra Bremner (Helicon)

The Guiness UK Data Book (Guiness Publishing)

*How to be a Brit, George Mikes (Andre Deutsch)

The New British State (The Times)

*Notes From a Small island, Bill Bryson (Doubleday)

*Residence in Britain: Notes for People from Overseas (Central Office of Information)

Statlas UK (Ordnance Survey)

*Time Out London Guide (Time Out Magazine Ltd.)

*Top Towns (Guiness Publishing)

*We British: Britain Under the Moriscope, Erik Jacobs & Robert Worcester (Weidenfeld & Nicholson)

*Whitaker's Almanack (The Stationery Office)

APPENDIX C: WEIGHTS & MEASURES

Officially Britain converted to the international metric system of measurement on 1st October 1995, although many goods have been sold in metric sizes for many years. The use of imperial measures was officially due to finish at the end of 1999 but has been given a reprieve until end of 2009. Therefore you can expect to find goods sold in imperial (and other old British measures), metric or marked in both metric and British measures. Many foreigners will find the tables on the following pages useful. Some comparisons shown are approximate only, but are close enough for most everyday uses.

In addition to the variety of measurement systems used, clothes sizes often vary considerably depending on the manufacturer – as we all know only too well! Try all clothes on before buying and don't be afraid to return something if, when you try it on at home, you decide it doesn't fit or it's a different colour from what you imagined. The vast majority of British shops will exchange most goods or give a refund, unless they were purchased at a reduced price during a sale.

Women's clothes:

Continental	34	36	38	40	42	44	46	48	50	52
UK	8	10	12	14	16	18	20	22	24	26
USA	6	8	10	12	14	16	18	20	22	24

Pullovers:

	Women's						Mens					
Continental	40	42	44	46	48	50	44	46	48	50	52	54
UK	34	36	38	40	42	44	34	36	38	40	42	44
USA	34	36	38	40	42	44	Sm	Medium		large		exl

Note: sm = small, exl = extra large

Men's Shirts

Continental	36	37	38	39	40	41	42	43	44	46
UK/USA	14	14	15	15	16	16	17	17	18	

Men's Underwear

Continental	5	6	7	8	9	10
UK	34	36	38	40	42	44
USA	small	medium	large	extra large		

Children's Clothes

Continental	92	104	116	128	140	152
UK	16/18	20/22	24/26	28/30	32/34	36/38
USA	2	4	6	8	10	12

Children's Shoes

Continental	18	19	20	21	22	23	24	25	26	27	28
UK/USA	2	3	4	4	5	6	7	7	8	9	10

Continental	29	30	31	32	33	34	35	36	37	38
UK/USA	11	11	12	13	1	2	2	3	4	5

Shoes (Women's and Men's)

Continental	35	35	36	37	37	38	39	39	40	40
UK	2	3	3	4	4	5	5	6	6	7
USA	4	4	5	5	6	6	7	7	8	8

Continental	41	42	42	43	44	44
UK	7	8	8	9	9	10
USA	9	9	10	10	11	11

Weights:

Avoirdupois	Metric	Metric	Avoirdupois
1 oz	28.35 g	1 g	0.035 oz
1 pound	454 g	100 g	3.5 oz
1 cwt	50.8 kg	250 g	9 oz
1 ton	1,016 kg	1 kg	2.2 pounds
1 tonne	2,205 pounds		

Note: g = gramme, kg = kilogramme

Length:

British/US	Metric	Metric	British/US
1 inch =	2.54 cm	1 cm =	0.39 inch
1 foot =	30.48 cm	1 m =	3.28 feet
1 yard =	91.44 cm	1 km =	0.62 mile
1 mile =	1.6 km	8 km =	5 miles

Note: cm = centimetre, m = metre, km = kilometre

Capacity:

Imperial	Metric	Metric	Imperial
1 pint (USA)	0.47 l	1 l	1.76 UK pints
1 pint (UK)	0.568 l	1 l	0.265 US gallons
1 gallon (USA)	3.78 l	1 l	0.22 UK gallons
1 gallon (UK)	4.54 l	1 l	35.211 fluid oz

Note: l = litre

Temperature:

Celsius	Fahrenheit	
0	32	freezing point of water
5	41	
10	50	
15	59	
20	68	
25	77	
30	86	
35	95	
40	104	

The Boiling point of water is 100° Celsius, 212° Fahrenheit.

Oven temperature:

Gas	Electric	
	°F	°C
-	225-250	110-120
1	275	140
2	300	150
3	325	160
4	350	180
5	375	190
6	400	200
7	425	220
8	450	230
9	475	240

For a quick conversion, the Celsius temperature is approximately half the Fahrenheit temperature.

Temperature Conversion:

Celsius to Fahrenheit: multiply by 9, divide by 5 and add 32.
Fahrenheit to Celsius: subtract 32, multiply by 5 and divide by 9.

Body Temperature:

Normal body temperature (if you're alive and well) is 98.4° Fahrenheit, which equals 37° Celsius.

APPENDIX D: MAP OF BRITAIN

The map of Britain opposite shows the counties of England, Wales, Scotland and Northern Ireland (listed below). The list shows the abbreviations (in brackets) in common use for many English counties.

England

Avon
Bedfordshire (Beds)
Berkshire (Berks)
Buckinghamshire (Bucks)
Cambridgeshire (Cambs)
Cheshire
Cleveland
Cornwall
Cumbria
Derbyshire (Derby)
Devon
Dorset
Durham
East Sussex
Essex
Gloucestershire (Gloucs)
Greater Manchester
Hampshire (Hants)
Hereford & Worcestershire (Worcs)
Hertfordshire (Herts)
Isle of Wight
Kent
Lancashire (Lancs)
Leicestershire (Leics)
Lincolnshire (Lincs)
London
Merseyside
Norfolk
North Yorkshire (Yorks)
Northamptonshire (Northants)
Northumberland
Nottinghamshire (Notts)
Oxfordshire (Oxon)
Shropshire (Salop)
Somerset
South Yorkshire (Yorks)
Staffordshire (Staffs)
Suffolk

Surrey
Tyne & Wear
Warwickshire (Warwicks)
West Midlands
West Sussex
West Yorkshire (Yorks)
Wiltshire (Wilts)

Wales

Clwyd
Dyfed
Glamorgan
Gwent
Gwynedd
Powys

Scotland

Borders
Central
Dumfries & Galloway
Fife
Grampian
Highland
Lothian
Orkney Islands
Shetland Islands
Strathclyde
Tayside
Western Isles

Northern Ireland

Antrim
Armagh
Down
Fermanagh
Londonderry
Tyrone

APPENDIX E: SERVICE DIRECTORY

This **Service Directory** is to help you find businesses and services in Britain serving both residents and visitors. Note that when calling Britain from abroad you must dial your international access number (e.g. 00) followed by 44 (the country code for the Britain), the area code (without the first zero) and the subscriber's number. Please mention *Living and Working in Britain* when contacting companies.

ACCOMMODATION

The Apartment Service, London SW19 4DT, UK (☎ 0181-944 1444, fax 0181-944 6744). Contact: Charles McCrow.

PUBLICATIONS

World of Property, Outbound Publishing, 1 Commercial Road, Eastbourne, East Sussex BN21 3XQ, UK (☎ 01323-412001).

RELOCATION AGENTS

Focus Information Services, 13 Prince of Wales Terrace, London W8 5PG (☎ 0171-937 7799).

Homefinder Relocation, First Floor, 33 High Bridge, Newcastle-upon-Tyne, NE1 1EW (☎ 0191-222 0900/0860 252849, fax 0191-233 1264, e-mail: homefinder@ homefinder.demon.co.uk). Contact: Christopher O'Doherty (Managing Director). Homesearch, area tours, schoolsearch throughout the Northeast to client's specific requirements. Established for over 15 years.

Karen Deane Relocations, Plaza, 535 Kings Road, London SW10 0SZ (☎ 0171-352 4144).

UK Relocation Services Ltd., 58 Grand Avenue, London N10 3BP (☎ 0181-442 0044, fax 0181-442 1404, e-mail: ukrelocation@compuserve.com). Contact: Paulene Grant (Managing Director). Home finding, schools advice and settling-in programme throughout the UK.

SCHOOLS

American Community Schools, England, Heywood, Portsmouth Road, Cobham, Surrey KT11 1BL (☎ 01932-867251, fax 01932-869798, e-mail: jscruton@acs-england.co.uk). Contact: Judson Scruton (Director of Development). ACS has three superbly equipped stately campuses and offers American and International education for students aged 3 to 19.

TRAVEL

Flightclub, Guildbourne Centre, Chapel Road, Worthing, West Sussex BN11 1LZ, UK (☎ 01903-231857, fax 01903-201225, e-mail: flightclub@clubs.itsnet.co.uk). Offers low cost flights worldwide from all UK airports. Incentives for overseas property owners/managers.

INDEX

A

Accident Insurance · 313
Accommodation · 98
  Bed & Breakfast · 374
  Buying Property · 100
  Home Contents Insurance · 321
  Hotels · 372
  Relocation Consultants · 98
  Rental Contracts · 106
  Rental Costs · 104
  Rented · 101
  Self-Catering · 375
  Singles · 103
  Youth Hostels · 376
Address
  Change · 130
  Style · 124
Aerial Sports · 411
Aids · 295
Airline Services · 223
  Airports · 224
  Baggage · 227
  Fares · 225
Airports · 224
Alcohol Abuse · 294
Angling · 412
Appendices
  A: Useful Addresses · 484
  B: Further Reading · 490
  C: Weights & Measures · 492
  D: Map of Britain · 496
  E: Service Directory · 498
Arrival · 86
  Checklists · 94
  Customs · 89
  Embassy Registration · 93
  Entry Refusal · 87
  Finding Help · 93
  Immigration · 86
  Passport Stamps · 88
  Police Registration · 92
Art Galleries · 378

Au Pairs
  Finding a Job · 37
  Permits & Visas · 79

B

Badminton · 408
Ballet · 381
Banks · 332
  Business Hours · 334
  Cash Cards · 338
  Credit Cards · 340
  Current Accounts · 334
  Debit Cards · 338
  Loans · 343
  Mortgages · 345
  Opening an Account · 334
  Overdrafts · 343
  Savings Accounts · 336
Bars · 388
BBC Radio · 167
Bed & Breakfast · 374
Billiards · 402
Bills
  Electricity & Gas · 112
  Telephone · 143
  Water · 115
Births · 296
Books · 429
  Further Reading · 490
British
  Citizenship · 440
  Currency · 329
  Drivers · 253
  Government · 444
  People · 466
  Roads · 255
BSkyB · 164
BT · 134
Building Societies · 333
  Mortgages · 345
Buildings Insurance · 319

Buses · 215
  Long-Distance · 216
  Rural & City · 217
  Timetables · 221
Business Hours
  Banks · 334
  Post Office · 121
  Shops · 423
Buying a Car · 234
  Abroad · 236
  New · 234
  Used · 237
Buying Property · 100

C

Cable TV · 166
Cafés · 390
Camping · 378
Capital Gains Tax · 362
Car Insurance · 243
  No Claims Discount · 246
  Premiums · 244
Caravans · 378
Cars
  Accidents · 257
  Buying · 234
  Drinking & Driving · 259
  Driving Licence · 241
  Garages & Servicing · 265
  General Road Rules · 248
  Hire · 267
  Importation · 231
  Insurance · 243
  Motoring Organisations · 269
  Parking · 270
  Petrol · 262
  Registration · 232
  Rental · 267
  Road Tax · 247
  Selling · 240
  Speed Limits · 263
  Test Certificate · 239
  Theft · 260
  Used · 237
  Vehicle Licence · 247
Cash Cards · 338
Casinos · 386
Caving · 406

Chemists · 285
Childbirth · 289
Cinemas · 380
Citizens Advice Bureau (CAB) · 450
Citizenship · 440
Climate · 441
Clinics · 287
Clothes · 428
Concerts · 383
Consumers' Association · 437
Contracts
  Accommodation · 106
  Employment · 46
  Insurance · 303
Cost of Living · 366
Council Tax · 350
  Registration · 93
Credit & Charge Cards · 340
Credit Rating · 331
Cricket · 401
Crime · 442
  Car Theft · 260
  Drinking & Driving · 259
Currency
  British · 329
  Foreign · 330
Current Accounts · 334
Customs · 89
  Duty-Free Allowances · 436
  Prohibited Goods · 92
Cycling · 403

D

Deaths · 296
Debit Cards · 338
Dentist · 290
  Insurance · 318
Department & Chain Stores · 427
Deportation · 82
Discotheques · 385
Divorce · 452
Doctors · 282
  Emergency · 278
Driving · 230
  Licence · 241
Drug Abuse · 294
Duty-Free Allowances · 436

E

Education · 172
  Curriculum · 182
  Employment · 57
  Examinations · 184
  Further · 197
  Higher · 192
  Kindergarten · 180
  Language Schools · 198
  Nursery School · 180
  Primary · 180
  Private · 187
  School Hours · 178
  School Terms · 178
  Secondary · 181
  Special · 186
  State or Private? · 173
  State · 174
  University · 192
EEA · 22
Electricity · 108
  Bills · 112
Embassies
  List of · 484
  Registration · 93
Emergencies
  Car Accidents · 257
  Health · 278
  Telephone Numbers · 154
Employment · 20
  Contract Jobs · 26
  Job Hunting · 31
  JobCentres · 25
  Language · 39
  Part-Time · 27
  Personal Applications · 32
  Recruitment Consultants · 25
  Salary · 33
  Terms · 42
  Trainees & Work Experience · 36
  Voluntary Work · 29
  Women · 30
  Work Permits · 69
  Working Conditions · 42
  Working Illegally · 38
Employment Conditions · 48
  Acceptance of Gifts · 58
  Accident Insurance · 52

Annual Holidays · 53
Cars & Driving Licence · 52
Changing Jobs · 58
Commission & Bonuses · 49
Company Pension Fund · 52
Confidentiality · 58
Discipline · 59
Dismissal · 59
Education & Training · 57
Flexi-Time Rules · 50
Income Protection · 53
Long Service Awards · 58
Medical Examination · 51
Miscellaneous Insurance · 53
National Insurance · 51
Notice Period · 56
Overtime & Compensation · 50
Paid Expenses · 55
Part-Time Job Restrictions · 58
Place of Work · 48
Pregnancy & Confinement · 57
Public Holidays · 54
Redundancy · 60
References · 61
Relocation Expenses · 51
Retirement · 59
Salary & Benefits · 48
Sickness or Accident · 53
Special Leave of Absence · 55
Trade Union Membership · 61
Travel Expenses · 51
Validity & Applicability · 48
Working Hours · 49
Employment Service · 24
English · 39
  Learning · 198
Entry
  Certificate · 68
  Clearance · 65
European Economic Area (EEA) · 22
European Union (EU) · 15, 22
Eurostar · 213
Eurotunnel · 220

F

Fax · 150
Ferries · 219
Finance · 328
  Banks · 332
  British Currency · 329
  Building Societies · 333
  Capital Gains Tax · 362
  Cash & Debit Cards · 338
  Cost of Living · 366
  Council Tax · 350
  Credit & Charge Cards · 340
  Credit Rating · 331
  Foreign Currency · 330
  Income Tax · 352
  Inheritance Tax · 363
  Loans · 343
  Mortgages · 345
  Overdrafts · 343
  Savings Accounts · 336
  VAT · 351
  Wills · 364
Finding a Job · 20
Fishing · 412
Food · 424
Furniture · 431
Further
  Education · 197
  Further · 490

G

Gambling · 386
Garages · 265
Gas · 111
  Bills · 112
Gasoline · 262
Geography · 444
Golf · 413
Government · 444
GPs · 282
Gymnasiums · 414

H

Health · 276
  Births & Deaths · 296
  Childbirth · 289
  Clubs · 414
  Counselling · 293
  Dentist · 290
  Doctors · 282
  Drug Abuse · 294
  Drugs & Medicines · 285
  Emergencies · 278
  Hospitals · 287
  Insurance · 315
  NHS · 279
  Optician/Optometrist · 292
  Private Treatment · 281
  Sexually-Transmitted Diseases · 295
  Smoking · 295
  Social Services · 293
Heating · 116
Help
  Consumer Advice · 437
  Counselling · 293
  Emergency Telephone Numbers · 154
  On Arrival · 93
Higher Education · 192
Hiking · 405
Holidays
  Annual · 53
  Compassionate Leave · 55
  Public · 54
  Schools · 178
Home Contents Insurance · 321
Home Loans · 345
Hospitals · 287
  Childbirth · 289
Hotels · 372
Hours
  Banks · 334
  Post Office · 121
  Shops · 423
  Working · 49
Household Appliances · 432
Housing
  See Accommodation

I

Immigration · 86
Income Tax · 352
  Allowances · 359
  Independent Taxation · 355
  PAYE · 355
  PAYE Tax Code · 356
  Returns · 361
  Self-Assessment · 361
  Self-Employed · 358
Inheritance Tax · 363
Insurance · 300
  Accidents · 313
  Buildings · 319
  Car · 243
  Companies · 301
  Contracts · 303
  Dental · 318
  Health · 315
  Holiday · 323
  Home · 319
  Home-Contents · 321
  Long-Term Care · 318
  Medical · 315
  Motor Breakdown · 269
  National · 306
  Pensions · 308
  Permanent Health · 314
  Personal Liability · 323
  Social Security · 303
  Travel · 323
Internet · 153
  Shopping · 434

J

JobCentres · 25
Jobs
  Contract · 26
  Employment · 20
  Employment Service · 24
  European Employment Services · 24
  Holiday · 28
  Hunting · 31
  Part-Time · 27
  Qualifications · 23
  Self-Employment · 34

  Short-Term · 28
  Temporary & Casual · 27
  Trainees · 36
  Work Experience · 36

K

Kindergarten · 180

L

Language
  English · 39
  Schools · 198
Le Shuttle · 220
Leaving Britain
  Checklist · 479
Legal System · 448
  Small Claims Court · 451
Leisure · 370
  Caravans & Camping · 378
  Casinos · 386
  Centres · 397
  Cinemas · 380
  Concerts · 383
  Discotheques & Nightclubs · 385
  Gambling · 386
  Gardens · 379
  Libraries · 393
  Museums & Art Galleries · 378
  Pubs · 388
  Restaurants & Cafés · 390
  Social Clubs · 385
  Stately Homes · 379
  Theatre, Opera & Ballet · 381
  Theme Parks · 379
  Tourist Information · 371
  Youth Hostels · 376
  Zoos · 379
Letter of Consent · 68
Libraries · 393
Licence
  Car · 241
  Motorcycles · 256
  Television · 163
  Vehicle · 247
Loans · 343

M

Magazines · 429
Mail · 120
  Collection · 129
  Important Documents · 127
  Letters · 121
  Parcels · 125
  Shopping · 433
  Valuables · 127
Mail-Order · 433
Map of Britain · 496
Markets · 424
Marriage · 451
Medicines · 285
Metric Tables · 492
Metro · 213
Military Service · 452
Miscellaneous · 440
Mobile Phones · 148
Monarchy · 453
Money · 328
Mortgages · 345
MOT · 239
Motorcycles · 256
  Importation · 231
  Registration · 232
Motoring · 230
  Accidents · 257
  British Drivers · 253
  Buying a Car · 234
  Car Hire · 267
  Car Insurance · 243
  Car Theft · 260
  Cars · 230
  Company Cars · 52
  Drinking & Driving · 259
  Driving Licence · 241
  Garages & Servicing · 265
  General Road Rules · 248
  Motorcycles · 256
  Organisations · 269
  Parking · 270
  Petrol · 262
  Road Maps · 266
  Roads · 255
  Selling a Car · 240
  Speed Limits · 263
  Test Certificate · 239

  Traffic Police · 256
  Vehicle Excise Duty · 247
  Vehicle Importation · 231
  Vehicle Registration · 232
Motorsports · 402
Mountaineering · 406
Movie Theatres · 380
Moving House
  Checklist · 478
  Expenses · 51
Museums · 378
Music · 383

N

National Health Service (NHS) · 279
  Today · 280
National Insurance · 306
National Lottery · 386
National Savings Accounts · 131
Newspapers · 429
Nightclubs · 385
Nursery School · 180

O

Odds & Ends · 440
Opera · 381
Optician/Optometrist · 292
Orienteering · 405
Overdrafts · 343

P

Pagers · 148
Parcel Post · 125
Parking · 270
Part-Time Employment
  Permits & Visas · 76
Passports
  Stamps · 88
  Visas · 67
Payphones · 146

Pensions · 308
  Company · 309
  Personal · 311
  State · 306
Permits & Visas · 64
  Au Pairs · 79
  Children · 75
  Deportation · 82
  EEA Nationals · 72
  Entry Certificate · 68
  Entry Clearance · 65
  Entry Refusal · 87
  Fiancé(e)s · 75
  Investors · 74
  Letter of Consent · 68
  Medical Treatment · 80
  Other British Nationals · 72
  Part-Time Employment · 76
  Permit-Free Categories · 71
  Persons of Independent Means · 79
  Police Registration · 92
  Political Asylum · 81
  Refugees · 81
  Relatives · 76
  Self-Employed Persons · 73
  Settlement · 82
  Spouses · 74
  Students · 77
  Trainees & Work Experience · 76
  Visitors · 80
  Work Permits · 69
  Working Holidaymakers · 73
Personal Pensions · 311
Petrol · 262
Pets · 454
  Quarantine · 454
Phone Books · 151
Phones · 134
Police · 457
  Registration · 92
  Traffic · 256
Pool · 402
Population · 458
Post Office · 120
  Business Hours · 121
  Change of Address · 130
  Letter Post · 121
  Mail Collection · 129
  Miscellaneous Services · 129
  National Savings Accounts · 131

Parcel Post · 125
Postal Orders · 130
Pot-Holing · 406
Prescriptions · 285
Primary School · 180
Private Schools · 187
  Choosing · 190
Public Holidays · 54
Public Transport · 204
  Airline Services · 223
  Buses · 215
  Ferries · 219
  Le Shuttle · 220
  Long-Distance Buses · 216
  Taxis · 221
  Timetables & Maps · 221
  Trains · 205
  Underground Trains · 213
Pubs · 388

Q

Quarantine · 454

R

Racquet Sports · 407
Radio · 167
Railways · 205
Rambling · 405
Recreation Centres · 397
Recruitment Consultants · 25
Redundancy · 60
Refugees · 81
Religion · 459
Relocation Consultants · 98
Removals
  Checklist · 478
Rented Accommodation · 101
  Contracts · 106
  Costs · 104
  Singles · 103
Restaurants · 390
Road Tax · 247
Rock-Climbing · 406
Royal Family · 453
Rugby · 400

S

Salaries · 33
  Employment Conditions · 48
Satellite TV · 164
Savings Accounts · 336
Schools · 172
  Further Education · 197
  Holidays · 178
  Kindergarten · 180
  Language · 198
  Nursery · 180
  Pre-School · 180
  Primary · 180
  Private · 187
  Secondary · 181
  State · 174
  State or Private? · 173
  University · 192
Secondary Schools · 181
Self-Catering · 375
Self-Employment · 34
  Permits & Visas · 73
Service Directory · 498
Settlement · 82
Shopping · 420
  Abroad · 435
  Antiques · 432
  By Mail · 433
  By Phone · 433
  Centres & Markets · 423
  Chain Stores · 427
  Clothes · 428
  Competition · 422
  Consumers' Association · 437
  Department Stores · 427
  Duty-Free · 436
  Food · 424
  Furniture · 431
  Home · 433
  Hours · 423
  Household Appliances · 432
  Internet · 434
  Newspapers & Books · 429
  Secondhand · 432
  Supermarkets · 424
Skiing · 403
Small Claims Court · 451
Snooker · 402

Soccer · 398
Social
  Clubs · 385
  Customs · 460
Social Security · 303
  Benefits · 305
Special Education · 186
Sports · 396
  Aerial · 411
  Badminton · 408
  Board Sailing · 410
  Canoeing · 410
  Caving & Pot-Holing · 406
  Centres · 397
  Cricket · 401
  Cycling · 403
  Fishing · 412
  Flying · 411
  Football · 398
  Gliding · 411
  Golf · 413
  Gymnasiums · 414
  Hang-gliding · 411
  Health Clubs · 414
  Hiking · 405
  Hot-Air Ballooning · 411
  Miscellaneous · 415
  Motor · 402
  Mountaineering · 406
  Orienteering · 405
  Paragliding · 411
  Racquet · 407
  Rock Climbing · 406
  Rowing · 410
  Rugby · 400
  Skiing · 403
  Sky-Diving · 411
  Snooker & Billiards · 402
  Soccer · 398
  Squash · 408
  Subaquatic · 410
  Surfing · 410
  Swimming · 409
  Table Tennis · 408
  Tennis · 407
  Water · 410
  Waterskiing · 410
  Windsurfing · 410
  Yachting · 410
Squash · 408

Starting A Business · 34
State Schools · 174
   Admissions · 178
   Choosing · 177
   Curriculum · 182
   Examinations · 184
   Hours · 178
   Primary · 180
   Provisions · 179
   Secondary · 181
   Special Education · 186
   Uniforms · 179
Students
   Accommodation · 103
   College Accommodation · 196
   Grants · 192
   Holiday Jobs · 28
   Loans · 193
   Permits & Visas · 77
   Voluntary Work · 29
Subway · 213
Supermarkets · 424
Swimming · 409

T

Table Tennis · 408
Tax
   Capital Gains · 362
   Council · 350
   Income · 352
   Inheritance · 363
   Returns · 361
   Road · 247
   Value Added · 351
Taxis · 221
Telegrams · 150
Telephone · 134
   Bills · 143
   BT Call Rates · 142
   Choosing a Phone · 136
   Companies · 134
   Deposit · 136
   Directories · 151
   Emergency Numbers · 154
   Entertainment Numbers · 141
   Information Numbers · 141
   Installation & Registration · 135
   International Calls · 144
   Internet · 153
   Malicious Calls · 153
   Mobile · 148
   Moving House · 153
   Network Services · 140
   Payphones · 146
   Public · 146
   Service Numbers · 155
   Shopping · 433
   Standard Tones · 137
   Using the · 138
Teletext · 159
Television · 158
   Cable · 166
   Licence · 163
   Satellite · 164
   Standards · 159
   Stations · 160
   Videos · 166
Telex · 150
Tennis · 407
Terms of Employment · 42
   General Positions · 42
   Managerial & Executive Positions · 46
Theatre · 381
Time Difference · 461
Tipping · 462
Toilets · 463
Tourist Information · 371
Trade Unions · 61
Trains · 205
   Eurostar · 213
   General Information · 207
   Rail & Network Cards · 211
   Season Tickets · 209
   Special Tickets · 209
   Tickets · 208
   Timetables · 221
   Underground · 213
Travel Insurance · 323
Tube · 213

U

Universities · 192
Useful Addresses · 484
Utilities · 107
  Electricity · 108
  Gas · 111
  Telephone · 134
  Water · 114

V

Value Added Tax (VAT) · 351
Vehicle
  Importation · 231
  Licence · 247
  Registration · 232
Videos · 166
Visas · 67
Voluntary Work · 29

W

Walking · 405
Water · 114
Watersports · 410
Weather · 441
Weights & Measures · 492
Which? Magazine · 437
Wills · 364
Work Permits · 69
Working Conditions · 42
  Contracts · 46
  Terms of Employment · 42
Working Hours · 49
Working Illegally · 38

Y

Youth Hostels · 376

Z

Zoos · 380

SUGGESTIONS

Please write to us with any comments or suggestions you have regarding the contents of this book (preferably complimentary!). We are particularly interested in proposals for improvements that can be included in future editions. For example did you find any important subjects were omitted or weren't covered in sufficient detail? What difficulties or obstacles have you encountered which aren't covered here? What other subjects would you like to see included?

If your suggestions are used in the next edition of *Living and Working in Britain*, you will receive a free copy of the Survival Book of your choice as a token of our appreciation.

NAME: _____

ADDRESS: _____

_____

_____

Send to: Survival Books, PO Box 146, Wetherby, West Yorks. LS23 6XZ, United Kingdom.

My suggestions are as follows (please use additional pages if necessary):

OTHER SURVIVAL BOOKS

There are other 'Living and Working' books in this series including America, Australia, Canada (summer '99), France, London (autumn '99), New Zealand, Spain and Switzerland, all of which represent the most comprehensive and up-to-date source of practical information available about everyday life in these cities and countries. We also publish a best-selling series of 'Buying a Home' books that include Buying a Home Abroad plus buying a home in Britain (autumn '99), Florida, France, Ireland, Italy, Portugal and Spain.

Survival Books are available from good bookshops throughout the world or direct from Survival Books. If you aren't entirely satisfied simply return them to us within 14 days of receipt for a full and unconditional refund. Order your copies today by phone, fax, mail, e-mail from: Survival Books, PO Box 146, Wetherby, West Yorks. LS23 6XZ, United Kingdom (tel/fax: +44-1937-843523, e-mail: orders@survival books.net, Internet: survivalbooks.net).

BUYING A HOME IN . . .

Survival Book's 'Buying a Home' series of books are essential reading for anyone planning to purchase a home abroad and are designed to guide you through the jungle and make it a pleasant and rewarding experience. Most importantly, they are packed with valuable information to help you avoid the sort of disasters that can turn your dream home into a nightmare! Topics covered include:

- Homework & Avoiding Problems
- Choosing the Region
- Finding the Right Home & Location
- Real Estate Agents
- Finance, Mortgages & Taxes

- Home Security
- Utilities, Heating & Air-Conditioning
- Moving House & Settling In
- Renting & Letting
- Permits & Visas

- Retirement, Working & Starting a Business
- Travelling & Communications
- Health & Insurance
- Renting a Car & Driving
- And Much, Much More!

Survival Books are the most comprehensive and up-to-date source of practical information available about buying a home abroad. Whether you're seeking a mansion, villa, farmhouse, townhouse or apartment, a holiday or permanent home, these books will help make your dreams come true. Buy them today and save yourself time, trouble <u>and</u> money?

ORDER FORM

Qty	Title	Price*			Total
		UK	Europe	World	
	Buying a Home Abroad	£11.45	£12.95	£14.95	
	Buying a Home in Britain (summer 1999)	£11.45	£12.95	£14.95	
	Buying a Home in Florida	£11.45	£12.95	£14.95	
	Buying a Home in France	£11.45	£12.95	£14.95	
	Buying a Home in Greece/Cyprus (winter 1999)	£11.45	£12.95	£14.95	
	Buying a Home in Ireland	£11.45	£12.95	£14.95	
	Buying a Home in Italy	£11.45	£12.95	£14.95	
	Buying a Home in Portugal	£11.45	£12.95	£14.95	
	Buying a Home in Spain	£11.45	£12.95	£14.95	
	Living and Working in America	£14.95	£16.95	£20.45	
	Living and Working in Australia	£14.95	£16.95	£20.45	
	Living and Working in Britain	£14.95	£16.95	£20.45	
	Living and Working in Canada (summer 1999)	£14.95	£16.95	£20.45	
	Living and Working in France	£14.95	£16.95	£20.45	
	Living and Working in London (autumn 1999)	£11.45	£12.95	£14.95	
	Living and Working in NZ	£14.95	£16.95	£20.45	
	Living and Working in Spain	£14.95	£16.95	£20.45	
	Living and Working in Switzerland	£14.95	£16.95	£20.45	
	The Alien's Guide to France	£5.95	£6.95	£8.45	
				TOTAL	

Cheque enclosed/Please charge my Access/Delta/Mastercard/Switch/Visa* card,

Expiry date _____ No. __ __ __ __ __ __ __ __ __ __ __ __ __ __ __ __

Issue number (Switch only) _____ Signature: _____

* Delete as applicable (price for Europe/World includes airmail postage)

NAME: _____

ADDRESS: _____

_____

_____

Send to: Survival Books, PO Box 146, Wetherby, West Yorks. LS23 6XZ, United Kingdom **or tel/fax/e-mail credit card orders to 44-1937-843523.**